ENCYCLOPEDIA
OF MEDIA AND POLITICS

ENCYCLOPEDIA OF MEDIA AND POLITICS

Edited by

Todd M. Schaefer
Central Washington University

Thomas A. Birkland
University at Albany, State University of New York
Center for Policy Research

A Division of Congressional Quarterly Inc.
Washington, D.C.

CQ Press
1255 22nd Street, NW, Suite 400
Washington, DC 20037

Phone: 202-729-1900; toll-free, 1-866-4CQ-PRESS (1-866-427-7737)
Web: www.cqpress.com

Cover design: McGaughy Design, Centreville, Virginia

Cover photo credits: Photographers, Library of Congress; George W. Bush, AP Images; Richard M. Nixon, Library of Congress; Bill Clinton, AP Images; Stevenson-Kennedy supporters, AP Images; Carl Bernstein and Bob Woodward, AP Images.

♾ The paper used in this publication exceeds the requirements of the American National Standard for Information Sciences—Permanence of Paper for Printed Library Materials, ANSI Z39.48-1992.

Printed and bound in the United States of America

10 09 08 07 06   1 2 3 4 5

LIBRARY OF CONGRESS CATALOGING-IN-PUBLICATION DATA
Encyclopedia of media and politics / edited by Todd M. Schaefer, Thomas
A. Birkland.
    p. cm.
  Includes bibliographical references and index.
  ISBN 13: 978-1-56802-835-4 (alk. paper)
  ISBN 10: 1-56802-835-0 (alk. paper)
    1. Mass media—Political aspects—United States—Encyclopedias.   2.
Press and politics—United States—Encyclopedias. I. Schaefer, Todd M.
(Todd Michael)   II. Birkland, Thomas A.   III. Title.

P95.82.U6E47 2006
302.230973—dc22   2006031567

Contents

About This Book

Debate about the role of the media and its influence on the U.S. political system has never been greater than it is today. With the ascendancy of the World Wide Web and the ongoing evolution of print and broadcast journalism, new questions have arisen as older ones remain topics of discussion about the role of the so-called fourth estate in U.S. democracy. Although the media play a vital role in informing the public about the government and political leaders, they find themselves under increasing scrutiny as the ever-more-informed and media-savvy audience questions the way in which they depict and shape political discourse.

The *Encyclopedia of Media and Politics* is the first encyclopedic reference to focus on the intersection of media and politics. Students, scholars, and others interested in this timely topic will find it a useful resource. It explores such topics as the evolution and influence of different media, including new technologies; press relations with the White House, Congress, political parties, and other political institutions; the role of the media in covering elections, issues, policies, war, and crises; and media regulations, legislation, and court cases. The *Encyclopedia* features more than 300 entries written by some fifty scholars and researchers in a wide range of fields, including political science; mass communication; television and radio; speech communications; public affairs; ethnic studies; public opinion; technology; and journalism. Entries range from brief biographies and topical entries of a few hundred words to essays of several thousand words that discuss complex topics and concepts in depth. Most entries feature brief bibliographies listing titles useful in pursuing further study.

In an introductory essay, Doris A. Graber, professor of political science at the University of Illinois–Chicago and a noted expert on media, politics, and public opinion, explains why media are important to contemporary politics and vice versa. She also provides an overview of the array of topics and issues that comprise the study of the relationship between media and politics. Her essay sets the stage for the entries that follow by framing the major questions and research agendas in the field.

Acknowledgments

The *Encyclopedia of Media and Politics* is the culmination of the work of many people. We especially thank Mary Carpenter, the acquisitions editor at CQ Press who recognized the potential of this project, was an enthusiastic proponent of it, and brought us on board. David Arthur provided quick and adept development assistance, including issuing and reissuing contracts for the many contributors. The copyediting and production skills of Katharine Miller, Lorna Notsch, and Robin Surratt were essential.

For agreeing to run a "recruitment ad" for contributors, we are grateful to David M. Ryfe, a professor at the University of Nevada–Reno and the editor of the *Political Communication Report,* the newsletter of the Political Communication Section of the American Political Science Association and the International Communication Association. Professors Scott Althaus (University of Illinois at Champaign-Urbana), Jill Edy (University of Oklahoma), and Ken Kollman (University of Michigan), along with Doris A. Graber and Jarol Manheim (George Washington University), also kindly passed along our call.

We also thank all of the scholars and writers who contributed to the volume, without whom this work would not have been published. Last but not least, as always we sincerely express our thanks for the support of our families during the sometimes-long hours occupied by this project.

Todd M. Schaefer

Thomas A. Birkland

Articles and Contributors

Chronology of Major Media and Political Events, 1690–2006

1690   *Publick Occurrences,* the first newspaper, published in Boston (lasts one issue)

1704   *Boston News-Letter,* the first continuously published newspaper, issued as a weekly

1706   Benjamin Franklin—printer, publisher, inventor, and diplomat—is born

1734   John Peter Zenger, a New York publisher, acquitted by a jury of "seditious libel," signaling emerging values of press freedom

1764   *Connecticut Courant* first published, precursor to the *Hartford Courant,* the oldest continuously published newspaper in the United States

1774   First shots of the Revolutionary War fired at the Battle of Lexington and Concord

1776   Declaration of Independence signed in Philadelphia

1789   Federalist Papers—published in newspapers in New York State—are influential in the ratification of the Constitution

       Gazette of the United States founded (published until 1793)

1791   Enactment of the Bill of Rights, which includes the First Amendment, providing for speech and press freedoms

1798   Alien and Sedition Acts enacted, severely limiting speech and press rights, particularly those of President John Adams's opponents

1801   *New York Post* founded

1826   The first photograph, a heliograph, produced in France

1831   William Lloyd Garrison, abolitionist, founds one of the earliest and most influential of the abolitionist newspapers, the *Liberator,* in Boston (published until 1866)

1833   *New York Sun* founded (merged into *New York World-Telegram and Sun* in 1950)

1836   Louis Daguerre of France invents the daguerreotype, a silver- and copper-based photograph

1841   *New York Tribune* founded by Horace Greeley

1843   The rotary press, invented by Richard M. Hoe, makes it possible to mass-produce newspapers, leading to the penny press and making newspapers a true mass medium

1844   The first telegram transmitted, from Baltimore to Washington; the message, "What hath God wrought?"

1846   Associated Press, the first U.S. wire service, is founded

1851   *New York Times* founded

1860   Republican Abraham Lincoln elected president; the Republican Party replaces the Whig Party

1861   U.S. Civil War begins; is extensively covered by newspapers, particularly using the new technologies of telegraphy and photography to an extent never before employed

1866   First successful transatlantic submarine cable laid, allowing for rapid communication between North America and Europe

1872   *Boston Globe* founded

1876   Alexander Graham Bell receives first patent on the telephone, the first device that transmits voices over great distances

1877   *Washington Post* founded

1880   First news photograph printed

       Washington Post becomes first daily newspaper in Washington, D.C.

1881   *Los Angeles Times* founded

1886   Linotype machine produced by Ottmar Mergenthaler, allowing for more rapid typesetting

1888   George Eastman markets the first popularly useable camera that does not require the consumer to develop the film

1892   Thomas Edison receives patent for the duplex (two-way) telegraph

1896   Adolph Ochs acquires the *New York Times*

1897   *New York Times* adopts "all the news that's fit to print" as slogan

       William Randolph Hearst takes over operation of the *San Francisco Examiner,* starting the Hearst newspaper chain

1898   Battleship *Maine* explodes in Havana harbor, an event closely associated with the yellow journalism of the Hearst papers that precipitates the Spanish-American War

1899   *Wall Street Journal* founded

1900   Various successes in radiotelegraphy lay the groundwork for radio

1904   *New York Globe* founded (published until 1923)

1906   President Theodore Roosevelt uses the term *muckraker* in a positive way to describe investigative journalists of the late nineteenth and early twentieth centuries

1908   *Christian Science Monitor* founded

1909   *New York Amsterdam News* founded by James Anderson (continues today as an important source of news and comment aimed at the African American community in the city)

1914   World War I begins in Europe

1917   United States enters World War I, joining Allies against Germany and its allies, the Central Powers

Pulitzer Prize established; becomes the most prestigious journalism award in the United States

1918   World War I ends with an armistice on November 11

1919   *Schenck v. United States*: holds that speech can be regulated if it poses a "clear and present danger" to the nation or to social order

New York Daily News publishes first issue

1920   American Civil Liberties Union (ACLU) is founded, taking the role of earlier civil liberties groups; original mission is to protect citizens and immigrants accused of sedition

First commercial radio station, KDKA Pittsburgh, takes to the air on election day

1922   First radio advertisement airs in New York City

1923   *Gitlow v. New York*: holds that the First Amendment applies to the states via the Fourteenth Amendment, but upholds the conviction of the petitioner, a socialist claimed to be advocating the violent overthrow of the state

Nielsen Media Research founded to measure radio audiences (in 1950 begins TV ratings)

Time magazine founded

1924   Hearst establishes *New York Daily Mirror*

1926   *New York Herald Tribune* first published (closes in 1966)

The NBC (National Broadcasting Company) network created

1927   Radio Act of 1927 creates the Federal Radio Commission; precursors to the Communications Act of 1934 and the FCC

CBS network created (originally the Columbia Phonographic Broadcasting System)

1929   Black Tuesday stock market crash, signaling the beginning of the Great Depression

1932   President Franklin D. Roosevelt elected; claims a mandate to take aggressive steps against the Great Depression

Roosevelt's first fireside chat is broadcast (one of at least thirty-eight)

Newsweek magazine founded

1934   Communications Act of 1934 creates the Federal Communications Commission

1935   Associated Press begins its wirephoto service, transmitting halftone photos to clients, based on technologies pioneered by AT&T, RCA, and Western Union in the early 1920s

George Gallup establishes the American Institute for Public Opinion while at the Young and Rubicam advertising agency

1936   A *Literary Digest* poll makes a wildly inaccurate prediction that Alf Landon would win the presidential election; gaffe illustrates the dangers of poor survey methods; a Gallup poll correctly forecasts the winner

Hearst loses control of his publishing chain in wake of bankruptcy during the Great Depression

1937   Roosevelt suffers largest political defeat of his career over his "Court-packing" plan to replace older Supreme Court justices with ones he would appoint and who would rule favorably on New Deal legislation

1939   First television broadcast (not widely expanded until after World War II)

1940   Edward R. Murrow broadcasts from London during the German "blitz" bombing campaign

1941   *Bridges v. California*: upholds free speech of a union leader who commented on a pending legal case; Supreme Court holds that restricting speech when no "clear and present danger" exists is unconstitutional

Japan bombs Pearl Harbor, Hawaii, leading to U.S. entry into World War II

NBC television network takes to the air

1942   Voice of America founded under the Office of War Information

1943   ABC network created from former NBC Blue network relinquished by NBC due to antitrust issues

1945   World War II ends with the defeat of Germany and, later, Japan; weeks before Germany capitulates, Roosevelt dies and is succeeded by Vice President Harry S. Truman

Congressional Quarterly, later *CQ Weekly*, founded

1946   CBS resumes regularly scheduled television service; first station was all but shut down during World War II

1947   *Meet the Press* debuts on NBC

1948   President Harry S. Truman defeats New York governor Thomas Dewey, despite a Gallup prediction of a Dewey victory and premature announcements of Dewey's "victory"

First cable (CATV) system installed

U.S. News & World Report formed in the merger of *United States News* (established 1933) and *World Report* (established 1946)

CBS Television News debuts as a daily evening news broadcast (renamed *Douglas Edwards with the News* in 1950)

1949   Camel News Caravan, early network news broadcast on NBC

1950   Korean War begins with North Korea crossing into South Korea; U.S. and UN forces intervene

1951	*Douglas Edwards with the News* (CBS) becomes the first evening news broadcast on both coasts via coaxial cable
1954	Army-McCarthy hearings widely televised to the nation, hastening the political demise of ardent anti-communist Joseph McCarthy (R-Wis.) by revealing his often brutal tactics
	Face the Nation debuts on CBS
1955	*Village Voice* founded in New York City, becoming one of the earliest examples of alternative media
1956	*Huntley-Brinkley Report* broadcast on NBC
1957	Little Rock, Arkansas, schools are racially integrated when President Dwight D. Eisenhower sends federal troops to enforce the provisions of *Brown v. Board of Education* (1954), making "separate but equal" schools unconstitutional
	Soviet Union launches *Sputnik,* the first artificial satellite
1958	United Press merges with International Press Service to create United Press International (UPI)
1959	Section 315 of the Communications Act of 1934 exempts incidental appearances of candidates in news coverage, allowing stations to cover candidates as subjects of news stories not limited by the equal time provision
1960	Kennedy-Nixon presidential debates viewed or heard by an audience of millions
1961	Berlin Wall constructed to prevent East Germans from escaping to West Berlin
1962	Communications Satellite Act of 1962 regulates the emerging field of satellite communication
	The first "active" telecommunications satellite, *Telestar,* launched
	Walter Cronkite takes to the air on *CBS Evening News*
1963	President John F. Kennedy assassinated in Dallas; Vice President Lyndon B. Johnson of Texas assumes the presidency
	Katharine Graham takes over leadership of the *Washington Post*
1964	"Daisy girl" commercial aired by the Johnson campaign, suggests that Republican candidate Barry Goldwater would likely lead the nation into nuclear war
1965	Beginning of most active U.S. involvement in the Vietnam War, known as the "television war" because images from it aired nationally on evening network news shows
1967	Public Broadcasting Act of 1967 creates the Corporation for Public Broadcasting (CPB)
1968	Tet offensive—North Vietnamese and Viet Cong forces penetrate deep into South Vietnam; offensive is a tactical failure, but the media portray it as a major challenge to U.S. policy in South Vietnam
	60 Minutes, CBS's highly successful news magazine show, debuts
1969	Neil Armstrong and Buzz Aldrin become the first people to walk on the moon; moonwalk is televised to a worldwide audience
	PBS founded (first program broadcast in 1970)
1970	Advent of phototypesetting ("cold type"), which replaces the "hot type" method (linotype)
	Gary Trudeau's *Doonesbury* comic strip—which blurs the distinction between comics and editorial cartoons—first published
	National Public Radio founded (first broadcast in 1971)
1971	*Pentagon Papers Case:* firms the doctrine against prior restraint; the Supreme Court rules that the federal government could not restrict the *New York Times's* and *Washington Post's* publication of the papers
1972	*Branzburg v. Hayes:* holds that compelling reporters to testify before grand juries does not violate journalists' First Amendment rights
	The "Muskie incident," in which Sen. Edmund Muskie (D-Maine), candidate for president, appeared to weep about a smear leveled at his wife by the *Manchester Union Leader*
	First geostationary communications satellite, *Anik I,* launched by Canada
	Watergate scandal starts with break-in at Democratic National Committee headquarters in the Watergate complex
1974	President Richard M. Nixon resigns as a result of the Watergate scandal and congressional moves toward impeachment
1976	Carter-Ford debates, first presidential debates since 1960; Gerald R. Ford's apparent gaffe (on Soviet domination of Poland) greatly aids Jimmy Carter's campaign
	New York Post purchased by Rupert Murdoch
1978	*Federal Communications Commission v. Pacifica Foundation:* upholds FCC's power to regulate radio content, particularly at certain times of the day when children are likely to listen
	World News Tonight debuts on ABC using a three-anchor format
1979	C-SPAN, the Cable Satellite Public Affairs Network, first broadcasts
1980	ABC's *Nightline* debuts as *America Held Hostage*
1981	IBM PC popularizes personal computers
	Walter Cronkite retires from *CBS Evening News* and is replaced by Dan Rather
1982	*USA Today* first published as a "national" newspaper; printing and distribution system establishes the state of the art for national newspaper distribution
1983	First "internet"—the TCP/IP network—forming as NSFNet
	World News Tonight adopts traditional single-anchor format (with Peter Jennings as anchor until 2005)

1984   Cable Communication Policy Act of 1984 enacted, creating a comprehensive regulatory system for cable television

Apple Macintosh revolutionizes computer interfaces and creates desktop publishing

1985   General Electric acquires NBC through its acquisition of RCA

1986   Space shuttle *Challenger* explodes 71 seconds after liftoff; millions worldwide witness the event on television

Fox Broadcasting Corporation debuts

1987   Iran-contra scandal, in which aides to President Ronald Reagan illegally sold weapons to Iran and used the proceeds to fund the contras fighting the Sandinista government of Nicaragua

1988   Willie Horton ad aired by the George H. W. Bush campaign to criticize Gov. Michael Dukakis of Massachusetts during 1988 presidential campaign; highly controversial ad is condemned as racist by many

1989   The fall of communism in Europe as Eastern European countries ease travel restrictions and East Germany allows passage through the Berlin Wall

1990   Iraq invades Kuwait; Iraq's failure to leave Kuwait precipitates huge U.S.-led military buildup in anticipation of the Persian Gulf War

1991   Persian Gulf War begins; extensive CNN coverage is closely followed by millions of viewers worldwide, particularly in nations participating in the U.S.-led coalition to drive Iraqi forces out of Kuwait

CERN (European Particle Physics Laboratory) and Tim Berners Lee popularize the Web, HTML (hypertext markup language), and HTTP (hypertext transfer protocol)

1992   Texas entrepreneur H. Ross Perot announces his independent candidacy for president on CNN's *Larry King Live*

1993   First graphical Web browser, NCSA Mosaic, is released, the forerunner of HTML-based Web browsers

1995   Internet opened to commercial users; marks the beginning of rapid growth of the medium

Westinghouse Electric Corp. buys CBS

1996   Communications Decency Act of 1996 seeks to regulate content on the Internet

Disney purchases Cap-Cities/ABC

1997   *Reno v. American Civil Liberties Union:* invalidates large parts of the Communications Decency Act as unconstitutional for its content-based blanket restrictions on speech

1998   President Bill Clinton impeached in the House of Representatives (Senate fails to convict him in early 1999)

2000   Confusion reigns on election night, as several networks prematurely declare Al Gore winner of the presidential election based on exit poll data supplied by Voter Research and Surveys

The "Internet bust" unfolds, as many firms seeking to make money through various means on the Internet go out of business

Viacom completes acquisition of CBS

2002   FCC mandates that all television sets be able to receive signals in high-definition (HD) format by 2007

2003   Print and broadcast journalists are "embedded" in military units in the U.S.-led invasion of Iraq

2004   The Super Bowl "wardrobe malfunction," in which singer Janet Jackson's breast is exposed on nationwide television, leading to crackdowns on "indecency" in radio and television and to substantial increases in the fines the FCC can impose for broadcast indecency

2005   Judith Miller, writer for the *New York Times,* is jailed for contempt of court for not revealing a source involved in the leak of the identity of a CIA agent; obtains release after 85 days when her source releases her from her promise of confidentiality

Congress passes legislation that requires analog TV stations to switch to all digital broadcasting by 2009

Mort Zuckerman buys *Daily News*

Dan Rather steps down as the anchor of the *CBS Evening News*

2006   NBC buys Vivendi's Universal unit, becoming NBC Universal

Katie Couric takes over as anchor of the *CBS Evening News*

Introduction: The Intersection of Media and Politics

We live in a political world, where much is constantly happening. Some things we experience directly, but over a lifetime, most things, by necessity, come to us indirectly. Someone else experiences them or is informed about them and then relays information to others, individually or collectively. In complex societies, that "someone" is the media—institutions created to dispense information to large numbers of people. In essence, we see most of the world through the eyes of others. Their perceptions, transmitted to us, influence how we view the world of politics.

The *Encyclopedia of Media and Politics* explores the role of the mass media in the information creation and transmission process in the United States. Long and short essays describe the mass-mediated pictures of the political world that are presented daily to U.S. audiences. Some essays explain how and why journalists pick the stories that they tell and how and why people concerned with these stories try to influence these choices. Many of the essays analyze the consequences that flow from seeing the world through the particular prisms through which the U.S. media present it.

There is of course a history to this process. The world has changed in major ways since the founding of the United States in 1776, as have the methods for collecting and transmitting stories, the training and orientation of the storytellers and the people they interview, as well as the audiences exposed to the media. Many of the essays in this encyclopedia detail what was then and what is now, documenting giant leaps in technology, audience size, and media impact. This introductory essay sets the stage by presenting an overview of the interplay between media and politics that illustrates how crucial the media are to U.S. political life and the life of every citizen.

Media as a Window on the World

Reflect for a moment on images of the political world. Who are the political leaders locally, nationally, and on the world scene? What significant events are occurring? What do they mean for you, for the United States, for people in other parts of the world? The information needed to answer such questions can be found in the print, audio, and audiovisual news media that report it directly or to others who relayed it.

How persuasive are media images? It is well known that most adults are loath to alter the views of the political world that they have formed and reinforced over their lifetime. Nevertheless, they frequently do change their opinion based on what they learn from the news media. Media images are most persuasive when they involve situations that people are apt to experience only indirectly through the media, rather than personally.

The perspectives from which news stories depict the political world provide much of the reality that people living in the United States, including political leaders, know. News stories create the contexts in which political activities that affect you take place, irrespective of the accuracy of these stories. The fact that stories featured prominently arouse the attention of the public and political leaders points to the media's agenda-setting power (Agenda setting, pp. 9–10). Publicity puts events on the public's agenda of concerns and politicians' agenda of discussion and possible action. Because news stories circulate widely, they become shared political experiences, forming the basis of widely shared opinions about public policies and political issues.

News stories inform millions of people from all walks of life about whatever domestic or foreign sites and events journalists have chosen to report. For every site and event that they choose to cover, however, thousands of others are left outside the gates of publicity, dooming them to remain largely unknown (Gatekeeping, p. 97; Newsgathering process, pp. 180–181; News management, pp. 181–183). The failure to report certain stories is often more consequential than directing the limelight toward others. The lack of media coverage can foreclose opportunities for action that could potentially change the flow of political events. What does not happen also has consequences.

Media as Pace Setters

Besides calling attention to matters of potential public concern, the media also provide cues to the public about the degree of importance of an issue. In general, journalists prominently cover stories that they deem important. In newspapers, these stories are likely to appear on the front page with big headlines and pictures. On television or radio, they are presented as lead stories or lengthy features. Matters deemed less important get "buried" in the back pages or are given brief exposure in the later portions of television or radio shows.

Nearly all coverage, however, even when brief and comparatively inconspicuous, lends an aura of significance to publicized topics. The mere fact that a particular story is told suggests to many people that the issue or people covered are out of the ordinary in some way. Political candidates whose efforts to win an election are widely publicized, social crusaders whose goals become front-page news, or convicted murderers or terrorists whose story wins a hearing on radio or television often become instant celebrities. Their unpublicized counterparts remain obscure and bereft of political influence. The media thus confer status on individuals and organizations through the sheer fact of coverage. They serve as agencies of social legitimation.

Standards and Frames

The tenor of news stories suggests acceptable standards of private and public behavior. News audiences learn repeatedly which views and behaviors are acceptable and which are unacceptable or outside the mainstream, reinforcing prevailing cultural values and the status quo. This situation troubles people who want to change society radically, but it pleases people who want to maintain the established social and political system.

By identifying acceptable standards, media stories determine the criteria by which the public evaluates public policies and the performance of public officials. The perspectives, or "frames," into which news stories are cast similarly shape the judgments that people are likely to make about political situations and policies designed to cope with them (Framing, p. 89). For instance, news stories can be framed to blame juvenile crime on criminal justice policies, on race and class inequalities, on individuals' bad character traits and upbringing, or on the accidental conjuncture of events that tempt adolescents to misbehave. The framing of stories about juvenile crime then suggests not only the causes but also the kinds of remedies that are needed to cope with the problem.

Media stories often create skewed impressions. In fact, in many respects, the news is inherently misleading. Events that are publicized inevitably loom larger than life, distorting real world conditions. Even films and photographs deceive the eye. A small group of demonstrators may look like an invading army when cameras zoom in on them or shoot them with distorting lenses. Misperceptions also arise because journalists cannot provide the context of most stories in sufficient detail or because their reports contain errors. Misperceptions created by media stories can cause serious harm, such as undermining confidence in good policies and practices, in good people, and in good products. For example, the frequency of violent crime stories in the news and entertainment media exaggerates the incidence of these events and exacerbates fears of becoming a crime victim. People then take unnecessary precautions, including avoiding entire neighborhoods and shunning certain people or groups of people.

Megaphone Effect

The proliferation of broadcast media, including the development of the Internet, has vastly enhanced the reach of media and hence their influence. Millions of people worldwide can now see and hear the same news stories in their homes on television and computer screens. In the past, audiences were much smaller and far more geographically limited. In combination, the new venues bring a much broader spectrum of political views to the fore and offer many new opportunities for interested citizens to learn about and participate in politics. Roughly two-thirds of U.S. residents currently can easily access Internet sources either from home or from work. By 2010, access within the United States is expected to be nearly universal (New media, pp. 175–178).

Not only are the media the chief source of most Americans' views of the world, but they are also the fastest way to disperse information throughout the entire society. Major political news broadcasters, such as CNN (Cable News Network) and other round-the-clock news providers, can diffuse breaking stories throughout the country (and around the world) within minutes or hours of an event occurring. People hear the stories, either directly from radio or television or secondhand from other people who received mass media messages. The news about al-Qaida's attack on New York City and outside Washington, D.C., in September 2001 reached a majority of U.S. residents in less than an hour.

Political Socialization

Given the media's role as a window on the world, with journalists calling attention to specific events and explaining their significance, it is not surprising that news media have become major agents of political socialization for children as well as adults (Children and the media, pp. 43–46; Socialization, p. 269). Children learn basic political facts, values, and orientations from readily available stories in news and entertainment television and educational shows designed especially for them. Children may encounter media offerings directly or they may learn about their messages from their parents, peers, and teachers. They then use this information to model their behavior to help them fit into their cultural milieu. Exposure to politically relevant information is especially crucial for young people just beginning to develop and establish political attitudes and behavior patterns.

Most of the new opinions that grown-ups form during their adult life also are based on information supplied by the mass media. That does not mean that adult news audiences necessarily adopt the precise attitudes and opinions suggested in the news about politics. Rather, the information that news and entertainment media supply provides the ingredients that adults use in adjusting their existing attitudes and opinions to keep pace with a constantly changing world. Significant recent changes in the balance of public opinion facilitated by news and entertainment stories include shifts in societal prejudices against certain ethnic and religious groups, greater tolerance for homosexuals, and changed attitudes toward mainland China and Russia.

Average Americans absorb a great deal of diverse information from day to day, week to week, and year to year. How do they sort through this reservoir of information to make discrete political decisions? As a rule, people will use the most recently encountered versions of the news as reference points to guide their thinking and judgments. That happens because the newest information "primes" people's memory so that it is uppermost in their mind when considering subsequent events. For example, after people have been exposed to stories about increasing unemployment in a state, most will give negative ratings to the performance of state leaders because they have been primed to blame leaders for lagging employment. If, instead, people have most recently noticed stories about reductions in taxes, they will give the same leaders positive ratings because tax reductions are viewed favorably (Framing, p. 89).

The media's importance in shaping political opinions is magnified vastly by their pervasiveness in U.S. homes. Average high school graduates today have spent more time in front of a television than in school. Much of the content of their lessons and textbooks is based on information provided by the media. By the time most adults have finished schooling, they have spent nearly half of their leisure time watching television, listening to the radio, or reading newspapers and magazines. Various forms of television—including broadcast and cable programming, Internet downloads, and recorded entertainment—occupy three-fourths of this time.

Besides wanting to stay informed about happenings that may affect them, many people also use the mass media to satisfy the need for entertainment, companionship, and relief of tension. Watching television is a way to pass the time cheaply and with minimal physical or mental exertion. The ability to create a product that attracts huge audiences, including political elites of all types as well as ordinary people, is a major ingredient in the news media's power.

Shaping Public Opinion

The media's power to shape news presentations and thereby influence public opinion lies at the heart of the tensions between media and government, because the media have more influence than governments prefer. Politicians and other leaders are keenly aware of the consequences of the media's power to call attention to people, issues, and policies. Journalists can pick and choose from among the available facts about government and are predisposed to accentuate negative news that puts politicians in an unfavorable light. They can select spokespeople for specific points of view and structure questions to elicit answers that run counter to politicians' desired scripts. Journalists routinely chop lengthy official statements into brief quotes and then weave them into an account that is often supplemented with information gathered from sources hostile to political incumbents. The length of sound bites that express public officials' views on political matters in their own words has been shrinking. With the exception of major presidential speeches, they average less than ten seconds and rarely exceed twenty seconds (Sound bite, p. 270).

Because getting the public's attention is so crucial for winning political battles in a democracy, most politicians try mightily to time and structure events to yield favorable publicity for themselves and their causes. They are especially eager to forestall damaging coverage because they know that unfavorable stories can seriously hurt their political career and the policies they espouse. In fact, the prospects of media scrutiny routinely influence their behavior. For instance, they often avoid or conceal activities likely to receive negative press. If they have misbehaved, they may atone for their misdeeds through public confessions of guilt and regret.

Although complaints about negative media coverage have received the lion's share of attention, positive coverage that helps political leaders is also common. It can increase public support for them and their favored policies. It can also be crucial in determining whether a chief executive's appointees will be confirmed by the legislature. Media support is particularly important for political leaders during national emergencies, such as wars and other man-made and natural disasters, when unity within the government and public backing can be vital. Television coverage may allow politicians to visit constituents in their homes, thereby creating emotional ties akin to meeting them in person. In fact, in the United States, the concentration of news coverage on the president has tipped the political scales of power among the three branches of government in favor of the presidency.

From a philosophical perspective, the power of the media to set the political agenda is a matter of concern because it is not controlled by a system of formal checks and balances as is power at various levels of government. It is not subject to periodic review through the electoral process because the public does not vote for reporters and their superiors and media owners. Except when media emphases or claims are patently wrong, remedies are few. In the United States, citizens are protected from false advertising of consumer goods through truth in advertising laws, but there is no way to protect them from false political claims or questionable news selection by media personnel without threatening the rights to free speech and a free press guaranteed by the Constitution (First Amendment, pp. 83–87; Prior restraint, p. 228).

Institutionalization

In the context of the United States, "media" refers to thousands of institutions. There are close to 1,500 daily newspapers in the country and many thousands of over-the-air and cable television stations, not to mention radio stations, Web sites, magazines, trade journals, and the like. That makes it important to keep in mind that generalizations about media cover a large number of individual variations. Nonetheless, it is possible to point to general characteristics that provide a reasonably accurate image of how the U.S. media, considered as a whole, are organized and how that affects patterns of news coverage.

The News Business

Media ownership patterns. American mass media are predominantly privately owned and operated as for-profit business enterprises. That characteristic explains a lot about news coverage patterns (Competition, pp. 55–56; Cross-ownership, pp. 60–61; Ownership of media, pp. 198–201). Typologies range from ownership of a single media outlet by one individual to ownership of multiple outlets, including a variety of print and electronic media, by huge corporate conglomerates that may also own and operate non-media businesses. Owners and the people and organizations that run media enterprises are a varied lot as well. They may be media experts or business tycoons or special interest organizations representing various economic, ethnic, and religious groups. Their primary goal may be to present the best news possible or to foster special political and non-political interests or to earn high profits for shareholders. Political goals may include promoting or defeating particular candidates or policies. Most media enterprises combine a mix of such goals.

Most Americans prefer to have operation of U.S. media enterprises in private hands because they like the idea that content choices reflect the tastes of diverse owners and because they fear that government ownership and controls could make the media powerful propaganda weapons that administrations would use to keep themselves in power. Is private control of this powerful institution really safer in private hands, especially when huge conglomerates dominate the media scene? What are the consequences of concentrating control over media enterprises in the hands of a few very large corporations (First Amendment, pp. 83–87; News management, pp. 181–183; Ownership of media, pp. 198–201)?

Privately owned media must generate sufficient income to pay for their business expenses and earn a profit. In the United States, most of the media earn income from advertising revenues rather than fees charged to audiences for receiving news and other offerings. Advertisers are willing to pay high fees in return for the opportunity to reach large audiences with their sales messages. News media accordingly attempt to tailor their programs to maximize their attractiveness to key groups desired by advertisers.

Audience preferences. Media feature an endless succession of dramatic stories with human interest themes, such as crimes and disasters, rags-to-riches lives, love-and-hate relationships and the like, because audience research shows that such stories attract and hold the largest audiences. Should they? Is this really the type of information that most Americans want, or do they flock to this type of news because regular news offerings are overloaded with facts and are boring?

Many critics of media performance contend that viewers would choose educational offerings over entertaining stories if the press would make them available. The evidence indicates otherwise. Large numbers of average Americans, along with many intellectual elites, like tabloid news and sensational programming (Hard and soft news, pp. 106–107). Tabloid newspapers and magazines featuring sex or violence far outsell publications that concentrate on serious analysis of political and social issues. Movies featuring heinous crimes and explicit sex become huge box office successes. The same holds for pornographic Web sites. In response to audience tastes, they are the most plentiful type of offering on the Internet (Obscenity and pornography, pp. 194–196).

What these complaints about low-brow media fare tend to ignore is that much high-brow fare currently offered to the public is unappealing and confusing. It is overloaded with facts that are meaningless to average people who lack essential contextual information. The language used to tell stories is often difficult to comprehend, and the lengthy reports of conflicting opinions and interpretations confuse viewers. People are quite ready to consume hard news when its significance to their own lives is made clear and when they understand the context that gives the event its meaning. The upswing in attention to serious news in the months following the September 11 attacks is one of many examples (Terrorism and the media, pp. 284–285).

Philosophies of News Production

Thus far, we have focused broadly on the social significance of news, especially its political aspects, and on some of the economic factors that explain the forms it takes in the United States. We now turn to a closer look at the role that journalists play in news production and on the areas of politics that they cover.

Mirror Models

One common philosophy of news production is that it is and should be a "mirror" on the world, depicting everything that is happening. That, of course, is impossible. Millions of significant events take place daily, forcing journalists to choose which they wish to observe and report. There are neither enough reporters to tell the stories nor enough news space to report them nor enough interested news consumers to make a complete record a sound investment of precious resources. Instead, why not make the news a representative sample of reality? The answer is because various groups in the United States disagree about the types of stories that are truly important or interesting and therefore deserve publication. Time and space for reporting the news are limited, so that many individual stories and types of stories are poorly covered or not covered at all. Neglected stories include the myriad of ordinary events that happen every day. News does not normally portray routine rush hour traffic or youngsters at a playground or a congregation assembled for church services unless something very unusual has happened (Newsworthiness, pp. 186–188; Objectivity, pp. 193–194).

Social Responsibility Models

Journalists who espouse social responsibility philosophies believe that they must do more than merely observe and report the flow of events. They believe that they should strive to better society by alerting media audiences to the problems that society needs to solve. As guardians of public interests, journalists should foster political action when necessary by publicizing social problems. Social responsibility theories may lead journalists to become major players in the game of politics, rather than acting in their traditional role as impartial chroniclers of information provided by others. It may also garner them journalism honors, like Pulitzer Prizes (Objectivity, pp. 193–194; Public/Civic journalism, pp. 233–234; Social responsibility, pp. 269–270)

The desire to influence political events in areas where social malfunctions are evident often takes the form of investigative journalism (Investigative reporting, pp. 115–116; Muckraking, pp. 163–164). Major print and electronic media may devote substantial resources to expose corruption and wrongdoing in the hope of stimulating reforms and correction. The most prominent "villains" targeted for exposure are big government, big business, and organized crime. At times, the goals of investigations are less lofty. The chief purpose may be to present sensational information that attracts large audiences or to affect the course of politics in line with a particular journalist's or news medium's political preferences.

Proponents of the public, or civic, journalism model also favor abandoning traditional news reporting roles in favor of active participation in political affairs (Public/Civic journalism, pp. 233–234). Instead of taking the lead themselves, however, they favor taking their cues from citizens. According to this model, journalists should ascertain people's concerns and then write stories that help citizens play an active and successful role in public life to deal with these concerns. The press then spurs public dialogue that brings out a diversity of views. After consensus has been reached among the clients of a particular news venue, that enterprise then should vigorously champion appropriate public policies.

Blending Models

There are many other guiding principles for reporting events besides those already mentioned. Each represents judgments about the role that news offerings should play in society, including the nation's political life. Moreover, none of the models discussed thus far fully explains the news-making process; rather, the process reflects all of them in varying degrees. Which system is best must be judged in the context of the needs of particular communities and their visions of a wholesome society. No plan works equally well everywhere.

What becomes "news"? How do journalists identify the stories that they want to publicize as "news"? What is "news"? The not-so-simple answer to this seemingly simple question is that news is whatever different journalists in various communities, operating under unique sociopolitical conditions, consider to be "news." In other words, the determination of what stories are newsworthy enough to be included in mass media offerings hinges on the choices that journalists make in light of their social environment, their journalism conventions, and their own inclinations (Newsgathering process, pp. 180–181; Newsworthiness, pp. 186–188).

Various philosophies about news come into play in these choices. In the United States, when people talk about what ought to be news, the demands of democratic political life have traditionally tended to be uppermost. Accordingly, the news dwells on politics. Stories that inform citizens about their government and help them to perform their civic duties are deemed most essential. Critics charge, however, that civic needs are poorly served. They say the same about the media's performance of their watchdog role, which requires media to scrutinize government activities to detect failures in performance or illegalities (Watchdog role, pp. 300–301). Neither journalists nor government officials are completely at ease with the media's watchdog role because the media have not been elected to serve as a supervisory

fourth branch of government (Fourth estate, pp. 87–88). Media owners are self-selected, and the journalists whom they hire do not reflect the socioeconomic differences and diverse partisan orientations represented in the country as a whole. This raises questions about the impartiality of their judgment of the performance of elected officials (Media bias, pp. 149–153; Objectivity, pp. 193–194).

Objectivity and sources. News philosophies that advocate using reporting to foster political goals run afoul of several important tenets that hold sway in U.S. journalism, among them the hallowed principles of neutrality and objectivity. According to these principles, the choice of facts to be reported should depend entirely on their intrinsic importance rather than any preferences that reporters or their sources or employers might have. Journalists should be nonjudgmental in their reports; they should offer nothing but the facts, without any evaluations or subjective interpretations (Reporting events, p. 251). Furthermore, news should be reported quickly and accurately. It should provide information about the who, what, where, when, how, and why of the story: who are the actors, what did they do, and where, when, and how did the situation happen? One of the most serious threats to neutral and objective reporting springs from journalists' nearly exclusive reliance on established government elites as their sources of news about government (Objectivity, pp. 193–194).

Access to major political news is gained primarily through interviews with public officials or through news releases by government departments and agencies. Even when reporters personally observe events and investigate problematic aspects of the situation, they still usually validate their own views by soliciting comments from public officials. Reliance on government sources often is a matter of necessity rather than choice. For instance, when reporters want to enter military zones or nuclear production facilities or prisons, they need government permission. Some forms of cooperation between journalists and public officials are universally applauded. In times of crises, such as major natural or man-made disasters, the media, particularly radio and television, become vital arms of public and private crisis control (Crisis journalism, pp. 57–59; Pseudo-crisis, p. 232). Besides reporting about developments in the situation, journalists provide crisis workers quick access to the public by allowing them to use media channels to deliver their messages personally or through media personnel.

Public relations experts are another pool of news sources. They represent a wide range of organizations, interest groups, and business enterprises and seek publicity for their concerns; they might work for political parties, groups interested in a single issue (such as protecting a rare species of birds or promoting a new series of postal stamps), or ethnic and religious groups who believe that their civil rights are threatened. Experienced public relations experts know the deadlines of important publications and network television news. Therefore they schedule events and news releases so that they are fresh and enticing at the time when journalists make their final news choices for the paper or journal or broadcast. Most public relations releases are discarded, but many are published verbatim or in an edited version (Media consultants, pp. 153–154; Press secretaries, pp. 227–228).

Gathering the News

To understand what information makes it into the all-important stream of news that journalists consider for inclusion in their reports, it is important to know how the newsgathering process works (Newsgathering process, pp. 180–181).

The Beat System

News organizations establish regular listening posts, or "beats," in those places in which events of interest to the public are most likely to happen. In the United States, beats cover major political executives, legislative bodies, court systems, and international organizations (Media and Congress, pp. 140–143; Media and the courts, pp. 143–145; Media and the presidency, pp. 145–149). Places in which dramatic out-of-the-ordinary behaviors are most apt to occur, such as police stations and hospitals, are monitored. Media record fluctuations in economic trends at stock and commodity markets and at institutions designed to check the pulse of the nation's business. Some beats, such as health or education, are functionally defined, and reporters assigned to them generally cover a wider array of institutions on a less regular schedule than is the case with institutional beats.

Given the consensus about the types of stories that must be covered, the styles of coverage, and the similarity in news beats, overall news patterns—the types of stories that are covered and the relative prominence of various topics—are fairly uniform throughout the country. That does not mean, however, that the stories are reported from the same perspectives. When a variety of media cover the same story, as happens routinely, they often use sources representing different elites. When that happens, the thrust of the story may vary widely even though the underlying facts remain the same. A few highly respected national newspapers and a small number of newscasters have been extraordinarily influential in putting their versions of news events on the political agenda. News coverage in the *New York Times,* the *Washington Post,* and the *Wall Street Journal* is emulated nationwide (*New York Times,* pp. 189–190; *Wall Street Journal,* p. 295; *Washington Post,* p. 300). This phenomenon contributes to pack journalism, that is, the penchant of print and broadcast journalists to follow en masse the lead of elite media in terms of addressing the same topics and framing them in similar ways (Pack journalism, p. 203).

Pressures of Time and Space

Among the many constraints that prevent journalists from producing top-notch news, inadequacies of time and space rank high (Time pressures, pp. 287–288). To make time pressures worse, in the case of a developing story, journalists must use valuable space and time reintroducing it for audience members hearing about it for the first time. In addition, all of the media work with deadlines that keep them from preparing stories as carefully as they ideally might like. Television stations that broadcast around the clock generally have the least time to investigate most stories and to provide background and interpretation. This is why background or investigative stories on television frequently originate in the print media.

The problem of insufficient time pertains not only to preparing stories but also to presenting them. The average news story on television and radio takes about a minute, just enough time to announce an event and present a fact or two about it. Complex stories may be ignored entirely if they cannot be drastically condensed or, for television, if there is insufficient time to obtain attractive visuals. Aspects of the news that are visually appealing and readily available to film crews often unfortunately fail to shed light on the most important angles of the story.

Government Regulation of Media

All governments try to control the news media because they regard them as important political forces. Although control is universal, its extent, nature, and purposes vary, depending on political ideology and culture. The right of the press to criticize government flourishes when governments are deemed accountable to the people, and average citizens are deemed capable of forming sound opinions about the conduct of government and the merits of current and prospective officeholders.

First Amendment Guarantees

The First Amendment to the U.S. Constitution—which provides that "Congress shall make no law . . . abridging the freedom of speech, or of the press"—provides the news media their exceptionally strong basis for resisting government controls of news content (First Amendment, pp. 83–87). In fact, the press is the only private enterprise in the United States with a constitutionally protected status. The scope of this privilege and its application to broadcast media, however, have fluctuated since ratification of the First Amendment in 1791 because the Supreme Court has interpreted it in different ways in various court cases (*Red Lion Broadcasting Co., Inc. v. FCC,* p. 246, and other cases). Similar press freedom clauses in state constitutions have also yielded a broad range of interpretations that may be at odds with each other and with those on the national level.

The First Amendment freedoms granted to the press are not absolute, as the courts have ruled that certain social rights may at times be superior. For instance, the freedom to publish often must yield to the right to privacy or the right to a fair trial (*Sheppard v. Maxwell,* p. 265, and other cases). Other exceptions include prohibitions on publishing libelous or slanderous comments, publicizing obscene materials, or revealing the contents of materials shielded by the courts or by other government institutions (Obscenity and pornography, pp. 194–196). The United States, like all societies, also has laws that prohibit publication of information that would endanger national security and aid the nation's enemies (*New York Times v. United States,* pp. 190–191, and other cases). In democratic societies, media and the government are in perennial disagreement about the turning point at which disclosure of information poses a serious threat to the nation and when that danger is outweighed by the urgency to keep the public informed. Governments lean toward restraining publication of news that is potentially dangerous; the media lean toward publication.

The media's fight against government efforts to censor news has been strengthened immeasurably by freedom of information laws (Freedom of Information Act of 1966, pp. 92–93). These laws, in force at all levels of the U.S. government, provide that information must be disclosed to the media and citizens unless the government proves that exposure would cause substantial harm. That puts the heavy burden of securing incontrovertible proof for the need for censorship on government officials, rather than forcing information seekers to prove that the information may safely be released. Still, much information remains secret because the government has classified it as too sensitive to release (Censorship, pp. 40–41).

Tools of Regulation

Aside from imposing direct curbs on publication, governments can use economic support in the form of direct and indirect subsidies to exert control over the media. For example, postage and telephone rates, which are subject to government control, have been kept low to encourage wide dissemination of news. The government has also provided revenue to some news media by paying them for publishing official government information, such as lists of tax-delinquent properties or announcements of election-related information. The power of presidents and other high-ranking officials to grant or refuse interviews and to leak information to favored reporters can be used to influence journalists. In times of war, when government censorship increases and is more readily tolerated, most journalists avoid difficulties with laws that restrain press freedom by refraining from publishing material likely to be considered objectionable (Censorship, pp. 40–41). In such cases, self-censorship largely replaces government censorship. Encouraging self-censorship has become the government's most potent control over information because tight control over potentially sensitive information has become well nigh impossible in the Internet age (New media, pp. 175–178).

The Federal Communications Commission (FCC) administers broadcasting rules for the U.S. government (Federal Communications Commission, pp. 79–80). The commission, with members appointed by the president and confirmed by the Senate, is supposedly independent in its judgments and free of partisanship. The reality is, however, different. Congressional control over the FCC budget, pressures by multiple interest groups, and presidential control over the appointment of members greatly curtail the FCC's freedom of operation. Furthermore, its rulings can be appealed to the courts, which frequently have overturned them. The FCC is prohibited from controlling the content of news offerings, but it can use its power to license new stations and renew existing licenses for stations as a way of influencing the quality of content. The FCC can deny a license to stations whose programs do not meet its public interest standards.

Topics

Journalists' control over the selection of news topics is not absolute. Aside from the constraints mentioned above, there are times when what to publish and thereby put on the agenda for public discussion and possible action may be beyond the discretion of media personnel. When events are crucial to the lives of large numbers of people or when an important story is reported by competing media, journalists may feel compelled to cover the situation. Nonetheless, there remains an extremely wide range of topics for which coverage is discretionary. How is that discretion used? What patterns, if any, are discernable?

Primary Contenders

Election campaigns. Journalists cover election campaigns extensively, especially at the presidential level (Campaigns, elections, and the media, pp. 34–37). Candidates need to get their stories out to the public to impress prospective voters with their talents and programs, and citizens need adequate information to make choices that may have profound political consequences. The battle over campaign news selection and framing is intense because the stakes are so high. Who gets covered, how, and how often and which issues and events are stressed may determine the winner. Coverage becomes most intense for key events, such as debates between the candidates or the results of polls tracking a race (Exit polls, pp. 74–76; Polls and media, pp. 219–220; Presidential debates, pp. 221–224). News stories are also important in shaping the images of the political parties, although that part of the coverage is usually incidental, rather than a straightforward analysis of party policies and activities (Political parties and the press, pp. 212–215).

In recent years, candidates, assisted by professional consultants, have turned increasingly to advertisements to present their positions in their own words and with their own selection of images, rather than leaving such matters to the not-so-tender mercy of reporters (Political content in advertising, pp. 206–209). In turn, news media have paid increasing attention to the content of advertisements and the strategies that candidates adopt in creating and placing these advertisements. Negative advertising has become a popular news focus. To what extent does it lure voters away from par-

ticular candidates and assure votes for their opponents? Does it generate cynicism about candidates and elections that turns potential voters into non-voters? How do these messages affect what voters think, and how does that vary by gender, age, and education? These are key questions for which scholars continually try to find answers. Given the instability of political life, definitive answers remain elusive.

Interest groups. The game of politics in the United States and elsewhere is played by groups whose interests are diverse and often at odds. Many groups therefore need extensive publicity to reach their goals (Civil society and the media, pp. 48–50). Journalists' decisions to grant or withhold publicity can be crucial for a group's success. This scenario forces groups to compete for media attention by making their stories more interesting and exciting than others' and by creating newsworthy events. Groups working for goals that resonate with journalists' sympathies have a better than average chance of obtaining publicity. Examples are protest movements that have objected to U.S. military ventures abroad, to the use of nuclear energy, to environmental pollution, and to various forms of discrimination against minority groups.

The need to offer journalists interesting, well-crafted stories often makes it difficult for low-status groups who lack professional public relations guidance to get their causes before large publics. This problem has harmed the image of some politically disadvantaged groups, such as people of color, women, homosexuals, and homeless people (Minority portrayals, pp. 161–162). These groups are largely ignored by the media except when unusual circumstances arise, which are apt to portray them negatively (African Americans and the media, pp. 6–9; Asian Americans and the media, pp. 16–18; Latinos and the media, pp. 126–128; Native Americans and the media, pp. 171–173; Women in politics and the media, pp. 305–307). This is one area where the Internet has made a significant difference because it provides an inexpensive way for disadvantaged groups to tell their story to large audiences (Alternative media, pp. 12–13; New media, pp. 175–178).

Executives, legislators, and judges. As mentioned, stories about the national political scene are staples of U.S. news coverage (Media and Congress, pp. 140–143; Media and the courts, pp. 143–145; Media and the presidency, pp. 145–149). They are given substantially more time and space than other aspects of politics, such as state-level and international news. This means that, politically speaking, U.S. audiences tend to focus, above all, on the national scene. The presidency receives almost daily coverage. Coverage of Congress and its members and the high courts is far less plentiful. Even the Supreme Court makes the news only intermittently, generally when it issues important decisions or during confirmation hearings for new justices.

Special events. The media devote large amounts of space and time periodically to national celebrations and events, such as inaugurations and commemorations, and to important developments and technological triumphs, such as advances in the fight against killer diseases and space exploration. There are generally numerous stories involving conflicts among public figures about the merits of proposed legislation in an array of areas, including homeland security, energy scarcities, social benefits for veterans, senior citizens, the disabled, and children, and environmental legislation related to air and water quality. Government policies involving health care reform, education subsidies, or changes in tax rates also provide frequent story material. These stories usually report the political maneuvering leading to policy decisions, rather than the substance of the policy and its likely societal impact. Inadequate health insurance then becomes a human-interest drama about a working-class family who has to skimp on medicine and visits to a doctor. The larger issues involved in health care insurance are apt to be slighted.

The activities of governors and mayors from large states and cities become newsworthy primarily if they involve major public policy issues or if an incumbent stands out because of race, gender, or prior newsworthy activities. News about crime and law enforcement is also plentiful because audiences want to know about such events, in part out of curiosity and also because of fear and a desire to avoid victimization. A few regular features, such as weather bulletins and sports reports, receive a substantial portion of scarce space as well. At times, a single dramatic story—for example, al-Qaida's attack on the United States or the death of former president Ronald Reagan or the fraud convictions of major business leaders—can preempt coverage of news that would otherwise be reported.

In general, the news media, especially in big cities, emphasize negative events and conflict. The unending litany of bad news has alienated and chased away many news consumers. Some social scientists believe that the cynicism created by news that dwells on human failures undermines support for the government and its leaders and generates political apathy. If that is the cost, should the media sharply reduce or shun tales of woe?

International news. As in the case of news about domestic affairs, the major problem in covering news about the world beyond the United States is that there is far more than can be published. International news also suffers from other deterrents to coverage. Most important, the public's interest in foreign news fluctuates. In addition, international news is expensive to produce, and media entrepreneurs are often unwilling to provide adequate staff and research resources for it. Language barriers can be troublesome and transmission difficulties can be enormous. For television news, which presents the bulk of foreign news for average Americans, restrictions on access to foreign locations and inadequate technical facilities often frustrate the quest for good visuals. Meaningful pictures are especially important for foreign news because they offer viewers unfamiliar sights that are difficult to imagine or describe.

International stories tend to focus on those countries with which the United States has its most significant good or bad relations. In recent years, these have usually included England, France, Germany, Italy, and Russia in Europe; Israel, Egypt, Saudi Arabia, Iran, and Iraq in the Middle East; and China, Japan, India, North Korea, and Pakistan in Asia. Aside from Canada and Mexico, the Western Hemisphere receives light coverage, except for news about illicit drug exports or civil strife or international business issues.

International coverage is not only unevenly distributed geographically, but is also uneven in substance. For countries that are familiar to many Americans, like England or Germany or Italy, foreign correspondents report about ordinary political life akin to their stories about U.S. domestic politics. When news media turn to areas of the world that they rarely cover, they do so mostly when these areas suffer major disasters, such as military conflicts, famines, earthquakes, or floods. This type of coverage conveys the faulty impression that these foreign countries are always in serious disarray (Media diplomacy, p. 154; Public diplomacy, pp. 234–236). Except during U.S. military involvement abroad, international news stories average less than 10 percent of the stories in the daily press.

Most foreign news stories, like their domestic counterparts, provide support for administration policies. The media usually report official views about the policies required to serve U.S. national interests and about the motivations of friendly and hostile countries. This changes only when numerous respected sources in Congress and elsewhere voice strong disagreement with the policies. That has happened occasionally with support for military ventures, such as the war in Vietnam and hostilities in Iraq. Media scholars refer to this phenomenon as "indexing" the news to the occurrence of publicly expressed dissent in high places (War and the media, pp. 296–300).

Social issues. Criticism of the mass media for what they do not cover is a reminder of their importance. Publicity matters. Aside from occasional feature stories, the news media slight many serious and persistent societal problems, such as alcoholism, teen pregnancy, deteriorating urban infrastructure, water pollution, and the like. The turn toward softer, human-interest-oriented news that began in the 1970s has led to heavy emphasis on a few problems, for instance, racism and AIDS, but many others remain slighted (Hard and soft news, pp. 106–107). It is important, however, to remember that entertainment venues cover many of the social issues neglected by news media. The fact that these stories appear in a fictional format does not decrease their political relevance, though it may reduce their political impact. Entertainment television has become a significant source of most Americans' knowledge about social institutions, including the criminal justice system, emergency medical services, or explorations of outer space.

Criticism of the Media

What should one make of the criticism leveled against U.S. news media? Although they have earned great praise from many audiences as well as from scholars and pundits, they have also been condemned as a scourge that debases social and political life in the United States. Their performance as a civics tutor and monitor of government has also been labeled a colossal failure (Fourth estate, pp. 87–88; Watchdog role, pp. 300–301).

The Impact of Expectations

The nature of the judgments passed on the media hinges heavily on the critics' expectations about the role that mass media should play. Harsh assessments tend to reflect an inclination to focus single-mindedly either on the media's flaws or their worthwhile achievements. In a world where dramatic pronouncements attract attention, pale, nuanced judgments are likely to be ignored. The controversy over the news media's performance as providers of civic information illustrates quite well the problem of clashing expectations. Scholars and pundits disagree about the requirements of democratic citizenship and citizens' ability and willingness

to meet them. Some expect citizens to have detailed knowledge about the major aspects of important political issues, yet others believe that a general understanding suffices for making sound voting decisions. Of course, views about what constitutes adequate civic information will differ depending on which view of knowledge requirements one shares. Similarly, different appraisals about citizens' interest in consuming political information bear on judgments about how news should be presented to entice the audience to pay attention to it.

Regardless of the critics' expectations, the evidence does not support a blanket indictment of the media's performance. First and foremost, *news media,* a collective noun, covers a broad range of enterprises, including newspapers, news magazines, television, radio, and the Internet. It also refers to individual institutions within these broad categories. In terms of supplying civic information to citizens, there exists a wide gulf between serious, politically oriented print media and television and radio programs on the one hand and the scores of tabloids and entertainment-oriented broadcasts on the other. Any citizen willing to make the effort to obtain in-depth political information about the major issues of the day can find it more readily than ever in U.S. media. The traditional media's Web sites, with their links to additional information sources, are veritable goldmines. The breadth of perspectives available on the Internet is mind-boggling.

The Dearth of Specialized News

Besides the ever-present constraints of scarce space and time, inadequate training of media staff is also a major reason for the inadequate coverage of many issues. For instance, social problems generally involve a plethora of interrelated complex issues that can be assessed quite differently by various experts. Most reporters are generalists who do not feel qualified to appraise the merits of health care plans or prison reform or water purity standards. They therefore shy away from such stories. The same holds for economic issues, although they might be of interest to average people because they affect their standard of living. There is a dearth of coverage of such issues in television broadcasts and most newspapers because employment trends, pricing structures, tax policies, and the like are difficult to understand and to simplify and report in an interesting and clear style. It may also be difficult to locate acceptable sources for such stories because business and labor leaders are far less inclined to cultivate press relations than are their counterparts in government or in academia.

Besides being criticized for sparse coverage of many crucial issues, U.S. media have also been condemned for ignoring the unique problems of disadvantaged social groups. Among the groups left out are the United States' ethnic and racial minorities, women, labor unions, left- and right-wing revolutionaries, as well as people with nontraditional lifestyles and orientations. These groups complain that lack of coverage or skewed coverage is counterproductive for their interests. It keeps them socially isolated and prevents issues that they care about and their problems from receiving sufficient attention from politicians and the public.

Complaints about lack of coverage are well-founded, but they must be put into the context of a media system flooded with far more information than it can possibly present. The addition of new beats must be balanced by removing or decreasing existing areas of coverage. Which ones should be sacrificed? No answer will satisfy most everyone because no consensus exists among media watchers about the criteria for determining what is newsworthy.

New technologies have made it possible to expand the number of news venues. If some of these devoted themselves to covering slighted people and issues, more problems could be aired and more viewpoints expressed. Would these media, however, reach the kinds of audiences that currently underrepresented groups desire? The answer is moot because the time resources available to most people are already extremely strained, so that little room remains to add more information venues without eliminating current ones considered essential for work and home life.

The Bias Issue

When the news media address controversial public policy issues—such as the dangers of nuclear energy generation or the merits of a new health care system—or when they cover political campaigns or demonstrations some critics charge that political bias dictated the choice of stories as well as their focus and tone (Media bias, pp. 149–153; Media elitism, pp. 154–157). If bias is defined as deliberately lopsided coverage or intentional slanting of news, the preponderance of research shows that bias is the exception rather than the rule. Most reporters in the mainstream press try to cover issues in a neutral manner, and most try to include a variety of viewpoints, although they rarely stray far from the political center. Many non-ideological factors influence the thrust of the

news. These spring from interpersonal relations among journalists and between them and their information providers, from professional norms within news organizations, and from constraints arising from news production processes, cost-benefit considerations, and legal regulations. As mentioned, economic concerns weigh heavily.

Given journalistic conventions, like the beat system, and resource constraints for collecting data and writing stories, it is not surprising that the end product rarely reflects all elite viewpoints and all shades of public opinion. Press output inevitably represents a small, unsystematic sample of the news of the day. To attract large, heterogeneous audiences—and keep news profitable—media enterprises dilute serious news to a greater or lesser degree with entertainment fare and with features that help people with daily activities. The economic imperative to produce profits for the parent organization accounts for many of the excesses of negativism and voyeuristic journalism.

The multiplication of news channels in the United States and elsewhere, and the ease with which audiences can tap them, have forced electronic as well as print media to compete more fiercely for audiences and for the advertisers whose payments cover much of the cost of news production. Shrinking profit margins in individual enterprises have forced cutbacks in staffs that put additional workloads on the remaining workforce. Although databases that can provide context for stories have grown exponentially, the time available to individual reporters to search them has shrunk. Besides, the traditional media's news turf has been eroded by new media's ability to broadcast twenty-four hours a day and thus immediately publish breaking stories.

Historical Perspectives

One must put complaints about the media into historical perspective (History of American journalism, pp. 109–112). They are occurring at a period in history when regard for most major institutions in the United States is at a low ebb, and it is fashionable to express cynicism. Nonetheless, when people are asked whether they are satisfied with their own daily newspaper or with the nightly television news broadcasts that they select, most respond positively. People like the products of the mass media well enough to consume them on a scale unheard of in the past. Three of every four adults claim that they read newspapers regularly; nearly all homes have radio and television and tune in extensively. In the average household, the radio is turned on for three hours a day and television for seven. Millions of people, by choice, have switched from pre-television sources of diversion to watching shows condemned as trash by social critics and often even by the viewers themselves. These same people ignore shows and newspaper stories with the critics' seal of approval.

History also shows that politicians and the general public are fickle and schizoid in their condemnation as well as their praise. They may applaud the media one day and condemn them the next depending on their satisfaction with the daily crop of news and entertainment. They may also split their judgments, hailing some offerings and damning others. On one hand, the nation's founders were the first to complain about the venal, lying press, but on the other the first to agree that, warts and all, it is the bedrock on which democratic freedoms rest. As the French say, "Plus ça change, plus c'est la même chose"—the more things change, the more they remain the same.

Doris A. Graber
University of Illinois–Chicago

ENCYCLOPEDIA
OF MEDIA AND POLITICS

A

ABC

The American Broadcasting Company (ABC) emerged in 1943, after the Federal Communications Commission ordered the National Broadcasting Company (NBC) to sell one of its two radio networks. In response, NBC sold the less-popular Blue Network, which became ABC. After World War II, ABC evolved into an early pioneer in television, acquiring Channel 7 in five major markets and making a big push to bring TV to the air. While it struggled to find successful programming, the network had some early hits with *Disneyland* and *The Mickey Mouse Club*. The DuMont network's exit from television broadcasting in 1955 supplied another boost to the network, as it allowed more affiliates to join ABC. Still, ABC remained the third-ranked TV network until the 1970s.

In the 1970s, ABC's appointment of Harry Reasoner and Howard K. Smith to the anchor desk of its evening news represented the network's first success in broadcast news. Throughout the decade, ABC's stature rose with its introduction of innovative sports and entertainment programming. Roone Arledge, chief of the sports division, received credit for many innovations, including instant replay, the popular *Wide World of Sports* and Olympics coverage, and the premiere of *Monday Night Football* in 1971. As head of programming, Fred Silverman introduced such hits as *Happy Days, Laverne and Shirley,* and *The Love Boat*. Later, under Arledge's management of the news division, the network applied sports programming techniques to news programs, including shorter segments and flashy graphics.

In the late 1970s, the network strengthened its news division with the introduction of *World News Tonight*. Originally featuring an unusual three-anchor format—with Peter Jennings in London, Frank Reynolds in New York, and Max Robinson, the first regular African American national news anchor, in Chicago—the program later adopted the more traditional one-anchor format, featuring Jennings. The Iran hostage crisis, which began in 1979 after Iranians took American diplomats captive in Tehran, spawned the development of *Nightline,* the successor to "America Held Hostage," which ABC put on air to provide viewers with late-night updates on the crisis. *Nightline* launched anchor Ted Koppel to a highly visible role in news reporting.

In 1985 Capital Cities, Inc. purchased ABC and its cable holdings, including the widely distributed ESPN sports networks, for $3.5 billion. The firm, renamed Capital Cities/ABC, was in turn bought by the Walt Disney Company in early 1996 for $19 billion. The company's name reverted to ABC, which took over Disney's TV operations. In buying Capital Cities/ABC, Disney acquired the network, cable networks, and local stations, thereby achieving a considerable degree of vertical integration. Disney, for example, owned the National Hockey League's Anaheim Mighty Ducks (until 2005) and broadcast hockey games on ESPN through the 2003–2004 season. Some critics of the ABC/Disney merger raised concerns about whether ABC would be able to exercise independent news judgment. Meanwhile, the company failed to fully realize sought-after synergies in entertainment and sports programming. ABC's poor ratings performance in the early 2000s contributed in part to calls for Disney chief Michael Eisner to relinquish power in 2004. Eisner did so, just as ABC's entertainment division scored big hits with *Lost* and *Desperate Housewives,* and the news division's *Good Morning America* finally caught up to long-time ratings leader *Today* on NBC.

See also *Arledge, Roone; Jennings, Peter; Koppel, Ted.*

REFERENCES

Holson, Laura M., and Geraldine Fabrikant. "Disney Chief to Leave, Setting Off Race for Job." *New York Times,* September 11, 2004, A1.

Quinn, Sterling. *Inside ABC: American Broadcasting Company's Rise to Power.* New York: Hastings House, 1979.

Slide, Anthony. *The Television Industry: A Historical Dictionary.* Westport, Conn.: Greenwood, 1991.

Walker, James, and Douglas Furguson. *The Broadcast Television Industry.* Boston: Allyn and Bacon, 1997.

Abell, Arunah Shepherdson

Arunah Shepherdson Abell (1806–1888), a journeyman printer from Rhode Island, founded the *Baltimore Sun* in 1837 as a four-page penny tabloid, in marked contrast to the six-cent "literary" dailies of the time. Abell most likely set the type himself. He went on to transform the paper into a respected chronicle of national and international news. Abell's newspaper innovations include the first use of rotary-impression, high-speed presses in the United States; a "pony express" system of telegraph and underwater cable for rapid transmission of stories; and use of railroads for gathering dispatches from correspondents as well as for distributing newspapers.

In 1847 the *Sun* broke the story of Vera Cruz city's surrender, which assured U.S. victory in the Mexican-American War. As Maryland teetered on the fence during the Civil War, Abell fought to remain politically independent and favored stories that he felt mattered in people's lives. Abell did not allow by-lines, forgoing the "glory of the writers" and focusing on continuity and quality of the paper's news and analysis. Three generations of Abell's descendants managed the *Sun* papers until they were sold in 1910.

REFERENCE

Williams, Harold A. *The Baltimore Sun, 1837–1987.* Baltimore, Md.: Johns Hopkins University Press, 1999.

Accuracy in Media

Accuracy in Media (AIM) is a watchdog group with the stated mission of encouraging members of the media to report news fairly and objectively without partisanship. Founded in 1969 by Reed Irvine, a popular lecturer and frequent guest on radio and television, AIM has worked against what Irvine believes is the news media's liberal bias. To accomplish AIM's mission, its members frequently attend the annual shareholder meetings of large media organizations. In addition, they participate in letter-writing campaigns to news organizations and newsrooms to voice their dissatisfaction with stories they believe to be incorrectly or unfairly reported. AIM publishes a twice-monthly newsletter, broadcasts a daily radio commentary, promotes a speaker's bureau, and syndicates a weekly newspaper column. It is the conservative ideological counterpart to Fairness and Accuracy in Reporting (FAIR).

See also *Fairness and Accuracy in Reporting.*

REFERENCES

Accuracy in Media, www.aim.org.

Gomery, Douglas. *Media in America: The Wilson Quarterly Reader.* Washington, D.C.: Woodrow Wilson Center Press, 1998.

Action for Children's Television

Action for Children's Television (ACT) was a grassroots activist group concerned about the lack of quality television programming offered to children. Founded by Peggy Charren and other suburban Boston homemakers in 1968, the group petitioned the Federal Communications Commission (FCC) in 1970 to require that broadcasters provide more programming suitable for children. ACT also concerned itself with advertising during children's programming. Although unsuccessful in its attempts to have the FCC ban commercials aimed at children, the group successfully lobbied the agency to reduce the amount of time allowed for commercials on children's television from sixteen to nine-and-a-half minutes per hour. The passage of the Children's Television Act of 1990, which mandates the FCC to increase the quantity and quality of children's programming, is considered one of ACT's major successes. In

1992 Charren disbanded ACT because she believed that the time had arrived for other citizens' groups to monitor the airwaves and pressure broadcasters.

See also *Children and the media.*

REFERENCES

Alperowicz, C., and R. Krock. *Rocking the Boat: Celebrating Fifteen Years of Action for Children's Television.* Newtonville, Mass.: Action for Children's Television, 1983.
Cole, B. G., and M. Oettinger. *Reluctant Regulators: The FCC and the Broadcast Audience.* Reading, Mass.: Addison-Wesley, 1978.

Adams, John

John Adams (1735–1826)—a lawyer, political philosopher, and one of the founders—was the first vice president of the United States and its second president. After graduating from Harvard College in 1755, Adams accepted a teaching position in Worcester, Massachusetts, while he pondered his future. In 1758 he changed course, apprenticing as a lawyer. His practice often took him to Boston, where he joined with a distant cousin, Samuel, in a group of professionals debating such topics of law as the Stamp Act of 1765. Based on these discussions, Adams wrote a series of anonymous articles for the *Boston Gazette* that was later reprinted as "A Dissertation on Canon and Feudal Law," tracing the origins of freedom and the natural rights of man. He moved to Boston in 1768 and continued to speak out in favor of the liberty of colonists within the British Empire. Adams gained considerable notoriety when in 1770 he defended British soldiers accused of murder in the Boston Massacre.

Adams served as a delegate to the First Continental Congress, held in 1774 in Philadelphia. During his subsequent years in Philadelphia, Adams argued for the decisive separation of the colonies from Britain, the appointment of George Washington as commander in chief of the Continental Army, and the formation of a naval force to challenge British supremacy at sea. Adams's extensive writings, including "Novanglus Papers" (1774–1775) and "Thoughts on Government" (1776), outlined the principles of liberty and order for the new American nation; his political writings contributed significantly to the foundation principles of the new republic.

During 1776–1777, Adams was appointed chairman of the Board of War and Ordnance, tasked with equipping the Continental Army. In 1778 he traveled to Paris as a diplomatic agent of the new United States to seek French commercial and military support. On his return to Massachusetts, Adams was selected to be a member of the state's constitutional convention, held in 1780. Later chosen as a delegate to the Paris peace negotiations between the United States and Britain, Adams alienated Benjamin Franklin and therefore withdrew to Holland, where he secured Dutch recognition of U.S. independence. He returned to Paris in 1782, joining Franklin and John Jay to secure the peace by concluding the Treaty of Paris of 1783. Adams negotiated loans for the United States from the Netherlands and commercial treaties in France before becoming the first U.S. minister to Britain in 1785. While in London, he expanded his political writings with *A Defence of the Constitutions of Government of the United States* (3 vols., 1787), which was influential in the deliberations of the Constitutional Convention in 1787.

In the United States' first presidential elections, Adams, the runner-up, was elected vice president in 1788 and was reelected in 1792. By the end of Washington's term as president, U.S. politics had developed a two-party system of Federalists and Republicans (later Democratic-Republicans). By a mere three electoral votes, in 1796 the Federalist Adams became the second U.S. president elected. As president, he tried to steer a moderate, nonpartisan path to bridge the differences between Thomas Jefferson's Republicans and Alexander Hamilton's Federalists. As tensions rose, Adams signed the Alien and Sedition Act of 1798, which threatened freedom of the press and freedom of speech by imposing harsh penalties on anyone who criticized the government. Enforcement of the act was selective, targeting the president's enemies, and led to Adams's defeat in the 1800 election. He retired to Quincy, Massachusetts, where he remained until his death.

See also *Alien and Sedition Acts of 1798; Hamilton, Alexander; Jefferson, Thomas.*

REFERENCES

Brown, Ralph Adams. *The Presidency of John Adams.* Lawrence: University Press of Kansas, 1975.
McCullough, David. *John Adams.* New York: Simon and Schuster, 2001.
Peterson, Merrill D. *Adams and Jefferson: A Revolutionary Dialogue.* New York: Oxford University Press, 1978.

Adversarial journalism

See *Watchdog role*

Advertising

See *Political content in advertising*

Advocacy journalism

In advocacy journalism, members of the media serve as advocates on behalf of groups or issues. The early American press was extremely partisan; newspapers during the revolutionary era only presented "their side" of the issues, reflecting the perspective of a political party or a social group. Such advocacy dominated journalism until the early twentieth century, when objective reporting became the professional norm. Advocacy journalism, however, continues to be practiced today.

Advocacy journalists believe that it is impossible to achieve true objectivity, so journalists have an obligation to use their expertise to interpret events. Those who practice advocacy journalism think of themselves as representing the public interest by transmitting political party or group perspectives. Public journalism, or civic journalism—favoring public rather than partisan or ideological advocacy—represents a new variant that puts the citizen at the center of the news process. It emphasizes news that encourages civic participation and engagement, and uses ordinary citizens as sources more than reliance on government officials.

Advocacy journalists have most often been party journalists, but they have also represented social movements, religious organizations, and other interests. Many ethnic and community publications operate under the advocacy model. Advocacy journalism is often grouped with muckraking journalism and literacy journalism under the category of new journalism.

See also *Muckraking.*

REFERENCES

Applegate, Edd. *Journalistic Advocates and Muckrakers.* Jefferson, N.C.: McFarland and Company, 1997.

Janowitz, Morris. "Professional Models in Journalism: The Gatekeeper and the Advocate." *Journalism Quarterly* 52 (1975).
Newman, Andy. "Is It Opinion, or Is It Expertise?" *American Journalism Review* 15, no. 2 (March 1993).
Schudson, Michael. "The Public Journalism Movement and Its Problems." In *The Politics of News: The News of Politics,* edited by Doris Graber et al. Washington, D.C.: CQ Press, 1998.

African Americans and the media

The absence of extensive social contact between blacks and whites increases the power of the mass media to improve the opportunities of African Americans to further the quality of their lives. For the many whites who live their lives detached from those of blacks, television, movies, and newspapers have become the default sources of information about African Americans. The images and information that flow through these channels have the capacity to destroy stereotypes that encourage discrimination or to reinforce them. The media both reflect the position of blacks in U.S. society and provide a means for changing policies to further reduce racial inequality. White political attitudes are a critical component of the mechanisms for policy change.

The mass media are far from being the primary determinants of the quality of life for African Americans, but they can play an important part in selecting and emphasizing the information that influences the mental maps of its consumers. During the civil rights movement of the 1960s, print and broadcast media sympathetically conveyed horrific images of injustice that prodded Congress to pass landmark legislation that continues today to aid African American political influence and social mobility. The mass media, like other major institutions, are susceptible to political and economic pressures that shape their agendas. There is nothing inevitable about the selection of criteria for shaping mass media content, but the criteria chosen—whether motivated by social justice or a ratings-driven profit motive—can have indirect but tangible effects on the lives of African Americans.

The civil rights legislation of the 1960s not only provided legal protection for African Americans and other minorities and broadened opportunities for them, it also changed the way the country talks about race. Powerful norms against the public expression of racist opinion accompanied the legal

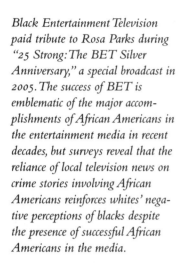

Black Entertainment Television paid tribute to Rosa Parks during "25 Strong: The BET Silver Anniversary," a special broadcast in 2005. The success of BET is emblematic of the major accomplishments of African Americans in the entertainment media in recent decades, but surveys reveal that the reliance of local television news on crime stories involving African Americans reinforces whites' negative perceptions of blacks despite the presence of successful African Americans in the media.

commitments to the ideals of racial equality. According to studies of public opinion, among white Americans near-universal support exists on such issues as equal access to jobs, public accommodations, and education. There remains a gap, however, between the stated commitment to such ideals and their implementation. Examples of the gap include the resistance by some whites to busing and affirmative action. In response to some scholars who assert nearly universal affirmation among whites of principles of equality as evidence of the virtual disappearance of racial prejudice and discrimination from the lives of African Americans, others point to continuing disparities between blacks and whites as evidence of white resistance and continuing racial discrimination.

Opportunities for African Americans have improved since the civil rights revolution, but inequalities remain. For example, the *Statistical Abstract of the United States* reveals median black household income to have been 65 percent that of white household income in 2003 and black unemployment to have been twice that of white unemployment, a ratio that has varied little since 1970. Meanwhile, the level of segregation, arguably the most influential factor in racial inequality, has fallen, albeit unevenly. For example, the 2000 census revealed a decrease in segregation in the West and the South, the fastest growing parts of the United States, but continuing high levels in the rust belts of the Northeast and Midwest.

These changes have led political scholars to differing conclusions about the extent and significance of change in white American racial attitudes. While some see a complete turnaround, others point to continuing racism disguised by other, more acceptable means. For example, a few scholars argue that political ideology rather than racial animus drives white Americans' opinion on race-targeted social policy. According to this view, opposition to affirmative action is based more on adherence to core American beliefs and values—for instance, individualism—rather than underlying prejudice. Other scholars argue that appeals to such beliefs and values are simply a ruse for rationalizing racial inequality (or "laissez-faire racism"). One way of resolving such differences is by examining research that points to the continuing political influence of race-based appeals, as in the Willie Horton ad during the 1988 Bush presidential campaign.

The success of such racial appeals depends on eliciting an unconscious response based on the continued presence and influence of racial stereotypes among whites. Powerful social norms may prevent public expressions of agreement with such stereotypes, but the sentiment behind such beliefs can be activated at an unconscious level and influence perceptions and behavior nonetheless. For example, social psychological research shows that although most Americans reject racial stereotypes, they can be influenced nonetheless by images or issues paired repeatedly in mass media content. This explains, for example, how a politician can plausibly deny talking about race but still manage to raise the issue through the language he or she uses, such as raising the topic of "urban" crime. Although whites are statistically much less likely to become victims of crime, news reports that focus heavily on black-on-black crimes can elicit fear and thereby reinforce negative images of African Americans in general.

Much of the research on mainstream mass media content shows positive changes in increased levels of black visibility and near elimination of the negative stereotypes common before the civil rights movement. For example, it would be inconceivable today for a mainstream television show or movie to depict blacks in the subordinate role of a handservant to whites. Today blacks appear as prominent characters in highly rated prime-time programming, playing professionals and executives among other roles. In some ways, these changes reflect (and perhaps exaggerate) the real-world success of that fraction of the black population who have experienced upward social mobility following the civil rights revolution.

At the same time, however, reflecting the relatively low number of interracial relationships compared to same-race coupling in real life, television and motion pictures continue to treat black and white romantic intimacy as somewhat taboo. This convention is sometimes violated for dramatic effect, but the larger pattern reflects the lack of close contact that prevents interracial relationships from being treated as an afterthought. *The Jeffersons* and *Six Feet Under* aside, there have been few successful television series with an interracial couple or more than a handful of commercials depicting such a relationship. One might object to such a critique based on the necessity of the mass media to adhere to conventions of reality, but close examination of media content—particularly prime-time television and movies—reveals less than a reliance on such fidelity concerning other issues, even among the wave of prime-time "reality" series.

The prominence of black success in television entertainment may ironically have unintended negative consequences in terms of white attitudes about race. Whereas studies of national surveys of racial attitudes show that during the mid-1940s most whites believed blacks to be intellectually inferior to whites, today less than 10 percent believe so. Instead, recent national surveys reveal that two out of three whites believe blacks could do better if they "tried harder." In short, moral weakness has replaced biological inferiority as the widely accepted explanation among whites for continuing black disadvantage. This supposed lack of effort seems a natural conclusion given the belief among whites that passage of civil rights legislation eliminated discrimination against blacks. Racial discrimination being less visible in the real world today and the prominence of successful blacks in the mass media (for example, Bill Cosby, Oprah Winfrey, Tiger Woods), in politics (Barack Obama, Colin Powell, Condoleezza Rice), and as anchors on national and local news programs makes all the more compelling the explanation of perceived black moral weakness. If these blacks have achieved prominence and success, the reason for the failures of others must be their lack of effort.

Meanwhile, in contrast to the pictures of success in prime time, crime committed by blacks has become a staple of many local evening newscasts. Studies of local news content reveal a consistent emphasis on seemingly random violence committed by anonymous black lawbreakers. Without providing the contexts of history, continuing economic disadvantage, poor educational opportunities, and discrimination, local news reinforces white attitudes of black moral failure.

A distinctly African American media has existed, albeit unevenly, for some time. It developed in part in response to the tradition of unflattering portrayals of blacks in the broader media as well as an effort to express and reflect this unique subculture within American society. *Freedom's Journal,* the first newspaper aimed at African Americans, was founded in 1827, and other notable papers, such as Frederick Douglass's *North Star* and its successors, filled a niche. A fledgling abolitionist press published in the North up through the Civil War. In subsequent years, black newspapers, including Marcus Garvey's *Negro World* in Harlem (1918–1933), chronicled the changing circumstances of African Americans while at the same time promoting their causes and speaking out on such issues as lynching, segregation, and inequality. Many black newspapers lasted only a few years, falling victim to the lack of education and economic status of their target population. Nevertheless, in the period before and just after World War II, the black press grew in circulation and in stridency in support of civil rights.

The success of the civil rights movement and the diversification of the mainstream media since the 1970s contributed to a decline in the circulation and prominence of papers like the *Chicago Defender* and Baltimore's *Afro-American,* though they have by no means disappeared. African American magazines such as *Ebony* and *Jet* along with Black

Entertainment Television (BET) continue to provide minority perspectives and an outlet for the black community and others. To some extent, these media have survived by imitating some aspects of mainstream media while retaining an ethnic tint to their coverage. Like other specialty, "narrowcasting" outlets, African American media represent a platform from which politicians can reach black audiences; take for example the appearances on BET by Bill Clinton during the 1996 presidential campaign and by Sen. Trent Lott (R-Miss.) to apologize for racially insensitive remarks he made in 2002. Despite gains made by African Americans within the media and without in the decades since the 1950s, the number of blacks in the mainstream media remains relatively small and the coverage of issues affecting African Americans fairly limited.

REFERENCES

Bobo, L. Race, "Public Opinion, and the Social Sphere." *Public Opinion Quarterly* 61, no. 1 (Spring, 1997): 1–15.

Entman, R. M., and A. Rojecki. *The Black Image in the White Mind: Media and Race in America.* Chicago: University of Chicago Press, 2000.

Glaeser, E. L., and J. L. Vigdor. "Racial Segregation in the 2000 Census: Promising News." Brookings Institution, Washington, D.C., 2001, www.brook.edu/es/urban/census/glaeser.pdf.

Jackman, M. R. "Individualism, Self-Interest, and Racism." *Social Science Quarterly* 77, no. 4 (December 1996): 760–767.

Kinder, D. R., and L. M. Sanders. *Divided by Color: Racial Politics and Democratic Ideals.* Chicago: University of Chicago Press, 1996.

Massey, D., and N. Denton. *American Apartheid: Segregation and the Making of the Underclass.* Cambridge, Mass.: Harvard University Press, 1993.

Mendelberg, T. "Executing Hortons: Racial Crime in the 1988 Presidential Campaign." *Public Opinion Quarterly* 61, no. 1 (Spring 1997): 134–157.

———. *The Race Card: Campaign Strategy, Implicit Messages, and the Norm of Equality.* Princeton, N.J.: Princeton University Press, 2001.

Newkirk, Pamela. "The Minority Press: Pleading Our Own Cause." In *Institutions of American Democracy: The Press,* edited by Geneva Overholser and Kathleen Hall Jamieson. New York: Oxford University Press, 2005.

Schuman, H., C. Steeh, L. Bobo, and M. Krysan, eds. *Racial Attitudes in America: Trends and Interpretations.* Cambridge, Mass.: Harvard University Press, 1998.

Thernstrom, S., and A. Thernstrom. *America in Black and White.* New York: Simon and Schuster, 1997.

Agenda setting

Agenda setting is the process through which the issues that receive prominent attention from political actors and the news media become the issues that the public believes are most important. Although powerful leaders, such as the president or members of Congress, are often considered agenda-setters, the heart of agenda setting lies with the media. In particular, the media's ability to focus the attention of the public on a small set of pertinent issues to the essential omission of others is what makes the agenda-setting effect important.

To determine whether the focus on an issue or set of issues results from the agenda-setting effect, it is essential to show how the issue or issues receiving prominent media coverage for a period of time (usually a month or more) become increasingly important to members of the public. Thus, the media's agenda—the amount of news coverage or political advertising afforded an issue during a specific time period—is the first variable that must be measured. The second variable is the public's agenda, which is typically measured by charting over time the response to the survey question "What is the most important problem facing this country today?" The agenda-setting hypothesis is confirmed if an increasing amount of coverage about an issue corresponds to an increase in the percentage of people who believe that that issue is the nation's most important problem.

Theoretical and empirical demonstrations of agenda setting are somewhat new to the study of political science, journalism, and psychology. Maxwell McCombs and Donald Shaw provided the first major evidence of agenda setting by illustrating how the agendas of nine major news outlets in Chapel Hill, North Carolina, during the 1968 elections correlated with the issues that the residents of that area came to believe were most important. In the 1980s, Shanto Iyengar and Donald Kinder used experimental analysis to show that by focusing on a few key issues, the news media can set the public's agenda. These studies provide evidence for what is sometimes referred to as first-level agenda setting—that is, when the news media are able to exert influence over what issues people think about without necessarily affecting what people think.

Second-level agenda setting, more commonly called framing, affects how people think about issues. For example, do people think of the abortion issue as being about the "right to life" or the "right to choose"? Competing lawmakers or candidates for political office will typically frame issues in different ways, hoping to sway public support in their favor. Although first-level agenda setting effects have been widely confirmed in the United States and other countries, scholarly analysis of second-level agenda-setting effects have received mixed results. On the one hand, changing how an issue is framed consistently alters people's opinions about the issue. On the other hand, the effects diminish significantly when issue framings compete with each other, as they often do in media coverage of political events or in the context of the two-party system. Nevertheless, agenda setting at either the first or second level can influence public opinion and voting behavior.

REFERENCES

Druckman, James N. "Political Preference Formation: Competition, Deliberation, and the (Ir)relevance of Framing Effects." *American Political Science Review* 98, no. 4 (November 2004): 671–686.

Iyengar, Shanto, and Donald R. Kinder. *News That Matters: Television and American Opinion.* Chicago: University of Chicago Press. 1987.

McCombs, Maxwell, and Donald Shaw. "The Agenda-Setting Function of the Mass Media." *Public Opinion Quarterly* 36 (1972): 176–187.

Sniderman, Paul M., and Sean M. Theriault. "The Structure of Political Argument and the Logic of Issue Framing." In *Studies in Public Opinion,* edited by William Saris and Paul M. Sniderman. Princeton, N.J.: Princeton University Press, 2005.

Agnew, Spiro T.

Spiro Theodore Agnew (née Anagnostopoulos, 1918–1996) was the thirty-ninth vice president of the United States, serving under President Richard M. Nixon from 1969 to 1973. He previously had been governor of Maryland from 1967 to 1969. A World War II and Korean War veteran, Agnew had also held the post of Baltimore County chief executive, to which he was elected in 1962.

As vice president, Agnew accepted the role of lightning rod for the Nixon administration and delivered direct assaults against administration critics, including the media and liberal politicians. He branded those opposed to the Vietnam War "an effete corps of impudent snobs" and the media as "a small and unelected elite" unrepresentative of the American people. In 1973 Agnew resigned the vice presidency—when he pled no contest to federal income tax evasion stemming from his role in state politics. The only other vice president to have resigned was John C. Calhoun of South Carolina, who did so to join the U.S. Senate in 1832.

REFERENCE

Witcover, Jules. *A Heartbeat Away: The Investigation and Resignation of Spiro T. Agnew.* New York: Viking, 1974.

Vice President Spiro T. Agnew (left) with President Richard M. Nixon in 1968. Agnew, who developed a reputation for bashing the media, was forced to resign over a tax-evasion scandal in 1973, ending a career in politics that included serving as governor of Maryland.

Ailes, Roger

Roger Eugene Ailes (1940–) is a television executive and media consultant widely acknowledged for his work with political campaigns. Ailes began his television career in 1962 as a property assistant for *The Mike Douglas Show,* which was at the time a local Cleveland talk show. He eventually became the show's executive producer, receiving two Emmy Awards for it in 1967 and 1968.

In 1967 Ailes had chided Republican candidate Richard M. Nixon, making his second run for the presidency, "Television is not a gimmick, and if you think it is, you'll lose again." Nixon selected Ailes to be his media adviser for his 1968 campaign. In 1969 Ailes founded Ailes Communications, a media production and consulting firm based in New York City. He would go on to serve as a media consultant for the successful presidential campaigns of Republicans Ronald Reagan and George H. W. Bush, garnering him the status of a political media "genius." Ailes was a key force behind the controversial "Willie Horton ad" that severely damaged Democrat Michael Dukakis's presidential candidacy in 1988.

Ailes won a third Emmy as executive producer and director of "Television and the Presidency" (1984), a television special. He became president of CNBC, NBC's cable channel, in 1993 and chairman and chief executive officer of Fox News and the Fox News Channel in 1996. Ailes is a co-author, with Jon Kraushar, of *You Are the Message: Secrets of the Master Communicators* (1988).

REFERENCES

Barnes, Fred. "Pulling the Strings." *New Republic,* February 22, 1988, 11–14.

Collins, Scott. *Crazy Like a Fox: The Inside Story of How Fox News Beat CNN.* New York: Portfolio, 2004.

Hayden, Thomas. "Natural-Born Networker." *U.S. News & World Report,* October 21, 2005, 56–58, "Roger Ailes—Packaging Images." *U.S. News & World Report,* February 8, 1988, 58–59.

Stengel, Richard. "The Man behind the Message—If Anyone Can Build a Better Candidate, It Is Roger Ailes." *Time,* August 22, 1988, 28–29.

Alien and Sedition Acts of 1798

The Federalist-controlled Congress passed the Alien and Sedition Acts of 1798 in response to a potential war with France. The Alien Act allowed the president in times of war

This 1798 engraving depicts the congressional melee over Republican congressman Matthew Lyon being punished for "seditious libel" after criticizing President John Adams and his Federalist Party.

to detain and deport foreign nationals believed to be a threat to the government. Although the Federalists declared the law necessary to protect the nation from French sympathizers and saboteurs, it was applied to political opponents of the Federalist Party. In particular, authorities used the act to stifle dissent among English and Irish aliens who opposed the Federalist Party's support of Great Britain and identified with the Democratic-Republican Party.

The Sedition Act allowed authorities to charge with seditious libel any person who published an article containing "false, scandalous, and malicious" writings about the U.S. government or President John Adams, a Federalist. Under this law, numerous Republicans—including newspaper editors, writers, and Representative Matthew Lyon of Vermont—were sent to prison or fined for criticizing the president or the Federalist Party. Many viewed the act as purely partisan, because it failed to punish criticism of the vice president, Republican Thomas Jefferson, thus allowing Federalist newspapers to attack Jefferson with impunity. In addition, both laws were drafted to expire in 1801, at the end of President Adams's term.

See also *Adams, John; Jefferson, Thomas.*

REFERENCES

Miller, John C. *Crisis in Freedom: The Alien and Sedition Acts.* Boston: Little, Brown, and Company, 1951.

Rosenfeld, Richard. *American Aurora.* New York: St. Martin's Press, 1997.

Stone, Geoffrey R. *Perilous Times: Free Speech in Wartime.* New York: W. W. Norton and Company, 2004.

Alternative media

On a basic level, the term *alternative media* covers a wide range of media—from community radio to fan 'zines to news Web sites—that challenge the status quo. At the same time, however, the concept remains a slippery one, fraught with multiple meanings. Defining precisely what the alternative media are is problematic. Defining it too broadly or narrowly risks conceptual imprecision and limits the term's usefulness. Complicating this issue are the various modifiers frequently folded into or used interchangeably with "alternative media," including "citizens'," "community," "participatory," "radical," and "independent." Labeling as "alternative" all of these subgroups may lead to overlooking significant nuances.

The most expansive and popular use of "alternative media" includes all media that are somehow opposed to or are in tension with mainstream media. The communications scholar James Hamilton argues that most definitions of alternative media cast mainstream media as "maximizing audiences by appealing to safe, conventional formulas, and [alternative media foregoes] the comfortable, depoliticizing formulas to advocate programs of social change." Hamilton and others have suggested, however, that this dichotomy is oversimplified. The radical media theorist John Downing argues that to speak of alternative media in this way is almost oxymoronic. "Everything, at some point," he notes, "is alter-native to something else." As with many cultural objects and practices, today's alternative may be co-opted and reappropriated to become tomorrow's mainstream. For example, the commercial penny press began as an alternative medium to the partisan press.

Despite the generic qualities associated with so-called alternative media, a number of recurring themes across competing definitions fortunately help clarify it (though there are exceptions). For example, several prominent theorists of alternative media define it as much by organizational processes as by front-end content. In other words, the ways in which the media are produced and the social relations they assist can be as important as the final media product. Oftentimes, these social relations stress participatory processes and community involvement in media making. Chris Atton argues, "Alternative media … are crucially about offering the means for democratic communication to people who are normally excluded from media production." James Hamilton similarly synthesizes a number of theoretical threads: "[Alternative media's] collective value is in their exploration of new forms of organizing more participatory techniques of media and more inclusive, democratic forms of communication." According to this definition, alternative media allow those who are most often underrepresented or misrepresented in mainstream media to tell their own stories through their own media. Atton argues that such characteristics as noncommercial sites for distribution, transformed

The rise of blogs, such as Bill Nowling's "Lunch Bucket Conservative," illustrates the power of alternative media as a means for private individuals to engage in political advocacy and media discourse.

social relations, roles, and responsibilities, and transformed communication processes comprise this democratization of the media. A community radio station with rotating leadership roles or a public access channel produced by a cooperatively run organization exemplifies these qualities.

Alternative media have historically been a crucial resource for social movements and marginalized groups in the United States. Revolutionary pamphleteers helped fan the flames of independence against the British. A vibrant abolitionist press kept alive the antislavery movement for decades preceding the Civil War. A popular working-class press proved similarly integral to the burgeoning labor movement during the first half of the twentieth century. In the early 1900s, *Appeal to Reason,* the advertising-supported socialist newspaper, reached nearly a million subscribers and helped advance the socialist candidate Eugene Debs's presidential ambitions. During the nineteenth and twentieth centuries, an ethnic press provided sustenance for various marginalized cultural groups. Likewise, an underground press helped sustain the civil rights movement and other activist groups during the 1960s.

More recently, the Internet has complicated the distinction between alternative and mass media by lowering barriers to entry and enabling new network-based forms of media organizing. In the broader sense of alternative media, this simply may mean a wider distribution for non-mainstream political points of views, such as those found on Alternet or Commondreams.org. In other cases, the political opportunities enhanced by the Internet are far more radical and democratizing. A classic example of the latter is Indymedia.org. Founded during the November 1999 World Trade Organization protests in Seattle, Indymedia allows anyone with Internet access to "be the media" by uploading news content (print, photos, audio, or video) to the Web site. Operated according to such anarchic and radical democratic principles as consensus-based decision making, as of early 2006 there were more than 150 Indymedia sites across six continents. With the explosion of the blogosphere, this type of do-it-yourself (diy) media is increasingly commonplace. As a whole, this subgroup of alternative media is sometimes called cyberactivism, or simply Internet activism. The conservative counter to Indymedia, a radical left-wing organization, is the grassroots site Free Republic. In fall 2004, the latter gained recognition during the "Rathergate" affair by targeting a news story by Dan Rather that relied on unveri-

fied documents criticizing President George W. Bush's military service.

The ways in which alternative media challenge mainstream assumptions and rearrange social relationships often places them consciously or by default under the rubric of progressive politics. Conservatives, however, produce alternative media as well. Christian Right groups increasingly use the Internet to organize constituents, as do right-wing white supremacist groups. By some measures of Internet sites and traffic, politically conservative groups and individuals dominate the blogosphere in terms of numbers and impact.

Other issues, such as institutional questions of ownership, participation, and funding, also touch on the porous boundaries between mainstream and alternative media. For example, there is an assumption that alternative media are small-scale nonprofit organizations independently owned and run on a volunteer and collective basis. Although many community media organizations do indeed operate in such a fashion, this standard fails based on any number of media organizations sometimes included in the expansive definition of "alternative media," including the *Village Voice,* the British *Guardian,* public broadcasting, and even conservative talk radio, with its audience of millions.

The debate over the exact meaning of "alternative media" promises to continue. Broadly speaking, alternative media counter mainstream representations and assumptions. More specifically, alternative media suggest democratized media production that tends toward the noncommercial, the community based, and the marginalized. Moreover, technological changes, such as the Internet, will continue to call into question any definition about what constitutes alternative media and mainstream media. In the end, one must remember that when discussing alternative media, as with all concepts and categories, the map is not the territory, but merely an approximation.

REFERENCES

Atton, Chris. *Alternative Media.* London: Sage Publications, 2002.
Downing, John. *Radical Media: Rebellious Communication and Social Movements.* Thousand Oaks, Calif.: Sage Publications, 2001.
Hamilton, James. "Alternative Media: Conceptual Difficulties, Critical Possibilities." *Journal of Communication Inquiry* 24 (2000): 357–378.

American Society of Newspaper Editors

The American Society of Newspaper Editors (ASNE) was founded in 1922 as a forum for directing editors of U.S. newspapers to address problems and issues in promoting the general interests of the newspaper editing profession. ASNE established as its principles the encouragement of ethical and professional performance; pursuit of journalistic responsibility; freedom of the press; independence, truth, and accuracy; impartiality; and fair play. In 1988 the organization adopted a newsroom diversity mission statement with the goal of hiring and promoting people of color in the newsroom and increasing the number of women in management. Along with the National Newspaper Publishers Association and the National Press Club, ASNE reflects the institutionalized professionalism of modern journalism, and like these other organizations, is sometimes the target of appeals or complaints about coverage by politicians.

REFERENCE

American Society of Newspaper Editors, www.asne.org.

American Spectator

The *American Spectator* is a magazine of opinion and investigative journalism on the conservative side of the political spectrum. R. Emmett Tyrell Jr. founded the magazine in Bloomington, Indiana, in 1967 as the *Alternative,* a right-leaning response to the leftist publications prevalent on college campuses. It became the *Alternative: An American Spectator* in 1974 and three years later adopted its current name. Libertarian and sometimes even liberal voices have appeared in its pages along with conservative ones.

The *American Spectator* rose to prominence and wide circulation in the early 1990s with hard-hitting exposés of Anita Hill, who accused Supreme Court Justice Clarence Thomas of sexual harassment, and by breaking the "troopergate" story of former president Bill Clinton's sexual escapades, including the sexual harassment charges of Paula Jones that eventually led to Clinton's impeachment. The magazine's very success in some ways, however, led to its decline. Financial difficulties from legal and staff problems arising from its Arkansas Project—an investigation of Clinton and other matters—led Tyrell to sell the magazine in 2000; its circulation plummeted. He and others bought it back in 2003. Tyrell assumed the mantle of editor in chief and has since tried to return the magazine to its origins.

REFERENCES

American Spectator, www.spectator.org.
York, Byron. "The Life and Death of *The American Spectator.*" *Atlantic Monthly,* November 2001, 91–110.

Anderson, Jack

Jackson Northman Anderson (1922–2005) was a Pulitzer Prize–winning and sometimes controversial newspaper columnist. Anderson began his journalistic career writing for his local Utah newspaper, the *Murray Eagle,* and then joined the *Salt Lake Tribune* in 1940 before serving as a Mormon missionary from 1941 to 1944 and as a World War II correspondent in 1945. He later joined Drew Pearson's "Washington Merry-Go-Round" staff at the *Washington Post,* taking over the column after Pearson's death in 1969. Along with other liberal journalists, he became a strong opponent of Sen. Joseph McCarthy and helped bring him down.

Anderson sparked controversy with his unorthodox methods of finding news and a penchant toward sensationalism that *Time* described as an "uneven mixture of muckraking and kiss-and-tell gossip." He broke many important news stories, including some related to the Watergate scandal, the CIA plot to assassinate Fidel Castro, and the secret relationship between the United States and Pakistan. His work on this last story won him a Pulitzer Prize for journalism in 1972. Anderson also wrote *Confessions of a Muckraker* (1979) and *The Washington Money-Go-Round* (1997). He died of complications from Parkinson's disease in December 2005. In 2006 Anderson made headlines posthumously when it was reported that the FBI wanted to search his files in a hunt for classified documents from his days as an investigative reporter. His family rejected the agency's request.

REFERENCES

Anderson, Jack, and James Boyd. *Confessions of a Muckraker: The Inside Story of Life in Washington during the Truman, Eisenhower, Kennedy and Johnson Years.* New York: Random House, 1979.
"Anderson's Brass Ring." *Time,* January 17, 1972, 34.
Buckley, William F., Jr. "The Theory of Jack Anderson." *National Review,* May 12, 1972, 545.
Martin, Douglas. "Jack Anderson, Investigative Journalist Who Angered the Powerful, Dies at 83," *New York Times,* December 18, 2005, 58.

Anonymous sources

See *Ethics and the media; First Amendment*

Apple, R. W., Jr.

Raymond Walker Apple Jr. (1934–2006) was an award-winning *New York Times* journalist and editor. He published under the name R. W. Apple Jr. (and was known as Johnny Apple among colleagues and media observers). Apple served in the U.S. Army, working as a speechwriter for the commanding general of the Continental Army Command, and later graduated from Columbia University in 1961. He went to work as a reporter for the *Wall Street Journal* before moving to NBC News as a television writer and correspondent in 1961. Apple joined the *New York Times* in 1963, eventually becoming a chief correspondent and an associate editor. He was the *Times'* chief Washington correspondent from 1985 to 1997 and its Washington bureau chief from 1992 to 1997.

Apple traveled to more than 100 countries, writing about their art, culture, foreign and domestic affairs, and politics. He covered major international events, including the Vietnam War, the Iranian Revolution and hostage crisis, the collapse of the Soviet Union and communism, and the 1991 Persian Gulf War. He interviewed every U.S. president from Lyndon B. Johnson to George W. Bush. Later in his career, Apple served as an associate editor at the *New York Times* while continuing to write front-page news analysis as well as stories on travel and food. He died in October 2006.

REFERENCES

Apple, R. W., Jr. *Apple's America: The Discriminating Traveler's Guide to 40 Great Cities in the United States and Canada.* New York: North Point Press, 2005.

Apple, R. W., Jr. *Apple's Europe: An Uncommon Guide.* New York: Atheneum, 1986.

Trillin, Calvin. "Profiles: Newshound—The Triumph, Travels and Movable Feasts of R. W. Apple, Jr." *New Yorker,* September 29, 2003, 70–81.

Arledge, Roone

Roone Pinkney Arledge (1931–2002), a pioneering television producer and executive, revolutionized televised sports and news broadcasting and was responsible for some of television's best-known programs. Arledge began his television career at the DuMont network in 1952, served in the army from 1953 to 1955, and also in 1955 landed a stage manager's assignment at New York's WRCA-TV (NBC), where he advanced to producer.

In 1960 Arledge joined ABC to produce a ten-minute weekly sports segment covering NCAA football. He shortly thereafter introduced *ABC's Wide World of Sports,* in 1961, and in 1970 launched *Monday Night Football.* Arledge pioneered many innovative changes, including instant replay. He had advanced rapidly at ABC, getting promoted to network vice president in 1964 and president of ABC Sports in 1968. He promoted one of sport's most famous phrases—"the thrill of victory, the agony of defeat"—as the tagline for ABC Sports and produced all ten ABC Olympics broadcasts, including the 1972 Munich games.

Arledge took on the additional responsibility of president of ABC News in 1977. He applied the same energy and creativity to the network's news programming that had proved so successful in its sports division. From nightly updates on the Iranian hostage crisis that began in 1979, Arledge developed the late night news program *Nightline* in 1980 and chose Ted Koppel as its anchor. He also created and added *20/20* and *Prime Time Live* to ABC's prime-time broadcast lineup. When the industry discounted David Brinkley as past his prime, Arledge thought otherwise and rejuvenated the veteran journalist's career with *This Week with David Brinkley* in 1981. Arledge ran ABC Sports until 1986 and ABC News until 1998.

REFERENCES

Arledge, Roone. *Roone.* New York: HarperCollins, 2003.

Gunther, Marc. *The House That Roone Built: The Inside Story of ABC News.* Boston: Little, Brown, 1994.

O'Neil, Terry. *The Game behind the Game: High Pressure, High Stakes in Television Sports.* New York: Harper and Row, 1989.

Sugar, Bert Randolph. *The Thrill of Victory: The Inside Story of ABC Sports.* New York: Hawthorne, 1978.

Asian Americans and the media

Like many other ethnic groups, the growing Asian American communities in the United States often see themselves represented in mainstream media portrayals as stereotypes, but they have also created ethnic-specific and pan-ethnic media that cater to their needs and tastes. Moreover, their struggles to obtain media access have resulted in changes in advertising, Hollywood representations, and campaign advertising.

Asian Americans in the United States number 15 million, representing 4.5 percent of the population. By 2050, they are expected to represent more than 8 percent of the total U.S. population. Three-fifths of Asian Americans are foreign born, of which 52 percent are naturalized citizens. Some 2.3 million Asian Americans speak another language at home, and they speak more languages than any other ethnic group. More than 80 percent of Asian Americans claim to speak English "very well." Though largely first generation, some Asian Americans—in particular those among Chinese Americans, Filipino Americans, and Japanese Americans—are now into their fifth generation in the United States.

Asian Americans are overall more educated than the general U.S. population. They have the highest proportion of college graduates of any race or ethnic group: 49 percent have a bachelor's degree or higher, 87 percent of those above 25 years of age are high school graduates, and 20 percent hold an advanced degree. Asian Americans have become a vital force in the U.S. economy. They have the highest median household income in the country—$57,518 in 2004—and they earn an overall per capita income that is 84 percent that of non-Hispanic whites and have poverty rates between that of whites and other racial minorities. Asian Americans represent the highest proportion of small business owners, with 1.1 million businesses in 2002. Their business receipts totaled $343.3 billion in 2002. Combined Asian American buying power in 2005 was $397 billion and is forecast to reach $579 billion by 2010. By 2007 Asian Americans will have investment holdings in excess of $1 trillion.

The state of relations between Asia and the United States continually affects Asian Americans. For example, during the nineteenth and early twentieth centuries, U.S. involvement in Asia led to massive changes, disruptions, and dislocations in China, Korea, Japan, and the Philippines that were accompanied by large-scale migrations of workers to the United States and its colonial possessions. Asian labor, being cheap

Addressing stereotypical depictions of Asian Americans has been a central theme in Margaret Cho's career as an actor and comedian.

and widely available, became essential to U.S. business interests and contributed to the economic development of the West Coast and Hawaii. Many Asian immigrants who came to the United States faced rampant racism and perceptions of a perpetual foreignness. For example, responding to growing numbers of Chinese in California, Congress passed the Chinese Exclusion Act of 1882, legislation targeting for the first time a specific race for exclusion and deportation. Even now, discrimination lingers, and remarkably some Asian Americans—among them Los Alamos Laboratory physicist Wen Ho Lee and U.S. Marine Corps officer candidate Bruce Yamashita—have recently been accused of disloyalty and misconduct and subjected to unfounded governmental prosecution and persecution.

Stereotypes and Media Presence

As in the past, the mainstream U.S. media continue to portray Asian Americans in stereotypical roles. The racial, gender, and class stereotypes surrounding Asian Americans revolve around four Gs: gooks, geishas, gung fu, and geeks. The media stereotype Asians and Asian Americans typically as foreigners, family oriented, clannish, and overachieving. Seldom are Asians and Asian Americans differentiated or distinctions made among Asian Americans' ethnic groups. Asian women are typically portrayed as exotic, subservient, and sometimes devious and sexually manipulative of white men. Asian men are variously depicted as sexually castrated or abusive, socially inept and undesirable, gangsterish and group oriented, subservient and kowtowing, sexist and misogynistic, wise but asexual, hardworking but humorless, devious and evil, sneaky and disloyal, and plotting secretively for the overthrow of white men to gain access to white women.

Films depicting classic Asian stereotypes include *The Cheat* (1915), *The Good Earth* (1937), *The World of Suzy Wong* (1961), *The Deer Hunter* (1978), *The Year of the Dragon* (1985), *The Joy Luck Club* (1993), and *Memoirs of a Geisha* (2005). Tied to U.S. relations with Asia and Western ideas about the exotic "Orient," Asian stereotypes—like all stereotypes—tend to dehumanize and belittle. Although they help to sell newspapers, magazines, and movies, they also engender an atmosphere for open discrimination against Asian Americans.

Asian Americans, keenly aware of the U.S. media's influence on the way society views and treats them, have actively criticized their depiction and treatment. American media lack any real understanding of Asian Americans and underrepresent their issues and concerns in print and on screen. Actions against Asian and Asian American stereotypes include demonstrations held against the Madame Butterfly imagery and "white-face" casting of *Miss Saigon*; a campaign to hold accountable those who used the word "Chinaman" in the "Tsunami Song" issued by a radio station shortly after Hurricane Katrina; and a boycott of Abercrombie and Fitch for selling T-shirts stating "Two Wongs don't make a White." The motion picture release of *Memoirs of a Geisha,* which portrays the life of a Japanese geisha but uses actors of Chinese ancestry, stirred controversy and debate, implying that all Asians are "the same."

In a survey of TV and newspaper managers in August 2004, the Asian American Journalist Association (AAJA) found Asian Americans to be severely underrepresented in newsroom management at newspapers and in broadcast television stations. Moreover, a subsequent AAJA study in 2005 found that U.S. mainstream newspapers that lacked Asian American staff also had a corresponding lack of coverage of Asians, Asian Americans, and Asian American issues. The same study found disproportionately fewer Asian Americans at the top twenty-five newspapers. Another AAJA study conducted by the Annenberg School of Communications at the University of Southern California found that Asian American male broadcasters were substantially underrepresented in all major television markets. Of the top twenty-five markets, there were twenty on-air Asian American males and eighty-six Asian American females.

Another study, commissioned by the National Asian Pacific American Legal Consortium, reported that Asian American actors in prime time represent less than half of the Asian American proportion of the population. Such actors were primarily relegated to playing stereotypical roles, such as "technology geeks," martial artists, and passive victims, according to a study by the Leadership Conference on Civil Rights. The "2005 Asian American Justice Center Report Card on Television Diversity" also found that only seventeen Asian American actors appeared in regular roles in prime time. The number of Asian American actors with regularly recurring roles had fallen precipitously from the preceding years' figures. The center gave the networks a grade of C+ for television diversity.

Media Consumption, Ownership, and Politics

Asian Americans are avid consumers of media. Like the average American reader, three-quarters of Asian American adults are magazine readers. Compared to most readers, Asian American magazine readers have a higher household income, are more educated, and are more likely to have children at home. Admerasia estimated that advertisers, responding to the substantial per capita investments and purchasing power of Asian Americans, have spent between $200 million to $300 million per year on the Asian American market. The top ten advertisers targeting Asian Americans include iconic representatives of corporate and governmental America (in order): AT&T, MCI, Verizon, Ford Motor Company, General Motors, New York Life, HSBC, Office of National Drug Control Policy, Asiana, and China Airlines.

Although overall minority media ownership remains low nationwide, holding less than 4 percent of television and radio broadcast licenses, there are signs of progress among Asian Americans in this area. According to a market research study commissioned by the Magazine Publishers of America in 2005, more than 120 ethnic-specific and pan-ethnic magazines target Asian Americans. Sixty-nine ethnic-specific and pan-ethnic television and radio stations cater to Asian Americans, as do more than a dozen cable television companies and providers. Examples include Azn Television, the ImaginAsian Network, the International Channel, MTV China/Korea/India, and TV Japan. According to Mike Sherman of the International Channel, the pan-ethnic audience of second-generation Asian Americans is driving this growth in media interest and holds tremendous potential because of their substantial buying power, desire to see relevant images of themselves in media, and their youthful demographics.

In contrast, in the area of political advertising, Republicans and Democrats both neglect Asian Americans in their media campaigns. Of the $20 million spent on ethnic media during the 2004 presidential elections, little was spent on advertising directly targeting Asian American voters. Democratic candidate John Kerry failed to spend *any* advertising dollars to campaign for Asian American votes. Asian Americans have founded several organizations, including Campaign Advantage and API-Vote, to encourage the mainstream to take the Asian American electorate seriously and to fund media projects encouraging their voter participation. These organizations actively promote minority and Asian American candidates and attempt to create opportunities for non–Asian American candidates to reach out to Asian Americans.

Asian Americans realize that any substantial change in their depiction and treatment will require collaboration, advocacy, and legislation as well as new entrepreneurial initiatives in the nonprofit and corporate sectors. Among the primary advocates of media change are the Asian Media Watch, Asian American Journalists Association, Asian American Justice Center, Asian Pacific American Media Coalition, Center for Asian American Media, and the Media Action Network for Asian Americans. Their efforts as well as others aim to improve the depiction, representation, and participation of Asian Americans in U.S. media in the future.

REFERENCES

Entman, Robert M. "Persons of Color in the Media: Images and Impacts." Briefing by the Leadership Conference on Civil Rights Education Fund for the U.S. House of Representatives, based on a report prepared for the Dellums Commission of the Joint Center for Political and Economic Studies, December 6, 2005.

Feng, Peter. "In Search of Asian American Cinema." *Cineaste* 21, no. 1–2 (Winter–Spring 1995).

Hamamoto, Darrell Y. *Monitored Peril: Asian Americans and the Politics of TV Representation.* Minneapolis: University of Minnesota Press, 1994.

Magazine Publishers of America. "Asian-American Market Profile." New York, 2005.

Narasaki, Karen K. "The 2005 Asian Pacific American Report Card on Television Diversity." Asian American Justice Center, Washington, D.C., 2005.

Stuelpnagel, Larry, et al. "Asian Americans in Newsroom Management: A Survey of TV and Newspaper Managers." Asian American Journalists Association, San Francisco, 2004.

U.S. Bureau of the Census. "Facts for Features: Asian Pacific American Heritage Month, May 2006." Report no. CB065-FF-06, 2006.

Wing, Bob. "The Racial Formation of Asian Americans, 1852–1965." *Monthly Review,* December 2005.

Wu, Denis, and Ralph Izard. "Representing the Total Community: Relationships between Asian-American Staff and Asian-American Coverage in U.S. Newspapers." Asian American Journalists Association, San Francisco, 2005.

Xing, Jun. *Asian America through the Lens: History, Representations, and Identity.* Walnut Creek, Calif.: Altamira, 1998.

Associated Press

The Associated Press (AP) is a nonprofit cooperative membership association that collects and delivers news to thousands of newspapers and radio and television stations. Its member organizations use and contribute stories to the AP's news services. The organization is governed by a twenty-one-member board of directors elected by its membership. The board elects a president from among its members and appoints a chief executive.

In 1846 five New York City newspapers formed the first regional Associated Press to pool their resources and reduce the costs of gathering and transmitting news along telegraph lines. Other regional associations followed their example. In 1893 a nationwide Associated Press emerged from the Western Associated Press. This new organization signed exclusive arrangements with Reuters of England and other European news organizations.

In 1925 Kent Cooper became the general manager of the AP. During his forty-one-year tenure, the AP grew into a huge outfit. Developing state bureaus as the primary unit of the AP represents one of Cooper's greatest successes. In recent decades, the broadcast media have become a significant part of the organization's membership. The AP has approximately 1,700 contributing member newspapers and

5,500 member television and radio stations. It operates some 150 bureaus in the United States with a total of 242 worldwide. It has won twenty-nine Pulitzer Prizes for photography and eighteen for writing.

REFERENCES

Associated Press, www.ap.org.

Cooper, Kent. *Kent Cooper and the Associated Press: An Autobiography.* New York: Random House, 1959.

Gramling, Oliver. *AP: The Story of News.* Port Washington, N.Y.: Kennikat Press, 1969.

Attack journalism

Attack journalism refers to the idea that the news media are too harsh and unduly critical in their treatment of public figures, particularly those in government. It has become common for politicians to lament adverse treatment by the media, a state of affairs stretching from the partisan-owned-and-operated penny presses of the eighteenth and early nineteenth centuries to the muckrakers of the early twentieth century to the investigative reporting and "feeding frenzies" of recent decades. Today, however, consensus exists among at least some journalists that coverage of politics and politicians has become too cynical and too confrontational and has resulted in an uninformed and apathetic public.

Political analyst Larry Sabato asserts in *Feeding Frenzy* that from the time of Franklin D. Roosevelt to that of John F. Kennedy, the overwhelmingly male Washington press corps enjoyed reasonably close relationships with presidents, which led them to be more tolerant of their peccadilloes and, Sabato asserts, during Kennedy's administration to feign blindness in the case of the president's numerous extramarital affairs. As women joined the press corps in greater numbers, standards of personal behavior began to change for politicians and for the press, with previously unreported behaviors being deemed newsworthy. In addition, the evolution of television news into the fast, superficial treatment of numerous stories in one broadcast encouraged reporters to focus mainly on the "horse race" aspects of politics, such as who's ahead, who's up, who's down, instant poll numbers, and so on. News executives came to view in-depth treatments of complex policy issues as "boring" to the public and the cause of viewers tuning out, leading to declining advertising revenue. Thus, an adversarial journalism based on

Fox News Channel's Bill O'Reilly and other talk show hosts and commentators have become famous for their combative treatment of politicians and others whose positions on issues they dislike.

political gaffes and blunders supplanted insightful coverage of substantive issues.

Critics and reform-minded journalists have called for a return to civility and substantive coverage of legitimate political events, warning of possible repercussions—including attempts to restrict freedom of the press—if enough private citizens and public officials become too disenchanted with the news media. Supporters of the status quo, however, are reluctant to engage in the kind of compliant, uncritical journalism that predominated in the past.

REFERENCES

Modern Media Institute. *The Adversary Press.* St. Petersburg: Modern Media Institute, 1983.

Sabato, Larry. *Feeding Frenzy.* New York: Free Press, 1991.

Atwater, Lee

Harvey LeRoy Atwater (1951–1991), a self-proclaimed "dirty tricks" political strategist, rose to prominence as an advisor to Republican presidential candidates and to notoriety for injecting convicted felon Willie Horton into the 1988 presidential campaign. Born and raised in South Carolina, Atwater developed a taste for politics at an early age along with an affinity for the Republican Party. He became the darling of various state politicians and adopted a campaign style heavy on ad hominem attacks in promoting what became known as divisive, or wedge, issues.

Supported by Sen. Strom Thurmond (R–S.C.), Atwater moved to Washington to join President Ronald Reagan's staff, where he contributed to Reagan's reelection in 1984 and became a major player in George H. W. Bush's victory over Massachusetts governor and Democratic presidential candidate Michael Dukakis in 1988. Atwater championed the use of the political ad featuring Horton, an African American prisoner in Massachusetts who committed an armed rape and robbery while on a weekend furlough. Atwater used this to attack Dukakis as being soft on crime.

In recognition for his contribution to Bush's election, as well as his prowess in the increasingly rough-and-tumble environment of national politics, Atwater was appointed chairman of the Republican National Committee, where he served from 1988 to 1990. Before succumbing to brain cancer in 1991, Atwater expressed contrition for his bare knuckle and, to some, offensive style of campaigning.

See also *Horton, Willie; Political consultants; Reagan, Ronald.*

REFERENCE

Brady, John Joseph. *Bad Boy: The Life and Politics of Lee Atwater.* New York: Perseus Publishing, 1996.

B

Background

News sources sometimes transmit information to journalists on a "background" basis, meaning that the source will be identified by title or a broad descriptive phrase rather than by name. For example, a reporter may refer to the secretary of state as "a senior administration official." This type of attribution allows both parties to present information that otherwise might not be revealed because of the unwillingness, for any number of reasons, of the official to be identified as the source. Reporters covering diplomatic and national security stories rely heavily on information reported on background.

Backgrounders—an interview in which information is conveyed on a background basis to one or more journalists—are particularly useful for officials wanting to make anonymous attacks against political rivals or for attacking opposing viewpoints. Backgrounders also allow officials to float "trial balloons" to monitor public responses to potentially controversial policy initiatives. Lower-level officials can "blow the whistle" on a background basis to expose alleged wrongdoings by superiors from whom they fear retribution if identified by name. Journalists often consent to such terms if it is the only way to report the information.

Backgrounders are important instruments in the press-government relationship. Perhaps the most spectacular use of background involved a figure dubbed "Deep Throat," the source who confirmed information for *Washington Post* reporters Bob Woodward and Carl Bernstein during their reporting of the Watergate scandal. In 2005 W. Mark Felt, a high-ranking official in the FBI during the scandal, stepped forward to acknowledge that he had been Deep Throat. Previously, during the Kennedy and Johnson administrations, "deep background," a distinct form of background attribution, had evolved. Deep background refers to information being reported without any attribution whatsoever. Hence, a journalist might say, "It was learned today that ... " and omit any reference to the source.

REFERENCE

Abel, Elie. *Leaking: Who Does It? Who Benefits? At What Cost?* New York: Priority Press, 1987.

Bandwagon effect

The bandwagon effect occurs when the electorate perceives most people leaning toward a particular candidate or cause and decide to do the same—that is, "jump on the bandwagon." Opinion polls are often blamed for creating a bandwagon effect in politics, and politicians who criticize this phenomenon are often guilty of attempting to manipulate their own polls to create it.

The use of polling in U.S. newspapers started in 1824. Magazines began using polling techniques in the 1900s, with scientific polling techniques appearing in the 1930s. As polls grew in sophistication, some political observers began to think that they influenced the way people voted. The 1948 election of Harry S Truman over Thomas E. Dewey represents a victory over the bandwagon effect. The polls erroneously predicted Dewey the winner over Truman, the underdog. Nevertheless, concern continues to this day about the effect of media reports of poll results on the electorate.

Evidence documenting the bandwagon effect—and its opposite, the "underdog effect," in which voters switch their allegiance to a candidate trailing in pre-election polls—is inconclusive and difficult to test. Experimental studies in which respondents are told of real or hypothetical candidate poll standings before they announce their choice have found some influence of polls on voters. Michael Traugott and Paul Lavrakas argue that the bandwagon and underdog effects are likely to exist simultaneously among different subsets of voters. Because these effects require public awareness of polls, and such knowledge varies greatly among the electorate, its actual impact on elections is difficult to judge.

See also *Exit polls; Horse race journalism.*

REFERENCES

Cantril, Albert H., *The Opinion Connection: Polling, Politics, and the Press.* Washington, D.C.: CQ Press, 1991.
Traugott, Michael W., and Paul J. Lavrakas, *The Voter's Guide to Election Polls.* 3rd ed. Lanham, Md.: Rowman and Littlefield, 2004.

Bantam Books v. Sullivan (1963)

In *Bantam Books v. Sullivan* (1963), the Supreme Court declared a Rhode Island law imposing informal censorship unconstitutional. The 1956 law created a state commission to examine books and magazines to determine whether they were obscene, contained "indecent or impure language," or "manifestly tend[ed] to the corruption of the youth." The commission's findings were to be circulated to local police. Publishers and distributors of books and magazines were to be warned that prosecution might be recommended. Bantam Books and other publishers and book distributors filed a state court action to have the law declared unconstitutional. The trial court refused to find the law unconstitutional, but granted an injunction preventing members of the commission from acting in their official capacity. The Rhode Island Supreme Court agreed with the trial court's decision on the statute's constitutionality and reversed the trial court's injunction. Bantam appealed to the U.S. Supreme Court.

Justice William Brennan wrote the majority opinion, in which the Court ruled the Rhode Island law unconstitutional, holding that it created prior censorship. Although the notices of the Rhode Island commission were only advisory, they were issued as the pronouncements of state authority, in violation of the Fourteenth Amendment, and had the effect of discouraging publication, sometimes of materials that could not have been successfully prosecuted under obscenity statutes. Justice John Marshall Harlan dissented, arguing that the advisory nature of the Rhode Island notices did not subject publishers or retailers to a direct penalty.

REFERENCES

Bantam Books v. Sullivan, 372 U.S. 58 (1963).
Elias, James, et al., eds. *Porn 101: Eroticism, Pornography, and the First Amendment.* Amherst, N.Y.: Prometheus Books, 1999.
Hixson, Richard F. *Pornography and the Justices: The Supreme Court and the Intractable Obscenity Problem.* Carbondale: Southern Illinois University Press, 1996.

Bennett, James Gordon

James Gordon Bennett (1795–1872), a pioneering newspaper publisher, founded the *New York Herald* and cofounded the Associated Press. Bennett immigrated to the United States from his native Scotland in 1819. While working as a teacher, he began writing on assorted cultural, economic, and political issues for newspapers in Charleston, South Carolina, and New York City. Bennett started the *New York Herald* in 1835, breaking from the norm by publishing his paper daily and covering stories that appealed to "the great masses of the community." He invested heavily to increase accurate news content as well as boost circulation. In 1848 Bennett, along with his New York City colleagues, created the first cooperative news collection service—the Associated Press.

Bennett's son, James Gordon Bennett Jr., assumed management of the *Herald* in 1867, but did not share his father's innate curiosity or enthusiasm for the newspaper business. He financed circulation-building expeditions, such as Harry Stanley's search for Livingstone and G. W. De Long's ill-fated expedition to the Arctic. In 1922, after the younger Bennett's death, the *Herald* merged with the *New York Tribune.*

REFERENCES

Crouthamel, James L. *Bennett's* New York Herald *and the Rise of the Popular Press.* Syracuse: Syracuse University Press, 1989.
Fermer, Douglas. *James Gordon Bennett and the* New York Herald: *A Study of Editorial Opinion in the Civil War Era, 1854–1867.* New York: Palgrave Macmillan, 1986.

Bernays, Eddie

Edward L. Bernays (1891–1995) pioneered the field of managing public images and perceptions, making him the father of public relations. Bernays, born in Vienna, Austria, into an influential family, was the nephew of Sigmund Freud, the father of psychoanalysis whose work would influence Bernays's professional life. He began his career in 1917 with the Committee on Public Information (CPI), which was charged with controlling information during World War I and selling the U.S. effort to "make the world safe for democracy." After the war, in 1919, Bernays founded the first public relations firm in New York City and began defining the profession. He viewed public relations as an essential element in affecting public opinion, whether to sell a product or an idea.

Bernays combined psychology and other social and behavioral sciences to create image campaigns and shape public opinion for his clients, which included CBS, General Electric, and Proctor and Gamble. His success in corporate public relations transferred naturally to the political arena, where he tailored the public images of political candidates and policies. Such was Bernays's influence that Joseph Goebbels, Nazi Germany's minister of information, referred to his ideas and approach as a guiding influence in the development of the fascist state's propaganda methods and apparatus. Bernays's concepts, methods, and approach also became the blueprint for the efforts of today's "spin doctors" to manage information at all levels. Bernays wrote *Crystallizing Public Opinion* (1923), *Propaganda* (1928), *The Engineering of Consent* (1947), and *Biography of an Idea: Memoirs of a Public Relations Counsel* (1965).

See also *Spin; Spin doctors.*

REFERENCES

Bernays, Edward L. *Biography of an Idea: Memoirs of Public Relations Counsel.* New York: Simon and Schuster, 1965.

Cutlip, Scott. *The Unseen Power: Public Relations: A History.* Hillsdale, N.J.: L. Erlbaum Associates, 1994.

Ewen, Stuart. *PR! A Social History of Spin.* New York: Basic Books, 1996.

Tye, Larry. *The Father of Spin: Edward L. Bernays and the Birth of Public Relation.* New York: Henry Holt, 1998.

Bernstein, Carl

Carl Bernstein (1944–), a journalist and author, is best known for his Pulitzer Prize–winning reporting on the Watergate scandal. Bernstein began his journalism career as a copyboy with the *Washington Star* in 1960 and worked his way up to reporter. He worked for the *Elizabeth Daily Journal* in New Jersey during 1965–1966 and joined the *Washington Post* in 1966 as a reporter. When notice of a break-in at the Watergate headquarters of the Democratic National Committee raised interest, Bernstein joined with his *Post* colleague Bob Woodward to investigate it for the metropolitan desk. They benefited enormously from a highly placed anonymous source known as Deep Throat and eventually linked the so-called third-rate burglary to President Richard

Washington Post *reporter Carl Bernstein (left) and his colleague Bob Woodward in 1973 during the Watergate investigation that eventually led to President Richard M. Nixon's resignation. They won a Pulitzer Prize that year for their reporting, and their book* All the President's Men *was made into an Oscar-winning movie.*

M. Nixon's closest White House advisors. Their reporting of the story won them a 1973 Pulitzer Prize and contributed to a parallel congressional inquiry that led to the only resignation of a sitting U.S. president and prison terms for his key aides. With Woodward, Bernstein co-authored *All the President's Men* (1974), documenting their experience of reporting the Watergate scandal; the book was made into an Oscar-winning movie by the same title.

Bernstein worked as the Washington bureau chief and senior correspondent for ABC News on national security matters from 1980 to 1984, contributing editor for *Time* during 1991–1992, and moved to *Vanity Fair* as a contributing editor in 1977. He became a frequent political commentator on network television and has written feature articles on the relationship between the intelligence community and the press, discontent in Iraq under Saddam Hussein, and a critical assessment of the trend toward sensationalism in journalism. Bernstein also wrote *The Final Days* (1976), *Loyalties: A Son's Memoir* (1989), and *His Holiness: John Paul II and the History of Our Time* (1996). After Mark Felt revealed himself to be Deep Throat in 2005, Bernstein contributed to *The Secret Man* (2005), Woodward's book about the famous source.

See also *Investigative reporting; Nixon, Richard M.; Washington Post; Watergate.*

REFERENCES

Bernstein, Carl. "The Idiot Culture." *New Republic,* June 8, 1992, 22–28.

Bernstein, Carl, and Bob Woodward. *All the President's Men.* New York: Simon and Schuster, 1974.

Havill, Adrian. *Deep Truth: The Lives of Bob Woodward and Carl Bernstein.* New York: Birch Lane Press, 1993.

Block, Herbert Lawrence

Herbert Lawrence Block (1909–2001), who signed his work as "Herblock," was a renowned Pulitzer Prize–winning political cartoonist whose career spanned more than sixty years. Block began as a staff cartoonist working with the *Chicago Daily News* in 1929. His cartoons initially reflected the conservative views of the newspaper, but the Great Depression transformed Block's perspective. In 1933 he joined Edward Scripps's Newspaper Enterprise Association in Cleveland. Observing President Franklin D. Roosevelt and

his New Deal heal the wounds of the Great Depression taught him "that government can do the things that need to be done."

Block turned his pen on Hitler and fascism as well as the America First Committee for its isolationist stance. While many liberals saw Stalin as a savior, Block saw the Soviet leader as a dictator. Block joined the *Washington Post* in 1946 and in the early 1950s took on Sen. Joseph McCarthy when it was unpopular to do so. Many of his most famous cartoons were about the scandal-plagued Nixon administration. Block won Pulitzer Prizes in 1942, 1954, and 1979 for his cartoons.

See also *Cartoons, editorial.*

REFERENCES

Block, Herbert. *Herblock: A Cartoonist's Life.* New York: MacMillan Publishing Company, 1993.

"Herblock's History: Political Cartoons from the Crash to the Millennium," http://www.loc.gov/rr/print/swann/herblock.

Blogs, Web logs

See *New media*

Blumenthal, Sidney

Sidney S. Blumenthal (1948–) is a former Clinton White House staffer and a journalist and author whose work has appeared in the *New Yorker,* the *Washington Post,* the *New Republic,* and *Vanity Fair.* In the 1980s, Blumenthal met Bill and Hillary Clinton at a Renaissance Weekend and would grow close to them while covering the 1992 presidential campaign. In 1997 he joined the Clinton administration's White House communications team and soon thereafter filed a $30 million defamation suit against Matt Drudge, of the Drudge Report, and America Online for publishing statements that he beat his wife. (He dropped the suit after Drudge issued an apology.) As the public relations point man for the Clintons, Blumenthal drew considerable fire from conservatives and a subpoena from independent counsel Kenneth Starr, who was assigned to investigate a number of incidents involving the Clintons.

In March 2004, Blumenthal became the Washington bureau chief for Salon.com. He continues to write articles for national and international publications. He is the author of *The Permanent Campaign* (1982), *The Rise of the Counter-Establishment* (1986), *Our Long National Daydream* (1988), *Pledging Allegiance* (1990), and *The Clinton Wars* (2003), a voluminous defense of the Clintons.

REFERENCES

Greenberg, David. "The Clinton Warrior." *Washington Monthly,* June 2003, 44–48.

Tomasky, Michael. "Lib Liberation." *New York Magazine,* June 23, 2003, 18–20.

Bly withdrew from journalism after marrying Robert Seaman in 1895. Upon her husband's death in 1904, she ran his companies. Bly, on holiday in Europe at the outbreak of World War I, reported on eastern front operations for the *New York Evening Journal.*

See also *Investigative reporting.*

REFERENCES

Ehrlich, Elizabeth. *Nellie Bly.* New York: Chelsea House Publishers, 1989.

Kendall, Martha. *Nellie Bly: Reporter for the World.* New York: Houghton-Mifflin, 1992.

Kroeger, Brooke. *Nellie Bly: Daredevil Reporter, Feminist.* New York: Random House, 1994.

Bly, Nelly

Born Elizabeth Jane Cochran (1864–1922), the journalist Nellie Bly pioneered the field of investigative reporting and in the process evolved as a champion of human rights. At the age of sixteen, Cochran left home in search of work in Pittsburgh, arriving only to find that the jobs available to women paid very little. "What Girls Are Good For" (1885), an article in the *Pittsburgh Dispatch,* enraged Cochran, inspiring her to write a letter of protest to editor George Madden, who in turn challenged her to write about the lives of women. Following the practice of the day, Cochran chose a pseudonym—Nellie Bly. She wrote about divorce from the perspective of women she interviewed and argued for changes in marriage and divorce laws. Madden was sufficiently impressed that he hired Bly as a full-time reporter.

Bly's writing style reflected her inclination to become immersed in a story and to report her experiences. Joseph Pulitzer hired her in 1887 to write for his newspaper, the *New York World.* Bly launched the practice of investigative journalism as she exposed and examined child labor, poverty, and inadequate housing and poor working conditions. She feigned insanity to illuminate the abhorrent conditions at the Blackwell's Island asylum in New York, including committing healthy family members and patients with physical rather than mental ailments; her reports led to much-needed reform. In a sensational journalistic exercise, during 1889 and 1890 Bly reported in a travelogue as she circled the world more quickly than Phileas Fogg, the protagonist of Jules Verne's *Around the World in Eighty Days.*

Bradlee, Ben

Benjamin Crowninshield Bradlee (1921–) is a journalist, author, and former managing editor of the *Washington Post.* Bradlee graduated from Harvard University in 1942 and served in the U.S. Navy for three years during World War II. After the war, he worked briefly for the American Civil Liberties Union before co-founding the *New Hampshire Sunday News* (1946). In 1952–1953, Bradlee served at the State Department in its Office of U.S. Information and Educational Exchange (USIE), a precursor to the United States Information Agency. He moved to *Newsweek* in 1953. His coverage of the 1960 presidential election pitting Democrat John F. Kennedy against Republican Richard M. Nixon marked the beginning of a long-time interest in these two politicians' lives and careers. Bradlee wrote *That Special Grace* (1964) and *Conversations with Kennedy* (1975) to preserve his observations of the senator from Massachusetts and thirty-fifth president of the United States.

Washington Post publisher Katharine Graham hired Bradlee as managing editor in 1968 and eventually as executive editor. He encouraged aggressive investigative reporting by *Post* journalists and led the newspaper during some of the most turbulent years in U.S. history as he helped build the paper's reputation and circulation. Defying the Nixon administration, in 1971 Bradlee decided to publish the Pentagon Papers, documents detailing the secret history of the events leading up to and contributing to the Vietnam War. He provided essential support for *Post* reporters Bob Woodward and Carl Bernstein as they investigated the "third-rate burglary" that launched the Watergate scandal and the first resignation of a sitting U.S. president. For three decades, the three men kept secret the identity of Deep Throat—Mark Felt, former assistant director of the FBI—confirming it only after Felt's self-disclosure in 2005. Bradlee retired as managing editor in 1991 but remains a vice president of the paper.

See also *Washington Post; Watergate.*

REFERENCES

Bradlee, Ben. *A Good Life: Newspapering and Other Adventures.* New York: Simon and Schuster, 1995.
Halberstam, David. *The Powers That Be.* New York: A. A. Knopf, 1979.
Mathews, Tom. "The Bradlee Treatment." *Newsweek,* July 1, 1991, 69.

Branzburg v. Hayes (1972)

Branzburg v. Hayes (1972) established that journalists may not use the First Amendment as a defense for shielding sources. During the course of writing a story, Paul Branzburg, a journalist for the Louisville *Courier-Journal,* witnessed people manufacturing and using illegal drugs. Branzburg resisted efforts by Judge Hayes to compel him to reveal confidential information concerning those involved to a grand jury. Branzburg claimed that to testify would damage his credibility with his sources and compromise reporters' ability to perform their jobs.

The Supreme Court took up *Branzburg v. Hayes* together with *In re Pappas* and *United States v. Caldwell,* two other cases in which reporters refused to reveal information to a grand jury about possible illegal activities. In a 5-4 opinion, the Court ruled that reporters must respond in good faith to the questions of a grand jury because the First Amendment does not relieve them of their duty as citizens, like all other citizens, to do so in a criminal matter. In addition, the reporters' testimony serves a "compelling" and "paramount" state interest. Since *Branzburg,* the courts have tended to examine cases involving reporters' privilege on a case-by-case basis and to adhere to a three-part rule derived from Justice Lewis Powell's dissent in *Branzburg*: that the government must show that the information sought is highly material and relevant to the case; it is necessary or critical to the claim; and it cannot be obtained from other sources.

REFERENCES

Adams, Julian. *Freedom and Ethics in the Press.* New York: Richards Rosen Press, 1983.
Branzburg v. Hayes, 408 U.S. 665 (1972).
Francois, William E. *Mass Media Law and Regulation.* Ames: Iowa State University Press, 1990.
Gora, Joel M. *The Rights of Reporters: The Basic ACLU Guide to a Reporter's Rights.* New York: Discus Books, 1974.

Bridges v. California (1941)

The landmark decision in *Bridges v. California* (1941) severely limits a judge's authority to cite individuals for indirect contempt of court, an act of disrespect that occurs outside the courtroom. The decision resulted from two unrelated cases. In one case, Longshoremen's Union leader Harry Bridges had been cited for contempt after he sent a telegram to the secretary of labor threatening a Pacific Coast dock workers' strike if a lower court enforced a ruling unfavorable to him and his organization. In the other case, a court had found the *Los Angeles Times* in contempt for publishing several editorials—including one titled "Probation for Gorillas?"—that the court believed was an attempt to influence the judge to impose stiffer sentences on convicted labor leaders.

Supreme Court Justice Hugo Black, writing for the 5-4 majority, cited constitutional framer James Madison in asserting that the First Amendment is the standard for press and speech protection. Black held that contempt citations are enforceable only if the publication or statements create a "clear and present danger" to the criminal justice system. The Court held that the power to impose contempt citations is rooted in English common law and relies on an "inherent tendency" or "reasonable tendency" for the publications or statements to hurt the administration of justice.

REFERENCES

Bridges v. California, 314 U.S. 252 (1941).
Calvert, Clay, and Don R. Pember. *Mass Media Law.* Boston: McGraw Hill, 2005.

Brinkley, David

David McClure Brinkley (1920–2003), a preeminent broadcast journalist, helped define network news. Brinkley began his journalism career as a reporter for the *Star-News* of Wilmington, North Carolina, where he worked from 1938 to 1941. He served in the army during World War II and as a reporter for United Press news service. Brinkley joined NBC Radio in 1943, went to NBC-TV in 1946, and became NBC's first White House correspondent in 1951, supporting the Camel News Caravan—NBC-TV's early news effort— from 1951 to 1956. During the 1956 presidential election, NBC producer Reuven Frank teamed Brinkley with Chet Huntley to cover the party conventions. The combination worked, leading NBC to introduce *The Huntley-Brinkley Report* in October 1956, with Huntley in New York and Brinkley in Washington, D.C. Theirs remained the dominant news program until Huntley retired in 1970. Brinkley was then paired with John Chancellor, but they lacked chemistry. Brinkley's dissatisfaction mounted, in part because he disliked going to New York.

In 1981 Roone Arledge hired Brinkley for ABC News and built a weekly public affairs program—*This Week with David Brinkley*—around Brinkley's distinctive style. He asked George Will to lend his conservative perspective and Sam Donaldson to bring a liberal leaning to a freewheeling discussion with Washington's powerful and influential. The format suited Brinkley, and he remained the program's host until retiring in 1998.

See also *Arledge, Roone; Camel News Caravan; Evening Network News; Sunday news shows.*

REFERENCES

Brinkley, David. *David Brinkley: A Memoir.* New York: A. A. Knopf, 1995).

Frank, Reuven. *Out of Thin Air: The Brief Wonderful Life of Network News.* New York: Simon and Schuster, 1991.

Gunther, Marc. *The House That Roone Built: The Inside Story of ABC News.* Boston: Little, Brown, 1994.

Broder, David S.

David Salzer Broder (1929–) is a journalist, Pulitzer Prize–winning columnist, and political commentator. Broder received his bachelor's and master's degrees in politi-

David Brinkley (left) with co-anchor Chet Huntley in 1961 after winning Emmys for NBC's Huntley-Brinkley Report. *Their evening news program ran for fourteen years, with Huntley reporting from New York and Brinkley stationed in Washington, D.C.*

cal science from the University of Chicago and served two years in the U.S. Army. He began his newspaper career as a reporter for the *Bloomington Pantagraph* in Illinois. Broder reported on national politics for *Congressional Quarterly* from 1955 to 1960, the *Washington Star* from 1960 to 1965, and the *New York Times* from 1965 to 1966. He joined the *Washington Post* in 1966. Broder was awarded the Pulitzer Prize for distinguished commentary in May 1973 and was promoted to associate editor at the *Post* in 1975.

Broder writes a nationally syndicated political column for the Washington Post Writers Group and is a regular commentator on CNN's *Inside Politics* and also makes appearances on NBC's *Meet the Press* and PBS's *Washington Week in Review.* He has been a fellow at the Institute of Politics at the John F. Kennedy School of Government at Harvard University and a fellow of the Institute of Policy Sciences and Public Affairs at Duke University. Broder has written numerous books, including *The Party's Over: The Failure of Politics in*

America (1972), *Changing of the Guard: Power and Leadership in America* (1980), *A Candid Look at How the News Is Made* (1987), and *Democracy Derailed: Initiative Campaigns and the Power of Money* (2000).

REFERENCES

Alterman, Eric. "The News from Quinn-Broderville." *Nation,* December 14, 1998, 10.
Astor, Dave. "Friedman & Broder Are Editors' Faves." *Editor and Publisher,* July 15, 2002, 29.
Strupp, Joe. "The 'Dean' Still Laying Shoe Leather." *Editor and Publisher,* November 2005, 12–13.
Wilson, James Q. "Liberalism and Purpose." *Commentary,* May 1972, 74–76.

Brokaw, Tom

Thomas John Brokaw (1940–) is an award-winning broadcast journalist and former national network news anchor. He began his career as a newscaster, weatherman, and staff announcer at KTIV-TV in Sioux City, Iowa, in 1960. He joined NBC News in 1966 with stints on *Saturday Night News* and the *Today Show* before becoming the sole anchor of *NBC Nightly News* in 1983. He won seven Emmy Awards for his broadcasting and reportedly served as the model for William Hurt's Tom Grunick, the protagonist in James L. Brooks's 1987 film *Broadcast News.* He retired from his anchor seat in 2005.

In addition to his work in broadcasting, Brokaw has written articles, essays, and commentary for numerous publications, including *Life,* the *Los Angeles Times, Newsweek,* the *New York Times,* and the *Washington Post.* He also authored several books, most notably *The Greatest Generation* (1998)—about those Americans who grew up during the Great Depression, fought in World War II, and came home to help build the United States into an economic and political superpower. He also wrote *The Greatest Generation Speaks* (1999) and *An Album of Memories* (2001).

REFERENCES

Brokaw, Tom. *A long way from home: growing up in the American heartland.* New York: Random House, 2002.
Brokaw, Tom. *The greatest generation.* New York: Random House, 2005.
Goldberg, Robert, and Gerald Jay Goldberg. *Anchors: Brokaw, Jennings, Rather and the Evening News.* New York: Birch Lane, 1990.
Westin, A. V. *Newswatch: How Television Decides the News.* New York: Simon and Schuster, 1982.

Bryant, William Cullen

William Cullen Bryant (1794–1878), the first major American poet, helped define American journalism and literature. His first published work, *The Embargo* (1807), attacked President Thomas Jefferson and called for his resignation. Bryant was admitted to the bar in 1815 in Massachusetts and practiced law from 1816 to 1825. His first collection of poems was published in 1821 to wide acclaim. He then moved to New York and with a friend established and became co-editor of the *New York Review* in 1825. His poetry circulated widely, through his newspapers, and the quality of his writing earned him a broad readership, including a following across the Atlantic.

Bryant joined the *New York Evening Post* in 1826 and became part owner and editor in chief from 1829 to 1878. He made use of his position to advocate for human rights, free trade, and the abolition of slavery as well as to support abolitionist settlers in Kansas, deride the *Dred Scott* decision, and laud John Brown's resistance. He also used his writing skills and success to give voice as a member of the emerging American literati, which included James Fenimore Cooper, Samuel F. B. Morse, and Thomas Cole. An outspoken supporter of President Abraham Lincoln and a prominent founder of the modern Republican Party, Bryant encouraged Lincoln to issue the Emancipation Proclamation through his writing and his newspaper. In his later years, Bryant traveled widely, gave speeches, and returned to his poetry. He produced blank verse translations of the *Iliad* (1870) and the *Odyssey* (1872).

REFERENCES

Brown, Charles Henry. *William Cullen Bryant.* New York: Scribner, 1971.
Bryant, William Cullen. *Power for Sanity: Selected Editorials of William Cullen Bryant, 1832–1861.* New York: Fordham University Press, 1994.

Buchanan, Pat

Patrick Joseph Buchanan (1938–) is an author, politician, and commentator. Buchanan began his career as a reporter working for the *St. Louis Globe-Democrat* after completing graduate school at the Columbia University School of Journalism in 1962. He was promoted to editorial writer and

Conservative Pat Buchanan's long political career has included advising and speechwriting for Presidents Nixon, Ford, and Reagan and running on three occasions for the presidency.

assistant editorial editor in 1964. Seeking new challenges, Buchanan arranged a meeting with former vice president Richard M. Nixon, then a partner in a New York City law firm, in 1966. Buchanan's ability impressed Nixon, so he hired the young reporter as an assistant and speechwriter in preparation for his 1968 presidential campaign.

After Nixon's election, Buchanan became a special assistant to the president. He wrote speeches for Nixon and Vice President Spiro T. Agnew and contributed to planning the president's successful 1972 reelection campaign. In Nixon's second administration, Buchanan became special consultant to the president, with much of his attention focused on the developing Watergate scandal. After Nixon's resignation in 1974, Buchanan stayed on in the Ford administration until the following year, when he returned to journalism as a syndicated columnist, commentator, and lecturer.

Buchanan joined the second administration of President Ronald Reagan as director of communications in 1985, serving for two years before returning once again to journalism. An outspoken critic of Reagan's vice president and successor, George H. W. Bush, Buchanan campaigned against him for the Republican Party nomination in 1992 and ran again in 1996. In 1993 he founded the American Cause, an educational foundation dedicated to the principles of freedom, federalism, limited government, traditional values, and a foreign policy that puts the United States first. He chaired the group until 1999.

In the 2000 presidential election, Buchanan launched his third attempt at the Republican nomination. Advocating an America First platform and a staunchly conservative and partially populist agenda, Buchanan accused Republicans of having moved too far toward the center of the political spectrum. With his campaign stalled by October 1999, Buchanan abandoned the Republican Party to join the Reform Party, a move that caused considerable conflict within the organization founded by Ross Perot.

As a traditional conservative, Buchanan has been a vocal critic of the neoconservative administration of George W. Bush and its interventionist foreign policy. He appeared on CNN's *Crossfire,* continues to appear regularly on the syndicated *McLaughlin Group,* and has hosted his own radio program, Mutual Radio's *Buchanan & Co.* He wrote *The New Majority* (1973), *Right from the Beginning* (1988), *The Great Betrayal* (1998), *A Republic, Not an Empire* (1999), and *The Death of the West* (2001).

REFERENCES

Buchanan, Patrick J. *The Death of the West: How Dying Populations and Immigrant Invasions Imperil our Country and Civilization.* New York: Thomas Dunne Books/St. Martin's Press, 2002.

———. *The Great Betrayal: How American Sovereignty and Social Justice Are Being Sacrificed to the Gods of the Global Economy.* Boston: Little, Brown, 1998.

Grant, George. *Buchanan: Caught in the Crossfire.* Nashville, Tenn.: Thomas Nelson, 1996.

Nadler, Richard. *The Perils of Pat.* Kansas City, Mo.: Nadler Publishing, 1996.

Stern, Kenneth S. *Backgrounder—Patrick Joseph Buchanan.* New York: American Jewish Committee, Institute of Human Relations, 1990.

Buckley, William F., Jr.

William F. Buckley Jr. (1925–) is the founder and long-time editor of the *National Review* known for his acerbic, polysyllabic wit. Shortly after graduating from Yale University, Buckley wrote his first book, *God and Man at Yale: The Superstitions of Academic Freedom* (1951), a critical assessment of his education. He was an editor of the *American Mercury* during 1951–1952 and founded the *National Review* in 1955.

Buckley used his platform and intellect to promote modern American conservatism, with his magazine becoming the leading journal of conservative thinkers. He was an unsuccessful candidate for New York City mayor in 1965 and recounted his experience and views of the campaign in *The Unmaking of a Mayor* (1966). Buckley hosted *Firing Line,* which aired on PBS from 1966 to 1999. He also wrote numerous articles for a wide range of publications. Buckley relinquished control of the *National Review* to a nonprofit corporation in 2004, and in his retirement writes a twice-weekly syndicated column and serves as a political commentator on a variety of political affairs television programs. He remains the magazine's editor at large.

Buckley has written a series of spy novels and *The Redhunter: A Novel Life and Times of Senator Joe McCarthy* (1999), a fictionalized biography of Sen. Joseph McCarthy that paints the 1950s anticommunist "witch hunts" in a favorable light. Buckley's autobiographical *Nearer, My God: An Autobiography of Faith* (1997) reflects on his life and Roman Catholic faith. He also produced an autobiographical compendium of fifty essays titled *Miles Gone By* (2004).

See also *National Review.*

William F. Buckley Jr. is the founder and editor at large of the National Review, *a leading conservative publication. Here he addresses the National Press Club in 1965 during a failed bid for New York City mayor.*

REFERENCES

Buckley, William F. *Miles Gone By: A Literary Autobiography.* Washington, D.C., and Lanham, Md.: Regnery, 2004.

——— *Nearer, My God: An Autobiography of Faith.* New York: Doubleday, 1997.

Judis, John B. *William F. Buckley, Jr.: Patron Saint of the Conservatives.* New York: Simon and Schuster, 1988.

McManus, John F. *William F. Buckley, Jr.: Pied Piper for the Establishment.* Appleton, Wis.: John Birch Society, 2002.

Cable Communication Policy Act of 1984

Before enactment of the Cable Communication Policy Act of 1984, the Federal Communications Commission (FCC) heavily regulated the cable TV industry. The 1984 legislation swept away a great deal of the regulatory infrastructure that the industry claimed fettered its growth and penetration into previously unserved and underserved markets. The primary purpose of the law was to allow market forces, not regulation, to determine cable TV rates.

The Cable Communication Policy Act represented an attempt by the federal government to reconcile telecommunications law with the new mass media environment, which included broadcast TV, VCRs, and cable TV. Although the act's intent was to spur competition among various entertainment media, the immediate result was a rise in rates for cable TV. Providers of cable had long sought regulatory relief so that they could increase rates and return to levels of profitability that had prevailed in the early 1980s. According to the U.S. General Accounting Office, cable rates increased 43 percent between 1986 and 1989.

A large part of the rate increase resulted from the law's provisions for the award of local franchises by municipal government—the prevailing method of allocating local cable franchises. Under this system, local governments allow cable TV operators to be the exclusive provider of cable service. The 1984 act, however, gave local governments little recourse against operators whose rates were considered too high or who provided poor service. The Cable Act of 1992 gave local governments more regulatory power over cable providers, but rates continued to rise for approximately one-third of cable subscribers even after the 1992 legislation. Although the 1984 act created controversy and prompted an FCC evaluation of its outcomes in 1990, the act did produce some positive results. Cable TV's subscriber base, market share, and number of channels offered grew substantially after the 1984 deregulation of the industry.

REFERENCES

Bishop, Ronald. "Cable Television." In *Mass Media and Society,* edited by Alan Wells and Ernest A. Hakanen. Greenwich, Conn.: Ablex Publishing, 1997.

Crandall, Robert W., and Harold Furchtgott-Roth. *Cable TV: Regulation or Competition?* Washington, D.C.: Brookings Institution, 1996.

Cable television

As television became more popular in the late 1940s and early 1950s, many communities, even some reasonably close to TV transmitters, could not receive TV broadcast signals. Oftentimes, hilly terrain blocked their signals. The first primitive cable television systems, initially called Community Antenna Television (CATV), were built in the late 1940s to retransmit signals to inaccessible communities. The first cable system based on subscriber fees was built in Lansford, Pennsylvania, in 1950. With only a small number of signals available for broadcast, the low channel capacities of early CATV systems proved not to be an issue.

Turner Broadcasting chairman and president Ted Turner (left), here with Time Warner chairman and CEO Gerald Levin in 1995, began a media empire and revolution with his founding of TBS in 1976 and the launch of CNN in 1981.

In the late 1950s and early 1960s, however, CATV systems began expanding their services. Using microwave relays and large antennas that picked up increasingly distant signals, such as from other cities, the new cable services came into conflict with the Federal Communications Commission's (FCC) goals of expanding TV service through ultra-high frequency (UHF) services (channels 14 through 83). The FCC began to require CATV operators to demonstrate that "signal importation" was in the "public interest." Overall, however, providers operated unfettered by the FCC. In 1966 the FCC began to regulate more actively, halting the installation of new systems and the growth of existing ones in the top 100 urban television markets. This effectively squelched signal importation and cable TV growth for several years.

Although the cable television industry complained that the freeze on new cable systems inhibited its growth, the freeze also benefited it. During that period, the industry strengthened its financial standing and technical prowess in the smaller markets in which it was most active. The industry also learned how to work with local governments and citizens to establish cable systems. The de facto moratorium also introduced a period of industry consolidation, in which some large firms bought or established cable systems in several different cities, making them so-called multiple system operators (MSOs). MSOs, which include such companies as Time Warner Cable and TeleCommunctions Inc. (TCI), today own most of the nation's cable systems.

In 1972 the FCC issued the cable television "Report and Order," thereby fully recognizing cable as an important mass communications medium and providing a regulatory framework for its growth. This acknowledgment was driven in part by the FCC's awareness that for various technical reasons, UHF worked poorly for large numbers of users. Many viewers subscribed to cable for its increased offerings and to improve the reception of over-the-air local broadcasts. With this in mind, the FCC allowed cable system operators to enter urban markets, initiating a new growth period for cable TV. The FCC harnessed the industry to further what it determined to be the public interest, requiring, among other things, that cable systems provide local access facilities and that franchises be awarded by local governments.

Satellites and the Growth of Cable

Growth of the cable TV industry remained relatively slow in the early 1970s, with demand largely limited to areas distant from major urban TV markets. Some urban users subscribed to cable primarily to improve their signal reception. The relatively few channel choices pale by comparison to those available today. Some local operators began offering local access for cable programming or other system-produced local programming and such services as continuous weather information, stock tickers, and clocks.

What became known as "premium" (extra-cost) cable began in earnest in 1972 with the first broadcast of a film by the Home Box Office Company (HBO). HBO started modestly as a local pay-television outlet in Wilkes Barre, Pennsylvania. Its services expanded to other cable television operators, but its program distribution system remained primitive, consisting of terrestrial microwave relays and tapes shipped via courier to local systems. This made for cumbersome and expensive service.

Technical innovations involving telecommunications satellites are primarily responsible for the explosive growth of cable TV and subsequent direct delivery TV systems. Communications satellites were first used for network television relays between continents. The FCC began licensing domestic satellite communications (DOMSATs) in 1975 with the launch of SATCOM I, the first DOMSAT. HBO committed to a five-year deal to use a transponder on SATCOM I. Although DOMSATs were initially expensive, HBO's status as a premium channel allowed it to recoup the costs of satellite transmission. Indeed, satellite transmission is considerably less expensive than a network of terrestrial relays and has become even less expensive with improvements in technology and carrying capacity. For example, costs decreased when the FCC licensed the use of small, receive-only antennas at the cable "head-end." WTBS, an Atlanta television station owned by Ted Turner, became the second satellite-delivered service in December 1976. WTBS became TBS—the first "super station," providing a variety of syndicated entertainment shows and sporting events from Turner-owned Atlanta sports teams.

Two factors contributed to making the 1980s the age of growth in the cable television industry: the burgeoning growth of satellite program distribution and deregulation of the cable industry. With greater possibilities for satellite distribution, and greater system channel capacity, the market for cable TV programs and channels grew rapidly into the mid-1990s. The most widely distributed cable network is ESPN, which started in 1979. Other networks followed, among them the Cable News Network (CNN), MTV, and various Turner networks, including TBS, CNN Headline News, and TNT. WTBS became the TBS channel, which set the standard for what became known as "basic cable" services. Basic cable services, which include TNT, CNN, ESPN, and MTV, are financed by a combination of advertising and per-subscriber fees, often less than one dollar per subscriber, paid by the cable operator to the network. Premium (pay) channels, such as HBO and Cinemax, require that subscribers pay additional fees for these services. Some pay channels are combined into one-price packages, while other channels are distributed free to cable systems. C-SPAN's channels, for example, carry public affairs programming. The cable industry funds these relatively low-cost channels in large part to demonstrate its commitment to public service. Educational and public access channels are similarly included in order to satisfy national and community desires for community-oriented television. Several cable networks, such as Nickelodeon and the History Channel, carry programs that are not only commercially successful but are sometimes of high quality.

Pay-per-view (PPV) services have become an important revenue source for programmers in recent years with the advent of greater channel capacity and addressable cable TV boxes, which allow two-way communication between the box and the main cable office. With greater channel capacity, however, many operators have introduced multiple channels of PPV movies, sports, and adult-oriented entertainment.

The Future of Cable TV

With passage of the Telecommunications Act of 1996 and rapid technological developments, the market for at-home information and entertainment continues to change almost daily. New technologies, consumer preferences, and delivery systems are altering the nature and function of cable television. Direct-satellite television systems (DSS), in which television signals are delivered directly to the home via a small satellite dish antenna, perhaps pose the most immediate threat to cable TV operators. DSS systems often fill gaps in service, particularly in hard-to-serve rural areas. Because DSS antennas require unobstructed views of the southern horizon, they are not well suited to urban areas or to extreme northern areas, such as in Alaska and Canada.

Cable TV operators are responding to the satellite threat by improving service and choice and by emphasizing the supposed ease of cable installation versus the installation of satellite TV. With the popularity of the Internet, the cable industry has used its growing capacity to offer connections to it at speeds far faster than those through telephone lines. Cable's increasing bandwidth—that is, its capacity to carry a signal—allows cable TV operators (particularly where fiber optic cable is widely used) to offer business and residential telephone services, computer data networking, and centrally monitored burglar alarm systems. Rapid technological and regulatory change is accelerating the convergence between the Internet, telephone, and cable TV, as computer software and hardware companies, MSOs, and telephone companies cross each other's domains and offer multiple services. Cable operators sell access to high-definition television (HDTV) at prices and with ease of installation competitive with satellite. Cable TV is currently the preeminent delivery system for information and entertainment in urban and suburban North America. In 1998 basic cable viewership exceeded that of the four major broadcast networks for the first time.

See also *Cable Communication Policy Act of 1984.*

REFERENCES

Bishop, Ronald. "Cable Television." In *Mass Media and Society,* edited by Alan Wells and Ernest A. Hakanen. Greenwich, Conn.: Ablex Publishing, 1997.

Clayton, Kathy. "The 1980s, A Decade in Review: Cable Leaps and Bounds into the 1980s." *Electronic Media,* January 1, 1990, 25.

Crandall, Robert W., and Harold Furchtgott-Roth. *Cable TV: Regulation or Competition?* Washington, D.C.: Brookings Institution, 1996.

Hazlett, Thomas W., and Matthew L. Spitzer. *Public Policy toward Cable Television: The Economics of Rate Controls.* Cambridge, Mass., and Washington, D.C.: MIT Press and AEI Press, 1997.

Hollins, Timothy. *Beyond Broadcasting: Into the Cable Age.* London: BFI, 1984.

Le Duc, Don R. *Cable Television and the FCC: A Crisis in Media Control.* Philadelphia: Temple University Press, 1973.

Moeller, Philip. "The Age of Convergence." *American Journalism Review,* January/February 1994, 22–28.

Parsons, Patrick R., and Robert M. Frieden. *The Cable and Satellite Television Industries.* Boston: Allyn and Bacon, 1991.

Camel News Caravan

On February 16, 1949, the Camel News Caravan, an early version of television news, premiered on the NBC network. The program greatly influenced television news reporting in its formative years. John Cameron Swayze anchored the broadcasts from their initial airing until 1956, when he was replaced by Chet Huntley and David Brinkley.

R. J. Reynolds—the manufacturer of Camel cigarettes—sponsored the Camel News Caravan. Some critics raised questions about the exclusive sponsorship of a news broadcast by an advertiser, suggesting that news judgments might be compromised by the need to satisfy the sponsor. Other critics voiced concerns about the program's emphasis on the visual aspects of stories—which were usually drawn from newsreel-style film—rather than on the substantive issues that supposedly made the stories worth reporting. The use of imagery was, however, a conscious effort to differentiate television news from radio and print news; this distinction continues today, and remains central to criticisms of the actual news substance, or lack thereof, in television news.

REFERENCES

Karnick, Kristine Brunovska. "NBC and the Innovation of Television News, 1945–1953." *Journalism History* 15, no. 1 (Spring 1988): 26–34.

Campaign advertising

See *Political content in advertising*

Campaigns, elections, and the media

Without the mass media, only a few Americans would actually "experience" a presidential campaign. Modern campaigns—at least those for national and statewide office—exist mainly in the form of media ads and media coverage. Yet only recently has the nature, content, and influence of the media in covering campaigns been closely examined.

Most early studies reported that media coverage only minimally affected public opinion. Researchers found that most people chose a candidate at the beginning of a campaign and by election day had not changed their minds. These studies suggested that individuals consumed the media that supported their existing views—"selective exposure"—and paid attention only to information confirming what they already believed—"selective perception." Researchers have since developed additional tools to measure the profound as well as subtle effects of the media and have uncovered a range of fascinating ways in which media coverage influences political campaigns.

How Campaigns Are Covered

That news reporting displays a partisan bias is perhaps the most widespread suspicion about media coverage of politics. Many Americans seem to believe that the media are slanted against their views. Yet when researchers measure the evaluative content of news stories and the number of column inches or broadcast minutes devoted to particular candidates, they find relatively little evidence of partisan bias. Of course, some newspapers endorse candidates on their editorial pages, though fewer do so now than in the past. Evidence is mixed on the extent to which or whether these editorial endorsements spill over into the news columns, though most major newspapers have a policy of maintaining a separation between the two areas. Researchers have found even less evaluative content in network television coverage of campaigns, probably because of the history of extensive government regulation of the broadcast media and the networks' need to maintain a broad, national audience. It is in the interest of broadcasters and most newspaper publishers to publish straight news with as little bias as possible in order to appeal to the broad audience sought by advertisers.

What kind of news appeals to a broad audience? In general, high ratings are linked to a particular "definition of news" that stresses excitement, drama, and conflict; timeliness and novelty; compelling pictures, and a focus on human interest and personalities rather than on the actions of faceless institutions. Campaign charges and countercharges are more likely to attract viewers and readers than will detailed stories about a candidate's policy positions. Thus, the media adopt a market-driven definition of "news" in attempting to appeal to the most people.

Yet dramatic, exciting, novel, and timely stories may not be the type of news most important to citizens of a democracy. Stories about lurid murders, for example, get more attention than stories about, say, the Federal Reserve Board, although the Fed's decisions directly affect interest rates, home mortgages, and employment. Economics is poorly understood among the general populace and requires more of an effort to present in an entertaining manner. As a result, a ratings-driven definition of news results in the underreporting of policy issues and institutional trends that affect lives every day but are hard to make exciting.

The market-driven definition of news leads journalists to report most campaign events in the style of a horse race: who's ahead, who's falling behind, who's emerging from the pack. This style of coverage far outweighs the attention paid to policies and issues because it is exciting and dramatic; the polling results are timely; it involves individual success and tragedy; and shifting poll numbers make for reliable graphics. More important, when a news story about a campaign focuses on the horse race, voters do too. Emphasis on poll standings, however, does little to inform voters how the candidates might approach the issues of taxes, defense, or job opportunities.

Ratings affect even that small portion of campaign news that actually deals with political issues. For example, human interest stories about the families of soldiers figured prominently in the reporting on the Iraq War as a campaign issue in 2004, because audiences are more interested in individual personalities than in big, abstract events. Such stories, although compelling, do not help viewers put events and actions into context.

Candidates learn quickly, of course, that they have a better chance of attracting news coverage if they provide stories that conform to the media's need to appeal to a broad audience. Researchers have found that although presidential candidates issue press releases discussing substantive policy issues from the start of a campaign, these news releases are less likely to be picked up, especially by the national media, than are releases attacking an opponent. In this way, media values guide campaign strategy.

Media Agenda Setting, Priming, and Framing in Elections

Media coverage rarely switches people's minds on issues. Changes in opinion usually occur when an issue is new to the viewer or listener and when coverage consistently emphasizes one view. Evidence exists, however, that the media do affect the priorities people assign to various issues and the criteria they use in forming judgments about candidates. Research using edited newscasts found that when TV news highlights a particular problem, viewers come to see that problem as more important than they did before. This is the phenomenon known as agenda setting. Similarly, when TV news draws attention to an issue in a campaign, such as the economy or a candidate's likeability, it keeps that element in viewers' minds. The result is to "prime" it, or cause the viewer to give it greater weight in evaluating the candidates than they otherwise might. For example, when economic issues are primed in campaign coverage, the candidate who does better in the polls on those issues often has a better chance of winning the election.

Framing is another technique that might affect people's opinions. The media can interpret, or "frame," any event in a number of different ways. When George W. Bush won reelection in 2004, for example, the president, other Republicans, and some media presented and interpreted the event as a Republican sweep because his party won the presidency, the House, and the Senate, all by increased margins. Others, however, interpreted it as a hair's breadth victory because

Bush won only 51 percent of the vote. Both interpretations have some validity in that there is supporting evidence for each. Media coverage, however, provides a story only one "lead," not two, and the choice of this lead, interpretation, or frame—or as political practitioners call it, spin—can make a difference in how audiences perceive the election results.

One example of how the framing of a story can affect public opinion involves the Ku Klux Klan. Researchers showed university students two different versions of a local TV story about a Klan rally—one presenting the rally as a free speech issue and the other raising questions about possible violence and disorder. The students who saw the "free speech" frame expressed greater tolerance of such rallies than did those who saw the "disorder" frame. Media coverage affects attitudes in part by focusing on one or two aspects of a complicated story, an inevitable result of the limits on broadcast time, press space, and viewers' attention. Its impact is limited, however, when news sources present multiple or different frames and when citizens have other sources of information, such as interpersonal discussion.

The effects of media coverage are also moderated by aspects of individuals' social identities. People's party identification and other prior attitudes, educational levels, age, and affluence all affect their perceptions of a news story. Individuals receive information not only from mass media, but also from family members, friends, and co-workers. Their level of trust in media sources can also affect their perception of media content.

Media coverage of campaigns tends to elevate a relatively few people as prime sources of news about the campaign. Certain individuals, such as the candidates' press representatives, become reliable sources of information about the strategies and other elements of the operation. They attain this status because they have good information, they are willing to talk, and they tend to present their ideas dramatically and effectively. Journalists are heavily dependent on these sources for "insider information," so it seems only natural for journalists to treat these sources with care; they do not want to bite the hand that feeds them. This situation can result in gentle treatment of incumbents' campaigns, because incumbents are major sources of news. This emphasis on a few sources can limit the range of interpretations citizens receive. The public is much more likely to hear the interpretations and spin of major party activists than those of Libertarians or Greens and more likely to understand the perspectives of well-paid, highly educated campaign professionals than those of people closer to the average voter.

The media emphasis on conflict and drama has increased the focus on negative ads, which encourages campaigns to air more of them. Often, such ads are aired simply to create a media buzz around them, which can benefit the campaign that released it even if it is quickly pulled off the air. Debate continues over the effects of such ads on U.S. politics: Do they make people cynical, turning them away from politics, or do they lead people to become involved? The best recent evidence favors the latter view. Negative ads stimulate emotion, are memorable, and raise the stakes in the campaign, so they tend to increase voter turnout.

Conclusion

Pinpointing the effects of the media on campaigns is a challenging task. Measures of media exposure are not foolproof. If people are asked how much they watch or listen to various types of media, they may not remember accurately or they may "mis-remember," for instance by overestimating how much time they spend watching the news and underestimating the time they spend watching *Survivor*. Determining the amount of change produced by media exposure requires that we learn exactly what information and beliefs people had *before* they were exposed to media news and other programming; that is not easy to do. Researchers also deal with the problem of disentangling the impact of events from the effect of the coverage of those events. For instance, was the Bush campaign in 2004 highly negative in that it operated in attack mode or was it a largely positive campaign that journalists portrayed as negative?

Many other aspects of the media's influence are only now beginning to be examined. These include the effects of "soft news," such as network news magazines and talk shows, as well as pure entertainment programs with the occasional political content. Episodes of police dramas dealing with victims' or suspects' rights or the experiences of gays and lesbians and even war-related commentary on football broadcasts can affect people uninterested in politics but who pick up political information as a byproduct of watching such entertainment programs. The challenge of studying nonverbal communication, including pictures and the facial expressions of actors and news broadcasters, is another area awaiting further study. New research along these lines will deepen our understanding of media effects in campaigns and elections as well.

See also *Horse race journalism; Political content in advertising.*

REFERENCES

Bartels, Larry M. "Messages Received: The Political Impact of Media Exposure." *American Political Science Review* 87, no. 2 (June 1993).

Bennett, W. Lance. *News: The Politics of Illusion.* 6th ed. New York: Pearson/Longman, 2005.

Dalton, Russell J., Paul A. Beck, and Robert Huckfeldt. "Partisan Cues and the Media: Information Flows in the 1992 Presidential Election." *American Political Science Review* 92, no. 1 (March 1998): 121–125.

Graber, Doris A. *Mass Media and American Politics.* 6th ed. Washington, D.C.: CQ Press, 2002.

Iyengar, Shanto, and Donald R. Kinder. *News That Matters.* Chicago: University of Chicago Press, 1987.

Jamieson, Kathleen Hall, and Paul Waldman. *The Press Effect.* Oxford: Oxford University Press, 2003.

Leighley, Jan E. *Mass Media and Politics.* Boston: Houghton Mifflin, 2004.

Page, Benjamin I., Robert Y. Shapiro, and Glenn R. Dempsey. "What Moves Public Opinion?" *American Political Science Review* 81, no. 1 (March 1987): 23–43.

Patterson, Thomas E. *Out of Order.* New York: A. A. Knopf, 1993.

West, Darrell M. *Air Wars.* 3rd ed. Washington, D.C.: CQ Press, 2001.

Cartoons, editorial

Editorial cartoons use wit, irony, hyperbole, humor, and caricature to comment on politics and society. As social critics, editorial cartoonists direct their sense of incredulity or morality at events and trends in the news. They are not compelled or required to present both or all sides of an issue. "The best cartoons," said Boardman Robinson, who worked as an editorial cartoonist during the early decades of the twentieth century, "often grow out of a sense of indignation. They express one's reaction from the meanness and futilities of life, one's feeling of resentment at social wrong and oppression."

For an editorial cartoon to effectively convey its message, it must resonate with readers in an intimate or personal way, perhaps by even making the reader uncomfortable. Editorial cartoonists attempt to hit at the heart of something that is wrong, unjust, or absurd, often by making it appear ridiculous or even sinister. This sometimes requires a startling image. "In a democratic society—where apathy and ignorance lurk as sources of constant danger—there are few instruments as powerful as editorial cartoons," John Kuenster wrote in 1961. "Sometimes, free people have to be punched, figuratively speaking, between the eyes to awaken them to their heritage . . . to remind them freedom thrives best in an informed, alert society."

In 1754 the Pennsylvania Gazette *published this cartoon depicting Benjamin Franklin's revolutionary sentiments in an effort to rally colonial support for independence from Britain.*

The most memorable editorial cartoons tend to be simple and to the point. Like a switchblade, they cut deeply and leave an impression. The *Washington Post*'s Herbert Block—or Herblock as he signed his cartoons—once drew a stubbly faced Vice President Richard M. Nixon, who years later told his advisers, "I have to erase the Herblock image." Few articles or photographs during the Vietnam War era are as memorable as David Levine's drawing of President Lyndon B. Johnson lifting his shirt to reveal a scar shaped like Vietnam. (Johnson had earlier emerged from surgery to show reporters and photographers his gallbladder scar.) Levine used this instance to capture Johnson's legacy in a way that transcends the written word. In contrast, in making complex issues simple, editorial cartoons may sometimes employ trite and hackneyed symbols or resort to ethnic or sexist stereotypes. Poorly conceived cartoons can be confusing or unclear, rendering them ineffective.

Editorial cartoonists have contributed to the political and social fabric of the United States since Benjamin Franklin called for a united front against England in his crude drawing "Join, or Die." In 1812 an editorial cartoon depicted a salamander as a newly created political district devised by Massachusetts governor Elbridge Gerry, introducing the world *gerrymander* into the American lexicon. A late nineteenth-century comic strip called "The Yellow Kid" served as inspiration for the term *yellow journalism*. In the 1950s, Herblock coined the term *McCarthyism* in associating the abuses of the "red scare" with Sen. Joseph McCarthy (R-Wis.), the outspoken chairman of the Senate hearings investigating communism in the United States. Critics of McCarthy accused him and other conservatives of using politics to curtail civil liberties. In one drawing, Herblock depicts a man labeled "hysteria" carrying a bucket of water up a ladder to extinguish the Statue of Liberty's flame.

William M. "Boss" Tweed, the ignominious political figure of the 1870s, summarized the simple potency of editorial cartoons in reportedly saying, "I don't care what they print about me. Most of my constituents can't read. But them damn pictures!" *Harper's Weekly* cartoonist Thomas Nast thus helped shine greater light on Tweed's dealings with drawings that included "The Brain," an illustration of Tweed's body with a bag of money for a head. Nast became the first cartoonist to demonstrate the potential impact of cartoons on society, first during the Civil War, when President Abraham Lincoln called him "our best recruiting sergeant" for his attacks on the Confederacy, and then during his series of attacks against Tweed and New York City's Tammany Hall. Nast is credited with popularizing the symbols of a donkey to represent the Democratic Party, the elephant as the Republican Party, and the tiger to stand for Tammany Hall. In his use of powerful imagery, Nast set the standard against which future cartoonists would be measured.

Nast's criticism of Tweed demonstrates the lengths to which some politicians might go to suppress cartoonists. Tweed reportedly once tried to intimidate and even bribe Nast so that the artist would quit criticizing him. In 1903 the Pennsylvania legislature passed a law aimed at suppressing cartoons, but the measure had the opposite effect, leading cartoonists throughout the country to condemn it. During World War I, the U.S. government prosecuted a number of cartoonists for drawings critical of the war, and during the 1960s, President Nixon ordered the Internal Revenue Service to audit *Los Angeles Times* cartoonist Paul Conrad, a frequent Nixon critic.

Editorial cartoons also of course can provoke angry responses from readers. For instance, Edmund Duffy of the *Baltimore Sun* was fearless in condemning the Ku Klux Klan in the 1920s and early 1930s. After one lynching, Duffy drew a black man dangling from a rope accompanied by the state song, "Maryland, My Maryland!" Incensed readers attacked the newspaper's delivery trucks and beat its drivers. Nevertheless, the cartoon contributed to the state passing an anti-lynching law. H. L. Mencken, Duffy's editor at the *Baltimore Sun,* once said, "Give me a good cartoonist and I can throw out half the editorial staff."

Editorial cartoonists often connect with their readers by finding the humor in tragedy and suffering. During World War II, cartoonist Bill Mauldin poignantly captured the solder's life in his "Willie and Joe" strip. Mauldin later produced the image of the Lincoln Memorial weeping after the assassination of President John F. Kennedy, one of the most poignant cartoons in U.S. history. Editorial cartoonists tried to capture the aftermath of al-Qaida's September 11, 2001, attacks with images reminiscent of the Lincoln illustration, such as a weeping Statue of Liberty, a determined Uncle Sam, or a bald eagle sharpening its talons. Later, many of the country's best editorial cartoonists—among them Clay Bennett, Steve Benson, Jeff Danziger, Kevin Kallaugher, Pat Oliphant, Joel Pett, Ann Telnaes, and Garry Trudeau—emerged as vocal critics of the war against Iraq. Like Mauldin during World War II, Trudeau, the author of *Doonesbury,* sends one of his characters, B.D., to war in Iraq, where he loses a leg. The strip then chronicles B.D.'s struggles with physical, mental, and emotional pain, which evocatively resonates with large numbers of soldiers and their families.

Editorial cartoonists have made their greatest impact under conditions involving social unrest, charismatic politicians, appropriate technology, and a healthy newspaper industry and supportive editors. They are least likely to succeed under state-sanctioned repression, a content or fearful status quo, an abundance of banal politicians, poor or unavailable technology, and a struggling newspaper industry. During the last twenty-five years, the number of editorial cartoonists working for daily newspapers has been steadily shrinking, a reflection of the declining influence of the newspaper industry in the United States. Editorial cartoonists have therefore begun adapting to other media, including television, the Internet, and animation.

See also *Thomas, Nast; Block, Herbert Lawrence*

REFERENCES

Fischer, Roger. *Them Damned Pictures!* North Haven, Conn.: Archon Books, 1996.

Hess, Stephen, and Sandy Northrop. *Drawn and Quartered: The History of American Political Cartoons.* Montgomery, Ala.: Elliott and Clark, 1996.

Hodgart, Matthew. *Satire.* New York: McGraw-Hill, 1969.

Kuenster, John. "The Responsible Editorial Cartoonist." *Voice of St. Jude,* March 1961, 10.

Lamb, Chris. "Pulitzer-Prize-Winning Cartoonist Still Draws His Own Conclusions." *The Daily Iowan,* November 2, 1988.

———. "Drawing the Limits of Political Cartoons in the U.S.: The Courtroom and the Newsroom." Ph.D. diss., Bowling Green State University, 1995.

———. *Drawn to Extremes: The Use and Abuse of Editorial Cartoons.* New York: Columbia University Press, 2004.

Paine, Albert Bigelow. *T.–H. Nast: His Period and His Pictures.* New York: Macmillan, 1904.

Press, Charles. *The Political Cartoon.* London: Macmillan, 1981.

Robinson, Boardman. "The Cartoon as a Means of Artisitic Expression." *Current Literature* 53 (October 1912): 462.

Carville, James

James Carville (1944–), a political consultant and commentator, rose to national prominence as a political advisor to Democrat Bill Clinton's 1992 presidential campaign. Having difficulties in college, Carville dropped out of school and served for two years in the Marine Corps before returning to Louisiana State University to obtain undergraduate and law degrees. He worked as a litigator at a law firm in Baton Rouge from 1973 to 1979.

Dissatisfied with a legal career, Carville began freelancing as a political consultant and in 1982 managed his first campaign, for a Virginia senatorial candidate. The following year, he managed a Texas gubernatorial campaign and was nicknamed the "Ragin' Cajun," because of his sharp repartee and intellect. His first major victory came with the 1986 election of Robert Casey to the governorship of Pennsylvania. During this time, Carville had begun collaborating with Paul Begala, with whom he formed a political consulting firm. Among their other successes are the 1990 gubernatorial victory of Zell Miller in Georgia, the 1991 election of Harris Wofford to represent Pennsylvania in the Senate, and the reelection of Sen. Frank Lautenberg of New Jersey in 1998. In 1997 he co-founded the international consulting firm Gould, Greenberg, Carville, NOP.

While advising Clinton's 1992 campaign, Carville courted controversy when his personal relationship with Republican strategist Mary Matalin, his counterpart in the Bush campaign, became public. Carville and Matalin married in 1993. Carville co-hosted CNN's *Crossfire* from April 2003 until its cancellation in 2005. Carville is the author of *We're Right, They're Wrong* (1996) and *And the Horse He Rode In On: The People v. Kenneth Starr* (1998). He is co-author, with Paul Begala, of *Buck Up, Suck Up—and Come Back When You Foul Up* (2002).

REFERENCES

Matalin, Mary, and James Carville. *All's Fair: Love, War, and Running for President.* New York: Random House Value Publishing, 1997.

Office of James Carville, www.carville.info.

Cater, Douglass

S. Douglass Cater (1923–1995), a journalist and public official, was instrumental in the creation of the Public Broadcasting Service (PBS). Cater served as an analyst in the Office of Strategic Services (OSS) during World War II and began his journalism career as an editor of Harvard University's *Crimson* while completing his education after the war. He joined the *Reporter* magazine, serving as its Washington editor from 1950 to 1963 and its national affairs editor from 1963 to 1964, and then left to work in government.

Cater served as special assistant to President Lyndon B. Johnson from 1964 to 1968, specializing in health, education, and welfare matters. He is credited with convincing Johnson to endorse the Public Broadcasting Act of 1967 with the argument that "our security depends on the enlightenment of our citizens" and became known as the "godfather to public broadcasting." He worked for Hubert Humphrey's 1968 presidential campaign and then moved into teaching and leadership positions in higher education. He also served several years as vice chairman of the *Sunday Observer* of London and chairman of the *Observer International.* Cater authored *The Fourth Branch of Government* (1959), *Power in Washington* (1964), and *Dana: The Irrelevant Man* (1970), and with Marques Childs co-authored *Ethics in a Business Society* (1963).

See also *Fourth estate; Corporation for Public Broadcasting.*

REFERENCE

"An Interview with Douglass Cater." *American Education* 2 (October 1966): 20–21.

CBS

CBS is a leading broadcast television and radio network. It began in 1927 as the United Independent Broadcasters, which struggled financially until later that year, when the owners of Columbia Records bought the network and renamed it the Columbia Phonographic Broadcasting System. The company began broadcasting in 1928 with sixteen stations. Also in 1928, William "Bill" Paley, who would do more than anyone to shape the network's identity, bought Columbia Phonographic's stake in the network and renamed the company the Columbia Broadcasting System, CBS. Paley emphasized quality programming that earned the network the nickname the "Tiffany network."

CBS became a leader in early radio news, hiring the legendary Edward R. Murrow. The most famous journalist during CBS's early days, Murrow became known for his reports from a besieged London during the German blitzkrieg bombings of 1940. His reports, which started, "This is London" (emphasis on *This*, followed by a slight pause), brought home the reality of the war to Americans. Perhaps most important, however, was Murrow's skill in hiring excellent print reporters to serve in CBS's news division. These reporters worked under trying technical and political constraints to beam world news to Americans during a particularly turbulent period of history.

CBS, not as quick as other networks to move into television, was eventually forced into the medium by market pressures, but after doing so established one of the three major broadcast television networks. The network continued to distinguish itself in news. Some conservatives called it the "Communist Broadcasting System" because of Murrow's critical reporting on the activities of Sen. Joseph McCarthy (R–Wis). Murrow's public affairs program, *See It Now* (first aired on March 9, 1954), along with the nationally televised Army-McCarthy hearings led to McCarthy's downfall. CBS ironically required staff to take loyalty oaths, for which it was criticized, though perhaps this policy was a reaction to the criticism of its news reporting. Murrow left the network in 1961 to join the United States Information Agency.

Fred W. Friendly, CBS's widely respected news division president, resigned in 1966, when it became clear that profit and entertainment had become more important than the news division as reflected in the emphasis on such shows as *Beverly Hillbillies* and *Petticoat Junction*. In the early 1970s, however, the network once again distinguished itself by airing quality programming. By 1973, CBS arguably had the most critically hailed lineup in the history of the medium: *M*A*S*H*, *All in the Family*, the *Mary Tyler Moore Show*, the *Bob Newhart Show*, and the *Carole Burnette Show* dominated Saturday night programming.

The *CBS Evening News*, the network's flagship news program, was anchored for eighteen years by Walter Cronkite, "the most trusted man in America." Cronkite's shift toward more critical reporting of the Vietnam War after the 1968 Tet offensive signaled the emergence of opposition to the war as a mainstream position. It was also in the late 1960s that the *CBS Evening News* overtook NBC's *Huntley-Brinkley Report* in the ratings. In 1968 the news division debuted *60 Minutes,* the award-winning and long-running weekly newsmagazine. Dan Rather, who joined CBS News in 1962, worked as a reporter and co-editor on *60 Minutes* and anchored the *CBS Evening News* from 1981 to 2005. Katie Couric, former co-host of NBC's *Today Show,* was tapped to replace Rather as its evening news anchor in September 2006.

CBS has experienced ownership changes after Paley's death in 1990. The Westinghouse Electric Corporation bought it in 1995, and in 2000 Viacom acquired CBS in the largest media merger at the time. In 2005 Viacom spun off CBS into the CBS Corporation, which includes the broadcast television network and radio, as well as publishing (including Simon and Schuster), TV production, cable television, outdoor advertising, and theme parks.

REFERENCES

Kisseloff, Jeff. *The Box: An Oral History of Television, 1920–1961.* New York: Viking, 1995.
Paley, William. *As It Happened, A Memoir.* Garden City, N.Y.: Doubleday, 1979.
Smith, Sally Bedell. *In All His Glory: The Life of William S. Paley, the Legendary Tycoon and His Brilliant Circle.* New York: Simon and Schuster, 1990.

Censorship

Censorship is the control of expression and communication, particularly the control of mass communication, which includes television, radio, cinema, the press, and the Internet. Governments have practiced censorship since antiquity as a means of promoting cultural norms and maintaining social and political order. The word derives from the Roman office of the censor, which was established in 443 BCE.

In 1789 James Madison, the author of the Bill of Rights, sought in the First Amendment of the Constitution to protect individual freedoms, including freedom of speech and freedom of the press. Thus, publishing became the only private enterprise given explicit constitutional protection. With this protection, the press could serve as an additional check on the three official branches of government; the press is therefore sometimes called the "fourth branch." Despite this protection, freedom of the press to publish was and is by no means absolute. The Alien and Sedition Acts of 1798 targeted opponents of the John Adams administration, including those in the media, and censorship by state and local governments was not unheard of as the First Amendment was initially only applied to federal, but not state, abridgement of press and speech rights. In the early twentieth century, however, the Supreme Court, through various rulings, interpreted the Fourteenth Amendment to enforce the power of the First Amendment against government censorship at the national, state, and local levels. Of special interest was prior restraint, or censorship before publication.

Despite the Court's ruling, federal, state, and local governments continued to practice explicit forms of censorship by setting significant legal limits on expression. For example, the Federal Communications Commission established rules governing the use of broadcast media; some local ordinances required advance registration for mass demonstrations on public property and sometimes restricted them to particular venues; criminal prosecution remained a possibility for actions involving sexual obscenity, solicitation, fraud, threats of violence, or disclosure of classified information; defamation, fraud, and workplace harassment were civil offenses.

In addition, in times of war and national crisis, the government has restricted the freedom of the press to publish or broadcast, sometimes through the acquiescence of the media themselves. In World War I, the government imposed censorship on coverage of the war at home and abroad through the Espionage Act, the Trading-with-the-Enemy Act, and the Sedition Act. During the "red scare" of the 1920s, the Supreme Court upheld the jailing of communist publishers on the ground that they threatened national security. During World War II, journalists and media organizations readily cooperated with the government and submitted material to military reviewers, largely because of a consensus that certain information could harm the war effort. The media had more freedom to cover the Korean War and, especially, the Vietnam War, but the government still sought to restrict the flow of information. Since then the media have grudgingly accepted restrictions on information in exchange for access by joining more readily controlled press pools, for example during the Panama invasion in 1989 and the 1991 Persian Gulf War. They did so again by cooperating with the Pentagon in "embedding" journalists with military units during the 2003 Iraq War.

Although formal censorship is relatively rare, it is not the only variety. Implicit, or socially imposed, forms of censorship are more sophisticated. Because they are less obvious, they may be just as powerful as legal forms. Journalists may use restriction, omission, obfuscation, ambiguity, suppression, sanitization, distraction, and manipulation to divert attention from issues that they prefer not to be discussed or to exclude others from discussion. For example, journalists may choose not to cover certain issues or views because they go against "politically correct" attitudes or are too far outside mainstream values. Media self-censorship may also occur in matters of economic self-interest, such as when coverage involves media monopolies, advertising revenue, or business practices of media parent corporations.

REFERENCES

Chomsky, Noam. *Necessary Illusions: Thought Control in Democratic Societies.* Boston: South End Press, 1989.
Foerstel, Herbert. *Banned in the Media: A Reference Guide to Censorship in the Press, Motion Pictures, Broadcasting, and the Internet.* Westport, Conn.: Greenwood Press, 1998.
Phelan, John, ed. *Communications Control: Readings in the Motives and Structures of Censorship.* New York: Sheed and Ward, 1969.

Center for Investigative Reporting

The Center for Investigative Reporting (CIR), founded in 1977, is an independent news organization committed to high-quality reporting in the public interest. The center's mission is to strengthen democracy by exposing injustice and abuses of power. To do so, CIR investigates critical and underreported issues, produces in-depth stories, and provides its reporting to citizens and decision makers. It markets its stories to news outlets for publication or broadcast, but also provides raw information and documentation to the outlets. CIR primarily focuses on social and criminal justice, the environment, and science and technology. The center is staffed by reporters and editors working in San Francisco and Washington, D.C., and freelancers throughout the country.

REFERENCES

Center for Investigative Reporting, www.muckraker.org.

Center for Media and Public Affairs

The Center for Media and Public Affairs (CMPA), a nonprofit research center, conducts studies of news and entertainment media. Founded in 1985, CMPA uses surveys and content analysis to evaluate public controversies about the media and is best known for its reports on news media coverage of controversial issues, government officials, and political candidates. It has also studied sex and violence in entertainment media. Unlike some media watchdog groups, CMPA does not charge the media with biased or inaccurate reporting, but provides statistical breakdowns of "positive" and "negative" coverage, letting readers interpret the results. Nonetheless, some critics charge that CMPA's studies reflect a conservative agenda. CMPA counters that it uses scientific methods and that liberals as well as conservatives cite its studies. In 2004 CMPA affiliated with George Mason University in Fairfax, Virginia.

REFERENCE

Center for Media and Public Affairs, www.cmpa.com.

Center for Media Literacy

The Center for Media Literacy promotes the skills needed to select and critically consume information from the media with the goal of creating a more democratic society. In 1977 Elizabeth Thoman founded *Media & Values,* a graduate school newsletter project that grew into a magazine advancing media literacy. The Center for Media and Values followed in 1989. The center distributed media literacy resources on such topics as sexism in the media and alcohol and tobacco advertising. In 1994 the Center for Media and Values became the nonprofit Center for Media Literacy. The center focuses its resources on national leadership, community outreach, and teacher training for the U.S. media literacy movement. It conducts literacy workshops, publishes the magazine *Connect,* distributes educational materials on media literacy, and promotes alliances with organizations interested in the education of children and adults.

REFERENCE

Center for Media Literacy, www.medialit.org.

Chancellor, John

John Chancellor (1927–1996), a broadcast journalist, served as an anchor for the *NBC Nightly News* for more than a decade. Chancellor developed a passion for journalism as a fourteen-year-old copyboy for the *Chicago Daily News.* He served two years in the U.S. Army and spent two years in college before dropping out and working for the *Chicago Sun Times.* Chancellor joined NBC as a reporter and rose to prominence when NBC chose him to replace Dave Garroway as host of the *Today Show* during 1961 and 1962. His frustration with the clash between journalism and the entertainment aspects of television news surfaced at this time and would concern him throughout his broadcasting career.

During the 1964 Republican National Convention, for unknown reasons police surrounded Chancellor on the floor and escorted him from the auditorium as he famously said, on air, "this is John Chancellor, somewhere in custody." He became NBC's chief White House correspondent during 1964 and 1965. President Lyndon B. Johnson persuaded Chancellor to join the government as the director of Voice of America, the broadcast unit of the U.S. Information Agency, from 1965 to 1967. Dissatisfied with government service, he returned to journalism and to NBC, where he served as an anchor for the *NBC Nightly News* from 1970 to 1982. During his career as anchor, Chancellor interviewed every U.S. president from Harry Truman to Ronald Reagan, every British prime minister from Clement Atlee to Margaret Thatcher, and every Israeli prime minister from Golda Meir to Menachem Begin. He also reported from the Berlin Wall when it was built in 1961 and when it was torn down in 1989. His struggle with changes to the nature and tone of television news is reflected in his parting words, "I think I've outlived the culture here." Chancellor wrote *The News Business* (1983), *Peril and Promise: A Commentary on America* (1990), and *The New News Business: A Guide to Writing and Reporting* (1995).

REFERENCES

Castro, Peter. "Sure Hand, Brave Heart." *People,* July 29, 1996, 67–68.
Chancellor, John. *Peril and Promise: A Commentary on America.* New York: Harper and Row, 1990.
Chancellor, John, and Walter R. Mears. *The New News Business: A Guide to Writing and Reporting.* New York: HarperPerennial, 1995.
"Covering It All." *Newsweek,* July 22, 1996, 67.

Chat rooms

See *New media*

Children and the media

Children spend more time engaged by television than with any other type of mass media. They view it an average of three hours per day, and by graduation from high school have spent more time in front of the television than in the classroom. It is well established that children's exposure to television influences many of their perceptions about social norms, beliefs, attitudes, and behaviors. Given the prominent role of television in the lives of children, it is not surprising that policymakers have devoted more attention to protecting children from its adverse effects than from those of any other medium of mass communication.

All regulations related to television content flow from the federal level. Although Congress can adopt legislation governing any aspect of television, it is more common for the Federal Communications Commission (FCC) to exercise its authority to regulate broadcast television and to a lesser extent cable television. Different rules apply to broadcast and cable television regarding what content they may or may not deliver, and they receive differing degrees of First Amend-

ment protection. Although the First Amendment guarantees freedom of speech and freedom of the press, the courts have held that the government may restrict these freedoms in cases in which there is a "compelling governmental interest" involving the protection of children.

Broadcast television stations are licensed by the FCC and, because they use public airwaves, are required to serve the "public interest, convenience, and necessity." The basis for many of the regulations related to children rests on this obligation. Broadcast stations are locally based, and most are affiliated with national broadcast networks, such as ABC, CBS, Fox, NBC, or PBS. In contrast, cable networks, such as HBO and MTV, by virtue of transmitting exclusively via cable, do not require use of the FCC-licensed, publicly owned airwaves. Also, they are available only to consumers who agree to pay a subscription fee. For these reasons, cable stations are not as heavily regulated as broadcast channels.

Print media receive the greatest degree of First Amendment protection from content-based government regulation. Few policy concerns, however, have been raised involving children and print media: their literacy skills limit early access to text-based materials, and their access to adult-oriented print media can be more easily restricted compared to that to television or film. The law is still evolving in terms of how the First Amendment applies to Internet material, but the courts appear to view the Internet as closer to print media than to television in terms of the government's

Lawrence Lien, CEO of Parental Guide Inc., explains how parents can use the "V-chip" to block television programs containing sensitive or inappropriate material. The FCC holds responsibility for regulating the broadcast industry, but the V-chip allows parents to further restrict the programming their children consume.

authority to regulate content for the protection of minors. In sum, the government can regulate broadcast television more actively to protect children from harm than is permissible concerning print media, the Internet, or cable television. Policy concerns involving children and media fall into three primary categories: (1) policies designed to protect children from adverse effects of exposure to potentially harmful program content; (2) policies designed to protect children from adverse advertising; and (3) policies designed to promote educational content beneficial to children. Law and regulation in all of these areas have focused primarily on broadcast television.

Harmful Content

Television violence is the area of children and media policy that has received the most public attention and debate over the years. Concern about television violence surfaced early in the medium's history, with Congress holding hearings on it in the mid-1950s. In the 1960s, 1970s, and 1980s, researchers began collecting evidence about the potential harmful psychological effects of viewing violence. Hundreds of studies have examined the topic, and their findings identify three primary types of effects on children: (1) learning of aggressive attitudes and behaviors; (2) desensitization (or increased callousness) toward victims of violence; and (3) exaggerated fear of being victimized by violence from others.

By the 1990s, a broad range of public health officials and organizations, including the surgeon general, the National Institute of Mental Health, the American Medical Association, and the American Psychological Association, had concluded that too much exposure to television violence posed a significant risk of negatively affecting children.

Despite policymakers, concerns about television violence from the 1950s to the 1990s, officials failed to formally consider any serious governmental regulation during this period. Rather, Congress and the FCC expressed their concern to television industry leaders by conducting hearings and voicing public complaints about the levels of violence broadcast. Such complaints, the "raised eyebrow approach" to regulation, were supposed to convey an implicit threat of regulation if the industry failed to "clean up its act." This approach enjoyed some success at limiting violence on television, but violent programming often increased during periods when policymakers turned their attention elsewhere. In 1996 in the State of the Union Address, President

Bill Clinton called on Congress to adopt the V-chip, an electronic filtering device that parents can use to block the reception of programming that contains violence or other material inappropriate for children. Congress included a provision in the Telecommunications Act of 1996 requiring that all television sets sold in the United States include a V-chip.

The legislators left it to the television industry to devise a program-rating system for use with the V-chip. In 1997 the industry adopted a system similar to the long-established motion picture ratings used to alert potential viewers and parents to films' content. Television programs intended for general audiences are rated according to one of four age-based categories: TV-G (general audience), TV-PG (parental guidance suggested), TV-14 (parents strongly cautioned; may be unsuitable for children under 14 years of age), and TV-MA (mature audiences only). Programs intended for children may also be rated TV-Y (appropriate for all youth) or TV-Y7 (designed for age 7 and above). In addition, the V-chip television ratings include content descriptors to indicate why a program received a particular rating. These include V for violence, S for sexual behavior, D for sexual dialogue, and L for adult language. Thus, a program rated TV-14 for intense violence and strong adult language would include the V and L content ratings along with the TV-14 designation. The television industry maintains a complete description of the V-chip rating system on the Internet at www.tvguidelines.org.

With the exception of sports events and newscasts, all other programs on broadcast and cable television are rated according to this system. The network or channel distributing the programming rates the content. With the V-chip technology, parents have the option of activating the filtering device to block certain categories of programming. Research suggests that only a small minority of parents use this capability, and when they do so it is primarily to protect younger children. Many more parents, however, report that they find the television ratings helpful in deciding which programs are appropriate for their children.

The second concern about the harmful effects of media on children involves content categorized as indecent. The FCC defines indecency as material that describes or depicts sexual or excretory activities or organs in terms that are patently offensive to contemporary community standards. This policy applies to broadcast radio and television, but not to cable television or other non-broadcast media. Indecent material may not be aired between the hours of 6:00 a.m.

and 10:00 p.m., when children are most likely to be watching. In *Federal Communications Commission v. Pacifica Foundation* (1978), the Supreme Court upheld the constitutionality of the FCC's indecency policy when the agency fined the New York radio station WBAI for airing George Carlin's "Filthy Words" monologue. In the skit, the comedian utters a series of four-letter words that the FCC had deemed indecent and jokes about their supposed harmfulness.

In the 1990s, Congress and the FCC attempted to extend the restriction on broadcast indecency to twenty-four hours a day, but the courts overturned their effort, ruling it a First Amendment violation. For the policy to be constitutional required allowing a period of time for adults to access indecent material, which receives a degree of constitutional protection. Thus, the "safe harbor" approach to regulating indecency remains in effect, with indecent material prohibited on broadcast channels between 6:00 a.m. and 10:00 p.m., but allowed late at night, when children are less likely to be watching or unsupervised by an adult. Indecency regulation does not apply to cable television channels, film, or other mass media. Thus, program content on cable networks may include more explicit sexual content than is allowed on broadcast channels or language considered by some to be offensive.

Congress has twice unsuccessfully sought to regulate indecent material on the Internet. In 1996 it adopted the Communications Decency Act, and in 1998 it approved the Child Online Protection Act (COPA). The courts overturned both laws as unconstitutional violations of the First Amendment. Although broadcasters are licensed to use the publicly owned airwaves and therefore are required by law to serve the public interest, the Internet is available to everyone for any purpose. As a result, the courts grant greater First Amendment protection to the Internet than to broadcast media.

Influence of Advertising

The average child is exposed to an estimated 40,000 television commercials annually. Unhealthy food products, such as candies, snacks, sugared cereals, and fast foods, account for as much as half of all television advertising aimed at children. Research has shown that children ages eight and under lack an awareness of the persuasive intent of advertising messages. As a result, they more readily accept advertising claims and appeals as accurate and truthful and are therefore

uniquely vulnerable to commercials' influence. To address this concern, policymakers adopted a number of regulations on television advertising to children, including restrictions on certain practices, such as host-selling and program-length commercials and limits on the amount of commercial time allowed in children's programming.

The FCC enacted regulations in the 1970s prohibiting host-selling, which is when a character who appears in a program also promotes a product in a commercial aired during that character's show. For example, it would be considered host-selling if Fred Flintstone appeared in a cereal commercial during a break from *The Flintstones*. Another FCC policy restricts the advertising of program-related products during a show regardless of whether a program-related character is involved. This regulation, the program-length commercial policy, would prohibit a commercial for Flintstones cereal from appearing during *The Flintstones* even if no program-related character was featured in the ad. Both of these regulations apply solely to broadcast television, but cable television channels follow them voluntarily. In 1990 Congress limited to 12 minutes per hour on weekdays and 10.5 minutes per hour on weekends the amount of time that broadcast and cable channels can devote to commercials in children's television programming. The FCC can fine stations that exceed these limits, and such incidents have occurred. For example, the agency fined the cable network Nickelodeon $1 million for airing excessive commercials 591 times.

Educational Media Content for Children

As the government has devoted substantial attention to protecting children from harm by the media, it has also taken steps to promote more positive options for children during the time they spend watching television. For many years, child advocates lobbied the FCC to require broadcast television stations to deliver children's educational programming as part of their public interest obligations. The FCC refused to act, preferring marketplace competition to government regulation, but because children's programming is not particularly profitable, few commercial stations chose on their own volition to air educational children's shows. In 1990 Congress finally adopted the Children's Television Act, which requires that broadcast stations serve the educational and informational needs of children in order to maintain their licenses. The FCC is responsible for enforcing the law.

Because the FCC can be uneasy with content-based

judgments, it initially allowed broadcast stations to liberally define what qualifies as educational programming. This led some stations to designate such programs as *The Jetsons* and *Yogi Bear* as educational. In 1996 the FCC tightened its enforcement of the law in several ways: educational programs must have a specifiable learning goal or objective; stations should normally provide three hours per week of children's educational programming; and stations must identify their educational and informational children's shows with an "E/I" on-screen logo to help parents identify beneficial programs. The E/I logo must remain on-screen at all times throughout a qualifying show.

Cable television channels are not required to serve the public interest by delivering educational children's shows, but some cable networks offer such content as part of their regular mix of programming. The federal government provides limited support for the children's educational programming that airs on public broadcasting stations, which have traditionally been the industry leader, introducing *Sesame Street* in 1969. Based on the history of the relationship between children and the media, it is clear that as children's use and exposure to the media change along with media technologies, political debates over the proper role of government in regulating that relationship will continue.

See also *Action for Children's Television; Federal Communications Commission v. Pacifica Foundation (1978); Telecommunications Act of 1996.*

REFERENCES

Calvert, Sandra, and Jennifer Kotler. "Lessons from Children's Television: The Impact of the Children's Television Act on Children's Learning." *Journal of Applied Developmental Psychology* 24 (2003): 275–335.

Gentile, Douglas, ed. *Media Violence and Children: A Complete Guide for Parents and Professionals.* Westport, Conn.: Praeger, 2003.

Gunter, Barrie, Caroline Oates, and Mark Blades. *Advertising to Children on TV: Content, Impact, and Regulation.* Mahwah, N.J.: Lawrence Erlbaum Associates, 2005.

Hamilton, James, ed. *Television Violence and Public Policy.* Ann Arbor: University of Michigan Press, 1998.

Kaiser Family Foundation. "Parents, Media, and Public Policy: A Kaiser Family Foundation Survey." Kaiser Family Foundation, Menlo Park, Calif., 2004, www.kff.org/entmedia/entmedia092304pkg.cfm.

Kunkel, Dale, and Brian Wilcox. "Children and Media Policy." In *Handbook of Children and the Media.* edited by Dorothy Singer and Jerome Singer. Thousand Oaks, Calif.: Sage Publications, 2001.

Minow, Newton, and Craig Lamay. *Abandoned in the Wasteland: Children, Television, and the First Amendment.* New York: Hill and Wang, 1995.

Palmer, Edward L., and Brian M. Young. *The Faces of Televisual Media: Teaching, Violence, Selling to Children.* Mahwah, N.J.: Lawrence Erlbaum Associates, 2003.

Roberts, Donald, and Ulla Foehr. *Kids and Media in America.* Cambridge: Oxford University Press, 2004.

Strausburger, Victor, and Barbara Wilson. *Children, Adolescents, and the Media.* Thousand Oaks, Calif.: Sage Publications, 2002.

Chomsky, Noam

Noam Avram Chomsky (1928–) is a prominent social and political theorist and educator. Chomsky earned his doctorate in linguistics in 1955 and began his teaching career at the Massachusetts Institute of Technology, where he was the Ferrari P. Ward Chair of Modern Languages and Linguistics from 1966 to 1976; he is currently Emeritus Institute Professor of linguistics. Over the years, he has advanced linguistics and the principles of education as well as the contribution of language in politics.

Chomsky is the creator of the Chomsky hierarchy, a classification system of formal languages. He has used his stature as a world-renowned academic and linguistics theoretician to speak out on political issues beyond his credentials. Since 1965, Chomsky has been a leading critic of U.S. foreign policy and has promoted a radical vision of U.S. social, political, and economic policies. He played a major role in the opposition to the Vietnam War.

Chomsky has directed his thinking and political writings at U.S. intervention in the developing world, the political economy of human rights, and the "propaganda" role of the corporate media. According to a model he and Edward Herman developed, media in democratic societies such as the United States' serve a propaganda function in maintaining support for the regime, not unlike in totalitarian systems, though the means differ. They argue that structural biases in how the news is produced—in particular, the influence of owners, advertisers, dominant interest groups, and government sources—greatly influence content and lead to media that help "manufacture the consent" of the population. Chomsky's ideas and activism involving media and politics have made him a controversial if significant figure, especially on the American Left.

See also *Media bias; Propaganda.*

In January 2006, MIT professor and political activist Noam Chomsky delivered the Annual Amnesty International Lecture "War on Terror." A vocal opponent of the Vietnam War, Chomsky continues to criticize U.S. foreign policy and the corporate media.

REFERENCES

Chomsky, Noam. "You Say You Want Devolution." *Progressive,* March 1996, 18–19.

Herman, Edward S., and Noam Chomsky. *Manufacturing Consent: The Political Economy of the Mass Media.* New York: Pantheon, 1988.

Lyons, John. *Modern Masters: Noam Chomsky.* New York: Viking Press, 1970.

MacFarquhar, Larissa. "The Devil's Accountant." *New Yorker.* March 31, 2003, 64-79.

Rai, Milan. *Chomsky's Politics.* London: Verso, 1995.

Christian Broadcasting Network

The United States' first Christian television station went on the air in October 1961. Incorporated as the Christian Broadcasting Network (CBN) and operated by Marion "Pat" Robertson, it grew into the world's largest Christian media enterprise and provided Robertson, a Baptist minister, a platform for airing his conservative religious and political views.

Robertson delivered his first political statement on CBN in 1974, when he lambasted President Richard M. Nixon for the "cruel hoax" he had foisted upon the American people.

In 1976 he supported Jimmy Carter for president, but disappointed by Carter's liberal social agenda, he became a Reagan supporter in the 1980s. Robertson himself sought the Republican presidential nomination in 1988, but following the Iowa caucus his campaign largely fizzled.

After his political defeat, Robertson built the Christian Coalition, a grassroots political movement for which he recruited a million supporters by using the CBN mailing list. The coalition mobilized a number of formerly inactive evangelical and Pentecostal Christians to get involved in politics. Robertson and the coalition's resulting political success and ties to the Republican Party led to increased scrutiny by Robertson's opponents and the Internal Revenue Service (IRS). In March 1998, CBN agreed to a settlement with the IRS for inappropriate political activity related to Robertson's 1988 presidential bid. The settlement revoked the CBN's tax-exempt nonprofit status for 1986 and 1987. The CBN also made an undisclosed "significant payment" to the IRS and promised not to engage in campaign activities. The CBN and Christian Coalition are officially separate entities, but Robertson continues to use his network, and its *700 Club* news and discussion show, to broadcast an evangelical viewpoint on the issues of the day.

See also *Robertson, Pat.*

Televangelist Pat Robertson founded the Christian Broadcasting Network, home of the 700 Club and other religious programming, in 1961. He has been the source of controversy over the years, such as here in August 2005 when he seemingly called for the assassination of Venezuelan president Hugo Chavez during a 700 Club broadcast.

REFERENCES

Foege, Alec. *The Empire God Built: Inside Pat Robertson's Media Machine.* New York: John Wiley and Sons, 1996.

Stafford, Tim, and Ted Olsen. "When Evangelicals Look in the Mirror, Do We See the Host of 'The 700 Club' Staring Back?" *Christianity Today,* August 12, 1996, 26–33.

Timmerman, David M., and Larry David Smith. "The World According to Pat: The Telepolitical Celebrity as Purveyor of Political Medicine." *Political Communication* July–September 1994, 233–248.

Christian Science Monitor

The *Christian Science Monitor* is a weekday newspaper published by the Church of Christ, Scientist. Mary Baker Eddy, the founder of Christian Science, established the paper in 1908. The *Monitor* began as an alternative to the sensational papers of the day and grew into a publication of national scope. The *Monitor* stood out as a fair, thoughtful, and in-depth publication that analyzed long-range political, social, and economic trends.

Soon after its launch, the *Monitor* attained a circulation exceeding 100,000. Under the leadership of Ervin D. Canham, managing editor and editor from 1940 to 1964, it became one of the world's leading newspapers. The *Monitor* chooses its personnel with great care and has employed some of the truly great reporters and editors of the twentieth century. Unlike other papers, it relies on an extensive network of reporters, rather than on wire services, for its content. While retaining a somewhat somber front, the paper has changed in format from time to time. In 1975 the *Monitor* adopted a tabloid style and in the late 1980s began running color photographs. It continues to choose its advertisers carefully, employing its own standards of morality and probity.

REFERENCES

The Christian Science Monitor, www.csmonitor.com.

The First 80 Years: The Christian Science Monitor, *1908–1988.* Boston: Christian Science Monitor Press, 1988.

Understanding Our Century. Boston: Christian Science Monitor Press, 1984.

Civic journalism

See *Public/Civic journalism*

Civil society and the media

Civil society consists of the associations of individuals and groups who volunteer or work cooperatively outside of formal governmental and business institutions. Often referred to as the third sector, civil society encompasses the activities of intermediary institutions, such as professional and trade associations, nonprofit organizations, religious groups, neighborhood associations, labor unions, political parties, citizen advocacy organizations, social groups, and sports clubs. Social capital—the networks that develop among friends, associates, and intermediary institutions—forms the foundation of civil society. Based on goodwill, trust, and a sense of mutual obligation, social capital allows people to work together to achieve common goals. Communities high in social capital typically have strong networks of volunteers to deal with problems and improve the quality of life for citizens. As people work toward mutually beneficial goals, they form attachments to their communities. Cooperation becomes a habit, and trust develops between citizens and their neighbors.

The United States has a long tradition of civil society. In the early 1800s, French philosopher Alexis de Tocqueville noted, "Americans of all ages, all stations in life, and all types of dispositions are forever forming associations." He maintained that this lively associational life provides a basis for social progress. Civil society cultivates democratic values, such as egalitarianism and tolerance of people unlike oneself, and promotes civic engagement, such as a willingness to take part in governmental affairs and community life. As societal groups come together, underrepresented interests can gain a voice in community decision making. Volunteer activities situate individuals within networks of people with similar interests who can work together. Participation in intermediary institutions can provide citizens with the experience and skills, such as voting, organizing, raising funds, and managing media relations, that are necessary for political and social activation.

Communication is essential for developing norms of cooperation. A public sphere where citizens come together to discuss societal values, issues, and events is an essential component of civil society. Public debate allows citizens to communicate with government officials and institutions and to engage in problem solving and policymaking. The mass media are integral to civil society. Citizens can make their positions known to leaders via the media in numerous ways, including writing letters to newspapers, calling in to radio and television talk shows, and appearing on community cable programs. In addition, the media help citizens establish community networks by generating awareness of issues and promoting voluntary or civic activities. By providing information in a timely and accessible form, the media theoretically enable people to make well-informed choices, thus contributing to democratic governance.

Not everyone agrees, however, that the mass media promote civil society. Some scholars contend that civil society thrives on face-to-face interactions between citizens. Robert Putnam argues that civil society in the United States has been eroding since the 1960s, when television became a fixture in American homes. As people spent more of their time watching televised programming, they became less committed to community-based or group activities. Putnam points out that membership in social clubs, such as bowling leagues and bridge clubs, has declined, and more people are "bowling alone." Fewer people take part in collective forms of civic engagement, such as attending town meetings and working for political parties.

Putnam identifies a variety of factors that coincide with the decline in civil society, including Americans' busy schedules, the pressure to attain financial security, and increased mobility, but he maintains that mass media are the primary culprits. As a result, public support for the political system has eroded, voter participation has declined, and political apathy has become widespread. In keeping with this argument, Roderick Hart contends that television allows citizens to experience the civic realm vicariously, rather than engaging directly in community affairs. That is, people feel that they fulfill their civic duty by monitoring politics via media. Voters who follow elections through the media may not be inclined to do field work for a candidate or political party, attend a rally, or even vote.

Other scholars disagree with the perspective that mass media are detrimental to civil society and take issue with Putnam's assessment of community activism in widespread decline. There is evidence of community activism thriving in media-saturated environments. Studies conducted by Pippa Norris indicate that societies with widespread access to mass media also have well-developed social and volunteer networks and are high in social capital and political trust. In the United States, the number of civic associations has increased over the past decade along with the range of issues they are concerned with. Associations publicize their activities through mass media, and as a result, people are likely to become involved with causes that interest them, such as promoting awareness of colon cancer or helping at-risk youth, and to join a group that is taking action. Younger people are especially likely to volunteer for a cause.

The significance of media content in promoting or inhibiting the development of civil society is also a subject of debate. On the one hand, the mass media offer ample news and public affairs programming that promotes political knowledge and can empower citizens to take action. People who read the newspaper or watch television news are exposed to people and organizations making a difference or attempting to do so in their communities. With such knowledge, people can join organizations that suit their interests. On the other hand, news coverage often focuses on the negative aspects of politics, such as scandal and corruption, which can be alienating and discourage people from becoming politically active. In addition, many citizens watch entertainment programming that emphasizes values antithetical to ideals that support community involvement. Situation comedies and dramas, the most popular shows on television, tend to concentrate on characters and stories that emphasize individualism. Story lines often show people acting alone to solve problems and overcome adversity and rarely depict associations or groups working to better society.

The Internet, as a technology of mass communication, has left its mark on civil society. Some observers argue that it has improved democratic representation by enhancing the ability to engage in civic life. Perhaps most representative is the ability of citizens to publish their ideas, opinions, and concerns in the online environment. Discussion boards, chat rooms, and Web logs (blogs) allow unprecedented access to the public sphere. Political leaders and the mainstream media have become attentive to the writings of "citizen journalists," who often provide insight into public opinion on issues and act as watchdogs monitoring government activities.

Online media also strengthen associations by allowing people with similar concerns to come together in virtual communities even if they live far apart. Relationships formed online can translate into participation offline, as virtual community members arrange to meet face-to-face. Online communication helps simplify the organizational aspects of community groups, as members can readily share logistical information, such as how to carry out particular tasks. Skeptics admit that the interactive communication facilitated by the Internet may be better than sitting passively in front of the television, but the connections between citizens and associations fostered online only go so far. The online environment does not automatically create citizens who give of their time to help others. Virtual communities cannot do the hands-on volunteer work needed to care for the poor and elderly, raise children, and staff community programs. Further, the digital divide separating those who have access to the technology and the skills to use it from those who do not threatens to exclude much of society from engaging online. Thus, community activism generated online is limited to those who already have the greatest resources in society.

Although opinions differ about the negative and positive effects of the mass media, it is clear that they play an important role in civil society that is increasing as media technologies, such as the Internet and personal digital appliances

(PDAs), proliferate. In an effort to strengthen civil society, schools, civic organizations, and community groups are implementing programs to teach citizens how the media can help them become engaged in their communities.

REFERENCES

Eberly, Don E. *America's Promise: Civil Society and the Renewal of American Culture.* Lanham, Md.: Rowman and Littlefield, 1998.

Hart, Roderick P., and Bartholomew H. Sparrow. *Politics, Discourse, and American Society: New Agendas.* Lanham, Md.: Rowman and Littlefield, 2001.

Johnson, Thomas J., Carol E. Hays, and Scott P. Hays, eds. *Engaging the Public: How Government and the Media Can Reinvigorate American Democracy.* Lanham, Md.: Rowman and Littlefield, 1998.

Norris, Pippa. "Does Television Erode Social Capital? A Reply to Putnam." *PS: Political Science and Politics* 29, no. 3 (September 1996): 474–480.

———. *Virtuous Circle: Political Communications in Post-Industrial Societies.* Cambridge: Cambridge University Press, 2000.

Putnam, Robert. *Bowling Alone: The Collapse and Revival of American Community.* New York: Simon and Schuster, 2000.

Rheingold, Howard. "Virtual Communities, Phony Civil Society?" *Rheingold's Brainstorms,* www.rheingold.com/texts/techpolitix/civil.html.

Skocpol, Theda, and Morris P. Fiorina, eds. *Civic Engagement in American Democracy.* Washington, D.C.: Brookings Institution Press, and New York: Russell Sage Foundation, 1999.

CNN

CNN, the Cable News Network, launched on June 1, 1981, as a creation of broadcaster Ted Turner and over the years evolved into a trailblazer in news broadcasting. Resource and technological constraints made CNN's first broadcasts relatively primitive. The network began to benefit from the penetration of cable into large numbers of households in the late 1980s, which is when it began to distinguish itself as a key source of breaking news during national and international events and crises.

CNN extensively covered the 1986 *Challenger* explosion, and its coverage of the collapse of communism in Eastern Europe and the protest movement in China in 1989 created CNN's reputation as a credible source of international news. The event that made CNN a key player in television news, however, was the 1991 Persian Gulf War. When the air war began in January of that year, CNN held an advantage over the other U.S. networks because it had a correspondent, journalist Peter Arnett, on the ground in Baghdad. Arnett's reporting eventually came under attack for allegedly being too sympathetic toward the Iraqi regime, but this seems in large part the result of his simply being there when other journalists were not.

Before CNN, information moved through the news day in a predictable rhythm. Officials and others in Washington once could release embarrassing or damaging information late in the day knowing that attention would be less than had the information been released before the evening news and newspaper deadlines. The advent of satellite technology and cheap video creation and transmission systems—pioneered by CNN—rendered almost moot the issues of timing and the strategic release of information. CNN's contributions in covering breaking news led to what is now known as the "CNN effect," in which people simultaneously learn of events around the world and just as quickly begin to demand answers and information from government and other responsible parties. Unlike the old "news cycle," it renders less time for those in front of the camera to hone their message. CNN has also helped create the "24-hour news cycle," which has since been adopted by other networks and print media, as the Internet allows for the coverage of constantly breaking news.

CNN's success has ironically led to the erosion of its dominance in cable news, with two all-news cable outlets, MSNBC and the Fox News Channel, debuting in the late 1990s. The former is a joint venture of the NBC television network and Microsoft and, like CNN, takes no overt ideological position. Fox, created by Rupert Murdoch's News Corp., takes an ideologically conservative line. Some of Fox's programming often outperforms CNN's programming. For breaking news, however, large numbers of viewers still turn to CNN, as they did on September 11, 2001, when CNN broke the story of the al-Qaida attacks on New York City and on the Pentagon. CNN has responded to new competition by introducing programming that some observers have criticized as gimmicky and valuing style over substance, such as the recently introduced *Situation Room,* hosted by Wolf Blitzer. This broadcast features "raw" footage, live interviews, and a fast pace that creates the illusion of unmediated information. Many respected journalists have worked or continue to work for CNN, including Judy Woodruff, Paula Zahn, Aaron Brown, and Bernard Shaw. CNN hired Soledad O'Brien, a popular journalist from NBC's *Today Show,* to co-anchor the network's early morning programming.

Some early critics of CNN expressed skepticism that a news network headquartered in Atlanta could become a serious enterprise. Today CNN has a major presence in New York, Washington, D.C., and overseas, with its primary studios still in Atlanta, at the CNN Center. Turner Broadcasting, of which CNN is a part, was purchased by Time Warner in 1996. CNN now encompasses multiple networks, including the domestic network, CNN International, CNN Headline News, and the CNN Airport Network, which broadcasts to television sets in airport departure lounges. CNNFn, a financial network, and CNNSI, a joint venture with *Sports Illustrated,* were discontinued in 2004 and 2002, respectively.

REFERENCES

Auletta, Ken. *Media Man: Ted Turner's Improbable Empire.* New York: Norton, 2004.

Pike, Sid. *We Changed the World: Memoirs of a CNN Global Satellite Pioneer.* St. Paul, Minn.: Paragon, 2005.

Schonfeld, Reese. *Me and Ted against the World: The Unauthorized Story of the Founding of CNN.* New York: Cliff Street, 2001.

Cochran, Elizabeth

See *Bly, Nelly*

Cohen, Richard

Richard M. Cohen (1941–) is a journalist and columnist. He served in the U.S. Army and graduated from New York University and the Columbia University Graduate School of Journalism. He worked as a copy aide at the *New York Herald Tribune* and a reporter for United Press International in New York before joining the *Washington Post* in 1968 as a reporter. He covered a wide range of assignments, including night police action, city hall, education, state government, and national politics and was the paper's chief Maryland correspondent. Cohen was one of two reporters who broke the story of the corruption investigation of Vice President Spiro T. Agnew that ultimately led to his resignation.

Cohen began writing a column for the Metro section of the *Post* in 1976, became a nationally syndicated columnist through the Washington Post Writers Group in 1981, and moved to the op-ed page in 1984. Cohen continues to write a twice-weekly, nationally syndicated op-ed column that often is a lightning rod for conservatives. With Jules Witcover, he co-wrote *A Heartbeat Away: The Investigation and Resignation of Spiro T. Agnew* (1974).

REFERENCES

Washington Post Writers Group, www.postwritersgroup.com.

Colonial press

See *History of American journalism*

Commentary

Commentary refers to the media genre in which journalists or experts in a field provide opinionated assessments on a topic. It differs from mainstream news coverage in that it is not supposed to be neutral and descriptive, suppressing the viewpoint of the reporter. In short, commentary is the broadcast media version of the op-ed column, though some newspapers also label their guest editorials "commentaries".

Commentary is sometimes delivered as a separate segment or essay, as was done by ABC's Howard K. Smith and CBS's Eric Sevareid at the end of their evening news broadcasts in the 1960s and 1970s. Today on *60 Minutes*, the CBS newsmagazine, Andy Rooney appears in a segment at the end of the program, offering commentary as often on mundane, everyday matters as on weighty political issues. On radio, Paul Harvey does much the same on his syndicated *News and Comment*. These types of commentaries have become less common in the contemporary media scene, having been surpassed by fiery punditry and debate-like shows, such as the *O'Reilly Factor* and *Crossfire*.

Commentary more often takes the form of guest or regular experts in a field appearing on a program to add depth or insight on a topic, such as when scholars or political professionals offer their assessments of a presidential speech or debate, a policy proposal being debated in Congress, an event in the news, and so on. For example, presidential historians Doris Kearns Goodwin and Michael Beschloss appear periodically on PBS's *Newshour*.

Commentaries are important to politics because of their potential effect on the audience. Some academic studies have found that experts and media commentators can significantly affect public opinion on political issues because of their generally credible status.

REFERENCES

Page, Benjamin I., Robert Y. Shapiro, and Glenn Dempsey. "What Moves Public Opinion?" *American Political Science Review* 81, no. 1 (March 1987): 23–43.
Soley, Lawrence. *The News Shapers: Sources Who Explain the News.* New York: Praeger, 1992.

Commercial speech

In *Pittsburgh Press Co. v. Pittsburgh Commission on Human Relations* (1973), the Supreme Court defined commercial speech as that which "does no more than propose a commercial transaction." Only well into the twentieth century, in *Valentine v. Chrestensen* (1942), did the Court first consider the issue of commercial speech; when it did, it upheld a ban on the distribution of commercial handbills on the ground that commercial speech lacked First Amendment protections.

Decisions in four Supreme Court cases between 1975 and 1980 have led to the formulation of the commercial speech doctrine. In *Bigelow v. Virginia* (1975), the Court declared that an advertisement published in a Virginia newspaper for an abortion service in New York fell under First Amendment protection despite being a paid message. Jeffrey Bigelow, the newspaper editor, had been convicted under a statute making it a misdemeanor to "encourage or promote the securing of an abortion." Virginia courts upheld the conviction based on *Chrestensen,* which involved "pure" commercial speech. In the Supreme Court's assessment, however, the ad "did more than simply propose a commercial transaction. It contained factual material of clear 'public interest.'"

A year later, in *Virginia State Board of Pharmacy v. Virginia Citizens Consumer Council, Inc.* (1976), the Court began to dismantle *Chrestensen* by ruling that a state law forbidding the advertising of prescription drug prices violated the First Amendment. Justice Harry Blackmun noted in the majority opinion that the Court had decided to abandon the "simplistic approach" of distinguishing between commerical and other speech. The justices held that speech rights are for the protection of the listener as well as for the speaker, and it was in the consumers' interest to know the price of drugs because they varied from store to store. In *Linmark Associates v. Township of Willingboro* (1977), the Court held that homeowners had First Amendment protection to place "for sale" signs on their front lawns. The case followed a New Jersey community's ban on such signs to discourage panic selling by white homeowners as the racial composition of the area changed.

In *Central Hudson Gas & Electric v. Public Service Commission* (1980), the Court struck down as a violation of the First Amendment a rule by the New York Public Service Commission prohibiting advertising by utilities that might encourage energy consumption rather than conservation. According to the Court's decision, commercial speech can be regulated based on a four-part test: (1) The message content is misleading or is for an illegal product, *or* (2) the government has a substantial interest, and (3) the regulation directly advances the government interest, and (4) the regulation is narrowly tailored to be no more extensive than needed. Setting part 1 aside, in other words, laws regulating advertisements must be the least restrictive means for achieving a substantial government goal; rather than banning advertisements outright, government must provide advertisers clear guidelines for them. For example, if government legitimately wants to protect the public against deceitful used car sales, it may not do so by forbidding used car lots to advertise. The Supreme Court has used the four-part test in striking down several laws regulating commercial speech. In *44 Liquormart, Inc. v. Rhode Island* (1996), the Court ruled as unconstitutional a Rhode Island law prohibiting the display of prices in advertisements for liquor. In *Lorillard Tobacco Co. v. Reilly* (2001), the Court struck down restrictions imposed in Massachusetts on outdoor and in-store tobacco product advertisements near playgrounds and schools; it held the restrictions to be unnecessarily broad.

The main focus of government policy and Court decisions on commercial speech is whether commercial advertising is misleading or whether it accurately informs the public. The Federal Trade Commission (FTC), the primary government body involved in monitoring and regulating advertising, is charged with protecting consumers from unfair, misleading, or deceptive advertising, countering

somewhat the tradition of "caveat emptor"—let the buyer beware. Actions taken by the FTC against advertisers include asking them to sign a consent agreement to discontinue the advertisement in question (without admitting wrongdoing) or to provide substantiation for the claims made in their advertisements.

Political advertising does not constitute commercial speech and therefore is not subject to regulation like other advertising. The Court has determined political advertising to be "political speech" and therefore protected under the First Amendment. In essence, commercial speech receives less protection than does political speech. The type of some information that might be considered "false advertising" in a product ad under the commercial speech doctrine would be allowed in a political one. Also, according to the Federal Communications Act of 1934 (Title 47, sec. 315), broadcasters who air candidate advertising must present it uncensored, even if the content is known to be false. Access to airtime for political advertising has also been regulated. Equal time rules require that if a broadcast station permits one legally qualified candidate for elective office to use its facilities or purchase time to air an advertisement, it must make available the same for other legally qualified candidates for that office.

REFERENCES

Finkelman, Paul, and Melvin I. Urofsky. *Landmark Decisions of the United States Supreme Court.* Washington, D.C.: CQ Press, 2003.

Overbeck, Wayne. *Major Principles of Media Law.* Belmont, Calif.: Thomson Wadsworth, 2005.

Pember, Don R., and C. Calvert. *Mass Media Law, 2005–2006.* New York: McGraw-Hill, 2005.

Tedford, Thomas L., and Dale A. Herbeck, *Freedom of Speech in the United States.* 5th ed. State College, Pa.: Strata Publishing, 2005.

Communications Act of 1934

Congress passed the Communications Act of 1934 to regulate the broadcast, telephone, and telegraph industries. The measure created the Federal Communications Commission, a permanent regulatory agency with five members appointed by the president and confirmed by the Senate. The act cites the "public interest, convenience and necessity" as the standard for licensing broadcasters. This phrase has been and continues to be a source of controversy and the basis of litigation concerning broadcast law. In spite of First Amendment protections, Congress chose to regulate radio and television based on the principle that broadcasters were making use of the electromagnetic spectrum, which belongs to the public. Licensees could use this valuable public resource as long as they served the interests of the people.

In the 1980s, Congress and the Reagan administration began to deregulate the broadcast industry through amendment of the Communications Act. The conservative-led government adopted the stance that the public is best served by greater competition among those who broadcast and those who seek broadcast licenses. Much of the deregulation involved excising the rules concerning broadcaster behavior. Among the rules that have been dropped by the FCC are the fairness doctrine, which required that broadcasters carry programming examining important community issues; limitations on the number of commercial minutes that can be broadcast each hour; and a process called ascertainment, which required broadcasters to determine the need and interests of the community in order to provide more useful programming.

REFERENCES

Creech, Kenneth C. *Electronic Media Law and Regulation.* Boston: Focal Press, 1996.
Domick, Joseph R., Barry L. Sherman, and Gary A. Copeland. *Broadcasting/Cable and Beyond: An Introduction to Modern Electronic Media.* 2nd ed. New York: McGraw-Hill, 1993.
Pember, Don R. *Mass Media Law.* New York: McGraw-Hill, 1999.

Communications Decency Act of 1996

The Communications Decency Act (CDA) of 1996 was signed into law as part of the Telecommunications Act of 1996. Sen. Jim Exon (D-Neb.) had presented the CDA more than two years earlier as a way to protect children from the dangers of technology. After failing to move the law forward, Exon introduced the CDA during the Senate Commerce Committee debate over the telecommunications bill. The CDA added Section 223(d) to the Communications Act of 1934, prohibiting the use of an interactive computer service to display to anyone under 18 "any comment, request, suggestion, proposal, image, or other communication that, in

context, depicts or describes, in terms patently offensive as measured by contemporary community standards, sexual or excretory activities or organs, regardless of whether the user of such service placed the call or initiated the communication." This language essentially applied the broadcast indecency standard set in *Federal Communications Commission v. Pacifica Foundation* (1978) to the Internet. Violating the CDA could result in fines or up to two years in prison.

During the floor debate, Senator Exon asserted the need for the CDA by presenting a blue binder filled with pornography that his staff had found on the Internet. Despite vocal opposition ranging ideologically from Sen. Patrick Leahy (D-Vt.) to House Speaker Newt Gingrich (R-Ga.), the Senate voted 84-16 in support of "protecting children." The roll call vote was broadcast live on C-SPAN. The following year, in *Reno v. ACLU* (1997), the U.S. Supreme Court declared unconstitutionally vague those CDA sections relating to the regulation of indecency on the Internet.

See also *Federal Communications Commission v. Pacifica Foundation (1978); Reno v. American Civil Liberties Union (1997).*

REFERENCES

Emeritz, Robert E., Jeffrey Tobias, Kathryn S. Berthot, Kathleen C. Dolan, and Michael M. Eisenstadt, eds. *The Telecommunication Act of 1996: Law and Legislative History.* Bethesda, Md.: Pike and Fischer, 1996.
Federal Communications Commission v. Pacifica Foundation, 438 U.S. 726 (1978).
Reno v. ACLU, 521 U.S. 844 (1997).
Zarkin, Kimberly, and Michael Zarkin. "Entrepreneurial Politics and Civil Liberties Policy: The Case of Communications Decency Legislation." *International Social Science Review* 77 nos. 3/4 (2002): 191–207.

Communications Satellite Act of 1962

The Communications Satellite Act of 1962 called for establishing a global satellite communications system and mandated creation of the Communications Satellite Company, or COMSAT, as a privately owned company with a charter to serve the public interest. A similar organization, INTELSAT, was formed separately as a consortium of international users of communication satellites.

In the 1960s, experiments with "passive" satellites, which reflect signals bounced off them, and "active" satellites, which receive and then relay a boosted signal, suggested the value of satellites as an adjunct to undersea cables or short-wave radio for global communication. The American Telephone and Telegraph Company (AT&T) sought approval from the Federal Communications Commission to launch an experimental communications satellite, or "comsat," in 1960, but the federal government had no policy for such an undertaking. The government later decided that the public interest would be best served by a government-chartered company to serve as a "carrier's carrier," thus leading to the Communications Satellite Company. As the private sector became more involved in launching comsats, COMSAT was fully privatized. In 2001 Lockheed Martin fully acquired its assets. By that time, at least five private companies operated comsats.

REFERENCES

Clarke, Arthur C. "Extra-terrestrial Relays: Can Rocket Stations Give World-wide Radio Coverage?" *Wireless World,* October 1945, 305–308, www.lsi.usp.br/~rbianchi/clarke/ACC.ETRelays.html.

Communications Satellite Act of 1962, Public Law 87-624, August 31, 1962, 76 Stat. 419, as amended; 47 U.S.C. 701 et seq.

Whalen, David J. *Communications Satellites: Making the Global Village Possible.* Washington, D.C.: National Aeronautics and Space Administration, 2006, www.hq.nasa.gov/office/pao/History/satcomhistory.html.

Competition

Competition refers to striving to be better than one's opponent(s) or the best in one's field. In the United States, a "free press" has meant both a media free from (most) government control and a privately owned one existing in a free market. Competition is one of the principles underlying this media system. In theory, the presence of competition among media outlets can be positive. Journalists vie with each other, encouraging better reporting and acting as checks on information. In the process, they create a "marketplace of ideas" that competes for the public's attention, thereby providing a range of perspectives.

Competition can also have negative ramifications. Firms vie to create the most attractive news product to capture the largest possible audience in order to maximize advertising revenue. An economic market produces winners and losers: those who lose go out of business, perhaps leaving the winners with little incentive to improve. Successful media firms sometimes divert increased profits elsewhere rather than reinvesting them to improve the quality of their journalistic products. Competition between journalists for stories and "scoops" can lead to sloppy reporting, hasty conclusions, or outright errors. Fierce competition for advertisers and the revenue they generate may influence the coverage an industry receives by favoring it or simply not offending it.

The increasing concentration of media ownership and cross-ownership in recent years has raised questions about a lack of competition and its adverse effects on the marketplace of ideas. Some argue that fewer owners do not necessarily lead to a narrowing of perspectives or decline in the quality of the news product. They hold that without the competition-driven temptation to sensationalize or produce only what sells, news media under monopoly or oligopoly conditions are freed to produce a product that better serves the public. Studies of local newspapers have found that in fact the quality of news in "one-paper towns" is not necessarily worse than in markets with multiple papers.

Beyond these issues, some critics question whether media competition benefits democracy. Media scholar Robert Entman argues that competition in the economic and political marketplaces limits rather than encourages news quality and diversity. Because the media tend to "give the people what they want"—and the public makes little demand for meaty political news—they emphasize entertainment over substance. On the supply side, economic competition encourages media organizations to minimize costs and risks to profits. This drive may encourage media to produce similar content, to avoid losing audiences to competitors, and lead them to cover news where it can be found cheaply, such as in the comments of official sources on beats. At this point the political market comes in: competition between elites for control of the news agenda may lead them to slant or manipulate news to best their opponents at the media game, emphasizing "spin" over truth. Media consequently fail to live up to free press ideals; in a less competitive environment, news might improve. Competition thus remains a significant if sticky issue in the world of media and politics.

See also *Cross-ownership; Ownership of media.*

REFERENCES

Compaine, Benjamin M., and Douglas Gomery. *Who Owns the Media? Competition and Concentration in the Mass Media Industry.* 3rd ed. Mahwah, N.J.: Lawrence Erlbaum, 2000.

Entman, Robert M. *Democracy without Citizens: Media and the Decay of American Politics.* New York: Oxford University Press, 1989.

Picard, Robert G. "Money, Media, and the Public Interest." In *Institutions of American Democracy: The Press,* edited by Geneva Overholser and Kathleen Hall Jamieson. New York: Oxford University Press, 2005.

Corporation for Public Broadcasting

The Corporation for Public Broadcasting (CPB) is a private nonprofit corporation formed by Congress in 1967 with the mission to promote non-commercial public telecommunications services, including television, radio, cable, and the Internet. The CPB is governed by a nine-member board of directors appointed by the president and confirmed by the Senate. The corporation has formed other organizations integral to public broadcasting, such as National Public Radio, the Public Broadcasting Service, and Public Radio International.

The CPB receives most of its funding from Congress, with additional support from corporate sponsors, foundations, and private donations. Its public subsidy has recently been under attack by conservative members of Congress. In June 2005, House Republicans on an Appropriations subcommittee proposed cutting its funding from $400 million to $200 million, with an eventual phasing-out of all public support. Although the latter is unlikely to occur, the trend toward decreased federal funding will probably continue.

REFERENCES

Ickes, L.-R. *Public Broadcasting in America.* New York: Nova Science Publishers, 2005.

McCauley, Michael P., et al. *Public Broadcasting and the Public Interest.* Armonk, N.Y.: M. E. Sharpe, 2003.

Rogers, Ralph B. *Splendid Torch.* West Kennebunk, Maine: Phoenix Publishers, 1993.

CQ Weekly

CQ Weekly, a flagship publication of Congressional Quarterly Inc., provides extensive coverage of federal policy issues, legislation, and politics with an emphasis on the inner workings of Capitol Hill. The magazine, established in 1945 as *Congressional Quarterly* to track the votes and actions of members of Congress, now offers news and analysis on the White House, federal agencies, the courts, and "K Street" lobbying efforts as well as Congress. It publishes forty-eight times a year.

Nelson Poynter founded the magazine as a quarterly publication to provide another check on government power by providing Americans information on congressional action, vote by vote. *CQ Weekly* continues to comprehensively track legislative activity in addition to presenting broad analysis of political events. It is relied upon in various quarters for its nonpartisan and analytical coverage. CQ subscribers include members of Congress and their staffs, White House and federal agency officials, corporate and nonprofit policy strategists, librarians, researchers and students, and political scientists who study the procedures and ramifications of federal action. It sells advertising to corporate entities and coalitions that have a stake in the outcome of legislation.

REFERENCE

CQ Weekly, www.cq.com/corp/show.do?page=products#cqweekly.
Merry, Robert W. "CQ at 60." *CQ Weekly,* September 26, 2005, p. 2534.

Credibility gap

A credibility gap is the difference between a government's or a politician's pronouncements and indicators of reality. The term was coined during the administration of President Lyndon B. Johnson to describe the gap between official government statements, especially about the relative success of the war in Vietnam, and the information from other sources.

"Credibility gap" flows from the term *missile gap,* which Democratic presidential candidate John F. Kennedy used in the 1960 campaign to describe the U.S. nuclear weapons deficit vis-à-vis the Soviet Union (which was later found to be inaccurate). Its roots probably stem most directly from earlier government manipulations of the press, such as the 1960 U-2 incident during the Eisenhower administration and the 1961 Bay of Pigs fiasco under Kennedy. The credibility gap further widened during the presidency of Richard M. Nixon, with the lies and revelations surrounding the Watergate scandal. Talk of a credibility gap resurfaced in the aftermath of the 2003 U.S.-led invasion of Iraq, when some of the claims made by President George W. Bush to justify the war were found to be false and possibly deceptive.

In part because of the credibility gap, during the 1970s the public's trust and confidence in government declined dramatically, but rebounded somewhat in the 1980s. Many observers argue that reporters likewise became more suspicious of political leaders and since Vietnam have been more analytical, critical, and even cynical, with these attitudes seeping into their coverage. In large measure, neither the press nor the public now places unquestioning faith in politicians to tell the truth or to solve problems.

REFERENCES

Grossman, Michael Baruch, and Martha Joynt Kumar. *Portraying the President: The White House and the News Media.* Baltimore, Md.: Johns Hopkins University Press, 1981.
Wise, David. *The Politics of Lying.* New York: Random House, 1973.

Crisis journalism

Crisis journalism refers to coverage by the news media of a dramatic, usually unexpected event of potentially significant consequence. It causes the public to pay attention, to buy newspapers and magazines, to watch television news, and to participate in chat rooms and on blog pages. For the media, crises generally involve four specific stages. Stage one consists of an announcement—commonly called "breaking news"—that the crisis has occurred, and usually, though not always, some reference to the most dramatic aspect of the event. Information at this stage tends to be sketchy, as the details, including the magnitude of the crisis, are likely not yet known.

Stage two reveals more concrete details of the story, including the details of the crisis and its implications. Stage three contains analyses of the crisis, such as how victims are coping. Stage four features an evaluation and critique of the crisis, which includes placing blame: Could the crisis have been avoided and how? What warning signs went unheeded? Could it happen again? Is there a return to normalcy? Were lessons learned?

Coverage of the 1999 Columbine High School shooting in Colorado illustrates this dynamic. Stage one revealed that children and faculty at the school had been shot. TV news reported the story as it evolved. The identities of the shooters or victims were not immediately known. The reporting focused on the drama of shots being fired and the children running from the school. The first print coverage, hours after police had stormed the school, revealed the shooters' names and the number of persons killed and injured. Whether the two shooters acted alone, the extent of the victims' injuries, and how the incident unfolded were still, however, unknown.

Breaking news constitutes the dramatic, first stage of crisis journalism reporting. Here CNN provides coverage of the Oklahoma City bombing on April 19, 1995.

Stage two brought more details, including descriptions of the personalities of the shooters, stories of survival, stories of bravery, and stories of doom. Stage three examined and analyzed the gunmen, including how they planned the attacks and their social adjustment problems, and memorials for the victims. Stage four highlighted the efforts of individuals, the school district, and the community to recover. Stages three and four are frequently the longest and may cover weeks or even years.

Hurricane Katrina in 2005 represents another example of the crisis dynamic. After stage one coverage of initial deaths and destruction, the remaining stages varied in the several Gulf Coast states hit by the storm. Florida, which was hit first, got stage one coverage of damage and death, but the greater damage in Alabama, Mississippi, and Louisiana overshadowed its later stages in national coverage. The flooding of New Orleans then overshadowed to a great deal the later stages of coverage in Alabama and Mississippi. Katrina's aftermath in New Orleans spawned numerous other crises and issues to report: miscommunication among governments and the failures of government, particularly those of the Federal Emergency Management Agency (FEMA) and President George W. Bush; the "blame game"; the political fallout; displaced persons; restoration of the city and its culture; and restoring levees to protect it. These and numerous other crises of the hurricane's aftermath point to years of stage three and stage four coverage.

FEMA head Michael Brown suffered severe criticism and was forced to resign during stage three. Six months later, during stage four—after investigations and the leaking of a videotape of a Bush administration meeting before the storm hit Louisiana—it came to light that Brown had warned the president and others of the danger of the levees being breached and was scapegoated by the administration for the federal government's poor performance and lack of preparedness. Brown's apparent engagement in the impending disaster, despite his obvious failings, lessened somewhat the lambasting he endured in the media. The news media are sometimes accused of rushing to judgment and assigning blame, as happened in the 1995 Oklahoma City bombing, when foreign terrorists were initially accused but the perpetrator turned out to be an American. In a similar manner, coverage of airplane crashes often contains considerable speculation about the cause, even as journalists, particularly on television, caution against making hasty judgments.

In covering the September 11, 2001, attacks by al-Qaida,

the Asian tsunami in 2004, and the aftermath of Hurricane Katrina, the media put forth varying estimates of how many people had died. In all three situations, their figures were much higher than the actual death tolls. Some see in this good news, but others see the practice as an effort to shock the public. Saturation is another frequent problem of recent years. It generally occurs when the news media cannot or will not move to the next stage of coverage and tend instead to repeat "hot" coverage, especially visuals. Critics of the news coverage of Hurricane Katrina's aftermath in New Orleans argue that once the media started the blame game, they could not stop, despite there being thousands of untold heartwarming and heart-wrenching stories of efforts to survive. The same refusal to "move on" occurred after the media reported widespread civil disorder, which later was revealed to have been greatly exaggerated. Saturation coverage usually pushes other stories out of the news cycle.

Although crisis journalism often contains errors, the news media are sometimes at their best during crises. Radio and television news provide immediate and even lifesaving information in storms and during other natural disasters. In numerous instances, these warnings have kept death tolls lower than they might otherwise have been. It was the news media that warned New Orleans residents and others to evacuate the city. The *Times-Picayune* had run stories months earlier warning that the levees would probably fail during a severe hurricane. Its warnings, however, were to no avail.

Newspapers offer more in-depth and investigative coverage than do television and radio news. In turn, news magazines can offer even greater depth. The Internet as a popular news medium provides more immediacy than newspapers and more depth than television. Organizations in crises now sometimes deliver their own bad news on their Web sites, providing the public their side of the story before the news media do. In fact, these organizations hope to inform the news media with their Web account to pre-empt questions asked by reporters. Blogs, or Web logs, offer varied and often valuable opinions and sometimes scoop the mainstream press on big stories. Bloggers can potentially be helpful or harmful during a crisis. Blogs can disseminate independent information to the public quickly, but they may also mislead, because blogs may or may not be accurate, and there is no institutionalized system of checks to confirm facts as with reputable newspapers.

During national emergencies and tragedies, the news media bring people together, helping them share the experience of shock and grief. This happened after the assassinations of President John F. Kennedy, the Rev. Dr. Martin Luther King Jr., and Sen. Robert Kennedy in the 1960s, after the explosion of the space shuttle *Challenger* in 1986, and during and following the September 11 attacks. Television news came into its own when following Lee Harvey Oswald's assassination of President Kennedy, rolling cameras made Jack Ruby's shooting of Oswald the first televised murder. Since that time, television news producers have attempted to position cameras wherever an event might yield a compelling story. Today, however, footage recorded by amateur videographers is as likely to be shown as professional footage.

Al-Qaida, no doubt, understood the media coverage it would garner in planning the September 11 attacks. News media continually rebroadcast the dramatic and tragic footage of the second plane hitting the South Tower of the World Trade Center and the resulting disintegration of both buildings. This devastating act grabbed the world's attention. The print media covered the story in greater detail than television could, although television news stayed on the air almost continuously that day.

As news outlets have become increasingly prone to chasing ever-higher ratings, basic journalism has begun to evolve into pseudo-crisis journalism to the detriment of a journalistic sense of substance. Today's audience is larger than ever, and with global twenty-four-hour news, more news needs to be produced (even as each outlet is under pressure to reduce news staffs to save money). To survive, the smaller staffs look for exciting and interesting news at the expense of more worthy topics. This business-driven phenomenon fuels a form of journalism in which the media makes an event a crisis by virtue of its coverage.

See also *Pseudo-crisis.*

REFERENCES

Fancher, Michael R. "Study of News Media Provides Disturbing Picture of Journalism," *Seattle Times,* March 21, 2004, A2.

Fearn-Banks, Kathleen. *Crisis Communications: A Casebook Approach.* Mahwah, N.J.: Lawrence Erlbaum and Associates, 2006.

Grossman, Lawrence K. "News Judgement, Professionalism Are Guides to Crisis Coverage." *Broadcasting,* February 17, 1986, 57.

Walter Cronkite delivers the news for CBS in 1952. Famous for his professionalism, Cronkite was known as "the most trusted man in America," as well as "Uncle Walter," for his assuring delivery of news of major events.

Cronkite, Walter

Walter Leland Cronkite Jr. (1916–), a renowned broadcast journalist, served as national news anchor for CBS for almost two decades. Cronkite began his journalistic career working as a campus correspondent for his high school newspaper, the *Houston Post,* from 1933 to 1935; he continued to work for it during his freshman year in college. He later dropped out of college and moved to Kansas City to become an announcer for KCMO radio. Cronkite worked for United Press International from 1937 to 1948 as a war correspondent during World War II covering major battles in North Africa and Europe, chief correspondent covering the Nuremberg Trials, and Moscow bureau chief. CBS hired him in 1950 as a broadcast journalist. There he hosted *Up to the Minute,* anchored numerous segments of *The Week in Review,* and *You Are There,* a series of historical vignettes. In 1962 Cronkite succeeded Douglas Edwards as the anchor of the *CBS Evening News,* where he would work until 1981.

His trademark signoff, "And that's the way it is," became a nationally recognized idiom. CBS briefly replaced Cronkite in 1964 because of low ratings against NBC's "Huntley and Brinkley," but it reinstated him after public protest. Cronkite eventually became the ratings leader from 1967 until 1981.

Cronkite took pride in his journalistic impartiality, but on rare occasions his emotions surfaced. His voice noticeably cracked as he announced the death of President John F. Kennedy in 1963, and he was visibly moved by the Apollo 11 moon landing in 1969. Beginning with the Tet Offensive in early 1968, his increasingly critical reporting on the Vietnam War may have contributed to President Lyndon B. Johnson's decision not to seek reelection. Cronkite's broadcast kept the unfolding Watergate scandal before national and international audiences.

In retirement, Cronkite has remained active, working on various documentary specials for PBS and the Discovery and Learning Channels, as well as writing a weekly syndicated column. In hindsight, Cronkite believed that he retired too early.

REFERENCES

Cronkite, Walter. *A Reporter's Life.* New York: A. A. Knopf, 1996.
James, Doug. *Walter Cronkite: His Life and Times.* Baltimore, Md.: JM Productions, 1991.
Westman, Paul. *Walter Cronkite: The Most Trusted Man in America.* New York: Dillon Press, 1980.

Crossfire

See *Pundit shows*

Cross-ownership

Cross-ownership refers to one conglomerate or corporation owning media outlets in more than one type of medium, such as when the same company owns a newspaper and a radio station. Cross-ownership among media firms in some locales has increased in recent decades and is a potentially important political matter, because it raises issues of media concentration, monopolization, and, most important, viewpoint domination across media. If the same company holds multiple outlets, theoretically it could stifle diversity in content and views and project a voice from the "soapbox" louder than others.

Responding to such concerns, the Federal Communications Commission (FCC) heavily restricted cross-ownership of a newspaper and a TV station within the same market in 1975. It "grandfathered" in those already in existence, such as the Tribune Company's ownership of the *Chicago Tribune* and WGN-TV. In 2003, however, the FCC undertook a sweeping revision of broadcast ownership regulations, including

News Corp. chairman Rupert Murdoch testifies in 2003 during Senate Commerce Committee hearings on media ownership. Murdoch called for easing media ownership restrictions, telling the committee that his ownership of dozens of TV stations improves local programming and does not reduce diverse viewpoints. Critics contended that the plan would further consolidate media ownership in the hands of a few corporate conglomerates and reduce the variety of content available.

loosening the ban on cross-ownership of newspapers and television stations, depending upon the size of the market.

Opponents of these measures attempted to thwart them in Congress but failed to receive legislative support to overturn these regulatory changes. Instead, a challenge to the rules made its way to the U.S. Supreme Court, which in June 2005 concurred with a lower-court decision striking down the FCC's action and instructing the agency to go back to the drawing board and conduct a review of all ownership rules.

Some argue that cross-ownership fears are misplaced because the advent and availability of new communications outlets, such as cable and satellite television and the Internet, give consumers a wide range of options for news and entertainment outside of local media. They also point out that rarely do newspapers and TV stations owned by the same company see eye to eye. Others respond that the old concerns remain valid, and given greater mergers within the media industry, localism and a wide range of perspectives will be lost if restrictions are loosened or removed.

REFERENCES

Compaine, Benjamin M., and Douglas Gomery, eds., *Who Owns the Media?: Competition and Concentration in the Mass Media Industry.* 3rd ed. Mahwah, N.J.: L. Erlbaum Associates, 2000.

Goldfarb, Charles B. "FCC Media Ownership Rules: Current Status and Issues for Congress." Congressional Research Service, Washington, D.C., updated June 16, 2005.

C-SPAN

C-SPAN, the Cable Satellite Public Affairs Network, a nonprofit educational organization, provides live, unedited coverage of American politics and political institutions, especially Congress. It is the brainchild of founder and CEO Brian Lamb, who in 1979 convinced cable executives to fund a channel to carry the unedited signal of the cameras of the U.S. House of Representatives into U.S. homes via cable TV. From its humble beginnings as one channel with limited programming, C-SPAN has grown to three channels with twenty-four-hour programming, a radio outlet, a Web site, and a student civic education outreach program. It reaches an estimated 85 million homes.

C-SPAN, the original and basic channel, provides live coverage of the House along with other public political events, such as press conferences, rallies, speeches, roundtable policy discussions, interviews, and the viewer call-in program *Washington Journal*. C-SPAN2, inaugurated in 1986 when the Senate allowed TV cameras into its chamber, focuses on live coverage of that body as well as coverage of current issues and *Book TV*, featuring forty-eight hours of weekend programming on nonfiction books. C-SPAN3, launched in 1997, supplements the public affairs offerings of the other two by covering press conferences, committee hearings, and the like, and by emphasizing U.S. history programming on weekends. C-SPAN radio is heard locally in the Washington, D.C., area and nationally via satellite radio. It consists of excerpts of the televised programming along with original programming.

C-SPAN differs from news organizations in that it supplies unfiltered political content, and even its hosted interview and call-in shows are notable for the neutrality and fact-based approach of the moderators. Its funding, derived from license fees from the cable systems that carry it, coupled with its nonprofit status free C-SPAN from commercial and competitive pressures. Lamb has, however, had to fight some battles over threatened cutbacks in its distribution. The cable industry had some political motives in its creation— namely, to provide a public service as defined by Federal Communications Commission regulations and thereby gain political support and preempt further possible regulatory efforts by Congress. Nevertheless, it is hard to argue that C-SPAN is not a public good.

The political influence of C-SPAN is difficult to judge, but it is important inside Washington as well as outside it. Members of Congress, administration officials, lobbyists, and even journalists rely on it for political surveillance and a platform for unmediated communication with the public. Its audience, estimated at 28 million viewers a week, is a small, narrow segment, but one highly interested in politics; one survey found that C-SPAN viewers voted at a rate of 90 percent in 2000.

C-SPAN provides an alternative to the journalist- and pundit-dominated discourse of mainstream media and political discussion programs. Some critics argue, however, that without interpretation or context, much of the public cannot understand some of its programs and may be susceptible to manipulation or slanted political rhetoric peddled by unmediated official voices. Regardless, at a minimum, it provides the citizenry an outlet for learning about and keeping track of their government.

See also *Cable television; Media and Congress; New media.*

REFERENCES

C-SPAN, www.cspan.org.

Frantzich, Stephen, and John Sullivan, *The C-SPAN Revolution*. Norman: University of Oklahoma Press, 1996.

Gruenwald, Juliana, "C-SPAN: From Novelty to Institution." *CQ Weekly,* November 29, 1997, 2948.

D

Daisy girl commercial

The "daisy girl" commercial is a classic negative advertisement run during the 1964 presidential campaign by Democratic incumbent Lyndon B. Johnson to raise doubts about his Republican challenger, Sen. Barry Goldwater of Arizona. Media consultant Tony Schwartz created the television ad, which features an image of a little girl awkwardly counting to ten as she picks petals off a daisy; her voice is then replaced with that of a deep-voiced announcer counting backwards to zero, whereupon the picture dissolves into an atomic mushroom cloud. Goldwater is never mentioned, but the commercial implies that he might start a nuclear war.

Senator Goldwater had accused the Johnson administration of neglecting U.S. nuclear defenses, suggesting the existence of a missile and manned-aircraft gap with the Soviet Union. In a 1963 congressional speech, Goldwater introduced a nuclear arms strategy meant to help reduce the United States' military presence in the North Atlantic Treaty Organization (NATO). The plan authorized the NATO commander to use atomic weapons in an emergency. With voters concerned about nuclear power, throughout the campaign Johnson kept Goldwater on the defensive about his nuclear defense plan, making him explain, restate, defend, and even change his positions. During this period, Johnson hired Schwartz, who created the powerful television advertisement now known as the daisy girl commercial.

Although the spot aired only once, newscasts around the country repeatedly ran it because of the tremendous public reaction it evoked. The commercial's impact got the attention of media consultants, alerting them to the potential "ripple effect" of negative ads. Some historians credit Johnson's wide margin of victory in the election to Goldwater's mention of nuclear war and the daisy girl commercial.

REFERENCES

Jamieson, Kathleen Hall. *Packaging the Presidency: A History and Criticism of Presidential Campaign Advertising.* New York: Oxford University Press, 1984.

West, Darrell M. *Air Wars: Television Advertising in Election Campaigns, 1952–2000.* 3rd ed. Washington, D.C.: CQ Press, 2001.

Davis, Richard Harding

Richard Harding Davis (1864-1916) was a celebrated, turn-of-the-century journalist well-known for his sensationalist writing, or "yellow" journalism. The son of renowned author Rebecca Harding Davis, Richard attended Lehigh and Johns Hopkins Universities before beginning his journalism career in Philadelphia in 1886. Davis then moved to New York City to report for the *New York Evening Sun.* He became managing editor of *Harper's Weekly* in 1890 and traveled widely, reporting on his adventures. His writing garnered popular attention with the publication of his *Gallegher and Other Stories* (1891).

Davis was the assignment reporter for William Randolph Hearst's *New York Journal* in 1896 in Cuba during the rebellious prelude to the Spanish-American War. By the outbreak of war, Davis had separated from Hearst because of editorial differences and had begun reporting for Joseph Pulitzer's

New York Herald, the *Times* (London), and *Scribner's Weekly.* Davis's dispatches from Santiago shot Theodore Roosevelt and the Rough Riders to national and international prominence. Roosevelt and Winston Churchill were his friends. Davis's other writings include the novels *Soldiers of Fortune* (1897) and *The Bar Sinister* (1903) and the plays *The Dictator* (1904) and *Miss Civilization* (1906).

REFERENCES

Davis, Richard Harding, and Charles Belmont Davis, eds. *The Adventures and Letters of Richard Harding Davis.* New York: Beekman Publishers, 1974.

Lubow, Arthur. *The Reporter Who Would Be King: A Biography of Richard Harding Davis.* New York: Scribner, 1992.

Miner, Lewis S. *Front Lines and Headlines: The Story of Richard Harding Davis.* New York: J. Messner, 1959.

O'Toole, G. J. A. *The Spanish War: An American Epic, 1898.* New York: W. W. Norton and Company, 1984.

Day, Benjamin Henry

Benjamin Henry Day (1810–1889) was a journalist and innovative newspaper publisher. Born in West Springfield, Massachusetts, Day learned the printer's trade while working for the *Springfield Republican.* He then moved to New York City and worked various jobs for the *Journal of Commerce,* the *Evening Post,* and the *Courier and Enquirer* before opening his own printing shop in 1830. He began publishing the *New York Sun* in 1833, writing and printing his own articles. He sold his papers for one cent, thus making them one of the first of the "penny dailies" tailored to a mass audience. He was also the first to employ newsboys to help sell his newspapers on the street. Day introduced steam power to drive his presses and within two years had expanded his paper's circulation to the point that he could claim the largest newspaper readership in the world.

In 1838 Day sold the *Sun* to his brother-in-law, Moses Yale Beach, for $40,000. Day used his proceeds from the sale to establish the *True Sun* and then the *Tatler* before starting the monthly *Brother Jonathan,* named for the fictional character symbolizing the early United States. *Brother Jonathan* would later become the first illustrated weekly in the United States. Day's son, Benjamin, followed in his father's professional footsteps, making his own contributions to the printing business.

REFERENCES

Whitlock, Francis Beacham. *Two New-Yorkers: Editor and Sea Captain, 1833.* New York: The Newcomen Society of England, American Branch, 1945.

Deaver, Michael K.

Michael K. Deaver (1940–) served as President Ronald Reagan's deputy chief of staff from 1981 to 1985 and as one part of a triumvirate of close presidential advisors (along with James Baker III and Edwin Meese). He had worked as a campaign staffer during Reagan's successful run for California governor in 1967 and remained with Reagan throughout his political career. Deaver designed the communications strategy for Reagan's successful presidential runs in 1980 and 1984, earning the moniker "the image maker" for his contributions to Reagan's public persona. Deaver's departure from the White House in 1985 after serving as deputy chief of staff coincided with an ethics investigation involving his wife, and he was later convicted of perjury related to influence peddling while in the White House.

As of mid-2006 Deaver held the positions of international vice chairman for the PR firm Edelman and executive vice president of corporate affairs for Edelman's Washington office, providing strategic counsel to clients on media relations. Deaver also makes television appearances to comment on politics, the media, and public affairs. He is the co-author, with Mickey Hershkowitz, of *Behind the Scenes* (1988) and the author of *A Different Drummer: Thirty Years with Ronald Reagan* (2001).

REFERENCES

"Exit the Californians." *Time,* January 14, 1985, 18.

"A New Round of Musical Chairs Claims Mike Deaver: The Last of Reagan's California Cronies." *People,* April 15, 1985, 40–41.

Thomas, Evan. "Who Is This Man Calling?" *Time,* March 3, 1986, 26–36.

Weisberg, Jacob. "He's Back." *New Yorker,* January 23, 1995, 22–24.

Deep Throat

See *Watergate*

Documentaries

Documentaries consist of non-fiction films based on or chronicling actual events, historical or social issues, or individuals' lives. Some documentaries have moved people to war, to peace, or to protest. Early American documentaries tended to avoid controversial themes, though a group of New York artists formed the Workers Film and Photo League and brought the Great Depression to celluloid in *Hunger* (1932), which used footage from the National Hunger March. The government also financed documentaries, such as Pare Lorentz's *The Plow That Broke the Plains* (1936), which was funded through the New Deal's Resettlement Agency. The U.S. government appointed Hollywood director Frank Capra to help prepare American soldiers and citizens for war after the outbreak of World War II. He excerpted the powerful imagery of German filmmaker Leni Riefenstahl's Nazi chronicle *Triumph of the Will* (1934) to inspire U.S. audiences to action through *Why We Fight.*

During the cold war in the 1950s, instructional and documentary films by the Civil Defense Administration prepared Americans (theoretically) for nuclear attack and were later satirized in Jayne Loader's *Atomic Café* (1982). The antiwar movement of the Vietnam era developed an oppositional documentary style in its dissent against the government's military positions in *Heart and Minds* (1974) and *Panama Deception* (1992).

Television documentaries ventured into controversy with *See It Now,* which starred Edward R. Murrow and premiered in 1951. Murrow's confrontation with Sen. Joseph McCarthy (R-Wis.) spelled the political epitaph of the politician who had devastated or destroyed the lives of U.S. citizens based on allegations of communist leanings. The plight of migrant workers in *CBS Reports'* "Harvest of Shame" and "The Selling of the Pentagon" (1971) also generated significant political consequences.

The Roosevelt Express, produced in 1944 by the AFL-CIO, was the first political documentary to tout a presidential candidate. Later, party convention films for presidential nominees touched on candidates' humble beginnings in small-town America and formed the visual core of presidential campaigns. Ronald Reagan's "Morning in America," for example, featured his hometown of Dixon, Illinois, and nostalgia of rural America. *The War Room* (1992), a behind-the-scenes documentary produced by D. A. Pennebaker and Chris Hegedus, unveiled the dark side of presidential campaigning and the strategizing behind them in its chronicling of Bill Clinton's 1992 run for the presidency.

Documentary filmmaker Michael Moore veered away from the mainstream political agenda in two humorous films, *Roger and Me* (1989) and *The Big One* (1997). Both take aim at corporate America's greed and the appalling lack of concern for employees displaced by foreign laborers hired to enhance a companys' profit margins. His *Bowling for Columbine* (2002), about school shootings and the gun culture in the United States, won widespread acclaim and an Oscar. *Fahrenheit 911* (2004) examined the George W. Bush administration's handling of the al-Qaida attacks of September 11, 2001, "war on terror," invasion of Iraq, and connections to oil interests and Saudi Arabia. Blatantly anti-Bush and popular in some circles, the film struck a dissonant chord in others, leading to counterefforts—such as *Michael Moore Hates America* (2004) and *Farenhype 911* (2004)—to debunk Moore's claims and stands.

The mass media recently have become the subject of documentaries. Notable examples include Robert Greenwald's *Outfoxed: Rupert Murdock's War on Journalism* (2004), about the Fox News Channel's conservative agenda, and *Control Room* (2004), which followed the behind-the-scenes operations and war reporting of al-Jazeera, the leading twenty-four-hour Arab news network, during the outbreak of the 2003 Iraq War.

New technologies have revolutionized the documentary genre. Digital technology allows filmmakers to more easily create films that can be easily and cheaply burned on DVDs and distributed through the Internet. These advancements have democratized the process, making it possible for more people with political axes to grind to get their message out into the media landscape.

REFERENCES

Barnouw, Erik. *Documentary—A History of Non-Fiction Film.* New York: Oxford University Press, 1988.

Combs, James E., and Sara T. Combs. *Film Propaganda and American Politics.* New York and London: Garland Publishing, 1994.

Donahue, Phil

Phillip John Donahue (1935–), an Emmy Award–winning television personality, pioneered the format of the issues-oriented talk show involving viewer participation and discussion. Donahue began his broadcasting career as an announcer at KYW-TV in Cleveland in 1957. He then worked as the news director for a Michigan radio station, a stringer for *CBS Evening News,* and a news anchor for WHIO-TV in Dayton before hosting his first, phone-in talk show, the *Conversation Piece,* from 1963 to 1967.

He debuted *The Phil Donahue Show* in Dayton, Ohio, in 1967 as a talk show aimed at "women who think." This pioneering show was syndicated two years later and went on to win several Emmys. Donahue and his talk show relocated to Chicago in 1974 and remained there until 1985, when it moved to New York City for the next eleven years.

Donahue's demeanor and some of the issues he tackled lead some to consider him the first "sensitive man" talk show personality. His popularity and the social and political content of his show led him to host such figures as Democratic presidential candidate Bill Clinton. With Vladimir Pozner, a former information chief for the Soviet Union, Donahue co-hosted the issues-oriented talk show *This Week with Pozner and Donahue* from 1991 to 1994. MSNBC coaxed Donahue out of retirement in 2002 to do a new *Donahue* show, but less than a year later, during the U.S. invasion of Iraq, the network abruptly canceled the program as Donahue tried to "break through the noisy drums of war." Donahue is the author of *Donahue: My Own Story* (1980) and *The Human Animal* (1985).

See also *Talk shows.*

REFERENCES

Carbaugh, Donald A. *Talking American: Cultural Discourses on Donahue.* Norwood, N.J.: Ablex Publishing, 1988.
Haley, Kathy. "From Dayton to the World: A History of the 'Donahue Show.'" *Broadcasting* (Washington, D.C.), November 2, 1992.
Nichols, John. "Donahue-War Casualty." *Nation,* March 22, 2003, 22.

Donaldson, Sam

Samuel Andrew Donaldson Jr. (1934–) is a broadcast journalist known in his prime for his persistence and aggressive style of questioning. Donaldson began his broadcast career as a disc jockey, announcer, and interviewer at local El Paso stations, transitioned to KRLD-TV in Dallas in 1959, and soon thereafter moved to WTOP-TV in Washington, D.C. He joined ABC News as its Capitol Hill correspondent in 1967 and became chief White House correspondent in 1977. Donaldson assumed the additional duties as the anchor of *World News Sunday* from 1979 to 1989 and occasional moderator of *Issues and Answers.* In late 1981, *Issues and Answers* had been replaced by *This Week with David Brinkley,* on which Donaldson served as a rotating correspondent and later as a permanent panelist. He continues to appear on the renamed *This Week* and work as a correspondent for ABC's *20/20.* Donaldson's autobiography is *Hold On, Mr. President* (1987).

REFERENCES

ABC News, www.abcnews.com.
Donaldson, Sam. *Hold on, Mr. President!* New York: Random House, 1987.
Fitzwater, Marlin. *Call the Briefing! Bush and Reagan, Sam and Helen: A Decade With Presidents and the Press.* New York: Times Books, 1995.

E

Editorials

Editorials are articles or pieces in media outlets that express the official position of the organization on an issue, event, or person. Far more common in newspapers than on radio or television, they are crafted by an editorial board or group of editors, although sometimes the owner or publisher may intervene in editorial writing. Editorials are unsigned, usually running under a paper's masthead on the editorial page. Some television and radio programs run editorials, which are usually presented by a news producer or the owner of a station. These characteristics distinguish editorials from news stories, which are supposed to be more objective and descriptive, and from opinion pieces, which are signed and written by either regular or guest columnists or commentators.

Editorials developed during the more independent era of the late nineteenth century as objective journalism replaced the blatantly partisan press. Their political role and effect is hard to assess. Because editorials explicitly express opinions and represent blatant attempts at persuasion, readers who come equipped with preconceived ideas and opinions may filter or blunt their messages more so than they might when processing news coverage thought to be neutral and credible. There is also the issue of whether significant numbers of people even read or watch them. Though difficult to document directly, editorials appear to influence opinion the most on local elections and ballot propositions. They likely provide important cues to so-called opinion leaders—educated and attentive members of the public, community leaders, politicians, and so on—about political matters of the day. They can also play the role of town crier by highlighting or raising certain topics.

The editorial stances of some news organizations have remained reliably stable over time, giving them a particular partisan or ideological cast. For example, the *New York Times* and the *Washington Post* are generally considered to be liberal leaning, while the *Wall Street Journal* and *Washington Times* are conservative. Because of the influence of editors or owners on editorial content, however, the positions of media outlets can and do sometimes change over time with changes in personnel.

See also *Commentary; Endorsements; Objectivity; Op-Ed.*

REFERENCES

Page, Benjamin I. "The Mass Media as Political Actors." *PS: Political Science and Politics* 29, no. 1 (March 1996): 20–24.

Vermeer, Jan P. *The View from the States: National Politics in Local Newspaper Editorials.* Lanham, Md.: Rowman and Littlefield, 2002.

Email

See *New media*

The U.S. military allowed members of the news media to "embed" with active military units during its 2003 invasion of Iraq. Although such arrangements enhanced media access, critics questioned whether journalists could report objectively while working with and being protected by combatants in the conflict. Here photographers traveling with the 1st Marine Expeditionary Force shoot images in the Kuwaiti desert prior to the invasion.

Embedding

Embedding refers to the placement of journalists among active military units, including when sent into combat. The practice evolved as a compromise experiment by the military and the media after complaints about government-imposed controls on coverage of conflicts. In particular, journalists felt too restricted and cut off by the "pool" system used in the Panama invasion in 1989 and the Persian Gulf crisis and war of 1990–1991. In such a system one or a few journalists are allowed to participate in a military operation or other news event with the expectation that they will then share information with other reporters. In one sense, embedding represents a return to the more open system of coverage used during the Vietnam War. After undergoing brief but rigorous training, journalists are approved as "embeds" for placement with units.

Supporters of embedding argue that this approach allows journalists to capture a closer, more realistic picture of the war as it happens as well as of the experiences of the troops on the ground. Because the journalists accept certain ground rules—such as not broadcasting troop locations, holding reports until it is safe to file them, and so on—the practice does not compromise the safety of the troops.

Critics contend that embedding can result in the media acting as a tool of government propaganda because journalists may become "too close" to their sources, naturally identifying with the troops with whom they work and who protect them. Another critique charges that embedding produces flashy, exciting coverage of combat, especially on television, giving only a "worm's eye view," lacking perspective. Members of the media as well as the military feel, however, that embedding has been a success, so it is likely to be used in future conflicts.

See also *Pool journalism; War and the media.*

REFERENCES

Friedman, Paul. "TV: A Missed Opportunity." *Columbia Journalism Review* 42, no. 1 (May/June 2003): 29.

Ricchiardi, Sherry. "Close to the Action." *American Journalism Review* 25, no. 4 (May 2003): 28.

Seib, Philip. *Beyond the Front Lines: How the News Media Cover a World Shaped by War.* New York: Palgrave MacMillan, 2004.

Endorsements

Endorsements are editorials in which media organizations, especially newspapers, formally take positions on candidates or ballot issues in an upcoming election. They represent a clear case of overt political favoritism by the media.

The editorial board or the owner of an outlet makes most endorsements. As perhaps the last vestige of the days of the partisan press, candidate endorsements align a newspaper or magazine with political figures, which is why in recent years a sizable number of papers have halted the practice. For example, surveys conducted by *Editor and Publisher* found that in the 1940 presidential election, only 13 percent of newspapers refused to endorse a candidate, whereas by 1996 28 percent did so.

Although endorsements can sometimes be surprising, most newspapers appear to be reliably predisposed toward candidates of a certain party or political philosophy. In the aggregate, studies show that since the 1930s the vast majority of newspapers have endorsed the Republican presidential candidate. This figure is used by those who accuse the media of a conservative bias. The exceptions include Democrats Lyndon B. Johnson in 1964, Bill Clinton in 1992, and (narrowly) John Kerry in 2004.

Endorsements are politically significant because of their potential effect on voters and the news itself. Studies have found that while endorsements seem to have little effect on opinion in presidential elections, they are more influential in state and local elections for candidates and ballot issues, because the electorate usually has less information on which to base a decision.

More controversial is the issue of whether endorsements, or the management that makes them, also subtly influence news coverage of elections or issues by media organizations. There is theoretically a "firewall" between news and editorial divisions so that the opinions expressed in editorials do not bias or influence the news. Some critics argue that, nonetheless, editorial stances may affect as well as reflect news coverage. While many communications scholars and media people dispute it, some academic studies seem to support this notion. Arthur Rowse, in *Slanted News,* found a close fit between thirty-one newspapers' handling of campaign-funding stories about presidential candidates Dwight Eisenhower and Adlai Stevenson in 1956 and the papers' endorsements. A study by Kim Kahn and Patrick Kenney examining newspaper coverage of more than sixty U.S. Sen-

ate campaigns found news stories to be biased in favor of the candidate endorsed on the editorial page and to appear to influence voters' assessments of the candidates as well. Todd Schaefer also found that editorial assessments of presidential State of the Union addresses appeared to be influenced by whom the paper endorsed in the previous election. Papers that endorsed the incumbent (that is, the winner) were more likely to praise the speech, while those that endorsed the loser in the previous election were more likely to criticize it.

See also *Editorials.*

REFERENCES

Kahn, Kim Fridkin, and Patrick J. Kenney. "The Slant of the News: How Editorial Endorsements Influence Campaign Coverage and Citizens' Views of Candidates." *American Political Science Review* 96, no. 3 (June 2002): 381–394.
Page, Benjamin I. "The Mass Media as Political Actors." *PS: Political Science and Politics* 29, no. 1 (March 1996): 20–24.
Rowse, Arthur Edward. *Slanted News: A Case Study of the Nixon and Stevenson Fund Stories.* Boston: Beacon Press, 1957.
Schaefer, Todd. "Persuading the Persuaders." *Political Communication* 14, no. 1 (January–March 1997): 97–111.

Equal time rule

The equal time rule is a provision of the Communications Act of 1934 that requires radio and television stations to treat candidates for federal office equally in selling or donating airtime. In other words, if a station offers to sell a certain amount of time to one candidate, it must offer the opportunity to another candidate to buy an equivalent amount of advertising time. Also, if the station gives a candidate advertising time, it must give other candidates the opportunity to use an equivalent amount of airtime. Broadcasters cannot censor the content of a candidate's message unless it violates federal law, and they face possible license revocation or fines for violating the equal opportunity provisions.

The equal time rule—codified in section 315 of the Communications Act—is often misunderstood to require "equal time" for candidates and for controversial opinions, but the regulation actually calls for "equal opportunities" regarding advertising for any "legally qualified candidate for any public office" (per a 1974 amendment). Although some mistaken citizens have demanded airtime to rebut viewpoints with which they disagree, the equal time provision does not provide for such public access to the airwaves.

Once a candidate makes "use" of airtime at a broadcast station, all other candidates for the same office must be given the same considerations at that facility. A 1959 amendment to the Communications Act exempted incidental appearances on some programs from the equal time rule, such as when radio and television stations broadcast news conferences, on-the-spot statements by or interviews with candidates, or documentaries. The equal time provision therefore does not limit the ability of stations to cover candidates as subjects of news stories.

Before 1971, no station was compelled to offer advertising time to any candidate; the section 315 provisions only applied when they offered time to one candidate. In 1971 Congress amended the Communications Act to require that radio and TV stations offer political advertising at their most favored advertising rates (that is, those offered to commercial advertisers that buy a lot of airtime) and encouraged stations to make reasonable amounts of advertising time available to federal candidates. Both of these provisions were deemed to further the concept that broadcasters are licensed to serve the broader public interest, and Congress considered political advertising to serve that interest.

REFERENCES

Communications Act of 1934, Public Law 416, 73rd Congress, 2nd sess. (June 19, 1934). Amended 47 U.S.C. Sec. 315.
Federal Communications Commission. *The Law of Political Broadcasting and Cablecasting: A Political Primer.* Washington, D.C.: Government Printing Office, 1980.
Klieman, Howard. "Equal Time Rule." Museum of Broadcast Communications, www.museum.tv/archives/etv/E/htmlE/equal-timeru/equaltimeru.htm.
Rowan, Ford. *Broadcast Fairness: Doctrine, Practice, Prospects. A Reappraisal of the Fairness Doctrine and Equal Time Rule.* New York: Longman, 1984.

Ethics and the media

The news media connect communities and disseminate information. They also provide a forum for opinions. Newspapers, magazines, radio, television, and Web sites all play a critical role in politics as well. What the media do, when they do it well, undergirds the democratic process. They serve as vehicles through which the public and political organizations intersect, and they provide insight into how the civic community operates. Their success, however, depends on their credibility, which rests upon trust between the news organization and the news consumer. The media, in most cases, seek to ensure this bond by adhering to accepted ethical standards.

Ethics build upon a foundation of principles and morals and involve the act of evaluating and selecting between good and bad options based on the principles and values in which people believe. Understanding the options that exist and choosing the most ethical course are critical for news organizations. Ethical guidelines help journalists decide how they gather and report the news, and ethical questions offer a way to test news coverage assumptions. Journalistic ethics are generally based on the purposes of the media within society, such as educating the public, providing a forum for opinion, and so on. For those in the news business, ignoring the damage that bad ethical choices might create can undermine trust, disillusion news consumers, and demoralize newsrooms. Selecting good options can help strengthen the bonds of trust between the news media and the public, improve civic conversation, and make for better journalism.

New York Times *reporter Judith Miller leaves a Washington, D.C., courthouse after testifying before a grand jury that she could not remember who revealed to her the name of covert CIA operative Valerie Plame. Events surrounding Plame's unmasking raised questions about the right of journalists to protect their sources.*

An Ethical Crisis?

The issue of press credibility, while always a factor for the press, came to the fore during the tumultuous 1960s, in part because of major events, including the war in Vietnam. Edwin Emery, a journalistic historian, wrote in *The Press and America,* "The credibility gap as an institution was painfully apparent in American life by 1970. There were gaps between the President and people, President and press, and press and people."

The following decades brought a widening of the gap between the public and press. In one gauge of this gap, a Gallup Poll survey on media credibility has asked over time, "In general, how much trust and confidence do you have in the mass media—such as newspapers, T.V. and radio—when it comes to reporting the news fully, accurately, and fairly: a great deal, a fair amount, not very much, or none at all?" By this measure, the news media's credibility fell to its lowest level in thirty years—declining from a high of 72 percent in June 1976 to a low of 44 percent in September 2004. (These percentages represent respondents who indicated that their trust and confidence ranged from "a fair amount" to "a great deal.") That trust and confidence have not rebounded, and may even remain in decline, as the public has come to view journalists as more interested in scoops and scandals than in serious reporting.

Since 2000, a number of news associations and professional organizations—among them the American Society of Newspaper Editors (ASNE), the National Press Photographers Association (NPPA), the Radio-Television News Directors Association (RTNDA), and the Society of Professional Journalists (SPJ)—have created or updated codes of ethics. Robert Steele, a journalistic ethics scholar at the Poynter Institute, developed guidelines and questions that journalists can use to help them think through the ethical implications of their news decisions. He encourages journalists to see the use of an ethical decision-making process as important to pursuing excellence in the craft, just as any other journalistic skill. According to Steele's "Guiding Principles for the Journalist," available on the Poynter Institute Web site, journalists should seek the truth and report it as fully as possible, act independently, and minimize harm.

In a series of ten questions that he developed, Steele provides a means for more fully exploring what journalists may cover, why they are covering it, and what the outcome of that coverage might be. The questions focus on what journalists know and need to know, journalistic purpose, ethical concerns, policies, different perspectives, stakeholders, role reversal, alternatives, and justification. The principles and questions play a part in a process that prompts journalists to examine the way they approach the news, and how the public perceives their approach, and helps lead to a better understanding of the perceptions, implications, and consequences of the actions taken by the news media.

Ethics and Political News Coverage

The value of an ethical decision-making process, and the consequences of not having such a process, can become especially evident during controversial political stories. A number of recent examples highlight the tension raised when ethical principles and questions collide with news coverage. One of them involved the public disclosure of a CIA operative, Valerie Plame, in 2003. Knowingly revealing the name of a CIA covert agent is against the law for federal employees. A number of journalists, however, became aware of Plame's status as an agent as a result of conversations with officials working in President George W. Bush's White House. Of the several journalists involved in the affair, at least three of them—Matthew Cooper of *Time,* Judith Miller, then with the *New York Times,* and syndicated columnist Robert Novak—played prominent roles involving ethical issues.

In a column in 2003, Novak cited an anonymous government source in identifying Plame by name as a CIA operative. That led to a grand jury investigation because of federal law against such disclosure. Novak, who promised his source confidentiality, refused to publicly name the individual. Should Novak have kept his promise or should he have considered it unnecessary to keep his promise of confidentiality because the source may have broken the law? Although some journalists believed that Novak should honor his original promise of confidentiality, others, such as Geneva Overholser, a University of Missouri professor, former *Washington Post* ombudsman, and former editor of the *Des Moines Register,* argued that he should reveal the source.

Honoring a promise to keep a source confidential is an important ethical issue for many journalists. If a journalist gives his or her word to someone, it must be kept. To renege on one's word could destroy a source's trust. If done often, it could make obtaining critical information—some of it important for the public to know—difficult, if not impossible. Some people believe, however, that exceptions exist to such a promise. In an op-ed for the *New York Times,*

Overholser wrote, "In this case ... journalists should call upon Mr. Novak to acknowledge his abuse of confidentiality and reveal his sources himself—thereby keeping the control of confidentiality in journalistic hands rather than in those of the legal system."

Before making a promise of non-disclosure and anonymity, journalists should understand fully the basis upon which they are making such a decision and its ethical implications. Some questions a journalist should ask before agreeing to confidentiality include the following:

- Why is the source requesting confidentiality? Is the reason valid?
- How important is the information to the story?
- How credible will the story seem if it relies on an unidentified source?
- How is anonymity justified?
- What happens if the information turns out to be a lie or illegally divulged?

Cooper and Miller faced a dilemma similar to Novak's. Cooper wrote about Plame in *Time*. Miller never wrote about the subject, but she had learned about Plame from government sources. Both journalists originally decided to maintain the confidentiality of their sources, were called before a grand jury, and were cited for contempt of court for not revealing their source during the grand jury investigation. Both also faced jail time, though Novak did not, raising much speculation about his testimony. Patrick Fitzgerald, the special prosecutor in the case, argued that neither Cooper nor Miller could claim confidentiality because all the relevant White House officials had signed waivers releasing reporters from any confidentiality agreement involving the investigation. Cooper and Miller, however, viewed these waivers as coercive, so they vowed to continue to honor their agreements unless they received personal releases from their sources.

Time and the *New York Times* filed suit to dismiss the contempt charges, but the U.S. Supreme Court refused to overturn lower court rulings affirming the contempt orders. After reviewing legal precedents on confidentiality, *Time* chief executive Norman Pearlstine decided that the magazine could not hold itself above the law and, therefore, gave Fitzgerald the notes compiled by Cooper, against the reporter's wishes. Shortly before Cooper was to report for jail, his source released him from the promise of confidentiality in testifying before the grand jury. Miller, with the

support of the *New York Times,* continued to refuse to reveal her source. In 2005 she went to jail for eighty-five days for doing so. She was released from jail after her source encouraged her to speak to the grand jury. Cooper and Miller's situations raised additional questions:

- What kind of release from a source frees a journalist from his or her promise of confidentiality?
- Is a journalist entitled to refuse a court order to testify?
- Is a journalist who gathers information but does not publish it subject to the same requirement to testify as a journalist who writes a story?
- Should journalists be shielded from such prosecution?

Miller also became embroiled in a controversy regarding her reporting on weapons of mass destruction prior to and during the Iraq War. In that case, Miller relied on confidential sources who assured her that such weapons existed in Iraq. These weapons, she reported, could be used against the United States, seeming to support a major part of the Bush administration's case for war. No such weapons were ever found. Many journalists felt that Miller had become too close to her sources, especially ones who may have had political motives for feeding her "privileged" information. Reporters' ethical duties are not, however, to their sources, but to the public. Miller also failed to verify the information or seek other views. This situation raised the following questions:

- What kind of guidelines should govern reporter-source relationships?
- How close can a reporter get to those with political power while maintaining his or her independence?
- How many points of view should a reporter seek for a story?
- How can a reporter report what government officials say without having others believe that they are a mouthpiece for the government?

Another ethical issue emerged in the form of the so-called Swift boat controversy, when during the 2004 presidential campaign members of a Swift boat veterans group accused Sen. John Kerry, the Democratic Party's presidential nominee, of having failed to tell the truth about the medals he had earned during the Vietnam War. The news media's coverage of the story focused initially on the allegations and counter-allegations in a barrage of stories that offered information— some of it questionable—without much context. It took several weeks before such newspapers as the *New York Times* and *Washington Post* provided comprehensive overviews of the allegations and the individuals behind them. The incident raised the following ethical and other questions:

- Who were the players in the story and what were their motivations?
- Was it a story that required immediate disclosure or should there have been more investigation before it was published or broadcast?
- How useful was the story in helping the public understand the candidate and the issues?
- What public records existed to verify or contradict the allegations being made?

A CBS News report that it had proof of President George W. Bush having received favored treatment while serving in the National Guard during the Vietnam War serves similarly as an ethical example. Dan Rather, the managing editor for CBS News, reported that his organization had obtained documents raising questions about the president's service in the guard, in particular whether he had served his full term of duty. Following the news reports, bloggers as well as mainstream news organizations began questioning the authenticity of the documents and their provenance. Rather said that he believed the documents to be authentic and the story true, but several days later, Rather and CBS News president Andrew Heyward apologized for airing the story and stated that they could not vouch for the documents. Rather also identified and interviewed the source, who admitted to misleading CBS about how he had obtained the documents.

The drive to be "first" with a juicy, scandalous story may have clouded the judgment of Rather and CBS. In this case, experienced journalists, including Mary Mapes, a veteran CBS producer, failed to ask ethical questions that might have precluded airing such a story prematurely:

- Who might be the best resource for authenticating such documents?
- What questions might the documents raise, and who could answer those questions?
- What was the motivation of the source who supplied the documents?
- How would viewers judge the source's motivation and veracity?
- What might be the impact on the story and the credibility of the news organization in airing such a story?

News organizations play an important role in helping the public understand and act upon the politics of the day, and political coverage benefits when the news media use an ethical decision-making model. A journalistic approach that makes ethics an indispensable tool enhances the credibility of the news it provides and ensures that the media's role as educator and critic in the democratic political process created by the founders functions as they intended.

See also *Media feeding frenzies; Scandal; Shield laws; Time pressures.*

REFERENCES

American Society of Newspaper Editors, www.asne.org/ideas/codes/codes.htm. For a list of news organizations' code of ethics.

Emery, Michael, Edwin Emery, and Mary Roberts. *The Press and America: An Interpretive History of the Mass Media.* 9th ed. Boston: Allyn and Bacon, 2000.

Fuller, Jack. *News Values: Ideas for an Information Age.* Chicago: University of Chicago Press, 1996.

Kovach, Bill, and Tom Rosentiel. *The Elements of Journalism: What Newspeople Should Know and What the Public Should Expect.* New York: Crown Publishers, 2001.

Lambeth, Edmund. *Committed Journalism: An Ethic for the Profession.* Bloomington: Indiana University Press, 1992.

Overholser, Geneva. "The Journalist and the Whistleblower," *New York Times,* February 6, 2004, A27.

Poynter Institute. Poynter Online, www.poynter.org or www.poynter.org/subject.asp?id=32.

Evening network news

In 1948 and 1949 CBS and NBC took initial steps toward nightly news broadcasting. ABC's first evening news broadcast aired in 1953. All three networks' news programs initially were limited to presenting newsreel footage to small markets, primarily in the eastern United States. An inability to gather video from a distance was among the major shortcomings of television news gathering in its infancy.

In mid-1963 CBS and NBC expanded their evening news programs—the *CBS Evening News* and the *Huntley-Brinkley Report*—from fifteen to thirty minutes. This longer format coincided with the tumultuous time in U.S. history that included the assassination of President Kennedy, the civil rights movement, and the Vietnam War. The events of the day made for dramatic imagery, but the evening news roughly held to the same format employed at its inception: News anchors rarely left the studio for on-the-spot reporting. Most news footage was shot on film, and the delay between an event and its airing could be considerable, depending on the amount of time it took to film the event, send the film to a studio, process it, and transport or transmit the video to New York. By the 1970s, communications satellites and smaller, more portable video cameras had significantly changed television news gathering. The two technologies complemented each other: video cameras dispensed with film that had to be developed, and satellites allowed for the inexpensive transmission of video from the point of origin to the broadcast studio.

In 1978 ABC News introduced an original format with *World News Tonight,* its revamped nightly news program. The format featured "news desks" in Washington, Chicago, and London, a situation made possible by relatively cheap satellite communications, which also allowed for more readily gathered news. ABC returned to a more traditional format from 1983 until 2005, with Peter Jennings anchoring the news solo from New York. All three major networks moved toward flashier graphics and more visually interesting reports to get viewer's attention, and by the late 1980s, story counts had increased while the typical news story had become shorter. In other words, news reporting became broad and shallow, instead of narrow and deep.

Cheap satellite and news-gathering technologies also explain why news audiences have declined since the late 1980s. Shrinking broadcast audiences are not a sign of waning interest in news, rather technological advancements now allow consumers to get their news from an array of media—cable news networks, radio, print, the Internet, podcasts, and so on—and around the clock. In addition, local television news has grown in popularity, as satellite hookups permit local stations to cover national and international stories.

Consumers who desire in-depth news are not likely to find it by watching network newscasts. The typical evening news, if set in print in a newspaper, would not fill the front page. Regardless, the evening news remains an important part of the networks' identity as evidenced by the media attention surrounding Katie Couric's decision in 2006 to anchor the *CBS Evening News.* Although network news audiences are proportionally smaller than they were in the 1980s, because they tend to be older and thus have relatively larger amounts of disposable income, advertisers still value them.

Networks continue to tinker with evening news formats in their efforts to reinvigorate news programming and get a leg up on the competition. After Peter Jennings departed from ABC in 2005, the network tried a two-anchor format,

featuring Bob Woodruff and Elizabeth Vargas, but shortly thereafter Woodruff was badly injured by an explosion while reporting from Iraq. Exposing a news anchor or a popular journalist to some risk is not new in broadcasting, but Iraq was one of the highest-risk assignments undertaken by an evening anchor. The incident involving Woodruff caused ABC and other networks considering such assignments to weigh the ratings rewards of sending high-profile journalists into high-risk situations versus the value of consistency at the anchor desk. Woodruff's injury and ABC's low ratings led it to appoint Charlie Gibson, a popular co-anchor of *Good Morning America,* to the anchor desk.

Media scholars and critics often debate whether and to what extent TV news and the evening news affect the political agenda. Their effects are unclear, but for at least twenty-five years the networks' news agenda was set by the stories that ran on the front page of the *New York Times.* Today, with other forms of news taking hold, nightly news programs have begun to run fewer and longer stories and more feature material than so-called spot news. This trend will continue if it stabilizes or increases viewership.

REFERENCES

Althaus, Scott L. "American News Consumption during Times of Crisis." *PS: Political Science and Politics* 35, no. 3 (2002): 517–521.

Frank, Reuven. *Out of Thin Air: The Brief Wonderful Life of Network News.* New York: Simon and Schuster, 1991.

Gans, Herbert. *Deciding What's News: A Study of* CBS Evening News, NBC Nightly News, Newsweek, *and* Time. New York: Pantheon, 1979.

Garner, Joe. *We Interrupt This Broadcast: The Events That Stopped Our Lives. From the Hindenburg Explosion to the Attacks of September 11.* 3rd ed. Naperville, Ill.: Sourcebooks MediaFusion, 2002.

Mickelson, Sig. *The Decade That Shaped Television News: CBS in the 1950s.* Westport, Conn.: Prager, 1998.

Shales, Tom. "Follow the Bouncing News with ABC," *Washington Post.* July 11, 1978, C1.

Exit polls

Exit polls survey a sampling of voters immediately after they cast their ballots in an attempt to discover how and why they voted as they did and in some cases to project the winner of an election. Harry Field and other researchers experimented with asking questions at polling places in the 1940s, but "exit polls" did not become a part of election day reporting until the 1960s. The use of exit polls as analytical

A man displays the four different headlines of the November 8, 2000, issue of the Chicago Sun-Times, *with three of the four concerning the outcome of the presidential election between Democratic candidate Al Gore and Republican George W. Bush. The news media had used random sampling exit polls as analytical tools since 1972, but the practice came under fire after the 2000 elections, when they led to confusion and erroneous projections.*

tools for projecting election-night results and understanding of voters' rationale began in 1972.

Throughout the 1980s, several news organizations competed in exit polling, using different questionnaires and methodologies. As a cost-cutting measure in 1990, the three major broadcast networks—ABC, NBC, and CBS—joined with CNN to form Voter Research and Surveys (VRS) to conduct "pooled" exit polls for use by all four organizations and for sale to interested local stations and newspapers. In 1993 VRS merged with the News Election Service (NES), which had been counting votes for news organizations on election days since 1964. The new organization, Voter News Service, added two more members, the Associated Press (which had been part of NES) and Fox News, to the consortium in 1996. All election-night reporting eventually became dependent on material from VRS exit polls. The

networks continued, however, to compete in analysis and interpretation, and many independently declared states won or lost.

The methodology of exit polls is a variation of random sampling: within each state, a random set of precincts are selected proportionate to size, after stratification by past vote and geographic location. Workers stationed at the polling places interview a designated percentage of voters. This could mean every other voter, every third voter, and so on, depending on the total number of voters. The questionnaire contains as many as thirty multiple-choice items. Results from individual questionnaires are transmitted to a central location three times during the day.

After the 1980 election, the state of Washington adopted legislation to limit the actions of exit poll interviewers, requiring them to maintain the same distance from the polling station as those electioneering for a candidate. The networks, as well as several newspapers, successfully sued the state, claiming that interviewers speaking to voters after they had cast their ballots, should not be viewed as electioneering and that the law violated the First Amendment protection of freedom of the press. Also in 1981, the broadcast networks promised Congress not to characterize the outcome in a state on election day before the majority of polling places in that state had closed. Because the majority of the population lives in the eastern time zones and states begin to close their polls as early as 6 p.m. EST, it is still possible in a presidential election for someone to have gained a majority of electoral votes long before the Pacific states close their polls at 11 p.m. EST.

Exit polls again became embroiled in controversy in the 2000 presidential election. The razor-thin margin between Republican George W. Bush and Democrat Al Gore nationally, and especially in Florida, which would ultimately decide the race, coupled with the networks using the same data from VRS to make projections, resulted in calls and miscalls. A premature announcement that Gore had won Florida had to be retracted. Hours later, Fox News, relying on vote count data, first made the projection for Bush. The other networks followed shortly after. Ties between a Fox analyst and the Bush family led to further controversy, especially as the Florida vote was (partially) recounted and the outcome ended up in the courts. Technical failures while updating the VRS system left the networks without exit poll data for the 2002 midterm elections. VRS disbanded soon thereafter.

In the 2004 election, the networks instituted a new service, and they were generally cautious in relying on exit polls to make projections. Nevertheless, controversies still arose over exit poll overestimates of the Democratic vote in key states, such as in Ohio. Despite the problems with exit polls, their utility in allowing networks to "scoop" the competition in announcing election projections and to explain the vote ensures their continued use.

REFERENCES

Frankovic, Kathleen A. "Public Opinion and Polling." In *The Politics of News, The News of Politics,* edited by Doris Graber, Denis McQuail, and Pippa Norris. Washington, D.C.: CQ Press, 1998.

Mitofsky, Warren J. "A Short History of Exit Polls." In *Polling and Presidential Election Coverage,* edited by Paul J. Lavrakas and Jack K. Holley. Los Angeles: Sage Publications, 1991.

Traugott, Michael W., and Paul J. Lavrakas. *The Voter's Guide to Election Polls.* 3rd ed. Lanham, Md.: Rowman and Littlefield, 2004.

F

Face the Nation

See *Sunday news shows*

Fairness and Accuracy in Reporting

Fairness and Accuracy in Reporting (FAIR), a national media watchdog group, strives to strengthen the First Amendment by advocating for greater diversity in the press and by scrutinizing media practices that marginalize the public interest and minority and dissenting viewpoints. Founded in 1986 by Jeff Cohen, FAIR operates not only as an anti-censorship organization but also works to expose neglected news stories and advocates the breakup of dominant media conglomerates.

FAIR publishes the magazine *Extra!,* a bimonthly examination of the media, and produces *CounterSpin,* a weekly radio program. FAIR's specialized research and advocacy desks work with media and activists on issues of interest to them. Its women's desk tracks sexism and homophobia in the media. The racism watch desk monitors the media's perception of people of color. FAIR is generally viewed as the ideological counterpart to the conservative Accuracy in Media (AIM).

See also *Accuracy in media.*

REFERENCES
Fairness and Accuracy in Reporting, www.fair.org.

Fairness doctrine

The fairness doctrine, which originated with a 1949 Federal Communications Commission (FCC) decision, stemmed from the situation that unlike publishing, only a finite number of radio and TV stations could operate in a given area. The "scarcity" of the broadcast spectrum led to empowering the FCC to regulate the broadcast media in the public interest.

The fairness doctrine began emerging in 1941 in an FCC ruling on the license renewal of Boston radio station WAAB. Although the commission renewed the station's license, it contended that many of the station's editorials were not objective or impartial. In the ruling, commonly referred to as the Mayflower decision (after a competing business that challenged the license application), the FCC chided the station's practice of editorializing and discouraged other stations from doing the same. The FCC viewed broadcasters as serving as "public trustees," who had an obligation to the public to air discussions of controversial public matters, provided that such discussions were balanced—that is, no one position could dominate the airwaves. Thus, in 1949 the FCC modified the Mayflower decision, allowing broadcasters to editorialize if they presented all sides of a controversy.

The fairness doctrine was just that—a regulatory doctrine, not a single regulation or law. One can discern in it a motivation—to balance viewpoints—similar to that which drove Congress to enact section 315, the "equal time" provision, of the Communication Act of 1934. Although an FCC doctrine does not have the legal force of a statutory enactment, the FCC took the doctrine seriously and enforced it and added to it throughout the life of the doctrine.

In the 1950s and 1960s, the FCC extended the fairness doctrine to public affairs programs, commercial advertising, and political advertising and appearances. It required broadcasters to balance the presentation of any controversial subject of public importance in overall programming and to take the initiative to produce controversial programming. Thus, the FCC viewed the fairness doctrine as a means by which the government could ensure that stations provide a reasonable opportunity for the presentation of contrasting viewpoints. The commission granted licensees discretion regarding the time devoted to a controversy, the issues covered, the viewpoints presented, the appropriate representatives, and the program format and other programming decisions.

Application of the fairness doctrine to advertising took place in 1963 under the Cullman doctrine. In 1966 the FCC determined that the broadcasting of cigarette commercials was a controversial issue and required anti-cigarette advertising in some reasonable proportion. In 1968 the U.S. Court of Appeals for the District of Columbia Circuit upheld this regulatory finding in *Banzhaf v. FCC*. Following *Banzhaf*, environmentalists and others attacked product advertisements for cars, snowmobiles, public utilities, and gasoline engines, arguing that the advertising raised controversial issues although the controversy might not be addressed in the advertisements. The FCC reversed itself in 1974, stating that its regulatory decision on cigarette advertising had been in error and that paid advertising should be exempt from the fairness doctrine.

In 1967 the FCC ruled that personal attacks trigger the fairness doctrine. The rule allowed a person attacked during discussion of a controversial topic to respond on the air; the station airing the attack was required to notify the person attacked within a week of the broadcast. The Supreme Court upheld the rule in *Red Lion Broadcasting Co. v. FCC* (1969), in which it declared as constitutional the concept of fairness, as interpreted by the FCC, because it was based on the scarcity of available frequencies, which limited the number of broadcast facilities. Print media, not being scarce, could not therefore be similarly regulated. Also in 1967, the FCC adopted the political editorial rule, which required that a station that editorialized for or against a candidate had to notify the opposing candidate within twenty-four hours and permit him or her to respond.

Despite the Supreme Court's ruling in *Red Lion*, several factors led to the fairness doctrine's demise. It eventually became too unwieldy, and in the early 1970s the FCC began to reverse its position, as it did following the numerous complaints stemming from *Banzhaf*. Some indications suggest that the fairness doctrine had "chilled" broadcast speech. That is, broadcasters avoided controversial programming to bypass government interference. In addition, the rise of media outlets, such as cable networks, undermined the scarcity argument. Deregulation of content controls, which began during the Carter administration, accelerated under the Reagan administration, and the fairness doctrine became a target. The FCC under Reagan suggested in 1985 that the doctrine be abolished, arguing that it had not served the public interest, rested on questionable regulatory assumptions, and might have a chilling effect on speech and violate the First Amendment. The FCC later officially determined that the doctrine was no longer necessary because of competition within each market, a situation that relieved broadcasters of the requirement that they present controversial issues of public importance in a balanced fashion. In August 1987, after almost forty years of enforcement of the fairness doctrine, the FCC abolished it. Prior to this action, Congress had attempted to enact the doctrine as law to prevent its imminent demise, but President Reagan vetoed the legislation. Congress again tried to reinstate it during the administration of George H. W. Bush, but that measure too was vetoed. In 2000 the U.S. Court of Appeals for the District of Columbia Circuit ordered the FCC to immediately repeal the personal attack and political editorial corollaries on procedural grounds stemming from First Amendment challenges to the rules. No action was taken to reinstate them.

See also *Red Lion Broadcasting Co., Inc. v. FCC (1969); Right to access.*

REFERENCES

Banzhaf v. FCC, 405 F.2d 1082 (1968), cert. denied, 396 U.S. 842 (1969).

Benson, Larry D. *The Fairness Doctrine: A Bibliography.* Public Administration Series. Bibliography, P-2809. Monticello, Ill.: Vance Bibliographies, 1990.

Corry, John, et al. *Speaking Freely: The Public Interest in Unfettered Speech. Essays from a Conservative Perspective.* Washington, D.C.: Media Institute, 1995.

Federal Communications Commission. *The Law of Political Broadcasting and Cablecasting: A Political Primer.* Washington, D.C.: FCC, 1984.

Friendly, Fred. *The Good Guys, the Bad Guys and the First Amendment.* New York: Random House, 1976.

Geller, Henry. *The Fairness Doctrine in Broadcasting: Problems and Suggested Courses of Action.* Santa Monica, Calif.: Rand, 1973.

Jung, Donald J. *The Federal Communications Commission, the Broadcast Industry, and the Fairness Doctrine, 1981–1987.* Lanham, Md.: University Press of America, 1996.

Krattenmaker, Thomas G., and Lucas A. Powe Jr. *Regulating Broadcast Programming.* Cambridge, Mass.: MIT Press; Washington, D.C.: AEI Press, 1994.

Limburg, Val E. "Fairness Doctrine." Museum of Broadcast Communications, www.museum.tv/archives/etv/F/htmlF/fairnessdoct/fairnessdoct.htm.

Pinkston, Will. *The Fairness Forecast: Free Speech, Fair Play, and Talk Radio.* Nashville: Freedom Forum First Amendment Center at Vanderbilt University, 1995.

Red Lion Broadcasting Co. v. FCC, 395 U.S. 367 (1969).

Rowan, Ford. *Broadcast Fairness: Doctrine, Practice, Prospects. A Reappraisal of the Fairness Doctrine and Equal Time Rule.* New York: Longman, 1984.

Simmons, Steven J. *The Fairness Doctrine and the Media.* Berkeley: University of California Press, 1978.

REFERENCES

Andersen, Kurt. "The Outsider." *New Yorker,* March 31, 1997.

"Drained of Zeal—A look at the President's Men." *Time,* May 28, 1979, 16.

Editorial. "A Change at the Helm." *Newsweek,* July 13, 1998, 5.

"Fallows' Fracas—How to Enrage Ex-Colleagues." *Time,* May 7, 1979, 25.

Miller, William Lee. "Match Point to the Media." *Christian Century,* November 21, 1979, 1153–55.

Fallows, James

James Mackenzie Fallows (1950–) is an award-winning author, correspondent, and commentator. Fallows began his journalism career as the editor of the Harvard University *Crimson.* He later wrote and edited for the *Washington Monthly* and *Texas Monthly* and served as President Jimmy Carter's chief speechwriter from 1977 to 1979. Fallows then worked as the national correspondent and Washington editor for the *Atlantic Monthly* from 1979 to 1996. Shortly after joining the *Atlantic,* he wrote "The Passionless President," an article critical of the Carter administration, especially the president's inner circle. During the 1980s and 1990s, he also wrote commentaries for National Public Radio.

Fallows again generated national attention for *Breaking the News: How the Media Undermine American Democracy* (1996), in which he criticizes journalism for its penchant toward sensationalism, negativism, and punditry, that is, opting for entertainment over content. He contends that the fourth estate's slide toward mediocrity is corroding the very essence of American democracy. From 1996 to 1998, Fallows held the position of editor of *U.S. News & World Report,* where he tried unsuccessfully to implement some of the ideas from his book.

Fallows, the national correspondent for the *Atlantic Monthly,* continues to write for a number of other magazines. He is the author of *National Defense* (1981), which won an American Book award, *More Like Us: Making America Great Again* (1989), *Looking at the Sun: The Rise of the New East Asian Economic and Political System* (1994), and *Free Flight: Inventing the Future of Travel* (2001).

Federal Communications Commission

The Federal Communications Commission (FCC) is the independent federal agency charged with regulating interstate and international communication by radio, television, wire, satellite, and cable. Established by the Communications Act of 1934, it reports directly to Congress.

The notion of regulating the nation's airwaves stems from the sinking of the RMS *Titanic* in 1912. The investigation into the disaster revealed that a radio station in Newfoundland had received the ship's distress signal, but as news broke of the accident, amateur radio operators filled the airwaves with interference, severely hindering radio communication and therefore response to it. Following that tragedy, Congress enacted the Radio Act of 1912, which cleared the airwaves for distress signals and also established several legal and regulatory principles that underlie current broadcast regulations. A key feature of the radio act is the allocation, through regulation, of the electromagnetic spectrum in such a way that all manner of wireless communications systems do not interfere with each other. Through its regulatory efforts, the government recognized the airwaves as a scarce good whose fate should not be left to the market, but should instead be regulated to serve the public interest.

By the 1920s, broadcast radio had become the fastest growing part of the wireless communications industry, so Congress enacted the Radio Act of 1927 to regulate radio stations, clarify that broadcasters did not own the radio spectrum, outline rules on frequency allocations and power, and make explicit the authority of the Federal Radio Commission, created under the radio act, to regulate content deemed to be obscene or profane. The act also made clear that radio stations received their license in pursuit of the "public interest, necessity, and convenience."

The Communications Act of 1934 created the FCC as the successor to the Federal Radio Commission and gave it regulatory power over interstate and intrastate communication via wireless and wired communication (such as telephone and telegraph). Wired communication had formerly been regulated by the Interstate Commerce Commission. The 1934 act retained the radio act's provisions regarding the public interest, necessity, and convenience and provisions allowing the FCC to regulate the content of broadcast communication. Today five commissioners—appointed to five-year terms by the president and subject to approval by the Senate—work to ensure that the communications facilities in the United States operate in the "public interest."

The FCC generally does not govern the selection of broadcast programming. Broadcasters may not, however, present obscene material, a ruling reinforced by the Supreme Court's decision in *Federal Communications Commission v. Pacifica Foundation* (1978) that a radio station could be sanctioned for broadcasting the famous George Carlin "seven dirty words" monologue. New technology has, however, changed the field considerably; while broadcasting still has the most limited First Amendment protections, a Supreme Court ruling limited the FCC's power in terms of emerging technology and obscenities. In *Reno v. American Civil Liberties Union* (1997), the Court struck down provisions of the Communications Decency Act of 1996 that would have made it a crime to post indecent and obscene materials on the Internet that minors might be able to access. The ruling extended First Amendment principles to the Internet and acknowledged it as a medium different from broadcast and cable communications.

In another arena, after the infamous 2004 Super Bowl halftime "wardrobe malfunction" involving popular singers Janet Jackson and Justin Timberlake, Congress pressured the FCC to more closely regulate broadcasting. Soon thereafter, the commission began taking more stringent action against radio's so-called shock jocks, such as Howard Stern, assessing fines and causing some radio chains to cancel some syndicated programming. Stern left terrestrial radio in 2006 to broadcast on the Sirius satellite radio system, a form of broadcasting, like cable TV, not subject to FCC content restrictions. Meanwhile, Congress enacted legislation that increased by a factor of ten the fines that the FCC can assess stations that violate obscenity rules. As of mid-2006, the legislation awaited the president's signature. That said, the failure of a TV or radio station to serve the "public interest,

necessity, and convenience" is hardly ever addressed by the commission, which routinely renews licenses in the vast majority of instances.

Obscenity issues aside, the FCC has been remarkably busy in the deregulation of the telecommunications sector under the provisions of the Telecommunications Act of 1996, which was designed to promote competition in telecommunications across a wide range of media, including radio and TV, and telephone and data communications, such as via the Internet. Even before deregulation, the FCC changed its practice of allocating spectrum based on "best public use" to auctions, in which users of the spectrum bid for the rights to slices of it. A notable exception was the granting of a digital TV license to every owner of an analog license, and the subsequent attempts by TV stations to use only part of their digital bandwidth for higher-definition TV (not true HD), reserving the remainder for data broadcasting and other services. The process of deregulation is not fully complete, and it will be years before the ultimate effect of the 1996 act becomes clear.

See also *Radio Act of 1927*.

REFERENCES

Caterinicchia, Dan. "House OKs Huge Raise in Indecency Fine; Violations Would Cost $325,000." *Washington Times,* June 8, 2006, A1.

Lasar's Letter on the Federal Communications Commission, www.lasarletter.com.

Quirk, Matthew. "Air Pollution: FCC Fines for Indecency and Obscenity." *Atlantic Monthly,* May 2004, 36.

U.S. Congress. House Committee on Energy and Commerce. *Federal Communications Commission Authorization Act of 1983: Report Together with Additional and Dissenting Views.* Washington, D.C.: GPO, 1983.

U.S. Congress. House Committee on Energy and Commerce. *Federal Communications Commission Authorization Act of 1991: Report to Accompany H.R. 1674 (Including Cost Estimates of the Congressional Budget Office).* Washington, D.C.: GPO, 1991.

Federal Communications Commission v. Pacifica Foundation (1978)

In *Federal Communications Commission v. Pacifica Foundation* (1978), the Supreme Court ruled in a 5-4 decision that the FCC had the authority to regulate indecent radio broadcasts and that doing so did not violate the First Amendment. The case revolved around the radio broadcast of George Carlin's "seven dirty words" monologue by WBAI, a Pacifica station. A New York citizen who heard the broadcast while driving with his young son filed a complaint with the FCC. The commission responded to the complaint by informing the Pacifica Foundation that the corporation could be subject to administrative fines if it received additional complaints. Pacifica challenged the FCC ruling in federal court.

The Supreme Court held the regulation of obscene radio broadcasts to be permissible for several reasons: First, the monologue was not political in nature, and, therefore, the FCC could not be accused of trying to censor political views with which it did not agree. Second, the broadcast was easily accessible by minors. Whereas theaters and bookstores can deny admission to children without restricting the access of adults, the unique accessibility of radio makes it a less protected form of communication. Third, the Court suggested the importance of "context" when deciding whether vulgar language can be regulated, noting, "We have not decided that an occasional expletive ... would justify prosecution. The Commission's decision rested entirely on a nuisance rationale under which context is all-important."

REFERENCES

Federal Communications Commission v. Pacifica Foundation, 438 U.S. 726 (1978).
O'Brien, David. *Constitutional Law and Politics: Civil Rights and Civil Liberties.* New York: W. W. Norton and Company, 2003.

Federal Radio Commission

The Radio Act of 1927 created the Federal Radio Commission to regulate the communication industry and to handle such issues as licensing, advertising, censorship, and freedom of speech. The act also authorized the commission to enforce commercial broadcasting issues not regulated in the Wireless Act of 1910 or the Radio Act of 1912.

Commercial broadcasting began with Westinghouse playing regular radio broadcasts funded by a local radio store selling the radio receivers necessary for listening to the programs. This marketing strategy became quite popular, and by 1922 more than 670 stations had licenses in the United States. Going a step further, AT&T began selling airtime to businesses willing to advertise on the radio. The American public, strongly opposed to the idea of radio advertisements,

wanted stricter broadcasting regulations. Because previous communications laws had not anticipated commercial broadcasting, stations were easily able to legally overpower or interfere with the signals of their competitors.

The Radio Act of 1912 authorized the secretary of commerce and labor, at the time Herbert Hoover, to issue radio licenses. Hoover, however, could not enforce the specific hours or the amount of power at which stations could broadcast. Four national conferences during the early 1920s attempted to deal with the radio interference problems, and in 1926 President Calvin Coolidge urged Congress to rewrite the law.

The Radio Act of 1927 was the first broadcast legislation to use the phrase "public interest, convenience and necessity," making that medium a utility responsible for informing the public. It also enacted censorship with the phrase "no person ... shall utter any obscene, indecent or profane language by means of radio communication." Congress founded the Federal Radio Commission to bring order to the airwaves and to stop the sabotage plaguing network broadcasts. Authorized by the 1927 act, President Coolidge appointed five members to the new commission "by and with the consent of the Senate" with no more than three representatives from the same political party. The commission had the power to enforce guidelines on licensing, censorship, and freedom of speech, bringing more order to the airwaves.

When Congress passed the Communications Act of 1934, it made the Federal Communications Commission the radio commission's successor and authorized the FCC to regulate interstate and foreign radio, television, wire, and cable communications.

See also *Communications Act of 1934; Federal Communications Commission; Radio; Radio Act of 1927.*

REFERENCES

Bliss, Norman, ed. *The FCC Rule Book: Complete Guide to the FCC Regulations Governing Amateur Radio.* Newington, Conn.: The American Radio Relay League, 1995–96.
Federal Regulatory Directory. 8th ed. Washington, D.C.: Congressional Quarterly, 1997, 92–93.

Federalist Papers

The Federalist Papers, a series of eighty-five letters, were published between October 1787 and August 1788 in an effort to persuade the citizens of New York to support the ratification of the U.S. Constitution. Published originally in New York City newspapers, the letters covered a range of topics concerning the powers and functions of the proposed national government. Although published under the pseudonym Publius, scholars generally attribute their authorship to Alexander Hamilton, John Jay, and James Madison. Soon after their newspaper appearance, the letters were reprinted as the *Federalist Papers* in a two-part edited volume and used as a debater's handbook of sorts by constitutional advocates in New York and Virginia. As such, they were an early and notable use of the mass media for political persuasion.

Although just one of the many voices in the debate over ratification, some of the Federalist Papers have come to be regarded as classics of American political thought. In particular, Madison's Federalist No. 10, "The Same Subject Continued: The Utility of the Union as a Safeguard against Domestic Faction and Insurrection," is considered by historians and political scientists as perhaps the most eloquent justification for the U.S. political system and is routinely reprinted in introductory texts on U.S. government. The Federalist Papers also continue to inform the practical workings of the U.S. government through their use by Supreme Court justices and legislators in defending their interpretations of the Constitution.

REFERENCES

Furtwangler, Albert. *The Authority of Publius: A Reading of the Federalist Papers.* Ithaca, N.Y.: Cornell University Press, 1984.
Hamilton, Alexander, James Madison, and John Jay. *The Federalist Papers.* New York: New American Library, 1961.

Fenno, John

John Fenno (1751–1798) was an early American printer and publisher. Born in Boston, Fenno came of age during the Revolutionary War and learned the printing trade in New York and Philadelphia. With the backing of Alexander Hamilton, between 1789 and 1798 in Philadelphia, Fenno developed, edited, and published the *Gazette of the United States,* often referred to as the *Federalist.*

As with many newspapers of the day, Fenno's *Gazette* promoted the political ideology of the editor and the papers' backers. As the mouthpiece of the Federalists, the *Gazette of the United States* competed directly with Philip Freneau's *National Gazette,* which was supported by Thomas Jefferson and the Democratic-Republicans. The newspapers' passionate partisanship contributed greatly to the alignment of the citizenry with the rival political parties.

Fenno received a contract from the new U.S. government to publish the *Journals of the Senate,* which became the public record of Senate actions and activities. He published the *Journals* from 1789 to 1797. After Fenno died of yellow fever in Philadelphia, his son, John Ward Fenno, succeeded him in the family printing business.

REFERENCE

Pasley, Jeffrey L. *The Tyranny of Printers: Newspaper Politics in the Early American Republic.* Charlottesville: University Press of Virginia, 2001.

Fireside chats

President Franklin D. Roosevelt used "fireside chats" to communicate to the public and generate support for his administration's actions. Roosevelt realized that he had to create a partnership with the people in order to make the fundamental economic and political reforms that he deemed necessary during the Great Depression and into World War II. To bring the people along, he decided to communicate his intentions to them directly and attempt to lend them comfort through the medium of radio. His concept was to speak to the people as if he were visiting them in their homes.

On March 12, 1933, barely a week into his first administration, Roosevelt delivered the first of his fireside chats. In this first broadcast, on the banking crisis, the president urged the public to stop hoarding cash. Later, with popular backing, Roosevelt pushed through the far-reaching New Deal, which included the Social Security program, price supports for farmers, unemployment insurance, and other safeguards taken for granted today in some quarters. A reporter coined the phrase "fireside chat" after Roosevelt's second such broadcast in May 1933.

President Franklin D. Roosevelt delivered weekly radio addresses to the public to build support for his policies and programs. After his second such address, a reporter dubbed these events "fireside chats." Roosevelt is pictured here on June 5, 1944, shortly before a chat on the liberation of Rome by Allied forces in World War II.

Roosevelt, an excellent speaker, was the first president to use the radio effectively to communicate with the masses. He held at least twenty-eight fireside chats (with debate continuing over whether additional speeches should be designated as such). His chats were essential in rallying the public around his sometimes controversial policies. Roosevelt used homely and simple examples that allowed the "average man" to understand complex government issues. The fireside chats not only enabled him to keep in touch with the public, but they also made the people feel a part of government decisions. The chats continue to influence politics and presidential media strategy, as presidents still often want to communicate directly with the people rather than have their thoughts and actions reported and interpreted through the media. Roosevelt's fireside chats likely are the inspiration for the contemporary practice of weekly presidential radio addresses.

REFERENCE

Buhite, Russell D. *FDR's Fireside Chats.* Tulsa: University of Oklahoma Press, 1992.

First Amendment

The First Amendment is one of the most cherished and yet most controversial elements of the Bill of Rights, the first ten amendments to the U.S. Constitution that were ratified in 1791. The scope of the rights set out in these first ten amendments—among them the Second Amendment's right to "keep and bear arms" and the Fourth Amendment's prohibition against "unreasonable" searches and seizures—has been highly contentious over the centuries. In outlining the rights of the people, the First Amendment denies Congress the authority to do the following:

- Establish a religion, meaning that the United States cannot create an official state church, such as the Anglican Church in the United Kingdom. This provision is known as the establishment clause.
- Prohibit the people from exercising their religion as their conscience dictates. This stems from the fact that early colonial settlers sought to escape religious persecution as well as from the experience of those who suffered persecution for their faith in the United States. This is known as the free exercise clause.
- Abridge the people's right to say or print what they wish.

Against the wishes of the Bush administration, in December 2005 the New York Times *revealed that the government had been conducting warrantless surveillance of phone calls. The* Times *revelation led to debate about freedom of the press, which is protected by the First Amendment, and government power. Here, students at Georgetown University Law School protest the administration's policy—an act also protected by the First Amendment—during a speech by Attorney General Alberto Gonzales in January 2006.*

• Prohibit the people from posing complaints or requests to the government. Even today in many nations, people who seek redress from the government can be and are punished. This part of the First Amendment forms the basis for freedom of association and is meant to prohibit government interference in the creation of groups.

Of course, the U.S. government has not adhered perfectly to what some argue is the plain language of the First Amendment that "Congress shall make no law" that would infringe these rights. Case law and practice suggest that the speech and press protections of the First Amendment are neither self-enforcing nor absolute, and the constitutional history of the First Amendment, which only started developing in full in the twentieth century, is a story of an attempt to balance the rights of free speech, press, and other expression with broader societal efforts to maintain an orderly and moral society.

Less than a decade after adoption of the Constitution, Congress passed the Sedition Act, in 1798, making it a crime to publish information about the president or Congress deemed to bring disrepute upon the government. Proponents of the law claimed that the people were sovereign, and therefore those publishing such information undermined the people and republican government. Because Congress represents the people, bringing it into disrepute represents an effort to delegitimize the people's electoral decisions. Opponents of the Sedition Act also claimed that the people were sovereign and should therefore always retain the right to criticize their representatives. Opponents further argued that people could be prosecuted for their opinions under the law given the potential blurring of fact and opinion.

As these two positions illustrate, the guarantees of freedom of speech and freedom of the press did not include a measure of their scope. The Sedition Act had been directed at stifling Thomas Jefferson's Democratic-Republican Party, whose members believed the legislation to be unconstitutional. Federalists, on the other hand, believed in the constitutionality of the law, and every judge who decided a case based on it was a Federalist.

In *Barron v. Baltimore* (1833), the Supreme Court held that the Constitution only restricts the ability of the *federal* government to abridge the liberties of the people as citizens of the United States. To the extent that individual rights were infringed by *state* governments, the Court held that citizens must seek redress from the state courts under state constitutions. Thus, while many states had free speech and free press provisions in their constitutions, these were only enforceable to the extent that the courts in the individual states enforced these laws. The Fourteenth Amendment, passed in 1868, was interpreted by some to apply the same constitutional standard of protection for individual liberties to citizens of the states as well as to citizens of the United States—the incorporation doctrine—but this interpretation did not begin to influence case law until the early twentieth century. The First Amendment proved central in this development.

As the United States prepared to draft men for World War I, Congress took the position that it could punish speech and writings deemed to hinder the war effort. This led to passage of the Espionage Act, a law intended to protect national security, but which also had the effect of restricting individual liberties. In operation, the Espionage Act made criticism of the decision to go to war a criminal offense. In *Schenk v. United States* (1919) and *Debs v. United States* (1919)—decided in the aftermath of the war—the Supreme Court upheld the government's power to restrict antiwar speech and publication under the Espionage Act. Whatever the First Amendment might otherwise mean, in times of war, the federal government felt it had the right to suppress antiwar dissent.

In another postwar case, *Abrams v. United States* (1919), the court sided with the government's argument that the government could punish anarchists who, in violation of the Espionage Act, distributed leaflets denouncing U.S. entry into World War I. In this case, Justices Oliver Wendell Holmes and Louis Brandeis dissented, with Holmes writing that opposing viewpoints should be allowed into the "marketplace of ideas" and that government interference with speech and press freedoms is tolerable only when there is a "clear and present danger" created by the material in question. These two justices also dissented in *Gitlow v. New York* (1925), a case involving a leaflet promoting general strikes, but in upholding Gitlow's conviction under

New York law, the majority noted that states must adhere to the First Amendment on the same basis as the federal government.

In *Near v. Minnesota* (1931), the Supreme Court made clear that states would indeed be held to a higher First Amendment standard than had existed previously. In *Near,* the Court invalidated a state statute allowing local government officials to prohibit the future publication of material alleged to be "malicious, scandalous and defamatory" based on previous editions. Thus was born the prohibition of prior restraint, an issue the Court would revisit in the Pentagon Papers cases.

These cases notwithstanding, free speech rights did not flower in the 1940s and 1950s, particularly during the "red scare" promoted by Sen. Joseph McCarthy and other prominent national figures. Indeed, membership in so-called subversive groups—which ranged from the Communist Party to some labor unions, professional organizations, and interest groups, such as the American Civil Liberties Union—was often cited as a cause for impugning one's patriotism and loyalty. By the 1960s, however, after the repudiation of McCarthy's movement, a fresh set of legal challenges were mounted against government suppression of speech and the press. During the 1960s and early 1970s, numerous cases involved determining whether a book or movie could be judged obscene and whether such materials enjoyed First Amendment protection.

For most of this period, the law on obscenity precluded any discussion of sex as necessarily obscene. Thus writings about birth control could be and were suppressed. In addition, the federal government forbade the importation of such books as James Joyce's *Ulysses* and D. H. Lawrence's *Lady Chatterly's Lover.* These actions underscored the first obscenity issue: Can government ban great (or serious) literature on the ground that it is obscene? In *Roth v. United States* (1957), the Supreme Court said no, although it would take seven more years and a 5–4 vote in *Grove Press v. Gerstein* (1964) for Henry Miller's *Tropic of Cancer* to be allowed to circulate freely. On the same day of the *Grove Press* decision, the Court, in *Jacobellis v. Ohio* (1964), held that a film, *Les Amants* (The Lovers), was not obscene and therefore the theater owner that showed it could not be prosecuted for obscenity. The basic legal test for whether something is, as a matter of law, obscene is found in *Miller v. California* (1973). The Miller test, according to the First Amendment Center, requires that a jury assess the following:

- whether the average person, applying contemporary community standards, would find that the work, taken as a whole, appeals to the prurient interest;
- whether the work depicts or describes, in a patently offensive way, sexual conduct specifically defined by the applicable state law; and
- whether the work, taken as a whole, lacks serious literary, artistic, political, or scientific value.

The "community standards" test has been particularly problematic, because something that a jury in one community might find obscene would not meet that standard in another. Thus, *Miller* did not create a national standard. Congress has attempted many times to limit sex on cable television and the Internet, typically claiming the need to protect children, but the Supreme Court has routinely invalidated such efforts, and the ready availability of "adult entertainment" on cable TV, the Internet, and on DVD has mainstreamed this material to the point where legal challenges to its distribution are usually fruitless.

The Court has also ruled on the somewhat weightier issues of constitutional rights and free speech. In *New York Times v. Sullivan* (1964), it held that citizens had the right to criticize their leaders as harshly as they wished. The only expressed limitation on this right is a prohibition on writing or speaking falsehoods known to be untrue or uttered in reckless disregard of the truth. In affirming the right to criticize government, the Court opened its institutions to scrutiny and attack in all circumstances, including dissent during wartime, thus repudiating the World War I cases. Adversarial journalism eventually came to dominate the relationship between government and the media. *Sullivan* also led the Court to constitutionalize the area of libel more generally. Over the next decade, the justices issued a set of rules distinguishing private libel from the more newsworthy public libel. In essence, for well-known individuals inside and outside government, winning a libel case—even when defamed—became almost impossible.

The 1971 effort to publish the Pentagon Papers—documents detailing early U.S. involvement in Vietnam—tested the right of the press to scrutinize the workings of government. The papers were provided to the *New York Times* and the *Washington Post* by Daniel Ellsberg, an analyst for the RAND Corporation who obtained them in the course of doing government contract work during the Vietnam War. The papers' content suggested that the military and political establishment had not been truthful about the goals and progress of the war. The Nixon administration opposed making the papers public and brought suit to enjoin the *New York Times* from publishing them on the grounds that their release would harm national security. The *Washington Post* then announced that it too would publish some of the papers. The issue was so controversial, in terms of policy and constitutional rights, that the case moved through the judicial system in two weeks, with the Supreme Court ruling the injunction unconstitutional.

Three years later, the Court considered the converse of the injunction debate: Could the press be forced to print something that it did not want to print? A Florida law required that candidates for public office be allowed to respond in instances in which their character or conduct is assailed in a newspaper column. In a pair of editorials, the *Miami Herald* had savaged a teacher's union head running for the state legislature, but then refused to print his reply. In *Miami Herald Pub. Co. v. Tornillo* (1974), the Court vindicated the newspaper, holding that freedom of the press also meant that editors could choose what not to print. Many have argued that government has no right at all to interfere in the publication of sexually explicit or politically controversial issues given the First Amendment's command that Congress shall make no law abridging these rights. Most jurists believe, however, that circumstances do exist in which government can abridge speech and press rights.

A major controversy in constitutional law revolves around what exactly constitutes speech. In some settings, expressive behavior constitutes speech and therefore is protected. In *Tinker v. Des Moines Independent Community School Dist.* (1969), the Supreme Court invalidated a school district's punishment of students who wore black armbands to school to protest the Vietnam War. The Court thus held that students had similar First Amendment rights as adults and that expression could not be limited unless it was disruptive to the school environment. Student newspapers are not, however, free from interference from schools, as the court ruled in *Hazelwood School District v. Kuhlmeier* (1988). In this case, the Court, citing *Bethel School District No. 403 v. Fraser* (1986), asserted, "We have ... recognized that the First Amendment rights of students in the public schools 'are not automatically coextensive with the rights of adults in other settings.'" The weight of the case law suggests that high school papers are thus not entitled to the same constitutional protections as other media.

Certain expressive behaviors—such as burning the U.S. flag—continue to be controversial. In *Texas v. Johnson* (1989), the Court held, 5-4, that burning the flag, in this case at the 1988 Republican National Convention, was a protected form of expression under the First Amendment. The debate over the outcome of this case continues today. In June 2006, the House of Representatives passed a constitutional amendment banning flag desecration. The Senate, however, failed to muster enough votes for passage (and thereafter submission to the states for ratification).

In recent years, concerns about government secrecy, the war on terrorism, and the ability of journalists to gather news have raised important legal questions. Of interest, the government never indicted anyone involved in the publication of the Pentagon Papers, but the person who leaked them was. In *Branzburg v. Hayes* (1972), the Supreme Court ruled that reporters are citizens, like everyone else, and that they therefore must comply with a summons to appear before a grand jury to testify about criminal matters about which they may have knowledge. Many states have, however, enacted shield laws that prevent courts from forcing journalists to reveal the identities of sources. No such federal law as yet exists, which is why former *New York Times* reporter Judith Miller spent twelve weeks in jail in 2005 for refusing to reveal her source in the White House who possibly leaked the name of a CIA operative to the press in violation of federal law. This CIA case triggered considerable debate in legal and political circles. During times of great national stress and conflict, and particularly during war, the First Amendment comes under pressure from those who place a high value on order and on security. Just as at the founding of the Republic, the debate will continue to focus on how the nation can balance one of its most cherished rights—freedom of expression—with the preservation of national security.

See also *Alien and Sedition Acts of 1798; Gitlow v. New York; Pentagon Papers; Miller v. California; Near v. Minnesota; New York Times Co. v. Sullivan; New York Times v. United States; Obscenity and pornography; Prior restraint.*

REFERENCES

Bezanson, Randall P. *How Free Can the Press Be?* Urbana: University of Illinois Press, 2003.

Franklin, Marc A., David A. Anderson, and Fred H. Cate. *Mass Media Law.* 6th ed. New York: Foundation Press, 2000.

Lewis, Anthony. *Make No Law.* New York: Random House, 1991.

Powe, Lucas A., Jr., *American Broadcasting and the First Amendment.* Berkeley: University of California Press, 1987.

———. *The Fourth Estate and the Constitution.* Berkeley: University of California Press, 1991.

Sunstein, Cass R. *Democracy and the Problem of Free Speech.* New York: Free Press, 1993.

Fleischer, Ari

Lawrence Ari Fleischer (1960–) held the position of White House press secretary from January 2001 through July 2003. Even before he took his official post, he served as spokesman for the Bush campaign during the 2000 Florida recount. His official career spanned the September 11, 2001, attacks on the Pentagon and World Trade Center, the war in Afghanistan, and the beginning of the U.S.-led war against Iraq. Other notable political positions held by Fleischer include press secretary for Reps. Norman Lent (R–N.Y.) and Joseph DioGuardi (R–N.Y.) and Sen. Pete Domenici (R–N.M.). He also served as communications director for the House Ways and Means Committee and for Republican Elizabeth Dole's 2000 presidential campaign. After resigning from the White House, he formed Ari Fleischer Communications.

REFERENCE

Fleischer, Ari. *Taking Heat: The President, the Press, and My Years in the White House.* New York: William Morrow, 2005.

Fourth estate

The "fourth estate" refers to the media in their role as an independent institution and as a check-and-balance to the executive, legislative, and judicial branches of government. The expression originated in nineteenth-century England, where the press was regarded as having power equal to the priesthood, aristocracy, and commons—the three estates within the British Parliament. The First Amendment to the Constitution established the legal foundation for the media to operate independently without government interference (although the phrase "fourth estate" was not used at that time). This protection allows the media to legally assume the role of an adversarial or watchdog press. The media represent the fourth estate in American government by monitoring its actions, exposing and deterring wrongdoing by it, and assessing public policy. A lively debate currently revolves around whether the media have lived up to these objectives.

Douglass Cater characterizes the media as the fourth branch of government that makes the three formal branches more transparent and is as well a major actor in the policy-making process. Timothy Cook, however, considers the fourth branch metaphor outdated and less useful today than in previous eras. Rather, Cook views the media as an "intermediary institution," because they do not possess formal governmental power. In addition, other political institutions—such as the bureaucracy, political parties, and interest groups—are also referred to as the fourth branch of government or fourth estate.

REFERENCES

Cater, Douglass, Jr. *The Fourth Branch of Government.* Boston: Houghton Mifflin, 1959.

Cook, Timothy E. *Governing with the News.* Chicago: University of Chicago Press, 1998.

Graber, Doris A. *Mass Media and American Politics.* 7th ed. Washington, D.C.: CQ Press, 2005.

Fox Broadcasting Corporation

The Fox Broadcasting Corporation (owner of the Fox Television Network) was established as a subsidiary of Rupert Murdoch's News Corporation, a multinational media firm with holdings in Australia, the United Kingdom, and the United States. The Fox Network went on the air in the United States on 1986 with two nights of entertainment programming. Among the network's early successes were *The Tracey Ullman Show, Married with Children, The Simpsons* (which reintroduced prime-time, adult-oriented animation to network TV), and *In Living Color,* a sketch comedy show. Later additions to the line-up included the popular *Beverly Hills 90210* and *X-Files.* The network spun off from News Corporation in 1998 into the Fox Entertainment Group, which includes the Fox Broadcasting Company, cable stations, and the Los Angeles Dodgers baseball team, among other holdings. Murdoch is the majority shareholder in this new firm.

Fox's small number of relatively low-power UHF affiliate stations initially hindered its growth, seeming to predestine it as the perennial "fourth network," after ABC, CBS, and NBC. Fox, however, gained attention out of proportion to its viewership for at least three reasons. First, although Fox affiliates were often obscure stations above Channel 13, local cable systems carried the Fox station, rendering differences in signal quality insignificant. Second, Fox also started with a business strategy that recognized its weaknesses in relation to the established networks. Third, its programming targeted eighteen- to forty-nine-year-olds, a key demographic for advertisers. Thus, while Fox's overall viewership lagged behind that of the big three networks, it targeted audiences most often watching cable TV networks.

Fox's climb in the ratings can also be attributed to a willingness to quickly follow trends and to invest in sports programming. Yet Fox remains a relatively small network, providing only fifteen hours of prime-time programming compared with the twenty-two offered by the other networks. This may actually represent a strength for Fox, allowing it to focus more on its target audience while allowing affiliates to program an hour of prime time and claim the advertising revenue. In recent years, this strategy has yielded some hit programming, including *American Idol.*

Fox created a news division in 1992. Several of its affiliates either have no nightly local news broadcast or one evening broadcast at 10 p.m., an hour earlier than most network affiliates' news programming. Through aggressive marketing and a clearly defined product, however, Fox's twenty-four-hour cable news channel, Fox News Channel, has overtaken CNN in viewership. Despite famously advertising itself as "fair and balanced," Fox airs a conservative line up which attracts viewers who agree with some of the network's pundits in decrying what they view as the liberal bent in other media outlets. Fox's mix of news and entertainment and unabashed patriotism after the al-Qaida attacks of September 11, 2001, and during the Iraq War likewise won it a growing audience.

REFERENCES

Carter, Bill. "A Wily Upstart That Did a Lot of Things Right." *New York Times,* January 4, 1998.

Collins, Scott. *Crazy Like a Fox: The Inside Story of How Fox News Beat CNN.* New York: Portfolio, 2004.

Rapping, Elayne. "The Year of the Young." *Progressive,* February 1993, 36–38.

Zoglin, Richard. "Fox's Growing Pains." *Time,* August 23, 1993, 66.

Fox News Sunday

See *Sunday news shows*

Framing

Framing refers to the ways in which media emphasize or de-emphasize aspects of the reality on which they are reporting. Frames can be found in the subtle messages embedded in news stories, strategies news sources use to influence the news, and interpretations of the news by the public.

The concept of framing is easily conveyed through a metaphor: When making a photograph, the photographer chooses whether to zoom in on particular elements of a scene, use a wide-angle shot that captures a broader view, or use sharp or soft focus and so on. Journalists—often somewhat automatically or unconsciously—similarly decide what aspects of a story to bring into focus and which to leave in the background or out of view altogether. Politicians often consciously emphasize certain dimensions of government programs, election-year issues, or embarrassing scandals while downplaying others. Interest groups, social activists, academics, and others whom reporters use as sources also typically "frame" the information they provide. For example, is the Abu Ghraib prisoner abuse scandal an example of a systematic U.S. policy of torture or the overzealous antics of low-level, rogue "bad apples" in the military? The news is inevitably shaped by framing, as is how the audience interprets the news. According to Russell Neuman, Marion Just, and Anne Crigler, "frames are conceptual tools which media and individuals rely on to convey, interpret, and evaluate information."

First systematized by Erving Goffman in *Frame Analysis,* the study of framing became so popular that scholars have tried to clarify its definition. Robert Entman argues convincingly that frames are identifiable by four common characteristics: they attempt to define problems, to diagnose causes, to make moral judgments, and to suggest remedies. In other words, frames offer explicit or implicit claims about reality.

The effects of frames on news consumers are not entirely clear. Research conducted by Shanto Iyengar demonstrates that news frames can influence how people think about such problems as terrorism, poverty, and racial inequality. In contrast, through in-depth interviews, Neuman, Just, and Crigler have mapped the "issue frames" used by the general public to understand the news, illustrating that the public does not always adopt the frames presented in the news. Despite uncertainty over the effect of news frames on the public, scholars believe that they are important because they are struggled over as journalists seek to report the news and their sources seek to shape it. They are also crucial to human communication and cognition.

See also *Agenda setting.*

REFERENCES

Entman, Robert M. "Framing: Toward Clarification of a Fractured Paradigm." *Journal of Communication* 43, no. 4 (Autumn 1993): 51–58.
Goffman, Erving. *Frame Analysis.* New York: Free Press, 1974.
Iyengar, Shanto. *Is Anyone Responsible?* Chicago: University of Chicago Press, 1991.
Neuman, W. Russell, Marion R. Just, and Anne N. Crigler. *Common Knowledge.* Chicago: University of Chicago Press, 1992.

Franken, Al

Al Franken (1951–) is an Emmy and Grammy Award–winner who made his mark as a television comedy writer and producer before becoming a best-selling author and radio personality known for using humor to satirize and ridicule politics and the media today. Working largely behind the scenes, Franken supplied a significant amount of the political humor of *Saturday Night Live,* where he worked as a writer and occasionally appeared as a performer from 1975 to 1980 and 1985 to 1995. He burst onto the political scene with his best-selling book of political satire *Rush Limbaugh Is a Big Fat Idiot and Other Observations* (1996). Franken's send-up of the claims made by Limbaugh and similar radio hosts, primarily on the political right, broke ground in the politically focused, hypocrisy-seeking humor that the *Daily Show* would later pursue. Franken's *Lies and the Lying Liars Who Tell Them: A Fair and Balanced Look at the Right* (2003) gained added notoriety when one of its targets, Fox News, sued to stop publication of the book because its title was close to that of Fox New's "Fair and Balanced" slogan. Fox's case was a notorious failure, and the publicity actually aided book

Al Franken, radio talk show host, comedian, author, and former writer for Saturday Night Live, *takes a call during his program, "The Al Franken Show," on Air America Radio. Franken uses provocative humor to address political issues and the media.*

sales. Franken followed up this effort with *The Truth (with Jokes)* (2005).

In 2004 Franken became the featured talent on Air America, the syndicated liberal radio talk show network launched that year. His show relies largely on interviews with political figures and reporters in which they skewer conservatives and the media.

REFERENCES

Franken, Al. *Rush Limbaugh Is a Big Fat Idiot and Other Observations.* New York: Delacorte Press, 1996.

Shales, Tom, and James Andrew Miller. *Live from New York: An Uncensored History of* Saturday Night Live. Boston: Little, Brown, 2002.

Franklin, Benjamin

Benjamin Franklin (1706–1790) was a printer, inventor, scientist, diplomat, and one of the founders of the United States. Franklin, a prolific reader and largely self-taught, began working at age ten in his father's Boston chandlery and then became an apprentice to his older brother, James Franklin, when the elder opened a print shop in 1721. He wrote a series of opinionated letters under the pseudonym Silence Dogood for his brother's newspaper, the *New England Courant.* When the British imprisoned his brother for

sedition, largely as a result of printing the Dogood letters, Benjamin kept the print shop open and published the newspaper. The experience shaped his views on key elements of the future republic, such as freedom of speech and freedom of the press, and set him on a course of public advocacy using his humor, folksy wisdom, and practical writing style.

James Franklin was not particularly grateful for Benjamin's efforts, however, and inflicted servile abuse on his brother. In 1723 Benjamin broke his apprenticeship, an illegal act at the time, and fled to New York and later to Philadelphia. After early struggles, he found quick success with his print shop and newspaper, the *Pennsylvania Gazette,* which circulated from 1730 to 1748. Franklin wrote under the pseudonym Richard Saunders and published the annual *Poor Richard's Almanac* from 1732 to 1758, offering homespun humor, advice, and helpful information that made him nationally famous; this was the voice he would use throughout his career.

In 1727 Franklin founded a discussion group called the Junta, which evolved into the American Philosophical Association, and helped establish the first U.S. lending library in 1731. He developed a taste for politics as a clerk in the Pennsylvania Assembly in 1736 and held a seat in the Assembly from 1751 to 1764. He also served as the Philadelphia deputy postmaster from 1737 to 1753 as well as joint deputy postmaster for the colonies from 1753 to 1774, helping to improve postal efficiency. By 1748 Franklin's businesses had become sufficiently successful to allow him to turn over operations to a foreman, so he could devote more time to his scientific pursuits and politics.

At the outbreak of the French and Indian Wars, Franklin represented Pennsylvania at the Albany Congress in 1754, when he first suggested uniting the colonies. He carried out diplomatic missions to Britain on behalf of Pennsylvania during the periods 1757 to 1762 and 1764 to 1775; he also represented Georgia, New Jersey, and Massachusetts. Franklin argued against the Stamp Act in the House of Commons and helped repeal the much-despised legislation. His practical wisdom and popular style contributed to his selection to the committee of five charged with drafting the Declaration of Independence in 1776. As they signed the declaration, Franklin declared, "We must indeed all hang together, or, most assuredly, we shall all hang separately."

Franklin carried out missions to France to secure treaties of commerce and alliance during 1776–1778 and joined John Adams for the peace negotiations and treaty with Great Britain in 1783. Franklin acted as a conciliatory influence among the competing factions during the Constitutional Convention in 1787 and signed the resulting Constitution. He corresponded widely and wrote essays during his last years. Franklin's *Autobiography and Other Writings*—written for his illegitimate son, William, a loyalist with whom he was estranged—was published posthumously.

REFERENCES

Brands, H. W. *The First American: The Life and Times of Benjamin Franklin.* New York: Doubleday, 2000.

Franklin, Benjamin. *Benjamin Franklin: His Life As He Wrote It,* edited by Esmond Wright. Cambridge, Mass.: Harvard University Press, 1989.

Isaacson, Walter. *Benjamin Franklin: An American Life.* New York: Simon and Schuster, 2003.

Middlekauff, Robert. *Benjamin Franklin and His Enemies.* Berkeley: University of California Press, 1996.

Morgan, David T. *The Devious Dr. Franklin, Colonial Agent: Benjamin Franklin's Years in London.* Macon, Ga.: Mercer University Press, 1996.

Morgan, Edmund S. *Benjamin Franklin.* New Haven, Conn.: Yale University Press, 2002.

Van Doren, Carl. *Benjamin Franklin.* New York: Book-of-the-Month Club, 1980. First published in 1938 by Viking Press.

Zall, Paul M., ed. *Ben Franklin Laughing: Anecdotes from Original Sources by and about Benjamin Franklin.* Berkeley: University of California Press, 1980.

Franklin, James

James Franklin (1697–1735) was a colonial American printer and older brother of Benjamin Franklin. After serving as a printer's apprentice in England, Franklin returned to Boston in 1717 with a printing press to begin his own operation. In 1721 he started the *New England Courant,* the first newspaper in the American colonies to print original material; it was the third paper to be established. Franklin's father placed Benjamin in his apprenticeship, an assignment of significant consequences. Benjamin used the *Courant* to express his strong political views, including through the publication of opinionated letters under the pseudonym Silence Dogood, a fictional widow he created. The opinions printed in the *Courant* drew the ire of Crown authorities in Boston and resulted in James's imprisonment for sedition (that is, a libel against the government).

During James's month-long incarceration and as a result of the government's prohibition on his printing the *Courant,* Benjamin ran the print shop and newspaper. Benjamin suffered such servile abuse, however, that in 1723 he illegally left his apprenticeship and ran away to New York and ultimately to Philadelphia. To avoid the restrictive environment of Massachusetts, in 1725 James moved his press to Newport, Rhode Island, where he began that colony's first newspaper, the *Rhode Island Gazette,* in 1732–1733.

Franklin was a prolific printer, producing the colony's currency and publishing *Acts and Resolves of the General Assembly* and numerous popular publications. The example set by Franklin and his experience contributed to galvanizing colonial public opinion regarding censorship, freedom of the press, and the individual rights of citizens. The brothers Franklin eventually reconciled their differences. Beyond his contributions to colonial society, Franklin can be credited with teaching his brother the printing trade and inadvertently shaping the political views of the younger Franklin that would help define a new republic. When Franklin died in 1735, his widow, Anne, and their daughters continued to run the press. Their son, James Jr., served his printer's apprenticeship under his uncle Benjamin in Philadelphia before returning to Rhode Island to carry on for his father.

REFERENCES

Brigham, Clarence S. *James Franklin and the Beginnings of Printing in Rhode Island.* Boston: The Society, 1936.

Franklin, Benjamin. *The Autobiography of Benjamin Franklin,* edited by John Bigelow. Philadelphia: J. B. Lippincott and Co., 1868.

Freedom Forum

The Freedom Forum is a nonpartisan foundation dedicated to the ideals of free speech and a free press and attempts to influence the world of media and politics by building general support for good journalism. Founded in 1991 by *USA Today* publisher Al Neuharth, the organization has no connection to the newspaper or its parent, the Gannett Company.

The Freedom Forum consists of the Newseum, the First Amendment Center, and the Diversity Institute. The Newseum is an interactive museum celebrating the history and contributions of the news media industry. It also sponsors panel discussions, video productions, and other events focusing on the media and First Amendment issues. (The Newseum, formerly located in Arlington, Virginia, is awaiting completion of its new building in Washington, D.C., where it is scheduled to reopen in 2007.) The First Amendment Center, located at Vanderbilt University in Nashville, Tennessee, with additional offices in Arlington, Virginia, is an educational and analytic organization that seeks to preserve and protect the First Amendment. It sponsors and promotes research and educational outreach efforts dealing with threats to free speech, press, assembly, and religion. Vanderbilt also houses the Diversity Institute, which actively attempts to identify, recruit, and train racial and ethnic minorities for media careers.

REFERENCE

Freedom Forum, www.freedomforum.org.

In response to a request under FOIA, the Freedom of Information Act, the Department of Defense released this photo of soldiers arranging flags over the caskets of helicopter crewmembers killed during a training mission in Kuwait. In March 2003, on the eve of the U.S.-led invasion of Iraq, the Bush administration issued directives for enforcing a ban on media coverage of the return of soldiers killed overseas. Congress passed FOIA in 1966 to ensure public access to certain government documents and information and placed the burden on the government to justify why information should not be released.

Freedom of Information Act of 1966

Congress passed the Freedom of Information Act of 1966 (FOIA) to guarantee the public's access to certain federal government documents and to place the burden of proof on the government concerning why documents requested should be withheld from the public. Although FOIA does not make every government document available, it gives reporters, average citizens, and organizations the right to seek information on how public funds are being spent and policies carried out. According to a 1967 memo by Attorney General Ramsey Clark, the philosophy behind the act was to make disclosure the general rule rather than the exception.

FOIA provides all individuals equal rights of access to certain information, but there are several exceptions for withholding requested information. For instance, disclosure would be denied for documents detailing internal personnel rules and agency practices, trade secrets or financial information obtained from confidential sources, and personnel records whose release would constitute an invasion of privacy. Each state has its own Freedom of Information Act similar to the federal law that allows access to state government records.

The number of FOIA-related document requests has grown exponentially since enactment of the legislation. The press quickly turned the act into a tool for easily accessing information on government activities. As requests began to increase at a high rate, the executive branch asked Congress to provide funding for human resources and material purchases needed for departments to comply with the act. In addition, Congress legislated that the individual or organization requesting information must pay for copies of the information.

FOIA has been tested in several court cases, with the judicial branch usually siding with reporters and citizens, provided the information sought is not included in the act's exemptions. The U.S. Supreme Court has recently tended to side with the government in matters dealing with national security. The definition of what constitutes "national security" has been interpreted differently at different times, and after the al-Qaida attacks of September 11, 2001, and the invasion of Iraq, the Bush administration has attempted to block the release of documents concerning these events on national security grounds.

REFERENCES

Brooke, Heather. *Your Right to Know: How to Use the Freedom of Information Act and Other Access Laws.* Ann Arbor, Mich.: Pluto Press, 2005.
Foerstel, Herbert N. *Freedom of Information and the Right To Know: The Origins and Applications of the Freedom of Information Act.* Westport, Conn.: Greenwood Press, 1999.
Francois, William E. *Mass Media Law and Regulation.* Ames: Iowa State University Press, 1990.
Henry, Christopher L. *Freedom of Information Act.* New York: Novinka Books, 2003.

Freedom of the press

See *First Amendment*

Freneau, Philip Morin

Philip Morin Freneau (1752–1832), a poet and eighteenth-century newspaper editor, used his pen and position to oppose British colonial rule and to support the views of founder Thomas Jefferson in the early days of the Republic. A roommate and close friend of James Madison at Princeton University, Freneau went on to gain a reputation as a man of letters. In 1780 the British captured and imprisoned him, inspiring his poem "The British Prison Ship" (1781), a bitter condemnation of British cruelties. He also wrote numerous other poems, including "The Rising Glory of America," "American Liberty," and "George the Third's Soliloquy," which brought him fame as the "poet of the American Revolution."

Freneau used his positions as the editor of and contributor to *The Freeman's Journal* (Philadelphia) from 1781 to 1784 to advocate the essence of what is now known as Jeffersonian democracy. He became the editor of the *Daily Advertiser* in New York in 1789, and later, backed by Jefferson, edited the *National Gazette* in Philadelphia from 1791 to 1793 in direct competition with John Fenno's *Gazette of the United States.* Jefferson would claim that Freneau's paper "saved our Constitution which was galloping fast into monarchy." During the last thirty years of his life, Freneau retired to his farm with occasional stints at sea and wrote poetry and essays attacking corrupt politicians.

REFERENCE

Leary, Lewis. *That Rascal Freneau: A Study in Literary Failure.* New York: Octagon Books, 1964.

G

Gag orders

Gag order is a media term for court orders forbidding the publication of information related to a trial in order to prevent publicity from biasing jurors. The U.S. Supreme Court generally considers barring the media from publishing information about a case as prior restraint and therefore does not support its regular use. Meeting with limited success in gagging the media, judges also issue gag orders for counsel and witnesses and other actors involved in a case.

The Court set the standard for prior restraint in *Nebraska Press Association v. Stuart* (1976). Prior restraint has never been ruled unconditionally unconstitutional, and there are no established conditions for its use, but the bar for applying it is significantly high. To issue a gag order, a judge must demonstrate prior to the trial that no other means exist for protecting the rights of the accused from potentially damaging publicity. In *Gannett Co. v. DePasquale* (1979), the court ruled that judges can ban the media from pretrial hearings as long as their action meets the condition of *Nebraska Press* of having no other recourse for protecting the accused.

In *Richmond Newspapers, Inc. v. Virginia* (1980), the Court ruled that the Constitution requires that criminal trials be open to the press and public except in limited circumstances. In two subsequent decisions—*Press-Enterprise Co. v. Superior Court* (1984) and *Press-Enterprise Co. v. Superior Court* (1986)—it extended the ruling to jury selection procedures and most preliminary hearings in criminal cases. Lower federal courts have applied the ruling to civil trials, but the Supreme Court has not ruled on the issue. In *Globe Newspaper Co. v. Superior Court* (1982), the Supreme Court had held that a judge must first provide the public an opportunity to present arguments for open judicial proceedings before denying the media access. Although trial judges continue to impose gag orders, no part of the judicial process is constitutionally protected from media coverage. Members of the press will continue to challenge gag orders.

See also *Gannett Co. v. DePasquale; Media and the courts.*

REFERENCES

McLean, Deckle. "A New Kind of Gag Order: Fortunately, the Appeals Courts Don't Like Them." *Communications and the Law* 18, no. 2 (June 1996): 43–58.
Wright, Jay. "Mass Media and the Law." In *Mass Media and Society,* edited by Alan Wells and Ernest A. Hakanen. Greenwich, Conn.: Ablex Publishing Company, 1997.

Gannett

Gannett is one of the world's largest media enterprises. The Gannett chain of newspapers was founded in 1906, when Frank Gannett and his business partners acquired a half interest in the *Elmira Gazette,* a small upstate New York publication. The company moved to Rochester in 1918 and by 1923 had acquired newspapers in Ithaca and Utica as well as in Rochester. Gannett became quite profitable by buying existing newspapers in one-paper cities, most of which were relatively small. The firm continued to grow and by 1947 operated throughout the northeast, with twenty-one newspapers and seven radio stations. It began to expand nationally in the 1960s, starting its own newspaper, *Today* (now

Florida Today), only in 1966; the paper became profitable in a remarkable thirty-three months. Today, Gannett has holdings across the United States and in Germany, Great Britain, Guam, and Hong Kong. It also operates its own wire service, the Gannett News Service, to supply national and international news to its local outlets. Since 1986, the company has operated in northern Virginia, just outside Washington, D.C.

In terms of total circulation, Gannett is the largest newspaper chain in the United States. Since 1982, it has published *USA Today,* the first national general-interest newspaper in the country. The weekday circulation of *USA Today* exceeds 2 million copies, the largest of any newspaper in the United States. Although derided as "McNews" and the "McPaper" by readers who disliked the newspaper's short stories, emphasis on sometimes quirky graphics, and use of color, *USA Today* has become a popular source of quick news for travelers in the United States and Europe, even as it has tackled longer, more complex stories. Its satellite transmission of page images to remote printing sites, concise stories, and liberal use of color and graphics profoundly influenced newspaper distribution, content, and design worldwide.

In all, Gannett publishes ninety daily newspapers in the United States and has extended the *USA Today* brand to its *USA Weekend* Sunday supplement, which is carried by most Gannett local papers and many others. It also owns Newsquest PLC, a regional newspaper publisher in Great Britain. Gannett divested itself of its radio holdings in 1996 but continues to own twenty-two television stations nationwide.

Allen Neuharth, founder of *USA Today* and former Gannett CEO and chairman, is one of the more prominent personalities in the U.S. media. He founded News 2000, a project to promote First Amendment and journalistic values, and has vigorously defended the quality of chain newspapers in general, and Gannett's in particular. In 1991 Neuharth founded the Freedom Forum to promote press freedom in the United States and the rest of the world. Under the forum's sponsorship, the Newseum, a museum of journalism history, opened near Gannett's former headquarters in Arlington, Virginia, in 1997. It has since closed pending construction of a much larger facility in Washington, D.C., that is scheduled to open in 2007.

See also *Freedom Forum; USA Today.*

REFERENCES

Cose, Ellis. *The Press.* New York: Morrow, 1989.
Endicott, R. Craig. "100 Leading Media Companies." *Advertising Age,* August 10, 1992, S1.
Myers, Steven Lee. "Museum Turns Cameras on the News Business." *New York Times,* April 13, 1997, sec. 5, p. 3.

Gannett Co. v. DePasquale (1979)

Gannett Co. v. DePasquale (1979) established that the press does not have a guaranteed right to attend a criminal pretrial hearing. In 1976 two defendants were charged with robbery, grand larceny, and second-degree murder in upstate New York. At the pretrial hearing, the defendants moved to exclude the press, anticipating that statements they had made during the police investigation might prejudice them from receiving a fair trial if they were published. Neither the district attorney nor the reporter from Gannett's newspapers in Rochester objected to the motion to exclude the press at the time of the pretrial hearing. Judge DePasquale, having determined that such access might result in prejudicial pretrial publicity, ordered the proceeding closed.

Later, in civil court, Gannett's counsel argued that DePasquale's closure order was unconstitutional on the grounds that it infringed on the press's First and Fourteenth Amendment rights to access to public hearings, including pretrial proceedings. The intermediate court of appeal in New York agreed with the trial judge, but the New York Court of Appeals, the highest court in New York, overturned the appellate court's decision on the ground that potentially prejudicial pretrial publicity could prevent the defendant from receiving a fair trial. In affirming the New York Court of Appeals decision, the U.S. Supreme Court held that members of the press cannot insist on being present at a pretrial hearing when both parties request that the hearing be closed to the media. In the majority opinion, Justice Stewart wrote, "The Constitution nowhere mentions any right of access to a criminal trial on the part of the public; its guarantee, like the others enumerated, is personal to the accused." Thus, in this case the Sixth Amendment's right to a fair trial outweighed the First Amendment right of the press to access to pretrial hearings.

REFERENCES

Gannett Co. v. DePasquale, 443 U.S. 368 (1979).
Sullivan, Kathleen, and Gerald Gunther. *Constitutional Law.* 15th ed. Westbury, N.Y.: Foundation Press, 2004.

Gatekeeping

Gatekeeping, according to media scholar Everett Rogers, "is controlling the flow of messages through a communication channel." As *Washington Post* reporter David Broder notes, "all of us know as journalists that what we are mainly engaged in deciding is not what to put in, but what to leave out." In this way, the gatekeeper participates in what others have called the construction of social reality.

David Manning White conducted the first gatekeeping research in 1950, studying a wire service news editor, "Mr. Gates," to see how he selected stories. In *Mediating the Message: Theories of Influence on Mass Media Content,* Pamela Shoemaker and Stephen Reese argue that traditional gatekeeping studies had focused on "individual rather than routinized judgment." Mr. Gates rejected stories if he found them uninteresting, but he also selected stories consistent with his news organization's policies.

Gatekeeping may take place anywhere along the news production chain, from the editors and producers who assign and later refine stories to reporters who choose how to cover a story and which sources to use. Gatekeeping has also been found to conform to the judgment of larger news organizations, such as networks and wire services. Given ambiguous circumstances, news editors seek cues for making safe decisions for themselves and their organizations. As a result, competing news organizations tend to make similar judgments about news selections based on fairly consistent norms of behavior.

The result of a media consensus in gatekeeping leads to agenda setting, reducing the large number of story possibilities to only a few. Media agendas shape the agendas of public officials and the public in regard to the stories considered most important. Gaye Tuchman says news people are like fishermen, casting their nets to the sea. The biggest stories get caught in the net, while smaller stories slip through. Still, media personnel have time and space to fill, and will fill it with events regardless of whether they warrant such treatment. In the end, news organizations are profit-centered and gravitate to coverage that helps them to attract and maintain an audience.

See also *Newsgathering process; Agenda setting.*

REFERENCES

Broder, David. *Behind the Front Page.* New York: Simon and Schuster, 1987.
Rogers, Everett M. *Diffusion of Innovations.* 3rd ed. New York: Free Press, 1983.
Shoemaker, Pamela, and Steven Reese. *Mediating the Message: Theories of Influence on Mass Media Content.* 2nd ed. White Plains, N.Y.: Longman, 1996.
Tuchman, Gaye. *Making News: A Study in the Construction of Reality.* New York: Free Press, 1978.
White, David M. "The 'Gatekeeper': A Case Study in the Selection of News." *Journalism Quarterly* 27 (Fall 1950): 383–390.

Gazette of the United States

The *Gazette of the United States* was one of three newspapers founded at the instigation of Alexander Hamilton, the others being Noah Webster's *American Minerva* and William Coleman's *New York Evening Post.* First published in April 15, 1789, the *Gazette* was the leading Federalist Party newspaper and functioned as Hamilton's personal mouthpiece during the earliest years of the U.S. government. The paper was often referred to as the *Federalist.*

Boston schoolteacher John Fenno edited the *Gazette* while simultaneously holding the position of the official printer at the Treasury Department, which Hamilton headed as secretary. In his prospectus, Fenno promised a comprehensive agenda: to publish congressional proceedings, including all debates, and essays on domestic, foreign, and economic political issues. Eager to publish as much news as possible, Fenno banned all advertisements for most of the first year.

By the end of 1789, the *Gazette* circulated in every state of the Union as well as in Canada, Europe, and the West Indies. Because much of the circulation was unpaid, Fenno at one point suspended publication for three months and appealed to Hamilton for more funds. The *Gazette*'s positive coverage of the Federalists led opposition leader Thomas Jefferson to establish his own party organ, Philip Morin Freneau's *National Gazette.* In 1818 the *Gazette of the United States* united with the *True American* to form the *Union.*

See *Fenno, John; Freneau, Philip Morin; National Gazette.*

REFERENCES

Bleyer, Willard Grosvenor. *Main Currents in the History of American Journalism.* New York: Houghton Mifflin, 1927.
Lee, James Melvin. *History of American Journalism.* Garden City, N.Y., Garden City Publishing, 1923.

Gergen, David

David Richmond Gergen (1942–) is a commentator, author, editor, professor, and advisor to presidents. Gergen served in the U.S. Navy before graduating from Yale University in 1963 and Harvard Law School in 1967. He worked as a speechwriter in the administration of President Richard Nixon, communications adviser to President Gerald Ford, and director of communications for President Ronald Reagan. He joined *U.S. News & World Report* in 1985 as editor, working to increase subscriber and advertising revenue. He became editor at-large in 1986.

In a controversial move, Gergen returned to government service during 1993–1994 as counselor on foreign policy and domestic affairs to President Bill Clinton and as special international advisor to the president and to Secretary of State Warren Christopher. Gergen then rejoined *U.S. News* as editor at-large. He accepted a teaching position in 1999 at Harvard University's John F. Kennedy School of Government as a professor of public service and in 2000 became director of the school's Center for Public Leadership.

Gergen hosted *The World @ Large,* a thirteen-part discussion series of world events for the Public Broadcasting Service from 2000 to 2002. Various media outlets, including CNN and MSNBC, call on Gergen for political insight, analysis, and commentary based on his White House and Washington experience. He has also appeared as a regular analyst on ABC's *Nightline* and for a time teamed with Mark Shields to provide political commentary for the *Newshour* on PBS. He wrote *Eyewitness to Power: The Essence of Leadership. Nixon to Clinton* (2000), focusing on observations gleaned from having served four presidents from both major political parties.

REFERENCES

Barnes, Fred. "Gergen, Gergen, Gone." *New Republic,* February 21, 1994, 10–12.

Clift, Eleanor. "Where Did David Gergen Go Wrong?" *Newsweek,* March 21, 1994, 36.

Cooper, Matthew. "Gergen's Dying Dream." *U.S. News & World Report,* March 21, 1994, 32.

Gitlow v. New York (1925)

Gitlow v. New York (1925) established the liberties of the First Amendment as "fundamental," and that as such, they must be protected by the states as well as by the federal government. Benjamin Gitlow had been indicted and convicted under a New York criminal anarchy statute. The state defined criminal anarchy as advocacy in speech or writing for the violent or forceful overthrow of the government. Gitlow, an officer of the Socialist Party, had distributed a manifesto in which he called for violent revolution. In 1925 the Supreme Court upheld Gitlow's conviction by a 7-2 vote and established the "bad tendency" test: speech or writing with a tendency to threaten the public peace—in this case foment violent revolution—was punishable under the criminal anarchy statute.

The real significance of the case, however, is the Court's holding on First Amendment rights. Its ruling meant that the Fourteenth Amendment's due process clause—"No state shall deprive any person of life, liberty, or property without due process of law"—requires that these liberties be upheld in state courts as well as in federal courts. Therefore, beginning in 1925, the press and other media received First Amendment protection against state as well as federal action. This signaled the beginning of the application of the incorporation doctrine, under which other freedoms in the Bill of Rights—written originally to restrict the power of the federal government—applied to state actions through the Fourteenth Amendment. A brilliant dissenting opinion by Justice Oliver Wendell Holmes Jr., in which Justice Louis Brandeis joined, became the basis for the Court's later rejection of the bad tendency test, thus making political discourse and the media freer than it had been.

REFERENCES

Gitlow v. New York, 268 U.S. 652 (1925).

Werhan, Keith. *Freedom of Speech: A Reference Guide to the United States Constitution.* Westport, Conn.: Praeger, 2004.

An al-Jazeera staffer searches for a tape while networks from around the globe broadcast world events. Al-Jazeera represents a powerful media force in the Middle East, where it serves as an alternative to Western media outlets.

Globalization of communication

Although the word *global* is more than 400 years old, use of the term *globalization* arose in the 1960s, but it was not until the 1980s that globalization as a concept gathered currency in academic and popular discussions. It was initially identified primarily with economic developments: the liberalization of trade rules and the consequent expansion of world trade, the opening of markets worldwide to foreign direct investment, and an increasingly internationalized system of manufacture and production. Globalization has since come to be associated with the emergence of political and economic organizations that operate across national boundaries, the migration of people from one part of the globe to others, and the increasingly widespread flows of media and culture, as well as the growing awareness of these trends. As Malcolm Waters puts it, "We can define globalization as a social process in which the constraints of geography on economic, political, social and cultural arrangements recede, in which people become increasingly aware that they are receding and in which people act accordingly." Thus defined, globalization implies a world over time fundamentally transformed, marked by heightened flows of commodities, capital, people, places, ideas, and images.

The notion of globalization has been deployed widely and frequently to describe and explain some recent changes in the realm of media and communication. These transformations include the growing transmission and distribution of media content produced in one country to audiences in others, the growth of transnational satellite channels, such as CNN International, BBC World, and al-Jazeera, and the emergence and expansion of media conglomerates, such as Rupert Murdoch's News Corporation, that operate on a global scale.

Not surprisingly, these developments have given rise to considerable debate. On one side of the media globalization discussion are those (usually drawing on neo-Marxist arguments) who view this force in deeply negative terms. They argue that the control of communication resources by companies in a few developed countries that aggressively market media products around the world, especially to developing countries, is leading to the destruction of diverse indigenous traditions, cultural identities, and ways of life. In their view, globalization is resulting in the cultural transformation of diverse contexts by major U.S.-based media players who dominate the global media marketplace. Indeed, to many scholars and others, globalization appears to be little more than yet another variant of Western domination.

On the other side of this debate are theorists who recognize the presence of Western media and cultural products associated with globalization, but who do not accept the notion that global media flows represent either a form of domination or even a type of one-way traffic. Instead, they point to the existence of cultural flows from the countries of the developing to the developed world as well as between cultural and linguistic markets, especially in television and film. According to Chris Barker, "Globalization is not to be seen as a one-way flow of influence from the west to the 'rest,' rather, globalization is a multi-directional and multi-dimensional set of processes." Scholars holding this position also question assumptions about homogenization resulting from the diffusion of Western culture and argue that the processes of globalization lead instead to the fragmentation and hybridization of all societies. John Tomlinson contends, "The effects of cultural globalization are to weaken the cultural coherence in all individual nation-states, including economically powerful ones." To this camp, varied and different cultural developments characterize globalization, and the phenomenon cannot be understood in terms of existing center-periphery models.

Considerable discussion about the influence of recent changes in the media sector has thus essentially been framed around the poles of cultural homogenization and cultural heterogenization, the global and the local. As early as 1990, Arjun Appadurai argued that the tension between cultural homogenization and heterogenization represented the central problem of contemporary global interactions. Fifteen years later, the issue remains deeply contested, with the battle lines still sharply drawn between those who view the media as the providers of homogenizing fare and those who see them as a force whose cultural impact transforms all societies. Although consensus remains elusive in this aspect, in the context of globalization in recent years, there have been undeniably profound structural and institutional changes in media systems worldwide. These changes typically involve movement toward liberal media policies by nation-states (particularly in the realm of broadcasting), the emergence of global, regional, and national media conglomerates, and the development of global formats that share certain stylistic conventions and characteristics while simultaneously reflecting local tastes and preferences.

Media Policies

A series of changes with roots traceable to the 1980s have resulted in a reevaluation of media policies the world over.

Among these are the emergence of satellite and cable technologies, the establishment of international free trade regimes, and the replacement of state-controlled media with privately owned media. These changes have proved to be particularly dramatic in countries where radio and television services historically had operated in a highly regulated environment, whether under public service broadcasting organizations or direct government control.

According to Graham Murdock and Peter Golding, the market-oriented policy shift has caused countries to adopt a variety of strategies, including the following: the privatization or sale of public communication assets to private investors; liberalization or the introduction of competition into what were once state or public monopoly broadcast markets; and corporatization, or the adoption of a more profit-oriented style of functioning by public service organizations. In addition, there has been a parallel effort to encourage greater commercialization, with the result that government and public broadcasters are forced to decrease their traditional reliance on public funding and instead generate revenue through advertising, program sales, and sponsorship. Such policies have collectively resulted in the breakdown of the long-standing monopoly of government and public service broadcasters, an explosion of private commercial channels, growth in entertainment-based programming, and emergence of a dual system of broadcasting characterized by public and private broadcasters across the world.

Media Conglomerates

Another significant aspect of globalization-related media developments has been the emergence of vast media conglomerates whose reach extends around the globe. Although the globalization of media and markets is not an entirely new development, its current scope and scale are unprecedented. Underlying this global expansion are economic factors, namely, the low reproduction costs of media products and their potential for resale without requiring additional outlays by producers. In the risky environment of media production, where the profitability of a product can only be assessed after its completion, these factors, combined with technological changes, have played a key role in pushing companies to distribute their products on the largest scale possible. By 2002, the top ten media companies and at least 25 percent of the top twenty-five media groups were engaged in some type of overseas activity.

Much of the attention regarding the growth of media conglomerates has focused on the activities of the big few, such as AOL-Time Warner, ABC-Disney, Bertelsmann, News Corporation, and Sony. These firms moved aggressively in becoming global actors based on the considerable advantages that they enjoyed in terms of access to large domestic markets (such as the United States) as well as the ability to benefit from the so-called synergies that exist between the companies that they own.

The evidence also points to the simultaneous emergence of regional and national multimedia conglomerates engaged not only in the consolidation of their positions at home, but also in expansion into cultural-linguistic markets abroad. The growth of such conglomerates—which often form alliances with global companies or emulate their operational style—is significant. They not only share some of the aspects of the global giants' growth, such as access to large markets and thus the ability to generate advertising revenues, but they also benefit from their closeness to governments and political elites as well as their ability to provide audiences with culturally and linguistically relevant programming. Prime examples of such conglomerates include Brazil's O Globo, Mexico's Grupo Televisa, India's Zee TV, and Hong Kong's Television Broadcasts (TVB). The rise of consolidated media companies at the global and national-regional level (albeit on a relatively small scale) has significant implications. In fact, many scholars argue that the growing dominance of profit-oriented companies that control content and means of distribution poses a real challenge not only to the marketplace of ideas, but also to the range of available media products, with undue emphasis on commercial, entertainment-based programming.

Media Formats

Within the last decade, another major development associated with globalization has been the adoption and sometimes outright imitation of media formats first developed in the West (usually in the United States). These range from television news, soaps, talk shows, quiz shows, and most recently reality television translated into varied local contexts. This trend has resurrected concerns about the influence of globalization. Some scholars view it as yet another example of Western cultural imposition, while others argue that contemporary global culture makes possible unique appropriations of media products all over the world, resulting in the emergence of hybrid forms that synthesize the global and the local.

While debate on the influence of these formats continues, "global" media formats are undergoing a process of adaptation within national-regional contexts, whereby they maintain certain genre-specific characteristics while simultaneously reflecting their particular cultural and linguistic contexts. For instance, Who Wants To Be a Millionaire? in India, while retaining some of the stylistic conventions of the original show, was hosted in Hindi by a leading Indian film star asking India-specific questions. In a similar manner, although MTV operates globally, it is characterized by considerable linguistic and cultural adaptation. For instance, in East Asian countries, MTV-Asia avoids violent and sexually explicit videos, while in South Asia the channel devotes a considerable amount of time to programming related to Hindi films and music.

In addition to such domestications of media formats, as Michael Richards and David French point out, numerous other examples exist of the complex adaptation of Western television formats to fit indigenous viewing appeal, such as China's culturally specific version of Sesame Street or Taiwan's popular epic drama Pao the Judge, which while drawing on the stylistic conventions of Western serials are nevertheless based in terms of content on national folklore and historical myths. Indeed, even in Japan, the most Westernized of the Asian countries, shows, including Survivor, have been significantly adapted. As the producer of the Japanese version explains, "While the main feature of the U.S. version is the exposure of naked human nature, as witnessed in betrayals and plots forged among contestants to expel a particular rival, the Japanese version places more focus on the inner mental conflicts of each challenger." The U.S. version of Survivor was itself adapted from a Swedish program. In other words, while there exists a widespread diffusion of successful "Western" formats, the overwhelming preference of audiences for culturally and linguistically resonant programming results in the adaptation of these formats based on the cultural sensibilities of the context into which they are imported.

Media and globalization are closely intertwined and exhibit an interplay resulting in far-reaching structural and institutional changes within media landscapes worldwide. These changes include a pattern of liberalization and commercialization of electronic media systems and policies, the emergence of multimedia conglomerates, and the adaptation of media formats. These developments are manifest in a range of local contexts and underscore the necessity of undertaking an analysis of media globalization in a way that conceptualizes the phenomenon in terms of a convergence of policy orientations, market developments, and programming trends within countries, rather than the somewhat limited homogenization versus heterogenization debate, which does little to illuminate the complexities of contemporary developments in global media.

REFERENCES

Albrow, M. "Globalization, Knowledge and Society." In *Globalization, Knowledge and Society,* edited by M. Albrow and E. King. London: Sage, 1990.

Amin, S. *Capitalism in the Age of Globalization.* London: Zed Books, 1997.

Appadurai, A. "Disjuncture and Difference in the Global Cultural Economy." In *Global Culture: Nationalism, Globalization and Modernity,* edited by M. Featherstone. Newbury Park, Calif.: Sage, 1990.

Barker, C. *Global Television.* Malden, Mass.: Blackwell Publishers, 1997.

Chadha, K., and A. Kavoori. "Media Imperialism Revisited: Some Findings from the Asian Case." *Media, Culture and Society* 22 (2000).

Featherstone, M. *Undoing Culture: Globalization, Postmodernism and Identity.* London: Sage, 1995.

Iwabuichi, Koichi. "Feeling Glocal: Japan in the Global Television Format Business." In *Television across Asia: Television Industries, Program Formats and Globalization,* edited by Michael Keane and Albert Moran. London: RoutledgeCurzon, 2003.

King, A. D. Introduction. In *Culture, Globalization and the World System: Contemporary Conditions for the Representation of Identity,* edited by A. D. King. Binghamton: Department of Art and Art History, State University of New York, 1991.

Latouche, S. *The Westernization of the World: The Significance, Scope and Limits of the Drive towards Global Uniformity,* translated by R. Morris. Cambridge: Polity Press, 1996.

McChesney, R. "The New Global Media." *Nation,* November 29, 1999.

Moran, A. "Television Formats in the World." In *Television across Asia: Television Industries, Program Formats and Globalization,* edited by A. Moran and M. Keane. London: RoutledgeCurzon, 2004.

Murdock, G., and P. Golding. "Common Markets: Corporate Ambitions and Communications Trends in the UK and Europe." *Journal of Media Economics* 12, no. 2 (1999): 117–132.

Richards, M., and D. French. "Globalization and Television: Comparative Perspectives." *Cyprus Review* 12 (2000).

Schiller, H. *Communication and Cultural Domination.* New York: International Arts and Sciences Press, 1976.

Silj, A., and M. Alvarado, eds. *East of Dallas: The European Challenge to American Television.* London: British Film Institute, 1988.

Silj, A. "Italy: An Introduction." In *The New Television in Europe,* edited by A. Silj. London: Libbey, 1992.

Sinclair, J., E. Jacka, and S. Cunningham, eds. *New Patterns in Global Television: Peripheral Vision.* New York: Oxford University Press, 1996.

Straubhaar, J. "(Re)asserting National Television and National Identity against the Global, Regional and Local Levels of World Television." In *In Search of Boundaries,* edited by J. M. Chan and B. McIntyre. Westport, Conn.: Ablex Publishing, 2002.

Thussu, D. K. *International Communication. Continuity and Change.* London: Arnold, 2000.

Tomlinson, J. *Cultural Imperialism: A Critical Introduction.* London: Pinter, 1991.

Waters, M. *Globalization.* Routledge: London, 2001.

Wilkinson, K. "Where Culture, Language and Communication Converge: The Latin-American Cultural Linguistic Market." PhD diss., University of Texas, Austin, 1995.

Graham, Katharine

Katharine Graham (1917–2001), former publisher of the *Washington Post,* was arguably for a time the most powerful woman in the publishing business. Her interest in publishing began early, as she worked on the student newspaper at the Madeira School in northern Virginia, outside Washington. She went on to attend Vassar College and the University of Chicago, working summers at the *Washington Post,* which her father, Eugene Meyer, had bought in 1933. After graduating from the University of Chicago in 1938, Graham moved west to take a job as a waterfront reporter for the *San Francisco News.* She returned to Washington the following year to join the editorial staff at the *Post.* In 1940 she married Philip L. Graham, a clerk for Supreme Court Justice Felix Frankfurter.

Katharine Graham, pictured here in 1997, served as chairman, CEO, and publisher of the Washington Post *during challenging times, including publication of the Pentagon Papers and revelation of the Watergate scandal. She is recognized as having been a trailblazing female executive in an industry dominated by men. Her autobiography,* Personal History, *won a 1998 Pulitzer Prize.*

Eugene Meyer died in 1946, and controlling interest in the *Post* transferred to the Grahams in 1948. They acquired the *Washington Times Herald* in 1954 and *Newsweek* in 1961 and expanded their radio and television operations. Philip Graham committed suicide in 1963, at which point Katharine took over as president of the Washington Post Company. She hired Ben Bradlee as managing editor of the *Post* in 1965. In addition to being chief executive officer and chairman of the board, Graham became the publisher of the *Post* in 1969 and led the company during some of the paper's most turbulent times, including publication of the Pentagon Papers and the Watergate scandal in the 1970s. She relinquished her title as publisher in 1979 and chief executive officer and board chairman in 1991, but remained chairman of the Executive Committee until her death. Graham's autobiography, *Personal History* (1997), won her a 1998 Pulitzer Prize.

REFERENCES

Davis, Deborah. *Katharine the Great: Katharine Graham and Her* Washington Post *Empire.* New York: Sheridan Square Press, 1991.

Felsenthal, Carol. *Power, Privilege and the* Post: *The Katharine Graham Story.* New York: Putnam Pub Group, 1993.

Graham, Katharine. *Personal History.* New York: Knopf, 1997.

Halberstam, David. *The Powers That Be.* New York: Knopf, 1983.

Greeley, Horace

Horace Greeley (1811–1872) was a journalist, editor, politician, and publisher of the *New York Tribune.* Greeley began working at age fourteen as an apprentice to a Vermont newspaper editor. Starting in 1831, he found various jobs, as a printer, typesetter, and journalist in New York and Pennsylvania. In 1834 he founded the *New Yorker,* a literary and news journal, and wrote for it. From 1838 to 1840 he edited two Whig Party publications: the *Jeffersonian* and the *Log Cabin.* In 1841 he combined these papers as the *New York Tribune,* one of the first penny daily newspapers, and built it into a respected and prosperous platform for his generally liberal and abolitionist views. He hired talented writers and editors, including Charles Dana (as managing editor), George Ripley, and Margaret Fuller. He employed Karl Marx as a European correspondent for the *Tribune* during the 1850s.

Horace Greeley, founder of the New York Tribune, *was also an original member of the Republican Party who fervently opposed the extension of slavery. Following the Civil War, he joined the Liberal Republican Party, which nominated him as its presidential candidate.*

Greeley served for a short period in the U.S. House of Representatives in 1848 as a replacement for an indicted congressman. Having acquired a taste for politics, he later repeatedly ran for office, particularly after the Civil War, but failed to win election. He also failed to curry favor with members of Congress by publishing daily exposés on the peculiar activities of Capitol Hill. Greeley traveled to California in 1859, reporting on his experience while criticizing the haphazard settlement process and giving wide voice to Indiana editor John Soule's counsel to "Go west, young man, go west."

Greeley's support of the Free-Soil Movement, antislavery rhetoric, and his influential newspaper brought him to prominence as a founding member of the Republican Party in 1856. He opposed fellow New Yorker William Henry Seward's bid to become the first Republican president of the United States in 1860, and instead, with the aid of other anti-Seward forces in and around New York City, encouraged Abraham Lincoln to speak in New York. Lincoln's speech to the Cooper Union in Manhattan in 1860, and his speaking tour of New England in the following weeks, launched him to national prominence. Greeley was an advocate for women's suffrage and for a time flirted with collectivism.

Greeley opposed the secessionist activities of the Southern states and concessions to the maintenance of slavery, believing the rebellion to be the work of an unscrupulous minority. Differences about the national approach toward dealing with slavery and secession led to a split with Dana. Although Greeley campaigned for Lincoln in 1860, he later criticized him for moving too slowly on emancipation of the slaves. In the process, he and Lincoln engaged in the famous open exchange of letters that revealed Lincoln's primary objective to be the preservation of the Union, not the abolition of slavery. Greeley eventually withheld his support for Lincoln's reelection in 1864.

Often setting his own course, Greeley went against northern public opinion when in 1867 he posted bond for Jefferson Davis, the imprisoned Confederate president. Highly critical of President Ulysses S. Grant, Greeley helped form the Liberal Republican Party and then stood for election as its presidential candidate in 1872. The Democratic Party endorsed him, but he was badly defeated in a bitter campaign. In addition to this setback, Greeley was devastated by the death of his wife and lost effective control of the *Tribune* to Whitelaw Reid. Greeley died a short time later, in November 1872.

Greeley wrote numerous books, including *Glances at Europe* (1851); *An Overland Journey* (1860); a two-volume history of the Civil War, *The American Conflict* (1865); *What I Know about Farming* (1871); and an autobiography, *Recollections of a Busy Life* (1868).

REFERENCES

Granberg, Wilbur J. *Spread the Truth: The Life of Horace Greeley.* New York: Dutton, 1959.

Hale, William Harlan. *Horace Greeley: Voice of the People.* New York: Harper, 1950.

Ingersoll, Lurton Dunham. *The Life of Horace Greeley.* New York: Beekman Publishers, 1974.

Linn, William Alexander. *Horace Greeley: Founder of the* New York Tribune. New York: Beekman Publishers, 1974.

Van Duesen, Glyndon Garlock. *Horace Greeley: Nineteenth-Century Crusader.* Philadelphia: University of Pennsylvania Press, 1953.

H

Haig v. Agee (1981)

Haig v. Agee (1981), a First Amendment case, established the precedent that when an author's work is shown to directly threaten the national interest, the government may refuse to issue the author a passport or revoke his or her existing passport.

Philip Agee worked for the Central Intelligence Agency from 1957 to 1969. After his resignation, he announced a campaign "to expose CIA officers and agents and to take the measures necessary to drive them out of the countries where they are operating." Agee's actions stemmed from his disagreement with the United States' broad application of anticommunist policies toward all left-leaning governments and political movements, regardless of whether such groups or entities were avowedly communist. In 1975 Agee published *Inside the Company: CIA Diary*, detailing his experiences at the agency. In it, he revealed the names of numerous clandestine agents, which the Cuban and Soviet intelligence services likely noted. Two of the agents he named were later killed, and others suffered assaults.

In 1979 Secretary of State Cyrus Vance revoked Agee's passport, and Agee challenged the measure in court. The issue was straightforward: Does the secretary of state have the power under the Passport Act of 1926 to revoke a passport? A federal district court overturned Vance's revocation (*Agee v. Vance,* 483 F. Supp. 729 (DC 1980)), and the court of appeals for the D.C. Circuit agreed with the lower court's decision (*Agee v. Muskie,* 629 F.2d 80 (1980); Edmund Muskie had by that time been appointed secretary of state). After Alexander Haig assumed the helm at the State Depart-

ment, the Supreme Court heard the case and ruled 7-2 that the secretary of state does have the power to deny passports to persons whose actions are likely to compromise national security.

The justices decided the case on narrow statutory grounds, but acknowledged the First Amendment claim that the revocation of Agee's passport inhibited his action—that is, his freedom of movement. It did not, however, infringe on his speech or press freedoms. In essence, when an author's work can be shown to directly threaten the national interest, the government may refuse to issue a passport or revoke an existing passport although denial or revocation could effectually prevent a writer from traveling. Indeed, Agee, deported from several European countries after the ruling, was unable to travel freely. Cuba ultimately offered him asylum, and he has lived there for many years.

REFERENCES

Agee, Philip. *Inside the Company: CIA Diary.* New York: Stonehill Press, 1975.
———. *On the Run.* Secaucus, N.J.: Lyle Stuart, 1987.
Haig v. Agee, 453 U.S. 280 (1981).

Hamilton, Alexander

Alexander Hamilton (1757–1804) was a general, cabinet officer, influential political thinker, and one of the founders of the United States. Born in Nevis, British West Indies, Hamilton began working in the family store at eleven years of age. His family sent him to New York City in 1772 with letters of introduction. The following year he entered King's College (now Columbia University). Hamilton soon aligned himself with the anti-British patriots amid the revolutionary fervor. He wrote several lengthy essays that impressed readers with his writing skill, knowledge, and insight. At the outbreak of the war, Hamilton joined the Continental Army as a captain of artillery. By 1777, he had become aide-de-camp to Gen. George Washington and by that association soon assumed progressively greater responsibilities. Hamilton participated in the first postwar Continental Congress held during 1782–1783.

Hamilton then returned to New York City to open a private law practice and was chosen as a New York delegate to the Annapolis Convention of 1786. He also represented the state at the 1787 Constitutional Convention in Philadelphia, but he failed to exert much influence because of his very conservative views. Hamilton signed the Constitution, however, and then campaigned widely in New York to gain the state's ratification despite his personal reservations about several aspects of the document. In October 1787, Hamilton published the first of what would become the Federalist Papers, the eighty-five letters advocating ratification of the Constitution by setting out the ideals behind the document and the new republic. Hamilton wrote fifty-one of the papers, many as open letters signed by "Publius," and collaborated with James Madison on three others. Madison and John Jay wrote the remaining thirty-one essays.

President George Washington chose Hamilton to serve as the United States' first secretary of the Treasury, from 1789 to 1795. Hamilton wrote a series of reports during 1790–1791 on a program to stabilize the new nation's finances as well as lay the foundation for a strong, industrial country. In 1791 Hamilton and John Adams organized the Federalist Party, which advocated a strong central government, and he masterfully used various print media to voice the agenda of the party. Most notable among these was John Fenno's *Gazette of the United States*. Despite his many contributions to the formation of the United States, Hamilton's confrontational style, strong views on the necessity of a powerful central government, distrust of the common man, and aggressive intellect alienated some of his colleagues, particularly Adams and Thomas Jefferson.

Hamilton resigned from the government in 1795 and returned to New York City to practice law. He was commissioned as a major general and served as inspector general of the army from 1798 to 1800, during tensions with France,

and supported the controversial Alien and Sedition Acts of 1798. Hamilton remained politically active and used his influence to sway the House of Representatives to select Jefferson when he tied with Aaron Burr during the 1800 presidential election. He again opposed Burr and aided in his defeat in a run for governor of New York. The conflict between the two men led Burr to challenge Hamilton to a duel. Burr fatally wounded Hamilton, who died the next day.

See also *Fenno, John; Gazette of the United States; Jefferson, Thomas.*

REFERENCES

Brookhiser, Richard. *Alexander Hamilton, American.* New York: Free Press, 1999.

Cooke, Jacob E. *Alexander Hamilton.* New York: Charles Scribner's Sons, 1982.

——, ed. *The Reports of Alexander Hamilton.* New York: Harper and Row, 1964.

Daniels, Jonathan. *Ordeal of Ambition: Jefferson, Hamilton, Burr.* Garden City, N.Y.: Doubleday, 1970.

Elkins, Stanley, and Eric McKitrick. *The Age of Federalism.* New York: Oxford University Press, 1993.

Frisch, Morton J. *Alexander Hamilton and the Political Order.* Lanham. Md.: University Press of America, 1991.

Miller, John C. *Alexander Hamilton: Portrait in Paradox.* New York: Harper and Brothers, 1959.

Hard and soft news

Many people believe that the press has a fundamental responsibility to provide the public with the information they need to carry out their responsibilities as citizens in a democracy. Although this view remains subject to debate, it nevertheless raises the question of what sort of information these citizens need. The answer, according to many scholars and journalists, among them W. Lance Bennett and Thomas Patterson, is hard news, such as coverage of events involving top leaders, major issues, or significant disruptions in the routines of daily life. News organizations, however, have shifted their news coverage markedly over the past two decades away from traditional hard news topics and themes and toward an increasing emphasis on soft news, which is characterized by sensationalized presentation, human-interest and dramatic subject matter (like crime and disasters), and the absence of a public policy component. As John Zaller states, "soft news is information that is either personally useful or merely entertaining."

Today, virtually all media outlets that present any information about public affairs offer a mix of soft and hard news content. Yet some clearly offer more soft news than others. Matthew Baum defines as the soft news media those outlets that focus primarily on such material, including entertainment and tabloid newsmagazines and shows (*Entertainment Tonight, Inside Edition, People* magazine, *The Howard Stern Show*), network television newsmagazines (*Dateline, 20/20*), and daytime (*Oprah*) and late night (*The Tonight Show with Jay Leno, Late Night with David Letterman*) talk shows. These outlets differ in many respects, but in contrast to the quintessentially hard news outlets—such as the *New York Times,* National Public Radio, and network evening newscasts—they all focus primarily on soft news themes. They tend to cover similar types of political issues—scandals, wars, and natural disasters, for example—in similar ways. Their audiences tend to be less educated or interested in politics than those of most traditional news outlets.

Although soft news contains less public policy content than hard news, and people consume it primarily to be entertained, soft news outlets do cover politics, especially when it involves sensational human drama. Political sex scandals (the Monica Lewinsky affair) and military conflicts (the two Iraq wars) are cases in point. Both involve issues of substantial national importance—the impeachment of a president and war—and each is easy to cover in dramatic and entertaining fashion. In fact, soft news outlets covered all three issues extensively, at times rivaling coverage by traditional news outlets.

Soft news outlets emphasize different aspects of political issues than do their hard news counterparts. In war, for instance, where hard news highlights military tactics and strategies and political ramifications, soft news stories are more likely to focus on the struggles of military families to cope while their loved ones risk life and limb. In other words, where hard news focuses on geopolitics, soft news focuses on body bags. Matthew Baum contends that consumers—particularly politically inattentive ones—can nevertheless learn about select aspects of at least some of the major issues facing the nation via soft news outlets. Zaller argues that "the question of news quality is whether news provides a sufficiently rich and engaging ration of political information to make democracy work." Though narrower in scope in its political coverage than hard news, the soft news media may, at least for some individuals and for some political issues, fulfill this requirement.

REFERENCES

Baum, Matthew A. "Sex, Lies and War: How Soft News Brings Foreign Policy to the Inattentive Public." *American Political Science Review* 96 (March 2002): 91–109.
———. *Soft News Goes to War: Public Opinion and American Foreign Policy in the New Media Age.* Princeton, N.J.: Princeton University Press, 2003.
Bennett, W. Lance. *News: The Politics of Illusion.* 3rd ed. New York: Longman, 1997.
———. "The Burglar Alarm That Just Keeps Ringing: A Response to Zaller." *Political Communication* 20 (April–June 2003): 131–138.
Hamilton, James T. *All the News That's Fit to Sell: How the Market Transforms Information into News.* Princeton, N.J.: Princeton University Press, 2004.
Patterson, Thomas. "Doing Well and Doing Good." Research Report. Joan Shorenstein Center on the Press, Politics and Public Policy, Harvard University, 2000.
———. "The Search for a Standard: Markets and the Media." *Political Communication* 20 (April–June 2003): 139–143.
Zaller, John. "A New Standard of News Quality: Burglar Alarms for the Monitorial Citizen." *Political Communication* 20 (April–June 2003): 109–103.

Hart, Gary

Gary Hart (1936–), a former U.S. senator from Colorado, was widely considered an early frontrunner and the likely presidential nominee for the Democratic Party in 1988 until he dropped from the race after media reports about his private life and possible extramarital affairs. The stories and Hart's decision to withdraw before the primaries were widely debated by the public and the media. At one point, reporters from the *Miami Herald* had kept Hart's Washington, D.C., residence under surveillance after receiving an anonymous tip about his having affairs. Some observers criticized the *Miami Herald, Washington Post,* and other outlets that reported on Hart's private life because they believed that whatever affairs he might have had should be of concern only to his wife. Defenders of the stories argued that Hart's personal actions went to his credibility, because he had repeatedly denied having an affair and, indeed, had explicitly invited reporters' scrutiny of his private activities.

See *Scandal.*

REFERENCES

Taylor, Paul. *See How They Run.* New York: Alfred A. Knopf, 1990.
Zoglin, Richard. "Political Journalism May Never Be the Same." *Time,* May 18, 1987.

Hearst, William Randolph

William Randolph Hearst (1863–1951) was a powerful and controversial newspaper publisher and media empire builder. Hearst grew up in a privileged California family and began his journalism career as a student at Harvard University working on the *Harvard Lampoon* and later apprenticing with *New York World* owner Joseph Pulitzer. Within two years of being expelled from Harvard in 1885, Hearst's father established him as the publisher of the *San Francisco Examiner*. The newspaper became Hearst's journalistic laboratory, where he indulged a desire to publish fake news and stage "real" news to heighten reader shock and attraction—a practice that became known as yellow journalism—in the pattern of Pulitzer's *World*.

Hearst, called The Chief, moved his headquarters to New York City in 1895 to gain a broader audience. After receiving a large cash infusion from his father's estate, he purchased the nearly defunct *New York Journal* that year to directly challenge Pulitzer. Within a year, Hearst had built a circulation that exceeded the ailing Pulitzer's *New York World* in the sensationalist journalism game by hiring top-rung writers and illustrators, including Stephen Crane, Jack London, Frederic Remington, and Mark Twain.

Having shaken up San Francisco and New York City, Hearst took his blueprint to other major U.S. markets, establishing the *Chicago American* in 1900, the *Chicago Examiner* in 1902, and the *Boston American* and *Los Angeles Examiner* in 1904. He also acquired numerous magazines, including *Cosmopolitan* and *Harper's Bazaar*. The competition between Hearst and Pulitzer reached outrageous levels during the prelude to the Spanish-American War, which began in 1898. Hearst graphically illustrated the drive to sell papers and spread American values across the globe when he supposedly wired illustrator Frederick Remington, who wanted to leave Cuba because there was not yet any action, and told him, "You furnish the pictures. I'll furnish the war."

Hearst sought to translate his publishing success into politics. He was elected to the U.S. House of Representatives in 1902 and 1904 as a Democrat representing New York, but later made unsuccessful bids for the Democratic Party nomination for president in 1904, mayor of New York City in 1905 and 1909, and governor of New York in 1906. Hearst wielded considerable power over the information disseminated to the public, and his newspapers reflected his politics. He was an outspoken opponent of the British and U.S.

Engaged in a circulation war with publisher Joseph Pulitzer, William Randolph Hearst transformed the New York Journal *into a highly competitive paper through the use of sensationalism, yellow journalism, and dramatic images to attract readers. He hired top-notch writers and illustrators and built a media empire. New Yorkers twice elected Hearst to the House of Representatives in the early 1900s.*

involvement in World War I and the formation of the League of Nations. He was pro-Nazi in the 1930s and a staunch anticommunist in the 1940s.

Orson Welles's *Citizen Kane* (1941) was a not-so-subtle, fictional portrayal of Hearst and a not-so-flattering depiction of the ruthless methods he used to gain power. Hearst mustered all his power and influence to quash the film but eventually failed to do so. At the peak of his career, Hearst owned twenty-eight major newspapers in thirteen cities and eighteen magazines, along with several radio stations and movie companies. The Great Depression substantially weakened his financial position, forcing Hearst to relinquish control of his publishing empire to a seven-member committee in 1937 that managed to stave off bankruptcy. Hearst never regained the communications power he once held.

REFERENCES

Littlefield, Roy Everett. *William Randolph Hearst: His Role in American Progressivism.* Lanham, Md.: University Press of America, 1980.

Lundberg, Ferdinand. *Imperial Hearst: A Social Biography.* New York: Equinox Cooperative Press, 1936.

Nasaw, David. *The Chief: The Life of William Randolph Hearst.* Boston: Houghton Mifflin, 2000.

Pizzitola, Louis. *Hearst over Hollywood: Power, Passion, and Propaganda in the Movies.* New York: Columbia University Press, 2002.

Swanberg, W. A. *Citizen Hearst: A Biography of William Randolph Hearst.* New York: Scribner, 1961.

Winkler, John K. *W. R. Hearst: An American Phenomenon.* New York: Simon and Schuster, 1928.

Herblock

See *Block, Herbert Lawrence*

Hewitt, Don

Don Hewitt (1922–) is the network producer best known for having created *60 Minutes,* the long-running CBS television news magazine. Hewitt's first job, in 1942, was as an office boy (and eventually a copy boy) for the *New York Herald Tribune.* From 1943 to 1945, he served as a merchant marine correspondent and a war correspondent for *Stars and Stripes* covering World War II. He later held several newspaper assignments, including for the Associated Press and the *Pelham Sun* in New York. Hewitt joined CBS News as an associate director in 1948 and produced *Douglas Edwards with the News* from 1950 to 1962, the *CBS Evening News with Walter Cronkite* during 1963–1964, and CBS documentaries from 1965 to 1968.

In 1968 Hewitt created and began producing *60 Minutes,* which pioneered the television news magazine format featuring segments with recognized reporters. The early hosts of *60 Minutes* became known as Hewitt's "anchor monsters" and included Mike Wallace, Harry Reasoner, and Morley Safer. The program's appealing presentation led it to become the first news program to enter the Nielsen Top Ten. It has remained the highest rated public news program for more than thirty years. Hewitt is the author of *Minute by Minute* (1985) and *Tell Me a Story: Fifty Years and 60 Minutes in Television* (2001).

REFERENCES

Campbell, R. *60 Minutes and the News.* Urbana: University of Illinois Press, 1991.

Madsen, A. *60 Minutes: The Power and The Politics of America's Most Popular TV News Show.* New York: Dodd, Mead, 1984.

History of American journalism

The history of American journalism is one of political and social turmoil and European influence. Most early settlers found that they got all the information they needed from British newspapers brought to the colonies by ship. In September 1690, the four-page *Publick Occurrences, both Foreign and Domestick* appeared in Massachusetts, but authorities suppressed further publication after the first issue because it criticized the British government. The political landscape made it nearly impossible for a newspaper to print anything negative about the crown and survive, and it took time for colonial society to demand newspapers focusing on their immediate community rather than their heritage.

The weekly *Boston News-Letter* became the first continuously published paper in April 1704, eighty years after the establishment of the first colony. It held a monopoly for fifteen years, until founder and editor John Campbell, who also served as postmaster, lost political clout (and his job as postmaster). Campbell held on to the *News-Letter,* which encouraged the new postmaster, William Brooker, to start his own newspaper, the *Boston Gazette.* Thus for the first time, there existed competing papers, though the competition remained far from fierce. Both outfits had access to basically the same news, and their publishers feared possible government reprimand. In 1721 in Boston, James Franklin, the older brother of Benjamin Franklin, began publishing the *New England Courant,* the first newspaper to print news as well as editorials. He used the publication to crusade for change in the colonies, making him the first publisher to use a newspaper as a persuasive tool, not just an informational device. Franklin set the tone for the form and content of later U.S. newspapers.

After 1725 newspapers popped up throughout the colonies, especially in New York and Philadelphia. Each colony had dozens of new newspapers publishing each year, but few lasted more than one year. The *New England Weekly Journal,* one of the more notable newspapers, began publishing in 1727 in Boston and differed from its competitors in being the first to hire community correspondents to write original stories. In Philadelphia in 1729, Benjamin Franklin assumed management of the *Pennsylvania Gazette,* the first newspaper to take advantage of advertising. Franklin, a popular member of the community, had no trouble boosting ad sales. He is often referred to as the father of printing and to a lesser extent of advertising. Franklin's knowledge of printing and instincts about the information people not only needed but wanted helped make him a successful publisher. In 1732 he founded *Poor Richard's Almanac,* an eclectic mix of poetry and weather facts and other types of information. When he retired from publishing, Franklin helped others start newspapers, advising them on how to manage a paper and advertising.

Newspapers as a product improved with time. Printing technology evolved, and the newspapers' content became more critical. As publishers began to feel responsible for the content of their publications, they would often apologize for unfair or inaccurate information, foreshadowing today's corrections column. Many early newspapers were short-lived, but growth of the press can be credited in part to better transportation and communication facilities, an exponentially increasing population, and tensions between political factions. Also, as newspapers began to saturate the colonies, their potential economic value became apparent, as businessmen realized that advertising in them was a cheap way to pitch their products. As the country grew in prosperity, so did disposable income. The newspapers were a medium that entrepreneurs welcomed.

As newspapers found their footing, they assumed an important role in the fight for independence by providing an arena for communication for politically aligned groups and organizing against the crown. Publishers, wary of suppression, had an economic self-interest in being rid of British rule, as well as political incentives. The *Boston Gazette* became the nerve center for local radicals and published writings by famous revolutionaries, among them Sam Adams. An expert news gatherer, Adams used his skills to help not only organize the resistance, but also to foster an alliance among the American revolutionaries. He understood that the press could be instrumental in rallying troops and public support through news and editorials explaining why the colonies should declare independence. Revolutionary Isaiah Thomas wrote in the *Gazette* that if the liberty of the press were to be destroyed, the same fate would befall the personal liberties that originally brought the colonists to America. In 1776 Thomas Paine wrote the pamphlet *Common Sense,* which laid out reasons for breaking with Britain. More than 120,000 copies of the pamphlet were distributed in a three-month period, and newspapers reprinted it. Paine understood not only the political and economic ramifications of the independence war, but also the social ones. Many Americans learned about the Declaration of Independence through newspaper reports. The newspaper in these ways came to be an important tool in the founding of the United States.

After the war, a struggle emerged between political factions over how to write a constitution for the new nation and what to include in it. A number of state governments reported that they would not ratify a constitution without a provision for freedom of the press. The Bill of Rights was ratified in 1791, and the first of its initial ten amendments afforded protection to the press and limited government interference. The First Amendment was tested from its inception with the passage of the Alien and Sedition Acts of 1798 by the Federalist-controlled Congress in an attempt to stifle the Anti-Federalist press. The act did not prohibit criticism of the government per se, but rather malicious and false criticism of individuals. Upon Thomas Jefferson's election to the presidency in 1801, he and his partisans in Congress allowed the acts to expire, thereby loosening restrictions on the press.

During the first several decades of the 1800s, newspapers became instruments of persuasion associated with political parties and were often economically dependent on their political and partisan benefactors. In 1801 Federalist leader Alexander Hamilton established the *New York Evening Post* to bolster his party's position. Having lost the 1800 presidential election, Federalists planned to use the newspaper as a tool for attacking the Democratic-Republican administration of Thomas Jefferson. Although the media often attacked Jefferson, he defended the right of the press to freedom. Along with Jefferson, other presidents, including Adams and Jackson, actively courted and supported certain outlets and even aided their publishing allies by giving them government printing contracts. In essence, the job of an editor was partisan political hack first, newsman second. The era of the partisan press eventually waned, but it continues to resonate, as seen in editorial endorsements of political candidates.

Mass media began to take shape during the 1800s, as the public became more literate and the price of newspapers decreased. The first penny press newspaper appeared in 1833, spreading news considered sensational for the time. (This form of news inevitably led to the time, in the 1890s, when photos and newspaper stories became even more sensational.) One of the best examples of how the press matured is the founding of the *New York Tribune* by Horace Greeley in 1841. In 1833 Greeley had established the *New Yorker* as a respected literary magazine. He understood more than most the role the media could play as an opinion leader. Feeling a responsibility toward readers, Greeley believed that the news should reflect what they wanted and needed. In 1851 Henry Raymond started the *New York Times,* claiming to publish "all the news that's fit to print."

While the penny press increased newspaper circulation, it also started the race for news. Several other developments influenced the press's growth into the 1900s. As the news became more affordable, readers' choices increased, which led to more competition and therefore an increased effort to grab the public's attention. In this respect, the reading public became a factor shaping publications, and communications and productions systems continued to improve. In 1822 with the establishment of the Washington press corps, publishers realized that they needed reporters to specialize in covering parts of the government important to readers. The invention of the telegraph in 1844 made it easier to report news of events from across the country and changed the way the press gathered news. With this new capability, newspapers reorganized so that central agencies gathered news from around the nation and distributed it to regional outlets. By the 1860s, newspapers had become regionally focused in their news and advertising. When the Civil War erupted in 1861, newspapers naturally sought to inform the public, but did not want to reveal too much, lest they provide the opposing side an advantage. The military tried and often proved successful at silencing newspapers, citing the need for military secrecy. Reporters, however, were allowed much more freedom to travel and interact with troops than they are today. The on-the-spot news story developed at this time.

The growth of telegraph wire services along with the rise of newspaper chains and the desire to sell newspapers to all readers, not just adherents of one party or another, changed the nature of American media in the mid-to-late 1800s. These developments led to a more objective or descriptive style of reporting that relied heavily on interviews, named sources, and appeared in a standardized format. They also reinforced the political independence of newspapers and resulted in the separation of "straight" news from opinion on the editorial page. Technological advancements in the early part of the nineteenth century allowed newspapers to become a more visual medium, the most important development being the ability to easily reproduce photographs. Until this time, illustrations were carved into a piece of wood, inked, and stamped onto a page—a painstakingly slow process. The photograph became an important part of the age of yellow journalism. As the press developed into more of a mass medium, the need to entertain often outweighed the need to inform. There is no better example of this type of news than that produced by William Randolph Hearst, who in his sixty-four-year career sold newspapers trumpeting sensational stories, precursors to the supermarket tabloids.

Societal and economic changes after World War II again altered the media landscape. Television arose and came to dominate American media habits, influencing print journalism with its focus on visuals, emotion, and shorter story formats. In the 1960s, as the United States became increasingly divided over civil rights and the war in Vietnam, alternative and underground journalism took root, giving voice to ideologies outside the mainstream press. These underground papers could be printed cheaply, but circulation tended to be erratic. At the same time, proponents of a more adversarial, interpretive "new" and "advocacy" journalism led to a more analytical and interpretive style of reporting rather than a merely descriptive one. Investigative techniques, epitomized by the reporting of the Watergate scandal, gained new life. At the same time, proliferation of types and outlets of media and greater competition for audience attention led to the development of "soft news" and "infotainment," the merging of hard factual news with more sensationalistic entertainment.

Starting in the late 1970s, the public grew increasingly less trustful of the media. The press attempted to combat this trend by encouraging community involvement, such as through "civic" journalism. For example, newspapers and television stations invited citizens to serve on advisory boards, and the media afforded more opportunities to citizens to have their opinions printed. Today, the press is still adjusting to the Internet, with its effect on the print, audio, and visual broadcast industries continuing to evolve, not unlike previous eras involving groundbreaking technological advances.

REFERENCES

Allan, Stuart, ed. *Journalism after September 11*. New York: Routledge, 2003.

Barnhurst, Kevin, and John Nerone. *The Form of News: A History*. New York: Guilford Press, 2001.

Emery, Edwin. *The Press and America: An Interpretive History of the Mass Media*. Englewood Cliffs, N.J.: Prentice-Hall, 1984.

Hudson, Frederic. *Journalism in the United States, from 1690 to 1872*. New York: Harper and Brothers, 1873.

McMurtie, Douglas. *A History of Printing in the United States: The Story of the Introduction of the Press and of Its History and Influence during the Pioneer Period in Each State of the Union*. Vol. 2. New York: R. R. Bowker, 1936.

Sloan, W. David. *The Early American Press, 1690–1783*. Westport, Conn.: Greenwood Press, 1994.

Streitmatter, Rodger. *Mightier Than the Sword: How the News Media Have Shaped American History*. Boulder, Colo.: Westview Press, 1997.

Holmes, Oliver Wendell, Jr.

Oliver Wendell Holmes Jr. (1841–1935) is among the most renowned justices of the U.S. Supreme Court. He became known as "The Great Dissenter" for the weight of his arguments even in the minority.

Holmes had served in the 20th Massachusetts Regiment of the Union Army during the Civil War and later graduated from Harvard Law School (1866). He then went on to practice commercial law in Massachusetts before returning to his alma mater to teach constitutional law. Holmes edited the *American Law Review* from 1870 to 1873 and in 1881 published *The Common Law*, a treatise on "sociological jurisprudence." In it, he urged his colleagues to support the doctrine of "judicial restraint" by not allowing their personal opinions to affect their legal decisions.

Holmes became an associate justice of the Supreme Judicial Court of Massachusetts in 1883 and was promoted to chief justice in 1899. President Theodore Roosevelt appointed Holmes to the U.S. Supreme Court, where he served from 1902 to 1932. Holmes wrote the opinion for a unanimous court in *Schenck v. United States* (1919), establishing the criteria of a "clear and present danger" to the peace and order of society concerning "substantive evils that Congress has a right to prevent." The decision effectively limited First Amendment speech protections in wartime. In contrast to his position in *Schenck,* in *Abrams v. United States* (1919), Holmes dissented with perhaps his most impassioned defense of free speech. He asserted that only words so immi-

nently threatening to the nation should warrant "an immediate check ... to save the country." In his view, banning seemingly dangerous ideas is tempting, but "the ultimate good desired is better reached by free trade in ideas—that the best test of truth is the power of thought to get accepted in the competition of the market."

REFERENCES

Alschuler, Albert W. *Law without Values: The Life, Work, and Legacy of Justice Holmes*. Chicago: University of Chicago Press, 2000.

Burton, Steven J., ed. *The Path of the Law and Its Influence: The Legacy of Oliver Wendell Holmes, Jr*. New York: Cambridge University Press, 2000.

Howe, Mark De Wolfe, ed. *Touched with Fire: Civil War Letters and Diary of Oliver Wendell Holmes, Jr., 1861–1864*. New York: Fordham University Press, 2000.

White, G. Edward. *Justice Oliver Wendell Holmes: Law and the Inner Self*. New York: Oxford University Press, 1993.

Horse race journalism

Horse race journalism refers to media coverage—especially though not exclusively of election campaigns—that focuses on winning and losing, who's ahead or behind in polls or fund raising, politicians' strategy and tactics, and so on. The reporting is analogous to commentary on horse races, hence the name. Critics assert that such coverage comes at the expense of policy issues and candidates' positions, which are more important to democracy. Regardless, numerous academic studies show that media coverage of the horse race outweighs coverage of other campaign elements, a trend that has been increasing over time.

Explanations for the existence and prevalence of horse race journalism generally point to news organizations' gathering and production routines. Horse race aspects more readily fit their news values, because they are predictable, concrete elements that change over time, thus remaining "fresh" and new. Also, they are easy to report and explain to audiences. With the campaign and struggle between politicians providing the backdrop, they fit easily within the dramatic, narrative-driven plot of a story. Journalists, moreover, can make concrete evaluations of such matters without appearing to be biased or violating objectivity guidelines. Policy issues, on the other hand, provide none of these advantages. Instead, they rarely offer any drama, often are difficult to explain, and seldom change. Journalists are less able to competently critique them and risk exposing themselves to charges of bias if they do. The public, more concerned with policy issues, is arguably ill-served by such coverage.

REFERENCES

Patterson, Thomas. *Out of Order*. New York: Knopf, 1993.
Robinson, Michael, and Margaret Sheehan. *Over the Wire and on TV*. New York: Russell Sage Foundation, 1983.

Hustler v. Falwell (1988)

In *Hustler v. Falwell* (1988), the U.S. Supreme Court set forth a precedent defining libel that makes it difficult for public figures to prove the charge. The case stems from a parody of the Rev. Jerry Falwell, a conservative evangelist, published in *Hustler* magazine. In an ad ostensibly selling Campari Liqueur, Falwell is portrayed having incestuous relations with his mother in an outhouse. Falwell sued the magazine, citing emotional distress and libel. Lower courts awarded Falwell monetary damages, and Larry Flynt, the magazine's publisher, appealed.

The Supreme Court ruled in *Hustler*'s favor. The justices held that for libel to occur, the public figure must prove that the published statements contain a false statement of fact made with actual malice. According to the court, because the *Hustler* piece stated in several places that the ad was a parody and it ran in the fiction section of the magazine, it could not be construed as an assertion of fact. The ruling made it easier for media to parody public figures and harder for such figures to prove libel. The case provides a way for media to state opinion without fear of reprisal from public figures.

REFERENCES

Adams, Julian. *Freedom and Ethics in the Press*. New York: Richards Rosen Press, 1983.
Francois, William E. *Mass Media Law and Regulation*. Ames: Iowa State University Press, 1990.
Gora, Joel M. *The Rights of Reporters: The Basic ACLU Guide to a Reporter's Rights*. New York: Discus Books, 1974.

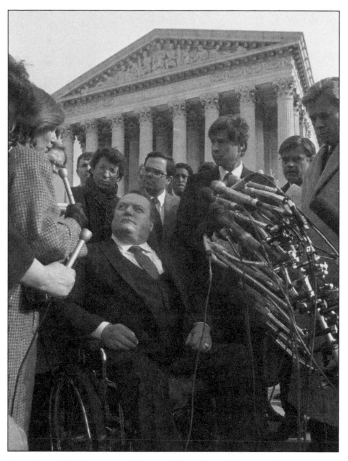

Hustler publisher Larry Flynt speaks with reporters in December 1987 about the libel suit filed against the magazine by Rev. Jerry Falwell stemming from a parody it ran involving Falwell and his mother. The Supreme Court ruled in favor of *Hustler. The justices' decision made it extremely difficult for public figures to prove libel.*

I

Imus, Don

John Donald Imus Jr. (1940–), a radio talk show host, began his career in the 1970s as a shock jock, but evolved into an acerbic interviewer who influenced the nature of political campaigning. He gained popularity in the 1980s and 1990s with sarcasm, rudeness, and wit aimed at his guests, mostly politicians, headline newsmakers, and journalists.

Imus achieved political prominence in 1992 by interviewing Bill Clinton, then governor of Arkansas, during the New York primary campaign. Clinton's friendliness, joking manner, and saxophone playing helped counter the effects of a media frenzy over charges that he had smoked marijuana as a college student. During the general election campaign, an Imus interview enabled Clinton to defend against accusations that he had avoided the Vietnam draft. Appearances on shows like Imus's changed political campaigning by making the personal public. In 1997 *Time* named Imus one of the twenty-five most influential people in the United States by moving politics into the realm of pop culture.

REFERENCES

Reed, Jim. *Everything Imus: All You Ever Wanted to Know about Don Imus.* Secaucus, N.J.: Birch Lane Press, 1999.
Tracy, Kathleen. *Imus: America's Cowboy.* New York: Carroll and Graf, 1999.

Infotainment

See *Hard and soft news*

Interest groups and media

See *Special interest groups and political advertising*

Internet

See *New media*

Interpretation

See *Commentary; News analysis*

Investigative reporting

Investigative reporting is a journalistic style in which reporters go beyond normal, official sources and use in-depth research and other techniques to uncover information usually intentionally hidden from public view. Journalists involved in investigative reporting primarily work in the public interest to bring to light private and government actions that effect communities and nations.

The tradition of investigative reporting dates back to the nineteenth century. As newspapers, and especially magazines, became more of a "mass" medium, some publishers and journalists, such as Joseph Pulitzer, S. S. McClure, Ida Tarbell, and Lincoln Steffens, began crusading, or "muckraking," efforts to uncover public wrongdoing by politicians and corporations, as much to distinguish themselves in the marketplace as to perform a public service.

Two prominent examples of investigative reporting involve the Cuban missile crisis and the Watergate scandal. During the missile crisis, the United States and the Soviet Union appeared headed toward nuclear war when a journalist broke the news of the confrontation over the Soviets positioning nuclear weapons in Cuba. In the Watergate scandal, the *New York Times* and *Washington Post* took what began as a break-in at the Watergate building in Washington, D.C., and through dogged research and reporting uncovered evidence of illegal wiretapping, sabotage, and political "dirty tricks" that led to the resignation of President Richard Nixon. The goal in both instances was to find and report the truth to the people and to uphold the integrity of the press.

Because of the time, effort, and resources necessary to conduct investigative reporting, its practice is sometimes limited by economic and other factors and has been in decline in recent years. In some instances, the media have opted for sensationalism rather than news of broad importance to sell papers and magazines. Investigative journalism continues, however, to play an important role in politics and society. For example, in 2005 the *New York Times* revealed that President George W. Bush had approved a secret government operation allowing the National Security Agency to eavesdrop on Americans' foreign phone calls without warrants from a judge, in apparent violation of a federal law. Investigative reporting thus performs a potentially important democratic function.

See also *Center for Investigative Reporting; Mother Jones; Muckraking; Watchdog role; Watergate.*

REFERENCES

Aramao, Rosemary. "The History of Investigative Reporting." In *The Big Chill: Investigative Reporting in the Current Media Environment,* ed. Marilyn Greenwald and Joseph Bernt. Ames: Iowa State University Press, 2000.

Center for Investigative Reporting, www.muckraker.org.

Protess, David L., et al. *The Journalism of Outrage: Investigative Reporting and Agenda Building in America.* New York: Guilford, 1991.

Issue advocacy

See *Special interest groups and political advertising*

Issue coverage

Scholars have long criticized the amount and depth of issue coverage provided by mass media outlets in the United States. Much of this criticism stems from studies of campaign coverage that reveal that news coverage during elections typically provides less substantial information about issues than does candidate advertising. Rather than focusing on issues, the media instead preoccupy themselves with the breaking events of the campaigns, as reporters cover the "horse race" elements—focusing on who's ahead in the polls, in fundraising, and so on—and frame stories around the strategy, or the "game," of the election. Some scholars argue that this approach to campaign coverage has become entrenched to the point that reporters are so accustomed to this frame that they fail to cover information that does not fit into it.

Although game frames dominate campaign coverage, the media also use them in stories about public policy issues, especially when the issues are discussed within the context of a national election or when policymakers are engaged in a clear-cut legislative conflict. Many argue that the diversification of media outlets, stemming from cable television and new technology, has exacerbated such concerns. In order to maintain ratings, the media have sensationalized news, repackaging it as entertainment and presenting it as soft news, all at the expense of the detailed information about policy issues found in traditional hard news.

The paucity and framing of issue coverage in the news have been criticized as the root of a number of problems facing U.S. democracy, including widespread ignorance of public affairs, cynicism toward government, declining political efficacy, and low voter turnout. Yet others contend that the diversification of media has increased access to hard news; that despite shortcomings, the news plays an important role in facilitating issue voting; and that the consumption of news is still linked to civic engagement.

See also *Campaigns, elections, and the media; Horse race journalism.*

REFERENCES

Cappella, Joseph N., and Kathleen Hall Jamieson. *Spiral of Cynicism: The Press and the Public Good.* Oxford: Oxford University Press, 1997.

Norris, Pippa. *A Virtuous Circle: Political Communications in Postindustrial Societies.* Cambridge: Cambridge University Press, 2000.

Patterson, Thomas E. *Out of Order.* New York: Knopf, 1993.

J

Jefferson, Thomas

Thomas Jefferson (1743–1826), the influential political thinker and founder, drafted the Declaration of Independence and served as the third president of the United States. After becoming a lawyer, in 1768 he was elected to the Virginia House of Burgesses, where he gained a wide following voicing opposition to Britain's taxation and governance policies toward the colonies. His *Summary View of the Rights of British America* (1774), published without his permission, put forth the revolutionary argument that the colonists' connection to Great Britain was wholly voluntary. Jefferson was appointed a delegate to the Second Continental Congress in 1775 in Philadelphia. Attendees selected Jefferson, regarded as a good writer, for a five-delegate committee—along with John Adams, Benjamin Franklin, Robert Livingstone, and Roger Sherman—and charged them with drafting a statement of rationale for severing relations with Great Britain. Their effort resulted in the Declaration of Independence.

Virginians elected Jefferson governor in 1779, during which time he wrote *Notes on the State of Virginia* (1781), his thoughts on slavery. In 1782 he was chosen as a delegate to the Continental Congress. A few years later, Jefferson succeeded Franklin as minister to France, serving from 1784 to 1789, and bore witness to the philosophical debate during the prelude to the French Revolution. President George Washington chose Jefferson to be the new nation's first secretary of state, a position he held from 1790 until 1793; Jefferson pursued a decidedly anti-British stance in foreign policy.

Jefferson's sharp personal and political disagreements with Alexander Hamilton over the power and role of the national government and U.S. foreign relations led him to become the face and voice of the anti-Federalist movement, which included support for Philip Freneau's *National Gazette* (1791–1793). Jefferson claimed that Freneau's newspaper "saved our Constitution which was galloping fast into monarchy." He took part in the debate surrounding the new Constitution, which he felt gave the federal government too much power and needed a bill of rights to protect the rights of individuals and states from federal intrusion.

As political differences hardened, the leaders of these two philosophies established political parties in opposition. Jefferson joined James Madison to form the Democratic-Republican Party, while Hamilton and Adams established the Federalist Party. Jefferson reluctantly stood for president in 1796, narrowly losing to Adams. As the runner-up and according to the law at the time, Jefferson became vice president and continued his opposition of the Federalists. President Adams signed the contentious Alien and Sedition Acts in 1798 in an attempt to bring the power of the state against dissenters. The acts—drafted to expire in 1801, the end of Adams's term—broadly contributed to the demise of the Federalist Party and to Jefferson's benefit.

Jefferson again ran for president in the contentious and divisive election of 1800. Because of the closeness of the vote, the election reverted to the House of Representatives. Hamilton lobbied the representatives not so much in favor of Jefferson as against Aaron Burr, with whom he had strong disagreements. The debate lasted for several weeks before

Jefferson emerged victorious. The 1800 election was the first peaceful transfer of power from one political party to another in the United States. In his 1801 inaugural address, Jefferson sounded a conciliatory chord, stating, "We are all Republicans—we are all Federalists." He was reelected in a landslide in 1804. After his second term, Jefferson retired to Monticello. He served also as president of the American Philosophical Association from 1797 to 1815 and founded the University of Virginia in 1819.

See also *Alien and Sedition Acts of 1798; Freneau, Philip; Hamilton, Alexander.*

REFERENCES

Commager, Henry Steele. *Jefferson, Nationalism, and the Enlightenment.* New York: G. Braziller, 1975.

Lehmann, Karl. *Thomas Jefferson, American Humanist.* Chicago: University of Chicago Press, 1965.

Malone, Dumas. *Jefferson and His Time,* 6 vols. Boston: Little, Brown, 1948–1981.

Matthews, Richard K. *The Radical Politics of Thomas Jefferson: A Revisionist View.* Lawrence: University Press of Kansas, 1984.

Peterson, Merrill D. *Thomas Jefferson and the New Nation: A Biography.* New York: Oxford University Press, 1970.

Randall, Henry S. *The Life of Thomas Jefferson,* 3 vols. New York: Da Capo Press, 1972.

Tucker, Robert W., and David C. Hendrickson. *Empire of Liberty: The Statecraft of Thomas Jefferson.* New York: Oxford University Press, 1990.

Jennings, Peter

Peter Charles Jennings (1938–2005) served as national anchor for ABC News for more than twenty-five years, bringing to the job many years of experience as a journalist. At age ten, Jennings hosted his first radio show, "Peter's Program," a children's talent showcase. He began his professional career as a disc jockey and news reporter for a small radio station in Brockton, Ontario, and worked his way up in Canadian radio and television. In 1964 Jennings joined ABC News as the anchor of a fifteen-minute evening news segment. A year later, at the age of twenty-seven, Jennings became the youngest television news anchor in history. He counted among his competitors none other than the legendary Walter Cronkite (CBS) and the team of Chet Huntley and David Brinkley (NBC).

From 1968 to 1978, Jennings took on several foreign correspondent assignments for ABC News and served as a news reporter for *AM America,* the predecessor to *Good Morning America.* In 1978 Jennings returned to the newsroom as a co-anchor, and in 1983 became the sole anchor of *ABC World News Tonight.* He left his job as ABC anchor in 2005 after being diagnosed with lung cancer. Jennings co-authored *The Century* (1998), *The Century for Young People* (1999), and *In Search of America* (2002).

REFERENCES

Goldberg, Robert, and Gerald Jay Goldberg. *Anchors: Brokaw, Jennings, Rather and the Evening News.* New York: Birch Lane, 1990.

Goldenson, Leonard. *Beating the Odds.* New York: Scribners, 1991.

K

Kennedy-Nixon debates

The four Kennedy-Nixon debates of 1960 are widely considered a landmark in the history of American political campaigning. These events between Democratic senator John F. Kennedy and Republican vice president Richard M. Nixon marked the first time that major party candidates for president debated during a general election campaign. The next presidential debate would not take place until 1976, after which such events would become a regular feature of the fall presidential campaign. The lapse between 1960 and 1976 may have stemmed in part from a myth that those who watched the debate on television thought that Kennedy had won, while those who listened to the debate on the radio thought that Nixon had won. Such a difference presumably demonstrates the power of visual imagery over the spoken word, and suggests that candidates who do not believe that they will look good on television will avoid televised debates. Evidence in support of this belief remains primarily limited to sketchy reports about a market survey conducted by Sindlinger & Company in which 49 percent of those who listened to the debates on radio said Nixon had won compared to 21 percent who said Kennedy, while 30 percent of those who watched the debates on television said Kennedy had won compared to 29 percent who said Nixon. Contrary to popular belief, the Sindlinger poll suggests not that Kennedy had won in the minds of television viewers, but that the candidates tied on television while Nixon won on radio.

Sindlinger and Company never released details about the sample, so it is unclear whether the survey results can be

The 1960 presidential debates between Democrat John F. Kennedy and Republican Richard M. Nixon illustrated the power of the media. Unscientific polling indicated that radio listeners believed Nixon had won, but television viewers sided with Kennedy because he appeared tanned and attractive while Nixon seemed pale and sickly.

applied to a broader population. Moreover, because 87 percent of American households had a television in 1960, most people could watch the debates if they chose to do so. The fraction of people lacking access to television in 1960 lived mainly in rural areas, and particularly in southern and western states, places that were unlikely to be home to significant proportions of presumably pro-Democrat and pro-Kennedy Catholic voters. This casts further doubt on whether the Sindlinger survey results speak to the effects of television or merely of the urban-rural split in Nixon's support.

See also *Presidential debates.*

REFERENCES

Jamieson, Kathleen Hall, and David S. Birdsell. *Presidential Debates: The Challenge of Creating an Informed Electorate.* New York: Oxford University Press, 1988.

Krause, Sidney. "Winners of the First 1960 Televised Presidential Debate between Kennedy and Nixon." *Journal of Communication* 46, no. 4 (August 1996): 78–96.

Kilpatrick, James J.

James Jackson Kilpatrick (1920–) is a journalist, editor, columnist, and commentator. Kilpatrick began his professional career as a reporter for the *Richmond News Leader* of Virginia in 1941 and eight years later became its editorial page editor. In 1962 he began writing a column, "A Conservative View," that went into national syndication and eventually ran for twenty-eight years. Kilpatrick also penned a weekly column, "The Writer's Art," on the use and abuse of the English language, beginning in 1981. "Covering the Courts" is a nationally syndicated column offering Kilpatrick's views and opinions on U.S. Supreme Court decisions and other court activities.

Kilpatrick appeared for eleven years as a regular debater for the "Point-Counterpoint" segment on CBS's *60 Minutes,* on which he offered a conservative perspective, and political analysis programs, such as *Meet the Press.* He is a trustee of the Supreme Court Historical Society, a founding trustee of the Thomas Jefferson Center for the Protection of Free Expression, and a frequent writer in defense of freedom of the press. Kilpatrick has authored or edited eleven books, including *The Writer's Art* (1984) and *Fine Print: Reflections on the Writing Art* (1993) as well as *Political Bestiary* (1978) with Eugene J. McCarthy.

REFERENCE

"Spoofing the Despots." *Time,* January 21, 1966, 47.

Kissinger, Henry

Henry Alfred Kissinger (1923–) was the powerful secretary of state and national security advisor in the Nixon and Ford administrations. Born in Fuerth, Germany, he fled with his parents to New York City in 1938 to escape persecution under the Nazis. He served in the U.S. Army Counter-Intelligence Corps from 1943 to 1946 and in the military intelligence reserve from 1946 to 1949. Kissinger spent his entire academic career, from 1954 to 1971, at Harvard, where he earned his doctorate and then became a professor of government. He gained national attention with the publication of *Nuclear Weapons and Foreign Policy* (1957).

Henry Kissinger (left) greets Chinese premier Chou En-lai in 1971 in Beijing while serving as national security advisor for President Richard M. Nixon. Kissinger served in the administrations of five U.S. presidents, from Eisenhower to Ford.

Kissinger served in several advisory positions in the Eisenhower, Kennedy, and Johnson administrations on issues of national security and foreign policy. President Richard M. Nixon chose him to be national security advisor, a position he held from 1969 to 1975, and secretary of state from 1973 to 1977. Kissinger was the chief architect of U.S. foreign policy in the Nixon and Ford administrations, helping to craft the rapprochement with the People's Republic of China, détente with the Soviet Union, and negotiations with the Arabs and Israelis to produce a cease-fire in the October 1973 War. Kissinger made common the term *shuttle diplomacy* with his public and secret travels and negotiations in advancing the administration's foreign policy, particularly in the Middle East. He took controversial positions in foreign relations with Cambodia, Chile, and Vietnam. Although some have argued that his positions reflect a classic realist approach to foreign relations, also known as *realpolitik,* others, most notably Christopher Hitchens, consider his actions, such as support for the rightist coup in Chile in 1973, to have been criminal.

Kissinger mastered interacting with the press, serving as a source and working to set the agenda in furtherance of U.S. policy, the administration's objectives, and his status in the administration. Kissinger was awarded the 1973 Nobel Peace Prize—along with Le Duc Tho, his counterpart from North Vietnam—for his contributions toward achieving a cease-fire in the Vietnam War. He continues to work as a consultant, lecturer, and commentator on foreign policy issues. Kissinger was originally named to co-chair the September 11 Commission but resigned when controversy arose over potential conflicts between the national interest and those of his clients. Kissinger has written numerous books, including *The Necessity for Choice* (1960), *The White House Years* (1979), *Years of Upheaval* (1982), *Diplomacy* (1994), and *Ending the Vietnam War* (2003).

REFERENCES

Hersh, Seymour M. *The Price of Power: Kissinger in the Nixon White House.* New York: Summit Books, 1983.
Hitchens, Christopher. *The Trial of Henry Kissinger.* New York: Verso, 2001.
Isaacson, Walter. *Kissinger. A Biography.* London: Faber and Faber, 1992.
Kissinger, Henry A. *Ending the Vietnam War: A History of America's Involvement in and Extrication from the Vietnam War.* New York: Simon and Schuster, 2003.

Knight Ridder

Knight Ridder, a newspaper publishing conglomerate and international telecommunications company, provides services to more than 100 million people in more than 150 countries. The corporation evolved in 1974 with the merger of two established newspaper groups.

Herman Ridder had bought *Staats-Zeitung,* a New York–based German-language paper, in 1892. (Ridder was a founder and president of the Associated Press and a supporter of the American Newspaper Publishers Association, becoming its president in 1907.) Ridder Publications incorporated in 1942 and continued to purchase additional media-related businesses. Charles Landon (C.L.) Knight had founded the Knight Group in 1903, when he bought the *Akron Beacon Journal* in Ohio. Knight's son, John, bought the *Miami Herald* in 1937, and his brother, James, worked as the operations manager. The Knights later bought its competitor, the *Miami Tribune.* Knight Newspapers incorporated in 1941.

In 1974 the two groups merged to become Knight Ridder Newspapers, which as of early 2006 owned thirty-two papers throughout the United States. Some critics argue that cost-cutting measures and standardization of content in large chains like Knight Ridder have hurt papers' ability to inform their local audiences. In March 2006, Knight Ridder was purchased by the rival McClatchy Company for $6.5 billion, making it the second-largest chain in the United States.

See also *Newspapers; Ownership of media.*

REFERENCES

Grant, Tina, ed. *International Directory of Company Histories.* Vol. 15. New York: St. James Press, 1996, 262–266.
Knight Ridder, www.knightridder.com.
Merritt, Davis. *Knightfall: Knight-Ridder and How the Erosion of News Is Putting Democracy at Risk.* New York: AMACOM, 2005.

Koppel, Ted

Edward James Koppel (1940–) is a broadcast journalist and was the host of ABC's Emmy Award–winning *Nightline* news program for twenty-five years. Koppel began his career as a radio news reporter with WMCA in New York. He joined ABC News in 1963 as a radio news reporter and served in a variety of reporting and commentary positions in Miami, Hong Kong, and Vietnam. Koppel became ABC News's chief diplomatic correspondent in 1971, during which time he covered Secretary of State Henry Kissinger's shuttle diplomacy. He also delivered numerous special programs for ABC News in the 1970s, including one on Kissinger (1974), the People of People's China (1973), and the award-winning "American Military Strength: Second to None" (1979).

In 1980 Koppel hosted the first *Nightline*, which evolved from late-night weekday updates on the Iranian hostage crisis. He was the sole anchor and became managing editor as well, until his departure in 2005. Koppel now writes and contributes to a variety of National Public Radio programs and hosts and produces Discovery Channel programs on global topics and events. He is the author of *Off Camera: Private Thoughts Made Public* (2000) and the co-author of *In the National Interest* (1977) with Marvin Kalb and *Nightline: History in the Making and the Making of Television* (1996) with Kyle Gibson.

REFERENCES

Gunther, Marc. *The House That Roone Built: The Inside Story of ABC News.* Boston: Little, Brown, 1994.
Koppel, Ted, and Kyle Gibson. *Nightline: History in the Making and the Making of Television.* New York: Times Books, 1996.

Kristol, William

William Kristol (1952–), also known as Bill Kristol, is an editor, author, political commentator, and a leader of the so-called neoconservative movement. He graduated from Harvard University with a bachelor's degree in government in 1973 and a doctorate in political science in 1979. He taught politics at the University of Pennsylvania from 1978 to 1983 and at Harvard University's John F. Kennedy School of Government from 1983 to 1985. Kristol then served as chief of staff to Secretary of Education William Bennett in the Reagan administration from 1985 to 1988, and chief of staff for Vice President Dan Quayle from 1989 to 1993, during the Bush administration. He is sometimes referred to as "Dan Quayle's brain."

Kristol made his mark as chairman of the Project for the Republican Future during 1993–1994, when the organiza-

tion contributed to the Republican Party's gaining control of Congress in 1994. He founded the *Weekly Standard* in 1995 and continues to serve as the magazine's editor and publisher. Kristol co-founded the Project for the New American Century in 1997, a neoconservative endeavor supported by the New Citizenship Project, of which Kristol is the chair. He is a member of the American Enterprise Institute.

Kristol regularly appears as a political analyst, commentator, and pundit on *This Week*, the *Newshour with Jim Lehrer*, and Fox News channel. He writes on political philosophy and American political thought and public policy for popular and academic publications. Kristol is the co-author of several books, including *Present Dangers: Crisis and Opportunity in American Foreign and Defense Policy* (with Robert Kagan, 2000), *Bush v. Gore: The Court Cases and the Commentary* (with E. J. Dionne Jr., 2001), *The Future Is Now: America Confronts the New Genetics* (with Eric Cohen, 2002), and *The War over Iraq: America's Mission and Saddam's Tyranny* (with Lawrence F. Kaplan, 2003).

REFERENCES

Bethell, Tom. "The Warrior Class: Bill Kristol and the National Greatness Crowd Would Love to Have a War." *American Spectator,* July–August 2001, 10–12.
Foer, Franklin. "Great Escape: How Bill Kristol Ditched Conservatism." *New Republic,* May 28, 2001, 17–20.
Kaylin, Lucy. "The Trouble with Bill." *GQ,* September 2001, 205–213.
Tanenhaus, Sam. "Bush's Brain Trust." *Vanity Fair,* July 2003.

Krock, Arthur

Arthur Bernard Krock (1886–1974) was an influential Pulitzer Prize–winning journalist and commentator. Krock attended Princeton University for a year before leaving for financial reasons and began his journalism career in 1907 as a cub reporter for the *Louisville Herald* of Kentucky. Krock moved to Washington, D.C., as a correspondent for the *Louisville Times* in 1910 and returned to Louisville in 1915 as the editorial director for both the *Times* and *Courier-Journal.* He traveled to Paris to cover the 1919 peace conference that ended World War I.

In 1923 Krock left Louisville for New York City to join the *New York World* as an editorial writer. When Walter Lippmann took over as editor of the *World,* Krock left, in 1927, to join the *New York Times* as a reporter; he became that paper's Washington correspondent and bureau chief in 1932. From 1933 to 1966, he wrote the highly regarded "In the Nation," a column that generally espoused a conservative line. Because of mounting tensions with publisher Arthur Hays Sulzberger, Krock was relieved of his position as bureau chief and replaced in 1953 by James Reston. He continued with his column and as an editorial commentator until 1967.

Krock won four Pulitzers, including two, in 1935 and 1938, for his writing, along with a special commendation and a special citation from the Pulitzer Committee. He received the Presidential Medal of Freedom in 1970. He stated in *Time* that he found the real reward of journalism to be "perceiving in a news event the hidden factors that are really the important roots of the action." Krock's autobiography is *Memoirs: Sixty Years on the Firing Line* (1968). He also wrote *In the Nation: 1932–1966* (1969), *The Consent of the Governed and Other Deceits* (1971), and *Myself When Young: Growing Up in the 1890s* (1973).

REFERENCES

"A Critical Look at U.S.—Size-Up by a Veteran Writer." *U.S. News & World Report,* October 10, 1966, 23.

Freeman, Neal B. "Gentleman Journalist of the Old School." *National Review,* November 19, 1968, 1176–1177.

Little, Stuart W. "Krock and the Presidents." *Saturday Review,* October 12, 1968, 84–85.

"Mr. Krock Retires." *Time,* October 7, 1966, 61–62.

"Old-School Ties." *Newsweek,* April 22, 1974, 73–74.

L

Landmark Communications, Inc. v. Virginia (1978)

In *Landmark Communications, Inc. v. Virginia* (1978), the U.S. Supreme Court ruled that criminal sanctions against a third party for disclosing confidential government proceedings were unconstitutional.

In accordance with a Virginia statute, Landmark Communications was charged with a misdemeanor after one of its newspapers, the *Virginia Pilot,* published a newspaper article revealing the identity of a state judge undergoing disciplinary investigation by the Virginia Judicial Inquiry and Review Commission. The Virginia legislature had enacted a statute making such disclosures a crime, believing that criminal sanctions were the only means of ensuring that commission proceedings remained confidential. Landmark Communications argued that they had a responsibility under the First Amendment to publish the article because its readers should be made aware of the judicial proceedings. The Virginia Supreme Court upheld Landmark's conviction. The company appealed.

The U.S. Supreme Court unanimously reversed and remanded the decision by the Virginia court. It held, instead, that the First Amendment right to freedom of expression extended to third parties who accurately reported on the confidential inquiry proceedings of state judges. Chief Justice Warren Burger, writing for the majority, asserted that free discussion of such governmental affairs is an essential function of the First Amendment. Therefore, Landmark Communications had a constitutional right to publish the article because it served "the interests of public scrutiny" as intended by the Constitution.

REFERENCES

Landmark Communications, Inc. v. Virginia, 435 U.S. 829 (1978).
Sullivan, Kathleen, and Gerald Gunther. *Constitutional Law.* 15th ed. Westbury, N.Y.: Foundation Press, 2004.

Larry King Live

See *Talk shows*

Late night talk shows

The opening monologues of late night television talk shows have evolved into a prime source of humorous political commentary. Once treated as mere entertainment, they are now regarded as an indicator of audience opinions and voting choices and perhaps a factor in them. Presidential candidates routinely appear on these shows to banter with the hosts and be interrogated by them.

From the mid-1960s through the mid-1980s, Johnny Carson began the NBC *Tonight Show* with a monologue of jokes and impressions, taking some of his material from current news events. Few public officials or journalists took notice of the jokes aimed at political figures that he interspersed among his comments. This situation changed in 1988, when Lee Atwater, the media consultant for George H. W. Bush's presidential campaign, said that he listened to audience responses to Carson's jokes to get a sense of what the public really thought about Bush and his competitors. Reporters then began to impute political significance to late night humor as Carson, his frequent guest host Jay Leno, and CBS *Late Night* host David Letterman regularly lampooned candidates and other political figures for their verbal gaffes, physical appearance, and personal foibles (though rarely for their policies and proposals.)

This type of hazing came to a head in August 1988, when gaffes by newly chosen Republican vice presidential nominee Dan Quayle elicited a torrent of jokes portraying him as stupid and out of his depth. Regardless of the accuracy or inaccuracy of these jabs, the damage to Quayle's public image was permanent, as he remained a favorite target of the late night comics throughout the Bush presidency. Moreover, the proportion of jokes about politicians only increased after the campaign ended. When Leno took over from Carson in 1992, he increased the political material in the *Tonight Show* monologues.

Meanwhile, journalists and politicians began to treat late night TV as a serious political phenomenon. Pew Research Center polls showed that by 2000, more than one out of four voters, and nearly half of those under the age of thirty, got their information about the presidential campaign from these shows. Scholars also began to debate the significance of late night political humor, and the Center for Media and Public Affairs at George Mason University established a continuously updated archive of late night political jokes, which now number more than ten thousand.

Some candidates eventually decided that if they were going to get needled by the talk shows, they might as well join them. In 1992 Democratic presidential candidate Bill Clinton took the lead by famously playing the saxophone on the *Arsenio Hall Show*. During the 2000 presidential campaign, Republican challenger George W. Bush and Democratic candidate Al Gore were interviewed by Jay Leno and David Letterman, comedians functioning as journalists.

In 2004 the late night talk shows had competition from the political humor of Comedy Central's *Daily Show*, a program built on "fake news" satirizing politics and politicians. Democratic presidential candidate John Kerry appeared on the show during the general election to rebut criticism of his Vietnam War record, but a defining moment in the merger of politics and entertainment had occurred earlier that year, when Democratic senator John Edwards declared his candidacy for president on the program. This prompted the host, Jon Stewart, to remind Edwards that he was on a "fake news" show. The episode serves as a reminder of how

the line between parody and reality is being blurred, as is the line between political news and entertainment.

REFERENCES

Niven, David, S. Robert Lichter, and Daniel Amundson. "The Political Content of Late Night Comedy." *Harvard International Journal of Press/Politics* 8, no. 3 (Fall 2003): 118–133.

"Politics Is a Joking Matter." *Media Monitor,* March–April 2006.

Young, Dannagal G. "Late-Night Comedy in Election 2000: Its Influence on Candidate Trait Ratings and the Moderating Effects of Political Knowledge and Partisanship." *Journal of Broadcasting and Electronic Media* 48, no. 1 (March 2004): 1–22.

Latinos and the media

While mainstream media in the United States have continued to either exclude Latinos from news and entertainment coverage or negatively stereotype them, Spanish-language media have provided a popular alternative for Latino media consumers. The 2000 census estimated the Latino population of the United States at no less than 40 million, with an annual buying power of $715 billion. The census also found that Latinos comprise 12 percent of the population and are increasing in number six times faster than any other group. As the fastest growing population in the United States, Latinos are an appealing market for media content, advertisers, and political hopefuls.

Nearly 59 percent of Latinos in the United States are of Mexican descent, 9 percent Central and South American, 10 percent Puerto Rican, and 3.5 percent Cuban. The remaining 18.5 percent come from or trace their families to other Spanish-speaking countries. Regardless, the news and entertainment often treat Latinos as one homogenous ethnic group, when in actuality they differ in history, tradition, customs, and concerns. Latinos also differ in their media usage, which varies by generations. First-generation Latinos, who have the strongest ties to their countries of origin, prefer Spanish-language media over English-language sources. Second-generation Latinos are more likely to be bilingual, speaking Spanish at home but English elsewhere, and consume Spanish- as well as English-language media. Third-generation Latinos consume mostly English-language media, but also take in Spanish-language media because of cultural ties. When attempting to appeal to and reach potential Latino audiences, one needs to consider these factors in

California governor Arnold Schwarzenegger speaks during a break at a 2005 taping of Voz y Voto *at Univision studios in Sacramento. Univision, a Spanish-language television network, provides an alternative to mainstream media for the country's large and growing Latino population.*

media placement of advertising or attracting Latino audiences through content.

Mainstream news coverage of Latinos has been criticized for a lack of attention toward them and concentration of negative portrayals. The infrequent coverage of Latinos primarily involves crime, gangs, poverty, and immigration issues. Prominent coverage focused on the death of the singer Selena in 1995 and the fate of Elian Gonzalez, the young Cuban refugee, in 1999 and 2000. Although news coverage often focuses on crimes involving Latinos, it neglects the presence of Latinos in law enforcement. A study by Travis Dixon and Daniel Linz on Los Angeles television crime coverage found that only 10 percent of police officers shown were Latino, while Latinos comprised 25 percent of law enforcement in the area.

Some Spanish-language papers dating to the 1830s conveyed messages of empowerment to their readers. Among them were the weekly *El Crepusculo de la Libertad,* published in 1835, and *El Clamor Público,* published in the 1850s. Today a thriving Latino press provides an alternative to mainstream coverage. More than 500 Spanish-language newspapers were in circulation in the late 1990s. Some English-language papers in metropolitan areas with sizable Latino populations offer Spanish-language inserts, like the *Miami Herald* and its *El Nuevo Herald.* As might be suspected, Spanish-language news cites substantially more Latino authorities as sources for quotes and sound bites than does the mainstream news.

Latinos have also been consistently underrepresented in entertainment, even as their population has continued to increase. The media even sometimes cast white actors to play Latino characters. For example, Natalie Wood and George Chakiris played *West Side Story*'s Puerto Rican leads, and Nicholas Turturro played *NYPD Blue*'s Detective James Martinez. Latinos have historically appeared primarily in westerns and crime dramas and often in supporting or background roles. In television, Latinos appear more often in comedies than in dramas, acting as gang members, drug lords, or characters with little education and low-skilled jobs. Latinos playing leading characters usually lack cultural identifiers that peg them as Latino, so the role could as easily be played by a non-Latino actor as by a Latino. Noteworthy Latino milestones in entertainment include the popularity of Cuban American bandleader Desi Arnez Jr. in *I Love Lucy* and the airing of the Mexican American family drama *American Family* on PBS and the *George Lopez Show* on ABC.

According to estimates by Jack Glascock and Thomas Ruggiero, one-third to one-half of U.S. Latinos who watch prime-time television tune in to Spanish-language networks, such as Azteca America, Telemundo, and Univision. Spanish-language networks have experienced considerable growth in recent years. In 2000, 87 television stations in 44 U.S. cities were affiliated with one of these three Latino networks, and by 2005 that number had grown to 151 stations in 53 cities. Through local affiliates and cable television, Univision—the powerhouse in Spanish-language television founded in 1961—reaches 98 percent of Latino households, including some 30 percent of adults ages eighteen to forty-nine during prime time. Univision's popularity stems from its Mexican-produced programs, specifically its *telenovelas,* such as *Rubi, Amor Real,* and *La Madrasta.* Univision has an agreement through 2017 with Mexico Televisa to produce and provide 80 percent of its prime-time content. In contrast to Univision, Telemundo reaches about 8 percent of that same viewing-age audience and is available in 93 percent of Latino households. Telemundo emerged in the late 1980s and was newsworthy in its purchase by NBC in 2002. In contrast to Univision, Telemundo is known for offering U.S.-produced telenovelas, such as *Tierra de pasiones* and *El Cuerpo del Deso.*

The telenovelas—Spanish-language television's most popular offerings—are comparable to soap operas, but most stories conclude in 150 to 200 episodes rather than continuing year after year. One study of novelas by Glascock and Ruggiero revealed that men and women appeared equally often in novelas, but female characters tended to have lower job status than the male characters, more childcare duties, and more attention focused on their attractiveness. Also, light-skinned Latinos were more likely to play major roles than were darker-skinned Latino actors, be younger, and be portrayed as upper class.

In addition to airing telenovelas, Univision and Telemundo also offer reality television programs, as well as broadcasts of such sporting events as the World Cup and the Olympics. The majority of Latino households prefer news and entertainment in Spanish, but these two networks also provide some programming in English aimed primarily at Latino cultures. In contrast to the predominantly Spanish-language networks Telemundo and Univision, the cable network SíTV provides all-English-language programming, and mun2 (of Telemundo) features mostly English content. These may appeal to U.S.-born Latino youths who consider English their primary language. The majority of money spent on advertising in Latino media goes to Spanish-language television.

The importance of the Latino population has not been lost on politicians. During the 1950 election, Republican Dwight D. Eisenhower became the first presidential candidate to attempt to court Latino voters. Republican Richard M. Nixon's campaign published brochures in Spanish aimed at the Cuban American, Mexican American, and Puerto Rican communities. The Democratic Party also organized in reaching out to Latino voters, and in 1994 the Democratic National Committee devised its first Latino communication strategy, reinforcing the growing importance of Latino voters in U.S. politics. Campaign Web sites during the 2000 elections offered text and information in Spanish for prospective voters and donors. George W. Bush openly appealed to Latino voters in Texas gubernatorial elections, and did so again when running for the presidency in 2000 and 2004. The concentration of Latino voters can influence the outcome of elections in the key states of Arizona, California, Colorado, New Mexico, New York, and

Texas and perhaps a few other places. As voters, Latinos have proved to be more unpredictable than other populations; some 40 percent do not identify with either major political party. Mobilizing the Latino vote may therefore be the key to electoral success in some cases, making media-based appeals to them increasingly important.

REFERENCES

Connaughton, Stacey L. *Inviting Latino Voters: Party Messages and Latino Party Identification.* New York: Routledge, 2005.

Dixon, Travis L., and Daniel Linz. "Overrepresentation and Underrepresentation of African Americans and Latinos as Lawbreakers on Television News." *Journal of Communication* 50, no. 2 (Spring 2000): 131–154.

Glascock, Jack, and Thomas E. Ruggiero. "Representations of Class and Gender on Primetime Spanish-Language Television in the United States." *Communication Quarterly* 52, no. 4 (Fall 2004): 390–402.

Larson, Stephanie Greco. *Media and Minorities: The Politics of Race in News and Entertainment.* Lanham, Md.: Rowman and Littlefield, 2006.

Len-Rios, Maria E. "The Bush and Gore Presidential Web Sites: Identifying with Hispanic Voters during the 2000 Iowa Caucuses and New Hampshire Primary." *Journalism and Mass Communication Quarterly* 79, no. 4 (Winter 2002): 887–904.

Pieraccini, Cristina, and Douglass L. Alligood. *Color Television: Fifty Years of African American and Latino Images on Prime Time Television.* Dubuque, Iowa: Kendall/Hunt Publishing, 2005.

Rodriguez, Clara E. *Latin Looks: Images of Latinas and Latinos in the U.S. Media.* Boulder, Colo.: Westview Press, 1997.

Lawrence, David, Jr.

David Lawrence Jr. (1942–) is a former publisher for the *Miami Herald* known for his commitment to journalistic standards and community service. He began his journalism career as a student at the University of Florida. While serving as the editor of the campus newspaper, he decided to address the slow pace of integration at the university, a move that drew the ire of the school's president and made him one of two editors in the school's ninety-one-year history to be removed from that position. When Lawrence completed his studies at the university in 1963, he was named Outstanding Journalism Graduate.

Lawrence went to work at the *St. Petersburg Times, Washington Post,* and *Palm Beach Post* before joining Knight Newspapers (now Knight-Ridder) as assistant to the editor of the *Philadelphia Daily News* in 1971. Lawrence then served as the editor of the *Charlotte Observer* before becoming the publisher and executive editor of the *Detroit Free Press* from 1978 to 1989. He became the publisher and chief executive officer of the *Miami Herald* in 1989. During his ten-year tenure at the *Herald,* the paper won five Pulitzer Prizes, and he resisted corporate pressures to downsize to cut costs while increasing revenues. Lawrence retired from the *Herald* in 1999, ending a long-standing battle to maintain a foundation of good journalism in the face of a changing community and corporate pressures emphasizing profitability.

Lawrence used his position to support community improvement efforts, especially in education and childhood development, serving on numerous boards, councils, and committees. He has received a variety of awards for his community service and leadership. He also chaired the national Task Force on Minorities in the Newspaper Business for two terms and served as the president of the American Society of Newspaper Editors for 1991–1992 and the president of the Inter American Press Association for 1995–1996. In retirement, he has focused on his interest in childhood development, serving as the president of the Early Childhood Initiative Foundation and becoming the University Scholar for Early Childhood Development and Readiness at the University of Florida. He chairs the Children's Services Council of Miami-Dade County. In 2005 the university announced the creation of the David Lawrence Jr. Endowed Professorship in Early Childhood Studies.

REFERENCES

Swartz, Mimi. "The *Herald's* Cuban Revolution." *New Yorker,* June 7, 1999, 36–43.

Lewis, Anthony

Joseph Anthony Lewis (1927–), also known as Tony Lewis, is a Pulitzer Prize–winning journalist, author, and lecturer. He attended Harvard, graduating in 1948, and while there edited the *Harvard Crimson.* He began his career working as a deskman, processing and copyediting news items written by other reporters for the Sunday *New York Times* from 1948 to 1952. In 1952 he went to work for the Democratic National Committee and joined the staff of the *Washington Daily News.* Lewis then returned to the *New York Times,* reporting from its Washington, D.C., bureau from 1955 to 1964, from London as bureau chief from 1965 to 1972, and as a columnist from 1969 to 2001.

Lewis won his first Pulitzer Prize in 1955 for a series of articles on the federal government's loyalty security program and the dismissal of a naval employee as a result of it. Lewis was selected as a Nieman fellow and studied at Harvard Law School during 1956–1957. He won a second Pulitzer Prize in 1963 for his coverage of the Supreme Court. Lewis wrote several books stemming from his observations and analysis of Court decisions, the first being *The Supreme Court: Process and Change* (1963). In *Gideon's Trumpet* (1964), he addressed the landmark case of *Gideon v. Wainwright* (1963), in which Florida petty thief Clarence Earl Gideon won the right to legal counsel and guaranteed representation for indigent defendants. *Portrait of a Decade: The Second American Revolution* (1964) concerns developments in U.S. civil rights and race relations in the postwar years. *The Supreme Court and How It Works: The Story of the Gideon Case* (1966), as the title suggests, offers Lewis's insight into the operations of the Court and how it reached its decision in *Gideon. Make No Law: The Sullivan Case and the First Amendment* (1991) chronicles and analyzes the Warren Court's landmark decision in *New York Times v. Sullivan* (1964), which expanded the freedom of the press and substantially raised the standard for libel involving public officials. Lewis is the editor of *Written into History: Pulitzer Prize Reporting of the Twentieth Century from the New York Times* (2001), a compendium of award-winning writing.

Lewis taught on the Constitution, the law, and the press at Harvard from 1974 to 1989 and was a visiting lecturer at universities in Arizona, California, Illinois, and Oregon. In 1983 he received the James Madison Visiting Professorship of First Amendment Issues at Columbia University.

REFERENCES

"Conversations/The Long View: 50 Years of Covering War, Looking for Peace, and Honoring Law." *New York Times,* December 16, 2001, sec. 4, p. 9.

"Lewis's Trumpet." *Newsweek,* August 24, 1964, 53.

Wenner, Kathryn. "Long Run." *American Journalism Review,* February 2002, 8.

Libel law

Libel is the communication of a false or misleading statement concerning a person that subjects them to public hatred, contempt, ridicule, or financial injury. Libel and slander are types of defamation, which consists of false statements that cause injury to a living person's name or reputation. One cannot defame the dead. Libel is distinguished from slander by its more permanent form of communication, such as in writing, painting, voice recording, or film. A false statement made in a television or radio broadcast is also treated as libel because of its dissemination to potentially large groups of people. Truth is an absolute defense to all claims of defamation. The person who originally makes a libelous statement is liable for any re-publication of the statement if it is foreseeable that the false statement will be repeated by someone else. People who repeat the libelous statement are also held liable.

Where defamatory statements involve public officials, public figures, and matters of public concern, plaintiffs have the additional burden of proving fault and falsity elements because defendants' statements are afforded certain constitutional protections under the First Amendment freedom of speech and press. Public officials are such higher-ranking government employees as mayors and judges, who are substantially responsible for governmental affairs. Public figures are such people as heads of major corporations, celebrities, and television personalities who wield great power and are heavily involved in societal affairs or have deliberately thrust themselves into public controversies. Matters of public concern are issues that interest or affect the community or general public.

Under the fault or "actual malice" requirement, plaintiffs must prove that defendants made the defamatory statements intentionally, recklessly, or negligently. Under the falsity requirement, plaintiffs must prove that the statements are false. In *New York Times v. Sullivan* (1964), the U.S. Supreme Court held that in addition to the general elements of libel, public officials must additionally meet the constitutional requirement of proving that the defamatory statement was made with "actual malice." This standard requires that the statement be made with the knowledge that it is false or made with reckless disregard for the truth, but not necessarily that it is made with hatred, ill will, or a desire to injure. In *Gertz v. Robert Welch, Inc.* (1974), the Court extended the public officials burden of proof to those who have voluntarily put themselves in the public's eye, requiring such public figures to prove "actual malice" as well, in part because they have more access to the media to rebut allegations against them. The First Amendment actual malice standard, however, is not required where the plaintiff is a private figure.

To prevail in a defamation suit requires injury to plaintiff's reputation. This requirement varies depending on whether the suit is based on libel *per se* or libel *per quod*. In ordinary libel per se cases, because of the more permanent nature of the explicitly defamatory statement and the corresponding extensive damage to the plaintiff's reputation, the plaintiff is not required to prove damage to his reputation in order to collect a damage award. In libel per quod cases, however, where the defamatory statement is libelous only when additional surrounding facts or circumstances are known, the plaintiff must prove that the additional facts or circumstances were known.

See also *Hustler v. Falwell (1988); New York Times v. Sullivan (1964)*.

REFERENCES

Amponsah, Peter Nkrumah. *Libel Law, Political Criticism, and Defamation of Public Figures: The United States, Europe, and Australia.* New York: LFB Scholarly Publishing, 2004.

Dry, Murray. *Civil Peace and the Quest for Truth: The First Amendment Freedoms in Political Philosophy and American Constitutionalism.* Lanham, Md.: Lexington Books, 2004.

Lawhorne, Clifton O. *Defamation and Public Officials: The Evolving Law of Libel.* Carbondale: Southern Illinois University Press, 1971.

Liddy, G. Gordon

George Gordon Battle Liddy (1930–), a syndicated radio host, first came to prominence in 1972, when it became clear that he had led a break-in at the headquarters of the Democratic National Committee in the Watergate complex in Washington, D.C. The burglary, eventually traced back to the White House, evolved into the Watergate scandal that led to the resignation of President Richard M. Nixon in August 1974.

After serving two years in the army during the Korean War, Liddy obtained a law degree from Fordham University in 1957 and joined the Federal Bureau of Investigation as a special agent that same year. He resigned from the agency in 1962 to practice international law in New York. Liddy then served as a prosecutor, ran unsuccessfully for Congress in 1968, and campaigned for the Nixon-Agnew Republican ticket in 1968. He joined the Nixon administration as special assistant to the secretary of the Treasury and in 1971 transferred to the White House as staff assistant to the president.

In 1972 Liddy resigned his White House position to work on Nixon's reelection campaign. Using a group code named the "plumbers," he organized the 1971 burglary of the office of Daniel Ellsberg's psychiatrist. Ellsberg was the analyst at the Central Intelligence Agency who leaked the Pentagon Papers; the burglary was intended to find embarrassing evidence to discredit Ellsberg. Liddy was a central planner of the so-called "third-rate burglary" at the DNC offices. For his role in Watergate and his refusal to implicate his co-conspirators, Liddy was convicted of burglary, conspiracy in the Ellsberg case, and contempt of court. He served five years of a twenty-year prison sentence beginning in 1974. No other conspirator received such a harsh punishment. President Jimmy Carter released him "in the interest of justice" in 1979.

After prison, Liddy became a popular speaker on college campuses, sometimes engaging in debates with well-known figures from the Left. He went on to host the *G. Gordon Liddy Show,* a nationally syndicated radio program, contribute commentary to newspapers and periodicals, and appear in movies and on assorted television programs. Liddy is the author of several books, including *When I Was a Kid, This Was a Free Country* (2002).

REFERENCE

Liddy, G. Gordon. *Will: The Autobiography of G. Gordon Liddy.* New York: St. Martin's Press, 1997.

Limbaugh, Rush

Rush Hudson Limbaugh III (1951–) is a political commentator, author, and radio and television broadcaster. He developed a passion for broadcasting in 1967, starting at his hometown radio station in Cape Girardeau, Missouri. After dropping out of college, Limbaugh began his professional career at KQV radio in Pittsburgh as a disk jockey. After being fired for controversial and inflammatory commentary, he worked as the director of group ticket sales in the box office of the Kansas City Royals baseball franchise from 1979 until landing another radio job as a political commentator

for KMBZ in Kansas City in 1983. He was again fired for inflammatory speech.

KFBK radio in Sacramento, California, hired Limbaugh in 1984 to replace the often-offensive Morton Downey Jr. Within a year, Limbaugh had become the most-listened-to talk radio host in the Sacramento area. Limbaugh signed a two-year contract with EFM Media Management in New York City in 1988 to enter the national market. By 1993 the nationally syndicated *Rush Limbaugh Show* was being broadcast by more than 600 radio stations.

As an unabashed conservative broadcaster, Limbaugh positioned himself as the vanguard against the liberal bias he proclaimed to exist in the media, especially in television and newspaper reporting: "I am equal time," he asserted. He is largely credited with the emergence of AM talk radio programming and with being the public voice of the conservative movement. As a prominent conservative voice, Limbaugh has attracted considerable attention from liberals, including a 1994 Fairness and Accuracy in Reporting (FAIR) report alleging errors in Limbaugh's statements. Comedian and political satirist Al Franken targeted him and other conservatives in *Rush Limbaugh Is a Big Fat Idiot and Other Observations* (1996).

In 2001 Limbaugh became the highest-paid radio personality in history when he signed an eight-year, $250 million contract with Premiere Radio Networks, a subsidiary of Clear Channel Communications. That same year, he acknowledged having near-total hearing loss—possibly because of his declared abuse of powerful prescription pain medications—and underwent cochlear implant surgery that partially restored his hearing. In 2003, while working as an ESPN commentator on *NFL Countdown,* Limbaugh sparked considerable controversy with race-based remarks about the performance of a quarterback. The event led to his resignation and a week later to his admission of being addicted to painkillers, which led to his being investigated for prescription fraud. In May 2006, he agreed to a deal that would dismiss the charge if he tested free of drugs for eighteen months.

Limbaugh is the author of *The Way Things Ought to Be* (1992) and *See, I Told You So* (1993).

REFERENCES

Arkush, Michael. *Rush!* New York: Avon Books, 1993.

Colford, Paul D. *The Rush Limbaugh Story: Talent on Loan from God. An Unauthorized Biography.* New York: St. Martin's Press, 1993.

Green, Joshua. "The Air America Plan." *Atlantic Monthly,* April 2005, 32–35 .

King, D. Howard, and Geoffrey Morris. *Rush to Us.* New York: Windsor Publishing, 1994.

Seib, Philip M., and Mike Towle, ed. *Rush Hour: Talk Radio, Politics, and the Rise of Rush Limbaugh.* Ottawa: Summit Publishing Group, 1993.

Lippmann, Walter

Walter Lippmann (1889–1974) was an influential journalist, author, political commentator, editor, and essayist. He began developing his political thought and career in journalism at Harvard University, where he co-founded the Harvard Socialist Club and edited the *Harvard Monthly.* He became a secretary for and apprentice to the editor and journalist Lincoln Steffens in 1911 and, like his mentor, supported Theodore Roosevelt and the Progressive Party in the 1912 presidential election. Lippmann's first book, *A Preface to Politics* (1913), was well received, christening his emergence on the stage of political commentary. A year later, he joined Herbert Croly and Walter Weyl in founding the *New Republic,* the political weekly.

In *Drift and Mastery* (1914), Lippmann rejected his earlier embrace of socialism in presenting a brilliant analysis of society, power, and humanism. He became an ardent supporter of Woodrow Wilson and the Democratic Party in the 1916 elections, served during World War I as assistant secretary of war under Newton Baker, and worked closely with Wilson and Col. Edward House in the drafting of the Fourteen Points. Lippmann was a delegate to the Paris Peace Conference in 1919 and helped draft the Covenant of the League of Nations. He, however, was so appalled by the severity of the retribution imposed on Germany by the Treaty of Versailles that he distanced himself from Wilson and argued against ratification of the treaty and U.S. participation in the league.

In 1920 Lippmann left the *New Republic* to join the *New York World,* the newspaper founded by Joseph Pulitzer. He was editorial page editor from 1923 to 1929 and became the newspaper's editor in 1929 until it folded in 1931. From there he moved to the *New York Herald Tribune,* wrote "Today and Tomorrow," a nationally syndicated column, for the next thirty years, won two Pulitzer Prizes, and became one of the most influential journalists in the United States during the turbulent mid-century.

Lippmann's pragmatic style and view of politics resonated with his readers and led him to support six Republican and seven Democratic presidential candidates during his professional life. He was an early supporter of Franklin D. Roosevelt and the New Deal and advocated a pragmatic liberalism; he, however, would ultimately condemn collectivism in *An Inquiry into the Principles of the Good Society* (1937). After World War II, Lippmann returned to the liberal views of his youth and at different times upset leaders of both major political parties by opposing the Korean War, the activities of Sen. Joseph McCarthy, and the Vietnam War.

Lippmann received a Pulitzer Prize citation in 1958 for his news analysis as demonstrated by *U.S. War Aims* (1944), *The Cold War* (1947), *Isolation and Alliances* (1952), and *Western Unity and the Common Market* (1962). Two of his more controversial books, *Public Opinion* (1922) and *The Phantom Public* (1925), written early in his career, questioned the public's ability to evaluate complex issues and expressed his doubts about the development of a true democracy in a complex, modern society. He also wrote *A Preface to Morals* (1929) and *Essays in the Public Philosophy* (1955). Lippmann's newspaper column moved to the *Washington Post* in 1961 until he ceased writing a regular contribution in 1967. Regarded as the first real political pundit, Lippmann significantly influenced public opinion and political thought.

REFERENCES

Luskin, John. *Lippmann, Liberty, and the Press.* Tuscaloosa: University of Alabama Press, 1972.

Riccio, Barry Daniel. *Walter Lippmann: Odyssey of a Liberal.* New Brunswick, N.J.: Transaction Publishers, 1994.

Steel, Ronald. *Walter Lippmann and the American Century.* Boston: Little, Brown, 1980.

Listservs

See *New media*

Los Angeles Times

The *Los Angeles Times* debuted as a publication of the Mirror Printing Book Bindery in 1881. As of 2005, it had a circulation of approximately 900,000 Monday through Saturday and more than 1,000,000 on Sunday. The *Times'* reputation as a major daily is evidenced by the more than thirty Pulitzer Prizes won by the paper and its staff since 1942 in fields including editorial cartooning, international reporting, and criticism. It received widespread acclaim for its in-depth coverage of the Los Angeles riots in 1992. Such accolades were not always the case.

Under the dominance of the Chandler family, the paper was run primarily as a family business that promoted policies and politicians the Chandlers favored, especially property rights, development, and conservative Republicans. The *Times* proved instrumental in the rise of Richard M. Nixon as a prominent state and national politician in the 1940s and 1950s. "Prodigal son" Otis Chandler, however, vowed to make the *Times* a great newspaper by greatly increasing its news budget, hiring good reporters, and promoting balanced, professional journalism. It was so even-handed in covering the 1962 governor's race between Nixon and Democrat Pat Brown that Nixon vowed to quit politics after facing its reporters' tough questioning. The *Times'* prestige and circulation grew as a result, in tandem with Los Angeles.

After Otis Chandler's retirement, his cousins attempted to steer the paper back toward its pro-business and conservative past. Their efforts led to turmoil and reductions in news budgets and staff. The paper went through a series of editors. In 1999 the *Times* made a deal to share profits from a special feature section on the new Staples Center with the arena and otherwise encouraged policies that blurred lines between its advertising and news divisions. The resulting controversy led to resignations and staff infighting. Circulation also suffered during this period. In 2000 the Tribune Company purchased Times-Mirror, owner of the *Times*. The new management set out to revive the *Times'* journalistic quality, bringing in Dean Baquet, formerly of the *New York Times,* as editor.

REFERENCES

Diehl, Digby. *Front Page: 100 Years of the Los Angeles Times.* New York: H. N. Abrams, 1981.
Gottlieg, Robert, and Irene Wolt. *Thinking Big: The Story of the* Los Angeles Times, *Its Publishers, and Their Influence on Southern California.* New York: G. P. Putnam's Sons, 1977.
The Los Angeles Times, www.latimes.com.
Meyerson, Harold. "The Life and Times of Otis Chandler." *Washington Post,* March 1, 2006, A17.

Luce, Henry R.

Henry Robinson Luce (1898–1967), an editor and magazine publisher, built the Time Inc. communications empire. He was born in Tengchow, China, the son of a Presbyterian missionary and called "Harry." Luce began his career in journalism as a reporter on the *Chicago Daily News* and the *Baltimore News* during 1921–1922 after graduating from Yale and Oxford Universities. With his Yale classmate Briton Hadden, Luce in 1923 founded *Time,* the weekly news magazine, the first of its kind written in a succinct, brisk style. Thus began a communications empire that would carry the name of its vanguard magazine.

After Hadden's premature death in 1929, Luce became editor in chief of *Time,* a position he held until 1964. He also launched the upscale business magazine *Fortune* in 1930 in the face of the Great Depression, acquired *Architectural Digest* in 1932, and began *Life* in 1936, ushering in the era of photojournalism. Luce saw his magazines in terms relative to their place in American society: "I always thought it was the business of *Time* to make enemies and the business of *Life* to make friends." During World War II, Time Inc. produced the "March of Time" newsreels providing war-related information to movie audiences. Luce developed *Sports Illustrated* in 1954 to expand his reach into the burgeoning domain of athletics.

During his long professional life, Luce built a magazine export business and Time-Life Books, a publishing company that incorporated such innovative practices as direct mail-order bookselling. His magazines drove innovations in printing technology of the day. Though never impressed or comfortable with the broadcast media of television and radio, he eventually though reluctantly added broadcasting stations to his communications holdings. Television doomed *Life,* a magazine that like its contemporary *Look* relied on images more than words.

Luce attempted to use his publications to educate the American public, whom he viewed as poorly informed on national and international affairs. He was an active editor of his magazines, which reflected his life-long conservative Republican views, anticommunism, internationalism, and singular focus on nationalist China (Taiwan), a position that often generated criticism because of its unrepentant bias. In the face of protests that *Time* should not claim to be a news magazine given that the views expressed were predominantly Luce's, he replied, "Well, I invented the idea, so I guess I can call it anything I like."

Luce was considered the most influential magazine publisher since S. S. McClure, and he used his clout to gain access to the circles of political power. His second wife was the journalist and playwright Clare Boothe Luce. Luce wrote *The American Century* (1941), *The Ethical Problems Facing America* (1946), *Bread and Liberty* (1946), *The Dangerous Age of Abundance* (1959), and *The Ideas of Henry Luce* (1969), published posthumously and edited by John K. Jessup.

REFERENCES

Halberstam, David. *The Powers That Be.* New York: Knopf, 1979.

Kobler, John. *Luce: His Time, Life, and Fortune.* Garden City, N.Y.: Doubleday, 1968.

Swanberg, W. A. *Luce and His Empire.* New York: Charles Scribner's Sons, 1972.

M

Magazines

Magazines are soft-cover publications usually printed in color and on glossy paper and typically published weekly, monthly, or quarterly with the purpose of informing or entertaining. They traditionally focus on a particular subject or are aimed at a specific demographic. Magazines serve as important vehicles for the diverse political, religious, and social perspectives and ideas of various groups.

Although general interest magazines exist, most concentrate on specific issues, such as current events, science, technology, sports, health, fashion, business, and women's issues. Some of the larger newspapers, such as the *New York Times* and the *Washington Post,* publish magazines that they include as supplements in their Sunday editions and feature more detailed, special-interest stories than would be found in a standard newspaper. While some magazine articles may be written by specialists, many do not require subject expertise.

Magazines differ from scientific or academic journals in that although journals also carry articles that explore particular topics in great detail, journal articles are written by scholars in particular academic fields, usually peer reviewed, and geared toward an audience of scholars and professionals. Academic journals also tend to be published less frequently and are financed almost exclusively through subscriptions, rather than the sale of advertising space. In contrast, some magazines, such as *People* or *US Weekly,* are intended to reach the broadest possible audience and focus on such topics as celebrity gossip, which is a trait often associated with tabloid publications. Unlike tabloids, however, magazines forego sensationalist journalism.

Popular news magazines, such as *Time, Newsweek,* and *U.S. News & World Report,* are published weekly and typically feature one major news story per issue that covers a topic in greater depth than do the other stories. These magazines often choose a prominent issue in the news for this central piece of reporting. Consumer magazines run the gamut from general-interest publications, such as *Reader's Digest,* to magazines tailored to a specific demographic, such as *Esquire, Cosmopolitan,* or *Parents;* and to specialized interests, such as *Car and Driver.* There is a magazine published for nearly every interest imaginable, for instance hunting, computers, hair, weddings, music, science fiction, tennis, and travel.

Business magazines, for example, *Business 2.0, DIRECT Magazine,* and *Forbes,* represent another group of special focus publications. They cover a range of topics, from general business and finance to sector- or industry-specific reporting. Some narrowly focused business magazines even practice "controlled circulation," whereby readers who meet certain criteria are provided free subscriptions. This guarantees advertisers that their ads will be read by their target relevant audience.

Political magazines constitute a substantial portion of the types of magazines published in the United States. Political opinion publications can be found that represent all degrees of the political spectrum, from the far Left to the far Right and points in between. A few examples are illustrative. *Foreign Policy,* founded in 1970 by Samuel Huntington, is a prominent bimonthly political magazine covering topics related to global politics and economics. Among politically oriented magazines, however, a more common style of publication is that which adopts, or even promotes, a particular political stance. The *International Socialist Review* and *Monthly Review* are two examples of magazines that cover events and issues as varied as labor struggles, U.S. foreign policy, gender discrimination, and Latin American economics, all from a socialist perspective. *Ms.,* currently owned by the Feminist Majority Foundation, is a politically motivated magazine that speaks to a particular demographic, considering itself the voice of the women's movement in the United States since its founding in 1972. *Islamica,* a quarterly magazine, is by far the most widely distributed English-language magazine addressing Muslim concerns and perspectives.

Political magazines such as the *National Review* and the *New Republic* are at the forefront of conservative and liberal magazines in the United States, respectively. The *National Review,* a biweekly magazine founded by William Buckley Jr. in 1955, boasts a broad readership that at times has included such politically conservative icons as former president Ronald Reagan and former Arizona senator Barry Goldwater. On the opposite end of the political spectrum, the *New Republic,* which publishes articles in support of "new democratic" policies, has been endorsed by many liberal politicians, including former president Bill Clinton and Connecticut senator Joseph Lieberman. Both magazines are cited by liberal and conservative commentators in the media for either accolades or criticism.

The history of magazines in the United States dates to the late nineteenth century, when they were purely an upper-class luxury. Because of the high cost of publication and printing, only the affluent, who also typically were the well educated, could afford to buy magazines. Most of the American populace only had access to newspapers and tabloids until the early 1880s. Two changes changed this dynamic: First, in 1879 Congress created second-class mail, which allowed for the wide circulation of materials at a significantly lower cost than first-class mail. Second, the price of magazines decreased dramatically when the publisher S. S. McClure lowered the price of his famous general-interest *McClure's Magazine* to 15 cents an issue and publisher Frank Munsey, McClure's primary rival, responded by lowering the price of *Munsey's Magazine* to 10 cents an issue. This prompted a nationwide price war in the magazine industry and ended the era of an elite-only readership of magazines.

McClure's Magazine and *Munsey's Magazine* quickly became popular and circulated widely. They bore little resemblance to the magazines on retailers' shelves today. The technology of the time limited the number of images to a few, and headlines were small; in fact, magazines at the turn of the century closely approximated soft-cover books. As technology advanced, however, publications gradually incorporated more graphics. Pictures, etched from images carved into wood or metal blocks, were used increasingly frequently to the point that publishers dispatched artists to sketch a news event as photographers are sent on assignment today.

The quality of images in magazines increased at the same time that printing costs decreased, making it possible for magazines to earn money by selling advertising space. Advertisements in magazines, while limited at first, proved to be lucrative, and their gradual inclusion fundamentally altered the magazine industry. No longer was competition between magazines based exclusively on the sale of information to its readers; instead, magazines competed for the attention of advertisers. In addition, the revenue from ads permitted publishers to further lower the prices of their magazines, including to levels below the cost of production. These developments coincided with the expansion of railroads and telecommunications technology, setting the stage for today's far-reaching system of mass media.

Fashion magazines in the 1920s were the first to employ the familiar "slick" look that magazines have today, but that format did not become common until advertisers began to adopt it for its attention-grabbing value in the 1950s. The years between the 1920s and 1950s proved to be formative ones in terms of style: images appeared increasingly regularly in magazines and more catchy full-page images (or "bleeds") gradually pushed out conventional margins, resulting in the abandonment of the book-like style of earlier magazines. Publishers also began to "jump the gutter," meaning to run headlines spanning the two pages of a magazine's spread.

As the media and communications industries have expanded globally, magazines have become important vehicles for defining and disseminating national and transnational cultures and identities, making the influence of magazines on domestic as well as international politics undeniable. Not only are magazines published in one country distributed in others, but some magazines publish each edition in a number of languages. In addition to responding to the demand for voices from a variety of political and social perspectives, magazines also act as purveyors of political ideas. The prevalence of magazines in the United States that cater to extreme left-wing and ultra-right-wing perspectives are a mixed blessing: on the one hand these magazines provide readers access to the types of news in which they have an interest, as well as to opinions with which they likely agree; on the other hand, however, such publications can serve to widen the political divide between liberal or conservative sympathies. Either way, because the availability of magazines expanded so greatly at the turn of the twentieth century and again at the end of the century, in part because of the Internet, magazines have become a profoundly influential medium of communications in the political and cultural realms in the United States and abroad.

REFERENCES

Bagdikian, Ben H. *The New Media Monopoly.* Boston, Mass.: Beacon Press, 2004.

Chomsky, Noam. *Media Control: The Spectacular Achievements of Propaganda* 2nd ed. New York: Seven Stories Press, 2002.

De Zengotita, Thomas. *Mediated: How the Media Shapes Your World and the Way You Live in It.* New York: Bloomsbury Publishing, 2005.

McChesney, Robert W. *The Problem of the Media: U.S. Communication Politics in the Twenty-first Century.* New York: Monthly Review Press, 2004.

Mott, Frank L. *A History of American Magazines.* Vol. 3. Cambridge, Mass.: Harvard University Press, 1960.

Starr, Paul. *The Creation of the Media: Political Origins of Modern Communications.* New York: Basic Books, 2004.

Manipulation

See *News management; Propaganda.*

Matalin, Mary

Mary Joe Matalin (1953–), a political consultant and commentator, began her career in grassroots politics before making her way to Washington, D.C. In the nation's capital, she worked for the Republican National Committee, rising to become chief of staff to Chairman Lee Atwater in 1985 and then serving as deputy campaign manager for political operations for President George H. W. Bush's 1992 reelection campaign. Matalin's relationship with James Carville, the chief campaign strategist for the Clinton-Gore campaign in 1992, received much publicity and became the subject of considerable speculation concerning bedroom cross-talk between the strategists. They eventually married.

In 1993 Matalin became a political commentator, hosting her own radio show on CBS and co-hosting CNBC's *Equal Time* and CNN's *Crossfire* in 1999. Matalin later served as counselor to Vice President Dick Cheney and assistant to President George W. Bush. She has written for various magazines and newspapers, including *Cosmopolitan, Newsweek,* and the *Los Angeles Times.*

See also *Carville, James.*

REFERENCE

Matalin, Mary, and James Carville. *All's Fair: Love, War, and Running for President.* New York: Random House Value Publishing, 1995.

Republican political consultant Mary Matalin, pictured here with Democratic strategist James Carville, who is also her husband, has served as an assistant to President George W. Bush and counselor to Vice President Dick Cheney. In addition, she has hosted a number of radio and television programs.

McCarthy, Joseph

In the aftermath of World War II, Joseph Raymond McCarthy (1908–1957) used his position as a U.S. senator and the accessibility of the media to publicly pursue alleged communists, creating in the process an atmosphere of fear and distrust amongst the public. He began his career as a lawyer in his native Wisconsin, was elected a circuit court judge in 1939, and served as a marine in World War II from 1942 to 1945. McCarthy was elected to the U.S. Senate in 1946 and reelected in 1952. In a 1950 speech in Wheeling, West Virginia, he dramatically held up a piece of paper that he claimed contained a list of 205 known communists then working in the State Department, giving voice to the "red scare," as the country feared the rise of communism abroad and at home. As chairman of the Committee on Government Operations and its Permanent Subcommittee on Investigations, McCarthy used the media, and especially the burgeoning television news, in making wild accusations with little substance. He coerced witnesses to expose or condemn colleagues. Resentment over McCarthy's methods mounted, but few publicly objected.

The public witnessed his tactics in the first televised Senate hearings in January 1954 in which McCarthy confronted Secretary of the Army Robert Stevens, attacking him for allegedly covering up espionage in the service, and accused and intimidated many others. Two months later on *See It Now*, broadcast journalist Edward R. Murrow became the most prominent voice to take on McCarthy for his abusive methods, helping turn the tide against the senator. In December 1954, by a vote of 65-22, the Senate censured McCarthy for behavior "contrary to senatorial traditions." In some respects, the media made and unmade McCarthy.

See also *Murrow, Edward R.*

REFERENCES

Griffith, Robert. *The Politics of Fear: Joseph R. McCarthy and the Senate.* Lexington: University of Kentucky Press, 1970.

Oshinsky, David M. *A Conspiracy So Immense: The World of Joseph McCarthy.* New York: Free Press, 1983.

Republican senator Joseph McCarthy of Wisconsin aggressively used the media to exploit the "red scare." He gained notoriety after a 1950 speech in which he produced a list of allegedly communist State Department employees. In 1954, in the nation's first televised congressional hearings, he interrogated and intimidated scores of people accused of being communist sympathizers. McCarthy acted virtually without reproach from critics, who feared similar accusations being levied against them.

McClellan, Scott

Scott McClellan (1968–) was the second White House press secretary for George W. Bush as well as a presidential assistant. He replaced Ari Fleischer as press secretary in July 2003. Prior to his White House experience, McClellan served as chief of staff for a Texas state senator. He then worked for Bush as deputy communications director while Bush was governor and later became the press secretary for the Bush-Cheney campaign in 2000. McClellan, a member of a Texas political family, had managed the campaigns of his mother, Texas comptroller Carol Keeton Strayhorn, in three of her elections. As Bush's press secretary McClellan became known for his unrelenting "on message" responses and non-responses to reporters' queries. He announced his resignation on April 19, 2006.

See also *Press secretaries.*

REFERENCES

Leibovich, Mark. "Unanswer Man." *Washington Post,* December 22, 2005, C1.

Wolff, Michael. "Words Fail Him." *Vanity Fair,* April 2006, http://www.vanityfair.com/features/general/060404fege01.

McClure, S. S.

Samuel Sidney McClure (1857–1949)—editor, publisher, and author—popularized magazines in the United States and promoted muckraking, an investigative style of journalism that continues to influence the media in the twenty-first century. Born in Ireland, McClure emigrated to the United States with his mother in 1866, two years after the death of his father. He worked his way through high school and from 1874 to 1877 attended Knox College, in Illinois, where he edited the *Knox Student*. McClure began his professional journalism career editing the *Wheelman* during 1882–1883. In 1884 he formed the McClure Syndicate, the first newspaper syndicate in the United States.

In 1893 McClure founded *McClure's Magazine,* spawning the so-called golden age of magazines. It was as the magazine's editor that McClure introduced muckraking in 1903. The first such articles published included those by Lincoln Steffens on corruption in U.S. cities, an installment of Ida Tarbell's exposé on Standard Oil, and a contribution by Ray Stannard Baker on labor union violence. McClure also joined Frank Doubleday in a book-publishing firm from 1897 to 1899. In 1906, at the height of *McClure's Magazine's* power, the core of McClure's writing staff split with him, largely over some of McClure's proclivities; the split began the magazine's slow decline. McClure became co-owner of *The Evening Mail* in 1915 and ten years later sold a diminished *McClure's Magazine* to William Randolph Hearst. The magazine ceased publication in 1929.

McClure led a more subdued and withdrawn life in his later years. He was awarded the Order of Merit of the National Institute of Arts and Letters in 1944. McClure wrote numerous articles and books, including *Obstacles to Peace* (1917), *The Achievements of Liberty* (1935), and *What Freedom Means to Man* (1938).

See also *Hearst, William Randolph; Muckraking; Steffens, Lincoln.*

REFERENCES

Cather, Willa. *The Autobiography of S. S. McClure.* Lincoln: University of Nebraska Press, 1997.
Lyon, Peter. *Success Story: The Life and Times of S. S. McClure.* New York: Scribner, 1963.
Muelder, Hermann R. *Missionaries and Muckrakers: The First Hundred Years of Knox College.* Urbana: University of Illinois Press, 1984.
McClure, S. S. *My Autobiography.* New York: Frederick A. Stokes Company, 1914.
Wilson, Harold S. *McClure's Magazine and the Muckrakers.* Princeton, N.J.: Princeton University Press, 1970.

McCurry, Mike

Michael D. McCurry (1954–) served as press secretary for President Bill Clinton from 1995 until 1998. As the president's representative to the press, McCurry handled many of the questions regarding the Monica Lewinsky scandal, the Paula Jones case, and the president's subsequent impeachment.

McCurry introduced a number of new features to the White House press office, including live television broadcasts of the daily press briefings. He proved to be popular with the Washington press corps and is largely credited with improving Clinton's relationship with reporters. McCurry's style, a combination of deflection and a quick wit, was influenced by his previous experience working for New Jersey senator Harrison Williams, who was convicted in the 1980s Abscam scandal. McCurry also worked for senators Daniel Patrick Moynihan of New York and Bob Kerry of Nebraska and had been the spokesperson for the Democratic National Committee.

See also *Press secretaries.*

REFERENCES

Kurtz, Howard. *Spin Cycle: Inside the Clinton Propaganda Machine.* New York: Free Press, 1998.
Purdum, Todd S. "Man in the News: Michael Demaree McCurry." *New York Times,* January 5, 1995.

McGrory, Mary

Mary McGrory (1918–2004), a journalist known for her provocative, distinctive, and often irreverent political commentary, reported on many of the biggest political stories of the twentieth century. She began her professional career as a secretary at Houghton–Mifflin in 1941 and a few years later, in 1947, entered the newspaper business as a secretary for the *Washington Star–News,* where she began her writing career. She occasionally wrote book reviews for the *Star* before debuting as a reporter covering the 1954 Army–McCarthy hearings. Impressed with McGrory's writing, *Star* editor Newbold Noyes asked her to pen a periodic column, which entered national syndication in 1960.

McGrory touched millions with her words following John F. Kennedy's assassination in 1963 and was respected for her no-nonsense style as a political reporter on the Vietnam War and the 1968 presidential election, her Pulitzer Prize

–winning commentary in 1974 on the Watergate scandal, and her perspective on the human dimension of the 1979 Three Mile Island nuclear reactor accident. McGrory made the Nixon White House's "enemies list," which was a measure of her professionalism as a journalist in the face of an administration known for its intimidation tactics. When the *Star* folded in 1981, McGrory joined the *Washington Post* as a columnist.

REFERENCES

Anon. "Mary." *Newsweek,* April 1, 1968, 64.

Opinions: Mary McGrory, www.washingtonpost.com/wp-dyn/opinion/columns/mcgrorymary.

Sanborn, Sara. "Byline Mary McGrory: Choice Words for Bullies, Fatheads, and Self-Righteous Rogues." *Ms,* May 1975.

McLaughlin, John

John McLaughlin (1927–) has made careers as a presidential speechwriter, a columnist, and a broadcast commentator. McLaughlin obtained a doctorate from Columbia University and two master's degrees from Boston College. He served as a speechwriter and special assistant to Presidents Richard Nixon and Gerald Ford. McLaughlin was associate editor of *America,* a weekly opinion journal, and has taught and lectured throughout the United States and abroad. He served as Washington editor and columnist for the *National Review* from 1981 to 1989, where he wrote "From Washington Straight," a column providing the inside story on politics and world affairs.

McLaughlin created, produces, and hosts two weekly public affairs programs: *The McLaughlin Group,* the political punditry talk-show created in 1982, and *John McLaughlin's One on One,* which features in-depth interviews and has been on the air since 1984. From 1989 to 1994, McLaughlin also produced and hosted *McLaughlin,* a CNBC one-hour, nightly talk show. McLaughlin mixes his political insight with humor to illuminate leaders and issues.

See also *Pundit shows.*

REFERENCES

Alterman, Eric. *Sound and Fury: The Making of the Punditocracy.* Rev. ed. Ithaca, N.Y.: Cornell University Press, 2000.

Media and Congress

Over the years, media coverage of Congress as an institution has mirrored the relative power of the institution vis à vis the president. In the seventeenth and eighteenth centuries, Congress commanded more coverage than the president, reflecting the legislature's dominance over the executive branch. This situation prevailed until President Theodore Roosevelt began to actively court reporters and cultivate media attention in the early twentieth century. In general, today's news coverage of Congress is declining in quantity, and it usually frames Congress in a negative light.

Journalistic norms in the early years of the Republic differed greatly from those of today, and this naturally affected the relationship between Congress and the media. Congress contracted with newspapers, such as the *National Intelligencer,* to provide journals of floor proceedings. These same papers also covered the legislature for their readers. Newspapers and particular political parties were affiliated, and reporting reflected the partisan bent of the paper. Individual reporters felt no need to distance themselves from members of Congress; in fact, many augmented their meager salaries by working as clerks for individual members or committees.

The modern era of congressional-executive relations dates from World War II (1938–1945), with the consolidation of power in the presidency and the emergence of the United States as a superpower. Political scientist Mark Rozell divides news coverage of Congress since 1945 into three eras: the Era of Neglect (1945–1965), characterized by objective journalism and silence on the editorial pages although Congress enacted important reforms, including the Legislative Reorganization Act of 1946, and Sen. Joe McCarthy (R-Wis.) held hearings during the 'red scare' to expose alleged communists; the Era of Discovery (1965–1977), characterized by positive coverage and editorial assessments of an activist Congress; and the Age of Cynicism (1977–present), in which Congress is variously portrayed as a collection of arrogant incompetents, crooks, and blowhards. The government scandals of the 1970s left a lasting impression on congressional coverage.

Today Congress comes in second to the president in the competition for news coverage, and when it is covered, it is often in reaction to the president's proposals or to unfolding events. In recent years, national news organizations have in general deemphasized coverage of Washington, and this decline in political news comes almost entirely at the

Democrat Robert C. Byrd speaks during the Senate debate on Condoleezza Rice's nomination as secretary of state in January 2005. Despite coverage of Congress by such specialized media as C-SPAN, many citizens and others lament the quality of political coverage in the mainstream media.

expense of Congress. Technological issues have compounded the decline, as Congress is particularly ill-suited for the medium of television, which depends on compelling pictures to augment reporters' comments. Congress comes across as a collection of visually uninteresting "talking heads," whether engaged in committee hearings, floor debates, or an impromptu interview.

Modern journalistic norms and definitions of newsworthiness emphasize conflict over consensus and unusual events over the routine. Coverage of Congress consequently focuses on political conflict—House versus Senate, Democrats versus Republicans, and Congress versus the White House. The media appear not to consider the normal legislative process to be particularly newsworthy. In addition, legislation is frequently complex, and differences between competing versions of bills can be subtle. Summarizing legislation and nuances in bills is difficult within the format of newspaper coverage and even more so in television or radio reporting. Political conflict becomes the more interesting aspect of congressional action.

In a paradoxical twist, another reason for the poor coverage of Congress as an institution is that so much of what occurs on Capitol Hill in any given day is potentially newsworthy. The dozens of committee hearings, independent investigations, meetings with administration officials, briefings, news conferences, confirmation hearings, and floor debates all represent candidates for coverage. Yet unlike the White House and executive agencies, Congress lacks a central communications office capable of coordinating a unified message of the day, shaping news coverage, or steering reporters toward the day's most important events. The atomistic nature of the modern Congress and each chamber's jealously guarded independence do not bode well for Congress creating such an office.

The national legislature does, however, occasionally dominate media coverage. Approximately once per decade in the postwar period, congressional proceedings have taken central stage: for example, during the "Kefauver Committee" hearings on organized crime (1950s), the Watergate and Iran-contra investigations (1970s and 1980s, respectively), the testimony of law professor Anita Hill before the Senate Judiciary Committee concerned with Clarence Thomas's Supreme Court nomination (1990s), the impeachment proceedings against President Bill Clinton (1990s), and congressional hearings on various aspects of the September 11, 2001, al-Qaida attacks and the "war on terror." Another notable exception to the "disappearing Congress" is the early months of the 104th Congress (1995), when the activities of the newly elected Republican majority in the House dominated news coverage of government. In this instance, the media focused on partisan political conflict, the personal conflicts between President Clinton and Speaker Newt Gingrich (R-Ga.), and the rivalry between Republicans in the House and Republicans in the Senate. The coverage failed to analyze in detail the structural changes underway in the House or the process by which many initiatives passed.

The proliferation of new media may also have contributed to the neglect of Congress by the mainstream media. For news of the legislative branch, one can access the Cable Satellite Public Affairs Networks (C-SPAN), which offer gavel-to-gavel coverage of floor debate, such publications as *The Hill* and *Roll Call* and those Congressional Quarterly publications that specialize in congressional coverage, and more than 600 official congressional Web sites, among other outlets. Nonetheless, the waning of congressional coverage in the mainstream media concerns proponents of a well-informed citizenry. Some media scholars argued that competition from C-SPAN might improve coverage of the institution, but their predictions have not been realized.

What are the implications of media coverage that either ignores Congress or consistently places it in a negative light? First, an informed citizenry represents the cornerstone of representative government, but without an understanding of the workings of government, citizens are ill-equipped to evaluate programs and claims made by policymakers, candidates, and parties. Second, coverage in the so-called Age of Cynicism produces declining public trust of Congress. Public opinion polls consistently peg public approval of Congress at less than 50 percent, where it has dwelled for decades. Only during periods of unusual national crisis, such as immediately after the September 11 attacks, have Congress's poll numbers improved considerably.

Individual members of Congress seek coverage in their home districts and states to enhance their electoral fortunes and to communicate with their constituents. Coverage of individual members by the national media predictably varies. For example, party leaders and committee chairs are more likely to receive national attention than are junior members. Aside from those in formal positions of power, some members of Congress become sought-after because of their expertise, willingness to comment, or penchant for sound bites. Senators comprise the majority of such notables. The Senate's small size relative to the House means that individual senators wield more power than do individual House members. In addition, Senate rules allow its members to become expert on more issues than do the workings of the House. Senators therefore are available to comment on a wider variety of subjects. Also, the Senate is a breeding ground for future presidential contenders (although very few actually succeed in winning the presidency) in a way that the House is not. The media therefore provide a platform for those looking to someday run for higher office.

House norms contribute to representatives' lower profiles. For many decades, the House Democratic leadership frowned upon members actively seeking media attention. "Show horses," so called by former Speaker Sam Rayburn

(D-Tex.), were considered legislative lightweights, whereas "work horses" eschewed media attention and were attentive to their legislative responsibilities. Recent studies have found that today those House members with the most prominent media profiles are also those most active on committees. The 1980s and 1990s saw the rise of House members who sought media attention as a means of influencing legislation as well as communicating with constituents. Many of these "media entrepreneurs" became quite skilled at garnering media attention, especially in specialized venues and in Washington newspapers. These members found that their presence in the media enhanced their reputations on the Hill, creating the perception of them as "players" on issues.

Political scientists David Niven and Jeremy Zilber have compared the media coverage of African American and women members of Congress to those of their white male counterparts. They found that reporters tend to feature African American members only in stories about racial issues and women members in stories about women's issues. These stereotypes persist although African American and women members do not present themselves as only narrowly interested in issues of race or gender.

Getting coverage in the national media is not easy for the institution or its individual members. Assessments involving local, "back home" coverage are mixed. For decades, scholars believed the local media to be friendly even if the national media were hostile. According to this theory, local reporters depend on members of Congress for story ideas and therefore are likely to depict them in a favorable light. Congress certainly has outfitted itself with ample resources to generate media attention: Both chambers provide radio and television studios for members to record and edit video or audio news releases and to conduct live interviews by satellite. Most members have a press secretary or media relations person on staff, and many member Web sites allow reporters to navigate with ease.

More recent scholarship indicates that generating favorable local media coverage is more difficult than initially believed. The country is divided into 50 states, 435 congressional districts, and 210 media markets. It is the rare, fortunate member whose district coincides with the boundaries of one or two media markets. More often, districts are divided between several media markets, which often cross state lines. In addition, in urban areas such as New York City or Los Angeles, several congressional districts share one media market, so fellow members must compete for a small, local news slot. Second, growing evidence reveals that local media coverage of Congress as an institution is negative, mirroring national trends, and coverage of individual members may also be hostile.

So if media coverage is difficult to attain, and likely to be negative even at the local level, why do members even try? Reelection. Despite Web sites and franking (free postage for official business), the media remain the principal means by which senators and representatives can communicate with their constituents. Of note, even negative coverage increases political knowledge, and with increased levels of political knowledge, voters are more likely to respect officeholders even when they disagree with them. Respect and name recognition translate into votes.

The lack of congruity between congressional district or state boundaries and media markets interferes with news coverage of congressional elections as well. Senate races, of course, generate more coverage because senators represent an entire state. House races are by comparison considered less newsworthy. Challengers and incumbents alike face the same difficulties generating media attention when they are campaigning in districts incongruent with media markets. In addition, challengers have the additional difficulty of establishing themselves as credible—and therefore newsworthy—candidates. Challengers are guaranteed more or less only four news stories during the campaign: announcement, primary victory, a candidate profile in a voters guide, and defeat. Other stories require significant effort to generate. The stories that attempt to predict who will win the election are likely to cast challengers in a bad light. Thus challengers may wish to turn to advertisements, but advertising, especially on television, is expensive. By contrast, incumbents have a somewhat easier time generating news coverage during election campaigns because they can parlay official duties and achievements into favorable media coverage.

News coverage exhibits distinct patterns when one of the candidates is a woman or a racial minority, often framing them as unusual, especially when paired against a white or a male. The issues that reporters tend to highlight when covering women and minorities are those they consider particularly important to women or minorities. Women especially are rarely depicted as knowledgeable on foreign affairs, defense, or other "men's issues."

See also *Media and the presidency*.

REFERENCES

Cook, Timothy. *Making Laws and Making News: Media Strategies in the U.S. House of Representatives.* Washington, D.C.: Brookings Institution, 1989.
Herrnson, Paul S. *Congressional Elections: Campaigning at Home and in Washington.* 2d ed. Washington, D.C.: CQ Press, 1998.
Hess, Stephen. *The Ultimate Insiders: U.S. Senators in the National Media.* Washington, D.C.: Brookings Institution, 1986.
Kahn, Kim Fridkin. *The Political Consequences of Being a Woman: How Stereotypes Influence the Conduct and Consequences of Political Campaigns.* New York: Columbia University Press, 1996.
Kedrowski, Karen M. *Media Entrepreneurs and the Media Enterprise in the U.S. Congress.* Cresskill, N.J.: Hampton Press, 1996.
Niven, David, and Jeremy Zilber. "'How Does She Have Time for Kids and Congress?' Views on Gender and Media Coverage from House Offices." *Women and Politics* 23, no. 1–2 (May–June 2001): 147–165.
Ritchie, Donald A. *Press Gallery: Congress and the Washington Correspondents.* Cambridge, Mass.: Harvard University Press, 1991.
Rozell, Mark J. *In Contempt of Congress: Postwar Press Coverage on Capitol Hill.* Westport, Conn.: Praeger Publishers, 1996.
Terkildson, Nayda, and David F. Damore. "The Dynamics of Racialized Media Coverage in Congressional Elections." *Journal of Politics* 61, no. 3 (August 1999): 680–699.
Vinson, Danielle. *Local Media Coverage of Congress and Its Members: Through Local Eyes.* Cresskill, N.J.: Hampton Press, 2003.
Zilber, Jeremy, and David Niven. *Racialized Coverage of Congress: The News in Black and White.* Westport, Conn.: Praeger Publishers, 2000.

Media and the courts

The media and the courts have had a strained relationship throughout history. Almost from the beginning, the courts and media have fought an ongoing battle, with the media struggling to maintain the flow of information to the public, and the courts attempting to fulfill their duty in the constitutional system, part of which is to protect individual and societal rights. These two very different objectives have played roles in shaping the structure of media organizations and the government.

The way the media cover the courts greatly affects the information disseminated to the public, from the cases it chooses to showcase to analyzing and interpreting complicated court decisions. The media create news about the courts through coverage of court rulings and activities, and the courts affect the way the media cover them through judicial decisions about freedom of the press. Both influence media portrayals of the judicial branch.

The courts have often sided with the media on First Amendment issues. Here Daniel Ellsberg addresses reporters in Los Angeles in 1973 about the Pentagon Papers trial. Ellsberg, while doing work for the Defense Department, leaked classified government documents to the New York Times *detailing U.S. military involvement in Vietnam. The Nixon administration attempted to halt publication of the documents. The case reached the Supreme Court, which ruled in favor of publishing them.*

Although the Constitution's singling out of the press for First Amendment protections provides it a status as one of the checks on government, the media sometimes have a difficult time covering the courts because of the differing objectives of the two institutions. The courts need to make sure that each party to a case receives a fair trial or hearing and that the dignity of the judicial process is maintained. The media need information to be able to inform the public. The process or secrecy of the courts can, however, sometimes leave the media without solid facts to report. This has led to a trend in which the media, specifically broadcast outlets, rely on experts and other analysts to assess court cases even if all the facts are not available.

Reporters who cover the Supreme Court collectively form the Supreme Court press corps. They act as gatekeepers of information concerning the highest court as well as interpreters of the Court's decisions. They also differ in some ways from other reporters who cover governmental agencies in that they must be able to quickly analyze Court decisions, as soon as they are handed down, and write simply and concisely about the often complex issues they involve. Although the Supreme Court press corps is not as influential (at least directly) as other government press corps, for instance the White House press corps, it still possesses the ability to affect the public's perception of the Court and the law by how its members frame issues, decisions, and other information.

Reporters involved in covering governmental agencies usually need to be aggressive and tend to employ an adversarial or at least detached posture toward their subjects. Supreme Court reporters, on the other hand, spend a good deal of their time reading and interpreting decisions. That the Court is fairly shielded from the public can cause problems of information flow. Justices decline requests for interviews and rarely make statements about their stance on an issue or case. Exceptions include when justices make public speeches or comments in various forums and hearings for confirmation to the Court, although in recent years nominees have been coached by administrations to reveal as little as possible about their views. The legal tradition of the courts not engaging in critical public debate relegates the media as the place where debate about the law and the courts' actions must take place, which produces the strange dynamic of one of the key players remaining silent.

Reporters must straddle a fine line between providing sufficient information to laypersons without oversimplifying it. The complicated nature of the law requires that reporters covering the courts be well informed about legal issues, case law, and the law in general. The need of court reporters to interpret rulings increases the possibility that the framing of issues may favor one political perspective or another. In covering the Supreme Court and lower appellate courts, journalists must often, to a certain extent passively, transmit what the courts do and say, treatment not generally afforded other political institutions. The courts also receive less coverage than the other two branches of government.

The evolution of the visual component of the media has in the past posed problems for the relationship between the courts and the media. Media coverage generated great interest in the 1937 trial of Bruno Richard Hauptmann for the alleged kidnapping and murder of the aviator Charles Lindbergh's baby. A newsreel camera recorded events in the courtroom until a judge discovered the taping and ordered it stopped. The aura surrounding the trial was likened to a circus. In response, the American Bar Association passed Canon 35 advising a ban of cameras and broadcasts in state courts. Sketch artists were, however, allowed. The association argued that courtroom proceedings be conducted with dignity. In 1952 it recommended banning television cameras as well. This trend began to be reversed in the 1960s, with states adopting statutes allowing audiovisual and photographic recordings of procedures in certain courts.

The premiere of the Courtroom Television Network (Court TV) in 1991 marked a turning point in the media coverage of trials. The network has aired more than 700 trials since its inception. In 1996 the Judicial Conference of the United States expanded the rules governing when cameras should be allowed in federal courtrooms, stating that each of the thirteen appeals courts should decide for itself whether to allow them in its courtroom. At least ninety federal cases have been televised. The Supreme Court, however, still forbids cameras for recording its proceedings, but it sometimes issues audio recordings.

The popularity of the Internet has also posed a challenge for media and the courts. The courts have ruled in various cases that netcasts of courtroom proceedings should receive the same protection as other media. In 1999 *Florida v. Eagan* became the first case to be shown over the Internet. With visual media increasingly present in courtrooms, the public can make judgments based on what they see for themselves, though the analytical and verbal skills of reporters are still needed to explain elements of cases and case law.

The courts have influenced the way the media do their job since the founding of the Republic, especially through its interpretations of the First Amendment's freedom of the press. The issue of private versus public has always been at the forefront of this struggle, with the courts deciding to what extent information can be made available to the public. Several landmark cases have determined the path the

media have taken and have also influenced the political landscape through the media. Defense of the First Amendment's freedom of speech and press is based on the value that society places on certain rights and the value of knowledge in a democratic system. The lack of free-flowing information hinders the encouragement of diversity of opinions. Free speech is also a requisite element of informed self-government and citizen participation in political decisions. A brief look at the history of the courts and the media demonstrates that the courts value the public's right to information and underpinnings of the First Amendment. They have argued that the First Amendment is not something to be taken lightly, and their interpretations have often sided with the media and their need for access to information.

See also *Censorship; First Amendment; Fourth estate; Gag orders; Media and Congress; Media and the presidency; Shield laws.*

REFERENCES

Alexander, S. L. *Media and American Courts: A Reference Handbook.* Santa Barbara: ABC-CLIO Publishing, 2004.
Bunker, Matthew D. *Justice and the Media: Reconciling Fair Trials and a Free Press.* Mahwah, N.J.: Lawrence Erlbaum Associates, 1997.
Carter, Charlotte A. *Media in the Courts.* Williamsburg, Va.: National Center for State Courts, 1981.
Davis, Richard. *Decisions and Images: The Supreme Court and the Press.* Englewood Cliffs, N.J.: Prentice-Hall, 1994.
Epstein, Lee, ed. *Contemplating Courts.* Washington, D.C.: CQ Press, 1995.
Freedman, Warren. *Press and Media Access to the Criminal Courtroom.* New York: Quorum Books, 1988.
Giles, Robert, and Robert W. Snyder, eds. *Covering the Courts: Free Press, Fair Trials and Journalistic Performance.* New Brunswick, N.J.: Transaction Publishers, 1999.
Paletz, David, and Robert Entman. *Media, Power, Politics.* New York: Free Press, 1981.
Robertson, Stuart M. *Courts and the Media.* Toronto: Butterworths, 1981.
Woodward, Bob, and Scott Armstrong. *The Brethren: Inside the U.S. Supreme Court.* New York: Simon and Schuster, 1979.

Media and the presidency

In addition to performing traditional constitutional duties, the modern president is also expected to act as "communicator in chief" in this era of the twenty-four-hour news cycle and technological developments that have greatly increased ways to access information. Presidents and their designees regularly make public appearances to maximize White House influence on public policy, drum up and

President Bill Clinton takes a question from Terence Hunt, the White House correspondent for the Associated Press, at an East Room press conference in 1997. Presidents use the media and such press conferences to defend their actions and to bolster support for their administration's policies.

sustain public approval of the administration, and in general represent the U.S. government to the nation and the world.

Changes in the technology of news delivery have vastly increased the pressure on presidential communications strategies, but presidents have always been able to rely on their unique position as the only nationally elected office-holder (apart from their vice presidents) to speak for the nation. From the start, presidents have used what Theodore Roosevelt called "a bully pulpit" to comfort and encourage Americans and to transform the country itself. For almost as long, the news media have provided an often dissonant counterpoint to presidential policies and pronouncements.

George Washington, the first U.S. president and a national hero, inspired great respect and support among the people of the newly independent colonies. During his administrations, political parties and a partisan press were in their nascent stages and thus did not wield a great deal of power or influence. This situation quickly changed, however, as Washington's immediate successors faced a far more hostile environment. John Adams and Thomas Jefferson headed opposing political factions that were supported by partisan

newspapers, creating a dynamic that rivals the contentious politics of today. Adams and his fellow Federalist Party members, angered by newspaper (and other) attacks on Adams's administration, criminalized criticism of the government by passing the Alien and Sedition Acts of 1798. Although newspapers in the postrevolutionary era had tiny circulations—the largest papers at the start of the nineteenth century printed only a few thousand copies—they were widely read by the most influential citizens.

When Jefferson took power after the 1800 election, he pardoned editors and public officials punished under the Alien and Sedition Acts' abridgement of free speech. The press's First Amendment rights, however, continued to be contested by presidents who saw criticism of them as destructive or unpatriotic. Even Abraham Lincoln, regarded by many historians as the greatest U.S. president, sent the army to close down newspapers and jail editors who criticized his leadership during the Civil War. Subsequent presidents sought, however, to promote policies through public discourse that increasingly flowed through the news media.

As the United States' role in the world expanded during the twentieth century, so did the apparent newsworthiness of its elected leader. Some presidents resisted becoming dependent on the media, while others found ways to turn it to their advantage. The expansionist vision for the United States espoused by Theodore Roosevelt made the modern White House the center of U.S. political communication. Roosevelt appreciated that presidents did not have to be detached policymakers, following congressional machinations from afar. If presidents became "characters" in stories that reporters wanted to write and readers wanted to learn about, the media could greatly enhance presidential influence on public opinion. (In fact, Theodore Roosevelt's widely covered military activities during the Spanish–American War helped launch his national political career.) Throughout Roosevelt's years in public life, and especially when he occupied the White House, reporters regularly sought out this larger-than-life and eminently quotable figure. The unprecedented mass readership of newspapers at the turn of the twentieth century followed few stories more avidly than that of Roosevelt, the nation's newsmaker in chief. In fact, studies show that the presidency consistently attracts more coverage than do Congress or the Supreme Court.

Franklin D. Roosevelt became the first president to master the new medium of radio, which emerged as a political instrument with the 1920 presidential election. His stirring first inaugural address in 1933 and his deceptively casual and optimistic "fireside chats" throughout his presidency helped calm a troubled nation deeply wounded by the Great Depression. Roosevelt, who enjoyed huge Democratic congressional majorities, used his media and political advantages to reshape the presidency as a dominating and publicly oriented institution. While many media owners bitterly opposed the New Deal, Roosevelt was popular with reporters—with whom he met regularly—and with ordinary citizens, who could follow his presidential activities through the increasing reach of radio broadcasting and newsreels.

Two decades later, television began to enhance the ability of political leaders to engage the electorate. President Dwight Eisenhower pioneered the use of television for campaign advertising and presenting policy initiatives. His understudy proved to be even more aggressive. When charges of improperly accepting gifts threatened Richard M. Nixon's position as "Ike's" running mate in 1952, Nixon responded with the famous "Checkers" speech, a nationally televised, emotionally charged appeal in which he painted his critics as so unreasonable that they had tried to prevent his little daughter from keeping a dog—a spaniel named Checkers—that she had received as a gift.

Nixon lost the 1960 election to the media-savvy John F. Kennedy, who used the first televised presidential debates to mold his public image as a fresh face representing youthful vigor and new perspectives. Nixon did not come across well to television audiences, but he learned the lessons of the new medium, building his 1968 campaign around an aggressive media management strategy that scripted his television appearances to create the public image of a "new Nixon," more trustworthy and empathetic than the Nixon the country thought it knew. By the early twenty-first century, nearly all White House officials had come to treat public communication as part of their job, through formal public appearances or informal background sessions with reporters. Three high-ranking officials—the press secretary, the chief of staff, and the director of communications—have taken the lead in helping the president disseminate the administration's message.

The press secretary is the official spokesperson for the White House, meeting with reporters regularly, sometimes several times a day, to answer questions about the latest issues and developments. The press secretary tries to direct reporters' attention toward the stories that the administration wants covered and away from those that it wants to avoid. In addition, the press secretary attempts to frame stories in ways that benefit the administration and selectively provides information designed to advance the president's legislative and political priorities. The position is a challenging one. A press secretary risks angering the president by saying too much, and he or she may anger reporters by saying too little. If a press secretary is thought to be uninformed or dishonest, reporters lose trust in administration pronouncements, which can lead to critical news coverage. Ron Zeigler, Nixon's press secretary, learned this lesson when he changed the administration's version of events related to the Watergate scandal by telling reporters that his previous statements to them were "inoperative."

Long-term communications planning is the job of the White House chief of staff and communications director. Their strategies ideally guide the process of showcasing the president's leadership, touting the administration's accomplishments, and emphasizing presidential priorities. For example, they devise public events designed to produce emotionally powerful pictures—such as Ronald Reagan speaking at Normandy to commemorate the fortieth anniversary of D-Day or George W. Bush speaking atop the rubble of the World Trade Center after the al-Qaida attacks of September 11, 2001. Meetings with foreign leaders similarly serve to remind citizens that the president is the head of state, not merely its most powerful politician. Indeed, every public meeting and "photo opportunity" with the president is scheduled with the intent of building political capital in some fashion. Without a strong media operation, presidents risk losing control over their public image and their administration's political agenda.

The office of the presidency, however, possesses certain natural advantages in dealings with the media. Research on the news coverage of several recent presidencies reveals a consistent institutional bias in favor of the White House. The executive branch, and the president in particular, receives far more coverage than does the legislative branch. In addition, coverage of the president is usually more positive than that of Congress, regardless of the partisan composition of the two branches. Indeed, most presidents devote great care to using the executive branch's advantages regarding the media. Another such advantage is that the administration speaks with a single voice while Capitol Hill can sound like a disorganized din of 535 disparate individuals. Even a unified party in Congress represents only part of the legislative branch, while the president personifies the executive branch. For these reasons, a president commands far greater media interest than the House Speaker or the Senate majority leader. Failure to manage the media effectively deprives a modern president of one of the greatest advantages over the divided legislative branch.

White House staff carefully script presidential events to play to a president's natural advantages. Ronald Reagan, a former actor and pitchman for General Electric, was a natural at delivering televised speeches that reached the public directly, without the intervention of reporters. Bill Clinton, who possesses a quick mind and engaging demeanor, frequently used town hall–style meetings to garner news coverage for his projects. George W. Bush, who is less comfortable and less articulate in unscripted settings than his predecessor, held only about half as many press conferences during his first term as did Clinton. Instead, Bush favors more planned events, such as appearances before crowds of military personnel, whose presence emphasizes the presi-

dent's responsibilities as commander in chief. Such appeals to the "symbolic politics" of the presidency were particularly effective in the emotionally charged political environment following the September 11 attacks.

Reporters do not simply accept whatever information they are given and then pass it along to their audience. White House reporters, who include some of the most experienced journalists in the country, can be quite aggressive in their questioning of the press secretary and the president. Journalists and scholars speak of a vigorous tug-of-war between the White House and the press corps over the release of information, particularly when it comes from the president. Several studies have shown that the bulk of presidential news coverage is of a critical tone and has become more negative over time (although Congress usually fares even worse). Opinion surveys and experimental evidence have suggested that the growing negativity in media coverage of government increases public cynicism about the country's elected officials. Such cynicism can make it difficult for presidents to alter the nation's direction in a significant way to deal with long-term challenges, such as federal budget and trade deficits and the potential financial crises involving Social Security and Medicare. News coverage of government overall has fallen considerably in recent decades, as the media have shifted their focus away from Washington and toward stories involving such less explicitly political topics as celebrity activities, crime, sports, business, and the weather. Researchers have found that the decrease in the coverage of politics has reduced public interest in government and exacerbated public cynicism toward political figures of both parties.

Despite some of the difficulties faced by modern presidents, they tend to retain the upper hand over journalists, particularly concerning military matters. Reporters, elected officials, and citizens are far more dependent on the president and the administration for military news than they are for domestic policy news, where there exist many readily available sources of information that cannot be tightly controlled. Through the media during wartime, presidents can equate criticism with disloyalty in an effort to reduce negative news coverage of administration policies. Since the military clashed with a skeptical media during the Vietnam War, every battle plan has included media management. For the Iraq War, launched in 2003, the Bush administration developed a plan to "embed" reporters with military units so they could cover the unfolding war from the battlefield.

This system probably resulted in quite sympathetic coverage during the active combat period early in the war. The failure, however, to find weapons of mass destruction—the administration's primary justification for invading Iraq—led to far more skeptical coverage of Bush's Iraq policies in the aftermath of active hostilities.

The development and growth of cable news and the Internet have dramatically increased the ability of the modern president to reach citizens without having to wrestle with journalists in setting the political agenda. Presidents, press secretaries, and other top administration officials can give speeches and hold news conferences carried live on C-SPAN, CNN, and a variety of Internet home pages, including the White House's own Web site. Citizens who want more than the sound bites that dominate conventional news media coverage and prefer their news unfiltered by reporters have never had an easier time watching, hearing, and reading White House messages.

On the Internet, bloggers use Web logs to level much harsher criticism against the White House and president than is generally found in the mainstream media. Of course, some bloggers defend the president just as single-mindedly, perhaps leveling the online playing field. Traditional news organizations are, however, permitting their reporters to engage in more commentary and subjective interpretation than in the past. Although this new media environment offers a mixed blessing to the modern White House, the clearest advantage that online news has conferred thus far is an even greater focus on the president and presidential policy preferences than in earlier eras dominated in turn by newspapers, radio, and television.

See also *Media and Congress.*

REFERENCES

Bennett, W. Lance. *News: The Politics of Illusion.* 6th ed. New York: Pearson/Longman, 2005.

Campbell, Colin, and Bert A. Rockman, eds. *The George W. Bush Presidency: Appraisals and Prospects.* Washington, D.C.: CQ Press, 2004.

Cook, Timothy E. *Governing with the News: The News Media as a Political Institution.* 2nd ed. Chicago: University of Chicago Press, 2005.

Cronin, Thomas E., and Michael A. Genovese. *The Paradoxes of the American Presidency.* 2nd ed. New York: Oxford University Press, 2004.

Edwards, George C., III. *On Deaf Ears: The Limits of the Bully Pulpit.* New Haven, Conn.: Yale University Press, 2003.

Entman, Robert. *Projections of Power: Framing News, Public Opinion, and U.S. Foreign Policy.* Chicago: University of Chicago Press, 2004.

Farnsworth, Stephen J., and S. Robert Lichter. *The Mediated Presidency: Television News and Presidential Governance.* Lanham, Md.: Rowman and Littlefield, 2006.

Kernell, Samuel. *Going Public: New Strategies of Presidential Leadership.* 3rd ed. Washington, D.C.: CQ Press, 1997.

Kumar, Martha Joynt. "The Contemporary Presidency: Communications Operations in the White House of President George W. Bush. Making News on His Terms." *Presidential Studies Quarterly* 33, no. 2 (2003): 366–393.

———. "Source Material: The White House and the Press. News Organizations as a Presidential Resource and as a Source of Pressure." *Presidential Studies Quarterly* 33, no. 3 (2003): 669–683.

Nelson, Michael, ed. *The Presidency and the Political System.* 8th ed. Washington, D.C.: CQ Press, 2006.

Norris, Pippa, Montague Kern, and Marion Just, eds. *Framing Terrorism: The News Media, the Government and the Public.* New York: Routledge, 2003.

Tulis, Jeffrey K. *The Rhetorical Presidency.* Princeton, N.J.: Princeton University Press, 1987.

Media bias

Media bias occurs when coverage lacks fairness or accuracy because it favors a particular political perspective. Charges of such bias have been lodged against media professionals and outlets, as well as against an entire medium and the entire media.

Various voices from all directions have complained and continue to complain of media bias. For example, Republican senator John McCain of Arizona once called NBC news anchor Tom Brokaw a "Trotskyite . . . left wing, Communist, pinko," and Republican senator Bob Dole alleged that "the greatest political scandal of this campaign is the brazen manner in which, without benefit of clergy, the *Washington Post* has set up housekeeping" with the Democrats. Democratic senator Richard Durbin accused radio of being filled with "station after station (of) right wing screamers." Democratic president Bill Clinton said that the United States had an "increasingly right-wing and bellicose conservative press." Typically, liberals tend to see the media as too conservative, while conservatives see it as too liberal. Meanwhile, Democrats think Republicans get favorable treatment, while Republicans believe Democrats are favored.

As a defense against charges of bias and as a mechanism for producing legitimately fair news, professional journalists are trained to report objectively, that is, to produce news as it is, not as one person sees it. Another convention is to present opposing sides of a debate. For instance, when a leading Democrat makes a statement about an issue, the reporter will almost invariably ask a Republican for his or her view and reaction. Striving for objectivity in political reporting was initially an economic decision. In the first decades of the country, supporters of rival political parties associated with Thomas Jefferson and Alexander Hamilton produced newspapers that carried news articles and editorials supporting their positions and ignoring or ridiculing the opposition. Openly slanted news, not surprisingly, appealed only to those who supported the papers' positions. As newspaper publishers began to recognize the potential for advertising revenue, especially at the dawn of the twentieth century, their focus turned to increasing their papers' circulation, which would allow them to increase their advertising rates. In the process, the price of papers fell for readers. Objectivity became standard because it meant that any newspaper could potentially be sold to readers of any political persuasion.

Nevertheless, maintaining objective coverage every day and in every report is made difficult by the inherent subjectivity of the news process. That is, media outlets must choose which of any number of stories to cover. Then, for each story selected, media professionals must decide how to cover the story in presenting it to the public. Consider covering a presidential speech, which sounds relatively easy. In such cases, the media know exactly where and when the news will happen. A TV news segment might dedicate most of the report to showing portions of the speech, but this still leaves room for bias. Which parts of the speech are highlighted and in what order? What, if anything, was shown of the crowd's reaction? Why cover that particular speech at all, given that the president and the president's opponents deliver speeches all the time and not all of them garner media attention. Almost the entirety of the media's job is fundamentally based on subjective decisions. No calculation exists to determine newsworthiness or how to cover events. The subjectivity of the media's work leaves them open to charges of bias. Anyone can complain about almost any aspect of a story and tar the media with the accusation of bias.

Evidence of Bias

Every Republican presidential candidate since Dwight Eisenhower has called the media biased. Perhaps most notable among them is George H. W. Bush. During his 1992 campaign rallies, Bush regularly held up a bumper sticker that read, "Annoy the Media. Re-elect George Bush." In various campaign speeches that year, he referred to members of the media as "nutty," "crackpots," and "bleeding hearts," and admitted he "can't stand those people." Reporters, Bush said,

were obsessed with "gloom and doom" and did not "know enough to pound sand in a rat hole. That's true." Are the media actually biased?

S. Robert Lichter, Stanley Rothman, and Linda Lichter conducted one of the more well-known efforts to document the political proclivities of reporters. In *The Media Elite* (1986), they describe interviews with hundreds of journalists working at prominent media outlets and explore the background and political and social beliefs of media professionals. The authors found that 54 percent of media professionals considered themselves to be liberals, while 17 percent labeled themselves conservatives. In presidential voting, at least 80 percent of the respondents reported supporting the Democratic candidate in previous presidential races. On the issues, a majority supported affirmative action and abortion rights and espoused the principle that homosexuality is not wrong, indicated that environmental problems are important, and agreed that government should reduce the income gap between the rich and poor. Indeed, "only 18 percent believe that working wives whose husbands have jobs should be laid off first, and even fewer, 10 percent, agree that men are emotionally better suited for politics than women." Fifty percent of their media respondents said they had no religion. In sum, according to *The Media Elite,* "These attitudes mirror the traditional perspective of American liberals." Allegations of media bias were amplified in volume and fervor in the aftermath of the 1992 election. A survey of Washington journalists found 89 percent had voted for Democrat Bill Clinton in 1992, 7 percent for Republican George H. W. Bush, and 2 percent for independent Ross Perot. The vast majority of research on reporters concludes that they personally favor the Democratic Party and boast moderate to liberal ideas. Does that matter?

Many studies question the relevance of such findings for two primary reasons. First, journalists have a professional incentive to maintain the appearance of impartiality to advance their careers, and second, even as studies find journalists prefer Democrats, the leadership of the companies they work for heavily favors Republicans. Herbert Gans watched news being produced from within CBS, NBC, *Time,* and *Newsweek,* and discussed what he saw in *Deciding What's News* (1980). Gans describes a process that left little room for personal political bias in the news because of what amounts to a committee system in which everyone involved in producing the news seeks to satisfy the demands of their superiors. Moreover, he found reporters' top goal to be landing the coveted lead story, not getting their personal views across.

Studies that seek to document media bias in actual news coverage frequently focus on political campaigning. Given that only two parties consistently contest elections in the United States, researchers argue that the Democratic and Republican candidates for president, for example, should draw similar amounts and types of coverage. The evidence from these types of studies shows two main results. First, within a given election year, or a particular news media outlet, one candidate might be significantly favored. For example, Ronald Reagan in 1984 and Bill Clinton in 1992 received considerably more favorable press coverage than did their opponents. When looked at over time and across sources, however, there is no evidence that the media favor one party over the other. Dave D'Alessio and Mike Allen looked at the results from numerous independent studies of presidential campaign coverage from 1948 to 1996 and found that the overall trend in studies of newspaper, radio, and television coverage showed equal treatment of Democratic and Republican candidates.

Some, however, question whether this is a fair basis for comparison. If, for example, one candidate has a better record of accomplishments, should not that candidate receive more and better coverage? *Tilt? The Search for Media Bias,* David Niven's study of media coverage, uses situations in which Democrats and Republicans have produced the same results in office as a basis for comparing media coverage. For example, when President George H. W. Bush presided over a national unemployment rate of 5 percent, did he receive better or worse coverage than did President Bill Clinton when he had the same unemployment rate? When assessments involve coverage comparisons on crime, economics, and several other issues, the evidence suggests that when Democrats and Republicans produce comparable results in office, they receive comparable treatment from the media.

Belief in Bias

Even as most academic research questions the notion of widespread media bias based on party or ideology, public belief in media bias remains widespread. In fact, the media's credibility has been dropping steadily. Once considered a trustworthy profession, by the early twenty-first century, public trust in "newspaper reporters" had fallen beneath that in lawyers, real estate agents, labor union leaders, stockbro-

kers, and even politicians, and was heading in the direction of the unenviable territory occupied by the least trusted of all professions: car dealers. Moreover, nine in ten Americans believe that members of the media are regularly influenced by their personal views when covering politics. When Americans were asked for a one-word description of the national news media, the most frequent response was "biased."

Public feuds between political figures and news outlets are becoming more common and helping to fuel these beliefs. In 2000 several U.S. senators waged public campaigns against media outlets; one senator paid for his own poll to demonstrate the public's belief in media bias, while another banned a reporter from entering his campaign bus intended to ferry reporters to a series of campaign speeches. Of note, efforts such as these, as well as the many comments from leaders of both parties complaining of media bias, attract media attention. Indeed, this pattern represents one of the major challenges to media credibility: charges of bias are news, but assertions of fairness are not. That is, political figures are quick to point out incidents of coverage that they believe are unfair, and when they do they often attract coverage. Political figures rarely announce they wish to compliment the media for their fairness, so the public hears of few such instances. Niven found that newspapers carried more than six times as much coverage that called the media biased than that defended the media as fair. In effect, the media play a major role in making the case for media bias, not necessarily because their coverage is biased, but because of their coverage of bias.

Psychology also plays a significant role in making beliefs in media bias widespread. In short, people are more likely to pay attention to and to remember material that offends them. In other words, in an article with seven assertions, six of which met with approval and one that does not, it is the one not agreed with that will be most likely recalled. Several studies have demonstrated the implications of this process. For example, people on opposing sides of an issue can be shown the same newspaper article, and both sides can conclude that it is biased against their point of view.

Implications

The fact that most people consider the media biased is not merely a threat to journalists' self-esteem. People who do not trust their news sources are, not surprisingly, less likely to believe the news. Of even more alarm, people who distrust the media are more likely to distrust the government and to reduce their consumption of news. In the process, the growing distrust of the media can therefore serve to help make people politically isolated and ill-informed.

Despite a long-standing economic imperative to produce neutral news, media outlets in the twenty-first century find themselves facing the central question of whether they are perceived to be biased, rather than whether the media are indeed biased. An alienated constituency hungry for news is not going to endlessly consume newspapers and news shows that it considers to be slanted. No doubt this pattern has fueled the popularity of conservative-oriented talk radio. In addition, in an age where technology constantly opens new paths to news—such as on the Internet and via an ever-expanding roster of cable news channels—the move toward ideological news media outlets will likely continue.

Other Slants on Bias

The media can cover Democrats and Republicans equally without covering either fairly or usefully. Thomas Patterson argues in *Out of Order* (1994) that the media are prone toward negativity in their coverage of candidates such that the typical coverage of Democrats, Republicans, and third-party presidential candidates gives them little space to express themselves, places a major emphasis on their mistakes, and focuses on the strategy of their campaigns rather than on their qualifications for office. Lance Bennett concludes in *News: The Politics of Illusion* (2004) that the media present news in a personalized, fragmented, and dramatized fashion. In other words, most news coverage consists of stories about individuals told outside of the context of the larger issues involved and are hyped to focus on sensational aspects. Such coverage may entertain, but it fails to engage people in the political process because political effects are disconnected from causes.

Other researchers have considered whether the media treat women and other political minorities fairly. Most studies conclude that political figures who are not white men tend to receive distinctive coverage. For example, women receive attention for such frivolous matters as their appearance—for example, one newspaper article on Democratic representative Nancy Pelosi noted that she has a "high-beam smile," "high cheekbones, sharp features" and "small fists" and that if she has "a negative in her political career, it's that she's too attractive"—and are portrayed as having interests largely in what are perceived as women's issues. African Americans, on the other hand, are often portrayed in racial terms and as having interests almost exclusively limited to civil rights and race-related issues.

The Bias Debate Continues

Bias is a question of perspective. On any given day, any single story, any single word in a story can bespeak a bias to an individual consumer. The effort to systematically demonstrate bias, rather than idiosyncratically accuse the media, has revealed a media comprised of people with distinct political views who largely produce news that is neither Democratic nor Republican, liberal or conservative. That is not to say the news is always fair, or even generally fair to all views and perspectives, but rather, the news is not in the control of either of the mainstream political factions of U.S. politics. Nonetheless, the media are ceaselessly subject to allegations of bias. Some of those allegations, however, have nothing to do with actual bias. Rich Bond, former chair of the Republican National Committee, admitted that crying media bias has "some strategy to it. I'm a coach of a kids' basketball and little league team. If you watch any great coach, what they try to do is 'work the refs.' Maybe the ref will cut you a little slack on the next one." In other words, one reason to complain of bias is to see what advantage it might bring you in future coverage.

The media are left to protest against allegations of bias with what often seem to be silly attempts to demonstrate fairness. In 2000 a last-minute change in Republican George W. Bush's schedule left the *Kansas City Star* unable to provide details to its readers in advance of his campaign visit to town. When Democratic presidential candidate Al Gore subsequently came to town, providing media outlets with plenty of advance warning, the *Star* purposely chose to withhold the information to be fair to Bush. Later the *Star* admitted, "In an effort to be fair, the paper ended up with two misses."

In *Media Circus* (1994), Howard Kurtz notes that media outlets ranging from the most prominent—such as the *New York Times* and the *Washington Post*—to the obscure—for example, the *Fairfield Ledger*—have investigated and ultimately forbidden political activity by its reporters outside the office and on the reporters' own time. Editors of the *Washington Post* warned all of their reporters (even those with non-political beats) that political advocacy on their own time was "unprofessional" and that foregoing the right to political expression "is the choice we make when we choose to work in this business." Allegations of bias in the media may be similar in frequency to complaints about the weather, but while the weather never listens and the people seldom act on those complaints, dismay with the media is a very real factor in U.S. politics.

See also *Media elitism*.

REFERENCES

Bennett, W. Lance. *News: The Politics of Illusion.* 6th ed. New York: Pearson/Longman, 2004.

D'Alessio, Dave, and Mike Allen. "Media Bias in Presidential Elections: A Meta-Analysis." *Journal of Communication* 50, no. 3 (Autumn 2000): 133–156.

Gans, Herbert. *Deciding What's News: A Study of* CBS Evening News, NBC Nightly News, Newsweek, *and* Time. Evanston, Ill.: Northwestern University Press, 2004.

Kurtz, Howard. *Media Circus: The Trouble with America's Newspapers.* New York: Times Books, 1994.

Lichter, S. Robert, Stanely Rothman, and Linda S. Lichter. *The Media Elite: American's New Power Brokers.* New York: Hastings House, 1990.

Niven, David. *Tilt? The Search for Media Bias.* Westport, Conn.: Praeger, 2002.

Patterson, Thomas E. *Out of Order.* New York: Vintage, 1994.

Media consultants

Media consultants help politicians and organizations handle media relations and image management. Although advisors have provided services informally to politicians for centuries, in recent years the profession of political consulting has become increasingly formalized. Contemporary political consultants are professionals engaged primarily in the provision of advice and services—such as polling, media creation and production, and direct mail fundraising—to candidates, their campaigns, and other political committees.

Recent developments in politics have heightened the demand for specialized skills and expertise, especially concerning media. The explosive growth in campaign spending over the past few decades has fueled much of this phenomenon. Campaigns typically devote more than half of their entire budget to advertising. Moreover, changes in the media business, including the proliferation of media outlets, greater audience-targeting capabilities, and technological advances, further boosted the demand for specialized media expertise. In short, media consultants emerged to provide media competence to political enterprises. Some leading political media consultants began their careers in the corporate world as specialists in consumer marketing.

President George W. Bush poses with media advisor Mark McKinnon prior to the 2004 Republican National Convention. Media consultants are responsible for establishing an effective communications strategy to cultivate a positive image of the candidate who hires them.

Contemporary political campaigns routinely hire media consultants to develop and execute effective communications strategies. Media consultants often focus on either paid media (advertising) or earned media (publicity and public relations). Paid media consultants tend toward further specialization, for example, advising on radio and television, Internet, print media, or direct mail. They typically work closely with other campaign operatives, especially pollsters, to develop messages designed to appeal to targeted audiences. Paid media consultants generally produce political advertisements, design the overall media plan, and conduct the media buy on behalf of their clients. These services may include negotiating rates with various outlets, delivering ads, and tracking placements, known as trafficking. Media consultants negotiate various compensation structures with their clients, although many receive a percentage of the total media buy (5 to 15 percent) as payment for their services. Contemporary political campaigns rely heavily on the skills and services provided by media consultants to promote their candidacies and causes. Still, research shows that while they certainly help candidate images and issues, they by no means ensure victory. Once in office, officials may also hire media consultants to help them in their public and media relations.

REFERENCES

Dulio, David A. "The Effect of Political Consultants." In *The Electoral Challenge: Theory Meets Practice,* edited by Stephen C. Craig. Washington, D.C.: CQ Press, 2006.

Luntz, Frank I. *Candidates, Consultants and Campaigns: The Style and Substance of American Electioneering.* Oxford: Blackwell, 1988.

Sabato, Larry J. *The Rise of Political Consultants: New Ways of Winning Elections.* New York: Basic Books, 1981.

Wayne, Leslie. "Political Consultants Thrive in the Cash-Rich New Politics." *New York Times,* October 24, 2000.

Media diplomacy

Media diplomacy refers to diplomatic activities carried out through statements, signals, and messages in the mass media or propelled by the coverage of events. Political scientist Eytan Gilboa defines it as "the use of the mass media by policymakers ... to send signals and apply pressure on state and nonstate actors to build confidence and advance negotiations as well as mobilize public support for agreements." The rise of global television allows communications media for the first time to possibly determine the outcomes of diplomacy. In this era of "telediplomacy," television can influence world politics in high-visibility crises and other diplomatic events.

The first clear example of the ability of media coverage to drive international politics occurred in the aftermath of the 1991 Persian Gulf War, when Iraqi president Saddam Hussein moved to suppress uprisings by the Kurdish population in northern Iraq and precipitated a mass exodus of Kurds. The death toll rose to upwards of 100,000, while U.S. president George H. W. Bush issued no less than half a dozen categorical denials of any intention to get involved. Within the span of two weeks, however, his administration shifted policy as a persistent media drumbeat stirred up support for assisting the Kurds. This media pressure was driven largely by the hordes of journalists who had recently been freed by the war's end from other reporting assignments and who had easy access to the Kurdish refugees. As a result, Bush launched the largest humanitarian relief effort in U.S. history.

At nearly the same time, Shiite Muslims in southern Iraq rebelled. Some 500,000 Shiites died under the brutal repression, but virtually no journalists had access to the unfolding massacre. Perhaps not so coincidentally, no military or humanitarian effort was undertaken to aid them. The harsh reality is that the Kurds had the "good fortune" of dying in front of television lenses, whereas the Shiites did not.

The media have affected modern diplomacy in other ways as well. As some observers have noted, government leaders and international actors must now tailor their messages for audiences around the globe. Also, though more rare, members of the media sometimes act as diplomatic brokers or players themselves. The most famous example occurred in 1977 when CBS anchor Walter Cronkite, after subsequent interviews with Israeli prime minister Menachem Begin and Egyptian president Anwar Sadat, acted as a go-between in encouraging the two to meet in person. Today's increasing reliance on television with a global reach suggests that tomorrow might bring an increasing role for telediplomacy and, consequently, an increasing ability for the media to influence the conduct of world politics.

See also *Public diplomacy.*

REFERENCES

Ammon, Royce J. *Global Television and the Shaping of World Politics: CNN, Telediplomacy, and Foreign Policy.* Jefferson, N.C.: McFarland, 2001.

Baker, James A., III. "Report First, Check Later: Former Secretary of State James A. Baker, III Interview with Marvin Kalb." *Press/Politics* 1, no. 2 (Spring 1996): 3–9.

Gilboa, Eytan. "Media Diplomacy: Conceptual Divergence and Application." *Press/Politics* 3, no. 3 (Summer 1998): 56–75.

O'Heffernan, Patrick. *Mass Media and American Foreign Policy.* Norwood, N.J.: Ablex Publishing Corporation, 1991.

Media elitism

The media stand accused of many failings in the court of public opinion. They are charged with being too liberal or conservative, too negative or cynical, too superficial or sensationalist. One complaint that seems to resonate loudly with journalists, as well as with their critics, is the charge that the media are elitist. Elitism means different things to different people, which makes it a difficult accusation to evaluate. The charge of elitism against the media clearly stems from recent changes in their profession that have vastly increased their status and influence in society. These same changes have, however, led to growing public dissatisfaction and threaten to undermine journalists' identification with the audience they seek to represent.

Fifty years ago most journalists saw themselves as ordinary working people who churned out quickly forgotten reports on the events of the day. They might have been eyewitnesses to history, but they had no thought of trying to make history. Owners of local newspapers mainly exercised the "power of the press," along with a handful of influential columnists who counseled the powerful and a few radio commentators who commanded nationwide audiences. This began to change during the 1960s, when a new breed of journalists—better paid and more educated than their predecessors—began to bring news of social change and disruption to an increasingly divided nation. In some cases, they were blamed for bringing an unwelcome message to a hostile audience. To a considerable degree, they also became engaged with the social conflicts on which they reported.

Some reporters challenged the claims of military and political leaders concerning their conduct of the long and controversial war in Vietnam. Others reported on student demonstrations and the social and cultural schism between the protesters and their opponents, who held very different perspectives. Still others used their coverage of the civil rights movement to alert the country to its past sins and ongoing responsibilities involving race relations. The medium of television, which conveyed the news through the prism of individual personality, made many of these journalists celebrities in their own right while vastly increasing the visibility and influence of their reporting.

All of these conflicts pitted student activists, intellectuals, and liberal policymakers against more conservative representatives of traditional forms of patriotism and respect for authority. To the latter it seemed that the media had taken sides with the knowledge workers and East Coast "cosmopolitans" against "middle America." The administration of Richard M. Nixon skillfully played on this audience's growing estrangement from the press by attacking journalists, most memorably in a 1970 speech delivered by Vice President Spiro T. Agnew, who called them "nattering nabobs of negativism" and "an effete corps of impudent snobs." Other conservative politicians and commentators soon seconded these accusations, whose underlying theme held that journalists had abandoned their role as objective chroniclers to become agents of social and political change

by attacking traditional values and institutions. By portraying journalists as elitists out of touch with ordinary people, whose ideas they were bent on changing to conform to their own, the administration sought to neutralize the effects of their reporting.

The conflict came to a head in the early 1970s, when a newly emboldened press focused public scrutiny on the Watergate scandal. Thus, the Nixon administration's war against the press not only backfired; it ended in a rout. The media received credit for playing a major role in bringing down the Nixon presidency, and *Washington Post* reporters Bob Woodward and Carl Bernstein became national heroes. They also served as role models for a new generation of bright and idealistic young people who saw journalism as a way to exercise personal creativity and social influence with the possibility of finding fame and fortune as well.

The profession had come a long way since the days of the "ink-stained wretches" who functioned as observers and recorders of events, which they depicted in line with their bosses' biases. Increasingly journalists saw themselves as educated professionals and the intellectual and social peers of the newsmakers they covered. At the most influential news organizations, the heavy hand of the press lord gave way to a new doctrine of separating "church and state," that is, the boardroom and the newsroom.

The increased social stature and public profile of journalism ironically only broadened public concern that the media had become a new elite exercising growing political influence while claiming to be above politics. Journalists reacted defensively, in part because they saw such criticisms as attacks on their independence, but also possibly because, as with many stereotypes, they contained some truth. The conflict intensified when a series of social science surveys appeared to demonstrate that journalists in the national media had very different backgrounds and values from those of the "average" American.

One of these surveys was later incorporated into *The Media Elite,* which became a catchphrase for critics of the national media. It described journalists at the television networks and leading newspapers and news magazines as the products of predominantly urban, well-off, and well-educated families who were mainly Democratic voters with liberal opinions on such social issues as abortion, affirmative action, and gay rights. Other surveys, including some taken by news organizations, supported this portrait while noting that journalists were more conservative on some economic issues, perhaps reflecting their own improved economic circumstances; a *Los Angeles Times* survey dubbed them "yuppie liberals."

These studies caught journalists off guard because they were used to a very different sort of academic criticism. Even as conservatives popularized the notion of an out-of-control activist liberal media, most scholars had focused on the organizational restraints on journalists and the dangers of a growing concentration of newspapers in the hands of a few large chains. Any ideological criticism emphasized the media's role in legitimizing the policies of a conservative political and industrial "establishment," by failing to represent alternative voices and perspectives. This critique treated working journalists as the pawns of more conservative media executives and owners, who constituted the real media elite. In a variation on A. J. Liebling's famous maxim, they argued that the power of the press belongs to those who own one.

Meanwhile, conservative commentators quickly seized on the new surveys as scientific proof of their own criticisms that the media had become a self-appointed elite working toward their own ends under the guise of serving the public. The conflict escalated after Ronald Reagan's election as president in 1980 ushered in a new period of political dominance by Republicans and conservatives. After two decades of emphasizing their historic role as watchdogs protecting the public against abuses of power, journalists were soon clashing regularly with the new president and his policies. News audiences—and not only conservative ones—began to complain that the White House press corps was "disrespectful," after witnessing the pointed questions they shouted during televised presidential press conferences. The same reporters who prided themselves on challenging the arrogance of power were now being charged ironically with arrogance for acting as an unelected political opposition. Just as liberals had worried about an "imperial presidency" extending executive authority, now conservatives warned of an "imperial media" that viewed itself as the arbiter in disputes among all other sectors of society.

At the same time, liberals who were dissatisfied with the national media's criticism of Reagan and his conservative agenda began to paint a very different portrait, one of a compliant and self-satisfied press that had become part of the establishment. In so doing, they adapted the older academic tradition of media criticism. Just as conservatives had argued that the media watchdogs had turned into attack dogs, liberals now argued, in works such as Mark Hertsgaard's *On Bended Knee* (1989) that they had become lapdogs of the powerful. Where conservatives saw the media attacking traditional institutions as an adversary, liberals saw a defanged watchdog, a newly empowered profession that had gained the world but lost its soul. Attacking media elitism suddenly became an equal opportunity political sport.

More than ideological differences, however, led to growing public dissatisfaction with perceived media arrogance and elitism. Highly publicized controversies and misdeeds, at some of the profession's most respected institutions, left ordinary citizens to fear that journalists believed they could play by their own rules without being held accountable. The most notorious of these were acts of pure invention: *Washington Post* reporter Janet Cooke, *New York Times* reporter Jayson Blair, and *USA Today* correspondent Jack Kelley were caught fabricating stories, with Cooke being forced to return a Pulitzer Prize. In other cases, sensational stories had to be retracted when they could not be verified. Among these were a CNN/*Time* magazine report that the U.S. military had exposed its own troops to a nerve gas during the Vietnam War and a CBS *60 Minutes* report, aired during the heat of the 2004 presidential election campaign, claiming the existence of documents proving that President George W. Bush had received preferential treatment during his National Guard service.

As important as professional lapses were in shredding public support, the charge of elitism also reflected the more activist and socially engaged role journalists appeared to claim as their prerogative. A new willingness to probe into the private lives of public figures, particularly their sexual relationships, troubled many people. Others were made uneasy by the "ambush" journalism that became a staple of television newsmagazine shows, in which reporters went incognito and used hidden cameras and other questionable techniques to catch wrongdoers in the act. Some highly publicized libel suits revealed a willingness to cut corners or to simply ignore ethical restraints in order to get the story. The public feared that journalists not only were not getting the story right but that they were not getting it the right way.

Journalists' new assertiveness was perhaps most evident in election news. Believing that they had been manipulated by campaign consultants and media advisors during the 1988 presidential election, the national media—especially the television networks—launched their own campaign to take the election news agenda away from the candidates. For example, the Radio-TV News Directors Association exhorted its members to "take control of the political agenda in 1992." That year the networks and many newspapers introduced such features as "ad watches," "truth boxes," and "reality checks," all designed to expose the candidates' lies or misrepresentations, while presenting themselves as the truth-tellers. This movement attracted the label of "corrective journalism."

This tack also made journalists much more central to the campaign itself, increasing the media's role from that of chroniclers to referees and even players. Indeed, the fact that so many journalists believed that they, rather than the presidential candidates, were best equipped to present the campaign to the public indicates the heights to which their professional self-esteem had risen. The public, in whose name all this was done, was not, however, convinced. Postelection polls showed the public giving journalists lower ratings than the parties, candidates, campaign consultants, and even talk show hosts for their performance in the 1992 campaign. Campaign news has gotten low marks from the public in every national election since. When asked to grade the media's campaign performance on a scale from A to F, the average mark has varied only from C-minus to D-plus.

Public disaffection with a more aggressive press has not been limited to election years. Beginning in the late 1990s, a series of national surveys by the Pew Research Center, Harris Poll, and other research organizations established the extent of the public's dissatisfaction. These surveys revealed that majorities of Americans believed that journalists have too much influence, let their own biases influence their work, cover up their errors, and do not care about the people on whom they report. Some polls found the public evenly divided over whether the media mainly help or harm U.S. democracy. To the degree that these findings have changed over time, the levels of criticism have only increased.

Journalists are acutely aware of their alienation from their audience. This problem has been the topic of a stream of conferences and journalism review articles. In fact, Pew Center polls show that majorities of both national and local media journalists agree that their profession is out of touch with the public. If this awareness has done little to stem the tide of criticism, it is partly because it reflects structural changes in the media's role in American society.

Underlying much of the public's dissatisfaction is the overriding fact that the media have become a major player in U.S. politics. Public opinion in the United States reflects a strong populist streak, which includes suspicion of the leaders of big government, big business, and now big media. Journalists at national news organizations are treated as VIPs, and many have become celebrities. Television journalists in particular are often counted among society's rich and famous, which makes them objects of adulation as well as resentment.

At the core of the media elitism debate is a clash between journalists' self-perceptions as the public's defenders against the rich and powerful and the widespread public perception of journalists themselves as a wealthy and influential elite. Even though journalists are pleased to act as movers and shakers (on the public's behalf, as they see it), most continue to hold on to their longstanding self-image as the public's surrogates looking out for the interests of the little guy. Much of their audience, however, now sees them, fairly or not, as big shots who have forgotten their roots.

News organizations in the early twenty-first century have sought to allay such suspicions through such means as greater transparency in their operations and a more audience-oriented approach to the news called public, or civic, journalism. To a great degree, however, charges of elitism are an unavoidable downside of the media's vastly enhanced role in U.S. society.

See also *Media and Congress; Media and the presidency; Media bias; Media feeding frenzies.*

REFERENCES

Alterman, Eric. *What Liberal Media? The Truth about Bias in the News.* New York: Basic Books, 2003.

Fallows, James M. *Breaking the News: How the Media Undermine American Democracy.* New York: Pantheon, 1996.

Gans, Herbert J. *Deciding What's News: A Study of* CBS Evening News, NBC Nightly News, Newsweek, *and* Time. Evanston, Ill.: Northwestern University Press, 2004.

Goldberg, Bernard. *Arrogance: Rescuing America from the Media Elite.* New York: Warner Books, 2003.

Hertsgaard, Mark. *On Bended Knee: The Press and the Reagan Presidency.* New York: Schocken, 1989.

Lerner, Robert, Althea K. Nagai, and Stanley Rothman. *American Elites.* New Haven, Conn.: Yale University Press, 1996.

Lichter, S. Robert, Linda S. Lichter, and Stanley Rothman. *The Media Elite: America's New Power Brokers.* New York: Hastings House, 1990.

Patterson, Thomas E. *Out of Order.* New York: Knopf, 1993.

Rosenstiel, Thomas. *Strange Bedfellows: How Television and the Presidential Candidates Changed American Politics.* New York: Hyperion, 1993.

West, Darrell M. *The Rise and Fall of the Media Establishment.* Boston: St. Martin's Press, 2001.

Media feeding frenzies

Larry Sabato coined the expression "media feeding frenzy" in *Feeding Frenzy: How Attack Journalism Has Transformed American Politics* (1991), defining it as "the press coverage attending to any political event or circumstance where a critical mass of journalists leap to cover the same embarrassing or scandalous subject and pursue it intensely, often excessively, and sometimes uncontrollably." He describes such coverage of certain events as akin to sharks in a feeding frenzy over wounded prey. Sensational media coverage attracts even more coverage, resulting in excessive reporting that can alter the significance of the original event. Examples of media feeding frenzies include coverage of President Bill Clinton's affair with Monica Lewinsky, California representative Gary Condit's relationship with Chandra Levy, and presidential candidate Howard Dean's scream during the 2004 Democratic primaries.

Two related concepts that contribute to feeding frenzies are "pack journalism" and "fish schooling." Pack journalism occurs when media outlets quickly move from one story to the next en masse, like a pack of wild dogs. Fish schooling suggests that journalists act like fish that mimic and follow the behavior of other fish in order to stay in the school. These behaviors resemble what Timothy Cook describes as journalists' tendency to "follow the leader," using the same sources and following the same norms.

Media feeding frenzies are identifiable not only by excessive coverage, but also by content. "Feeding frenzy" has a negative connotation. It does not refer to the excessive coverage of stories that convey valuable government and foreign affairs information. One can identify a media feeding frenzy when nearly every news channel or newspaper is focused on the same story of questionable importance. The subject of feeding frenzies typically is a politician's personal life, particularly indiscretions, character flaws, and personality traits. The content is politically of little or no use to citizens and is classifiable as soft news rather than hard news. Soft news aims toward entertaining and tends to focus on personalities and drama rather than on factual information and serious analysis.

Numerous factors lead to media feeding frenzies. Technological advances have facilitated instantaneous, worldwide coverage of events. This, combined with the emergence of twenty-four-hour cable news channels, has led to increased needs to fill airtime with content, resulting in repetitious coverage of relatively insignificant political and

Democratic presidential candidate Howard Dean delivered a motivational speech to supporters after conceding the 2004 Iowa caucus. Dean ended his talk with an exuberant cry of "Yeahhh!" Television and radio replayed "the scream" for days, and it became the subject of endless satire. Dean opponents cited it as evidence of his lack of presidential character. Some who witnessed the speech live commented that his concluding exhortation only seemed outlandish on the television replay.

other events. The need to increase ratings and profits has led to diversification of media outlets and to an explosion of channels with news content. Increased market competition has forced media outlets to devise new strategies for remaining competitive, including covering soft news, which is often more exciting and interesting to viewers than hard news. In addition, soft news is typically cheaper to produce than hard news or in-depth investigative journalism on complex policy issues. According to Sabato, market pressures have also resulted in media outlets breaking stories prematurely in an attempt not to be "scooped" on a big story. Other media outlets then quickly join in on the coverage, one-upping the initial story by making their version juicier. Sabato argues moreover that since 1974 the press has engaged in "junkyard-dog" journalism—"harsh, aggressive, and intrusive" reporting. Together, these factors provide the ideal environment for media feeding frenzies to flourish.

Prior media feeding frenzies can set the standard for journalistic approaches toward future stories and may contribute to additional frenzies. For example, once a topic such as a politician's marital infidelity results in increased sales and ratings, the next occurrence of an infidelity by a politician will likely be covered more intensively. The more novel, sensational, or controversial the event, the more likely it is to result in a feeding frenzy. The private lives of presidents, vice presidents, and presidential candidates tend to be perfect fodder for frenzies because of these individuals' unique positions in U.S. politics.

Media scholars generally criticize feeding frenzies because they overemphasize stories, oftentimes through sensational coverage that replaces substance with personalized drama. Critics charge that this type of coverage weakens American democracy, because it focuses on politicians' private lives instead of providing the public with useful information, such as their stance on public policy, governing, and foreign affairs. Critics also charge feeding frenzies with trivializing campaigns and creating cynicism among the citizenry. Frenzies can also create an adversarial relationship between the media and politicians, thus decreasing the access politicians allow the media, further limiting the ability of the public to learn about candidates and their positions.

On the positive side, it is possible that the intense coverage characteristic of frenzies makes government and politicians more transparent. Darrell West notes that the media do not always engage in irresponsible frenzies, relaying an example about a rumor concerning Hillary Rodham Clinton that the media responsibly refrained from turning into a feeding frenzy. John Zaller claims that the addition of entertainment to political content has enlarged media outlets' audiences and delivers political content to people who would normally not receive it. Zaller also believes that frenzies can sound "burglar alarms" that alert the public to issues that may typically elude them. Other media scholars, however, have argued that the function of the news media is to inform rather than to entertain. Thomas Patterson charges that many citizens are tuning out political news in part because of feeding frenzies' excessive coverage of nonsubstantive matters. W. Lance Bennett has similarly criticized media coverage for being too alarmist and for not providing more responsible coverage that conveys useful political information to citizens.

Although Sabato coined the phrase "media feeding frenzy" more than a decade ago and detailed examples of frenzies from more than fifty years prior, one can argue that feeding frenzies have become more frequent and more prominent since the early 1990s. If the political culture continues to grow more contentious, coarse, and partisan and media outlets face increasing market pressures, it is likely that feeding frenzies will remain pervasive. With the current incentives and constraints on the media market, the only way frenzies will cease is when consumers stop tuning in to them.

See also *Pack journalism; Scandal.*

REFERENCES

Bennett, W. Lance. "The Burglar Alarm That Just Keeps Ringing: A Response to Zaller." *Political Communication* 20, no. 2 (April–June 2003): 131–138.

Cook, Timothy E. *Governing with the News: The News Media as a Political Institution.* Chicago: University of Chicago Press, 1998.

Patterson, Thomas E. *Doing Well and Doing Good: How Soft News and Critical Journalism Are Shrinking Audiences and Weakening Democracy—And What News Outlets Can Do about It.* Cambridge, Mass.: Harvard University, Joan Shorenstein Center on the Press, Politics, and Public Policy, 2000.

Sabato, Larry J. *Feeding Frenzy: How Attack Journalism Has Transformed American Politics.* New York: Free Press, 1991.

Sabato, Larry J., Mark Stencel, and S. Robert Lichter. *Peepshow: Media and Politics in an Age of Scandal.* Lanham, Md.: Rowman and Littlefield, 2001.

West, Darrell N. "Responsibility Frenzies in News Coverage: Dissecting a Hillary Clinton Rumor." *Harvard International Journal of Press/Politics* 8, no. 2 (2003): 104–114.

Zaller, John. "A New Standard of News Quality: Burglar Alarms for the Monitorial Citizen." *Political Communication* 20, no. 2 (April–June 2003): 109–130.

Meet the Press

See *Sunday news shows.*

Memoirs v. Massachusetts (1966)

Memoirs v. Massachusetts (1966) clarified the Supreme Court's definition of obscene material. A Massachusetts statute permitted the state attorney general to bring a civil action against a book or other publication to have it adjudged obscene. The state brought such a suit against *Memoirs of a Woman of Pleasure,* an erotic novel commonly known as *Fanny Hill,* which was first published in 1749.

A few years earlier, in *Roth v. United States* (1957), the Court had established obscenity to be determined by "whether, to the average person, applying contemporary community standards, the dominant theme of the material taken as a whole appeals to prurient interests." *Memoirs v. Massachusetts* represents one of the first attempts by the Supreme Court to apply *Roth*. The Court, in an opinion written by Justice William J. Brennan Jr., held that the book had sufficient redeeming literary and cultural value and therefore could not be suppressed. The case established "redeeming social value" as the criterion for courts to apply independent of a work's erotic content or offensiveness when judging obscenity cases. The decision in *Memoirs v. Massachusetts* made it much more difficult for states to suppress erotic or pornographic material.

See also *Miller v. California (1973); Obscenity and pornography; Roth v. United States (1957).*

REFERENCES

Elias, James E., et al., eds. *Porn 101: Eroticism, Pornography and the First Amendment.* Amherst, N.Y.: Prometheus Books, 1999.

Hixson, Richard F. *Pornography and the Justices: The Supreme Court and the Intractable Obscenity Problem.* Carbondale: Southern Illinois University Press, 1996.

Memoirs v. Massachusetts, 383 U.S. 413 (1966).

Roth v. United States, 354 U.S. 476 (1957).

Journalist H. L. Mencken, pictured here on the left with satirist George Jean Nathan, challenged middle-class morals and the religious and political establishments during the first half of the twentieth century. His writings, often out of step with contemporary norms, generated considerable controversy.

Mencken, H. L.

Henry Louis Mencken (1880–1956) was an influential writer, editor, and literary critic of the twentieth century. He began his career in 1899 as a reporter for the *Baltimore Morning Herald* and worked his way up to managing editor of the *Baltimore Evening Herald.* After the *Herald* folded in 1906, he moved to the *Baltimore Sun,* where he remained for the majority of his career while also writing for other publications.

Mencken, working as a war correspondent in Germany and Russia during World War I, reported with a decidedly pro-German bent that drew considerable criticism in the United States. In 1919 he wrote *The American Language,* a critically acclaimed and popular guide to expressions and idioms heard in the United States. Mencken also published literary studies of George Bernard Shaw and Friedrich Nietzsche. He and George Nathan co-edited a satirical magazine,

The Smart Set, from 1914 to 1923, and in the mid-1920s he co-founded *The American Mercury,* a cultural magazine for "a civilized minority." Throughout the 1920s and 1930s, he contributed to the *Chicago Tribune, New York American,* and *The Nation.* Mencken also wrote "The Free Lance," a column in the *Baltimore Sun* papers from 1919 to 1941.

Mencken artfully took on such subjects as middle-class morals, organized religion, and the political establishment, and he used his position to lift those authors in whom he saw promise and to berate those who failed to measure up. As an editor, Mencken helped and published authors including Sinclair Lewis, Eugene O'Neill, and Dorothy Parker, and served as a role model for a generation of journalists.

He attacked the New Deal politics of Franklin Roosevelt, placing him outside the mainstream of public opinion, while his pro-German sympathies isolated him even further. Mencken abandoned his famous *Evening Sun* Monday articles in 1938, and at the beginning of World War II stopped contributing regularly to the *Sun* all together. He wrote an autobiographical trilogy—*Happy Days* (1940); *Newspaper Days* (1941); and *Heathen Days* (1943)—before suffering a stroke that robbed him of the ability to communicate in 1948. He died of a heart attack in 1956. His last volume, *My Life as Author and Editor,* appeared posthumously in 1993.

REFERENCES

Fecher, Charles A. *Mencken: A Study of His Thought.* New York: Knopf, 1978.

Rodgers, Marion Elizabeth, ed. *The Impossible H. L. Mencken: A Selection of His Best Newspaper Stories.* New York: Doubleday, 1991.

Teachout, Terry. *The Skeptic: A Life of H. L. Mencken.* New York: HarperCollins, 2002.

Miller v. California (1973)

In *Miller v. California* (1973), the Supreme Court in a 5-4 decision established a three-prong test for determining obscenity, replacing an earlier, more permissive test. Miller had been convicted of disseminating unsolicited advertisements for "adult" books and films in violation of California's obscenity statutes, which were based on the Court's ruling in *Memoirs v. Massachusetts* (1966) establishing the constitutional standard for obscenity as material "utterly without redeeming social value." The Court ruled in *Miller* that "[t]he basic guidelines for the trier of fact must be: (a) whether 'the average person, applying contemporary community standards' would find that the work, taken as a whole, appeals to the prurient interest; (b) whether the work depicts or describes, in a patently offensive way, sexual conduct specifically defined by the applicable state law; and (c) whether the work, taken as a whole, lacks serious literary, artistic, political, or scientific value."

Since *Roth v. United States* (1957), the Court had struggled to create standards for defining obscenity. In *Roth* the justices had backed the "community standards" test: "whether to the average person, applying contemporary community standards, the dominant theme of the material taken as a whole appeals to prurient interests." Because obscenity is such a subjective matter, most of the standards the Court had developed over the years proved to be unworkable in the long run. *Miller* made it easier to suppress sexually explicit materials by requiring that a work have "serious" value to avoid a finding of obscenity. In addition, the Court took the unusual step of instructing state legislatures on how to craft obscenity statutes to pass constitutional muster. The justices suggested that legislators could ban "patently offensive representations or descriptions of ultimate sexual acts, normal or perverted, actual or simulated" and "patently offensive representations or descriptions of masturbation, excretory functions, and lewd exhibition of the genitals." The majority reasoned that the First Amendment was designed to promote the "unfettered exchange of ideas" and "political debate," but not obscenity.

See also *Memoirs v. Massachusetts (1966); Obscenity and pornography; Roth v. United States (1957).*

REFERENCES

Miller v. California, 413 U.S. 15 (1973).

Ducat, Craig R. *Constitutional Interpretation.* 8th ed. Belmont, Calif.: Thomson/West, 2004.

Minority portrayals

In the U.S. media, minorities tend to be little seen or largely stereotyped, according to most research. Political scientists Robert Entman and Andrew Rojecki found that relative to minorities, whites are more frequently depicted as persons of substance and consequence who have opinions and make decisions on matters of importance. African Americans, by contrast, are more likely to be portrayed as being of significance in certain realms, such as in sports and in entertainment. Within negative contexts, such as those involving crime, whites are more likely to be presented as individuals—whose behavior offers little or no lesson about whites in general—while African Americans are categorized and labeled by race, as if to suggest that the misdeeds of an individual are characteristic of the group.

Studies focusing specifically on the news medium and African Americans dominate this area of research. In a broader study, political scientist Stephanie Greco Larson found similar patterns of under-representation and stereotyping of African Americans, Asian Americans, Latinos, and Native Americans in television and film as well as news. Larson analyzed the portrayal of people, political movements, and political leaders and found that those involving minorities convey the notion that they are apt to be violent, poor, and dishonest. Larson utilized data on the poverty rate to show the lack of justification for the media's minority-skewed depiction of poverty. Robert Ferguson has concluded that the dominant message in coverage of minorities

The Cosby Show's *portrayal of upper-middle-class African Americans challenged typical depictions of minority characters on television. Research suggests, however, that such representations and appearances by successful blacks in the media lead some white viewers to believe that more African Americans could be as successful if they simply "tried harder."*

is "otherness." Whether in good or, more typically, bad contexts, minorities represent people different from whites. This difference may be in power, ability, or inclination.

Although the media's portrayal of minorities provides insight into the industry, researchers find the effect of minority portrayals on the audience to be of more significance. Larson argues that the media largely project the typical thoughts of the audience in their construction of minority images. In other words, to maximize profits, the media seek to present images acceptable to a predominantly white audience. Ferguson contends that the media have the potential to challenge established power relationships and concepts of identity and in the process challenge prevalent beliefs that fuel racism. He, however, finds little evidence of the media rising to this challenge.

Entman and Rojecki report finding ambivalence among most whites about minorities. That is, most whites hold a mix of positive and negative notions about minorities that add up to a conflicted overall assessment. Entman and Rojecki argue that for many of these whites, the media are the most significant source of their racial experience and knowledge. In sum, many whites' understanding of and feelings toward minority groups are susceptible to media influence. Entman and Rojecki conclude that rather than using this influence to dispel negative assumptions, the media pri-

marily perpetuate and reinforce stereotypes of minorities for many whites otherwise ambivalent about race.

See also *African Americans and the media; Asian Americans and the media; Latinos and the media; Native Americans and the media.*

REFERENCES

Entman, Robert M., and Andrew Rojecki. *The Black Image in the White Mind: Media and Race in America.* Chicago: University of Chicago Press, 2000.

Ferguson, Robert. *Representing "Race": Ideology, Identity, and the Media.* London: Arnold, 1998.

Larson, Stephanie Greco. *Media and Minorities: The Politics of Race in News and Entertainment.* Lanham, Md.: Rowman and Littlefield, 2006.

Mother Jones

Mother Jones, which appeared in 1976, is a magazine that addresses social justice issues through investigative reporting. Published by the nonprofit Foundation for National Progress, it has thus far received four National Magazine Awards for its investigative reporting.

The magazine is named after Mary Harris Jones, a pioneering champion of the labor movement and labor organizer, and devotes itself to progressive-leftist political commentary and to exposing abuses of power. *Mother Jones* is primarily funded through subscriptions and donations, allowing it relative freedom from corporate advertising interests. Mainstream media organizations pick up many of its investigations and make the information known to a wider audience. A Web-based version of the magazine debuted in 1993, and in 2005 a radio program based on the magazine began airing as part of the Air America network. In 1996 *Mother Jones* published its first annual Mother Jones 400, a survey and searchable database of the country's top 400 political donors.

REFERENCES

Mother Jones, www.motherjones.com.
Noyes, Dan. *Raising Hell: A Guide to the Fine Art of Uncovering Corporate Secrets, Government Lies and Other Dirty Tricks.* San Francisco: Mother Jones Magazine, 1978.

Moyers, Bill

William "Bill" Moyers (1934–) began his award-winning career as a journalist, author, and social commentator as a cub reporter for the *Marshall News Messenger* in Texas at the age of sixteen. After a broad education at, among other schools, the University of Texas, Austin, he joined KTBS-TV in Austin as an assistant news editor before becoming Democratic senator Lyndon B. Johnson's personal assistant, a position he held during 1960–1961. Moyers then went to work for the Peace Corps, including as associate director for public affairs and deputy director. From 1963 to 1965, Moyers served in the Johnson administration as special assistant to the president and between 1965 and 1967 as press secretary. He left government to become the publisher of *Newsday,* where he worked from 1967 to 1970. He returned to television in 1970 as the host of the PBS series *This Week.*

Moyers is a disciple of Edward R. Murrow's "deep-think" journalism, having written, hosted, and produced a variety of investigative programs for CBS, NBC, and PBS and offering social commentary. In 1986 Moyers formed Public Affairs Television to produce and distribute his programs, which are noted for their breadth, thoroughness, and writing. Between 2001 and 2004, Moyers hosted *NOW with Bill Moyers,* a television news journal program on PBS from which he retired amid disagreement with Corporation for Public Broadcasting chairman Kenneth Tomlinson over the political content of the program.

For his work, Moyers has been recognized with many awards and honors, including thirty Emmys. He has written numerous books, many based on his television programs, including *Listening to America* (1971), *The Secret Government* (1988), *The Power of Myth* (1988), *A World of Ideas* (1989), and *Healing and the Mind* (1993).

REFERENCES

Bethell, Tom. "The Living Hell of Bill Moyers." *American Spectator,* March 2004, 38–39.
Burns, Ken. "Moyers: A Second Look—More Than Meets the Eye." *New York Times,* May 14, 1989.
Katz, Jon. "Why Bill Moyers Shouldn't Run for President." *New York Times,* March 8, 1992.
Lindberg, Tod. "The World According to Moyers." *National Review,* March 10, 1989, 22–25.
Nichols, John. "Moyers Fights Back." *Nation,* June 6, 2005, 8.
Zurawik, David. "The Following Myth Is Made Possible by a Grant from Bill Moyers." *Esquire,* October 1989.

Muckraking

Muckraking evolved in the late nineteenth century as a form of journalism involving the exposure of wrongdoing through investigative reporting. It targeted or pursued real and alleged political, legal, business, and financial corruption and other illegal activities, scandal, and social problems with the objective of creating an interest in reform.

The movement is associated with the period between 1890 and 1914. Henry Demarest Lloyd is considered the first American investigative journalist, or "muckraker," because of a series of articles he published in 1880 exposing corruption in business and politics. The movement blossomed in the next two decades with efforts such as *Harper's* exposure of Boss Tweed's Tammany Hall machine in New York City, Ida Tarbell's rail against Standard Oil, and Lincoln Steffen's pieces on "Tweedism" in St. Louis, both featured in *McClure's Magazine.*

President Theodore Roosevelt introduced the term *muckraker* in a 1906 speech to the House of Representatives in which he compared the investigative journalists of the time with the muckraker in John Bunyan's *Pilgrim's Progress:* "the

Man with the Muck-rake, the man who could look no way but downward, with the muck-rake in his hand; who was offered a celestial crown for his muck-rake, but who would neither look up nor regard the crown he was offered, but continued to rake to himself the filth of the floor. . . . There should be relentless exposure of and attack upon every evil man whether politician or business man, every evil practice, whether in politics, in business, or in social life. I hail as a benefactor every writer or speaker, every man who, on the platform, or in book, magazine, or newspaper, with merciless severity makes such attack, provided always that he in his turn remembers that the attack is of use only if it is absolutely truthful."

That year represented a triumph for the Muckrakers, with works like Upton Sinclair's *The Jungle.* Roosevelt responded to some of the problems exposed by investigative journalists by initiating legislation, including the 1906 Pure Food and Drugs Act and the Meat Inspection Act. He was perceived as being of a similar mind as the journalists until David Graham Phillips wrote "The Treason of the Senate," a series of articles in *Cosmopolitan* in 1906 attacking some of Roosevelt's political allies. A backlash ensued after the articles' publication, and similar investigative reporters became known pejoratively as "muckrakers"; the demand for their style of journalism declined as the public lost interest. In *The Era of the Muckrakers,* C. C. Regier argues that before muckraking's fall from grace, the reforms it contributed to between 1900 and 1915 made an impressive list.

The development of the Internet has provided a new dimension to illuminating and exposing damaging truths behind corrupt ethical lapses of corporate and government entities. Ordinary citizens' access to online information and their ability to post information to it carry forward the spirit of the muckrakers, if not the mantle. Indeed, the term is still used to refer to crusading investigative journalists (and journalism) seeking reform.

See also *Hearst, William Randolph; Investigative reporting; McClure, S. S.; Watergate.*

REFERENCES

Regier, C.. *The Era of the Muckrakers.* Chapel Hill: University of North Carolina Press, 1932.
Center for Public Integrity. *Citizen Muckraking: How to Investigate and Right Wrongs in Your Community.* Monroe, Me.: Common Courage Media, 2000.
Serrin, Judith, and William Serrin, eds. *Muckraking! The Journalism That Changed America.* New York: New Press, 2002.

Mudd, Roger

Roger Harrison Mudd (1928–), made his career as a journalist and national television broadcaster. He graduated from Washington and Lee University in 1950 before obtaining a master's degree in history from the University of North Carolina. Mudd began his journalism career as a reporter for the *Richmond News Leader* in Virginia and then became the news editor at a local radio station. He worked as a congressional and national affairs correspondent for CBS News from 1961 to 1980. Mudd is noted for a particularly harsh interview of Massachusetts senator Edward Kennedy prior to the 1980 presidential campaign. As reported in the *Washingtonian,* Mudd justified the interview, noting, "I was in charge of the questions. He was in charge of the answers."

When CBS selected Dan Rather to succeed Walter Cronkite in 1981, Mudd moved to NBC News, where he served as chief Washington correspondent, chief political correspondent, and co-anchor of the *Nightly News.* Mudd was a frequent contributor to NBC's *Meet the Press.* When Tom Brokaw succeeded John Chancellor, Mudd joined the *MacNeil/Lehrer NewsHour* on PBS as an essayist and correspondent from 1987 to 1992.

Mudd edited *American Heritage Great Minds of History: Interviews by Roger Mudd* (1999), a collection of interviews with historians Stephen Ambrose, Gordon Wood, David McCullough, Richard White, and James McPherson. He also taught journalism at Princeton University and Washington and Lee University in the early and mid-1990s and hosted A&E's *Save Our History* and *History Alive* until he retired in 2004.

REFERENCES

"The Unmuddling of Mudd." *Time,* July 14, 1980, 75.
Buckley, William F., Jr. "Mud on His Face." *National Review,* December 7, 1979, 1580–1581.
McLellan, Diana. "Mudd in Your Eye." *Washingtonian,* August 1995.
Schardt, Arlie, with Lucy Howard. "CBS's Mudd Drops Anchor at NBC." *Newsweek,* July 14, 1980, 64.

Murdoch, Rupert

Keith Rupert Murdoch (1931–) is a mogul who built a media and publishing empire reaching from Australia to Europe to the United States. Murdoch, born in Adelaide,

Australia, obtained his education from Oxford University, graduating in 1952. He began his career on London's Fleet Street with the *Daily Express* but returned to Australia in 1954 after his father's death to run the family business, News Limited, which included the *News* in Adelaide.

In 1960 he began to acquire a string of newspapers, including the *Daily Mirror* in Sydney. Murdoch bought the Nine Network TV stations in 1962 and two years later launched a national newspaper, *The Australian.* He purchased the British *News of the World* and the *Sun* in 1969. In the 1970s, Murdoch entered the publishing and media markets in the United States with his acquisition of the *San Antonio Express, San Antonio News,* and *New York Post.* He continued his penetration of the British market with the 1976 acquisition of the *Times* and *Sunday Times.* In 1980 he established News Corporation as an umbrella company for all his holdings. Murdoch became a U.S. citizen in 1985 to meet a prerequisite for owning U.S.-based television stations. He then acquired Twentieth Century Fox, formed the Fox Network, and in the 1990s launched into satellite television in Asia and Great Britain. Murdoch purchased Hughes Electronics along with its DirecTV satellite television system in 2003, giving News Corporation a broad reach, from content to delivery. He has consolidated an international media empire that includes television, movies, newspapers, books, and delivery systems for these media.

See also *Fox Broadcasting Corporation.*

REFERENCES

Chenoweth, Neil. *Rupert Murdoch: The Untold Story of the World's Greatest Media Wizard.* New York: Crown Business, 2001.

Lashinsky, Adam. "Look Who's Online Now." *Fortune,* October 31, 2005, 56–65.

Rohm, Wendy Goldman. *The Murdoch Mission: The Digital Transformation of a Media Empire.* New York: J. Wiley, 2002.

Murrow, Edward R.

Edward (or Egbert) Roscoe Murrow (1908–1965) was a renowned radio and television journalist. He began his career in the early 1930s as assistant director of the Institute of International Education. He then moved into journalism at CBS, where in 1937 he became director of its European bureau in London. Murrow broadcast the events of World War II in Europe, notably the German blitzkrieg in 1940.

Edward R. Murrow gained national recognition as a World War II radio news broadcaster. In the 1950s, he was one of the few public figures willing to confront Sen. Joseph McCarthy about his tactics in his alleged hunt for communists.

During his career, he would hire a generation of electronic journalists, including Eric Sevareid and Howard K. Smith, who became known as Murrow's Boys.

Murrow transitioned into television as the host of *See It Now,* which ran from 1951 to 1958. His most memorable broadcast came on March 9, 1954, when he engaged Wisconsin senator Joseph McCarthy. After the appearance, McCarthy's credibility began to suffer, bringing to an end his ability to use 'red scare' tactics against Americans. Murrow also hosted *Person to Person* throughout the 1950s, chatting informally with an array of personalities, including Marilyn Monroe, John Steinbeck, and Harry Truman.

In a 1958 speech before the Radio and Television News Directors Association, Murrow denounced the broadcasting industry for being "fat, comfortable, and complacent" and television for "being used to detract, delude, amuse and insulate us." Murrow split with CBS in 1961, and President John F. Kennedy appointed him to head the U.S. Information Agency that same year. He worked at the agency until 1964.

See also *McCarthy, Joseph; Sevareid, Eric; Smith, Howard K.; U.S. Information Agency.*

REFERENCES

Halberstam, David. *The Powers That Be.* New York: Knopf, 1979.
Kendrick, Alexander. *Prime-Time: The Life of Edward R. Murrow.* Boston: Little, Brown, 1969.

Edmund Muskie, Maine senator and Democratic presidential hopeful, delivered a speech in February 1972 denouncing the publisher of the Manchester Union Leader, *which had printed an attack on Muskie's wife and a forged letter about him. Muskie appeared to shed tears during the speech, which led to his campaign's loss of momentum as the media, and then the public, began to doubt his ability to lead the nation. Many asserted that the "teardrops" were melted snowflakes.*

Muskie incident

The "Muskie incident" refers to an event during the 1972 presidential campaigns that destroyed Edmund Muskie's chances at winning the Democratic nomination. Muskie, a senator from Maine, had been considered the front-runner for his party's nomination throughout much of 1971. Before the New Hampshire primary, however, Muskie became enraged by a series of inflammatory letters in the *Manchester Union Leader.* One of the articles attacked Muskie's wife, while the other later proved to be a hoax planted by President Richard M. Nixon's campaign staff as part of ongoing attempts to embarrass other candidates. In the forged letter, Muskie was accused of condoning the use of a racial slur by calling American descendents of French Canadians "Canucks."

Muskie spoke out against the stories and the *Union Leader's* publisher, William Loeb, and during the speech appeared to be so overcome by emotion that he cried. The media immediately seized upon the story, and press accounts changed from describing Muskie as a solid, sturdy individual to questioning whether he was emotionally capable of leading the nation. Although Muskie won the New Hampshire primary, he lost momentum and positive press coverage and dropped out of the race following the Florida primary. After the media frenzy waned, some reporters acknowledged, as Muskie maintained, that the tears might have actually been snow melting on Muskie's face.

See also *Media feeding frenzies.*

REFERENCES

Lippman, Theo, Jr., and Donald C. Hansen. *Muskie.* New York: Norton, 1971.
White, Theodore H. *The Making of the President, 1972.* New York, Atheneum Publishers, 1973.

Myers, Dee Dee

Margaret Jane "Dee Dee" Myers (1961–) served as a political communications consultant and White House press secretary to President Bill Clinton. She was the first to hold the latter position under Clinton and the first and thus far the only woman appointed to it. Prior to working for Clinton as communications specialist in the 1992 campaign, she handled press relations for the California branches of Democratic presidential candidates Walter Mondale and Michael Dukakis, along with former Los Angeles mayor Tom Bradley. She worked more recently as a consultant to the NBC White House drama *The West Wing* and as a private public relations specialist and part-time political commentator for MSNBC covering the "revolving door" between politics and the media.

REFERENCE

Han, Lori Cox. *Governing from Center Stage: White House Communications Strategies during the Television Age of Politics.* Creskill, N.J.: Hampton Press, 2001.

N

Nast, Thomas

Thomas Nast (1840–1902) was a notable American political cartoonist. Nast emigrated to the United States from Germany with his family in 1846. Never comfortable with his education and yielding to the economic pressures on his family, Nast became a draftsman for Frank Leslie's *Illustrated Newspaper* (1855). While in Leslie's employ, Nast learned the art of wood carving. In 1858, when Leslie's newspaper experienced financial difficulties, many—including Nast—were let go. He found employment in an art studio and when he tried his hand as a freelance political cartoonist, his depiction of a New York City police scandal (1859) was published by *Harper's Weekly*.

Nast worked for *Harper's* for less than a year when he was hired by the *New York Illustrated News* to cover events in Europe. He was stranded in London, however, when the paper failed to pay him, so he found employment with the *London Illustrated News* to earn return passage to New York. When the Civil War broke out, Nast wanted to enlist in the Union army, but friends convinced him he could be of greater service applying his talent as an illustrator. He overcame his sense of shame about leaving *Harper's* two years earlier and asked his former employer for a job. Nast was rehired (1861) and spent the war years illustrating many battles and scenes for the magazine. During this same period, Nast began an annual illustration series that created the popular image of Santa Claus.

Nast extended his focus on American life scenes and eventually turned his art, skill, and pen on the corruption of Tammany Hall in New York City (1871), contributing to

"A LIVE JACKASS KICKING A DEAD LION."
And such a Lion! and such a Jackass!

Political cartoonist Thomas Nast created the iconic images of the donkey and elephant representing the Democratic and Republican Parties, respectively. The donkey appeared for the first time in this 1870 cartoon marking the death of Edwin Stanton, President Abraham Lincoln's secretary of war.

the downfall of William "Boss" Tweed and establishing the political cartoonist profession. He created via his cartoons the popular icons of the Republican Party's elephant and the Democratic Party's donkey. Nast's political cartoons channeled public attention, influencing the outcome of elections and the conduct of public servants. In seven presidential elections in which Nast took a position, he never picked a loser. He also started his own publication—*Nast Illustrated Almanac*—and produced illustrations for more than seventy books. Nast left *Harper's* after Fletcher Harper's death and in the wake of disagreements with the new editor. He published his own newspaper, *Nast's Weekly* (1890), and briefly served as consul general to Ecuador (1902) before he died of yellow fever. Nast is acknowledged as the most influential political cartoonist of his time.

REFERENCES

Keller, Morton. *The Art and Politics of Thomas Nast.* New York: Oxford University Press, 1968.

Paine, Albert Bigelow. *Thomas Nast: His Period and His Pictures.* Princeton, N.J.: Pyne Press, 1974.

Sydney, Hoff. *Boss Tweed and the Man Who Drew Him.* New York: Putnam, 1978.

Nation

The *Nation* is the oldest weekly magazine of political discourse. Founded in 1865 by E. L. Godkin (1831–1902), a radical abolitionist and immigrant journalist, *The Nation* was conceived as a nonaligned, weekly journal of political opinion. Godkin used his broad knowledge, political independence, moral purpose, and incisive style as he took on carpetbaggers, government corruption, free silver, organized labor, and high tariffs. He sold the financially strapped magazine in 1881 to Henry Villard's *New York Evening Post,* to which *The Nation* became a weekly supplement. Godkin assumed the role of editor in chief in 1883 and remained at the *Evening Post* until 1899. Villard's son, Oswald Garrison Villard, took over *The Nation* in 1918 and moved the magazine politically to the far left, where it remains today. *The Nation* took controversial political positions supporting Soviet-style communism, opposing the cold war policies of successive U.S. administrations since World War II, and opposing the Vietnam War and both Persian Gulf wars. In 1932 Freda Kirchwey became editor in chief, the post she held until she was replaced in 1955 by Carey McWilliams. Hamilton Fish V and a group of investors acquired the magazine in 1977. Eighteen years later, *The Nation's* editor, Victor Navasky, assembled a group of like-minded investors to acquire the magazine and decided to maintain its political posture, despite business counsel to do otherwise. The current publisher and editor is Katrina vanden Heuvel.

REFERENCES

The Nation, www.thenation.com.

Alpern, Sara. *Freda Kirchwey: A Woman of The Nation.* Cambridge: Harvard University Press, 1987.

Armstrong, William M. *E. L. Godkin: A Biography.* Albany: State University of New York Press, 1978.

Humes, Dollena Joy. *Oswald Garrison Villard: Liberal of the 1920s.* Syracuse: Syracuse University Press, 1960.

Ogden, Rollo. *Life and Letters of Edwin Lawrence Godkin.* New York: Macmillan Company, 1907.

Villard, Oswald Garrison. *Fighting Years: Memoirs of a Liberal Editor.* New York: Harcourt, Brace and Company, 1939.

Wreszin, Michael. *Oswald Garrison Villard: Pacifist at War.* Bloomington: Indiana University Press, 1965.

National Association of Broadcasters

The National Association of Broadcasters (NAB) is a lobbying organization started in 1923 representing the free, over-the-air radio and television industry. Its mission is to foster the development of broadcasting and to protect the interests of the industry, both radio and television. It also has an affiliated political action committee, the Television and Radio Political Action Committee (TARPAC), which raises funds from members and makes contributions to candidates.

The board of directors issues a statement of principles for radio and television broadcasters. The organization seeks quality programming, but the application and interpretation of the specific standards remain under the sole discretion of the individual radio or television licensee. This self-policing system has enabled the industry to avoid government regulation of content. The system includes the establishment of the industry's own codes that regulate the amount of sex, violence, nudity, and profanity that is allowed to air. The NAB releases several publications a year that examine industry issues.

REFERENCES

National Association of Broadcasters, www.nab.org.

Board of Directors of the National Association of Broadcasters, *Statement of Principles of Radio and Television Broadcasters.* Washington, D.C.: National Association of Broadcasters, n.d.

National Gazette

The *National Gazette* was a semi-weekly paper in Philadelphia, founded and published by Philip Freneau at the urging of Thomas Jefferson. Its goal was to promote a more Republican Party perspective on national affairs—one aligned with Jefferson's point of view—to counter the Federalist and Hamiltonian *Gazette of the United States*. The *National Gazette* defended then-secretary of state Jefferson against attacks by supporters of Alexander Hamilton, promoted the generally weaker role for the national government envisioned by him, and even made some cautious criticisms of President George Washington. Unlike its rival counterpart, however, the *National Gazette* never gained the same financial and political footing and its life was brief, closing soon after Jefferson resigned as secretary of state in 1793.

See also *Freneau, Philip Morin; Gazette of the United States.*

REFERENCES

Mott, Frank Luther. *Jefferson and the Press.* Baton Rouge: Louisiana State University Press, 1943.
Rubin, Richard. *Press, Party, and Presidency.* New York: W. W. Norton and Co., 1981.

National Journal

The *National Journal* is a nonpartisan, specialized weekly publication in Washington, D.C., focusing on national politics and government. First published in 1969, it specializes in the analysis of emerging issues, descriptions of legislative trends, and profiles of both major and minor players in the nation's capital. It is widely read by executive branch officials, journalists, legislative aids, lobbyists, and think tank analysts. The *National Journal* found its niche during the 1970s, when lobbyists created a demand for expensive, highly specialized, nonpartisan publications on pending policy issues. The *CQ Weekly,* published by Congressional Quarterly, is considered the *National Journal*'s competitor. The *National Journal* company also publishes the *Almanac of American Politics, The Capital Source, The Federal Technology Source,* and *The Manager's Edge.*

REFERENCES

National Journal, www.nationaljournal.com/aboutnjmag.htm.
Case, Tony. "National Journal Changes Hands." *Folio: The Magazine for Magazine Management,* July 1, 1997, 22.

National Public Radio

National Public Radio (NPR) is a nationwide public radio system that creates and disseminates news and cultural programs through live satellite distribution. In 1939 the U.S. government initiated the development of the frequency modulation radio band (FM radio) and reserved twenty out of the one hundred FM channels for noncommercial, educational purposes. The 88.1 megahertz to 91.9 MHz frequencies remain noncommercial throughout the nation. This system of frequencies formed the basis for the eventual creation of NPR.

The Corporation for Public Broadcasting (CPB) was founded in 1967 and established criteria by which it would grant funds to build a national public radio system. The CPB established National Public Radio to distribute programs to public radio stations in the same way that the Public Broadcasting Service (PBS) would for television.

In 2005 there were more than eight hundred member public radio stations—almost half being licensed to higher

National Public Radio was founded by the Corporation for Public Broadcasting in 1971 and today reaches an audience of more than 26 million. Here reporter and commentator Daniel Schorr works out of NPR's Washington studio.

education institutions—reaching an audience of twenty-six million. The bulk of public radio station budgets are derived from membership or subscription contributions; only about 2 percent comes from grants from CPB and other foundations. NPR's Web site offers original programming, live audio feeds, and archived material.

REFERENCES

National Public Radio, www.npr.org.
Looker, Thomas. *The Sound and the Story: NPR and the Art of Radio.* Boston: Houghton Mifflin, 1995.
Witherspoon, John, Roselle Kovitz, Robert K. Avery, and Alan G. Stavistky. *A History of Public Broadcasting.* Washington, D.C.: Current Press, 1999.

National Review

The *National Review,* a political magazine first published in November 1955, represents a conservative counterpart to the more liberal *New Republic.* Under the guidance of William F. Buckley Jr., founder and long-time editor, the *National Review* has unified conservative intellectuals in their ideological struggle with American liberalism, moral relativism, and communism. Three distinct strains of American conservatism—libertarianism, anti-communism, and traditionalism—coalesce in the magazine's discussions, providing a forum previously unavailable to conservatives.

The magazine has criticized the growth of the national government, the increasing secularization of American life and institutions, and what it perceived as a lack of sufficient fervor in the fights against domestic and global communism. Many of the magazine's editors and writers participated in Barry Goldwater's 1964 Republican campaign for president, which struck many of the same themes as the *National Review.* In the post–cold war era, the magazine continued to push the same procapitalist, antisocialist, and traditionalist themes. During the 1980s, the *National Review* was a mouthpiece for the conservative establishment under Republican president Ronald Reagan, subsequently assuming the role of an opposition publication when Democrat Bill Clinton became president. At times, however, the magazine has criticized the two Bush administrations for not following conservative orthodoxy in perpetuating its role as a gatekeeper of American conservatism.

See also *Buckley, William F., Jr.*

REFERENCES

Judis, John. *William Buckley Jr.: Patron Saint of the Conservatives.* New York: Simon and Schuster, 1988.
Nash, George. *The Conservative Intellectual Movement in Modern America: Since 1945.* New York: Basic Books, 1996.
National Review, www.nationalreview.com.

National security

National security encompasses efforts to protect a nation-state's territorial integrity, sovereignty, and independence, especially from external threats. Governments ensure the survival and safety of the nation-state through the use of intelligence and counterintelligence, the exercise of military and economic power, and diplomacy in times of war and peace. The focus and breadth of issues considered to be of national security interest change as the nature of threats changes. For example, U.S. national security policy after the September 11, 2001, attacks found classic state-to-state approaches to security ill-suited to the emerging threat that nonstate actors such as al-Qaida pose. The Department of Homeland Security was created to coordinate the activities of previously autonomous government agencies to deal with the emerging threat of international terrorism.

The media influence national security in four broad ways: addressing issues properly considered threats (drug trafficking, economic and political migration, weapons of mass destruction, and so on); providing a forum for debate and discussion (to prioritize issues); serving as a vehicle through which policymakers seek to affect public opinion (as in airing the State of the Union address); and playing a role in the politics of censorship (as in the fight over the publication of the Pentagon Papers).

Presidents are expected to lead in national security matters more than in any other issue area, and a shrewd president utilizes the media to educate the public and garner policy support. The public may be skeptical of media reporting on national security events because reporters can be provided only limited access to security information and because the media may sometimes report the sensational in pursuit of profit. Trust in the media's objectivity in covering national security may suffer and add to the public's deference to executive authority in foreign policy matters.

On the other hand, critics of government may voice disfavor or alternative security strategies through the media, especially via an acknowledged expert in foreign policy.

After the al-Qaida attacks of September 2001 and the U.S. invasion of Afghanistan, the administration of George W. Bush established facilities at Guantanamo Bay, Cuba, to hold persons captured in the "war on terror." Media reporting on the treatment of prisoners and questions about their legal status has resulted in ongoing controversy about the administration's national security policies.

Government officials who disagree with national security policy may leak information to the media about the reasons for their disagreement and in this way influence the public, and in turn Congress and the executive, to reshape national security policy.

REFERENCES

Johnson, Douglas V. *The Impact of the Media on National Security Policy Decision Making.* Carlisle, Pa.: Strategic Studies Institute, U.S. Army War College, 1994.

Jordan, Donald L., and Benjamin I. Page. "Shaping Foreign Policy Options: The Role of TV News." *Journal of Conflict Resolution* 36, no. 2 (June 1992): 227–241.

Native Americans and the media

As noted at a 2006 symposium on Native American portrayals in the media, Indian Country is today a mystery to most people in large part because of the absence of U.S. media coverage about it. Myths persist about American Indians, and stereotypes about casinos and "rich tribes" pervade popular culture, but the realities and cultural strengths of American Indian and Alaska Native life remain hidden. Despite coverage of the Jack Abramoff lobbying scandal and the lawsuit over trust fund management (*Cobell v. Norton*), coverage of American Indians in the press continues to be scant.

The current way in which information is conveyed (or not) prevents non-Natives from more easily becoming knowledgeable about the lives of people of Indian nations. As a result, many non-Natives become upset when American Indians express their resentment of and protest distorted depictions of themselves in the media. For instance, residents of cities with sports teams with American Indian nicknames and mascots—such as Braves (Atlanta), Indians (Cleveland), Chiefs (Kansas City), and Redskins (Washington, D.C.)—and the regents, trustees, and alumni of such institutions as the University of Illinois (Chief Illiniwek), Florida State University (Seminoles), and the University of North Dakota (Fighting Sioux)—do not understand why members of most Native American tribes might object to these usages. Why might Native Americans be upset? Part of the answer, according to John Seigenthaler in his foreword to *Pictures of Our Nobler Selves,* is that "Native Americans, having been stripped of identity, dignity and distinction for more than two centuries, are convinced that false media caricatures have helped rob them of their history." Perhaps not surprisingly, the contributions of Native Americans to the news media in the United States—the same media that have played a key role in creating or perpetuating the flawed caricatures of America's Native peoples—have largely gone ignored.

From the beginning, Native American journalists have faced innumerable ordeals. Some resulted from conflicts with nontribal forces, others from tribal officials. Documenting this turbulent history in *Pictures of Our Nobler Selves,* Mark Trahant (Shoshone-Bannock) recounts the history of the *Cherokee Phoenix.* Elias Boudinot (Cherokee) was the founding editor of this publication, in 1827. The *Phoenix* was forced out of business in 1835, when the Georgia Guard, the state militia, destroyed its offices and dumped its lead type into a well. Not long afterward, the government forced the Cherokee themselves out of Georgia.

John Rollins Ridge (Cherokee) was a frequent contributor to the *Golden Era,* a literary magazine, and the founding editor of the *Sacramento Daily Bee,* in February 1857. The official history of the *Bee* begins, however, in July 1857, when it was sold to James McClatchy. Ridge had already moved on and would own and edit several newspapers in California, all of which were characterized by support for Native peoples and genuine concern about government policy toward American Indians. More recently, *Indian Country Today,* a weekly newspaper founded in 1981, has become a persuasive voice in American Indian journalism. It publishes more original journalistic content on Native American issues than any other news source, and its Web site, indiancountry.com, has the highest visitor traffic of any Native site. In 1998 Four Directions Media Inc., owned and operated by the Oneida Nation of New York, purchased *Indian Country Today* and established corporate headquarters in New York state.

Native American journalists have had their share of "firsts." Myrta Eddleman (Cherokee) became the first Native American woman to own a mainstream newspaper when her partners in the *Muskogee Daily Times* quit and she became sole receiver in 1897. After transferring ownership to her mother, Mary Eddleman, business improved, as the *Muskogee Daily Times* became the first newspaper in Indian Territory to contract with the Associated Press during the Spanish-American War. Reader interest at that time was high. Myrta Eddleman's younger daughter, Ora, grew up in the newsroom and later worked for her sister writing for *The Twin Territories,* a magazine. Ora later married Charles Reed, and the two of them moved to Casper, Wyoming. In 1924 a family friend launched KDFN, Wyoming's first radio station, and Ora proposed the idea of a "talk-type" program that could bring in revenue for the station. According to Trahant, Ora Eddleman Reed's half-hour talk show—also likely the first of its kind—proved to be a great success and was later expanded into a two-hour format in which she answered calls and letters from listeners, offering homespun and optimistic advice. The program ended when the Reed family moved to Tulsa in 1932.

No doubt aware of the opportunities presented by radio in reaching tribal communities, John Collier, commissioner of Indian affairs under President Franklin D. Roosevelt, budgeted federal money for radio communications in remote Alaskan villages and sponsored a national program to educate the nation about tribal history, culture, and current affairs that was carried on 170 stations from Alaska to Florida. According to Mary Ann Weston, author of *Native Americans in the News,* Collier advocated a philosophy of cultural pluralism and preservation of Indian cultures, which he asserted were valuable. Collier's "Indian New Deal" was the most sweeping change in Indian policy since the Dawes Act of 1887.

Few would deny that radio built on the traditions of Natives' oral storytelling society. Native peoples could listen to the radio as they would to an elder handing down a story from generation to generation. Today, there are more than twenty-five radio stations, mostly nonprofit public stations, serving tribal communities across the United States. Most are community stations. People call the station and share information about local government action, funerals, announcements of traditional ceremonies, and so on. The notion of community broadcasting best characterizes all tribal radio stations, but tribal radio is also, however, the only national medium in Indian Country. Once a day, *National Native News,* a five-minute newscast, is sent to public radio stations across the country. *Native America Calling* uses a toll-free number and a satellite consortium (American Indian Radio on Satellite, AIROS) to present issues directly to Native communities. It is also available through streaming on the Internet.

Few American Indians worked in television before 1970. Most of those who did were hosts of weekly public affairs programs in Minneapolis, Oklahoma City, and Phoenix, Arizona—cities with large Indian populations—or in smaller markets near reservations. Many of these shows still exist, often broadcast early on Sunday mornings to fulfill the station's public affairs commitment or, more likely, aired on public access cable channels. One of the first broadcast journalists to work in television was Tanna Beebe (Cowlitz and Quinault), who spent five years at KIRO-TV in Seattle. Another was Lorraine Edmo (Shoshone-Bannock), who worked for KID-TV in Idaho Falls. Perhaps the first Native American journalist to break a story on national television news was Hattie Kauffman (Nez Perce), working for ABC News in 1989 when she scooped the rest of the media with a story on the United Airlines Flight 811 accident at Honolulu International Airport.

Given the efforts of American Indians in journalism and the self-imposed mission of the media to provide fair and factual information, how successful have the media been in dealing with the imagery and the reality of Native Americans? A 2002 analysis of mainstream news coverage by nine leading newspapers found more articles about Native Americans than expected. Nonetheless, a content audit raised concerns about the gross inaccuracies and uninformed coverage that perpetuates stereotypes and incorrect perceptions. According to the *Reading Red Report,* the *Wall Street Journal* had the lowest number of articles (43) during the three-year period (1999–2002) under analysis, and the *New York Times* had the highest (519). Many of the articles, however, were about the same subjects—tribal casinos (145) and mascots (116). Although coverage of reservations (225) is appropriate, the report noted, "so many stories were datelined Pine Ridge that a reader might not have realized that New York City's 87,241 Native American residents make up the largest urban Indian community in the nation." While the *Washington Post* carried 33 articles on the multi-billion-dollar Indian land trust fund scandal involving the Department of the Interior, such extensive coverage of a priority issue for tribes is highly unusual. Recently, only four events of concern to American Indians received widespread coverage: the opening of the National Museum of the American Indian, the murder of classmates by a troubled teenager on Red Lake Reservation, the controversy surrounding University of Colorado professor Ward Churchill, and the investigation and indictment of high-priced, high-powered Washington insiders who bilked six tribes of millions by pretending to represent them, the coverage of which appeared to be fueled more by the involvement of nationally known personalities and politicians than by concern about the tribes. Getting national media coverage about the crucial concerns of tribes, even recognition of their existence, seems nearly impossible.

REFERENCES

"American Indian Radio on Satellite," www.airos.org.
Briggs, Kara, and Dan Lewerenz. "A Call for the News Media to Recognize Racism in Sports Team Nicknames and Mascots." *The Reading Red Report, 2003.* Vermillion, S.D.: Native American Journalists Association and News Watch, 2003, www.naja.com/resources/publications/2003_reading-red.pdf.
Briggs, Kara, Tom Arviso, Dennis McAuliffe, and Lori Edmo-Suppah. "Native Americans in the News: A 2002 Report and Content Analysis on Coverage by the Largest Newspapers in the United States." *The Reading Red Report.* Vermillion, S.D.: Native American Journalists Association and News Watch, 2002, www.naja.com/resources/publications/2002_reading-red.pdf.
"Message to Media: Hear the Indian Voice." *Indian Country Today,* March 10, 2006, www.indiancountry.com.
"Media Impact on American Indian Public Policy." *Indian Country Today,* January 12, 2006, www.indiancountry.com.
National Native News, www.nativenews.net.
Native America Calling, www.nativeamericacalling.com.
Reynolds, Jerry. "Communications Conference Calls for More Native Voice in Media." *Indian Country Today,* March 10, 2006, www.indiancountry.com.
Rolo, Mark Anthony, ed. *The American Indian and the Media,* 2nd ed. St. Paul, Minn.: National Conference for Community and Justice, 2000.
Rubin, Nan. *Report on the Findings and Concerns for Native American Public Radio.* New York: Community Media Services, 1987, http://nanrubin.com/nativeradio.pdf.
Singer, Beverly R. *Wiping the War Paint Off the Lens: Native American Film and Video.* Minneapolis: University of Minnesota Press, 2001.
Trahant, Mark N. *Pictures of Our Nobler Selves: A History of Native American Contributions to the Media.* Nashville, Tenn.: Freedom Forum First Amendment Center, 1995.
Weston, Mary Ann. *Native Americans in the News: Images of Indians in the Twentieth-Century Press.* Westport, Conn.: Greenwood Press, 1996.
Wieberg, Steve. "Mascots Create Divisiveness on Some Campuses." *USA Today,* May 16, 2005, C3.

NBC Universal

The National Broadcasting Company (NBC) was the first national broadcast network. NBC is still a major media outlet, with interests in network television, local stations, and cable broadcasting.

NBC was established by the Radio Corporation of America (RCA), itself the product of several companies' interest in promoting radio technology in the United States. The General Electric Company (GE) and Westinghouse also had interests in NBC, but RCA bought out those interests and by 1930 was the sole owner of NBC. In 1986 GE acquired RCA.

NBC's first radio broadcast, an entertainment show from New York City, came in 1926. The show was broadcast to twenty-five stations as far west as Kansas City. The first coast-to-coast broadcast was the 1927 Rose Bowl football game in California. NBC established its news division in 1933. NBC's broadcasts demonstrated the information and entertainment potential of radio, and demand for programming and station affiliation grew so quickly that NBC divided into two networks. NBC Red carried entertainment, and NBC Blue offered cultural and public affairs programming. Because of antitrust concerns, NBC in 1941 was forced to sell the Blue network, which became the American Broadcasting Company (ABC).

NBC's ties to RCA made the company a technological pioneer. NBC's founder, David Sarnoff, started work on TV in 1925, and the first regular telecast was of the New York World's Fair in 1939. World War II interrupted the emergence of TV, and radio was the primary medium through which Americans received immediate news bulletins. Meanwhile, NBC founded the long-running public affairs program "Meet the Press," first on radio and then on TV. NBC's radio experience helped build the first television network, linking four cities: New York City, Philadelphia, Washington, D.C., and Schenectady, N.Y. The viability of TV, however, became clearer when the number of TV households grew tenfold between 1947 and 1948.

NBC and RCA continued as the technical innovators throughout the 1950s and 1960s. RCA's color TV standard beat out CBS's for Federal Communications Commission approval in 1953, and by the mid-1960s, NBC introduced the colorful peacock symbol and "The Full Color Network" slogan. NBC was also a leader in news, with the nightly *Huntley-Brinkley Report* often running a close second behind Walter Cronkite on CBS.

NBC had many periods of ratings success. In the 1960s the network dominated the TV schedule with shows such as *Laugh-In*. In the 1970s it often lagged behind ABC but returned strong in the 1980s with shows such as *Cheers* and *Hill Street Blues*. *Seinfeld* and *ER* were among the most popular shows of the 1990s. In news, NBC enjoyed considerable success with its magazine show *Dateline NBC*. Its reality programming, particularly *Fear Factor* and *The Apprentice,* with Donald Trump, have also been hits.

NBC owns a business and public affairs channel, CNBC; a cable news channel with the Microsoft Corporation, MSNBC; and the Bravo cable network. It also owns the Spanish-language network Telemundo. The benefits of owning such a broad range of outlets were shown in coverage of the 2004 Athens Olympics, when NBC was able to show sports on all its affiliated broadcast and cable networks. Its most recent acquisition, Universal Studios, and the renaming of the company, NBC Universal, provide the company with

a movie studio base similar to its counterparts at other networks, particularly ABC.

REFERENCES

Auletta, Ken. *Three Blind Mice: How the Networks Lost Their Way.* New York: Random House, 1991.

Campbell, Robert. *The Golden Years of Broadcasting: A Celebration of the First 50 Years of Radio and Television on NBC.* New York: Charles Scribner's Sons, 1976.

Holson, Laura M. "Six Sigma: A Hollywood Studio Learns the G.E. Way." *New York Times,* September 27, 2004, C2.

Landler, Mark. "Microsoft and NBC's TV-Internet Service Trips in Debut." *New York Times,* July 16, 1996, D6.

McCarthy, Michael. "NBC Universal's Gamble on Olympics Pays Off Big." *USA Today,* August 30, 2004, 7B.

Near v. Minnesota (1931)

In *Near v. Minnesota* (1931) the U.S. Supreme Court, in a 5–4 decision, ruled prior restraint to be unconstitutional. In response to a profusion of yellow journalism, Minnesota law permitted state courts to issue injunctions prohibiting publication of any "malicious, scandalous and defamatory newspaper, or other periodical." A local prosecutor sought to suppress publication of the *Saturday Press,* a tabloid headed by Jay Near that had run articles about government corruption, including allegations that the Minneapolis police were in league with gangsters. Near was also known to publish articles attacking Catholics and Jews as well as blacks and labor. The state court issued an injunction against the *Press,* which appealed the order, ultimately to the Supreme Court.

The Court's opinion, written by Chief Justice Charles Evans Hughes, pointed out that the traditional conception of freedom of the press, in England as well as in the United States, consists of the absence of prior censorship. He called the Minnesota statute, the Public Nuisance Abatement Law, the "essence of censorship." Although a publisher might be legally liable for seditious or libelous material after the fact of publication, publication could not be prevented in advance. Hughes's opinion especially emphasized the role of the press in criticizing official misconduct, noting that prior restraint would silence such criticism. The precedent established in *Near v. Minnesota,* often cited and expanded in later decisions by the Supreme Court (most notably in *New York Times v. United States*), seeks to protect the press against attempts by government officials to conceal malfeasance in office or other governmental wrongdoing.

See also *New York Times v. United States (1971); Privacy Protection Act of 1980; Zurcher v. Stanford Daily (1978).*

REFERENCES

Harrison, Maureen, and Steve Gilbert, eds. *Freedom of the Press Decisions of the United States Supreme Court.* San Diego: Excellent Books, 1996.

Near v. Minnesota, 283 U.S. 697 (1931).

Parker, Richard A. *Free Speech on Trial: Communication Perspectives on Landmark Supreme Court Decisions.* Tuscaloosa: University of Alabama Press, 2003.

Negative ads

See *Daisy girl commercial; Political content in advertising; Willie Horton ad.*

New journalism

New journalism refers to two distinct periods in U.S. journalism history. The first period is that of Joseph Pulitzer and William Randolph Hearst and their efforts to boost newspaper circulation through aggressive newsgathering techniques, human interest stories, and sensationalism at a time that saw improvements in education, growth of an immigrant class, and social reforms during the transition from agrarian to urban economy in the post–Civil War era. The second period occurred a century later when some writers, less motivated by objectivity, adopted a style employing personal experience to convey a story. Jimmy Breslin, Truman Capote, Norman Mailer, Lillian Ross, Gay Talese, and Tom Wolfe were part of the movement toward the interpretation of real events in novel format.

Many editors scorned reporter involvement in the movement, but a few prominent examples emerged, including Tom Wicker of the *New York Times* and Haynes Johnson of the *Washington Post,* who utilized aggressive interviewing strategies in their work. Bob Woodward and Carl Bernstein's telling of the Watergate story is considered exemplary new journalism. In *All the President's Men,* personal involvement, interpretation, and graphic reporting of details are key to the

Writer and journalist Hunter S. Thompson insisted that objectivity in journalism was impossible. He pioneered "gonzo journalism," a form of new journalism that rejected pure objectivity in favor of personal interpretation and involvement.

story. Although new journalism as a movement waned, its notion of a more autonomous and interpretive press continues to influence journalistic practice.

REFERENCES

Dennis, Everette, and William L. Rivers. *Other Voices: The New Journalism in America.* San Francisco: Canfield, 1974.

Downie, Leonard. *The New Muckrakers.* Washington, D.C.: New Republic, 1977.

Wolfe, Tom. *The New Journalism.* New York: Harper and Row, 1973.

New media

New media refers to the forms of information creation, dissemination, and consumption that have become available largely because of the advent of the Internet and related

Politicians are increasingly turning to new media to communicate with constituents. Senate majority leader Bill Frist (R-Tenn.) records his weekly podcast for downloading to iPods and other portable electronic devices. Frist's podcast on avian flu was downloaded one million times.

technologies. Such proprietary networks as Compuserve, Prodigy, and America Online (AOL) anticipated the Internet's value to the general public as a source of information and entertainment. They provided services that allowed users to chat, use e-mail, and browse for information, but their e-mail systems were not interoperable, and pages of information on one system could not be shared among other systems. In the early 1990s, as personal computers became increasingly more powerful, and demand for new services on what was called the "information superhighway" grew, the Internet was put to broader commercial use. By 1994 it was available for widespread commercial applications.

Two other innovations made the Internet accessible to a mass audience: the Web browser and the proliferation of Internet service providers (ISPs) in the 1990s. The World Wide Web existed before browsers became popular. At that time, Web pages tended to be text-heavy, and users accessed them through text-only browsers, such as Lynx. Tim Berners-Lee along with Robert Cailliau and their colleagues at the European Particle Physics Laboratory (known by its French acronym, CERN) are considered to have been the driving force behind the Web. Berners-Lee developed hypertext systems for sharing information among scientists. In 1993 much of the underlying technologies of the Web entered the public domain. Key to the Web were and are HTTP (hypertext transfer protocol) and HTML (hypertext markup language).

In February 1993, the University of Illinois National Center for Supercomputing Applications (NCSA) developed the first graphical Web browser, NCSA Mosaic, for the Unix operating system, which was later that year used in the Macintosh system. This browser could display Web pages written in HTML 1.1. The fundamental features of Mosaic were licensed to Netscape and Microsoft, which later introduced the Netscape Navigator and Microsoft Internet Explorer browsers.

Before the Web browser and its underlying technologies, information on the Internet could be hard to find and difficult to use. The Web browser, HTML, and HTTP paralleled the rapid adoption of the Internet. In the late 1990s, high-speed home Internet connections over coaxial TV cable or through telephone companies' digital subscriber line (DSL) services made the Internet even more useful. High-speed Internet enabled content creators to post anything that could be digitized to the Web or the Internet, including audio, video, graphics, and text. Thus, much as the invention of radio and television created new technologies that allowed for new forms of media, the advent of the Internet created either a new medium or a set of new media that could serve as a replacement for or an adjunct to other forms of information. The current new media environment consists of, among other things, Web pages (sometimes called "the Internet" although Web servers are a part of the Internet, but not all of it); Web logs, or blogs; news delivery services through real simple syndication (RSS); and podcasting, a system for transmitting audio programs that can be downloaded.

Web pages are, in general, documents posted on the Internet in HTML that can be viewed by a Web browser. A collection of Web pages comprises a Web site. Because the systems for developing and posting Web pages are based on open standards, all one needs to create a Web site is access to a computer, a Web hosting account, and the codes with which to tag text in HTML or a program that will automatically do the coding. Web sites range from small personal sites, such those containing family pictures and news, to huge sites containing thousands of pages, such as the *New York Times*'s Web site, nytimes.com, or shopping sites, such as amazon.com, which is both the site name and the company name. All manner of uses have arisen from the Web, including booking airline and hotel reservations, listening to music, reading, and watching news and sports. The Web has become an essential element in the lives of many users.

Because the Web allows people and companies to broadcast information to large numbers of computers at a low cost per reader, many writers and publishers came to believe that such Internet sites as salon.com and slate.com represented the future of written communication and would overtake traditional print magazines. Many smaller sites that sought to reach mass audiences have come and gone, as subscription and advertising revenues fell short of these sites' ambitious writing and production plans. Slate, originally owned by Microsoft, is now a part of the Washington Post Company, while Salon continues as a well-regarded online journal of news and opinion, supported by a combination of subscriptions and advertising. Few sites, however, have successfully funded themselves from subscription revenue. The *Wall Street Journal* has been moderately successful because of the inherent value of the information the site contains, and the *New York Times* recently began to charge its readers for "premium" features, such as editorials and archived articles. The major political parties recognized the potential of the Web as early as the 1996 presidential and congressional elections, and by 2006 every party, political action committee, and candidate had a Web presence.

With the advent of the Web, other forms of information dissemination emerged. For instance, blogs have grown in popularity and attracted a great deal of media attention. They have been around for at least a decade and originally tended to consist of little more than a list of the Web pages that bloggers—the people who write and maintain blogs—posted on the Web that other people might find useful or of interest. Blogs link directly to the main strength of hypertext—the ability to form multiple links to and from disparate information. Around 2001, blogs began evolving into more complex sites. While most blogs serve small audiences, some have become widely read publications with distinctive voices that attract particular audiences. During the 2004 presidential campaign, the blogosphere, as the collectivity of blogs has become known, buzzed with discussions—some serious, some less so—about the key issues. In some instances, bloggers broke stories that the mainstream media then followed up. Some bloggers have gained minor celebrity status, among them Matt Drudge, Anna Marie Cox, and Markos Moulitsas Zúniga. At one time, serious journalists disdained blogs, but "old media" have now adapted the popular new media blog format to enliven their Web sites. The *New York Times* carries a blog by columnist Nicholas Kristoff, the *Washington Post* features blogs by several of its writers, and the Cable News Network (CNN) runs a blog by Anderson Cooper, who hosts some of its programs.

RSS is a technology that has grown slowly but may someday prove to be influential. With it, consumers use an RSS-compatible Web browser or an RSS newsreader to download and view stories based on keywords and sites that they select. Thus, instead of perusing the *New York Times, Rolling Stone,* and *Newsweek,* for example, for political news, one can simply set his or her RSS reader to download links to stories about a particular subject, such as stories on Medicare drug coverage, a U.S. representative, or a favorite sports team.

Streaming video, audio, and podcasting are the most recent technologies that promise to be disruptive to old media companies. In the late 1990s, the program Napster allowed users to "share" (or "steal," depending on one's perspective) music, most of it compressed in the MP3 format. Consumers shared millions of songs without the musicians or music labels being paid. Today, after much litigation, Napster and other outlets, such as Apple's iTunes, make music available for download on a pay-per-song basis. Streaming audio capabilities have existed for about ten years, and with broadband available in the home, many people can now listen to news, sports, and music broadcast from any radio station or Web site in the world that is connected to the Internet and that has the facilities to translate its analog broadcasts into digital media. This technology allows listeners to hear news from another city or from across the world. The British Broadcasting Company (BBC) adopted streaming audio early on, and many people turned to it for news about world events when they found their own country's broadcasts to be deficient or unreliable.

Streaming video has been a staple of such sites as CNN's, because the technology allows computer users to view news clips. Many sites, however, use streamed video to feature clips of offbeat human-interest stories and such events as accidents, disasters, and war, reflecting television's current predisposition for dramatic footage. Pay-per-view video is becoming increasingly popular, as TV networks begin to make their popular shows available, for a fee, for download and viewing on computers and portable video players. Along these lines, podcasting allows people to download audio files from an Internet site for listening on an iPod or similar portable MP3 player or computer. Podcasts also include collections of previously aired stories from radio, such as much of National Public Radio's content, or original programming generated by professional or amateur journalists or other "content providers."

All these new media have one thing in common: the Internet as distribution network. Among the major questions for scholars of the media's influence on politics and society, some of the most important concern whether and to what extent "old media" have adapted to "new media," whether and to what extent the new media have hastened already existing trends toward "narrowcasting" rather than broadcasting, and whether and to what extent new media are "new" or are just old media in new packaging. Accompanying these concerns is the so-called digital divide, the issue of access to new media and technology and how a lack of access affects certain peoples and communities.

Many observers thought that the new media would pose a major threat to the old media, represented by newspapers and television. So far, the threat has not been significant. Although newspaper readership and TV news viewing have fallen sharply in the past twenty years, one cannot attribute these changes entirely to the new media. New media's audience represents only a fraction of that of mainstream radio, TV, and newspapers. In addition, and more to the point, all the major news outlets—cable news providers, national and local newspapers, and the broadcast news networks—maintain their own extensive Web sites, which often carry video and audio features that they generate. The top-ranked news sites include bbc.co.uk, cnn.com, and nytimes.com. In many cases, the new media present the same information transmitted on radio and TV and printed in newspapers. Thus, the demise of the old media appears to have been greatly exaggerated. Over time, from the telegraph, to the telephone, to radio and TV, nearly every medium has changed, adapted, and continued to grow as media companies incorporated new technologies and changing popular tastes. The decline in broadcast news audiences may reflect a response to media trends (predating the popularity of the Internet) that promote narrowcasting to more precisely targeted audience segments. Evidence of this can be seen in the proliferation of various popular music formats in FM radio, narrowly focused blogs, and the use of search engines or RSS readers to obtain information.

For some years, it was believed that men were more likely to use the Internet and consume new media than were women. Although this situation no longer exists, a considerable disparity has been documented in use and access between young and financially comfortable people and those who are relatively older, poor, belong to ethnic or racial minorities, or are non-English speakers. This digital divide, exacerbated by narrowcasting, could mean that the great political issues and events typically held in common could be experienced differently by various, narrower population segments, undermining any sense of shared national community, interest, or purpose. Much of this concern remains speculative at this time, as many of these new media—particularly podcasting and RSS—may prove to be passing fads. The Internet platforms on which these technologies are based, however, will continue to shape and be shaped by innovations in information gathering, production, and delivery.

REFERENCES

Ahlers, Douglas. "News Consumption and the New Electronic Media." *Harvard International Journal of Press/Politics* 11, no. 1 (2006): 52–75.
Bosman, Julie. "First with the Scoop, If Not the Truth." *New York Times,* April 18, 2006, www.nytimes.com.
Bucy, E. Page. *Living in the Information Age: A New Media Reader.* 2nd ed. Belmont, Calif.: Wadsworth, Thomson Learning, 2005.
Davis, Richard A. *Politics Online: Blogs, Chatrooms, and Discussion Groups in American Democracy.* New York: Routledge, 2005.
Davis, Richard A., and Diana Owen. *New Media and American Politics.* New York: Oxford University Press, 1998.
Internet Society. "A Brief History of the Internet and Related Networks," www.isoc.org/internet/history/cerf.shtml.
Living Internet. "Living Internet," www.livinginternet.com.
Peter, Ian. "Ian Peter's History of the Internet," www.nethistory.info.
Wardrip-Fruin, Noah, and Nick Montfort. *The New Media Reader.* Cambridge, Mass.: MIT Press, 2003.

New Republic

The *New Republic* is a weekly political opinion magazine that has been published since 1914. It is aimed toward a relatively small but elite and influential audience. The magazine generally has been a voice on the left, though not the far left, of the U.S. political spectrum. The editorials and most of its articles have supported the agendas and aims of the Democratic Party, although it has also sharply criticized the party. The *New Republic* is an advocate of reform and a regulated economy since it was first published during the Progressive era. The magazine veered to the left during the 1930s and supported Socialist Norman Thomas for president in 1932. During the 1950s the *New Republic* gave more expansive coverage to cultural topics at the expense of political issues.

Since the mid-1970s, when Martin Peretz bought the magazine, it has displayed an interventionist spirit in foreign affairs but less consistency in domestic affairs. In general, the editors and many of the contributors have expressed a friendly dissatisfaction with the Democratic Party and its more progressive liberal agenda. It has generally been seen as a neoliberal magazine and has been sympathetic to the moderate Democratic Leadership Council's agenda that is more friendly to business, while still socially liberal.

REFERENCES

Seideman, David. *The New Republic: A Voice of Modern Liberalism.* New York: Praeger Publishers, 1986.

Sherrill, Robert. "The New Regime at the New Republic: Or, Much Ado about Martin Peretz." *Columbia Journalism Review,* March–April 1976, 23–28.

News analysis

News analysis refers to an interpretive genre of reporting that goes behind the headlines and puts news in context, helping to explain the why, how, and significance of news items instead of simply describing them. News analysis is a bridge between news reporting and editorializing. As an editor for the *Boston Globe* described it in a June 13, 1974, column, "News analysis explains the dynamics of a situation, background, options and the turn of events that could take place. The news analysis would stop short of saying what 'should' happen, what would be 'best,' whether a particular proposal should be supported or opposed."

News analysis developed in the move toward a more analytical, interpretive style in the post-Vietnam era, when the notion of straightforward reporting of what politicians do or say was viewed as ceding democratic control of the news to them, allowing them to potentially manipulate the populace. Analysis and interpretation is meant to help the audience make sense of the world.

On television, news analysis may be done by special correspondents or beat reporters who provide background and analysis of stories through their comments. Newspapers may explicitly label some stories as "news analysis," such as the *New York Times,* which runs such pieces on its front page, parallel to the top story of the day, written by venerable journalists such as R. W. Apple. For example, while the main story may be a straightforward description of a presidential speech, the news analysis would dissect what the president is trying to accomplish, why the president is giving the speech at a particular time, and the politics surrounding it. Furthermore, the news analysis may even critique the performance as a dramatic spectacle. News analysis generally focuses on analyzing the political context of a news event. News analysis may thus emphasize a "game frame" or politics as a competitive sport.

The effect of news analysis is difficult to judge. Some studies of televised "instant analyses" following presidential speeches showed that they did affect viewers' opinions of the speech. But these assumed heavy media exposure and a public that both trusted and watched the analysis and commentary, things that the public may not be likely to do. Others, such as Thomas Patterson, argue the more interpretive "game emphasis" of most news analyses may make the public more cynical about politics.

Nevertheless, the existence of news analysis itself is a clear change from the descriptive just-the-facts news media of the 1950s and earlier.

REFERENCES

Hage, George S., et al. *New Strategies for Public Affairs Reporting: Investigation, Interpretation, and Research.* 2nd ed. Englewood Cliffs, N.J.: Prentice-Hall, 1983.

Hill, Evan, and John J. Breen. *Reporting and Writing the News.* Boston: Little, Brown, 1977.

Paletz, David, and Richard Vinegar. "Presidents on Television: The Effects of Instant Analysis." *Public Opinion Quarterly* 41 (Winter 1977): 488–497.

Patterson, Thomas. *Out of Order.* New York: Vintage, 1994.

News blackouts

A news blackout is the purposive suspension of media coverage of a particular event. Blackouts may be ordered for security reasons or crises, such as hostage situations, or during sensitive meetings of political leaders when media coverage may be expected to adversely affect the outcome of the event. In most countries, these sorts of blackouts are often voluntary. During wartime, however, news blackouts can be used for strategic purposes, in which case they may be orchestrated by a country's government.

A more typical news blackout is that applied by some countries in the period leading up to or during political elections. Also called a reflection period, such a blackout prohibits media coverage of the candidates or even the issues at stake in the election. These blackouts can be mandatory or voluntary, and they vary in length. Because of a strong free press tradition and the First Amendment, such blackouts do not exist in the United States, though the Bipartisan Campaign Finance Reform Act of 2002 does limit the ability of noncandidate groups to buy and run political advertisements within thirty days of a primary or sixty days of a general election.

REFERENCES

Franklin, Bob, and David Murphy, eds. *Making the Local News: Local Journalism in Context.* New York: Routledge, 1998.
Gitlin, Todd. *The Whole World Is Watching: Mass Media in the Making and Unmaking.* Berkeley: University of California Press, 2003.

Newsgathering process

The term "newsgathering" refers to the techniques reporters use to acquire information. Because what the media report can affect people's issue preferences and political behavior, it is essential to understand the newsgathering process as an important element that influences how people view the world around them.

In an ideal world the media inform citizens about the major questions facing society while also reporting the potential policy alternatives that are aimed at solving them. But how do the media get the information that they provide?

Media scholar David L. Paletz describes the newsgathering process as containing three overlapping components: reporters originate, receive, and gather news. When journalists witness, and sometimes uncover, news and its consequences, they are originating information. For example, journalists originate news on location from war zones, natural disasters, and news conferences. Less often, reporters originate stories by conducting investigative, in-depth looks at a subject the way Bob Woodward and Carl Bernstein of the *Washington Post* did in the Watergate affair, which ultimately resulted in the resignation of President Richard M. Nixon in 1974. Reporters can also make the news, as ABC co-anchor Bob Woodruff and his camera operator did when they were badly wounded while in Iraq in early 2006.

Originating information takes a great deal of resources and effort, decreasing the likelihood that news organizations will give reporters the time they need to do thorough investigations. Meanwhile, reporters receive about one-third of all the content that ends up in the news from press releases. Because reporters have limited time and resources, they often rely on receiving information from governmental departments, legislators, and interest groups to produce stories. And because reporters are rarely experts in a particular policy area or research method, the information they receive from specialized sources is seldom scrutinized. For example, when data from a public opinion survey are released, the sponsoring organization's interpretation of the results is reported with little analysis. Some newspapers, mostly small papers with relatively few resources, print news releases from members of Congress word for word.

The third element of the newsgathering process highlights how reporters gather news by finding and interviewing second- and third-hand sources and by researching documents to reconstruct facts about newsworthy events. Gathering news in this way is facilitated when reporters cover regular beats such as the White House for the national news or crime for local news. Regular beats make it easier for journalists to cultivate sources, locate experts, and convince potential sources to speak with them.

Media critic Robert W. McChesney points out that routinized newsgathering strategies have some negative consequences, such as journalists' reliance on official sources, which can silence other perspectives on an issue. Some of these official sources themselves are critical of how institutionalized newsgathering processes encourage journalists to believe that cultivating and coddling official sources is more important than risking offending the sources. As former representative Lee H. Hamilton, D-Ind., wrote in 2006, "They follow the pack, rather than pursue stories that no one else has covered."

Increasing technological advances are beginning to change how reporters gather information. Journalists can search databases such as LexisNexis or use Internet search engines such as Google to increase both the speed and the volume of the information they gather. Although the validity of some Web-based sources and Web logs, or blogs, is doubtful at best, twenty-first-century journalism brings with it the opportunity to change how reporters get information and thus to affect how people engage with public life.

REFERENCES

Bennett, W. Lance. *News: The Politics of Illusion.* 6th ed. New York: Pearson/Longman, 2005.

McChesney, Robert W. *Rich Media, Poor Democracy: Communication Politics in Dubious Times.* New York: New Press, 2000.

Hamilton, Lee H. "The Press Is Good, but Not Good Enough." [Hillsboro, Ohio] *Times-Gazette,* February 1, 2006.

Paletz, David L. *The Media in Modern Politics: Contents and Consequences.* 2nd ed. New York: Longman, 2002.

News magazines

In the United States, news magazines are weekly magazines that focus on stories of national and international significance. The main outlets today within this subgenre are *Newsweek, Time,* and *U.S. News & World Report.* Some magazines, such as *The Nation* and *New Republic,* share their focus on political and social affairs but lean more toward opinion and commentary in their take on current events. Others—such as *Life, Look,* and *McClure's Magazine*—have ceased to exist.

News magazines developed in the early twentieth century, as the literate population expanded and as a response to the growing nationalization of politics and the role of the United States in world affairs. These trends called for a broader scope of coverage than that provided by some local newspapers. Coupled with the glossy, large-space visual power of photography, the magazines appealed to a mass market. They are important to media and politics because they provide a synthesizing and summarizing function on the week's events, in a sense offering a unifying narrative reflecting the major themes in the news. They are also able to offer more in-depth stories than newspapers or television outlets can provide.

However, because they come out late in the news cycle and cannot compete with broadcast sources such as television (especially with satellites and cable) and radio (which can provide breaking news), all three major magazines have suffered somewhat in their circulation and appeal in recent decades. Furthermore, with the advent of the Internet, the print versions of the magazines perhaps seem out of touch with today's media environment of specialized, on-demand news.

The major magazines have responded to this reality by coming out with Web versions and by moving more toward sensationalism or "infotainment." For example, they feature such items as lifestyle pieces and "news you can use" (heath trends, weight loss techniques, entertainment, changes in technology, and so on) on their covers. They also have joined in media conglomerates with other outlets with which they can cooperate, such as AOL–Time Warner. While the big weeklies do not seem to be going away, their role and nature in the contemporary world of media and politics remain to be seen.

REFERENCES

Gans, Herbert J. *Deciding What's News: A Study of* CBS Evening News, NBC Nightly News, Newsweek, *and* Time. New York: Pantheon, 1979.

Halberstam, David. *The Powers That Be.* New York: Knopf, 1979.

News management

News management is the set of techniques used by newsmakers, including government officials and politicians, to attract the attention of journalists and present images and information that are favorable to newsmakers' points of view. In recent years newsmakers have become increasingly skilled at managing news. They have developed techniques partly in response to the proliferation of news media outlets, advances in communications technologies, and the demands of the twenty-four-hour news cycle that now characterize news media. News management helps newsmakers shape and set the media agenda and to frame news items in favorable terms. Driving news management is a growing number of communications professionals who specialize in adapting public relations techniques for political purposes and who advise newsmakers on how to act—and react—strategically with journalists in an effort to control

President George W. Bush announced the end of major combat operations in Iraq aboard the aircraft carrier USS Lincoln *in May 2003. His appearance was stage managed to have a positive impact on public opinion.*

news situations. Current estimates suggest the number of such communications professionals in the United States (150,000) now exceeds the total number of journalists (130,000), and it is not uncommon for members of Congress and other government officials to employ several communications experts in their Capitol Hill offices to help manage the news process effectively.

Perhaps the best example of news management is the White House Office of Communications, created by President Richard M. Nixon to control the executive branch's press relations and external communications. The Office of Communications typically prepares press releases, news briefings, news conferences, and background documents to provide essential details about specific news and situations to journalists. The president also appoints a spokesperson, the press secretary, to respond directly to questions about policies and activities at daily news briefings and news conferences. The Office of Communications employs dozens of staff members to help manage relations with more than 1,700 reporters assigned to cover White House activities. Scholars have shown that both the size and sophistication of the White House press operation have experienced phenomenal growth over the past few decades.

In an effort to control the content and nature of external communications, newsmakers often attempt to fabricate news stories and to stage pseudo-events designed to attract media attention. Expertise in how the media work helps newsmakers achieve these goals. For example, newsmakers are aware of timing constraints on reporters and will manage communications in turn. One common strategy is to delay the announcement of potentially damaging news past the afternoon deadlines for newspaper reporters to minimize the attention the story gets in the next day's paper. Similarly, the announcement of bad news on a Friday afternoon or during the weekend can help to minimize attention because it will likely appear in low-circulation editions. Conversely, positive information may be released strategically to capitalize on opportunities for maximum exposure.

Newsmakers also take advantage of improvements in communications technologies that help to facilitate news management. A common technique is to package public relations materials in a news format using video news releases. These canned news stories are forwarded directly to newsrooms and other media outlets by satellite feed. Many understaffed stations simply air these prepackaged segments as they are received.

Another news management technique is staging pseudo-events. W. Lance Bennett describes pseudo-events as fully controlled media presentations designed to disguise actual political circumstances with realistic representations created to provide politically useful images to the media. Newsmakers take advantage of their access to writers, media consultants, costume consultants, and other professionals to carefully prepare events that become the key elements in a news story. Although these events often incorporate fragments of actual situations, they are planted primarily for the purpose of being reported and their relation to the underlying reality of the situation is ambiguous. Pseudo-events are characterized as self-fulfilling and nonspontaneous.

Politicians routinely stage pseudo-events to enhance their media images. Clever newsmakers often avoid staid events that are unlikely to attract media interest. Instead, they employ techniques designed to attract journalists' attention and need for visual content, especially television. To call attention to his initiatives to reform government by making the federal bureaucracy more efficient, for example, Vice President Al Gore stood with President Bill Clinton on the White House lawn in September 1993 in front of two forklifts piled high with federal regulations. Gore also punctuated his reform proposals by appearing on late-night television wearing safety goggles and shattering an ash tray with a hammer to poke fun at the Pentagon's requirement for an expensive ash receiver that would not break into more than thirty-five pieces. Both of these images enjoyed widespread television coverage.

In May 2003, amid war, dwindling popularity, and an impending presidential reelection campaign, President George W. Bush staged what has been described as "the mother of all photo opportunities." He landed on an aircraft carrier, fully clad in a flight suit, with a helmet tucked under his left arm, to salute sailors on the USS *Abraham Lincoln.* The dramatic image was covered in media around the world, and the powerful visual symbol of a strong commander in chief was replayed repeatedly in the American media.

Despite some criticism, the aircraft carrier landing was hailed by many as a triumphant example of news management. A *New York Times* article that reflected on the landing commented more generally on the Bush White House communications operation: "Bush's 'Top Gun' landing ... is only [the] latest example of how his administration is using [the] powers of television and technology to promote [the] presidency like never before." The *Times* article noted the White House's use of experts from network television, with sophisticated knowledge of lighting, camera angles, and backdrops.

To be sure, newsmakers are not always able to control news situations. Yet even during crises, news management techniques help newsmakers minimize the fallout by conducting damage control. Government officials and politicians often rely on communications experts to "spin" information in the media in an attempt to ensure that favorable messages are disseminated. Key features of strategic political communications and news management include simplification, repetition, and framing messages in a manner that accentuates the most positive information for the newsmaker.

Journalists are not oblivious to newsmakers' efforts to manage the news process. Nevertheless, despite their interest in reporting news in an objective and unbiased manner, time pressure, and close relations with the actors they cover often cause journalists to wittingly fall prey to news management techniques.

REFERENCES

Bennett, W. Lance. *News: The Politics of Illusion.* 6th ed. New York: Pearson/Longman, 2005.

Bumiller, Elisabeth. "Keepers of Bush Image Lift Stagecraft to New Heights." *New York Times,* May 16, 2003, 1A.

Manheim, Jarol. *All of the People, All the Time: Strategic Communication and American Politics.* Armonk, N.Y.: M. E. Sharpe, 1991.

Newspapers

Newspapers are cheaply printed publications generally intended for a mass audience. A newspaper may be of general or special interest, and it may be published daily, weekly, biweekly, monthly, bimonthly, or quarterly. Newspapers vary in presentation—broadsheet or tabloid— and how they are produced and delivered.

Although crude compared with today's newspapers, early newspapers were the first form of printed mass media. Their publishers sought to print relevant information for community members. Most early newspapers contained not only news stories but also advertisements, personal writings, such as poetry, and official governmental information.

Publick Occurrences, the first newspaper in the United States, appeared in Boston in 1690. The colonial government seized all copies, declaring that in the future anything in print would require a license, and its publisher was arrested. Not until 1704 was the first successful newspaper, the *Boston News-Letter,* founded by John Campbell, the city's postmaster. Campbell's paper culled much of its information from London newspapers and was used as a way to record governmental matters. The secrecy of government made it difficult

TEN CYLINDER TYPE-REVOLVING PRINTING MACHINE.

The first U.S. newspaper appeared in 1690, and the First Amendment guarantees freedom of the press, but the industry only boomed after technological advancements in the 1840s. The Hoe Web printing press was first used commercially in 1847 to produce thousands of newspapers every hour.

for the newspaper to report accurate accounts of meetings, and even if a publisher was able to determine what happened in meetings, he was dissuaded from publishing that information for fear of being jailed. It was not until much later that newspapers gained legal protection to freely report on governmental matters.

In 1729 Benjamin Franklin published the *Pennsylvania Gazette,* a newspaper geared toward literary, critical, and sometimes satirical journalism. Like *Publick Occurrences,* Franklin's paper focused on short local news items and European economic and political news from the London newspapers. In 1735 *New York Weekly Journal* publisher John Peter Zenger was jailed for publishing articles that belittled New York governor William Cosby. Zenger's attorney, Andrew Hamilton, argued that newspapers should be free to criticize the government as long as what they wrote was true. The jury found Zenger not guilty, and a precedent was set that shaped American attitudes toward press freedom.

By 1776 two dozen newspapers were being published, with Massachusetts, New York, and Pennsylvania dominating the newspaper market. The governments of these colonies substantially subsidized these papers, thus adding a measure of control to information flow. Publishers often worried about being jailed if information was considered a threat to the government. As a result, newspapers contained mundane and uncontroversial items. The American Revolu-

tion established the potential power of newspapers.

By the end of the Revolutionary War, there were forty-three newspapers in print, representative of the different politics of the time. Early journalistic style dictated that nothing was beyond printing, whether it was deemed true or not. In 1791 the government recognized the importance of a free press in a democracy, as reflected in the ratification of the Bill of Rights. The First Amendment provides Americans a right to a free press—that is, free from governmental control.

Although printing techniques had not changed much from 1436, when Johann Gutenberg invented the printing press, to the early 1800s, changes in technology allowed newspapers to become a mass medium. Advancements in printing technology—including mass-produced ink and paper, as well as the first machine-powered printing presses—allowed the newspaper publishing industry to grow rapidly.

As the population increased, so did the number of newspapers published. Cheaper paper and ink fostered the emergence of the "penny press"; newspapers were sold for a penny apiece and were published more often than ever before. The kind of information found in newspapers also evolved to include community news and to exclude bits and pieces of information gathered from anywhere. Newspapers shifted toward practicality and away from drama. It suddenly became fashionable for people to be knowledgeable about the world. With the emergence of the penny press and the spread of literacy, newspapers became available to most of society, not a luxury of the well-to-do. The penny press thus inspired, as William Gilmore put it, a newfound "citizen awareness."

The Industrial Revolution further changed the way newspapers were produced. Advances in technology made it easier for newspapers to quickly print tens of thousands of copies. Papers could also be reset and printed more often with the advent of typesetting machines. By 1850 there were 2,500 newspapers in existence in the United States alone. Illustrations added a visual element to newspapers.

During the Civil War people across the nation were eager for news from the battlefronts, and reporters began to change their reporting style from writing feature stories to producing immediate, hard news. This type of news was facilitated by the invention of the telegraph. Reporters became the recorders of history and were often admired by society. This led to the founding of even more newspapers. In 1880 there were about 11,000 different papers. By 1890, some newspapers' circulation exceeded one million copies daily. During this time the form of the newspaper took on the same characteristics seen in today's publications. Headlines became larger, photographs were commonly used, and community events, including sports, were covered.

By the early 1900s many large newspapers began to engage in what was known as "yellow journalism," a style of journalism that emphasized the shocking, scandalous, and sensational. One of the most famous photographs that ran in the New York Daily News was that of the execution of Ruth Snyder, a housewife who was convicted of murdering her husband. A reporter took the photo at the time of her death with a camera strapped to his leg. The photo allowed the Daily News to sell an extra 750,000 copies of the paper. Such practice became the norm for newspapers for many years before a wave of morality caused reporters and publishers to rethink their ideologies. Publishers and editors of the time used yellow journalism to further their political causes as well. There was little recourse for any misinformation that was printed. Publishers were powerful and often promoted their own political viewpoints. Few means were available to check whether information was in fact true. The introduction of television and radio and a wave of responsible journalism cut down on this practice. In 1896 Adolph Ochs bought the New York Times and vowed to provide news coverage that was impartial, distinguishing his publication from others at the time. He did not believe in sensational stories

to sell his newspaper and instead appealed to high culture for readership.

The addition of illustrations drastically changed the general format that newspapers had been using until the 1900s. They began to include more photographs and illustrations, thereby limiting the amount of words that were printed. This increased use of illustrations had a secondary effect. As newspapers became larger and more complicated in design, they relied more on advertising to support new and more expensive printing techniques. Newspapers tended to adapt their design and writing style to that of high-circulation papers. For example, during the 1980s, as USA Today became more powerful and its readership increased, other large newspapers began to mimic its style of having more graphics and ample white space, thereby further reducing the word count.

Media consolidation played a vital part in the way journalism evolved. In the 1980s newspapers began to consolidate or fold as bigger chains swallowed their competitors. Many media critics have argued that reporters are being pressured to write particular kinds of stories, but evidence of this phenomenon is contested. One certainty, however, is that many newspapers have become part of large media concerns whose focus often trends toward maximizing profits. As some newspaper chains flourished and turned into multimedia corporations, with holdings in TV, radio, and other media, smaller, local newspapers tended to struggle. The cost of printing was high, and the rising costs of paper and ink forced many smaller newspapers to link with larger companies.

Newspapers have had a profound effect on politics in the United States. One of their central roles is in exposing politicians who are involved in wrongdoing. Perhaps the most famous example of this is the Watergate scandal (1972–1974), in which Carl Bernstein and Bob Woodward, two reporters from the Washington Post, wrote a series of articles about crimes committed by members of President Richard M. Nixon's White House that ultimately led to the resignation of the president. This event briefly energized newspapers and journalists. However, public perceptions of the political neutrality of newspapers changed. More Americans found television news to be credible and less biased than newspapers through the latter part of the twentieth century (perhaps because, as a visual medium, people see what is presented on TV, as opposed to newspapers articles, which are written by someone).

When the Internet came into popular use in the late 1990s, newspapers adapted to the new medium. Newspapers became accessible not only through the standard print means but also through the Internet. Newspaper Web sites offered consumers a way to get breaking news or to find background information on stories published in the paper. It became easier to search newspapers and customize them for the type of news each consumer preferred. Some argument has arisen about whether the Internet will eventually replace the print version of newspapers. Thus far, although newspaper readership has declined, a large portion of the population still reads printed newspapers, just as people did after both radio and television became popular. As each new medium is introduced, newspapers have learned to adapt and survive.

REFERENCES

Alger, Dean E. *The Media and Politics.* Belmont, Calif.: Wadsworth, 1996.

Baldasty, Gerald. *The Commercialization of News in Nineteenth-Century America.* Madison: University of Wisconsin Press, 1993.

Barnhurst, Kevin, and John Nerone. *The Form of News.* New York: Guilford Press, 2001.

Brown, Richard D. *Knowledge Is Power: The Diffusion of Information in Early America, 1700–1865.* New York: Oxford University Press, 1989.

Cook, Timothy E. *Governing with the News: The News Media as a Political Institution.* Chicago: University of Chicago Press, 1998.

Gilmore, William J. *Reading Becomes a Necessity of Life.* Knoxville: University of Tennessee Press, 1989.

Leonard, Thomas C. *The Power of the Press: The Birth of American Political Reporting.* New York: Oxford University Press, 1986.

Nerone, John. *Violence against the Press: Policing the Public Sphere in U.S. History.* New York: Oxford University Press, 1994.

Schudson, Michael. *The Power of News.* Cambridge, Mass.: Harvard University Press, 1995.

Newsworthiness

Newsworthiness refers to the qualities by which journalists recognize some events and issues as significant. More than a list of specific qualities, newsworthiness rests upon reporters' and editors' sense of which daily developments deserve a slice of the always-limited "news hole." Deciding what is news is an important type of media power. Debates about newsworthiness have centered on several questions. Among them are, What drives journalists' decisions about what is newsworthy? and Do those decisions enhance or inhibit democracy and public understanding?

William Metz describes "news" as a slippery word: "If one asks, 'What is news?' there is no exact answer." Journalists tend to define the word not with abstract definitions but with lists of attributes that lend themselves to stories they believe audiences will find interesting and important. Scholars have attempted to identify the implicit rules that guide these decisions about newsworthiness. According to both journalists and scholars, news generally shares several characteristics. Most obviously, news is new. Newsworthy events and issues are those that are timely, that involve change, and that are unexpected or unprecedented. News is also dramatic. It involves conflict or the resolution of conflict, clear characters and strong story lines, and human tragedy or triumph. Often a story is newsworthy because it represents a new development in an ongoing news saga. More subtle but just as prevalent is a third characteristic: news is often defined by what government officials and other authorities say and do each day because their statements and actions can be indicators of a story's importance. Other criteria may include the geographic proximity of an event to the news organization producing the story (local or domestic topics generally receive more coverage than distant events) and the scope of the impact of an event or issue (events affecting large numbers of people generally receive more attention). These criteria are sometimes in conflict. For example, a story about a local murder in which the suspected killer is already apprehended and presents no danger to the wider community satisfies the "drama" criterion but not the "scope of impact" criterion (which is why some news organizations have begun to question how they cover crime). This kind of conflict illustrates the fact that newsworthiness is ultimately a matter of reporters' and editors' subjective, professionally honed judgment.

Many scholars have criticized journalists' decisions about newsworthiness. Their concern is that these criteria can, if overemphasized, crowd out other important news stories. For example, scholars criticize the news for overemphasizing the sensational (a complaint shared by much of the public). The news, they claim, is dominated by shocking crimes, natural disasters, political and celebrity scandals, and dramatic events such as missing children or whales trapped in arctic ice. Critics also charge that the news often chooses to tell simplistic stories about particular individuals and events instead of explaining the context and complexities of issues. Another criticism is that the media spotlight swings from event to event so often that the news becomes fragmented

Each day, CNN employees scan domestic and world news, analyzing the relevance, or newsworthiness, of the information before releasing it for mass consumption.

and difficult for the public to follow. Other scholars argue that the news emphasizes the "horse race" and "game" of politics, focusing on the means by which politicians win or lose elections instead of on the substance of policy debates. Media scholar Thomas Patterson, for example, has found a trend in reporting on presidential elections in the past three decades toward more news about the strategies and tactics by which politicians try to win office and less news about the substance of their policy positions.

Many scholars also criticize journalists for too readily taking their newsworthiness cues from political authorities. This "officialized" news, as W. Lance Bennett has labeled it, occurs because news organizations station reporters at official listening posts, such as the White House, the local city hall, and the police department, and report what is said and done there as news. It also occurs because most government institutions and agencies have press liaisons to provide news material to reporters. In a business that values producing reliable quantities of news on a daily basis, relying on officials makes it easier for reporters to meet deadlines and fill the daily quota of news. Institutional authorities such as White House spokespersons or the local police chief have another appeal for journalists: they are the most legitimate of news

sources. "Rank in governmental hierarchies" is, according to sociologist Herbert J. Gans, a primary indicator to reporters of a story's newsworthiness. Thus, issues that receive official attention (such as a presidential speech, a congressional hearing, or a prolonged police investigation) are more likely to receive sustained news attention than are issues that officials do not speak about or act upon.

Two other debates about newsworthiness should be mentioned. One involves the question of whether objectivity reigns in the newsroom or ideological bias distorts the news. Although this debate moves beyond strict questions of newsworthiness, it is worth discussing in this context. If the news is shaped by the ideological biases of journalists, inevitably their decisions about what is news will be biased as well. Do liberal reporters tend to focus on the shortcomings of Republican instead of Democratic politicians and on conservative instead of liberal ideals? Do large news organizations, as members of inherently conservative corporations, tend to promote the virtues of consumerism and to play down news about the downsides of capitalism? These debates are difficult, lively, and unresolved. While it seems clear that the editorial and ideological positions of some editors shape the news presented by some news organizations (with Fox News being a frequent current target of such criticisms), it is less clear whether a single ideological bias systematically shapes news across a majority of the mass media.

The other debate is over the tendency of news organizations to focus on bad news. Newsworthy events and issues tend to involve problems: things going wrong, officials not doing their jobs, government programs not working, companies ripping off consumers, and so on. As one top news executive told Herbert Gans, the role of journalists is to report "when things go awry, when institutions are not functioning normally." But rarely does the news link these problems to solutions. By focusing on when things go awry but not on what can be done in response, critics charge, the news disempowers the public.

Journalists often are uncomfortable with these criticisms of their news decisions. Their professional sense of what is news becomes so well developed that the choices they make can seem to them automatic and obvious. And because different news organizations tend to converge on the same top news stories every day, journalists are reassured that their decisions about newsworthiness are not arbitrary. (Critical scholars respond by arguing that this convergence simply illustrates journalists' shared sense of what constitutes news.) Journalists also charge that scholars do not adequately understand the constraints of the news business: ever-looming deadlines, demanding editors, and restricted time or space for the news. They protest that scholars want the news to look like a college text, when the news is, in fact, a product designed to be purchased by a large number of consumers who want their information to be interesting, not just educational. Some journalists are more open to these criticisms of their news decisions, however. A few contemporary journalism textbooks question the traditional criteria of newsworthiness that overemphasize novelty and drama. In his book *Breaking the News,* James Fallows, former editor of *U.S. News and World Report,* critiques many of the same patterns and trends in news coverage that media scholars have decried. And a growing movement within journalism called "civic journalism" or "public journalism" seeks to change news trends such as the overemphasis on problems instead of solutions.

Ultimately, the debates over newsworthiness hinge upon one crucial question: Do journalists exercise their power to decide what is news in ways that are helpful or harmful to the public and to democracy? After all, by focusing on certain issues or events, the media can have an agenda-setting effect on the public and on government itself. Some scholars and government officials have feared, for example, that when the media focus on dramatic and tragic international events, such as the killing of an American soldier in Somalia, they may inadvertently whip up the public's eagerness to resolve a situation quickly and thus increase the pressure on the government to act, whether or not action is in the national interest. But the opposite concerns are also important to consider. If the media overlook issues and events that do not meet the criteria of newsworthiness, they may marginalize important public issues simply because they do not qualify as news. Alternatively, through their reliance on official sources, the media can become extensions of those in power. Thus the media may help advance the current government's agenda, which may be desirable or undesirable for democracy, depending upon one's perspective.

One thing seems certain about the newsworthiness debate: journalists will continue to decide what is news, and critics will continue to question the decisions journalists make.

REFERENCES

Bennett, W. Lance. *News: The Politics of Illusion.* 6th ed. New York: Pearson/Longman, 2005.

Fallows, James. *Breaking the News.* New York: Vintage Books, 1996.

Gans, Herbert J. *Deciding What's News.* New York: Vintage Books, 1979.

Metz, William. *Newswriting: From Lead to 30.* Englewood Cliffs, N.J.: Prentice-Hall, 1991.

Patterson, Thomas. *Out of Order.* New York: Vintage Books, 1994.

New York *Evening Post*

Founded in 1801 by Alexander Hamilton as a Federalist organ, the *Evening Post* (now known as the *New York Post*) has always been a political newspaper. Its political slant has changed many times over the years along with its ownership. It has often been on the brink of folding but has always managed to survive. It is now the nation's oldest continuously published daily newspaper. Hamilton's editor, William Coleman, was a leading voice of the fading Federalist Party. Coleman's successor, William Cullen Bryant, shifted the newspaper's support to Jacksonian Democracy. In the 1850s Bryant broke with the Democrats over abolition and helped to found the Republican Party. In 1881 the paper was sold to Henry Villard, a railroad magnate who along with his editors waged war against Tammany Hall.

In 1977 Rupert Murdoch, the Australian publisher, took over control of the *Post*. He was able to increase circulation by using sensationalistic news stories. Murdoch was forced to sell the *Post* in 1988 when he established the Fox TV Network. It was purchased by real estate developer Peter S. Kalikow, who maintained the paper's conservatism, and it subsequently went through several other owners. Murdoch's News Corporation bought the paper back in 1993.

See also *Hamilton, Alexander; Murdoch, Rupert.*

REFERENCES

Nevins, Allan. *The Evening Post: A Century of Journalism.* New York: Boni and Liveright, 1922.

"Newspaper of Vision That's Helped to Make New York Great." *New York Post,* June 28, 1982.

Potter, Jeffrey. *Men, Money, and Magic: The Story of Dorothy Schiff.* New York: Coward, McCann and Geoghegan, 1976.

New York Sun

The *New York Sun* became the first successful "penny paper" in the United States under its founder, Benjamin H. Day. The daily police court column written by George Wisner was the most popular feature in any New York newspaper. Unlike other newspapers, the content of the *New York Sun* was barely political and focused more on local matters, ignoring the great national questions. In 1837 the newspaper was sold to Moses Beach, Day's brother-in-law, who hired such notable writers as Horatio Alger. Charles A. Dana became its editor in 1868, and the *Sun*'s politics became conservative. In 1897 Francis Pharcellus Church penned the famous editorial that answered a young reader's question, "Yes, Virginia, There Is a Santa Claus." Other *Sun* writers during this period were Julian Ralph, Will Irwin, and muckraker and social reformer Jacob A. Riis. In 1916 the *Sun* was acquired by Frank Munsey, the great "consolidator" of newspapers. By 1950 the *New York Sun* disappeared because of Munsey's business tactics. While there is now a new paper with the same name, it has no connection to the original.

REFERENCES

Dana, Charles A. *The Art of Newspaper Making.* New York: D. Appleton and Co., 1895.

O'Brien, Frank. *The Story of the Sun.* New York: D. Appleton, 1928.

Rosebault, Charles J. *When Dana Was the* Sun. New York: Robert M. McBride and Co., 1931.

New York Times

The *New York Times* is the most widely circulated newspaper in the United States and among the most respected, having won ninety-one Pulitzer Prizes—the most of any paper—since it began publication in September 1851. Henry Jarvis Raymond and George Jones founded the paper as the *New York Daily Times.* In 1897 the then-owner, Adolph Ochs, coined its slogan, "All the News That's Fit to Print," in an effort to distinguish his paper from those trading in the sensationalist, or "yellow," journalism of the time. The *Times* has since established a reputation for in-depth investigative reporting, breaking major stories, and reprinting transcripts of influential speeches and documents. It famously published the Pentagon Papers in the 1970s and revealed the Bush administration's secret wiretapping program in December 2005. In addition to breaking such stories, it also infamously issued a public apology and examination of its coverage of the lead-up to the 2003 Iraq War and a recounting of plagiarism committed by one of its reporters, Jayson Blair, that same year. The latter incident led the paper to create the position of public editor to regularly critique its work.

The *Times* is owned by the New York Times Company, which also publishes other major newspapers, including the *Boston Globe* and the *International Herald Tribune.* The *Times*'s status as a leading newspaper has resulted in its influencing media practices and First Amendment issues through its involvement in pivotal U.S. Supreme Court decisions, including *New York Times v. Sullivan* (1964), a First Amendment case that set a national standard for libel; *New York Times v. United States* (1971) (with *United States v. The Washington Post Company*), in which the Court rejected the U.S. government's attempt to halt publication of the Pentagon Papers; and *Caldwell v. United States (1972)* (consolidated with *In re Pappas* and *Branzburg v. Hayes*), in which the Supreme Court ruled that the First Amendment does not provide reporters privileges not afforded other citizens (in this case to quash a subpoena to appear before a grand jury in order to shield sources).

See also *Branzburg v. Hayes (1972); New York Times v. United States (1971); Pentagon Papers.*

REFERENCES

Diamond, Edwin. *Behind the Times: Inside the New York Times.* Chicago: University of Chicago Press, 1995.

Nicholas O., Berry. *Foreign Policy and the Press: An Analysis of the New York Times' Coverage of U.S. Foreign Policy.* New York: Greenwood, 1990.

Mnookin, Seth. *Hard News: The Scandals at the* New York Times *and Their Meaning for American Media.* New York: Random House, 2004.

New York Times Company. "Our Company: History," www.nytco.com/company timeline.html.

REFERENCES

Harrison, Maureen, and Steve Gilbert, eds. *Freedom of the Press Decisions of the United States Supreme Court.* San Diego: Excellent Books, 1996.

Hopkins, W. Wat. *Actual Malice: Twenty-five Years after* Times v. Sullivan. New York: Praeger, 1989.

New York Times Company v. Sullivan, 376 U.S. 254 (1964).

Parker, Richard A. *Free Speech on Trial: Communication Perspectives on Landmark Supreme Court Decisions.* Tuscaloosa: University of Alabama Press, 2003.

New York Times v. Sullivan (1964)

New York Times v. Sullivan (1964) established the precedent largely immunizing the media from charges of libel by public officials in the execution of their offices and limited the state courts' power in libel cases. The case arose in the early 1960s amid the political struggle over civil rights and stemmed from an advertisement published in the *New York Times* by the Committee to Defend Martin Luther King and the Struggle for Freedom in the South. The ad accused Montgomery, Alabama, police and other officials of conducting "a wave of terror" against blacks and asserted that King had been assaulted and arrested by the Montgomery police seven times. L. B. Sullivan, the Montgomery police commissioner, sued the *Times,* citing a number of factual inaccuracies in the ad—for example, King had been arrested four times, not seven. An Alabama trial court found that the *Times* had libeled Sullivan, even though his name did not appear in the ad. He was awarded $500,000 in damages. The Alabama Supreme Court affirmed the judgment, and the *Times* appealed to the Supreme Court.

The Court unanimously reversed the judgment against the *Times.* The majority opinion, written by Justice William Brennan, held the application of libel law to be "constitutionally deficient for failure to provide the safeguards for freedom of speech and of the press that are required by the First Amendment. . . . We further hold that under the proper safeguards the evidence presented in this case is constitutionally insufficient to support the judgment." Brennan's opinion relied heavily on the argument that repeated awards of damages for libel would inhibit open discussion of issues and of the performance of public officials. The resulting rule is that the media are liable for damages only if the official can show that false statements were made with "actual malice," that is, with knowledge that they were false or with reckless indifference to the truth.

See also *Libel law.*

New York Times v. United States (1971)

New York Times v. United States (1971)—with *United States v. The Washington Post Company* collectively known as the *Pentagon Papers Case*—reaffirms the principle, established in *Near v. Minnesota* (1931), that the First Amendment protects the press from government attempts at prior restraint, or censorship of material before publication.

In the mid-1960s, the Department of Defense ordered a classified study of the conduct of the Vietnam War that could be embarrassing to the government if made public. On June 13, 1971, the *New York Times* began publishing parts of "History of U.S. Decision-Making Process on Viet Nam Policy," popularly known as the Pentagon Papers. The newspaper had received a copy of the documents from Daniel Ellsberg, a former defense analyst who had worked on the project. The Nixon administration initially did nothing but then sought and obtained an injunction to halt further excerpts in the *Times* after it realized that the information could be damaging to its policies. A copy of the study was then leaked to the *Washington Post,* which printed the next installment. Between June 15 and June 23, three of the four courts reviewing the case ruled against the government. On June 25, the Supreme Court agreed to hear the cases. Oral arguments took place the next day.

The government argued that publication threatened to interfere with ongoing peace negotiations, put military personnel and prisoners of war at risk, and prolong the war. The newspapers argued that no statute authorized the suppression of classified material—such a provision had been struck from the Espionage Act while under consideration by Congress in 1917—and that they would publish material on past internal policy debates, not information that would interfere in peace efforts. The *Times* and the *Post* asserted that the government had not met the burden of showing that "irreparable harm" would result from publication of the documents. The Court agreed.

In a June 30, 1971, brief *per curiam* decision—that is, "for the court" as a whole, without attribution to any one justice—six members of the Court held that the government had failed to meet a standard that would justify restraint on publication. Three of the six held all forms of prior restraint to be unconstitutional. In its ruling, the Court affirmed the decision of the Court of Appeals for the D.C. Circuit in the case of the *Post* and ordered the Second Circuit Court of Appeals to affirm the decision of the federal district court in favor of the *Times,* thereby freeing the newspapers to continue publication of the papers. By the time of the decision, however, most of the documents had already appeared in U.S. as well as Canadian newspapers. The dissenting justices noted the haste with which the case had been decided, the difference between publishing secrets during wartime and peacetime, and the possibility of damage to national security. Another justice pointed out, however, that the study was essentially historical and therefore did not threaten conduct of the war or its operations.

See also *First Amendment; Near v. Minnesota (1931); Pentagon Papers.*

REFERENCES

Harrison, Maureen, and Steve Gilbert, eds. *Freedom of the Press Decisions of the United States Supreme Court.* San Diego, Calif.: Excellent Books, 1996.

Ellsberg, Daniel. *Secrets: A Memoir of Vietnam and the Pentagon Papers.* New York: Viking Press, 2002.

New York Times v. United States, 403 U.S. 713 (1971).

Parker, Richard A. *Free Speech on Trial: Communication Perspectives on Landmark Supreme Court Decisions.* Tuscaloosa: University of Alabama Press, 2003.

Rudenstine, David. *The Day the Presses Stopped: A History of the Pentagon Papers Case.* Berkeley: University of California Press, 1996.

Ungar, Sanford. *The Papers and the Papers: An Account of the Legal and Political Battle over the Pentagon Papers.* New York: Dutton, 1972.

Nixon, Richard M.

Richard Milhous Nixon (1913–1994), thirty-seventh president of the United States, was the only president to resign the office. After graduating from Duke University Law School in 1937, he failed to land a job with one of the big New York law firms—a fact that shaped his dislike for the so-called eastern establishment. Returning to his hometown of Whittier, California, Nixon joined a local law firm. He entered government service as a price regulator in the Office of Emergency Management, but then joined the Navy in 1942 and served through the remainder of World War II. Californians twice elected him to the House of Representatives (1947–1951) as a Republican, and he served on the House Un-American Activities Committee, leading the investigation of Alger Hiss, an alleged communist and spy who worked in the State Department.

Nixon was elected to the U.S. Senate in 1951. In 1952 Gen. Dwight D. Eisenhower chose him as his vice presidential running mate. During the campaign Nixon faced charges of accepting $18,000 from political supporters that he used for personal expenses. Nixon's televised response, known as the "Checkers speech" (for his discussion of the family's dog, Checkers, which he had received as a gift), demonstrated his political savvy by adroitly silencing the controversy. Nixon served as vice president throughout the Eisenhower administration (1953–1961).

In 1960 the Republican Party nominated him for president to run against the Democratic candidate, Massachusetts senator John F. Kennedy. The Kennedy–Nixon television debate, in which he appeared pale and tired opposite the youthful-looking Kennedy, taught him a lesson in public imagery. After losing a very close election, Nixon returned to a private law practice in California. He ran for governor in 1962 and lost, blaming it on the media and famously uttering: "You won't have Nixon to kick around any more, because, gentlemen, this is my last press conference." After his electoral defeat, Nixon joined a New York law firm as a partner, but never shed his political ambitions. After the Republican loss in the 1964 presidential election, he saw his opportunity. With the country sharply divided over the Vietnam War, Nixon and his running mate, Spiro T. Agnew, won the 1968 election, running on a promise of national reconciliation and defeating Hubert H. Humphrey, the Democratic nominee. In his administration, Agnew became the lightning rod and point man in confrontations with the "small and unelected elite" liberal media. He also established the White House Office of Communications to manage press interaction.

Over the years, Nixon developed a paranoia regarding anyone who opposed him. His "enemies list" reportedly numbered up to six hundred individuals and organizations.

Nixon and his aides distrusted and held contempt for the press, and he had rocky relations with the media throughout his tenure. During the 1972 election campaign against Democratic challenger George McGovern, members of his executive staff engaged G. Gordon Liddy in a "dirty tricks" operation that included a break-in at the Democratic National Committee offices in the Watergate complex. When investigative journalism revealed Nixon's involvement in the scandal, the resulting political pressure led him to resign from office in 1974 rather than risk impeachment. His successor, President Gerald R. Ford, subsequently pardoned him. In his later years, Nixon took on the role of elder statesman and wrote extensively, including *Six Crises* (1962), *RN: The Memoirs of Richard Nixon* (1978), *The Real War* (1980), *Leaders* (1982), *Real Peace* (1983), *No More Vietnams* (1985), *Nineteen Ninety-nine* (1989), and *Beyond Peace* (1994).

See also *Agnew, Spiro T.; Kennedy-Nixon debates; Liddy, G. Gordon; Watergate.*

REFERENCES

Aitken, Jonathan. *Nixon: A Life.* Washington, D.C.: Regnery Publishing, 1993.

Ambrose, Stephen E. *Nixon: The Education of a Politician, 1913–1962.* New York: Simon and Schuster, 1987.

Bernstein, Carl, and Bob Woodward. *The Final Days.* New York: Simon and Schuster, 1976.

Brodie, Fawn M. *Richard Nixon: The Shaping of His Character.* Cambridge, Mass.: Harvard University Press, 1983.

Emery, Fred. *Watergate: The Corruption of American Politics and the Fall of Richard Nixon.* New York: Times Books, 1994.

Genovese, Michael A. *The Nixon Presidency: Power and Politics in Turbulent Times.* New York: Greenwood Press, 1990.

Keogh, James. *President Nixon and the Press.* New York: Funk and Wagnalls, 1972.

Maltese, John Anthony. *Spin Control: The White House Office of Communications and the Management of Presidential News.* Chapel Hill: University of North Carolina Press, 1992.

Summers, Anthony. *The Arrogance of Power: The Secret World of Richard Nixon.* New York: Viking, 2000.

Nixon–Kennedy debates

See *Kennedy-Nixon debates.*

Objectivity

The notion of objectivity has been central to mainstream journalism in the United States for decades. Most analysts link its rise to changes in the news industry during the late nineteenth century that created the first true mass media system, reinforced by Progressive Era beliefs in the importance of neutral, professional journalism to democracy. As journalist and journalism critic Jay Rosen observes, "[At objectivity's] core [are] some key principles [such as] the notion of a disinterested truth, . . . the principled attempt to restrain your own biases, [and] looking at things from the other person's perspective." A simpler definition would be that objective news attempts only to inform, not to persuade, and avoids taking sides in any controversy. Simpler still, one could say that objective news is not "biased."

These definitions may raise more questions than they answer. Recent surveys show that sizable segments of the public doubt the objectivity of the news, even though such standard methods as editorial review of reporters' stories exist to correct for the biases and mistakes of individual reporters. As well, objectivity is difficult to measure, as is its opposite—bias. As research by the Pew Center for the People and the Press illustrates, people tend to recognize biases they disagree with more readily than biases with which they agree, so it may be almost impossible to produce news that all observers agree is objective. Journalists themselves, "tired of defending an embattled word," have increasingly favored notions such as accuracy instead. Meanwhile, the recent rise of blatantly partisan news outlets signals a move toward what some researchers with the Project for Excellence in Journal-ism have called a "journalism of affirmation": news "gathered with a point of view," attracting audiences who "come to have their preconceptions reinforced."

Broader concerns about objectivity include the critique that objectivity is often observed in a ritualistic way—reporting "both sides"—that obscures the facts of controversies. Media coverage of global warming and the greenhouse effect, in which the views of mainstream science and its less well-supported critics are presented on equal terms, is often cited as an example of this problem. Another critique of objectivity is that it ends up favoring the views of powerful people over the less powerful. Trying to be objective, as James Curran says, "can lead journalists to rely on established power holders and legitimated holders of knowledge as sources of news and comment." Some critics, such as Rosen, also contend that trying to be objective distances journalists from the communities they supposedly serve and obscures journalistic power, by demanding that journalists remain detached from the political and social struggles of which they are often at the very center.

Objectivity is arguably still a worthwhile goal for mainstream journalism. According to the Pew Research Center, although the public doubts objectivity's existence in practice, it continues to favor the ideal of an objective press. Moving toward a European-style partisan press, as some media critics have urged, could free journalists from the demands and problems of objectivity. The downside might be the loss of a still-valued ideal: that the news can provide a fact-based account of public debates that includes a variety of perspectives without openly advocating for any.

REFERENCES

Bennett, W. Lance. *News: The Politics of Illusion.* 6th ed. New York: Pearson/Longman, 2005.

Curran, James. "What Democracy Requires of the Media." In *Institutions of American Government: The Press,* edited by Geneva Overholser and Kathleen Hall Jamieson. New York: Oxford University Press, 2005.

Pew Research Center for the People and the Press. "Cable and Internet Loom Large in Fragmented Political News Universe: Perceptions of Partisan Bias Seen as Growing." January 11, 2004, http://people-press.org/reports/display.php3?ReportID=200.

———. "Terror Coverage Boosts News Media's Images." November 28, 2001, http://people-press.org/reports/display.php3?ReportID=143.

Rosen, Jay. *What Are Journalists For?* New Haven, Conn.: Yale University Press, 1999.

Janet Jackson and Justin Timberlake's performance at the 2004 Super Bowl caused an uproar when Timberlake snatched part of her outfit, briefly exposing her right breast to millions of television viewers. This infamous "wardrobe malfunction" outraged many people, who complained to the Federal Communications Commission. The FCC fined CBS, which had aired the program.

Obscenity and pornography

Although many people use the words *obscenity* and *pornography* interchangeably, in legal terms they are different. The word *pornography* derives from the Greek for "harlot writing" and refers to an array of sexually explicit material. Pornography generally has no legal meaning. *Obscenity* is a legal term that as defined by the courts refers to material that appeals to the prurient interest, is patently offensive, and lacks serious literary, artistic, political, or scientific value. The determination of whether material is obscene is left to local community standards, as defined by a jury in the case of a trial. Sexually explicit material has long been considered at the outside edge of the protections guaranteed by the First Amendment, and material found to be legally obscene receives no First Amendment protection. Obscenity is regulated at the state and federal levels, and disseminating it can lead to imprisonment, fines, and confiscation of property.

Prior to 1957, U.S. law was guided by an 1868 British ruling, *Regina v. Hicklin,* which declared material obscene based on the smallest sexually explicit excerpt. In 1957 the U.S. Supreme Court ruled in *Roth v. United States* that although obscenity stood outside the protection of the First Amendment, the social value of a work could mitigate whether material in question should be determined to be illegal. The Court's decision set off years of debate over the definition of obscenity.

Following *Roth,* the Supreme Court found itself inundated with obscenity cases. Because of the lack of a clear legal definition of obscenity, the justices were forced into the position of having to review material found to be obscene. In *Jacobellis v. Ohio* (1964), Justice Potter Stewart famously summed up his frustration in determining obscenity by stating, "I know it when I see it." In the sixteen years following *Roth,* the decisions handed down by the Court demonstrated the ongoing difficulty of defining obscenity. Ten cases, all decided in 1966, resulted in forty-five different opinions. In *Walker v. Ohio* (1970), Chief Justice Warren Burger complained that the Court had become a "supreme and unreviewable board of censorship."

The Court finally reached a modicum of consensus with its decision in *Miller v. California* (1973), though the justices remained far from united. They decided five obscenity cases that day by a 5–4 vote. The four dissenting justices concluded that seeking a legal definition of obscenity was a fruitless pursuit. Justice William O. Douglas argued that obscenity should be protected by the First Amendment with no further debate. Justices William Brennan, Thurgood Marshall, and Potter Stewart had come to believe that obscenity should be decriminalized because it could never be clearly defined. Despite the close vote, the Court's decision in *Miller* largely settled the conflict over the legal definition of obscenity. Although minor adjustments have been made over the years, the *Miller* test remains the definition of obscenity. Settling the legal debate, however, did little to silence the public debate over pornography.

The federal government has twice sponsored high-level investigations into the possible effects of pornography. In 1968 President Lyndon B. Johnson formed the President's Commission on Obscenity and Pornography. After two years of work, it concluded that neither hard-core nor soft-core pornography produced antisocial effects. The commission then recommended the repeal of all obscenity laws. In 1986 President Ronald Reagan formed the Attorney General's Commission on Pornography, the so-called Meese Commission, which after a year determined pornography to be pervasive and highly dangerous. It recommended more vigorous enforcement of obscenity laws.

The differences between the two commissions are instructive. The 1968 panel had a $2 million dollar budget (equivalent to $5 million in 1986 dollars) and twenty-two staff members. The Meese Commission received only $400,000 and had only nine staff members. The 1968 commission was chaired by the dean of the University of Minnesota Law School who was also a recognized expert on constitutional law with a reputation for fairness. The Meese Commission was led by a prosecutor who had won a presidential commendation for his zealous work on obscenity cases. While most of the members of the 1968 commission had not taken a public position on the issue, more than half of the appointees to the Meese Commission were well known for their opposition to pornography. It is thus not surprising that the commissions reached such disparate conclusions.

Regardless of what the government says or does, pornography is a big business. It is estimated that adult-oriented businesses generate between $10 billion and $14 billion a year. There are 700,000 adult videos rented each year. In 2004 *Playboy* reported a monthly circulation of three million and an ad rate of $141,620 for a full-page ad. The chief executive officer of Vivid Video lectures at business schools. In addition, even in conservative communities, pornography is becoming "normalized." In Utah County, Utah, recognized as one of the most conservative places in the United States, a local prosecutor charged the owner of a video store with violating obscenity laws, but he lost the case. During the trial, the defense attorney managed to convince the jury that the videos carried by the store were within community standards. He did so by presenting statistics establishing that pornography was common in the community. He showed that Utah County cable subscribers had ordered at least 20,000 explicit movies in the two years prior to the trial and that the Marriott across the street from the courthouse had recorded 3,448 adult pay-per-view movie rentals in one year.

In recognition of the constitutional issues and the complexity of regulating obscenity, two states—Hawaii and Oregon—have decriminalized the distribution of obscene materials to adults. Federal prosecutions of obscenity also declined with the end of the Reagan administration, but when Attorney General Alberto Gonzales took office in 2005, he cited prosecution for obscenity as one of his top priorities. Congress authorized a pornography task force within the Federal Bureau of Investigation, but the bureau is having difficulty getting agents to volunteer.

Although many Americans advocate loosening restrictions for adult-oriented pornography, child pornography remains an area that most agree continues to merit vigorous prosecution. Child pornography concerns the sale of sexually explicit media to children and the use of children in the making of sexually explicit material. In *Ginsberg v. New York* (1968), the Supreme Court agreed that material that is not obscene for adults could be considered obscene when sold to children. In *New York v. Ferber* (1982), the Court held that because children are physically harmed in the making of child pornography, all possession of such material is illegal. With the intent of criminalizing virtual child pornography, in 1996 Congress attempted to extend *Ferber* to make illegal anything that "conveys the impression" of a minor engaged in explicit conduct. The Court, however, ruled in *Ashcroft v. Free Speech Coalition* (2002) that because no children are harmed in the creation of computer-simulated child pornography, it failed to meet the *Ferber* standard.

See also *Memoirs v. Massachusetts (1966); Miller v. California (1973); Roth v. United States (1957).*

REFERENCES

Downs, Donald. "The Attorney General's Commission and the New Politics of Pornography." *American Bar Foundation Research Journal* 12, no. 4 (1987): 641–679.

Hale, F. Dennis. "Regulating Pornography." In *Communication and the Law,* edited by W. Wat Hopkins. Northport, Ala.: Vision Press, 2006.

MacKinnon, Catharine. *Only Words.* Cambridge: Harvard University Press, 1993.

Rich, Frank. "Naked Capitalists." *New York Times Magazine,* May 20, 2001.

Sebastian, Raymond F. "Obscenity and the Supreme Court: Nine Years of Confusion." *Stanford Law Review* 19, no. 1 (1966): 167–189.

Office of Communications

The Office of Communications is the section within the White House responsible for coordinating and disseminating the president's message. President Richard M. Nixon established it in 1969 to handle relations with the local and specialized media. Although its role varies with each administration, its primary responsibility is presidential public relations and "spin control."

The director of communications, a top presidential adviser, heads the office. Along with the press secretary and the Press Office, the communications director's main objective is to generate favorable coverage of the president. Although the Press Office and the Office of Communications share the same goals, they further them in different ways. The press secretary deals with the White House press corps on an almost daily, face-to-face basis, answering questions, responding to inquiries, providing briefings, and so on. The communications director and the Office of Communications focus more on long-range strategic planning, determining how to set the agenda, planning the president's public events, and ensuring that the media transmit the president's message as seamlessly as possible. As John Anthony Maltese describes it in *Spin Control,* "[T]he Press Office is primarily reactive, while the Office of Communications is primarily proactive." The development of the Office of Communications illustrates the increasing political importance of the mass media to the presidency and the desire of presidents to influence and control the media's portrayal of them.

REFERENCES

Kumar, Martha Joynt. "The Office of Communications." *Presidential Studies Quarterly* 31, no. 4 (December 2001): 609–634.

Maltese, John Anthony. *Spin Control: The White House Office of Communications and the Management of Presidential News,* 2nd ed. Chapel Hill: University of North Carolina Press, 1994.

The White House Office of Communications, established under President Richard M. Nixon in 1969, is responsible for coordinating interactions between the president and the mass media. Nicole Wallace, White House communications director under President George W. Bush, looks on as he conducts a news conference in 2006.

Office of Telecommunications Policy

President Richard M. Nixon created the Office of Telecommunications Policy (OTP) in 1970 to manage and address issues involving telephone and broadcasting regulations. The Federal Communications Commission, however, continued to be the final authority on regulatory issues. By 1972 White House officials were using the office and the license renewal process to apply pressure to commercial network news programming in an attempt to bring public broadcasting into line with the administration's political views. For instance, when a station sought to renew its license, it often had to defend itself against charges that its license should not be renewed because of "unfair" or "biased" news programs.

President Jimmy Carter reorganized OTP in fulfilling a campaign promise to reduce federal bureaucracy. In 1978 he merged OTP with the Treasury Department's Office of Telecommunications, creating the National Telecommunications and Information Administration within the Commerce Department.

REFERENCES

Carmody, John. "Query for a Carter Aide on Communications Role." *Washington Post,* April 13, 1978.

Grossman, Michael Baruch, and Martha Joynt Kumar. *Portraying the President: The White House and the News Media.* Baltimore: Johns Hopkins University Press, 1981.

Off the record

"Off the record" describes a situation in which information is provided to reporters and columnists that may not be published or broadcast in any form. Off-the-record information is given only after the source and the journalist mutually agree to the terms. Public officials commonly provide important information to reporters off the record for a variety of reasons. For example, while remaining anonymous, they can provide information that helps journalists better understand events, policies, or officials' behavior. Sources also may provide off-the-record information to discredit political rivals or opposing viewpoints or to silence a reporter who is getting too close to uncovering a story.

Controversy almost always occurs when sources attempt to claim off-the-record terms selectively during an interview or retroactively, following an interview. Reporters have angered sources by using information gained on an off-the-record basis from one official to get another source to confirm the information on the record. Reporters learning information on an off-the-record basis have also angered sources by repeating the information to a second reporter who then disseminates the story. The latter scenario is why one government press officer, as recounted by political media expert Stephen Hess, warned his colleagues that "nothing substantive should be discussed 'off the record' for the good and sufficient reason that nothing substantive ever stays off the record."

REFERENCES

Hess, Stephen. *The Government/Press Connection.* Washington, D.C.: Brookings Institution, 1984.

Press, Charles, and Kenneth Verburg. "Off-the Record Rules." In *American Politicians and Journalists,* edited by Charles Press and Kenneth Verburg. Glenview, Ill.: Scott, Foresman and Company, 1988.

Op-Ed

"Op-ed" is shorthand for "opposite the editorial page," referring to contributions in a newspaper that contain opinions distinct from the paper's own editorials. Such pieces have also been referred to as "opinion-editorials." In some papers, the op-ed page appears at the end of the main section, but in other papers it is in the middle. The op-ed section consists of articles by regular and guest columnists—usually journalists, experts, or notable figures, though not always—along with letters to the editor from readers.

Op-eds differ from regular news stories in that they take explicitly biased positions, rather than adopting a neutral and descriptive tone. They are politically significant because they, along with newspaper editorials, are thought to potentially influence public and, more important perhaps, elite opinion. Furthermore, because op-eds may be penned by syndicated columnists and run in a number of different newspapers, they potentially have an impact far beyond their home or host outlet. Such columnists may become influential with officials and other political insiders because of their political or policy acumen or because of their influence on the public. For example, Walter Lippmann, James "Scotty" Reston, William Safire, and Meg Greenfield, among others, were thought to wield great power with their pens.

Op-ed pages contribute to democratic societies through the variety of viewpoints they allow to be presented and for their potential to stimulate public thinking and deliberation. For example, Benjamin I. Page argues that the *New York Times* op-ed page is the United States' most prized soapbox and that the editors attempt to create a "mini-public sphere" around political issues, in part by running op-eds on both ideological or political sides of its own editorials. Because of its prestige and elite readership, the *Times*'s op-ed page can set the tone of national debate. Given the limited space on such a soapbox, the *Times*'s (and other papers') editorial decisions about which columnists and guest voices will appear perform a powerful gatekeeping function in the realm of public debate.

See also *Editorials; Gatekeeping.*

REFERENCES

Dewitt Wallace Center Op-Ed Resource, Duke University, www.pub-pol.duke.edu/courses/op-ed.

Benjamin I. Page. "The Mass Media as Political Actors." *PS: Political Science and Politics* 29, no. 1 (1996): 20–24.

Giant mass media conglomerations have largely supplanted family-owned publications. In this photo from 1969, an employee of the Marysville Journal-Tribune *in Ohio collects freshly pressed copies of the paper.*

O'Reilly Factor

See *Pundit shows*

Ownership of media

The notion of diversity of political opinion lies behind the press freedom protected by the First Amendment. The fear at the time of the American Revolution was that government might have the power to limit that diversity. Today, however, there is concern in some quarters that large media enterprises are limiting the range of opinions to which the public has access. These media businesses often consist of combinations of newspapers, magazines, book publishing, television, radio, music, World Wide Web sites, and film and video production.

The mass media industry is unique in the United States' private enterprise system because it deals in the politically and socially sensitive commodities of ideas, information, thought, and opinion. Especially since the development of the broadcast media, the power exists to simultaneously reach millions of individuals in the United States and increasingly the rest of the world with a message or an image. The mass media are widely perceived as opinion makers, image formers, and culture disseminators, as well as conduits for sales and marketing.

Such media companies as film studios and book publishers create content. Others, such as television stations and cable systems, transmit content. Firms have increasingly combined elements of both functions, much as newspaper publishers have long created the product and run their own distribution and circulation systems. The media have evolved into big businesses, just as other small businesses changed and expanded, spurred by the technologies of the Industrial Revolution, population growth, and a massive economy. In *Media Monopoly,* Ben H. Bagdikian contends that the media companies have grown too large. The implication, he believes, is that "[t]he American audience, having been exposed to a narrowing range of ideas over the decades, often assumes that what it sees and hears in the major media is all there is. It is no way to maintain a lively marketplace of ideas, which is to say that it is no way to maintain a democracy."

Studies by the Federal Communications Commission (FCC) and many academics suggest that there is less cause for alarm. In 2003 the FCC's Media Ownership Policy Working Group found that local television stations owned by large broadcast networks received awards for news excellence at three times the rate of stations owned by smaller groups, and they produced nearly 25 percent more news and public affairs programming than non-network-owned affiliates. Television stations owned by enterprises that also owned newspapers in the same community had higher news ratings, won more news awards, and offered more news shows than non-newspaper affiliates. In ten cities where the newspaper and a TV station had common ownership, half of the combinations had a similar editorial slant in the 2000 presidential election, while the other half had divergent slants.

Today, digital technologies and the Internet infrastructure undermine long-standing elements that differentiated media formats. Digital technology allows text, audio, and visual information to be transformed into the identical and interchangeable format of bits. Hundreds of thousands of entities own the Internet, but it works as a whole to connect hundreds of millions of users. Thus, the media industries, which in an earlier era could be described as encompassing sectors known as newspapers, books, television, and so on, today operate in an environment of blurred boundaries among media formats. For example, a television set may get its picture and audio at any given moment from a broadcast signal, a coaxial cable signal, a videocassette, an optical disk (DVD), or a satellite transmission. What then is the relevant medium? A person viewing the screen may not even know the conduit.

The changing media environment, which makes a precise definition of the media arena difficult to determine, also means that competition may be coming from diverse, new, and less traditional players, such as telephone companies, computer firms, financial institutions, and others involved in the information business. This suggests not only a broadened arena for conflict in the marketplace, but also in the regulatory environment as government agencies seek to identify their territory.

Horizontal and Vertical Integration

The most typical form of expansion is that of a single firm owning more than one entity in a single medium, such as multiple newspapers or radio stations. This is called horizontal integration. The firm then becomes a chain owner of newspapers, magazines, cable systems, and so on. This was traditionally the most frequently occurring form of media combination and has been the subject of the greatest share of scrutiny by regulators and economists. Examples would be a firm that owns television stations in Boston, Philadelphia, and Detroit or an enterprise that publishes magazines for skiers, for photographers, and for gourmet cooks. There are also media conglomerates, firms that are horizontally integrated in more than one medium, such as Time Warner, News Corporation, and Viacom. Firms that control all or part of the product or service from raw material to final distribution are vertically integrated. Vertical integration occurs when businesses representing several sequential stages of production that could be separately owned are instead directed by a single firm. An example is a publisher that owns a paper mill, has its own staff of writers and editors, performs its own typesetting, runs its own presses, and handles its own delivery to the customer.

Both the economic and social impact of vertical combinations are much more difficult to measure than are horizontal combinations. Many of the largest mergers in the media industry since the 1990s have been primarily vertical combinations, including Disney with Capital Cities/ABC and Time Inc. with Warner Communications. Most attention in the area of media ownership has traditionally focused on horizontal integration: large newspaper chains, the number of broadcasting stations under a single owner, the size of multiple system operators. The issue of the permissible degree of cross-ownership in a geographical area has been a long-time concern in the public policy arena. Vertical integration has become a central issue for debate, particularly in the combining of cable systems with programming sources, such as production studios.

Whether the media industry is more or less consolidated in ownership from some arbitrary time in the past depends on what is measured and how. The movie production and distribution business has had six major players for decades. Who they are has changed (Walt Disney Co.'s studios, previously minor players, have replaced MGM), and the owners of some studios have passed hands (Universal has been owned by MCA, Japan's Matsushita, Canada's Seagram's, France's Vivendi, and the United States' General Electric in the two decades prior to 2004). The number of companies that own daily newspapers has declined along with the fortunes of that industry. Daily newspaper circulation has declined 12 percent since 1985. Daily newspapers, which

Leading Media Companies, 2006

Corporate Parent (Home Country)	Selected Brands and Products (in the United States)	Major Areas of Media Operations
Bertelsmann A.G. (Germany)	Sony BMG Music, Random House	Music, publishing
CBS Corp. (United States)	CBS, MTV, Paramount TV, Showtime, Simon and Schuster, CW Network (50%)	Cable networks, publishing, TV and radio broadcasting, video production
Comcast (United States)	Comcast Cable, E! Entertainment, CN8	Cable networks, cable systems, Internet access, telephone
General Electric (United States)	Bravo, CNBC, NBC, Universal Studios	Broadcasting, cable networks, filmed entertainment
News Corp. (United States)	DirecTV, Fox Network, Fox News, HarperCollins, MySpace.com, *New York Post, TV Guide,* Twentieth Century Fox	Broadcasting, cable news, filmed entertainment, newspapers, online, satellite systems
Reed Elsevier (United Kingdom and the Netherlands)	Harcourt, Lexis/Nexis, *Publishers Weekly, Variety,* MD Consult	Publishing
Sony (Japan)	Columbia Pictures, Epic and Columbia Records, Playstation	Filmed entertainment, music, video games
Thomson (United States)	Sweet & Maxwell, First Call Datastream, Westlaw	Electronic information services
Time Warner (United States)	AOL, CNN, CW Network (50%), HBO, *People, Time,* Time Warner Cable, Warner Music, Warner Bros.	Cable systems, filmed entertainment, music, online, publishing
Viacom (United States)	BET, Comedy Central, MTV, Nickelodeon, Paramount Pictures	Cable networks, filmed entertainment
Walt Disney Company (United States)	ABC, Buena Vista Pictures, Disney Channel, ESPN, Miramax	Broadcasting, cable networks, filmed entertainment, online

accounted for 45 percent of all advertising expenditures in the 1930s, received only 17.7 percent of media ad budgets by 2004. Not surprisingly in this context, the newspaper industry has consolidated.

Meanwhile, the television industry has never been more competitive. From three networks gaining about 90 percent of prime-time audiences in the 1970s, there are now scores of networks, among them CNN, Fox, HBO, Nickelodeon, and C-SPAN. The original three networks—ABC, CBS, and NBC—now struggle to get 45 percent of the audience on a typical evening.

After several years of growing faster than the overall economy, the information industry overall grew 19.4 percent between 2000 and 2004, about the same rate as the gross domestic product in the same period. The information industry stayed at 4.7 percent of the economy. The growth rates of the economy and the media industries are critical data points for understanding some of the effects of industry mergers. Consolidation of players in an otherwise expanding industry may have a different outcome on pricing and market control than consolidation in a stagnant or declining industry sector. In *Who Owns the Media?,* Benjamin M. Compaine and Douglas Gomery examine a broad spectrum of data and conclude that the growth of the industry overall and the increased choices provided by newer technologies, such as cable, satellite, and the Internet, have largely neutralized the influence of high-profile media mergers.

Government Involvement

Over the decades, the three agencies of the U.S. government most regularly involved in monitoring the status of competition in the media industries have been the U.S. Department of Justice (DOJ), the Federal Trade Commission (FTC), and the Federal Communications Commission. The FCC has specific authority over broadcasting and cable through its mandate to safeguard "the public interest." DOJ and the FTC have statutory authority over antitrust issues.

The antitrust laws do not flatly prohibit media mergers any more than they prohibit other kinds of mergers. Under present law, some measurable impact on competition in some market must be proven before a merger or acquisition would be held to violate the antitrust laws. The courts generally have been reluctant to limit media mergers when such an impact has not been shown, regardless of the social or other objections that have been asserted. Perhaps the most important industry-wide action outside of film was *Associated Press v. United States* (1945), in which the Supreme Court clearly placed newspapers and other media within the jurisdiction of antitrust legislation. In 1979 the antitrust division of DOJ investigated the merger between newspaper publisher Gannett and broadcaster Combined Communications and ruled that because they were in two different "product markets," there was no antitrust issue despite the size of the merger.

In June 2003, the FCC proposed rules easing some of its long-standing regulations. Most controversial, under prodding from several federal court decisions, it raised the maximum national audience size a single television broadcaster would be allowed to reach from 35 percent to 45 percent, while liberalizing restrictions on common ownership of newspapers and TV stations in a single local market. They were met with much criticism in Congress and beyond.

One critical question that has faced the relevant agencies over the years is to what degree they could and should be more concerned about concentration in the media as compared with other industries. Should a stricter standard apply to the media because of the media's position in U.S. society and the importance of having many channels available for speech? Can free speech be separated from the economic structure that controls the media? Given the safeguards imposed by the First Amendment, the federal government has limited authority to apply stricter standards to media companies.

See also *Competition; Cross-ownership.*

REFERENCES

Albarran, Alan, and Sylvia Chan-Olmstead. *Global Media Economics: Commercialization, Concentration, and Integration of World Media.* Ames: Iowa State University Press, 1998.

Bagdikian, Ben H. *The Media Monopoly.* 6th ed. Boston: Beacon Press, 2000.

Compaine, Benjamin M., and Douglas Gomery. *Who Owns the Media? Competition and Concentration in the Mass Media Industry.* 3rd ed. Mahwah, N.J.: Lawrence Erlbaum Associates, 2000.

Federal Communication Commission, "Research Studies on Media Ownership," www.fcc.gov/ownership/studies.html.

Greco, Albert N. "The Impact of Horizontal Mergers and Acquisitions on Corporate Concentration in the U.S. Book Publishing Industry, 1989–1994." *Journal of Media Economics* 12, no. 3 (1999): 165–180.

Hamilton, James T. *All the News That's Fit to Sell: How the Market Transforms Information into News.* Princeton, N.J.: Princeton University Press, 2004.

Levy, Jonathan, Marcelino Ford-Livene, and Anne Levine. "Broadcast Television: Survivor in a Sea of Competition." Office of Strategic Planning and Policy Analysis working paper. Washington, D.C., September 2002, www.fcc.gov/osp/workingp.html.

P

Pack journalism

In pack journalism, or pack reporting, reporters take cues on events deemed newsworthy by reporters who regularly cover an issue, from each other, or from the wire services. This method of newsgathering partially grew from beat coverage whereby small groups of journalists report only on particular issues, or beats.

Timothy Crouse coined the term *pack journalism* in *The Boys on the Bus* to describe the journalistic activities of reporters during the 1972 presidential campaign. Crouse observed that campaign journalists followed candidates around in packs and often got the same information and wrote similar stories. The term also includes reporters from small newspapers following the reporting direction of experienced national political reporters, wire service reporters, and reporters from large newspapers.

Pack journalism tends to lead to a standardization of news coverage and to a relatively narrow range of topics being covered in the news. Such behavior can also contribute to "feeding frenzies" when political scandals break. The practice also encourages and facilitates the use of framing and thematic coverage in determining the shaping and sequence of news stories. For example, reporters might tend to cover one aspect of an issue while ignoring a range of other equally viable angles.

See also *Framing; Media feeding frenzies; Newsgathering process.*

REFERENCES

Crouse, Timothy. *The Boys on the Bus.* New York: Random House, 1972.

Killenberg, George M. *Public Affairs Reporting: Covering the News in the Information Age.* New York: St. Martin's Press, 1992.
Paletz, David L. *The Media in American Politics.* New York: Longman, 1999.
Soley, Lawrence C. *The News Shapers.* New York: Praeger, 1992.

Paine, Thomas

Thomas Paine (1737–1809), a revolutionary thinker, philosopher, and pamphleteer, published the influential pamphlet *Common Sense* (1776) advocating colonial independence in 1776 on the basis of reason. Paine began working as a corset maker at age thirteen and eventually pursued careers as a sailor, schoolmaster, and tax collector. He also took up writing; one of his earlier papers, "The Case of the Officers of Excise" (1772), argued for a pay raise for excise officers. After meeting Benjamin Franklin in London, Paine was convinced to emigrate to the colonies, with Franklin's letter of recommendation, and in 1774 found a job in Philadelphia as a publicist and later as the coeditor of *Pennsylvania Magazine*.

Paine quickly became involved in the controversial issues of the day. Paine's "African Slavery in America" (1775) condemned slavery in the colonies as unjust and inhumane. His *Common Sense* captured the revolutionary tension mounting after the Boston Tea Party and the beginning of hostilities at the Battles of Lexington and Concord. Paine argued that government represented a necessary evil that could only be mitigated by frequent, representative, and popular elections. He served in the Continental Army and wrote the highly influential *American Crisis,* a series of sixteen papers, between 1776 and 1783. His words, such as the famous "These are the times that try men's souls," were stimulating, invigorating, and encouraging for the new Americans.

In 1777 he was chosen secretary to the Committee of Foreign Affairs in the Continental Congress. Paine later returned to England, where he wrote *The Rights of Man* between 1791 and 1792. His support of the French Revolution led to his arraignment for treason and flight to Paris. The French made him an honorary citizen and elected him as a deputy to the National Convention. He was eventually arrested by Robespierre and imprisoned in 1793 for voting against the execution of the deposed king, Louis XVI, and proposing to offer the king asylum in the United States. While in prison, between 1794 and 1796 he drafted *The Age of Reason,* in which he advocates the controversial concept of deism, which denied the interference of a Creator in the universe and touted the achievements of the Age of Enlightenment.

Released from prison in 1796 through the efforts of James Monroe, then-U.S. minister to France, Paine returned to the United States after receiving an invitation from Thomas Jefferson in 1802. Despite his intellectual contributions to the Declaration of Independence and the Constitution, Paine was not received well. Many of his contemporaries had forgotten about Paine's service to the country, as well as his writings, and reviled him as a betrayer and infidel. He continued to produce critical writings on a variety of topics including the Federalists and religion. Paine envisioned a free society on a grand scale, adopted an aggressively antislavery stance, and was one of the first to suggest a world peace organization and social security for the poor. Nonetheless, his radical views on religion tarnished his image and alienated him from most of the fellow citizens who had once revered him.

REFERENCES

Aldridge, Alfred Owen. *Man of Reason: The Life of Thomas Paine.* Philadelphia: Lippincott, 1959.
Conway, Moncure Daniel. *The Life of Thomas Paine.* New York: B. Blom, 1969.
Foner, Eric. *Tom Paine and Revolutionary America.* New York: Oxford University Press, 1976.
Fruchtman, Jack, Jr. *Thomas Paine: Apostle of Freedom.* New York: Four Walls Eight Windows, 1994.
Hawke, David Freeman. *Paine.* New York: Harper and Row, 1974.
Keane, John. *Tom Paine: A Political Life.* Boston: Little, Brown, 1995.
Williamson, Audrey. *Thomas Paine: His Life, Work, and Times.* New York: St. Martin's Press, 1973.
Woll, Walter. *Thomas Paine: Motives for Rebellion.* New York: P. Lang, 1992.

Partisan press

See *History of American journalism; Political parties and the press*

PBS

PBS, the Public Broadcasting Service, a non-profit corporation, consists of more than 340 public television stations in the United States, Puerto Rico, the Virgin Islands, Guam, and American Samoa. PBS does not produce programming, but rather makes available programs produced by member stations or independent contractors. These productions generally are cultural, educational, or scientific in nature. They also include children's fare and news and public affairs. PBS offerings reach a total audience of approximately 90 million viewers each week.

Though a "public" network, the U.S. federal government, through the Corporation for Public Broadcasting and other departments and agencies, provides only about one-fourth of PBS's funding. Political battles in Congress over whether government should support a television network in an age of so many satellite and cable options, federal cutbacks, and controversies over the political content of some PBS programs have contributed to cuts in government support. Viewers—through fund-raising marathons, auctions, and other pledge drives—along with member station assessments and donations close the gap on budgetary shortfalls. PBS has also begun to allow "commercials" in the form of announcements by its sponsors.

See also *Coporation for Public Broadcasting.*

REFERENCES

Engelman, Ralph. *Public Radio and Television in America: A Political History.* Thousand Oaks, Calif: Sage, 1996.
Ledbetter, James. *Made Possible By . . . : The Death of Public Broadcasting in the United States.* New York: Verso, 1997.
Public Broadcasting Service, www.pbs.org.

Penny press

Beginning in the 1830s, the "penny press," newspapers sold for one cent a copy, represented the emergence of a nonpartisan and popularized mass medium. Among them were the *New York Sun,* the first penny paper, as well as the *New York Evening Transcript, Boston Daily Times,* and *Baltimore Sun.* The penny press represented a shift in U.S. journalism resulting from technological advances, increasing literacy, shifts in society toward a more democratic ethos, and growth of the market economy.

The penny press developed as an alternative to the highly partisan and largely party-controlled press of the time, sold primarily by subscription at six cents a copy. The emergence of the penny press sparked several changes in journalism. Advertising targeted popular consumers, increased sensationalism charges surfaced, and active newsgathering developed. The *New York Herald*'s coverage of Wall Street and "high society" prefigured modern financial and society pages. Although the penny press's early development is traditionally traced to the 1830s, Jeffrey Rutenbeck argues that such "independence"—if a switch in dependence from political parties to market forces can be labeled as such—did not become the norm in U.S. journalism until the 1870s. Although the penny press is of historical interest, it exhibited traits that have become issues in today's media environment, such as sensationalism and infotainment.

See also *History of American journalism; New York Sun; Pulitzer, Joseph; Yellow journalism.*

REFERENCES

Crouthamel, James L. *Bennett's* New York Herald *and the Rise of the Popular Press.* Syracuse: Syracuse University Press, 1989.

Mott, Frank Luther. *American Journalism: A History of Newspapers in the United States through 250 Years, 1690 to 1940.* New York: Macmillan, 1941.

Rutenbeck, Jeffrey B. "Newspaper Trends in the 1870s: Proliferation, Popularization, and Political Independence." *Journalism and Mass Communication Quarterly* 72, no. 2 (Summer 1995): 361–375.

Schudson, Michael. *Discovering the News: A Social History of American Newspapers.* New York: Basic Books, 1978.

Pentagon Papers

The Pentagon Papers refer to the once-confidential U.S. Defense Department documents that detail U.S. military involvement in Vietnam from 1945 to 1971. At a time of already low public support for the war, Daniel Ellsberg, working for the Defense Department, first leaked sections of these politically sensitive documents to the *New York Times* in 1971. In 1967 Secretary of Defense Robert McNamara had called for the compilation of U.S. military operations in Vietnam. The 7,000-page, forty-seven-volume report, *United States-Vietnam Relations, 1945–1967: A Study Prepared by the Department of Defense,* revealed U.S. military miscalculations and purposive deception of the American public regarding actual U.S. operations in Vietnam.

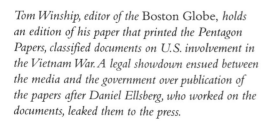

Tom Winship, editor of the Boston Globe, *holds an edition of his paper that printed the Pentagon Papers, classified documents on U.S. involvement in the Vietnam War. A legal showdown ensued between the media and the government over publication of the papers after Daniel Ellsberg, who worked on the documents, leaked them to the press.*

The publication of these documents, the Pentagon Papers, provoked the administration of President Richard M. Nixon to bring legal charges against the *Times* and Ellsberg. In 1971 the Supreme Court heard *New York Times v. United States* concerning the government's efforts to halt the publication of the papers. The Court ruled in the favor of the *Times*, marking a triumph for proponents of freedom of the press in the United States.

In the aftermath of the Supreme Court's ruling, large sections of the papers appeared in the *Times* and also in the *Washington Post*. Historians and political scientists consider the documents, now stored in the Lyndon Baines Johnson Library and Museum, to have contributed to ending U.S. military involvement in Vietnam.

See also *First Amendment; New York Times v. United States (1971); Prior restraint.*

REFERENCES

Ellsberg, Daniel. *Secrets: A Memoir of Vietnam and the Pentagon Papers.* New York: Viking Press, 2002.

Rudenstine, David. *The Day the Presses Stopped: A History of the Pentagon Papers Case.* Berkeley: University of California Press, 1996.

Ungar, Sanford. *The Papers and the Papers: An Account of the Legal and Political Battle over the Pentagon Papers.* New York: Dutton, 1972.

Pew Research Center for the People and the Press

The Pew Research Center for the People and the Press, an independent opinion research group funded by the Pew Charitable Trusts, studies public attitudes toward the press, politics, and public policy issues. Its research findings are widely distributed, but are particularly of interest to political leaders, journalists, scholars, and public interest organizations.

From 1990 to 1995, the Pew Research Center was known as the Times-Mirror Center for the People and the Press. Under the direction of Andrew Kohut, the center's research focuses on five areas of investigation: People and the Press, which explores public attitudes about the news media; People, the Press and Politics, which identifies the values and attitudes of the U.S. electorate; News Interest Index, which measures how closely the public follows major news stories; America's Place in the World, which provides in-depth surveys and analyses about international policy; and Media Use, which conducts surveys about people's use and attitude toward the Internet and traditional news outlets. The Pew Global Project Attitudes conducts public opinion polling on an international level.

REFERENCES

Pew Research Center for the People and the Press, www.people-press.org

Landler, Mark. "Times-Mirror Sets More Cuts and Closings." *New York Times,* July 20, 1995, D5.

Phillips, David Graham

David Graham Phillips (1867–1911), a critical journalist and author, was best known for a series of "muckraking" articles exposing corruption in the U.S. Senate that appeared in *Cosmopolitan* during 1906. Phillips began his career as a newspaper reporter for the *Cincinnati Times-Star,* the *New York Sun,* and eventually joined Joseph Pulitzer's *New York World,* where he worked from 1893 to 1902. In 1897 he went on assignment and covered the Greco-Turkish War. After the success of his first novel, *The Great God Success,* published in 1901, Phillips became a freelance writer for numerous publications, most notably the *Saturday Evening Post.* He was shot to death in 1911 by a deranged man angered by one of the author's novels that the assailant claimed had slandered his family. Phillips's novels include *The Conflict* (1911) and *Susan Lenox: Her Fall and Rise* (1917), the story of an illegitimate country girl's rise to success, which was published posthumously.

See also *Muckraking.*

REFERENCES

Filler, Louis. *Voice of the Democracy: A Critical Biography of David Graham Phillips, Journalist, Novelist, Progressive.* University Park: Pennsylvania State University Press, 1978.

Ravitz, Abe C. *David Graham Phillips.* New York: Twayne Publications, 1970.

Political content in advertising

Political advertising, particularly on television, is the dominant form of communication used by candidates to reach voters in the United States. In the first presidential election to use televised political advertising, in 1952 Dwight butions and expenditure reporting for federal elections remain subject to oversight by the Federal Election Commission, the law allows political candidates at all electoral levels to purchase almost unlimited amounts of advertising on commercial radio and television. The Federal Communications Commission enforces federal communication laws, which require television and radio stations to sell equal amounts of time to all "legally qualified candidates for federal office." Stations may not censor or impose content restrictions on federal candidates' advertising other than requiring sponsorship identification.

In 2002 Congress passed the Bipartisan Campaign Reform Act, also known as McCain-Feingold, which requires that candidates meet a more rigorous standard for sponsorship identification whereby candidates must appear in their advertising and explicitly state their approval of an advertisement. The legislation also placed new restrictions on fund-raising by candidates and parties and attempted to curb advertising by corporations and interests groups within sixty days of the election. Most observers agree that this legislation did not have the desired effect of reducing advertising expenditures by parties and, especially, by independent groups or of making candidates less likely to sponsor negative advertising.

Political advertising is often criticized for focusing campaigns more on a candidate's image than on substantive policy matters or issues and for being too negative. Research on political advertising content has shown that charges about the failure of political advertising to cover issues are unjustified. In fact, studies have shown that the content of political advertising is overwhelmingly devoted to issues. In presidential campaigns from 1952 through 2004, 69 percent of all campaign ads used by candidates in the general election focused on issues, rather than on candidate image. Although it is certainly the case that many candidates use their television spots to tell voters about their backgrounds, qualifications, character, and moral values, most television ads also give voters information about where the candidate stands on such issues as the economy, jobs, health care, international affairs, crime, education, and many other concerns. Other spots also provide specific policy proposals supported by the candidate.

The criticism that political advertising has become increasingly negative does have some basis in truth. Dwight Eisenhower's 1952 campaign commercials issued a great many negative attacks, but the attacks focused more on the

Journalist David Graham Phillips gained national attention in 1906 for his stories in Cosmopolitan *that exposed the corruption of powerful Rhode Island senator Nelson Aldrich.*

Eisenhower's campaign aired a series of short question-and-answer spots to personalize Eisenhower's image and to convince voters that he could handle their concerns. From this beginning, the importance of television advertising in electoral contests has steadily increased. Presidential candidates and candidates running for major statewide or congressional offices now spend millions of dollars to produce and air television and radio advertising in their campaigns. In the 2000 presidential campaign, Democrat Al Gore and Republican George W. Bush and their political parties spent more than $240 million on political advertising. In the 2004 presidential campaign expenditures for political advertising by candidates George W. Bush and John Kerry, their political parties, and various independent groups exceeded $600 million.

Political television advertising in the United States is subject to minimal regulatory control. While campaign contri-

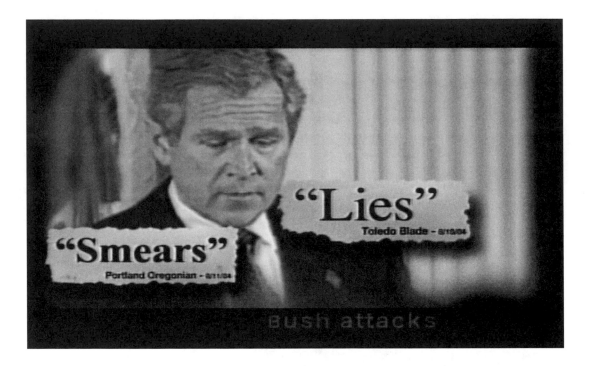

In the television age, political figures have used media advertising to establish an image, assert platforms, and secure votes. This 2004 advertisement, by the presidential campaign of Democratic challenger John Kerry, was in response to Republican attacks on Kerry's war record in Vietnam.

opposing Democratic Party than on Adlai Stevenson, Eisenhower's opponent. Lyndon B. Johnson's 1964 presidential campaign is often cited for its reliance on attack advertising aimed at the Republican challenger, Barry Goldwater. The Johnson campaign sponsored the well-known "daisy girl" commercial, in which a small girl picks petals from a daisy and an ominous countdown precedes the explosion of a nuclear bomb and the appearance of a mushroom cloud. The voice-over does not mention Goldwater, but viewers got the message that the election of Goldwater might mean nuclear disaster.

Overall, negative advertising characterizes only 38 percent of the ads in presidential campaigns from 1952 through 2004, but an increase in negativity is evident in the presidential campaign cycles from 1988 through 2004. Bill Clinton's advertising in his two presidential campaigns contains the highest percentage of negative ads in the history of political spot advertising: 69 percent of his 1992 ads and 68 percent of his 1996 ads were attack ads. In the 2004 campaign, the advertising sponsored by Bush and Kerry was balanced, with approximately half positive and half negative, but the overwhelming focus of independent advertising sponsored by such groups as the Media Fund, MoveOn.org, Swift Boat Veterans for Truth, the Progress for America Voter Fund, the AFL–CIO political action committee, and others was negative, with some estimates as high as 81 percent. Negative ads,

however, like all political advertising, heavily emphasize issues, not candidate image.

An important concern is what effect the content of political advertising has on voters. Research has shown that political advertising is an effective way of reaching voters and helping them to understand the issues in a campaign. Despite the criticisms about political advertising and the possibility that negative advertising can sometimes backfire or create a backlash against the sponsoring candidate, substantial research has shown that voters learn more information about campaign issues from political television ads than from television news or televised debates. This is particularly true of negative advertising, which is more memorable and more likely to increase voter issue learning and knowledge about candidates. Negative advertising is particularly effective when sponsored by someone independent of the candidate, such as an interest group that may be perceived as more credible and less self-interested than the candidate.

Political advertising appears to be especially effective at improving a candidate's evaluation levels, or lessening the opponent's evaluation in the case of negative ads, when the ad focuses on issues. Undecided voters and those with low involvement and low interest in a campaign may also be especially susceptible to the influence of political ads. One of the reasons that political ads are effective is that they often rely on emotional appeals.

Surveys of public opinion toward advertising repeatedly conclude that most voters say they do not like political advertising and that they are especially put off by negative advertising. Some political observers have argued that voters may be less likely to vote at all when exposed to a great deal of negative advertising. The evidence for this claim is limited, and other research suggests that negative advertising sometimes stimulates voter interest and involvement in politics.

Complaints that political advertising is too negative often have their basis in the concentration of the news media on controversial ads. As political advertising has grown more important to campaigning, newspapers and television have increased their coverage of the advertising, often monitoring ads and doing "ad watches" designed to provide voters with information about false and misleading claims in political ads. Media ad watches concentrate most of their attention on negative or controversial spots, and the results of such media scrutiny may do more to reinforce the claims in the advertisements than to lessen the effects on voters.

New technologies are opening additional venues for the distribution of political advertising. The growth of e-mail, the Web, text messaging, and other electronic distribution systems have led to changes in how political advertising is disseminated to voters. The use of the Web also provides more opportunities for voters to check claims made in political advertising and to engage in interactive responses, including chat rooms, forums, and blogs about campaigns and advertising messages.

REFERENCES

Ansolabehere, Stephen, and Shanto Iyengar. *Going Negative: How Attack Ads Shrink and Polarize the Electorate.* New York: Free Press, 1995.

Devlin, L. Patrick. "Contrasts in Presidential Campaign Commercials of 2000." *American Behavioral Scientist* 44 (August 2001): 2338–2369.

Diamond, Edwin, and Stephen Bates. *The Spot: The Rise of Political Advertising on Television.* 3rd ed. Cambridge, Mass.: MIT Press, 1992.

Jamieson, Kathleen Hall. *Packaging the Presidency.* 3d ed. New York: Oxford University Press, 1996.

Kaid, Lynda Lee. "Political Advertising." In *The Handbook of Political Communication Research,* edited by Lynda Lee Kaid. Mahwah, N.J.: Lawrence Erlbaum Associates, 2004.

Kaid, Lynda Lee, and Anne Johnston. *Videostyle in Presidential Campaigns.* Westport, Conn.: Praeger/Greenwood, 2001.

West, Darrell M. *Air Wars: Television Advertising in Election Campaigns, 1952–1992.* Washington, D.C.: Congressional Quarterly, 1993.

Political correspondents

Political correspondents, journalists assigned exclusively or primarily to cover politics, approach their work in a way that is different from the orientation of most journalists trained as generalists capable of reporting on virtually any topic. Most major news organizations assign political correspondents to cover beats, that is, specific aspects of national or state politics. Political correspondents' focus on politics allows them to develop expertise that can enhance the quality of their reporting. Major news bureaus often assign a political correspondent to each of the major branches of government in Washington, D.C. For example, there will be a political correspondent assigned to report on developments in Congress, at the Supreme Court, or at the White House. News organizations may also assign correspondents to report more generally on political developments at all levels of government.

Fueled primarily by the proliferation of news media outlets, the number of political correspondents has mushroomed over the past five decades. The White House press corps, a specialized group of political correspondents who report on the president, has increased almost seventy-fold since 1945. President Harry S Truman announced his decision to drop atomic bombs on Japan in 1945 to about twenty-five reporters. During the Clinton administration, more than 1,700 political correspondents were assigned to cover the White House.

Access to high-level political institutions and individuals remains restricted, even for members of the press. Reporters require clearances to gain access to Capitol Hill or to the White House, for example. From a practical viewpoint, news organizations that assign correspondents to report on these institutions can acquire such credentials. Designating specific reporters as political correspondents thus has its advantages, such as increased access to report on political news.

REFERENCES

Bennett, W. Lance. *News: The Politics of Illusion.* 6th ed. New York: Pearson/Longman, 2005.

Hess, Stephen. *The Washington Reporters.* Washington, D.C.: Brookings Institution, 1981.

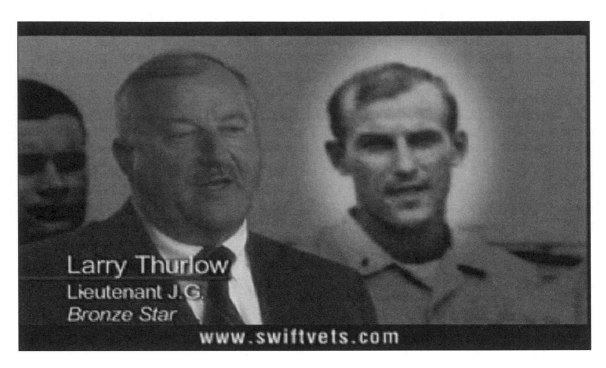

Vietnam veteran Larry Thurlow criticizes his former military commander and 2004 Democratic presidential candidate John Kerry. Swiftboat Veterans for Truth launched a series of negative campaign ads calling into question Kerry's military service in an effort to dissuade voters from electing him.

Political participation and the media

For the modern mass media, acting as a conduit of information between the political leadership and the citizens is a serious responsibility, because for any democracy to survive and flourish, the electorate needs to have a solid understanding of important issues and the ability to judge how its elected leaders are handling those issues. Because so few Americans have direct contact with their elected leaders, the media have the potential to affect political participation in a number of ways: by acting as a socializing agent that teaches people about democratic values and social norms; by serving as an agenda setter that gives some issues credibility and importance while discounting others; and playing the role of an informer that disseminates information about current issues and problems and alternatives. The media also affect political participation by covering campaigns and elections and providing information to voters.

For as long as there has been a modern mass media, concerns have been raised about their power to influence people. Many researchers feared initially that the media had a "hypodermic effect" on people, causing consumers to believe everything presented through the media. If this were indeed true, there could be profound consequences for allowing certain groups access or control of the media to influence an unsuspecting population. Studies during and after World War II, however, found no evidence to support the idea that people take everything they see and read at face value, losing the use of their critical reasoning skills. Because of these findings, many researchers refined their views and came to believe that the media had minimal effects on political participation and socialization; in other words, the media simply reinforced people's partisan views and were incapable of making them change their minds. People instead relied on their personal relations and on political elites for information that might alter their viewpoints in deciding political issues. According to the minimal effects model initially developed in the 1940s and 1950s, if the media had any impact on political views, it was a two-stage process: the media influenced local and national opinion makers, who in turn influenced voters. Recent research indicates, however, that the media have more subtle and complicated effects than previously believed when it comes to political socialization. This new theory, the contingent effects model, argues that certain types of media are capable at certain times of affecting some individuals, but the media are not capable of swaying the opinion of large segments of the population all of the time.

Most researchers also now believe that engagement with the mass media is one of the primary ways in which people, especially young adults, become socialized to political participation and democratic values. Among children not yet capable of complex reasoning, most political socialization comes from parents and other family members who explain ideas to them. This changes, however, as children mature. Most teenagers credit the media with exposing them to and teaching them about more complex issues, such as the economy, war, and race relations. The media become a critical socializing force because for many adolescents and teens using mass media—especially watching television, listening to the radio, and surfing the Internet—is the primary way they spend their leisure time. Some young people spend more time watching television than they do attending school. The media continue to socialize people even after they become adults, albeit in different ways. A person's political beliefs tend to be rather well established once he or she reaches adulthood. The media are only one factor in altering political perceptions. Most adults assess their personal political beliefs against the news they receive from the media, their life experiences, information from friends and relatives, and other sources. When they receive news that fails to conform to their currently held beliefs, they might reformulate their views taking into account this new information, or they might dismiss the information as unreliable or inaccurate.

In addition to informing adults and teaching young people about basic democratic values and other norms, the media affect political participation by discouraging it. When selecting which stories to cover and how to treat the actors involved, the media may dishearten people from joining particular political groups or revealing their beliefs in certain places. If the media frame a story in a way that casts a political opinion in a negative light, some politically active people holding that opinion may grow discouraged and abandon the cause, while others who share similar views but had not been politically active might choose to remain silent. In this way, the mass media can further marginalize ideas that are unpopular or already outside the mainstream. Simply put, the media help define acceptable political discourse and in the process delegitimize those views that fall outside these accepted boundaries.

In exploring media coverage of antiwar protests during the Vietnam War, some scholars found that news stories tended to highlight the internal divisions of the movement and trivialize the movement's goals and activities. The media also structured stories about the movement to present the protesters as marginalized individuals unrepresentative of the broader population. Using this frame, the media portrayed the student-led antiwar movement as a fringe element that did not subscribe to "traditional American values," and thus their protests were not bound to have any effect on the political process. These types of stories could have destroyed the morale of those already involved and could also have kept others from joining the movement.

Other researchers have found that media coverage can have a negative impact on the political participation of individuals by influencing public opinion. Because the media help to explain and define public opinion, they can also contribute to silencing minority viewpoints. Perhaps because of social norms or peer pressure, when people hold unpopular views, they are less likely to express those ideas in public and more likely to retreat from politics. This becomes cyclical, because once those who oppose a popular issue exit the public sphere, it appears that the popular view holds sway; with even less apparent dissent, people who might still disagree refrain from speaking out. Therefore, although necessary for a democratic society, the media can also depress turnout and participation by alienating people with unpopular views as well as by marginalizing groups by framing stories in negative ways.

Another, more positive, way the media influence political participation is by covering elections and informing the electorate about the candidates and the issues. In a country as large as the United States, it is impossible for candidates to meet with the voters face-to-face to explain their positions. Therefore an institution—the media—is needed to convey messages from candidates to the electorate. This is, perhaps, the most basic and critical aspect of the media's role in modern democracies. If the electorate is ignorant about current problems and available solutions, it cannot cast an informed vote. Many researchers have found that the decision to vote is related to the decision to pay attention to the news media. That is, avid readers of a newspaper are more likely to vote than those people who do not read a newspaper. In addition, people who closely follow the news through other media also are more likely to vote than those who do not keep current on events. There are many possible explanations for this connection.

Some scholars argue that people who follow the news have a better understanding of the issues and feel more capable of making informed political decisions. Other theories hold that people who follow the media feel more connected to society, believe that voting is a way to change or preserve society, and therefore take the responsibility seriously. In short, people who pay attention to the media feel more empowered than those who do not follow the news and are more likely to believe that they have a stake in the outcome of elections. Those who do not follow the news feel more disengaged from society and do not believe that they will have an impact on political issues. In this way, simply using the mass media positively correlates to political participation.

In addition to providing the public with information about elections and campaigns via news programming, the media also permit the public to learn about campaigns and candidates through political advertising, in which candidates tout their personal strengths and expose the weakness of the other candidates. Such advertising mutually benefits the media and the candidate, as well as the public. The media receive financial compensation for the advertisements, while the candidates speak directly to an audience without the interference of others interpreting their message or filtering their content. There is some indication that campaigns have a positive effect on political participation, as in non-presidential elections greater levels of campaign spending are positively associated with greater levels of voting. Because so many Americans spend their leisure time in front of the television, paid television advertisements present an opportunity for the candidates to directly present their arguments in 30-second spots.

Many social scientists and others are concerned about the prevalence of negative advertising. As the absolute number of political advertisements and the total number of negative advertisements, or attack ads, have increased dramatically over the past thirty years, some fear that the negativity of these advertisements has turned people away from the political process. Although the evidence remains incomplete, some research indicates that negative advertising might not keep people from voting and participating in elections. Rather, people who view these advertisements process them much like any other information from the media and evaluate them according to their already held beliefs. Therefore, people who view a negative ad attacking a candidate they support are more likely to discount the information in the ad and continue to support the candidate, while those who did not support the candidate are more likely to believe the information in the advertisement. Although negative commercials themselves might not depress voter turnout, some research indicates that negative campaigns depress voter turnout.

Overall, it can be concluded that the media have generally positive effects on citizen political participation.

Although some people contend that the media have had negative effects on some voters by increasing cynicism and apathy, the bulk of social science research shows that media use increases civic interest, engagement, learning, and involvement. Nevertheless, trends toward sensationalism and infotainment, coupled with political polarization and fragmentation of media audiences through cable television, talk radio, and the Internet, raise questions as to whether positive citizen involvement and engagement will continue to be the case.

See also *Political content in advertising; Political parties and the press.*

REFERENCES

Ansolabehere, Stephen, and Shanto Iyengar. *Going Negative: How Attack Ads Shrink and Polarize the Electorate.* New York: Free Press, 1995.

Gitlin, Todd. *The Whole World Is Watching: Mass Media in the Making and Unmaking of the New Left.* Berkeley: University of California Press, 2003.

Noelle-Neumann, Elisabeth. *The Spiral of Silence: Public Opinion—Our Social Skin.* Chicago: University of Chicago Press, 1993.

Norris, Pippa. *Virtuous Circle: Political Communications in Postindustrial Societies.* New York: Cambridge University Press, 2000.

Thorsen, Esser. "Moblizing Citizen Participation." In *Institutions of American Democracy: The Press,* edited by Geneva Overholser and Kathleen Hall Jamieson. New York: Oxford University Press, 2005.

Political parties and the press

From the earliest days of the United States, the link between political parties and the press was apparent in the pages of the partisan press and the relationships between leaders of party factions and the publishers they sponsored. Although that relationship has certainly changed, political parties and the press continue to rely on each other. Journalists use political parties to organize reporting on campaigns, governing, and policy and to appear balanced. Political parties and their leaders in government need the press to communicate with the public and with each other to influence elections and public policy. The result is that nearly 200 years after the heyday of the partisan press, it is hard to imagine the press and political parties functioning without one another.

The Rise and Fall of the Partisan Press

As the first partisan factions began to emerge inside

George Washington's administration and the new Congress, the leaders of these parties recognized the importance of communicating their political views to a wider audience. Thomas Jefferson and Alexander Hamilton, leaders of opposing partisan factions, formed alliances with sympathetic publishers. In exchange for the party leader securing government printing contracts or providing other financial support, the publishers produced party newspapers for their political sponsors. The partisan press frequently ran party speeches and debates verbatim, and unlike the mainstream journalism of today, made no attempt to be balanced or objective. The partisan press was a mouthpiece for the party.

By the 1830s, the direct connection between the parties and the press began to weaken. As publishers relied less on sponsorship and more on a mass audience to stay afloat financially, the content of their papers shifted away from partisan politics and toward local interest stories that would appeal to more people, and editors gained more independence to express their own views rather than those of their party patrons. The eventual evolution of the press into the independent, sometimes adversarial, journalism of today seems far removed from the partisan press and might lead to questions about whether there is any real link between the parties and the press today. Richard Davis points out that some scholars have even blamed the media for a perceived decline in party power over the last thirty years, as the media have usurped the parties' traditional role as intermediary between elected officials and the public. A closer look at the relationship between parties and the press, however, reveals that they do indeed continue to need and use each other though in very different ways than they did in the early days of the partisan press.

Why the Press Needs Political Parties

Political parties permeate coverage of campaigns and governing, but rarely do journalists today set out to make parties the primary subject of their stories. Three reasons, all related to news values and standards of the press, help explain why the media need parties for their coverage. First, parties help journalists organize and simplify political stories that sometimes involve complex issues and processes. Time and space constraints and the need to appeal to a mass audience encourage reporters to avoid issues or processes too complex to be explained in a short amount of space or in terms that most people will readily understand. Therefore, while campaigns are numerous and may involve a variety of issues or proposals, they can usually be reduced to which party wins and which party loses. Policy issues, for example, Social Security, are often difficult, and their details may not be easily understood by non-experts, but if Democrats and Republicans disagree on the issue or its solutions, the media can simplify the discussion to two partisan sides. For this reason, debate over Social Security reform in 2005 typically devolved to the Republicans' interest in creating personal savings accounts for citizens and the Democrats' contentions that Republicans wanted to "privatize" Social Security. Press coverage largely neglected other possible reforms. The ability to simplify politics and issues to two competing sides makes them easier to report and more accessible to the wider audience the press hopes to attract.

Second, parties are a consistent source of conflict and drama—two staples of media news values. Party conflict arises from differences over policy and competition to win seats in government. Jon Bond and Richard Fleisher have shown how Congress has become more ideological and partisan in the last twenty years. Journalists reflect this polarization in government as they distill everything from policy debates to confirmation hearings to partisan battles. As moderates in both parties disappear, there seems to be less common ground and fewer viable compromises that anyone is willing to entertain. Therefore, the media are able to find conflict on most issues by going to representatives of each party. Tim Groeling and Samuel Kernell have found that parties often oblige the media's desire for conflict by choosing to publicly criticize the opposing party, especially in times of divided government, rather than focusing on bipartisan messages or even praise for their own party.

The relatively narrow margins by which congressional majorities have held their power during the last decade have placed a premium on party unity and provided an endless source of partisan conflict for the media. This conflict is especially pronounced in the national media's coverage of campaigns, which often revolves around the horse race of whether the party in power can retain its majority or how many seats the minority will gain. In 2002, for example, coverage in the *Washington Post* and *New York Times* considered the impact of the troubled economy on Republicans' electoral fortunes and speculated about how the congressional debate and vote on military action in Iraq would affect the Democrats' chances of picking up seats in Congress.

Third, the parties offer the media a way to maintain the appearance of balance and journalistic norms of fairness.

Journalists are expected to be objective observers and not to be one-sided in their reporting. In practice, this means that reporters seek sources from different sides of an issue or controversy and that they use sources to express opinions or offer evaluations about issues, events, and actions rather than using their own voice. Because the public is generally aware that the two major parties oppose each other, journalists can include sources from each party as a way to maintain "balance" in their stories. Although this does not guarantee that all sides of an issue are represented in the news, it does appear to meet the journalistic standards of fairness. One sees this perhaps most clearly on political talk shows on television that invite a panel of guests usually equally divided between Republicans and Democrats.

Minor, or "third," parties are also affected by the media. In general, minor parties and their candidates receive far less coverage by the media, unless they are considered newsworthy by being unusual or likely to influence the race between the major party candidates. Attention to the two major parties in government may also help reinforce the two-party system in the public mind. Nevertheless, minor parties have been aided somewhat by the development of the Internet and other means of reaching voters disaffected with the Democrats and Republicans.

Why Parties Need the Press

The other side of the relationship between the press and political parties is the parties' reliance on the media to communicate not just with the public but with others in government. In recent campaigns, party organizations have joined candidates in buying advertising as a way to communicate to voters. Although the advertisements themselves are a way to take the parties' messages directly to voters, they also attract the attention of news media. The media's interest in covering the advertisements as news through stories on campaign strategies and through ad watches that evaluate the accuracy and effectiveness of the ads has allowed the parties to extend the reach of their paid advertising. The parties are increasingly expanding this tactic to influence policymaking and other political processes as well by placing ads on issues or events, such as confirmation hearings, in a few large markets with the hope of attracting additional coverage that will generate public support and pressure elected officials.

In Congress, the political parties have in the last fifteen years placed more emphasis on communicating a coherent message through the news media. Barbara Sinclair notes that

the expectation that party leaders in the Senate will further collective partisan concerns now encompasses the assumption that they must help coordinate and promote a party message. Dan Lipinski and Patrick Sellers have both discussed the institutionalized activities and efforts that leaders in the House and the Senate employ to accomplish this task. Party leaders encourage or instruct their members to use talking points that emphasize the goals and policies on which the party agrees, usually issues the party owns or is perceived as having an advantage over the other party on, as Sellers has revealed. In addition, as Lawrence Evans and Walter Oleszek discuss, party leaders in the Senate make use of parliamentary procedures, such as filibusters and cloture votes (attempts to end filibusters that require sixty votes), to draw attention to the party's message. For example, Republicans invoked cloture on some of George W. Bush's judicial nominations although they knew they did not have sixty votes, because they wanted simply to highlight the obstructionist tactics of the Democrats and to create an opportunity to discuss why they thought the judges were good choices.

Conclusion

Much has changed since party leaders and newspaper publishers worked together to further the parties' communication and interests, but even as the press has become independent from the parties, reporters continue to find it useful to cover them and to frame campaigns, issues, and political processes in terms of them. At the same time, the parties have learned how to cast their messages in ways that fit the news values of the press—highlighting conflict between the parties and creating simple labels to discuss issues and proposals—to communicate through the news to constituents and to each other to influence policymaking. Although the relationship between the press and the political parties has evolved, the two still rely on and benefit from each other.

See also *History of American journalism; Media bias.*

REFERENCES

Bond, Jon R., and Richard Fleisher, eds. *Polarized Politics: Congress and the President in a Partisan Era.* Washington, D.C.: CQ Press, 2000.

Cook, Timothy E. *Governing with the News: The News Media as a Political Institution.* Chicago: University of Chicago Press, 1998.

David, Richard. *The Press and American Politics: The New Mediator.* 3rd ed. Upper Saddle River, N.J.: Prentice-Hall, 2001.

Evans, C. Lawrence, and Walter J. Oleszek. "Message Politics and Senate Procedure." In *The Contentious Senate,* edited by Colton C. Campbell and Nicol C. Rae. Lanham, Md.: Rowman and Littlefield, 2001.

Groeling, Tim, and Samuel Kernell. "Congress, the President, and Party Competition via Network News." In *Polarized Politics: Congress and the President in a Partisan Era,* edited by Jon R. Bond and Richard Fleisher. Washington, D.C.: CQ Press, 2000.

Lipinski, Daniel. "The Outside Game: Communication as a Party Strategy in Congress." In *Communication and U.S. Elections: New Agendas,* edited by Roderick Hard and Daron Shaw. Lanham, Md.: Rowman and Littlefield, 2001.

Sellers, Patrick J. "Congress and the News Media: Manipulating the Message in the U.S. Congress." *Harvard International Journal of Press/Politics.* 5 (January 2000): 22–31.

Sinclair, Barbara. "The Senate Leadership Dilemma: Passing Bills and Pursuing Partisan Advantage in a Nonmajoritarian Chamber." In *The Contentious Senate,* edited by Colton C. Campbell and Nicol C. Rae. Lanham, Md.: Rowman and Littlefield, 2001.

Vinson, C. Danielle. "Political Parties and the Media." In *Media Power, Media Politics,* edited by Mark Rozell. Lanham, Md.: Rowman and Littlefield, 2003.

Political satire

Political satire—a form of critical inquiry that uses mockery, ridicule, and wit to make a moral point—blends humor, criticism, and even entertainment in addressing politics, politicians, and public affairs. The ridiculousness of political affairs is accentuated by attacking the vice and folly of politicians. Political satire is also a form of entertainment through which citizens who are not attentive to conventional political news outlets—and, therefore, may typically not encounter political content—can be exposed to politics.

Targets of political satire include governments, public affairs, politicians, politics, social order, law and order, the establishment, and hierarchies. Political satire employs irony, parody, caricature, juxtaposition, ridicule, mockery, wit, derision, sarcasm, and exaggeration in written, spoken, and visual forms to illuminate and question the conduct of politicians and public affairs. According to John Street and Geoffrey Baym, juxtaposing common sense and practicality against the rhetoric of politicians is a major tool of political satire. In doing so, political satire promotes a certain set of values and principles, such as populism, a belief in the wisdom of the common person over the elite. According to Baym, "Unlike traditional news, which claims an epistemological certainty, satire is a disclosure of *inquiry,* a rhetoric of challenge that seeks through the asking of unanswered questions to clarify the underlying morality of a situation." Political satire may not resonate with all citizens, as it requires an audience that understands its underlying assumptions.

Jon Stewart, host of Comedy Central's Daily Show, *has attracted a growing national audience with his delivery of satirized "fake news" as well as interviews with influential political figures.*

Political satire has a dual purpose: political reform and entertainment. Political satire is often motivated by intentions of reforming or changing politicians and conventions in politics, although it rarely offers substantive solutions to problems. It can foment dissent among the public, acting as a catalyst in altering public opinion toward the government, politicians, or policies. The primary purpose of political satire, however, is to entertain, often providing catharsis for those frustrated with politics and politicians. According to Dustin Griffin, political satire is subversive and may increase cynicism and skepticism toward government and political leaders, but by itself it does not produce revolutionary change.

Forms of political satire have existed as long as humans have submitted to governance and leaders have ruled. Benjamin Franklin was one of the first political satirists in the United States. The proliferation of the printing press and print media rapidly increased the amount and extent of political satire. Andrew Jackson was the first target of many cartoons. One of the most prominent political satirists during this time period was Samuel L. Clemens (Mark Twain), whose writings combined comedy and criticism of society and government. By the early 1900s, satire began to target technology and capitalism, as well as government. Examples include works by such entertainers as Will Rogers and movies like *Mr. Smith Goes to Washington*. According to John Street, contemporary political satire boomed in the 1960s with performers like Mort Sahl, Tom Lehrer, Bob Newhart, and Lenny Bruce in the United States and the British magazine *Private Eye* and the television show *That Was the Week That Was*. The increase in political satire is also partly attributable to the U.S. government's response to suspected communists during the 1950s and early 1960s.

More recently political satire has flourished as entertainment, such as live performance comedy by Chicago's Second City and Washington D.C.'s Capitol Steps; by late night comedians, including David Letterman and Jay Leno; and by "fake news" television shows like "Weekend Update" on *Saturday Night Live* and the *Daily Show*. Web sites and magazines, including www.whitehouse.org and *The Onion*, also produce popular satire. Many political leaders have acknowledged the popularity of political satire and have become hosts or guests on *Saturday Night Live* and the *Daily Show*. At times, leaders have even parodied themselves: Attorney General Janet Reno, New York mayor Rudy Giuliani, Arizona senator John McCain, and 2000 presidential candidates Al Gore and George Bush appeared in *Saturday Night Live* skits, and Senator Bob Dole, former secretary of state Colin Powell, and former presidents Bill Clinton and Jimmy Carter have appeared as guests on the *Daily Show*.

Many situations and attributes beget political satire. Rampant corruption and negligence in political affairs incite it, as do times when such conventional political outlets as print and broadcast news are uncritical of politicians and public affairs, or when free speech is restricted. According to Griffin, "It is difficult, or unnecessary, to satirize our political leaders when the newspapers are filled with open attacks on their integrity and intelligence."

See also *Block, Herbert Lawrence; Cartoons, editorial*.

REFERENCES

Baym, Geoffrey. "*The Daily Show*: Discursive Integration and the Reinvention of Political Journalism." *Political Communication* 22 (2005): 259–276.

Griffin, Dustin H. *Satire: A Critical Reintroduction*. Lexington: University Press of Kentucky, 1994.

Street, John. *Mass Media, Politics, and Democracy*. London: Palgrave, 2001.

Wagg, Stephen. "They Already Got a Comedian for Governor: Comedians and Politics in the United States and Great Britain." In *Because I Tell a Joke or Two: Comedy, Politics, and Social Difference*, edited by Stephen Wagg. New York: Routledge, 1998.

Politics and film

Producer Sam Goldwyn expressed a less-than-positive view of politics as the subject of films, stating, "Pictures are for entertainment; messages should be sent by Western Union." Director Alfred Hitchcock agreed, asserting, "Politics is bad box-office everywhere." Nevertheless, since D. W. Griffith's epic *Birth of a Nation* (1915), politics has been a staple of narrative filmmaking in the United States. One reason that filmmakers turn to political subjects is that political conflict offers drama. Uniting politics with film involves exploiting the conflict inherent in political life without preaching to or alienating the audience; in this respect Goldwyn and Hitchcock were correct. This unity must, however, be consistent with the primary goal of mass-market moviemaking—making money by telling a story.

Filmmakers must be cautious about embedding messages in films for two primary reasons. First, the production of feature films requires considerable time—often years—to create the screenplay and to assemble the production team of actors, writers, directors, and the hundreds of others necessary to create full-length films. To a great extent, producing a film today involves judging what an audience will want to see two years from today. Second, the cost of producing films invites caution. The average major Hollywood film of 2003 cost roughly $100 million to produce and market, and costs keep increasing. Filmmakers with that kind of investment to protect must be careful not to alienate significant segments of the mass audience they must attract to make a profit.

Over the years, filmmakers have developed several ways of exploiting the dramatic necessity of conflict—including political conflict—without having real-world political discord harm the box office. The most basic way to do this is to bend the content of a story to the requirements of narrative storytelling. The fundamental convention of the fiction film narrative is to personalize the narrative. The classic film story involves individuals struggling to overcome problems or achieve goals. The struggle may involve one character against another—sheriff versus outlaw—or against some imper-

Actor James Stewart plays Jefferson Smith in the 1939 Oscar-winning Mr. Smith Goes to Washington, *in which a naive young man completes the term of his dead senator and discovers widespread corruption in U.S. politics.*

sonal external force—an earthquake, for example. A character's goal may be simply to fall in love despite obstacles or for the honest politician to overcome the corrupt one. Whatever the struggle, it is ultimately resolved through the actions of the particular individuals involved. Orson Welles's *Citizen Kane* (1941), often ranked one of the greatest English-language films, embodies this individualism with a vengeance and does so with a strong political twist. The film's protagonist, Charles Foster Kane, based on publisher William Randolph Hearst, seeks power—political, economic, and personal—for classically psychological reasons, as a substitute for the love he lost as a child.

The upbeat resolution of most American films results in what is surely the most hallowed narrative convention of all in Hollywood filmmaking—the happy ending. The happy ending embodies what are the most important political lessons in all of American filmmaking: life is fair; life is just; everything will turn out fine. Most American films teach their audiences that a just outcome is the norm, and that it results from the work of good individuals. Beyond the classical narrative style used in most fiction films, filmmakers over the years have developed a set of characteristic ways of dealing with specifically political subjects:

Politics as Background

Filmmakers often use political conflict as background for the individual characters, whose stories and struggles inhabit the foreground. These characters bear the narrative burden and engage the audience. Consider the following films, all of which involve political conflict but place personal stories, often love stories, in the foreground: *Gone with the Wind* (1939), a love story in a Civil War setting; *Reds* (1981) and *Doctor Zhivago* (1965), love stories set during the Russian Revolution; *Casablanca* (1942), a World War II–era tale of love and sacrifice; *Coming Home* (1978), a love story during the Vietnam War era; *Born on the Fourth of July* (1989) and *Platoon* (1986), stories of young men coming of age in combat in Vietnam; *The Fountainhead* (1949), a love story with a libertarian theme; *Mr. Smith Goes to Washington* (1939), a love story resolved in a fight against political corruption; *The Way We Were* (1973), yet another love story, this one involving a couple from different social and political backgrounds.

In *The Last Hurrah* (1958), the story of Mayor Frank Skeffington unfolds in personal terms or in terms of the protagonist's position of mayor or in terms of the entire generation of politicians he represents. *Missing* (1982) primarily concerns family relationships rather than the background events of the CIA-backed coup to overthrow Salvador Allende, the popularly elected Marxist president of Chile. *The China Syndrome* (1979), though obviously anti-nuclear power, was also an effective thriller with an undercurrent of romance. *Norma Rae* (1979) and *Silkwood* (1983) both feature courageous female characters placed in highly dramatic and dangerous political settings. The German film

Good Bye Lenin! (2004) intertwines family drama with the reunification of East and West Germany.

Indirection and Allegory

Another way to address politics in a film is to structure a story so that it parallels political events and personalities, though at a considerable distance. This treatment inevitably renders the film's politics all but unseen. The classic *Wizard of Oz* (1939) was based on an explicit political allegory largely unperceived by its audience. Some film scholars interpret *Invasion of the Body Snatchers* (1956) as either an anti-communist statement or as an "anti-anti-communist" film critical of McCarthyism. The 1978 remake was a less thinly disguised attack on cults. One of a series, *Star Trek VI: The Undiscovered Country* (1991) plays out as an allegory of the end of the cold war. In such films there is little or no explicit reference to politics, therefore the audience may make the connections or it may not.

Consensus Subjects

Some political topics are controversial at one point, but by virtue of a consensus developed over time became safe to address. The spate of Vietnam films dealing with combat, starting with *Platoon* (1986), and the war's aftermath, in such films as *Running on Empty* (1988) and *In Country* (1989), are examples of movies that could not have been made ten or fifteen years earlier, when the audience's memory of the events depicted was fresher. *Mississippi Burning* (1988) and *Rosewood* (1997) are examples of films dealing with other controversial topics—violence during the civil rights era and the lives of former radicals. Such films are often criticized for rewriting history or narrating events from a privileged viewpoint. Critics reproached *Mississippi Burning* for telling its story from a predominantly white point of view and for portraying the FBI's vigor in investigating racial crimes more favorably than many thought justified. *Cry Freedom* (1987), set in South Africa, similarly presented a story of apartheid in South Africa from the point of view of the main white character, Donald Woods, rather than that of Steve Biko, a black South African.

A common way to deal with politicians is to avoid being politically specific about them. Frank Capra's *Mr. Smith Goes to Washington* (1939) is silent about the party affiliation of any character in the film or even the state from which the main characters come. In the 1992 remake, *The Distinguished Gentleman,* the main character is likewise not identified by party.

This permits the audience more easily to read its own political views into the characters and allows writers to portray political characters negatively, without concern about pleasing some of the audience but angering others.

Ambivalence

A common way to handle controversy in films, political or otherwise, is to treat the topic ambivalently by "balancing" contending sides so that partisans of any persuasion have something to applaud. In *Do the Right Thing* (1989), director Spike Lee ends the film with two quotations, one from Martin Luther King Jr. advocating nonviolence and the other from Malcolm X suggesting that violence may be necessary. The audience is left to draw its own conclusions from these divergent messages. *Dead Man Walking* (1995) contains similar balancing in its presentation of pro and con views on the death penalty.

A variation on the theme of ambivalence is to use satire to make everyone and everything look equally foolish, as in the Marx Brothers' *Duck Soup* (1933), in which Freedonia's prime minister, Rufus T. Firefly (played by Groucho Marx) declares war for the fun of it, and *The President's Analyst* (1967), in which politicians, corporations, the American middle class, and hippies are all satirized and U.S. and Soviet spies find themselves to be kindred spirits. Stanley Kubrick's *Dr. Strangelove, or: How I Learned to Stop Worrying and Love the Bomb* (1964) depicts a phone conversation between the president of the United States and the Soviet premier in which both appear as fools.

Political films shift subjects with the political times, typically in a pattern that moves from ignoring a subject entirely, to dealing with it obliquely, to finally addressing it directly when direct confrontation becomes commercially safe. Hollywood at first largely ignored the civil rights movement during the 1950s and 1960s. Mass-market films initially portrayed race relations in terms of melodramas of racial reconciliation, as in *Guess Who's Coming to Dinner* (1967). The all-black, much more commercially low-profile *Nothing but a Man* (1964) provided a less sunny version of the state of race relations. The arrival of aggressive—indeed over-the-top—black characters had to wait until the 1970s with films like *Sweet Sweetback's Badasssss Song* (1971).

The same pattern holds for the Great Depression. The 1930s were the heyday of so-called screwball comedies, many of which placed the depression in a comedic light involving a male and female from different economic and class backgrounds who nonetheless become attracted to each other and in so doing resolve personally through love what the country has been struggling to resolve economically and politically. *It Happened One Night* (1934) epitomizes the screwball comedy of mismatched lovers. Not until some years later does a film, *Grapes of Wrath* (1940), portray more realistically the lives of the depression-era poor. The depression-era filmmakers also pioneered the classic gangster film, such as *Little Caesar* (1930) and *Scarface* (1932), which portrayed an alternative system of power and success among poor and largely immigrant characters. The staying power of these stories of mobility among the politically and economically weak lives in the remake of *Scarface* in 1983 and in the three *Godfather* films (1972, 1974, and 1990).

Less profound political events than the Great Depression and race relations also can drive filmmaking. During the 1990s, for example, the presidency of Bill Clinton seemed to spark an unusually large number of films focused on the American presidency, with an average of nearly four films per year during that period, or roughly two and one-half times as many as during the 1980s and 1970s, including such films as *Dave* (1993), *Independence Day* (1996) *Air Force One* (1997), *The American President* (1995), *My Fellow Americans* (1996), *Wag the Dog* (1997), *Primary Colors* (1998), *Dick* (1999), *Murder at 1600* (1997), *Absolute Power* (1997), and *Nixon* (1995).

The history of American feature filmmaking makes clear that politics is not the box-office poison that Goldwyn and Hitchcock feared, but to understand the relationship between film and politics, it is important to realize that the profit-driven nature of mass-market commercial filmmaking bends political subjects into commercially viable stories. Politics is the raw material for a particular version—the movie version—of historic and monumental events that shape human lives.

See aslo *Documentaries*.

Polls and the media

Polling, the practice of asking a group of people an identical series of questions to assess their opinions or preferences, serves as an important source of information about the public's thinking on political leaders, candidates for public office, or controversial issues. News organizations, as well as major polling organizations, periodically conduct their own polls, on which they provide reports. Such polls range in size and scope from those conducted nationally by the polling organizations, such as Gallup, to those conducted within a strictly defined audience, such as the readership of a local or special interest magazine. During periods leading up to local or national elections, polls are often used to ascertain the likelihood of victory of the contending candidates or ballot items. Between elections, polls are useful for estimating the public's evaluation of political leaders' job performance.

Some polls may fit news values: they are timely and topical (thus being "new" and on issues of current interest); they give journalists bits of supposedly authoritative data that they can report "objectively" (scientifically gathered, straightforward information about "what the people think"); and their numbers can be simplified to explain a complex phenomenon (public opinion) in a short news story or segment.

Because it would take too long and be too costly to ask polling questions to the entire population, most polls, even those conducted by the large organizations, follow the principle of random sampling, in which a small group of people are randomly selected from the entire population to respond to questions. Their responses are then aggregated and projected to represent the population as a whole. Because of mathematical probability, random sampling allows a relatively accurate "guess" within a margin of error. For example, the final predictions of the Gallup poll for presidential elections from 1936 to 2000 have, on average, differed by only about 2 percent from the actual result.

Because polling purports to gauge public opinion—and what people think about politics is important to democratic government as well as inherently interesting—the mass media have long been in the business of publicizing poll results. Polling has evolved substantially since it was first used in the United States. The earliest U.S. poll on record is an 1824 local straw poll in Pennsylvania of 514 citizens that had Andrew Jackson defeating John Quincy Adams in the presidential election. Polling gradually became more popular but was for a long time limited to small-scale and unscientific surveys. Such polls were local and did not follow any formal practice or measure to guarantee accurate representation of the local population. The *Literary Digest* conducted the first national poll in 1916 by mailing questionnaires and counting the responses to correctly predict the election of Woodrow Wilson as president. The *Literary Digest* would go on to correctly predict four presidential elections in a row until 1936, when it incorrectly predicted that Alf Landon would defeat Franklin D. Roosevelt. Another poll conducted during the same election by George Gallup, however, correctly called Roosevelt's landslide victory.

The two polls reached different results because although the *Literary Digest's* sample of 2.3 million people was much larger than that of Gallup, the latter made an effort to poll a sample demographically representative of the population while the former drew only from its readers, who were primarily wealthy and pro-Republican. The *Literary Digest's* poll thus suffered from an inherent bias. This failure would put the publication out of business and would help secure the Gallup's reputation as the authority on polling in the United States as well as in many other countries. The Gallup Organization continues to be the most famous polling outfit in the United States. Other leading polling organizations include the Quinnipiac Polls, which are run by Quinnipiac University, the Pew Charitable Trusts, which focus on the media and political beliefs, and the Nielson Ratings, which track the popularity of different television programs.

The *Literary Digest's* disastrous prediction is far from the only case of incorrect forecasting. One of the most famous failures occurred when many national polls, including Gallup, predicted a landslide victory for Thomas Dewey over Harry S. Truman in the 1948 presidential election. Instead, Truman won. Despite potential problems with polls—stemming from flawed or biased sampling, poor wording of questions, and the difficulties of capturing public thinking on complex issues—the accuracy of random-sample polls in predicting elections and providing a snapshot of public thinking have made them highly attractive to news organizations. Indeed, since the 1940s, the number of polls taken and reported in mainstream media has increased markedly. By the 1970s, most major news organizations either sponsored their own polls or entered into joint agreements with polling firms or other news outlets. Examples of such collaborations include CBS News/*New York Times,* ABC News/*Washington Post,* and CNN/*USA Today*/Gallup.

Critics have noted some irony in public opinion polling—namely, the results of polls, when published or broadcast, may influence popular opinion. Some have argued that polls can produce a bandwagon effect, whereby people change their opinions to match the most popular opinion. Others have argued alternatively that polls have the opposite effect: people might adopt an opinion or support a candidate

precisely because it is less popular. Evidence has been found in support of both arguments, though it tends to more strongly support the bandwagon effect.

The reliance on polls to gauge candidates' popularity for campaign and election coverage has led some to charge the media with practicing horse race journalism, where they focus more on the competitive race between the candidates to win the election than on the candidates' stand on issues and qualifications. Some journalistic reformers have called for using polls as an antidote to politicians, interest groups, and party leaders' interpretations of "what the people want." Nevertheless, the increased practice and scope of polling has profoundly influenced U.S. politics and the media that cover it.

See also *Bandwagon effect; Exit polls; Horse race journalism; Pew Research Center for the People and the Press; Public/Civic journalism.*

REFERENCES

Cantril, Hadley, ed. *Gauging Public Opinion.* Princeton, N.J.: Princeton University Press, 1944.
Crespi, Irving. *Public Opinion, Polls, and Democracy.* Boulder, Colo.: Westview, 1989.
Frankovic, Kathleen. "Public Opinion and Polling." In *The Politics of News, the News of Politics,* edited by Doris Graber, Denis McQuail, and Pippa Norris. Washington, D.C.: CQ Press, 1998.
Oskamp, Stuart, and P. Wesley Schultz. *Attitudes and Opinions.* 3rd ed. Mahwah, N.J.: Lawrence Erlbaum Associates, 2005.

Pool journalism

Pool journalism describes several types of arrangements government officials use to provide broad media coverage of events that for various reasons they want covered by only a limited number of journalists. Pool arrangements are often used when the number of journalists interested in covering an event exceeds the space available to accommodate them, as sometimes happens in coverage of the presidency. Under such circumstances, news organizations enter into voluntary pool arrangements in which a small number of journalists are "deputized" by their peers to cover the event on behalf of a large number of news organizations. These pool journalists cover the event on the condition that they share their notes, images, and copy with the journalists unable to directly cover the event.

Journalists regard pool journalism, when used to cover routine governmental activities, as a necessary and desirable compromise that increases media access to newsworthy events by forgoing exclusive coverage. The use of pool journalism to cover wars, however, has been more controversial. In the mid-1980s, Pentagon planners envisioned pool arrangements as a way to provide for media coverage of conflicts at short notice while maintaining operational security during the early stages of a campaign. Officials first implemented pools to cover the 1990 invasion of Panama, and journalists considered it a dismal failure, as the pool representatives were not allowed to visit the scene of combat until late in the invasion. The most controversial use of reporting pools came during the 1990–1991 Persian Gulf crisis and war, in which pools were used as the standard means of covering the conflict. Because these pools had limited access to the theater of combat, quarters outside the military perceived them as a means of controlling, rather than facilitating, news coverage. The government has employed pools in subsequent conflicts, such as the 2001 invasion of Afghanistan, but their use has been more limited and provisional as the military has shifted to new systems, such as embedding, to manage coverage in time of war.

See also *Embedding.*

REFERENCES

Aukofer, Frank, and William P. Lawrence. *America's Team: The Odd Couple—A Report on the Relationship between the Media and the Military.* Nashville, Tenn.: Freedom Forum First Amendment Center, 1995.

Carruthers, Susan L. *The Media at War: Communication and Conflict in the Twentieth Century.* New York: St. Martin's Press, 2000.

Knightley, Phillip. *The First Casualty: The War Correspondent as Hero and Myth-maker from the Crimea to Iraq.* Baltimore, Md.: Johns Hopkins University Press, 2004.

Pornography

See *Obscenity and pornography*

Positive ads

See *Political content in advertising*

Presidential debates

Televised debates between presidential candidates have become a ritual of the U.S. electoral process. Various types of campaign debates had been held since the eighteenth century, but the televised 1960 Kennedy-Nixon debates represented a major innovation in campaign communication. As moderator Quincy Howe of ABC News concluded the fourth and final debate between John F. Kennedy and Richard M. Nixon, he praised the two presidential candidates, proclaiming, "The character and courage with which these two men have spoken sets a high standard for generations to come. Surely, they have set a new precedent. Perhaps they have established a new tradition." General election debates would not be held again until the Ford-Carter encounters sixteen years later, but a tradition of presidential debates is now firmly established with an unbroken chain of them since 1976.

The debate encounter, now a permanent fixture in contemporary presidential elections, functions within the context of electoral politics. Presidential candidates—not obligated to debate by force of law or campaign regulation—attempt to control risks, seeking to fashion a debate that will support their electoral strategy or complement their personal communicative strengths. Candidates also conversely attempt to negotiate debate particulars that will disadvantage their opponent. With public expectations for debates now firmly established, the struggle over these events has become not *if* debates will happen, but rather *how* they will occur, including when and where they take place, who will participate, and how they are structured.

In 1960 it literally took an act of Congress for Kennedy and Nixon to meet in debate. With the major TV networks arguing for televised debates and with Senator Kennedy thinking that such exchanges might be to his advantage, the Democratic-controlled Congress authorized a temporary suspension of Section 315 of the Federal Communications Act, the so-called equal time rule, to allow the networks to broadcast debates that included only Kennedy and Nixon, the two major-party candidates. These first-ever televised exchanges were sponsored jointly by the three networks—ABC, CBS, and NBC—which negotiated the debates' structure with the candidates. Both candidates sought to structure "safe" debate encounters, limiting the likelihood of candidate clash and spontaneity. In a speech to the Society of Professional Journalists in New York City just days following

Republican candidate George H. W. Bush, independent candidate Ross Perot, and Democratic candidate Bill Clinton take part in a nationally televised debate before the 1992 presidential election. The presidential debate has been a campaign tradition since 1976.

the debates, CBS president Frank Stanton recounted how a precedent had been set for the basic presidential debate design, later dubbed "the joint press conference," a model that would last until the 1990s:

> The format of the debates unquestionably had the limitations inevitable in any first breakthrough or major innovation. The interposition of the panel was at the firm insistence of the candidates and represented a compromise with which the networks were not too happy. The networks preferred the more traditional format in which each candidate would question the other. But we were eager to get on with the face-to-face broadcasts, even in the modified format, because we believed that whatever the imperfections, they could be eliminated as the debates evolved and it was important to take this first giant step forward.

In 1964 incumbent Democratic president Lyndon Johnson—no fan of the television camera and eminently aware of his shortcomings as a public communicator compared to the sophisticated Kennedy—stopped congressional attempts to again suspend Section 315 regulations to permit another installment of debates to be televised. Debates were also quashed in 1968 and in 1972 by Nixon, first as a candidate and then as an incumbent, believing his defeat in 1960 to be

due largely to his debate performance.

Televised debates finally resumed in 1976 because of a confluence of political and regulatory factors. First, an interpretation of Federal Communication Commission regulations allowed for independent debate sponsors to apply their own candidate selection criteria, so the networks could broadcast the affair as a bona fide news event. Second, the political environment in 1976 proved to be ripe for the resumption of presidential debates. With a weak incumbent Republican president—Gerald Ford—desiring to appear in command, and an anti-establishment Democratic challenger—Jimmy Carter—eager to appear side-by-side as a presidential equal, the televised debate option appeared to benefit both candidacies.

The League of Women Voters had assumed the role of independent debate sponsor when debates resumed, but it then became embroiled with candidates in a struggle for control. This battle became most apparent in 1984, when the organization tangled with the campaigns of Republican Ronald Reagan and Democrat Walter Mondale over the format to be used, and particularly over the selection of journalists who would serve as questioners. The league submitted an extensive list of potential questioners to the campaigns, seeking to impanel a group of four journalists. The candidates could agree on only three. At that point, the league publicly chastised both campaigns for their seeming petulance. Following this dust up, representatives of the Democratic and Republican Parties joined in 1987 to create an alternative debate sponsor, originally dubbed the "bipartisan" Commission on Presidential Debates (CPD), in 1988.

The candidates in 1988, Republican George H. W. Bush and Democrat Michael Dukakis, had originally agreed to debates sponsored by both the League of Women Voters and the CPD. Once again refusing to acquiesce to candidates' demands on debate structure and journalist selection, the league withdrew as debate sponsor. In a rather harsh indictment of the candidates' continued attempts to completely control the debates, league president Nancy Neuman, in explaining her organization's decision to step aside, stated, "The League ... is announcing today that we have no intention of becoming an accessory to the hoodwinking of the American public." Following the league's withdrawal, the CPD sponsored all of the 1988 debates and continues to serve as the only presidential debate sponsor.

This ongoing battle for control of what is perhaps the most important campaign communication event in a presidential contest might best be viewed as a struggle between candidates and the public interest. In short, do presidential debates serve the information needs of voters and contribute to a more informed electorate, or are these televised events controlled by and staged merely for the benefit of the two major-party candidates? The CPD continues to function with close ties to the two major parties. The founding and ongoing co-chairs of the commission are former national chairs of the Democratic and Republican Parties, and members of the CPD board of directors consist primarily of prominent party stalwarts. Despite its origins, the CPD has taken steps to shed its original "bipartisan" identity and function in ways that support the commission's current claim to be a "nonpartisan" organization. In fact, CPD actions, such as the inclusion of Independent presidential candidate Ross Perot in the 1992 debates, demonstrate its willingness to act as an independent arbiter of presidential debates.

An examination of debates of the past decade suggests that the CPD has been proactive in proposing alternate structures designed to serve public interests, and the CPD has more recently been quite successful in getting the candidates to accept their proposals without too much resistance. In fact, once the CPD assumed control of the debates, they steadily began evolving away from the original Kennedy-Nixon debate model—the much-criticized "joint press-conference" format—to encounters quite different in their design that incorporate elements advocated by debate scholars. The changes included the adoption of a single moderator, instead of a panel of journalists, to facilitate greater candidate interaction; extended and less-rigid candidate response sequences that allow for more in-depth discussion of issues; and more direct public participation, such as having undecided citizens participate in a town-hall format debate.

Perhaps the most often cited justification for televised presidential debates is their ability to reach large audiences. From their inception, presidential debates have attracted the largest viewing audiences of televised campaign events. In fact, approximately 80 percent of the adult population in the United States reported viewing or listening to at least one of the 1960 Kennedy-Nixon debates.

Debates and Average Viewership

Debate Year	Presidential Debates	Vice Presidential Debates	Average Viewers (in millions)
1960	4	0	63.1
1976	3	1	59.8
1980	1	0	80.6
1984	2	1	63.0
1988	2	1	59.7
1992	3	1	62.6
1996	2	1	36.3
2000	3	1	37.6
2004	3	1	50.9

Source: Data supplied by Nielsen Media Research. See www.debates.org.

For others, the measure of a debate's usefulness hinges on the question of whether they influence people's vote. On this matter, the empirical evidence is quite clear—there is little change in candidate preference following exposure to debates. Yet, whereas debates may not alter the voting choices of the vast majority of previously committed viewers, ample evidence has found that among the undecided, conflicted, and not-terribly-committed, the debates help in deciding voter preference and may even lead to a change in preference. Although the undecided and uncommitted citizens may constitute a small segment of the debate-viewing audience, it is exactly this slice of the electorate to which most campaigns target their message, and in close contests, these are the voters that may ultimately decide the outcome.

Indeed, from the nine presidential campaigns that have included general election debates, post-debate Gallup polling suggests that televised debates played a decisive role in the outcome of more than half of them, including the 1960, 1976, 1980, 2000, and 2004 debate series and elections.

Some observers argue that the very principle of democracy is perhaps best demonstrated in campaign debates in which those who desire to be president stand before the public and argue why the electorate should vote for them. The televised presidential debate has evolved significantly since 1960, and evidence suggests that the electorate benefits from their leaders' willingness to meet, face-to-face, in pursuit of the public's support.

See also *Kennedy-Nixon debates.*

REFERENCES

Benoit, William L., Mitchell S. McKinney, and R. Lance Holbert. "Beyond Learning and Persona: Extending the Scope of Presidential Debate Effects." *Communication Monographs* 66 (January 2001): 259–273.

Carlin, Diana B., and Mitchell S. McKinney, eds. *The 1992 Presidential Debates in Focus.* Westport, Conn.: Praeger, 1994.

Hellweg, Susan A., Michael Pfau, and Steven R. Brydon. *Televised Presidential Debates: Advocacy in Contemporary America.* Westport, Conn.: Greenwood, 1992.

Jamieson, Kathleen H., and David S. Birdsell. *Presidential Debate: The Challenges of Creating an Informed Electorate.* New York: Oxford University Press, 1988.

Kraus, Sidney, ed. *The Great Debates: Background, Perspective, Effects.* Bloomington: Indiana University Press, 1962.

———. *Televised Presidential Debates and Public Policy.* Mahwah, N.J.: Lawrence Erlbaum Associates, 2000.

Lanoue, David J., and Peter R. Schrott. *The Joint Press Conference: The History, Impact, and Prospects of American Presidential Debates.* Westport, Conn.: Greenwood Press, 1991.

McKinney, Mitchell S., and Diana B. Carlin. "Political Campaign Debates." In *Handbook of Political Communication Research,* edited by Lynda Lee Kaid. Mahwah, N.J.: Lawrence Erlbaum Associates, 2004.

McKinney, Mitchell S. "Let the People Speak: The Public's Agenda and Presidential Town Hall Debates." *American Behavioral Scientist* 49 (October 2005): 198–212.

The Racine Group. "White Paper on Televised Political Campaign Debates." *Argumentation and Advocacy* 38 (October 2002): 199–218.

Presidential press conferences

The presidential press conference, an organized, official meeting of the president of the United States and members of the news media, is perhaps one of the most important informal institutions in the country's system of political communication. Between elections, press conferences are the only occasions at which presidents must attempt to explain and defend their policies. Such events require that the president stay on top of the job. The presidential press conference has been equated with the British Parliament's "question time," when the prime minister must stand and answer questions from members of the opposition party. Because no similar practice exists in the United States, the media stand in as the opposition.

William McKinley was the first president to hold a formal press conference. Theodore Roosevelt continued this practice by inviting small, select groups to talk with him, and Woodrow Wilson further expanded the practice by allowing all accredited press representatives to attend his gatherings. Herbert Hoover insisted that journalists submit written questions in advance and distinguished between what could and could not be quoted. Franklin D. Roosevelt is said to have initiated the modern press conference, as he not only held regularly scheduled private meetings with the White House press corps, but also classified information into three categories: statements that could be directly quoted, statements that could be used for "background" but not directly attributed to him, and statements that were officially off the record. These ground rules, coupled with his power to decide which reporters would be allowed into these meetings, enabled Roosevelt to effectively control the news emanating from his conferences.

The press conference gradually became more open and public under Roosevelt's successors. The administration of Harry S. Truman made edited transcripts available for the first time. Dwight D. Eisenhower, albeit reluctantly, allowed the distribution of edited films for TV and radio transcripts after his press conferences. This approach was used in part because of Eisenhower's difficulties in communicating effectively and the fear, during the height of the cold war, that presidential misstatements might compromise national security.

President John F. Kennedy revolutionized presidential communication by holding live, nationally televised press conferences. Kennedy's youth, charm, and humor, along with his command of detail and rapport with reporters, attracted large audiences and enabled him to project an image of competence and confidence to the public. At the same time, television altered the nature of the press conference from a small, private, informal affair to a large, formal public gathering more akin to spectacle than an intimate and substantive briefing.

President George W. Bush takes questions from reporters during a January 2006 press conference at the White House. The presidential news conference, though varying in format, location, and frequency, has evolved since the McKinley administration of the late nineteenth century into an institution.

Presidents after Kennedy have also attempted to use press conferences to their advantage, although not always as effectively. Lyndon B. Johnson met the press more frequently and in a wide variety of formats, from barbeques at his Texas ranch to walks in the White House Rose Garden, and was known for calling conferences, even televised ones, on extremely short notice on almost any subject. Johnson's comfort with press conferences and their frequency declined as political problems with the Vietnam War increased. Richard Nixon's mistrust of the press and caution about his public performances led his conferences to be of a cold, formal quality, even as Nixon demonstrated clear understanding of subject matter. The conferences became openly hostile and confrontational as the administration's relationship with the press deteriorated during the Watergate scandal.

Gerald Ford and Jimmy Carter, while promising more access and openness to the media as symbolized by more regular conferences, also found the format less appealing and effective over time. They too soon favored alternative methods of communicating with the public. Ronald Reagan, though nicknamed the "Great Communicator," was uncomfortable and awkward answering questions at press conferences and was much better at speaking to the public through prepared speeches. Sometimes Reagan's aides had to clarify and correct his mistakes and misstatements in subsequent meetings with the media. Reagan consequently held fewer conferences than his predecessors and attempted to use them more strategically.

George H. W. Bush enjoyed bantering with reporters informally and initially held more formal press conferences than had Reagan. Yet, with his own public-speaking problems and conflicts with the press following the Persian Gulf War, he, too, became less open to them over time. Like Kennedy, Bill Clinton was seemingly well equipped to use press conferences to their full advantage. His rocky relations with the press early on and his desire for more control and experimentation with communications, however, led him to alternative methods, such as town hall meetings and talk shows. At times, Clinton's conferences became confrontational, echoing the days of Nixon, and he seemed to prefer to let his press secretary do battle with reporters, especially during the Monica Lewinsky scandal. George W. Bush, another president lacking strong public-speaking skills, downplayed formal meetings with the press in lieu of informal exchanges or focused interviews. He likewise chose to hold small numbers of press conferences and to use them to his advantage. For example, by early 2004, Bush had conducted only three live, "prime time" conferences, less than one per year. He more frequently appeared in joint sessions with foreign leaders, a practice begun by his father.

Just as there has been wide variation in the use, types, and formats of press conferences among presidents, there has also been wide variation in their frequency, related to presidents' news strategies and experiences in office. The variation in number and average does not reveal differences in the length of time between press conferences. Presidents interestingly do not appear to hold fewer conferences under difficult political circumstances, but in fact hold more—probably in as an attempt to improve their position through explanation or to prevent the impression that they are hiding from scrutiny.

Presidential Press Conferences, 1923–2002

President	Months in Office	Total	Yearly Average	Monthly Average
Coolidge	60	407	81	6.8
Hoover	48	268	67	5.6
Roosevelt	148	881	73	6.0
Truman	93	302	38	3.2
Eisenhower	96	193	25	2.0
Kennedy	34	65	23	1.9
Johnson	62	135	26	2.2
Nixon	66	39	7	0.6
Ford	30	40	16	1.3
Carter	48	59	15	1.2
Reagan	96	46	6	0.5
Bush	48	142	36	3.0
Clinton	96	193	24	2.0
Bush*	24	39	19	1.6

Source: Adapted from Lyn Ragsdale, *Vital Statistics on the Presidency* (Washington, D.C.: CQ Press, 1996), for Coolidge through Kennedy; and Martha Joynt Kumar, "'Does This Constitute a Press Conference?'" *Presidential Studies Quarterly* 33, no. 1 (March 2003), 230, for Johnson through W. Bush.
* Figures are for 2001–2002.

In general, the press conference has failed to live up to lofty expectations as an information system furthering democracy. Presidents view conferences not as an exercise in public information, but as part of an overall strategy of news management and public relations. Press conferences, as "uncontrolled" media events, present more risks for presidents, so they stack the deck to their advantage. Presidents control when, where, how, and, of course, if conferences occur, giving them an inherent edge over the press. Control over timing can be an effective way to ensure that a conference is not too damaging. Reporters are more likely to be unprepared to ask tough questions if called to a conference on extremely short notice. Long intervals between conferences usually lead to a variety of relatively superficial questions on a wide range of topics. Presidents can also set ground rules to limit the conference to certain issues or refuse to answer questions on some topics altogether. Presidents almost always begin conferences with an opening statement that allows them to get a certain amount of unmediated information out and that they hope sets the agenda for the conference.

Presidents can minimize damage and demonstrate competence through skillful preparation and anticipation of questions. They also can offer evasive or plausibly vague answers, a skill developed on the campaign trail. Sometimes they even go further by calling on or planting "softball" questions with friendly reporters. Still, mistakes are made, and reporters may ask something controversial or unexpected that catches the president off-guard.

For the press, not only does the president have the upper hand in these encounters, but there are other limits in holding the president to account. The need for drama and news means that reporters often adopt a more adversarial posture in style and tone than they do in substance. Editors may want them to ask questions of particular interest to hometown audiences or about certain subjects. Though a relatively small group, reporters competing for the president's attention by shouting questions reduce the coherence and dignity of the media. Often, the lack of follow-up questions limits the detail or quality of the content.

The public press conference has not been seen as overly effective or important by either side in recent years. For example, in 1995 two of the three major television networks refused to carry a live conference by President Clinton on welfare reform, citing the unlikelihood of useful "news," and more important, the loss of revenue from prime time entertainment programming. The rise of other media outlets, such as cable television talk shows, satellite feeds with local television stations, and so on, have given presidents other, often more friendly, ways of getting their message out to the public. The combination of these forces has led the press conference to decline in number and significance over time, creating uncertainty about its future role.

See also *Background; News management; Office of Communications; Off the record.*

REFERENCES

Edwards, George C. *The Public Presidency.* New York: St. Martin's Press, 1983.

Kumar, Martha Joynt. "The White House Beat at the Century Mark." *Harvard International Journal of Press/Politics* 2, no. 3 (Summer 1997): 10–30.

———. "'Does This Constitute a Press Conference?' Defining and Tabulating Modern Presidential Press Conferences." *Presidential Studies Quarterly* 33, no. 1 (March 2003): 221–237.

Presidential radio addresses

The rapidly expanding medium of radio in the 1920s and the 1930s offered presidents, beginning with Warren G. Harding—who in June 1922 delivered the first presidential address broadcast on radio—an effective way to communicate with the public. By 1936 there were more than 30 million radio sets across the nation—a tenfold increase since 1924—and by 1940 more than eight in ten households owned a radio.

President Franklin D. Roosevelt, a pioneer in the use of radio for directly communicating with the public, is widely regarded as a master of the medium. His experience with radio preceded his presidency, as he had strategically employed radio in his gubernatorial campaign in New York in 1930. During his tenure in the White House, Roosevelt's use of radio reached new levels of effectiveness and persuasiveness. Eight days after his twenty-seven-minute inaugural address—also broadcast via radio—Roosevelt delivered the first of his "fireside chats," to assuage concerns about a variety of national problems, including the economic crisis of the Great Depression. Roosevelt possessed a commanding and comforting tone, and the intimacy of the radio medium produced his virtual presence in American homes throughout the country. Roosevelt conducted fireside chats throughout his four terms as president, as radio became his principal means of communicating with the nation. Roosevelt's masterful oratory and rhetorical style coupled with his use of radio—delivering more than 300 radio addresses

during his presidency—are often credited for his unprecedented appeal and popularity among the public.

By the 1950s, television had eclipsed radio as the dominant form of mass communication, yet presidents since Roosevelt have maintained the tradition of regular, and some even weekly, radio addresses. Even as radio audiences have declined and become increasingly fragmented, radio remains popular for delivering messages directly to the public.

By the 1950s, television had eclipsed radio as the dominant form of mass communication, yet recent presidents have maintained the tradition of delivering radio addresses. Ronald Reagan, emulating FDR, revived the practice in 1982. A former radio broadcaster, Reagan took to the radio on Saturdays to counter what he felt was unfair coverage and filtering of his message by journalists. He planned originally to do eight to ten addresses to promote his economic program, but the positive response he received led him to continue the practice throughout his two terms. George H. W. Bush, Bill Clinton, and George W. Bush followed Reagan's lead, taking the opportunity to communicate directly with the public on a "slow" news day, when their message would not only be carried by radio, but also covered by other news outlets. These addresses have become such a part of the weekly media landscape that by tradition and fairness a member of the opposition party presents a response.

See also *Fireside chats; Radio.*

REFERENCES

Craig, Douglas B. *Fireside Politics.* Baltimore, Md.: Johns Hopkins University Press, 2000.

Rowland, Robert C., and John M. Jones. "'Until Next Week': The Saturday Radio Addresses of Ronald Reagan." *Presidential Studies Quarterly* 32, no. 1 (March 2002): 84–110.

Press secretaries

Press secretaries, appointees who operate as intermediaries and spokespersons for political figures, play a major role on the staffs of presidents, members of Congress, state governors, and high-profile political candidates. Every president since the days of Grover Cleveland and William McKinley in the late 1800s has relied on a staff member to handle relations with the media. President Herbert Hoover appointed the first official press secretary, but President Franklin Roosevelt's press secretary, Stephen Early, elevated the position to the level it enjoys today. Presidential press secretaries have become valuable assistants who serve as spokespersons, advisors on media strategies, and troubleshooters.

The appointment of James Haggerty by President Dwight D. Eisenhower as his press secretary marked the rise of this job to a high-profile position with considerable autonomy in dealing with the media. Prior to this time, presidents' relations with the press had been mostly informal and sporadic. Haggerty institutionalized the on-the-record press conference and broadcast coverage.

Presidential press secretaries are expected to serve three constituencies: the president, the White House staff, and the news media. Their worth is often judged by their access to the president, their credibility with the news media, and their status within the White House. Presidential press secretaries hold daily briefings, which are attended by members of the White House press corps.

Beginning in the 1950s, governors also began to rely heavily on press secretaries to speak for them and to deal with expanding media. Although press secretaries were rare on Capitol Hill during the 1960s, by the end of the 1970s, practically every member of Congress had one. Their duties ranged from being a surrogate spokesman to writing speeches and press releases and providing background and guidance to reporters. Most candidates for state and national office today have press secretaries on their campaign staffs.

See also *Fleischer, Ari; Myers, Dee Dee; McClellan, Scott; McCurry, Mike; Ziegler, Ron.*

REFERENCES

Ferrell, Robert H. *The Diary of James Haggerty.* Bloomington: Indiana University Press, 1983.
Tebel, John, and Sarah M. Watts *The Press and the Presidency.* New York: Oxford University Press, 1985.

Prior restraint

Prior restraint is the government prohibition of expression before it is made. The idea behind prior restraint is to prevent the publication of something so damaging that there would be no recourse for the parties affected to correct the damage. The two most important Supreme Court rulings on prior restraint reflect a wariness by the justices to block information, even if potentially damaging to society. In *Near v. Minnesota* (1931), the Court held attempts at prior restraint to be unconstitutional, setting a high standard for its application but leaving some room for exceptions, such as publication of the location of troops in wartime. Later, in *New York Times v. United States* (1971), the *Pentagon Papers Case,* the government sought to halt the publication of a Defense Department report on U.S. involvement in the Vietnam War. After several lower courts had issued injunctions, the Supreme Court ruled that the government had failed to meet the burden of proof to justify prior restraint.

The *Progressive* tested the concept of security issues as a possible reason to invoke prior restraint. A U.S. district court judge enjoined the magazine from publishing an article on an instructional guide for making a hydrogen bomb after determining that some of the information violated the secrecy provisions of the Atomic Energy Act. The judge stated that there was a likelihood of direct, immediate, and irreparable damage to the nation if the article were published. The government dropped its attempt to ban the article after portions of it appeared abroad.

The Court has afforded one segment of the press—students—less protection by the First Amendment than professional members of the media. Students have the right to freedom of expression, but only if their actions do not disrupt the work and discipline of the school. In 1988 the Court strengthened its position that protections for student journalists are not the same as those for professional reporters. In *Hazelwood School District v. Kuhlmeier* (1988), the Court held that public school officials could regulate the content of a school publication if that publication resulted from a supervised learning experience, since such activities were outside the realm of a public forum. Although the courts have recognized prior restraint as the antithesis of freedom of the press, it has not abolished its use entirely.

See also *Censorship; Near v. Minnesota (1931); New York Times v. United States (1971); Pentagon Papers; Zurcher v. Stanford Daily (1978).*

REFERENCES

Savage, David. *Guide to the U.S. Supreme Court.* 4th ed. Washington, D.C.: CQ Press, 2004.
Winston, Brian. *Messages: Free Expression, Media and the West from Gutenberg to Google.* London: Routledge, 2005.

Privacy

Although privacy, the absence or avoidance of publicity or display, has been sought, valued, and protected since the founding of the nation, it was not legally established at the federal level by Congress until the Privacy Act of 1974. The Supreme Court, however, had interpreted at least half of the Bill of Rights to guarantee a "right of privacy." In doing so it cited the First, Third, Fourth, Fifth, and Ninth Amendments, in addition to the post–Civil War Fourteenth Amendment, which applied federal constitutional standards to the states, and English common law tradition.

There are four recognized types of individual privacy rights: information, physical, decision, and propriety. Information privacy concerns the control of personal data, such as medical records. Physical privacy usually focuses on an individual's home and the right to solitude in a particular space. Decision privacy is the need to keep confidential one's thoughts in problem solving, and propriety privacy is the right to control one's visible attributes from the prying uses of others.

Competing social interests prevent privacy from attaining the status of an absolute right. These include the public's right to know about government, government officials, and government business; necessities of national defense and the military; criminal law enforcement; public health and safety concerns; and fiduciary values, such as trust, accountability, or loyalty. It is common, therefore, to balance privacy with these other social concerns. Though the courts have declared privacy a fundamental right, this right has also been superseded in court opinions by compelling state interests. State and federal courts have generally been lenient in allowing the mass media to publish information about the private affairs of "public figures," including public officials and celebrities. To strengthen privacy protection, some courts have allowed subjects of unsolicited media attention to use trespassing and private property laws to restrain the media, but as relatively few cases of privacy invasion have been taken to the courts, in practice protection of privacy for some categories of people falls to media discretion.

During the nineteenth century, legal scholars published several influential articles supporting explicit legal recognition of a right of privacy. Judge Thomas Cooley's *Treatise on the Law of Torts* (1880) extrapolated the existence of a right of personal immunity and a right to be let alone. That phrase, the "right to be let alone," was repeated in an often-cited *Harvard Law Review* article by Samuel D. Warren and Louis D. Brandeis, "The Right to Privacy" (1890), in which the authors discuss the right to enjoy life, a central tenet of the Declaration of Independence and the Constitution, as not only the right to liberty but also the right to be let alone. Although unwanted public scrutiny was often the result of media attention in the nineteenth century, the modern regulations that protect privacy frequently concern government activities.

The range of privacy laws covering many aspects of modern life enacted in the twentieth century includes, along with the 1974 Privacy Act, the Fair Credit Reporting Act of 1970, the Family Educational Rights and Privacy Act of 1974, the Right to Financial Privacy Act of 1978, the Privacy Protection Act of 1980, the Cable Communications Policy Act of 1984, the Electronic Communications Privacy Act of 1986, the Video Privacy Protection Act of 1988, the Telephone Consumer Protection Act of 1991, the Drivers' Privacy Protection Act of 1994, the Electronic Freedom of Information Act Amendments of 1996, the Children's Online Privacy Protection Act of 2000, the Financial Services Modernization Act of 2000, and the Health Insurance Portability and Accountability Act of 2000.

Many states' constitutions provided privacy protections modeled on the federal Bill of Rights, but during the last half of the twentieth century several states enacted explicit privacy provisions. For example, Florida's amended constitution, article 1, section 23, ensures that "[e]very natural person has the right to be let alone and free from governmental intrusion into his private life except as otherwise provided herein." California's revised constitution, article 1, section 1, declares, "All people are by nature free and independent and have inalienable rights. Among these are enjoying and defending life and liberty, acquiring, possessing and protecting property, and pursuing and obtaining safety, happiness and privacy."

Several international groups also have issued privacy guidelines and directives. In 1980 the Organization for Economic Co-operation and Development developed guidelines for the protection of personally identifying information transferred across national borders. The United Nations drafted Guidelines for Personal Files in 1990, and the European Union issued the Data Protection Directive in 1995. The EU issued a revised set of guidelines in 2002, the Privacy and Electronic Communication Directive.

European standards for protection of personal information have often exceeded those of the United States, thus some U.S. companies have been barred from some aspects of commerce in Europe. By the end of the twentieth century, the United States and the European Union negotiated an agreement enabling U.S. companies to do business otherwise prohibited, provided the Americans pledged to work toward the European standard of privacy.

The case law among U.S. courts reviewing privacy suits recognizes four kinds of common law rights protection: protection against intrusion, publication of embarrassing private facts, false light publicity, and appropriation of name, likeness, and identity. These were clarified by William L. Prosser in a 1960 *California Law Review* article and enumerated in the *Restatement of Torts* (1964). Intrusion is when someone intentionally breaks into the solitude or seclusion of another. Publication of embarrassing private facts occurs when publicity of matters concerning the private life of another is highly offensive to a reasonable person and is not of legitimate concern to the public. False light publicity occurs when erroneous personal facts that are highly offensive to a reasonable person are published in reckless disregard of the known falsity of the matters. Appropriation occurs when the name or likeness of another is used without permission for the benefit of someone else.

The early cases in formalizing the protection of privacy rights include *DeMay v. Roberts,* an 1881 Michigan opinion recognizing a right to privacy in childbirth; *Manola v. Stevens,* an 1890 New York injunction granted to an actress who wanted to stop the publication of a photograph; and *Pavesich v. New England Life Insurance Company,* in which a 1905 Georgia court asserted a man's right to privacy had been violated when an advertisement included his photograph without his consent.

In recent years, identity theft has become an even larger concern as more personal information is stored on computers. The most common forms of identity theft include credit card fraud, in which a consumer's name is used to open a new card account or an existing account is taken by another for purchasing use; communications services fraud, in which a utility service account is abused or new service is contracted; bank fraud, in which a checking or savings account is opened in the name of another in order to withdraw funds; fraudulent loans, in which agreements for deferred payment are made based on the name and credit report of someone else.

The California Public Research Interest Group and Privacy Rights Clearinghouse reported in May 2000 that it took victims, on average, nearly two years to resolve cases of identity theft. The victims usually spent some 175 hours and more than $800 out-of-pocket, excluding lawyers' fees, to reach a resolution. Almost half of the victims reported driver's license theft as the initial loss, and 15 percent of the victims discovered that there were criminal investigations or warrants for their arrest as a result of the identity theft.

As a result of findings such as these, many states have enacted laws requiring that credit reports be made available to residents at least once a year at no cost, and nearly all states passed legislation dealing with identity theft. The Federal Trade Commission also began providing information and advice on a Web site, www.consumer.gov/idtheft, and supported a consumer complaint hotline for people concerned about identity theft. A federal ID Theft Act was tested in two Delaware criminal cases in which the accused obtained from Web sites the names and social security numbers of military officers and used them to apply online for credit cards.

Increased computer use for communication as well as data storage has led to concerns in the workplace about the sanctity of personal space. *Smyth v. Pillsbury,* a 1996 Pennsylvania case, found that employees should harbor no expectation of privacy with respect to their workplace computers. Workplace monitoring of e-mail, for example, was found to be acceptable by the courts in several cases when a corporate-wide policy on such communication has been announced and instituted.

In 2001 the World Wide Web Consortium released a draft specification for its Platform for Privacy Preferences Project, or P3P. This technical solution was intended to provide information about the privacy practices of Web site servers so that users could decide knowledgeably about whether to release to these Web sites their personal information. The effectiveness of this tool was predicated on the swift and complete adoption by Web masters.

Ultimately privacy rights are only as strong as government protections for them. The conflict between freedom of the press and the public's "right to know" on the one hand and the citizen's right to privacy on the other continues to make privacy law in the United States contentious and controversial. The international community similarly varies so widely on privacy concerns that protecting privacy rights has largely fallen upon individuals who want to be left alone and shielded from public view.

See also *Stanley v. Georgia (1969)*.

REFERENCES

Alderman, Ellen, and Caroline Kennedy. *The Right to Privacy.* New York: Knopf, 1995.

Andrews, Sarah. *Privacy and Human Rights: An International Survey of Privacy Laws and Developments.* Washington, D.C.: EPIC, 2002.

Bahadur, Gary, William Chan, and Chris Weber. *Privacy Defended: Protecting Yourself Online.* Indianapolis, Ind.: Que, 2002

Garfinkel, Simson. *Database Nation.* Cambridge, Mass.: O'Reilly 2000.

Graber, Doris. *Mass Media and American Politics.* 6th ed. (Washington, D.C.: CQ Press).

Gutwirth, Serge. *Privacy and the Information Age.* Translated by Raf Casert. Lanham, Md.: Rowman and Littlefield, 2002.

Prosser, William. "Privacy." *California Law Journal* 48 (1960): 383–423.

Rosen, Jeffrey. *The Unwanted Gaze: The Destruction of Privacy in America.* New York: Random House, 2000.

Sykes, Charles. *The End of Privacy.* New York: St. Martin's Press, 2000.

Warren, Samuel, and Louis Brandeis. "The Right to Privacy." *Harvard Law Review* 4 (1890): 193–220.

Privacy Protection Act of 1980

Congress passed the Privacy Protection Act of 1980 in response to a 1971 warranted police search of the *Stanford Daily* student newspaper newsroom in search of unpublished photographs of a violent demonstration. The 1971 search raised fears among journalists of official and prosecutorial intimidation to reveal confidential sources and other material, and Stanford University sued on the grounds that the search had been illegal. The Supreme Court ruled against the university in *Zurcher v. Stanford Daily* (1978), prompting Congress to act. The Privacy Protection Act overrules the Court's decision and prevents law enforcement authorities from seizing materials from journalists before publication.

The act blocks most searches of newsrooms by requiring that authorities secure a subpoena for the evidence being sought. A search warrant permits an immediate and unannounced search of the premises, whereas a subpoena requires a court hearing, with both parties present. A judge may order an immediate search only if evidence exists that the person possessing the subpoenaed documents has committed a crime or seizure is necessary to prevent death or serious harm. A search warrant may be issued in two other circumstances: (1) there is valid concern that giving notice for obtaining a subpoena would result in the destruction or concealment of the materials sought or (2) legal remedies

have been exhausted but the required documents have not been produced.

See also *First Amendment; Zurcher v. Stanford Daily (1978)*.

REFERENCES

EPIC, "The Privacy Protection Act of 1980," www.epic.org/privacy/ppa.

Hopkins, W. Wat. *Communication and the Law.* Northport, Ala.: Vistion Press, 1999.

Pember, Don R. *Mass Media Law.* New York: McGraw-Hill, 1999.

Propaganda

In politics, propaganda—derived from the Latin word *propagate,*" meaning "to actively spread"—entails the deliberate and systematic dissemination of a philosophy or perspective intended to influence opinion and behavior. Propaganda need not involve a perversion of the truth—though it sometimes does—to serve a political agenda of government or other institution or group.

Propaganda is disseminated through mass media. Two factors—one borne of necessity, the other of convenience—have contributed to the use of mass media as such a tool. As populations and electorates have grown, their views have become more important in the governing process, and mass media provide the means to reach these large audiences. In addition, increased literacy has resulted in a greater reliance on the media for information, thus making mediated approaches to persuasion possible.

While the term *propaganda* is most closely associated with foreign affairs and wartime political efforts to gain support at home and abroad, this conception is too narrow. Policymakers and politicians now utilize the mass media to justify and sell all their policies to the public in order to garner public support. For example, the Clinton administration tried to sell the idea of national health care by highlighting the successes of such programs elsewhere in the world and asserting that access to universal health care was a right of every U.S. citizen. The proposal met with opposition, particularly from private insurance companies and the medical establishment, which argued that the United States had the most technologically advanced and highest-quality health care in the world. Opponents of Clinton's plan launched their own media blitz, claiming that nationalized health care would threaten continued superiority of care, highlighting U.S. leadership in medical research, and featuring instances of mismanagement under nationalized systems.

Proponents and opponents of the health care issue employed facts or elements of truth to bolster their claims. The health care example illustrates how the producers of propaganda serve their own political self-interests by highlighting only those aspects of an issue that promote their desired outcomes. In general, propaganda more often involves revealing only partial truths to the public, rather than disseminating deliberate lies. Institutions and public figures often try to avoid outright lying in the United States and other countries with an independent media and fierce competition between mass media providers for market share, as it places the credibility of information sources at risk.

REFERENCES

Combs, James E., and Dan Nimmo. *The New Propaganda: The Dictatorship of Palaver in Contemporary Politics.* White Plains, N.Y.: Longman, 1993.
Jowett, Garth S., and Victoria O'Donnell. *Propaganda and Persuasion.* Newbury Park, Calif.: Sage, 1986.

Pseudo-crisis

A pseudo-crisis is an apparent problem that has been fabricated or overstated to bring greater attention to an issue and to broaden demands to do something about the problem. The news media tend to focus their attention on an issue if it is considered a crisis, as such coverage satisfies some media's current preference for news as drama and conflict.

Beginning with the Tonkin Gulf crisis in 1964, the language of crisis has been used to promote various issues, such as the urban crisis, the environmental crisis, the energy crisis, the drug crisis, and the like. While these may be serious issues, the "crisis" label is consciously applied by advocates to foment or drum up a sense of urgency. The abundance of crisis claims may, however, have considerably eroded the rhetorical value of "crisis."

See also *Crisis journalism; Pseudo-events.*

REFERENCES

Boorstin, Daniel. *The Image: A Guide to Pseudo-Events in America.* New York: Vintage, 1992.
Stone, Deborah. *Policy Paradox.* New York: Norton, 1998.

Pseudo-events

A *pseudo-event,* a term coined by Daniel Boorstin in *The Image,* refers to an event, such as a press conference, demonstration, photo-op, or congressional hearing, that is conceived and executed to attract media coverage of an issue. A good example of such an issue is the "Grate American Sleep Out," organized by congressional Democrats, whereby members of Congress and Hollywood actors spent the night sleeping on grates in Washington, D.C., in the late 1980s to publicize the plight of the homeless. Many observers credited the publicity stunt with helping to secure the passage of legislation a week later to combat homelessness. In 1995 House Republican leaders counseled their members to hold pseudo-events to insulate themselves from political criticism that they were anti-environmental.

According to Doris Graber, pseudo-events "constitute more than half of all television news stories." Critics of these events lament the press's complicity in the manufacturing of news to the advantage of those staging the event. Some journalists, including Herbert Gans, defend the reporting of pseudo-events because not covering them would limit journalists to covering breaking news, of which there is not enough to fill the news time slots. Gans's defense suggests how strongly news organizations are dependent upon their subjects and sources to stage events and provide information.

See also *Pseudo-crisis; Reporting events.*

REFERENCES

Boorstin, Daniel. *The Image: A Guide to Pseudo-Events in America.* New York: Vintage, 1992.
Gans, Herbert. *Deciding What's News: A Study of* CBS Evening News, NBC Nightly News, Newsweek, *and* Time. New York: Vintage, 1980.
Graber, Doris A. *Mass Media and American Politics.* 5th ed. Washington, D.C.: CQ Press, 1997.

Public Broadcasting Act of 1967

The Public Broadcasting Act of 1967 provided an alternative to the programming available on commercial radio and television channels through its creation of the Corporation for Public Broadcasting (CPB) and mandated funding for public television and radio. The act, originally introduced as the Public Television Act of 1967, flowed from the Carnegie

Commission on Educational Television Report, which provided a blueprint for the role, activities, and programming of public television. Public radio would be included through the efforts and testimony of National Educational Radio (NER).

The act provided for year-to-year funding of public radio and television by Congress, until the Public Broadcasting Financing Act of 1975 offered a long-term solution to problems in funding for public broadcasting. In 1975 and 1978, Congress provided for multiyear advance funding authorization to reduce the potential of budgetary influence on public broadcasting. Congress also imposed special equal employment opportunity and community participation obligations on the recipients of these funds.

Public/Civic journalism

Public journalism, also known as civic or community journalism, is a movement advocating that journalists step beyond the mainstream practice of simply reporting the facts to engage the public in journalism and reporting in a way that encourages debate, presents views of community members beyond its leadership, and attempts to help communities move toward addressing the issues that concern them.

The conventional form of news that became dominant in the United States by the middle of the twentieth century focused on "chronicling"—reporting the who, what, when, and where of politics and other topics. Advocates of public journalism argue that conventional news too often distances the public from, or disillusions them with, civic life. Conventional journalism undermines civic engagement by focusing narrowly on "facts" and conflicts without providing adequate context or opportunity for citizen voices to be heard. In addition, public journalism's advocates charge that conventional news organizations had failed to serve the community because they did not think and act as if they belonged to the community.

Practitioners of public journalism do not follow the convention of simply depicting both sides of a political controversy. Instead, they write "explanatory" news stories that provide greater context and a wider range of viewpoints. They also look beyond the "golden rolodex" of officials, candidates, and their consultants as sources to present more of the views of average citizens. In addition, they favor

"problem-oriented" reporting that focuses on issues that citizens, not just politicians, perceive as important. This type of reporting considers the search for solutions as much as discussing the problems themselves. Indeed, according to the Community Journalism Project, one of many professional organizations promoting this approach to news, public journalism is "grounded in the concept that news organizations have a responsibility not just to report on local issues but, through their coverage, to actively facilitate their debate and resolution." According to Jay Rosen, one of the intellectual leaders of the public journalism movement, the goal is to reenvision journalism as "democracy's cultivator, as well as its chronicler," and to "restyle the work of the press so that it support[s] a healthier public climate."

Also setting public journalism apart from conventional news are such activities as the media convening—rather than simply attending and reporting on—"town hall" meetings on community issues or organizing citizen focus groups to help decide what issues to cover during an election campaign. In 1992, for example, the *Charlotte Observer* conducted polls to determine what issues the voters wanted addressed in that year's election. It then followed up with individual interviews and focus groups of poll respondents, who continued to serve as informal advisors to the editors and journalists throughout the campaign.

Public journalism is not just a notion of what should be in the news and how news should be determined. It is also a notion of what a journalist should be. Conventional journalism positions the journalist as a "neutral" outsider who observes but does not engage with the world. Advocates of public journalism argue that the journalist is rarely a mere observer and is, indeed, a political actor—one who influences as well as observes. Through the construction of images of the communities they cover, journalists inevitably exert influence on those communities. The key to better journalism, public journalists argue, is to abandon the pretence of neutral observation and embrace the reality of journalism's political influence, or in Rosen's words, to see the press "as a player in politics, an influential actor that could alter its actions without abandoning its role as truth teller." Public journalism also involves a particular view of the public. As the "Declaration for Public Journalism" proclaims, "[J]ournalism and democracy work best when ... public deliberation is encouraged and amplified; and when news helps people function as political actors and not just as political consumers."

Underlying public journalism is the belief, according to the Pew Center for Civic Journalism, that "journalism has an obligation to public life—an obligation that goes beyond just telling the news or unloading lots of facts," and that journalism "can help empower a community or it can help disable it." This notion of an obligation to something other than simply "reporting the facts" makes civic journalism unique—and controversial.

Numerous news organizations have begun to practice or at least experiment with forms of public journalism. One study sponsored by the Pew Center for Civic Journalism found that by 2001, at least one-fifth of all U.S. daily newspapers had tried some form of civic journalism. Moreover, the report found, "nearly all credit it with a positive impact on the community." Much of that experimentation was funded by the Pew Center, although that funding has since tapered off, leaving the future of the movement somewhat in doubt.

Public journalism has been controversial among many mainstream journalists, who take issue with the fundamental ideas and goals of the movement. Some critics see public journalism as little more than pandering to the public designed to increase market share in an era of tightening competition among news outlets. Some critics object strongly to the notion of surrendering control of the news agenda to polls and focus groups. The journalist's unique role, these critics argue, is to independently determine what is newsworthy by applying sound professional judgment. Allowing the public to decide the issue agenda, the critics claim, impinges on professional discretion and threatens the prized ideal of objectivity; in fact, they argue, public journalism replaces the ideal of objective news with journalism as advocacy for various community causes. As reporter Tim Porter, one critic of public journalism, puts it, "Good reporters instinctively connect to their communities.... Caring about crime, being concerned about education, sharing public outrage over lazy or corrupt elected officials doesn't interfere with good journalism. It causes it. But there is a line between empathy and advocacy that should not be blurred." For advocates of public journalism, however, the line between neutral observer and responsible community actor should indeed be crossed.

REFERENCES

Community Journalism Project. "Newsroom Resources," www.rtndf.org/resources/cj.shtml.

Friedland, Lewis A., and Sandy Nichols. "Measuring Civic Journalism's Progress: A Report across a Decade of Activity." Pew Center for Civic Journalism, September 2002, www.pewcenter.org/doingcj/research/measuringcj.pdf.

Porter, Tim. "An Uncivil Eulogy to Civic Journalism," www.tim-porter.com/firstdraft/archives/000105.html.

Public Journalism Network. "A Declaration for Public Journalism," January 25, 2003, www.pjnet.org/charter.shtml.

Rosen, Jay. *What Are Journalists For?* New Haven, Conn.: Yale University Press, 1999.

Schudson, Michael. "The Public Journalism Movement and Its Problems." In *The Politics of News, the News of Politics,* edited by Doris Graber, Denis McQuail, and Pippa Norris. Washington, D.C.: CQ Press, 1998.

Thames, Rick. "Covering Politics Civic Journalism Style," http://democracyplace.soundprint.org/thamesdf.html.

Public diplomacy

Public diplomacy seeks to build positive connections between a government and foreign populations, in contrast to traditional diplomacy, which concerns relations between governments. The goal of public diplomacy is to win the support or at least tolerance of constituencies whose opinions can enhance the functioning of foreign policy and whose opposition can impede policymakers' efforts. Proponents of public diplomacy argue that it differs from propaganda in that it is truthful rather than manipulative. Critics contend that such a distinction is more a matter of semantics than substance.

Public diplomacy endeavors proceed along various paths. According to diplomat Christopher Ross, U.S. public diplomacy involves "giving timely news to foreign journalists, providing information on America directly to foreign publics through pamphlets and books, sponsoring scholarships and exchanges to the United States, exhibiting art, broadcasting about U.S. values and policies in various languages, and simply transmitting balanced, independent news to captive people who have no information source independent of a repressive government." Public diplomacy may also use standard diplomatic mechanisms and the news media as part of its process, but it is not dependent on conventional diplomacy or news coverage. Joseph Duffey, who

A Lebanese viewer tunes in to al-Hurra, an Arabic satellite television station established and funded by the U.S. government to disseminate information and news to promote its interests in the Arab world. The launching of the station marked a massive public diplomacy effort to improve poor perceptions of U.S. policies in the Middle East.

served as director of the United States Information Agency (USIA), noted that public diplomacy is "an attempt to get over the heads or around diplomats and official spokesmen of countries and sometimes around the press to speak directly to the public in other countries and to provide an explanation of U.S. values and policies."

A government generally employs public diplomacy when it wants to improve its image. The United States initiated public diplomacy projects in the Middle East during and following the 2003 Iraq War. Public opinion surveys had found that in the Middle East and the rest of the Muslim world, only small minorities held favorable views of the United States. When American policymakers and others asked, "Why do they hate us?" the "they" in question referred to much of the population in the Muslim world, but people in other countries could be included as well. In Congress, House International Relations Committee chairman Henry Hyde (R-Ill.) reflected widespread frustration when he asked, "How has this state of affairs come about? How is it that the country that invented Hollywood and Madison Avenue has allowed such a destructive and parodied image of itself to become the intellectual coin of the realm overseas?"

A government's desire to counteract negative opinion is not simply a matter of wanting to be liked. Widespread antipathy obstructs the implementation of foreign policy, for better or for worse, and helps opponents of that policy build a constituency. A study conducted for the Council on Foreign Relations in 2003 found that anti-Americanism threatened U.S. security and that "by standing so powerful and alone, the United States becomes a lightning rod for the world's fears and resentment of modernity, inequality, secularism, and globalization." The State Department's Advisory Commission on Public Diplomacy reported in 2003 that "the United States today lacks the capabilities in public diplomacy to meet the national security threat emanating from political instability, economic deprivation, and extremism, especially in the Arab and Muslim world." Therefore, the task of the Bush administration's public diplomacy in the Middle East has been to convince the public there that the United States wants to encourage democracy, not create an empire.

Advocates of public diplomacy could make the case that international opinion polls on views of the United States point to the need for expanded efforts around the world similar to those in the Middle East. American policymakers must make their case in the face of anger and skepticism about U.S. intentions. Even citizens of traditional allies, such as France and Germany, resent what they perceive as the United States' unilateral approach to dealing with the rest of the world. In nations that have not had longstanding ties with the United States, public diplomacy could be used to help establish constructive relationships from the outset, rather than using public diplomacy for damage control after anti-American sentiments take hold.

The United States possesses the most sophisticated public diplomacy apparatus. Other nations also use public diplomacy to try to win international support for their policies, particularly controversial ones. Russia, for example, has used public diplomacy to present its case regarding the conflict in Chechnya. States have also long used public diplomacy as an instrument of foreign policy. During the American Revolution, for instance, the new nation's leaders courted French public opinion to elicit aid in the fight against England. As part of this effort, Benjamin Franklin was sent to France and personified American public diplomacy of that time. Public diplomacy assumed its contemporary form during the cold war, when it was a responsibility of USIA, which was created in 1953 with the mandate to counter anti-American propaganda disseminated by the Soviet Union. After the end of the cold war, Congress tightened USIA's budget, and in 1999 the agency ceased to exist as an independent body, instead becoming part of the State Department. In the aftermath of the September 11, 2001, attacks on the United States, the Bush administration decided to rejuvenate public diplomacy. As a result, the White House and several government agencies initiated global information projects.

The government emphasized Arabic-language broadcasting ventures to compete with indigenous programming that it viewed as biased against U.S. interests. Policymakers often cited the news shows of the Qatar-based al-Jazeera network as an example of slanted reporting. American government-sponsored Radio Sawa ("together" in Arabic) began broadcasting in 2002, and satellite television station al-Hurra ("the free one") went on the air in early 2004. Both feature a smoothly produced mix of news and pop culture in their efforts to attract an audience.

The ultimate success of public diplomacy is not, however, determined by production technique. If the audience dislikes the fundamental policies of the sponsoring government, slick media products will have little effect. That is an inherent limitation on the power of public diplomacy. Practitioners of public diplomacy must recognize the skepticism, and often the hostility, of much of the audience. In such instances, public antagonism is directed not at the packaging, but at the policy inside the package. Barry Fulton of George Washington University's Public Diplomacy Institute observed that "public diplomacy is not, and should not be, somehow considered as camouflage for public policy. Public diplomacy is describing public policy, but it doesn't improve on it, change it, or misrepresent it."

Public diplomacy is indispensable if a nation wants to rely on "soft" power, which international relations scholar Joseph Nye has defined as "getting others to want what you want. . . . [It] is also more than persuasion or the ability to move people by argument. It is the ability to entice and attract. And attraction often leads to acquiescence or imitation." To foster lasting international stability, some political theorists argue, soft power is likely to work better than "hard" coercive power, although some realists feel that coercive power, too, has its place as a policy option. Idealist theorists would argue that if public diplomacy reflects enlightened public policy, it is more likely to be successful and to allow soft power to become dominant in international affairs.

The key to understanding the importance of public diplomacy is to see it as more than simply a technique for delivering information. Rather, it is a way to alter perceptions that often underlie conflict. At its best, public diplomacy transcends the misrepresentations of propaganda and bridges the gap between a government and citizens throughout the world who are affected by that government's policies. It can nurture understanding among peoples and nations, and so can be a valuable instrument for peace.

REFERENCES

DeYoung, Karen. "Bush to Create Formal Office to Shape U.S. Image Abroad." *Washington Post,* July 30, 2002, A1.

Hess, Stephen, and Marvin Kalb, eds. *The Media and the War on Terrorism.* Washington, D.C.: Brookings Institution Press, 2003.

Kornblut, Anne E. "Problems of Image and Diplomacy Beset U.S." *Boston Globe,* March 9, 2003, A25.

MacFarquhar, Neil. "Washington's Arabic TV Effort Gets Mixed Reviews." *New York Times,* February 20, 2004, A3.

Nye, Joseph S., Jr. *The Paradox of American Power.* New York: Oxford University Press, 2002.

Ross, Christopher. "Pillars of Public Diplomacy." *Harvard International Review* 25, no. 2 (Summer 2003): 22–27.

Seib, Philip. *Beyond the Frontlines: How the News Media Cover a World Shaped by War.* New York: Palgrave Macmillan, 2004.

Telhami, Shibley. "The Need for Public Diplomacy." *Brookings Review* (Summer 2002): 47–48.

Public opinion

See *Polls and the media; Exit polls*

Public relations

See *Media consultants; News management; Office of Communications; Propaganda; Pseudo-events; Spin doctors*

Public Telecommunications Act of 1978

The Public Telecommunications Act of 1978 reflects several amendments made to the Communications Act of 1934, which established the Federal Communications Commission (FCC) and transferred to it the responsibility of supervising interstate telephone services. Although no major overhaul of the 1934 act would take place until the Telecom -munications Act of 1996, important modifications were made to the act in the Public Broadcasting Act of 1967 and again in the Telecommunications Act of 1978, largely to update the 1934 legislation to reflect advances in communications technology.

The central concern of the telecommunications acts has been to ensure the widespread, fair, and efficient distribution of public telecommunications services to all residents. This issue dates to a debate in the 1930s over how radio broadcasting facilities should be distributed between commercial and public stations. The 1934 act called for a compromise between these two types of broadcasting. In light of technological developments for the transmission of video programming, in 1978 Congress passed amendments specifying that educational public telecommunications services be made available to as much of the public as possible, via broadcast and non-broadcast technologies, such as cable, videotape, and videodisc.

More important, the law granted multiyear, advanced funding for public broadcasting to limit the influence of budgetary politics on its operations. It also placed new mandates on the operation of public television stations, such as requiring open meetings, public accounting procedures, and equal opportunity employment practices to increase minority involvement. The act led indirectly to the creation of a separate trade industry lobbying organization, the National Association of Public Television Stations.

REFERENCES

"In the Matter of Implementation of Section 301 of the Telecommunications Act of 1996." Comments of the Association of America's Public Television Stations. Washington, D.C.: Federal Communications Commission, 1996, www.fcc.gov/Bureaus/Cable/comments/csapts.txt.

Congress and the Nation, vol. 5, 1977–1980. Washington, D.C.: CQ Press, 1988.

Paglin, Max D. *A Legislative History of the Communications Act of 1934.* New York: Oxford University Press, 1989.

Pulitzer, Joseph

Joseph Pulitzer (1847–1911), the influential and innovative publisher of the *New York World* and benefactor of the Pulitzer Prize and the Columbia School of Journalism, was one of the driving forces behind the sensationalized yellow journalism of the late nineteenth century.

As a recent immigrant from Budapest via Germany and newly mustered out of the Union Army, Pulitzer began his journalism career in St. Louis, a city with a large German-speaking community. Pulitzer eventually landed a job as a reporter with the German *Westliche Post,* a nominally Republican paper critical of the corrupt Grant administration, a stance which helped shape Pulitzer's political views. Pulitzer joined a police commission board and became secretary of the liberal Republican convention that nominated newspaperman Horace Greeley for president in 1872. After disappointing election results, Pulitzer joined the Democratic Party and remained a faithful supporter for the rest of his life.

Pulitzer then studied law, renewed his interest in politics, and even gained admittance to the District of Columbia bar in 1876. He worked as a correspondent for the *New York Sun* during an extended trip to Europe. Pulitzer abandoned his short-lived law practice and returned to journalism full-time when he purchased the *St. Louis Dispatch* in 1878. To gain Associated Press membership, Pulitzer also bought the *St. Louis Post* and merged the two papers to form the *St. Louis Post and Dispatch,* later known as the *Post-Dispatch*. He committed his paper to attacking his favorite targets—corrupt politicians and government officials. Pulitzer declared his paper Democratic, yet announced that his paper "will serve no party but the people."

Joseph Pulitzer, publisher of the St. Louis Post-Dispatch *and* New York World, *was, along with William Randolph Hearst, an original purveyor of sensationalist yellow journalism. Pulitzer's revelation of the U.S. government's fraudulent $40 million payment to the French Panama Canal Company resulted in his indictment for libeling President Theodore Roosevelt and the banker J. P. Morgan. The subsequent dismissal of the case proved to be a landmark victory for freedom of the press.*

Pulitzer turned progressively to sensational journalism to attract readers. In 1883 he bought the *New York World* and promptly began to enliven the paper with the addition of cartoons, sketches, and the scandals and lurid crime investigations with sensational headlines that became known as yellow journalism. The sensationalism of Pulitzer's papers and his principal competition, William Randolph Hearst's *New York Journal,* reached notorious levels during the Cuban Revolution of 1895–1896 and the 1898 Spanish-American War.

Later, in a public tussle with the administration of President Theodore Roosevelt in 1909, Pulitzer's *World* exposed an allegedly fraudulent $40 million dollar payment to the French Panama Canal Company. The government indicted Pulitzer for libeling Roosevelt and financier J. P. Morgan—the first such state action against the press since the prosecutions under the Sedition Act of 1798. The dismissal of the case in 1911 constituted a major victory in establishing precedent for today's freedom of the press. Ironically perhaps, given his promotion of yellow journalism, Pulitzer's estate funded a new school of journalism at Columbia University—the first of its kind in the United States—and a trust for the Pulitzer Prize, awarded annually for excellence in journalism and authorship since 1917.

See also *Hearst, William Randolph; Pulitzer Prize; Yellow journalism.*

REFERENCES

Barrett, James Wyman. *Joseph Pulitzer and his World.* New York: Vanguard, 1941.

Bates, J. Douglas. *The Pulitzer Prize: The Inside Story of America's Most Prestigious Award.* New York: Carol Publishing, 1991.

Brian, Denis. *Pulitzer: A Life.* New York: Wiley, 2001.

Granberg, Wilbur J. *The World of Joseph Pulitzer.* London: Abelard-Schuman, 1965.

Juergens, George. *Joseph Pulitzer and the New York World.* Princeton, N.J.: Princeton University Press, 1966.

Swanberg, W. A. *Pulitzer.* New York: Scribner, 1967.

Seitz, Don Carlos. *Joseph Pulitzer: His Life and Letters.* New York: AMS Press, 1970.

Whitelaw, Nancy. *Joseph Pulitzer and the New York World.* Greensboro, N.C.: Morgan Reynolds, 2000.

Pulitzer Prize

The Pulitzer Prize acknowledges outstanding examples of journalism and literature in the United States. Named after its donor, Joseph Pulitzer, a Hungarian immigrant who came to the United States in 1864, the prizes were first awarded in 1917. Presented annually, Pulitzers are considered journalism's highest honor and are awarded in a number of categories, including reporting, editorial writing, photography, editorial cartoons, international correspondence, and feature writing. Magazines, radio, and television are not included in the journalism competition. Pulitzers also recognize achievements in the writing of fiction and nonfiction books, drama, and music.

Juries produce a list of nominees, and the Pulitzer Prize board makes the final decision, unless it deems the entries in a category for that year not meriting a prize. Until the 1980s,

The media have experienced an explosion of pundit shows because of their low production costs and popularity with viewers. Here Chris Matthews of MSNBC's Hardball *waits during a commercial break before going one-on-one with Republican Tom DeLay, the House majority leader who had recently announced his intent to resign from Congress under a cloud of scandals.*

white males dominated the awards, with most finalists and winners working for papers in the East. The prizes in recent years have become more geographically balanced, and more women and minority writers have received recognition.

See also *Pulitzer, Joseph.*

REFERENCES

Bates, J. Douglas. *The Pulitzer Prize: The Inside Story of America's Most Prestigious Award.* New York: Carol Publishing, 1991.

Holtenberg, John. *The Pulitzer Prizes.* New York: Columbia University Press, 1974.

Rothmyer, Karen. *Winning Pulitzers: The Stories behind Some of the Best News Coverage of Our Time.* New York: Columbia University Press, 1991.

Pundit shows

Pundit shows are programs in which journalists, politicians, and experts, self-proclaimed or otherwise, provide opinions about political events and issues. The term *pundit,* derived from the Hindi word *pandit,* meaning "wise man," implies an expertise, in this case in current affairs.

The pundit show originated in a series of interviews conducted by Walter Lippmann, the first Washington pundit. Beginning in 1960, CBS News paid Lippmann $10,000 for each of five annual appearances in which he presented his views on world events in response to questions by CBS reporters. NBC's *Meet the Press* had been giving journalists similar opportunities since 1947, but Lippmann was the first journalist to be invited to center stage.

A second milestone occurred in early 1968, when ABC News, trailing in the ratings and strapped for resources, introduced regular commentaries on the news by journalists and commentators such as Bill Moyers, Marya Mannes, James J. Kilpatrick, Gore Vidal, and Charles Evers. When polling indicated that viewers liked these segments, but did not see any of them frequently enough to develop any personal loyalty, ABC responded by dividing the job exclusively between Howard K. Smith, a conservative, and Frank Reynolds, a liberal. They became television's first daily pundits, paid not only to deliver the news, but also to tell audiences what to think about it. CBS's *60 Minutes* also adopted the point-counterpoint format of opposing viewpoints, making James J. Kilpatrick and Shana Alexander household names.

The debut of PBS's *Agronsky and Company* in December 1969 represents another important moment in pundit history. The show borrowed its format from PBS's *Washington Week in Review,* which had begun airing in February 1967. The latter simply asked beat reporters to explain their stories in detail, with the other members of the round table occasionally asking a question. Martin Agronsky improved the entertainment quotient of this formula by substituting opinionated pundits for the more neutral journalists and encouraging them to opine and disagree. *Agronsky* created a new kind of pundit stardom. The commentator George F. Will rode this vehicle to its ultimate destination.

The McLaughlin Group aired for the first time in April 1982, taking the *Agronsky* formula in a new direction. The show's success derived from its host's ability to lead the discussions in a fashion that owed more to a rough-and-tumble roller derby than to public affairs television. Guests ran through some topics in as few as thirty seconds. Each panelist represented a stock position, but all offered "inside opinions and forecasts."

The pundit world expanded shortly thereafter, as media corporations discovered that they could produce pundit programs more cheaply than almost any other kind of offering. The hosts commanded serious salaries, but more often than not the guests appeared for free. NBC News converted this insight into continuous news and punditry across one broadcast and two cable stations (CNBC and MSNBC) by 1996. Fox did much the same when it created the Fox News Channel shortly thereafter, with such programming as *The O'Reilly Factor* and *Hannity and Colmes*. The broadcast networks also expanded their pundit offerings on Sunday mornings and on their daily morning shows.

Pundit shows are not without controversy. Although they have increased political content on television, some observers ask at what cost. Critics argue that these shows have cheapened and harshened political discourse, turning public affairs into the political equivalent of professional wrestling.

See also *Lippmann, Walter; McLaughlin, John; Sunday news shows; Talk shows*

REFERENCES

Alterman, Eric. *Sound and Fury: The Making of the Punditocracy.* 2d ed. Ithaca, N.Y.: Cornell University Press, 2000.

Meyer, Karl E. *Pundits, Poets and Wits: An Omnibus of America Newpaper Columns.* New York: Oxford University Press, 1990.

Nimmo, Dan, and James E. Combs. *The Political Pundits.* New York: Praeger, 1992.

Steel, Ronald. *Walter Lippmann and the American Century.* Boston: Atlantic–Little Brown, 1980.

R

Radio

The introduction of radio, a wireless medium, for mass communications in the 1920s transformed politics. Until then, print media, primarily newspapers, dominated political communications. The advent of radio offered unprecedented levels of exposure to mass audiences, and the new medium rapidly became one of the most important and far-reaching vehicles for mass political communications and a key source of political news and information for Americans. The status of radio changed in the 1950s and 1960s, with the ascendance of television and its overtaking of radio in the market. Despite the growth of television, and the more recent growth and popularity of the Internet, radio remains an important medium for communication about politics and campaigns.

The Growth of Radio

During the early days of radio, only a few companies controlled the airwaves. As the number of Americans who owned radios increased into the millions, AT&T developed technology that would allow stations to network over phone lines so that a broadcast could be heard across multiple stations simultaneously. By 1924 AT&T could broadcast coast to coast. The Columbia Broadcasting System (CBS) and the National Broadcasting Company (NBC) quickly leased this technology from AT&T, and the number of radio stations in their combined networks grew into the hundreds. Initially, it seemed that NBC would dominate the airwaves, with two large networks under its control, known as Blue and Red (it later added a third, orange). By 1943, however, the Federal

Communications Commission (FCC) forced NBC to divest itself of some of its stations and, with the sale of its blue network, a third major network began, the American Broadcasting Company (ABC). Although many people were turning from their newspapers to their radios for the latest news, radio initially was not very skilled at news reporting. It took the medium almost a decade to find its footing in the news.

As advertising revenues were redirected from newspapers to radio, newspaper publishers fought back. Afraid that newspapers might not survive if "headline-minded" Americans became accustomed to radio's condensed version of events, newspaper owners began buying radio stations and preventing radio reporters from receiving Washington press passes. They also prevented radio reporters from using the wire services. Radio audiences, however, continued to grow rapidly, and politicians were eager to reach the public. Even the smallest radio network could boast ten million listeners during the evening news. By March 1933 forty million listeners tuned in to the radio to hear President Franklin D. Roosevelt's first "fireside chat." Eventually, in 1939, Congress allotted space for radio booths in both the House and the Senate press galleries. "Press conferences" became "news conferences." Radio journalism in politics had arrived in its own right.

Radio's Role in Politics

The first presidential speech broadcast on radio was Woodrow Wilson's "Fourteen Points," delivered to Congress on January 18, 1918, and relayed around the world by Navy radio stations. Wilson's speech, which came ten months before the signing of the armistice ending World War I, set out his plan for a lasting peace. Two years later the 1920 election results were announced via radio to a small listening audience of 500–1,000 people in Pittsburgh, Pennsylvania. Warren G. Harding, the first "radio president," won the election. His inauguration was broadcast live to a still growing audience. Americans' desire for political news on the radio grew rapidly, and nascent radio networks were eager to fill open airtime with political news.

Radio communications played a critical role in the 1924 presidential campaign. The proceedings of both major parties' nominating conventions were broadcast by radio, giving the public its first opportunity to listen in on the conventions and form early opinions about the candidates. Calvin Coolidge, a popular and effective radio communicator, claimed the Republican Party's nomination with ease, presenting a powerful and united image to listeners from the convention's site in Cleveland, Ohio. The Democrats, by contrast, who gathered at Madison Square Garden in New York City, had not fully recognized the importance of radio. As millions listened during the fifteen-day event, there were divisions and discord, culminating in fistfights that could be overheard on the air. After 102 contested ballots, the Democrats finally compromised and nominated John W. Davis. The party's image, however, was tarnished by perceptions of turmoil that had emerged in part as a result of the radio coverage. Discord in the Democratic Party, coupled with a prosperous economy, helped Coolidge sail to victory in the November election. It became clear that politicians could no longer get by in their campaigns without giving careful thought to their public impression, even at such an early stage. Radio and its vast audiences made it necessary for politicians to convey cogent arguments over the airways and to speak directly to audiences.

Few politicians were as masterful in their use of radio as Franklin D. Roosevelt. Roosevelt took office as president in 1933, during the Great Depression that began in 1929. During his twelve years in office, Roosevelt delivered three hundred "fireside chats" via radio. He believed that radio, by allowing him to speak directly to the people, enabled Democrats to bypass Republican-leaning newspapers. His messages were intended primarily to educate the public about his various policies, particularly during the early years of the New Deal, his program to help the country recover from the depression. Roosevelt spoke as if he were addressing friends by the fireplace, a practice that endeared him to the public. Roosevelt also used radio judiciously during his presidential

campaigns of 1936, 1940, and 1944. For example, in the 1936 election the Republican and Democratic Parties spent more than $2 million on radio, but Republican Alf Landon's use of the medium paled in comparison to Roosevelt's, who had honed his skills through his fireside chats and the like.

Market Changes

Radio's dominance of mass communication, however, was short-lived. As with newspapers before it, radio succumbed to the new ascendant medium—television. By 1960 the sales of radios were down 75 percent from their 1948 peak, and both audiences and advertisers migrated from radio to television.

The medium has never reclaimed its dominant position, but it remains a powerful vehicle for mass communication and politics. In the mid-2000s more than 10,000 local stations offered specialized content that continued to attract substantial audiences. Radio enjoys nearly universal penetration in the United States. Declines in newspaper readership over the last two decades have made radio audiences second only to television in terms of audience reach. Surveys consistently reveal that radio is the main source of campaign news and information for nearly one in ten Americans. The U.S. Census Bureau reported in 2003 that radio audiences exceed 84 million Americans, compared with 94 million for television and only 80 million for newspapers. A July 1998 Gallup Poll reported that approximately 40 percent of Americans turn to radio as a source of political news and information. Additionally, talk radio programming has attracted a growing number of listeners over the past two decades.

Radio remains an effective tool for political communications during campaigns as well. Because of its specialized outlets, such as stations that cater to country, classic rock, all talk, and so forth, radio permits nuanced targeting and "narrowcasting," which allows campaigns to design specific appeals that can be communicated relatively inexpensively to select audiences. Moreover, candidates' use of radio to promote their candidacies is widespread at both the federal and municipal levels. Studies of congressional campaigns reveal radio advertising to be as common, and in some cases more common, than the use of television advertising.

Technological advances and developments have required radio to evolve and adapt to new environments for nearly a century, yet radio remains a powerful medium for political communication. Today, radio faces new challenges from another potent new medium—the Internet. Internet penetration and audiences have expanded substantially in the late 1990s and early 2000s. Nevertheless, radio promises to remain an important medium for political communication in the years ahead.

See also *ABC; CBS; Fireside chats; NBC Universal; Roosevelt, Franklin D.; Talk radio.*

REFERENCES

Barnouw, Erik. *The Golden Web: A History of Broadcasting in the United States, 1933–1953.* New York: Oxford University Press, 1968.

Chester, Edward W. *Radio, Television, and American Politics.* New York: Sheed and Ward, 1969.

Greenfield Thomas Allen. *Radio: A Reference Guide.* New York: Greenwood Press, 1989.

Ritchie, Donald A. *Reporting from Washington: The History of the Washington Press Corps.* New York: Oxford University Press, 2005.

Strachan, J. Cherie. *High-Tech Grass Roots: The Professionalization of Local Elections.* Lanham, Md.: Rowman and Littlefield, 2003.

Radio Act of 1927

The Radio Act of 1927, passed by Congress to regulate issues such as licensing, censorship, and freedom of speech for the public airwaves, created the Federal Radio Commission and invested it with the responsibility of assigning each station its own frequency, power, and times of operation. With the growth in commercial broadcasting in the years after World War I, the commission was to bring order to the airwaves and to stop the sabotage plaguing network broadcasts. Networks were given some preference, as they constituted most of the first broadcast licenses.

The Radio Act also authorized the president to appoint five members to the commission "by and with the consent of the Senate," having no more than three representatives from the same political party. For the first time, broadcast legislature used the phrase "public interest, convenience, and necessity," indicating that, like public utilities, it was responsible for informing the public. It also enacted restrictions with the phrase "no person ... shall utter any obscene, indecent or profane language by means of radio communication," the boundaries of which are under regular debate.

Congress passed the Communications Act in 1934. Under this act, the commission's name was changed to the Federal Communications Commission. With amendments, the Communications Act continues to oversee broadcasting regulations in the United States.

See also *Censorship; Communications Act of 1934.*

REFERENCES

Bliss, Edward, Jr. *Now the News: The Story of Broadcast Journalism.* New York: Columbia University Press, 1991.

Federal Regulatory Directory. 12th ed. Washington, D.C.: CQ Press, 2006.

Raspberry, William

William James Raspberry (1935–) made a career in journalism that earned him a Pulitzer Prize. He began his career with the *Indianapolis Recorder,* before serving as an Army public information officer from 1960 to 1962. After joining the *Washington Post* as a teletypist in 1962, he worked his way up as an obituary writer, city desk reporter, and assistant editor. In 1966 he became the columnist of "Potomac Watch." The column began in the Metro section, was soon moved to the editorial page, and then became nationally syndicated. Raspberry first used the column to write about local issues, but then transitioned to urban and minority affairs, a change that garnered him the moniker of the "Lone Ranger of columnists."

William Raspberry began working at the Washington Post *as a teletypist and obituary writer in 1962. By his retirement in 2005, he had become the author of a nationally syndicated column and had won a Pulitzer Prize for commentary, in 1994.*

Raspberry's book *Looking Backward at Us* (1991), is a collection of his columns, primarily from the 1980s, covering such issues as race, family, education, and criminal justice. Raspberry won the Pulitzer Prize for commentary in 1994. He tells people who ask his political views that he is "a solutionist." He has taught at Howard University and is the Knight Professor of the Practice of Communications and Journalism at the DeWitt Wallace Center and the Terry Sanford Institute of Public Policy at Duke University. Raspberry retired from his column in 2005, after thirty-nine years of work, to devote his attention to educational and charity work for Baby Steps, a small Mississippi-based organization he developed to help teach parents how to provide their young children with the tools they will need for their education.

See also *Pulitzer Prize; Washington Post.*

REFERENCES

Fibich, L. "The Solutionist." *American Journalism Review,* May 16, 1994, 28–33.
Raspberry, William. "What I'll Do Next." *Washington Post,* December 26, 2005, A39.

Rather, Dan

Dan Rather (1931–) has had a long career as a national broadcast journalist and author, serving as anchor of CBS *Evening News* for twenty-four years. After teaching journalism at his alma mater, Sam Houston State Teachers College, he worked as a reporter in 1950 for the Associated Press. He worked at United Press International from 1950 to 1952 and simultaneously reported for KSAM Radio in Houston until 1953. The next year Rather began a one-year stint as a reporter for the *Houston Chronicle.* In 1956 he became the news director at KTRH-TV and in 1959 became a reporter for the station. Rather then joined KHOU-TV, the Houston CBS affiliate, as the news director, moving to CBS News in 1962.

When President John F. Kennedy was assassinated in Texas in 1963, Rather was on the scene and aired the first televised report of the event. His coverage earned such attention that he took on the post as CBS's White House correspondent later that same year. He soon became known for his confrontational and tenacious style. Most notably, at the 1974 National Association of Broadcasters convention in Hous-

ton, Rather asked President Richard Nixon a question to which Nixon replied, "Are you running for something?" Rather quipped, "No, sir, Mr. President. Are you?"

He joined CBS's *60 Minutes* in 1975. Six years later, Rather was chosen to be Walter Cronkite's successor as anchor of the *CBS Evening News.* He has contributed to the weekly news programs *48 Hours* and *60 Minutes II* since the beginning of both segments, in 1988 and 1999, respectively. Rather relinquished his anchor chair in 2005, amid a swirling controversy and accusations of political bias and inaccuracy regarding his reportage on President George W. Bush's military service record during the 2004 presidential campaign. He continued with *60 Minutes* and various public speaking engagements into 2006, when he contracted with a new cable channel, HDNet. Rather has written several books, including *The Palace Guard* (1974) and *Deadlines and Datelines* (1999).

See also *Cronkite, Walter; Evening network news.*

REFERENCES

Goldberg, Robert, and Gerald Jay Goldberg. *Anchors: Brokaw, Jennings, Rather and the Evening News.* Secaucus, N.J.: Carol Publishing Group, 1990.
Jones, Alex S. "The Anchors: Who They Are, What They Do, the Tests They Face." *New York Times,* July 27, 1986.
Matusow, Barbara. *The Evening Stars.* Boston: Houghton Mifflin, 1983.
Weisman, Alan. *The Extraordinary Life and Times of Dan Rather.* Hoboken, N.J.: Wiley, 2006.
Westin, Av. *Newswatch: How TV Decides the News.* New York: Simon and Schuster, 1982.

Raymond, Henry Jarvis

Henry Jarvis Raymond (1820–1869) was active in politics before making his mark in journalism and founding the *New York Times.* Raymond began his career as a contributing writer for Horace Greeley's *New Yorker,* while attending the University of Vermont. Upon graduation in 1840, he entered politics, campaigning for presidential candidate William Henry Harrison. The following year Raymond followed Greeley to launch the *New York Tribune.* He then moved to the *Morning Courier* and in 1843 to the *New York Enquirer.* Raymond joined other colleagues to form the Associated Press (AP) in 1848.

Despite his success in journalism, Raymond continued his political work, campaigning for Henry Clay and Zachary

Taylor. In 1849 he was elected as a state legislator. In 1851, with George Jones, he founded the *New York Times,* serving as the paper's first editor.

In 1854 Raymond returned to elected office as lieu-tenant-governor of New York. During this time he actively contributed to the organization of the Republican Party. He jumped into the national debate regarding a state's right to secede, arguing that the Constitution created a perpetual union that could not be dissolved. Raymond personally reported on some of the battles of the American Civil War (1861–1865). He was elected to the U.S. House of Representa-tives in 1864 and remained as editor of the *New York Times* until his death in 1869.

See also *Associated Press; New York Times.*

REFERENCES

Brown, Francis. *Raymond of the Times.* Westport, Conn.: Greenwood Press, 1970.

Maverick, Augustus. *Henry J. Raymond and the New York Press.* New York: Arno, 1970.

Reagan, Ronald

Ronald Wilson Reagan (1911–2004) received many nick-names over the course of his career as a film actor, California governor, and fortieth president of the United States, among them the "Great Communicator." After graduating from Eureka College, Illinois, in 1932, Reagan began his profes-sional career as a radio sportscaster for WOC in Davenport, Iowa, and then for WHO in Des Moines. At the time, he was an ardent supporter of President Franklin D. Roosevelt's New Deal and the Democratic Party. Reagan served in the Army Air Corps during World War II (1939–1945) and was assigned to make training films. After the war, he became a spokesman for the General Electric Company, a position he held for ten years beginning in 1952. Reagan hosted the tel-evision series *Death Valley Days* from 1962 to 1965. He twice held the position of president of the Screen Actors Guild, first from 1947 to 1952 and again in 1959–1960. During this time he became embroiled in the anticommunist investiga-tions of the House Un-American Activities Committee that led to the more public and controversial interrogations by Sen. Joseph McCarthy, R-Wis., and his committee.

It was at this time that Reagan switched his political affil-iation from the Democratic to the Republican Party. Now fully committed to his political ambitions, he was elected governor of California in 1966 and served two terms, ending in 1975. While governor, Reagan directly confronted the "free speech" movement at the University of California, which had formed in opposition to the Vietnam War. He also honed his skill at public speaking, blending it with a com-mitment to a conservative agenda in order to further his political standing. He campaigned unsuccessfully for the Republican presidential nomination, opposing Richard Nixon in 1968 and then, in 1976, Nixon's successor, Presi-dent Gerald Ford.

Reagan declined to run for a third term as California governor so that he could focus his efforts on the presidency. In 1980 he defeated incumbent president Jimmy Carter to become the fortieth president of the United States. Reagan relied on influential public relations advisors, including Michael Deaver and David Gergen, to orchestrate and con-trol public events, and to utilize the media, especially televi-sion, to enhance his public image and convey his message. After a decade of the Vietnam War, the Arab oil embargo, and the Iranian hostage crisis, Reagan used his upbeat rhetoric to invigorate the nation and unleash (in the words of his cam-paign) "the great, confident roar of American progress, and growth and optimism." These traits, coupled with the coun-try's relative prosperity and the orchestration of a successful media campaign, led to his landslide reelection in 1984.

Reagan's administration took a decidedly more militant posture in international relations with the 1983 invasion of Grenada, the Lebanese peacekeeping mission of 1984, the 1986 air raid on Libya, and the naval escort operations that took place in 1986 during the Iran–Iraq War. In a festering confrontation with Congress involving the anticommunist "contras" in Nicaragua, the Reagan administration became entangled in the Iran–contra scandal, which was uncovered to the public in 1986–1987.

Many of Reagan's critics suggested that he was only image—the clever and skilled face and voice of his conser-vative advisors—and yet even some of his critics credit Rea-gan with helping to end the four-decade cold war with the Soviet Union. After leaving office, Reagan began in 1994 to exhibit symptoms of Alzheimer's disease, and he withdrew from public appearances to his ranch in Santa Barbara, Cali-fornia. Reagan's autobiography, *Ronald Reagan: An American Life,* was published in 1990. He died in 2004.

REFERENCES

Cannon, Lou. *President Reagan: The Role of a Lifetime.* New York: Public Affairs, 2000.

Dallek, Robert. *Ronald Reagan: The Politics of Symbolism.* Cambridge, Mass.: Harvard University Press, 1999.

Deaver, Michael K. *A Different Drummer: My Thirty Years with Ronald Reagan.* New York: HarperCollins, 2001.

Denton, Robert E., Jr. *The Primetime Presidency of Ronald Reagan: The Era of the Television Presidency.* New York: Praeger, 1988.

Hertsgaard, Mark. *On Bended Knee: The Press and the Reagan Presidency.* New York: Schocken Books, 1989.

Stuckey, Mary E. *Playing the Game: The Presidential Rhetoric of Ronald Reagan.* New York: Praeger, 1990.

Reasoner, Harry

Harry Reasoner (1923–1991) achieved national attention as a network broadcast journalist in 1958 for his coverage of school desegregation in Little Rock, Arkansas. Reasoner, who had studied journalism at Stanford University and the University of Minnesota, began writing for the *Minneapolis Times* in 1942. His fledgling journalism career was interrupted by service during World War II (1939–1945). After the war Reasoner returned to journalism as a rewrite man and drama critic; he briefly worked at CBS Radio. He joined the United States Information Agency and was posted to Manila, Philippines, from 1948 to 1951. When he returned home, he worked as a Minneapolis television news director. CBS hired Reasoner in 1956 to be a commentator and special news broadcaster in New York City, where he quickly gained a reputation for his writing style and use of language. He gained national stature in 1958 for his coverage of the Little Rock, Arkansas, school desegregation confrontation. This recognition led to his selection to co-host the *Calendar,* a morning television show, a position he held from 1961 to 1963.

Don Hewitt selected Reasoner and Mike Wallace to be co-hosts of the new, weekly CBS journal program, *60 Minutes,* in 1968. Two years later ABC wooed Reasoner away from CBS to anchor the ABC evening news. In an effort to boost ratings, ABC attracted Barbara Walters, in 1976, and paired her with Reasoner as co-anchors of the evening news. The relationship, which lasted two years, was not successful, as Reasoner voiced criticism of Walters's position and salary. The rift led him to return to CBS and *60 Minutes* in 1979. He remained at CBS until he retired, shortly before his death. Reasoner wrote *Tell Me About Women* (1946), *The Reasoner Report* (1966), and *Before the Colors Fade* (1981).

See also *Evening network news; Walters, Barbara.*

REFERENCE

Hewitt, Don. *Tell Me a Story: Fifty Years and 60 Minutes in Television.* New York: Public Affairs, 2001.

Red Lion Broadcasting Co., Inc. v. FCC (1969)

In *Red Lion Broadcasting Co., Inc. v. FCC* (1969), the Supreme Court upheld the constitutionality of the "fairness doctrine," which required television and radio stations to present discussion of public issues and in so doing provide each side of an issue fair coverage. Fred Cook, author of *Barry Goldwater, Extremist on the Right,* brought the case when denied an opportunity by the Red Lion Broadcasting Company to rebut statements by Reverend Billy Hargis, who accused Cook of being a liar and a communist during a segment of a "Christian Crusade" series. The Federal Communications Commission (FCC), citing the fairness doctrine, ordered the station to allow Cook free airtime to respond. Red Lion Broadcasting decided to challenge the doctrine.

The Court unanimously held that the fairness doctrine contributed to a balanced and open discussion of public concerns, which was not only consistent with, but enhanced, the First Amendment. In the case of radio and television, it stated, the scarcity of spectrum space justified the provisions of the doctrine to ensure a diversity of voices. The growth of cable television and other types of programming, such as satellite, weakened this argument in subsequent years. The fairness doctrine remained in effect for nearly two decades after *Red Lion.* Despite efforts by Congress to save the fairness doctrine, the antiregulatory fervor of the Reagan administration led to its abolishment in August 1987, and the FCC citing its desire to extend to radio and television the same First Amendment protections guaranteed to the print media.

See also *Fairness doctrine; Right of access.*

REFERENCES

Red Lion Broadcasting Co., Inc. v. FCC, 395 U.S. 367 (1969).

Silber, Jerome S. *Broadcast Regulation and the First Amendment.* Lexington, Ky. Association for Education in Journalism, 1980.

Tillinghast, Charles H. *American Broadcast Regulation and the First Amendment: Another Look.* Ames: Iowa State University Press, 2000.

Reese, Matt

Matthew Anderson Reese (1927–1998) made significant contributions to politics as a political consultant and grassroots campaign organizer. After serving in the army during World War II, Reese graduated with a degree in political science from Marshall College in 1950. He returned to military service during the Korean War. After his discharge in 1953, he went to Washington, D.C., to become a staff assistant to Rep. Maurice Burnside (D-W.Va.). Through his work in Washington he acquired an affinity for politics and the intricacies of political campaigning. Reese came to national attention in political circles for his accomplishments in helping Sen. John F. Kennedy (D-Mass.) win the West Virginia presidential primary election in 1960. After Kennedy's election to the presidency, Reese ran the voter registration division of the Democratic National Committee (DNC). He also led Lyndon Johnson's 1964 voter registration effort.

In 1966 Reese left the DNC to form Matt Reese and Associates, which later became Reese Communications Companies, Inc. (RCC). The firm reportedly worked on more than 450 campaigns in the United States and in foreign countries, transitioning in the 1980s from helping political candidates to helping corporations. Reese defined grassroots voter organizing and was one of the first to focus on targeted voters—the undecided voter as well as the nonvoter who might favor his candidate or agenda. His approach to campaign operations, using customized plans, checklists, timelines, and organization charts, has been widely copied and imitated.

Reese sold RCC in 1986 and retired two years later. He was the founder and past president of the American Association of Political Consultants and taught at the Graduate School of Political Management at George Washington University. At the time of his death, Reese was writing an as yet unpublished book detailing his political experiences, tentatively titled, *Green Noses and Purple Ears*—his oftquoted description of the voters upon whom his efforts were focused.

REFERENCES

Sabato, Larry J. *The Rise of Political Consultants: New Ways of Winning Elections.* New York: Basic Books, 1981.
Strother, Raymond D. *Falling Up: How a Redneck Helped Invent Political Consulting.* Baton Rouge: Louisiana State University Press, 2003.

Regulation of the press

See *Communications Act of 1934; First Amendment*

Reid, Whitelaw

Whitelaw Reid (1837–1912) made his career as a journalist, newspaper editor, and diplomat. Before he reached adulthood, Reid displayed an active interest in journalism and politics that lasted throughout his life. He began his journalism career as editor of the *Xenia* (Ohio) *News.* He joined the *Cincinnati Gazette* as a reporter during the American Civil War (1861–1865), reporting predominantly from Washington, D.C. Reid served as aide-de-camp to General William Rosecrans, of the Union Army, during the 1861 Western Virginia campaigns and witnessed the battles of Shiloh and Gettysburg. He also served as librarian for the House of Representatives, from 1863 to 1866. Reid transcribed his wartime experiences into books—*After the War* (1866) and *Ohio in the War* (2 vols., 1868).

In 1868 Horace Greeley invited Reid to New York and hired him as an editorial writer for the *New York Tribune.* Reid became the paper's managing editor one year later. Reid and Greeley grew dissatisfied with the corruption of President Ulysses Grant's administration and became involved with the Liberal Republican movement. Reid orchestrated Greeley's Liberal Republican nomination for president in 1872. After Greeley's death later that year Reid gained financial as well as editorial control of the *Tribune* and continued to build the newspaper's reputation as a leading journal, expanding coverage of foreign affairs and government corruption.

While continuing to run the *Tribune,* Reid served as minister to France, from 1889 to 1892, and ambassador to Great Britain, from 1905 to 1912. He stood for election as the vice presidential candidate with Benjamin Harrison in 1892. After the Spanish–American War, in 1898, President William McKinley appointed Reid to the Peace Commission to assist with peace negotiations. Reid also wrote in the area of foreign affairs, including *Problems of Expansion* (1900). Generations of his family followed him into work at the *Tribune.*

See also *Greeley, Horace.*

REFERENCES

Duncan, Bingham. *Whitelaw Reid: Journalist, Politician, Diplomat.* Athens: University of Georgia Press, 1975.

Kluger, Richard. *The Paper: The Life and Death of the New York Herald Tribune.* New York: Knopf, 1986.

Reid, Whitelaw. *Rise to World Power: Selected Letters of Whitelaw Reid 1895–1912,* edited by David R. Contosta and Jessica R. Hawthorne. Philadelphia: American Philosophical Society, 1986.

Religion and the media

In the late twentieth and early twenty-first centuries, changes in communications media provided both challenges and opportunities for religious groups in the United States. Technical innovations such as radio, network television, cable television, and the Internet offered powerful, culturally plausible alternatives to religious perspectives on American political and social life. At the same time, the electronic media supplied religious leaders and interest groups with effective means of communication with actual and potential followers.

The Challenge to Religious Orthodoxy

Leaders of a number of religious denominations have often been critical of the mass media. Popular books, newspapers, magazines, cinema, and television have been characterized as fertile sources of corruption, in which sinful or ungodly values and lifestyles are presented in a positive light. In particular, television has been considered a medium in which violence, sexual promiscuity, and secularism are portrayed as desirable and even beneficial. Leaders of denominations such as Orthodox Judaism, the Southern Baptist Association, and the Church of Jesus Christ of Latter-day Saints have often encouraged their members either to avoid electronic media or to exercise extreme care and discretion in their media usage.

The most systematic challenge to the mass media has been posed by the Roman Catholic Church. The church has a long tradition of censorship (and has not shrunk from the use of that term). For much of its history the church published an *Index of Forbidden Books,* which ceased publication only in 1967, following the Second Vatican Council. In the United States, Catholic organizations such as the National Legion of Decency and the National Office for Decent Literature have monitored communications in the cinema and print media, respectively, and have attempted to guide

Radio evangelist James Dobson hosts the radio program Focus on the Family, *which reaches an estimated 200 million people in 164 countries daily. Through his program and organization of the same name, he encourages his followers to take stances on government social and cultural policies.*

Catholics' media usage. The Catholic Church in the United States has traditionally been regarded as a powerful social force, and the church has often been accorded great deference by film producers, in anticipation of possible negative reaction (and economic reprisal) by lay Catholics.

Although the mass media have posed challenges to Christian denominations in the United States, the existence and availability of such media have provided opportunities for religious groups to spread their own messages and values to wide audiences. For most of the twentieth century, religious publications such as the *National Catholic Reporter, First Things,* and *Commonweal,* among others, have provided religious viewpoints to mass readerships. Moreover, religious leaders and organizations have taken advantage of electronic media for much of the past century, and this trend shows no sign of abating.

Televangelism

Perhaps the most noteworthy recent development in the area of the media and religion is the rise of *televangelism,* a generic term that refers to explicitly religious broadcasting. The last two decades of the twentieth century were characterized by a virtual explosion in the use of television by religious groups.

There is nothing particularly novel about religious leaders using the most advanced technology to reach their audiences. Almost as quickly as radio became a popular medium in the 1920s, evangelist Billy Sunday made regular use of the airwaves to convey sermons to mass audiences. In the 1930s Father Charles E. Coughlin made similar use of radio to promulgate a theologically conservative, anti-Semitic, and politically populist version of Roman Catholicism that edged toward fascism. With the advent of television, religious leaders such as evangelical Protestant Rex Humbard and Roman Catholic bishop Fulton Sheen appeared on television to convey doctrinally conservative presentations of their respective theological traditions. Although the scarcity of air time during a period of dominance made it necessary for such shows to run during time periods when television viewership was relatively low, both informal impressions and a few systematic studies have suggested that such religious programming managed to attract rather large audiences. The manifest political content of such programming varied across religious leaders, with evangelical Protestants such as Humbard placing a much greater emphasis on inspiration and personal piety than did their Catholic counterparts.

The amount, extent, and scope of religious programming increased enormously with the spread of cable television. Cable made it technically and economically feasible to put highly specialized programming that did not require large national audiences or extraordinarily high capital investment on television. Accordingly, the late 1970s and early 1980s saw the advent of an entire cable network: The Christian Broadcasting Network (CBN) and a number of religious programs provided by various cable channels, including Jim Bakker's Trinity Broadcasting Network. Some of the most popular of these included Jerry Falwell's *Old Time Gospel Hour,* Marion "Pat" Robertson's *700 Club,* James and Tammy Bakker's *PTL Club* (the acronym stood for both "Praise the Lord" and "People That Love"), Jimmy Swaggert's *Ministries,* and Robert Schuller's *Hour of Power,* as well as regular programming offered by Billy Graham, Oral Roberts, and James Dobson. In addition to televised worship services, religious

television on cable provided alternative news programming, cartoons, and other programs for children (which always contained religious themes), and entertainment programming for adults. Most often, the latter consisted of reruns of such purportedly wholesome, family-friendly programs as *Bonanza* and *The Rifleman* (both of which were thought to illustrate the challenges of one-parent families) and *The Jack Benny Show.* Most conspicuously, televangelism in the 1980s had a distinctly and explicitly political cast. Televangelists such as Falwell and Robertson provided biblical frames for contemporary current events and supplied a distinctive, pro-Republican stance toward U.S. politics. Religious programming has been given partial credit for the voter mobilization of evangelical Christians, which resulted in the Republican takeover of the U.S. Senate in 1980 and Ronald Reagan's presidential victories in 1980 and 1984. Although the messages of televangelists have tended to focus on social issues, such as abortion, homosexuality, and feminism, evangelical spokespersons such as Falwell and Robertson have taken positions on a wide range of issues, such as apartheid in South Africa, the Panama Canal treaties, the gold standard, and the progressive income tax.

At its peak in the mid-1980s televangelists attracted very large audiences, although precise estimates varied from about 60 million viewers weekly (Gallup) to a more modest, but still impressive, 7 to 9 million weekly viewers (Arbitron). It is at least as difficult to estimate the effects of religious television on public attitudes as it is to determine the size of the audience itself. Clearly, much of the audience for televangelism is self-selected and thus predisposed to accept the politically and doctrinally conservative messages being offered. Ted Jelen and Clyde Wilcox found that the direct effects of religious television were greatest for viewers who were theologically mismatched with their congregations. That is, programs such as the *Old Time Gospel Hour* and *The 700 Club* attracted viewers whose personal theological views supported a literal interpretation of the Bible as the inerrant word of God, but who were members of theologically liberal or less orthodox congregations. For such viewers, religious programming provided a scripturally accredited alternative to the message offered by their own churches. It is also possible that there are many indirect effects of religious television, such as providing religious frames to ostensibly secular issues or mobilizing previously apolitical viewers.

Televangelism remains a prominent feature of cable television, although religious television underwent something of a decline during the 1990s. There were several reasons for this. First, prominent television ministers Jim Bakker and Jimmy Swaggert were involved in scandals occasioned by sexual misconduct, which limited the appeal of their programs and ultimately led to the demise of the *PTL Club* (and, ultimately, the Trinity Broadcasting Network). Second, Pat Robertson made an unsuccessful bid for the Republican presidential nomination in 1988, in which he attempted to put forth a more secular description of his television ministry. Robertson described himself as a television producer and businessman, rather than as a Christian minister. Moreover, the Robertson campaign exposed a cleavage within the religious right between Robertson's charismatic brand of evangelical Christianity and Jerry Falwell's more austere Christian fundamentalism. Finally, the apparent public indifference to sexual scandals associated with President Bill Clinton convinced a number of religious media spokespersons that religiously motivated political activity was unlikely to be fruitful and that religious media programming should return to the basics of encouraging individual conversions and to providing guidance for the private lives of the audience for religious electronic media.

Internet

Finally, no description of the relationship between religion and the media would be complete without mention of the use of the Internet by organized groups with religious foci. A number of interest groups have established Web sites by which they can communicate with members and potential members. These Web sites exist at all points along the religious and political spectrum: Conservative groups such as the Christian Coalition, the American Center for Law and Justice, and Jimmy Swaggert Ministries have established Web sites where supporters are provided with information, propaganda, and the opportunity to purchase goods and services. Such Internet sources, which have their counterparts among organizations of the Christian left, such as Sojourners, Pax Christi, and Bread for the World, are also efficient sources of fundraising. The Internet is also a valuable resource for organizations that seek to limit the role of religion in American public life, such as the American Civil Liberties Union and People for the American Way.

Again, it is difficult to assess the political effects of such electronic communications. It seems most likely that the audience for religious Web sites (indeed, for most Web sites) is highly self-selected and therefore composed of people already positively predisposed toward the group's message and ideology. Such Web sites seem unlikely sources of persuasion, but they may be extremely effective at political mobilization of potential activists and at raising resources, such as money and memberships. Taken as a whole, such Web sites may increase the balkanization of American politics at the mass level and reduce the potential for interaction among citizens with diverse viewpoints in the United States.

See also *Christian Broadcasting Network; Robertson, Pat.*

REFERENCES

Frankl, Razelle. *Televangelism: The Marketing of Popular Religion.* Carbondale: Southern Illinois University Press, 1987.

Frankl, Razelle, and Jeffrey K. Hadden. "A Critical Review of the Religion and Television Report." *Review of Religious Research* 29 (1987): 111–124.

Hadden, Jeffrey K., and Charles E. Swan. *Prime Time Preachers: The Rising Power of Televangelism.* Reading, Mass.: Addison-Wesley, 1981.

Jelen, Ted G., and Clyde Wilcox. "Preaching to the Converted: The Causes and Consequences of Viewing Religious Television." In *Rediscovering the Impact of Religion on Political Behavior,* edited by David C. Leege and Lyman A. Kellstedt. Armonk, N.Y.: M. E. Sharpe, 1993.

Wilcox, Clyde. *God's Warriors: The Christian Right in Twentieth Century America.* Baltimore, Md.: Johns Hopkins University Press, 1992.

Wills, Garry. *Reagan's America: Innocents at Home.* Garden City, N.J.: Doubleday, 1987.

Reno v. American Civil Liberties Union (1997)

In *Reno v. American Civil Liberties Union* (1997), the Supreme Court ruled that the Communications Decency Act (CDA) violated the First Amendment. The American Civil Liberties Union (ACLU) and dozens of other plaintiffs had challenged two provisions of the CDA, Title V of the Telecommunications Act of 1996, shortly after the bill became law. Section 223(a) of the CDA made it illegal to knowingly transmit via the Internet obscene or indecent material to anyone under age eighteen. Section 223(d) made it illegal to send or display patently offensive material in a manner that would be available to anyone under the age of eighteen, thus requiring close monitoring and proof of age. A U.S. district court in Pennsylvania issued an injunction, and the case was appealed directly to the Supreme Court under a provision of the act.

The government argued for the constitutionality of the CDA based on precedents established by *Ginsberg v. New York* (1968), *FCC v. Pacifica Foundation* (1978), and *Renton v. Playtime Theatres* (1986). The justices disagreed. The CDA failed to meet the First Amendment test on the grounds of vagueness and all tests for limits on free speech. The act included such words as *indecent* and *patently offensive* without defining them. It failed to provide the requisite government interest required to regulate content, and it discriminated on the basis of content. While acknowledging the authority of Congress to regulate the Internet under the Commerce Clause, the Court also noted that the legislature could not regulate its content in such a broad manner. In addition it found the requirements placed on Internet providers and users to be unreasonable. The 7-2 decision was for the most part unanimous, with Chief Justice William Rehnquist and Justice Sandra Day O'Connor dissenting in part.

See also *Censorship; Federal Communications Commission v. Pacifica Foundation (1978); Obscenity and pornography.*

REFERENCES

Finkelman, Paul, and Melvin I. Urofsky. *Landmark Decisions of the United States Supreme Court.* Washington, D.C.: CQ Press, 2003.
Reno v. ACLU, 521 U.S. 844 (1997).
Vick, Douglas W. "The Internet and the First Amendment." *Modern Law Review* 61, no. 3 (May 1998): 414–421.
Volokh, Eugene. "Freedom of Speech, Shielding Children, and Transcending Balancing." *Supreme Court Review* (1997): 141–197.

Reporting events

Events are the raw materials of the news, and the primary way journalists represent reality is through reporting on events. Trained to recognize events that are particularly newsworthy, journalists report the "who, what, when, where, and why" of events to the public. Indeed, the bulk of the daily news consists of reports on "what happened today." Journalists, however, do more than simply report events. They imbue events with meaning(s) in the process of converting them into news. If events are to make sense and seem meaningful to their audiences, journalists must often define and interpret events in addition to reporting objective facts about them (a process known as framing).

Different sorts of events provide different raw materials for journalists to work with. One important distinction, noted by media sociologists Harvey Molotch and Marilyn Lester, is between "routine" and "accidental" news events. Routine news events, such as a president signing a bill in the White House Rose Garden or a candidate delivering a campaign trail speech, are preplanned by politicians and other elites in order to manage the news and communicate effectively with the public. Accidental events, in contrast, occur unexpectedly: tornadoes and earthquakes, oil carriers running aground, the sudden death of a high-profile politician or businessperson. Such events, some of which become "news icons," or symbols of larger issues or trends, are particularly interesting because they can allow journalists greater interpretive license and can stimulate public discussion of political and social issues. For example, W. Lance Bennett and Regina Lawrence note that as the infamous garbage barge *Mobro* wandered the seas in 1987 looking for a port that would accept its cargo, journalists cast it as an indicator of a looming garbage crisis, stimulating news coverage of trash, the culture of wastefulness, and recycling.

Scholars have debated the value of event-focused news. Some have critiqued the journalistic habit of focusing on particular events rather than on the underlying forces in society that give rise to the events. Political psychologist Shanto Iyengar has demonstrated that event-centered, "episodic" news can encourage the public to view social problems as personal problems that have personal, individualized solutions (1991). In contrast, a study of news spanning one hundred years, conducted by communications scholars Kevin Barnhurst and Diana Mutz, discovered that modern journalists routinely "supply a context of social problems, interpretation, and themes" as they report newsworthy events (1997, 27). Whatever its value, event-centered news will undoubtedly remain the norm in mainstream American journalism.

See also *Framing; Newsworthiness.*

REFERENCES

Barnhurst, Kevin G., and Diana Mutz. "American Journalism and the Decline of Event-centered Reporting." *Journal of Communication* 47, no. 4 (1997): 27–53.
Bennett, W. Lance, and Regina G. Lawrence. "News Icons and the Mainstreaming of Social Change." *Journal of Communication* 45, no. 3 (1995): 20–39.
Iyengar, Shanto. *Is Anyone Responsible? How Television Frames Political Issues.* Chicago: University of Chicago Press, 1991.
Molotch, Harvey, and Marilyn Lester. "News as Purposive Behavior: On the Strategic Use of Routine Events, Accidents, and Scandals." *American Sociological Review* 39 (1974): 101–112.

Reston, James B.

James Barrett Reston (1909–1995), also known as Scotty Reston, made his mark as an influential columnist, editor, and journalist who had great access to the powerful politicians of his time. As a child, he emigrated with his family from Scotland to the United States in 1920 and settled in Dayton, Ohio. He began his journalism career in 1932, as a reporter for the *Springfield* (Ohio) *Daily News.* He then held a few positions in public relations before becoming an Associated Press reporter in New York City in 1934. Reston worked from New York City until 1937, when he transferred to London for the Associated Press. As World War II approached, Reston joined the London bureau of the *New York Times* as a reporter, covering the early years of the war in Europe. In 1941 he moved to Washington, D.C., where he remained throughout the rest his career. He progressed through the ranks of the *Times* and, from 1968, added the title of co-publisher of the *Martha's Vineyard Gazette,* a position he maintained until 1991.

From his position with the *New York Times,* Reston became a noted columnist and an insider with the political establishment. Although his writing garnered readership and praise, his methods drew criticism. His extraordinary access to and influence with the political powers of the day enabled him to write with some authority on topics of politics and foreign affairs. His detractors accused him of being a mouthpiece and apologist for the government, which they claimed compromised his objectivity as a journalist, especially during the Vietnam War and the Watergate scandal in the early 1970s.

Reston received two Pulitzer Prizes for his reporting, one in 1945 and the other in 1957. In addition to an autobiography, *Deadline: A Memoir* (1991), he wrote numerous other books, including *Prelude to Victory* (1942), *The Artillery of the Press: Its Influence on American Foreign Policy* (1966), *Sherman's March and Vietnam* (1987), and *Warriors of God: Richard the Lionheart and Saladin in the Third Crusade* (2001).

REFERENCES

Alterman, Eric. *Sound and Fury: The Washington Punditocracy and the Collapse of American Politics.* New York: HarperCollins, 1992.

Herman, Edward S., and Richard B. DuBoff. *America's Vietnam Policy: The Strategy of Deception.* Washington, D.C.: Public Affairs Press, 1966.

Reston, James, Jr. *Deadline: A Memoir.* New York: Random House, 1991.

Stacks, John F. *Scotty: James B. Reston and the Rise and Fall of American Journalism.* New York: Little, Brown, 2003.

Richmond Newspapers, Inc. v. Virginia (1980)

In *Richmond Newspapers, Inc. v. Virginia* (1980), the Supreme Court held 7-1 that the press and public have a right under the First and Fourteenth Amendments to be present at criminal trials, barring an extraordinary overriding interest, such as a clear threat to a fair trial. The case arose from a criminal trial in which the defendant, John Paul Stevenson, had been charged with second-degree murder for the fourth time. Having had the first conviction reversed on appeal and two mistrials, the defendant's lawyer moved that the trial be closed to the press and public. The prosecution did not object, so the judge agreed to the request. Richmond Newspapers submitted a motion to vacate the closure order as a violation of the First and Fourteenth Amendments.

The Court had held in *Gannett v. DePasquale* (1979) that the Sixth Amendment does not guarantee the press and public an independent right to attend criminal *pretrial* proceedings. Chief Justice Warren Burger's opinion in *Richmond Newspapers* focused on the significance and tradition of open courts. He noted, "[I]t is important that society's criminal process 'satisfy the appearance of justice' ... by allowing people to observe it." The Court acknowledged that although the right to attend criminal trials is not enumerated in the Constitution or the Bill of Rights, it is implicit in the First Amendment's guaranteed freedoms of speech, press, and assembly.

See also *Gannett Co. v. DePasquale (1979); Right of access.*

REFERENCES

Gannett Co. v. DePasquale, 443 U.S. 368 (1979).

Gunther, Gerald. *Constitutional Law.* Westbury, N.Y.: Foundation Press, 1991.

Richmond Newspapers, Inc. v. Virginia, 448 U.S. 555 (1980).

Right of access

Right of access relates to the media's right to obtain government-held information, the media's right of access to attend trials, and an individual's right to express views in the press against the publisher's will.

In general, although the First Amendment expressly grants freedom "of the press" in addition to freedom "of speech," the media has no greater or lesser First Amendment rights than do members of the public. Although it is recognized that the press generally has a First Amendment right to publish information it obtains, it has no constitutional right to compel governmental assistance to obtain that information. Certain laws, such as the Freedom of Information Act of 1966 (FOIA), however, allow the media, as well as the general public, access to information in the government's possession.

In a similar fashion, the media possess no greater right to attend trials than does the general public. The Supreme Court in *Richmond Newspapers, Inc. v. Virginia* (1980), however, held that although the Constitution or the Bill of Rights does not enumerate or expressly grant the media or the public's right of access to trials, certain factors, such as "satisfying the appearance of justice," justify allowing access to criminal and perhaps even civil trials. The right of access is implied in the First Amendment's guaranteed freedom of speech, press, and assembly.

Whether private individuals have a right to express their views in the media depends on whether print or broadcast media are involved. In cases involving print media, such as *Miami Herald Pub. Co. v. Tornillo* (1974), the Supreme Court did not recognize a First Amendment right to have one's views published against a publisher's will. On the other hand, in broadcast media, the Court held that the First Amendment allows the public certain rights of access to the airwaves. The rationale is that there is potentially no limit to the number of newspapers and magazines that can publish the viewpoint, but radio and television spectrums are limited and "technologically scarce." Because of modern technological advances in cable and satellite television as well as Internet-based streaming video, however, this distinction has been criticized as being obsolete. In general, the public does not have unfettered access to the media, and what limited rights it does have with broadcast media arise only after a station has broadcast some information.

See also *Fairness doctrine; Freedom of Information Act of 1966; Red Lion Broadcasting Co., Inc. v. FCC (1969); Richmond Newspapers, Inc. v. Virginia (1980).*

REFERENCES

Miami Herald Pub. Co. v. Tornillo, 418 U.S. 241 (1974).
Red Lion Broadcasting Co., Inc. v. FCC, 395 U.S. 367 (1969).
Richmond Newspapers, Inc. v. Virginia, 448 U.S. 555 (1980).

Right-of-rebuttal rule

The right-of-rebuttal rule was a subsidiary of the fairness doctrine established by the Federal Communications Commission (FCC). The rule reflected FCC concerns, dating back to the late 1930s, that the media had an obligation to present balanced and fair broadcasting on public issues. It provided that television and radio broadcasts make airtime available for an individual, particularly a public figure or candidate for public office, attacked on air to defend him- or herself. Formalized and shaped by *Red Lion Broadcasting Company, Inc. v. FCC* (1969) and *Miami Herald Publishing v. Tornillo* (1974), the rule was abolished with *Meredith v. FCC* (1987).

Although the FCC had been outspoken about its "fairness" concerns for several decades before *Red Lion,* this case provided it legal backing. In 1969 the Red Lion Broadcasting Company broadcast a "Christian Crusade" program during which Fred J. Cook, an author, was attacked. Cook invoked the fairness doctrine, declaring that he had the right to defend himself. When Red Lion refused his request for airtime, the FCC stepped in. The dispute between the FCC and Red Lion made its way to the Supreme Court, which ruled in the FCC's favor.

The second major case, *Miami Herald Pub. Co. v. Tornillo,* provided that non-broadcast media are not obligated to print a rebuttal by a candidate should that candidate be attacked in print. The justification was that broadcast media use a scarce public resource—radio/TV frequencies. Given this scarcity, it was considered acceptable that the government step in to ensure fair use of the resource. The same did not, however, hold for the print media, which existed in abundance; the First Amendment also put it beyond government regulation of content. As the number of cable television channels increased, however, the broadcast scarcity argument lost its strength. In 1987 a federal appeals court ruled that the fairness doctrine was not law and that it could therefore be repealed. In response to a court order in *Meredith,* in 1987 the FCC abolished the fairness doctrine.

See also *Fairness doctrine; Red Lion Broadcasting Co., Inc. v. FCC (1969); Right of access.*

REFERENCES

Rowan, Ford. *Broadcast Fairness: Doctrine, Practice, Prospects. A Reappraisal of the Fairness Doctrine and Equal Time Rule.* New York: Longmans, 1984.
Simmons, Steven J. *The Fairness Doctrine and the Media.* Berkeley: University of California Press, 1978.

Robertson, Pat

Pat Robertson (1930–), born Marion Gordon Robertson, is the founder and chairman of the Christian Broadcasting Network (CBN). The son of Absalom Willis Robertson, a U.S. senator, Pat Robertson graduated from Washington and Lee University in 1950 and served in the Marine Corps during the Korean War (1950–1953). After military service, he earned a law degree in 1955 and a master of divinity degree in 1959. One year later he bought a bankrupt UHF television station in Portsmouth, Virginia, and established the Christian Broadcasting Network. In 1968 he created the *700 Club*, a religious-based talk show, which became the foundation and platform for his political activities. Ten years later Robertson formed Operation Blessing, CBN's humanitarian unit. At the same time, he also founded CBN University (now Regent University) and, in 1988, the Christian Coalition, a political education organization, with the purpose of promoting a conservative Christian agenda.

Robertson has skillfully developed and used various media instruments to attempt to persuade the public about political and religious causes he supports. In 1988 he made an unsuccessful attempt to win the Republican Party nomination for president. He has at times made controversial statements about issues and world leaders not to his liking. For example, in an August 2005 broadcast of the *700 Club*, Robertson appeared to be supporting the assassination of Venezuelan president Hugo Chavez. Among the numerous books that he has written are *The Secret Kingdom* (1982), *Beyond Reason* (1984), *America's Date with Destiny* (1986), *The New World Order* (1991), *The Turning Tide* (1993), and *Bring It On* (2002). He also wrote an autobiography (1988; revised 1995).

See also *Christian Broadcasting Network; Religion and the media*.

REFERENCES

Boston, Rob. *The Most Dangerous Man in America? Pat Robertson and the Rise of the Christian Coalition*. Amherst, N.Y.: Prometheus, 1996.

Donovan, John B. *Pat Robertson: The Authorized Biography*. New York: Macmillan, 1988.

Peck, Janice. *The Gods of Televangelism*. Cresskill, N.J.: Hampton, 1993.

Straub, Gerard Thomas. *Salvation for Sale: An Insider's View of Pat Robertson*. Buffalo, N.Y.: Prometheus, 1988.

Timmerman, David M., and Larry D. Smith. "The World According to Pat: The Telepolitical Celebrity as Purveyor of Political Medicine." *Political Communication* 11 (1994): 233–248.

Roll Call

Roll Call, founded by Sid Yudain in 1955, has established itself as a leading print and online publication on congressional information and news. It is published Monday through Thursday when Congress is in session and on Monday only when Congress is in recess. *Roll Call* is delivered free to all congressional offices and is sold by subscription to others. In addition to political news and information about Capitol Hill, it publishes opinion articles by Washington analysts such as Morton Kondracke, Donna Brazile, and Norman Ornstein. *Roll Call* also provides coverage of congressional elections in every state.

REFERENCE

Roll Call, www.rollcall.com.

Rollins, Ed

Edward J. Rollins Jr. (1943–) is a Republican political strategist, political commentator, and communications expert. He received graduate degrees in political science and public administration from California State University. He began his career in the California legislature, where he served in several positions, including assistant to the speaker of the California state assembly. He managed President Ronald Reagan's 1984 landslide reelection campaign and then served as assistant to the president and deputy chief of staff for political and governmental affairs before resigning in 1985. He also managed many other campaigns at the state, local, and national levels, including Ross Perot's 1992 run for the presidency.

Rollins founded and chairs the Rollins Strategy Group, a communications and crisis management firm with offices in New York City and Washington, D.C., that works for corporations, governments, and political candidates around the world. He continues his political consulting and broadcast commentary on various television programs. Rollins wrote a memoir, *Bare Knuckles and Back Rooms* (1996), an appropriate title reflective of his political style.

REFERENCE

Thompson, Clifford, ed. "Rollins, Edward J." *Current Biography Yearbook, 2001*. New York: H. W. Wilson, 2001.

Roosevelt, Franklin D.

Franklin Delano Roosevelt (1882–1945), often referred to as FDR, was the thirty-second president of the United States, taking over management of the country in 1933, when it was in the grips of the Great Depression. Roosevelt attended Harvard University, where he was editor of the campus newspaper and where he developed his appreciation for journalism. He married his cousin, Eleanor Roosevelt, in 1905, and entered Columbia Law School. Although he did not graduate from law school, he passed the bar examination and began his professional career as a clerk for a Wall Street law firm. Roosevelt had an early eye for politics, and his opportunity came in 1910, when he was nominated by the Democratic Party to run for the New York state senate. He won that race but was defeated in 1914 in a bid for a U.S. Senate seat.

Roosevelt was chosen in 1912, during the administration of President Woodrow Wilson, to be an assistant secretary of the U.S. Navy. James Cox selected him as his running mate in the 1920 presidential campaign; the Democratic ticket was soundly defeated by Republican Party candidate Warren G. Harding. While vacationing in Canada in 1921, Roosevelt contracted poliomyelitis, a common ailment of his time, and lost the use of his legs.

In 1928 presidential candidate Al Smith convinced Roosevelt to campaign for governor of New York; he was elected and served in that position until 1932. With the Great Depression running the nation deeper into economic and social turmoil, Roosevelt decided to run for president in the 1932 election. He received the Democratic nomination and was elected in a landslide. He encouraged the nation with his rhetoric—"The only thing we have to fear is fear itself"—and mobilized the government to resolve the economic crisis with policies that became known as the New Deal.

Roosevelt was the first president to take his message directly to the citizenry in a series of live national radio broadcasts that became known as fireside chats. These broadcasts, intended to explain his policies to the public and encourage them, served his purposes well during the economic recovery and looming war. Roosevelt was also the first president skilled in journalism and media relations, and he aggressively used the press to further his governmental policies and objectives. That Roosevelt had polio was largely concealed from the public. At his request, the media agreed

The media-savvy Franklin D. Roosevelt is considered to have instituted the modern presidential press conference. The press largely respected his request not to print photographs of him in a wheelchair.

not to print photographs of him in his wheelchair or with braces on his legs.

As war pressure mounted in Europe and Asia in 1937–1938, Roosevelt skirted the law to support U.S. allies. He broke with the tradition of his presidential predecessors, running for a third term and easily winning reelection, despite the concerns over an imminent war. Japan's surprise attack on American forces at Pearl Harbor, on December 7, 1941, decided the issue, and shortly thereafter the United States entered World War II. Roosevelt and British prime minister Winston Churchill shaped the course of the war, as well as postwar politics, including the creation of the United Nations.

The rigors of wartime leadership took its toll on Roosevelt's health. He was reelected for an unprecedented fourth term in 1944, when the war was nearing its conclusion but far from over. He died April 12, 1945, while recuperating in Warm Springs, Georgia. Roosevelt had a lasting effect on both the office of the presidency and how it was covered by the mass media, increasing the importance of the office both in the government and in the public mind.

See also *Fireside chats; Presidential press conferences; Radio.*

REFERENCES

Burns, James MacGregor. *Roosevelt: The Soldier of Freedom.* Norwalk, Conn.: Easton Press, 1989.

Cole, Wayne S. *Roosevelt and the Isolationists: 1932–45.* Lincoln: University of Nebraska Press, 1983.

Freidel, Frank Burt. *Franklin D. Roosevelt.* 4 vols. Boston: Little, Brown, 1952–1973.

Goldberg, Richard Thayer. *The Making of Franklin D. Roosevelt: Triumph over Disability.* Lanham, Md.: University Press of America, 1984.

Graham, Otis L., Jr., and Meghan Robinson Wander, eds. *Franklin D. Roosevelt: His Life and Times.* New York: Da Capo Press, 1990.

Israel, Fred L. *Franklin Delano Roosevelt.* New York: Chelsea House, 1985.

Kernell, Samuel. *Going Public: New Strategies of Presidential Leadership.* 4th ed. Washington, D.C.: CQ Press, 2007.

Morgan, Ted. *FDR: A Biography.* New York: Simon and Schuster, 1985.

Schlesinger, Arthur M., Jr. *The Age of Roosevelt.* 3 vols. Boston: Houghton Mifflin, 1957–1960.

Roth v. United States (1957)

In *Roth v. United States* (1957), the Supreme Court established the "community standard" test for determining obscenity. Sam Roth, a New York publisher, was convicted for distributing obscene books and advertising by mail. A companion case, *Alberts v. California* (1957), also dealt with a state obscenity statute. The Court's decision upheld the convictions of Roth and Alberts by a 7–2 vote.

Although tightening the standards for what could be defined as obscene, the Court held such material to fall outside First Amendment protection because it had been historically viewed as being "without redeeming social value." It defined obscenity as "material which deals with sex in a manner appealing to prurient interest." According to the Court's new "community standards" test, material would be deemed obscene based on "whether to the average person, applying contemporary community standards, the dominant theme of the material taken as a whole appeals to the prurient interest." Justices Hugo Black and William O. Douglas dissented, arguing that under the First Amendment, the government should have no control over content. The *Roth* test, with refinement, remains the basis of contemporary obscenity law in the United States, though *Roth* itself was superseded by the more detailed three-pronged test set out in *Miller v. California* (1973).

See also *Censorship; Memoirs v. Massachusetts (1966); Miller v. California (1973); Obscenity and pornography.*

REFERENCES

Alberts v. California, 354 U.S. 476 (1957).

Elias, James, et al., eds. *Porn 101: Eroticism, Pornography and the First Amendment.* Amherst, N.Y.: Prometheus Books, 1999.

Hixson, Richard F. *Pornography and the Justices: The Supreme Court and the Intractable Obscenity Problem.* Carbondale: Southern Illinois University Press, 1996.

Roth v. United States, 354 U.S. 476 (1957).

Rusher, William

William A. Rusher (1923–) built a career as a publisher, author, and columnist. He graduated from Princeton University and served in the Army Air Corps during World War II. After graduating from Harvard Law School, he began his career as a Wall Street litigation lawyer and served as associate counsel to the U.S. Senate's Internal Security Subcommittee from 1956 to 1957. Rusher was the publisher of William F. Buckley's *National Review* magazine for thirty years, from its founding in 1957 until 1988. He wrote *The Coming Battle for the Media: Curbing the Power of the Media Elite* (1988) as a demonstration of what he perceived as the liberal philosophical bias of the media in general, as well as a call for conservatives to counter the alleged strident anticonservatism of the media establishment. In the book, Rusher also criticized the Supreme Court for broadening the media's First Amendment rights.

As a syndicated columnist, Rusher wrote opinion essays that appeared in some 250 newspapers nationwide, and his radio commentaries were broadcast on the Associated Press Radio Network. He is a distinguished fellow at the Claremont Institute in Claremont, California. Rusher's writings include *Special Counsel* (1968), *The Making of the New Majority Party* (1975), *How to Win Arguments* (1981), *The Meaning of Taiwan* (1989), and *The Rise of the Right.*

See also *National Review.*

REFERENCE

Rusher, William A. *The Rise of the Right.* New York: National Review Books, 1993.

Schoenwald, Jonathan. *A Time for Choosing: The Rise of Modern Conservatism.* New York: Oxford University Press, 2002.

S

Safire, William

William L. "Bill" Safire (1929–) is a Pulitzer Prize–winning political columnist, journalist, author, and historian. Safire attended Syracuse University for two years before taking a job as a copy boy at the *New York Herald Tribune*. He served in the U.S. Army as a public relations specialist during the Korean War.

In 1959, while representing a household products firm in Moscow, Safire helped to arrange the famous "kitchen debate" between Vice President Richard Nixon and Soviet Premier Nikita Khrushchev. He acted as chief of special projects for Nixon's 1960 presidential bid, worked for several Republican Party candidates in New York City and State, and supervised public relations for Nelson Rockefeller's 1964 presidential campaign. He also started his own public relations company in 1961.

In 1965 Safire began collaborating with Patrick Buchanan as an unpaid speechwriter for Nixon. He wrote Nixon's 1968 victory speech, then sold his company and joined Nixon's White House staff as an advisor and speechwriter. During his tenure, Safire crafted the words of explanation for public policy during the Vietnam War and coined Vice President Spiro Agnew's famous description of the liberal media, "nattering nabobs of negativism."

Leaving the White House prior to the Watergate scandal, Safire joined the *New York Times* editorial staff in 1973, penning a political column as well as a separate Sunday commentary on English usage, called "On Language." He was awarded the Pulitzer Prize for distinguished commentary in 1978, and, until his retirement in 2005, his words and insight carried considerable weight and influence among politicians, pundits, and readers. Safire continues to write, and he serves as chairman of the Dana Foundation. His numerous books include *Before the Fall: An Inside View of the Pre-Watergate White House* (1975), *Safire's Washington* (1980), *Take My Word for It* (1986), *The First Dissident* (1992), and *No Uncertain Terms* (2003), as well as several historical novels.

See also *Agnew, Spiro T.; Nixon, Richard M.*

REFERENCES

Alter, Jonathan. "Where There's Smoke, There's Safire." *Newsweek,* January 31, 1994, 41.
Jaffe, Harry. "No Bull Bill." *Washingtonian,* August 2003, 32–35ff.
Massie, Robert K. "Safire and Me." *Nation,* February 14, 1994, 184–185.
Pinker, Steven. "Grammar Puss." *New Republic,* January 31, 1994, 19–26.
Secules, S. "The Rise of the Conservative Voice." *Columbia Journalism Review* 40, no. 4 (November–December 2001): 84–85.

Salinger, Pierre

Pierre Emil George Salinger (1925–2004) was a journalist, author, White House press secretary, and expatriate political commentator. Salinger began his journalism career on the editorial staff of the *San Francisco Chronicle* in 1942 but soon enlisted in the navy and served in the Pacific theater during World War II.

In 1959 Salinger joined John F. Kennedy's presidential campaign, was later appointed White House press secretary, and served through Kennedy's assassination and President

Lyndon Johnson's accession administration. When Senator Claire Engle of California died in office in 1964, Salinger resigned from the White House staff and was appointed by Governor Edmund G. (Pat) Brown to fill the seat; when he stood for election in his own right, however, he lost. He later worked on Robert F. Kennedy's 1968 presidential campaign.

Moving to Paris, Salinger became a correspondent for the French news magazine *L'Express* before being appointed Paris bureau chief in 1978 and chief European correspondent for ABC News in 1983. He created considerable international controversy by making accusations of governmental conspiracy in the cases of two airline disasters, Pan Am Flight 103 (1988) and TWA Flight 800 (1996), and by offering an exposé of a purported Arabic transcript of a conversation between Saddam Hussein and U.S. ambassador to Iraq April Glaspie, who was allegedly "green lighting" the Iraqi invasion of Kuwait (1990)—a report that his own network initially refused to broadcast. His involvement in these controversies and his prominence as a journalist created a new term, "Pierre Salinger syndrome," describing Internet users who assume the accuracy of information distributed on the Web.

Salinger endured the criticism of journalistic colleagues and serious friction at ABC News, and with the support of his friend, Roone Arledge, he resigned from the network in 1993. Salinger wrote *With Kennedy* (1966), *Secret Dossier: The Hidden Agenda behind the Gulf War* (1991), *P.S., A Memoir* (1995), and *John F. Kennedy, Commander in Chief: A Profile in Leadership* (2000).

See also *Press secretaries.*

REFERENCES

"Au Revoir, Pierre." *Time,* December 18, 1964, 26.
Evans, D. "Salinger's Flight 800 Theory Draws Flak." *American Journalism Review* 19 (January–February 1997): 10.
McGrory, Mary. "Departure of Picturesque Pierre." *America,* April 4, 1964, 474.
Salinger, Pierre. *P.S., A Memoir.* New York: St. Martin's Press, 1995.

Sarnoff, David

David Sarnoff (1891–1971) was a pioneering radio and television executive, who instigated, stimulated, and supervised the burgeoning of radio, television, and electronics as information and entertainment media. In 1908 Sarnoff joined the Marconi Wireless Telegraph Company, where he became a junior operator. Working the night of the *Titanic* disaster, he collected the news details. Sarnoff advanced within Marconi and advocated a "radio music box" for public use. In 1919 General Electric formed Radio Corporation of America (RCA) to absorb Marconi's U.S. assets, and in 1921 Sarnoff convinced RCA to broadcast the Dempsey-Carpentier prizefight to demonstrate the potential demand for radio.

As general manager of RCA, Sarnoff formed the National Broadcasting Company (NBC)—the first radio network—in 1926. He became RCA president in 1930, introduced television broadcasting in 1939, and predicted that television would become an important factor in American economic life. During World War II, Sarnoff served as a communications consultant for General Dwight Eisenhower, who later made him a brigadier general. Known as "the General" within RCA, he became CEO of the company in 1947 and remained in that position until he retired in 1970.

See also *NBC Universal.*

REFERENCES

Bilby, Kenneth M. *The General: David Sarnoff and the Rise of the Communications Industry.* New York: Harper and Row, 1986.
Lyons, Eugene. *David Sarnoff: A Biography.* New York: Harper and Row, 1966.
Sobel, Robert. *RCA.* New York: Stein and Day Publishers, 1986.

Sawyer, Diane

Lila Diana Sawyer (1945–) is a broadcast journalist for ABC News, where she serves as co-anchor of *Good Morning America* and fills in as anchor on *World News Tonight.* In the 1970s she worked for White House press secretary Ron Ziegler in the Nixon administration. Hired by CBS News as a political correspondent in 1978, Sawyer was named co-anchor of the *CBS Morning News* in 1981. Three years later, she became a correspondent for the Sunday evening news magazine, *60 Minutes.* In 1989 she joined ABC News to co-anchor *Primetime Live.*

Sawyer gained a reputation as an enterprising reporter who is capable of producing excellent television journalism, such as her story on the treatment of women by the Taliban in Afghanistan, broadcast in 1996. Her notable interviews have included conversations with former defense secretary Robert McNamara, who apologized for his role in the Vietnam War; Panamanian president Manuel Noriega (in prison after his overthrow); and comedian Ellen DeGeneres, who announced her homosexuality.

REFERENCES

ABC News, http://abcnews.go.com/GMA/News/story?id=128165.

Gordon, Meryl. "Duel at Sunrise New York." *New York,* June 6, 2005, 22.

Scandal

The rise of 24/7 cable news programs and the Internet have created a blossoming of scandal coverage in recent years, intensifying the mainstream media's trend of increasing personal coverage of public figures in the aftermath of Watergate and Vietnam. The scandals of the 1960s and 1970s convinced many journalists that reporting on the character of political figures is an important public service, but the recent coverage trends harken back as well to the mudslinging, partisan press of the early nineteenth century.

At a televised news conference in January 1998, an apparently earnest President Bill Clinton uttered the defining sound bite of the Monica Lewinsky scandal: "I did not have sexual relations with that woman, Miss Lewinsky." Mr. Clinton's denial came a quarter of a century after a 1973 news conference in which a similarly embattled President Richard M. Nixon tried to stave off impeachment proceedings over the Watergate scandal with an equally memorable assertion: "I am not a crook."

The differences between the Watergate and "Monicagate" scandals are often cited to illustrate the debasement of our media-driven political culture. The former was concerned with grave matters of political corruption, the latter with salacious details of an extramarital affair. Watergate showed how intrepid investigative reporters could trace wrongdoing to the highest levels of government, and how televised hearings could let viewers everywhere follow the process of discovery. By contrast, the Lewinsky scandal came to represent much of what the public dislikes about the media—a rush to judgment spurred by competition, a reliance on leaked information and unnamed sources, and feeding frenzies by packs of reporters stalking a story at any

Newspapers trumpet President Bill Clinton's August 18, 1998, admission of his relationship with former White House intern Monica Lewinsky. The intense press coverage of the scandal highlighted the evolution of the media's relationship with top political figures from the days of President John F. Kennedy, whose alleged affairs the media did not report, to today's focus on the personal lives of politicians.

cost. Nonetheless, today's culture of scandal in political discourse can be traced back to Watergate and its aftermath in the 1970s.

To be sure, the idea of aggressive and partisan scandal reporting is as old as the Republic. The intensely partisan press of the early 1800s delighted in personal attacks on leading political figures, and battles between the first political parties were waged by means of partisan newspapers often called "scandal sheets." For example, in those years, Federalist-leaning papers spread allegations that Thomas Jefferson had attempted to seduce a neighbor's wife and kept a slave as a concubine. On a more elevated plane, the United States has a rich tradition of watchdog journalism that exposes abuses by the rich and powerful. Revelations about political and financial wrongdoing during the Progressive era of the early twentieth century helped reformers break up corporate monopolies, pass laws to reduce the influence of money in politics, and increase government regulation of food and drugs. This, however, was also the era of "yellow" journalism, in which tabloid newspapers built circulation with sensationalistic exposés and editorial crusades that sometimes bore little relation to the facts.

For much of the twentieth century, though, the news media shielded citizens from the personal foibles and human limitations of their political leaders. Mental and physical health issues were among the topics rarely broached. For example, a whole generation of reporters and photographers hid the nature and extent of Franklin D. Roosevelt's physical disability. Roosevelt lost the use of his legs after a bout of polio long before becoming president, but pictures showing his wheelchair were almost never published. In addition, his obvious physical deterioration was not widely reported prior to his death in office in 1945.

Other media cover-ups of personal matters that could have become White House scandals range from Grover Cleveland's secret operation for life-threatening jaw cancer in 1893 to Woodrow Wilson's extended incapacity to govern following a stroke in 1919, and Warren G. Harding's frequent womanizing in the White House during the early 1920s. More recently, John F. Kennedy's reckless dalliances—including a relationship with the girlfriend of an organized crime boss—were kept from the public despite the serious risk of blackmail and the extensive use of public funds, facilities, and personnel to facilitate his liaisons. It now appears that Kennedy's carefully cultivated image of physical vigor also masked serious health problems that were kept from the public. Nonetheless, presidents and lesser political figures were protected by a kind of "gentleman's agreement" that their private shortcomings would not be reported unless they seriously affected the conduct of their public duties.

All this changed in the wake of the Vietnam War and the Watergate scandal, when the political failures of Lyndon B. Johnson and Richard Nixon were traced in significant measure to flaws in personal character. By failing to report on personal matters that illuminate character and judgment, critics argued, reporters denied voters the information they needed to assess their political leaders properly. At a time of rapid social change and polarized politics, many journalists welcomed the opportunity to engage in more aggressive reporting. The story of the *Washington Post* investigation that helped to bring down the Nixon administration—and inspired both a best-selling book and a hit film—encouraged a generation of young reporters to try to become the next Bob Woodward or Carl Bernstein.

After Nixon resigned to avoid impeachment in 1974, a new generation of reformers descended on Washington, determined to elevate ethical standards in government. New ethics laws, public interest groups, congressional investigating committees, and special prosecutors all aimed to ferret out official wrongdoing. They were aided by an emboldened press, fresh from its Watergate victory and looking for new targets. Ironically, the better the system worked, the more skeptical the public became about government. As officials ran afoul of new ethics rules, scandal news proliferated, and it seemed to the public that ethical standards in government must be worse than ever.

Moreover, political battles were increasingly fought through the courts and the media, as politicians and interest groups learned to use the new scandal machinery to discredit their opponents. Even a failed ethics complaint guaranteed bad publicity for its target. Suzanne Garment describes this phenomenon as a "self-reinforcing scandal machine," whereby politicians learned to use scandals as politics by other means. For example, in 1987 Republican Newt Gingrich initiated ethics charges against Democratic Speaker of the House Jim Wright as a means of forcing Wright's resignation. Gingrich's success led to a kind of arms war of escalating ethics charges in Congress, as both parties searched for charges that would discredit members of the opposition. (The circle was completed in 1997, when then-Speaker Gingrich was himself gravely weakened by an ethics inquiry and resigned a year later.)

For journalists, the temptation was great to confuse the public interest with a personal interest in professional advancement; they seemed less likely to win promotions by dispassionate reporting than by bringing down powerful public figures. A wide variety of scholars have observed the pattern of greatly increased coverage of personal scandals since Watergate—a trend that has profoundly soured relations between journalists and politicians. *Washington Monthly* editor Charles Peters argues that the real journalistic lesson of Watergate was the importance of digging for information, but the lesson many political reporters took from it was to act tough. Also, where Woodward and Bernstein worked alone, the next generation of journalists developed a tendency to pile on. Larry Sabato coined the term "feeding frenzy" to describe those stories on "embarrassing or scandalous subjects" that attract a critical mass of journalists who pursue them "intensely, often excessively, and sometimes uncontrollably."

This aggressive stance served the public well in times of serious scandals, such as Watergate and Iran-*contra,* in which the Reagan administration illegally sold arms to Iran and used the proceeds to fund U.S.–backed forces fighting in Nicaragua. It also, however, led to heavy coverage of unfounded rumors on such topics as 1988 presidential candidate Michael Dukakis's mental health and 1984 vice presidential candidate Geraldine Ferraro's family ties to Mafia figures. In 1987 the scandal machinery took a great leap forward when a newspaper staked out the townhouse of Gary Hart, the front-runner for the Democratic presidential nomination, apparently in response to the candidate's challenge to the media mob that it substantiate any of the ethical lapses previously rumored about him. The subsequent report that he had spent the night with a young model then set off a feeding frenzy that destroyed the married Hart's political career and led a reporter to publicly ask the previously unthinkable question: "Have you ever committed adultery?" (Hart refused to answer.)

The Hart affair merged the high-minded rationale of the ethics watchdogs with the sensationalistic practices of the tabloids, and it opened the floodgates for media inquiries into the private lives of public figures. The headlines and airwaves were soon deluged with allegations about politicians' current and past extramarital affairs, illegitimate children, sexual orientations, mental health, and alcohol and drug use, as well as the foibles of their spouses and children. Some of the allegations proved false or were blown out of proportion, while others brought to light behavior that was clearly inappropriate, and the threat of exposure doubtless served as a deterrent to future instances.

However useful or titillating such revelations, the public has shown little gratitude to the messengers. Polls show that the increase in scandal reporting, and the Clinton scandals in particular, fed into the public's growing disillusionment with the press. For example, a 1998–1999 Pew Research Center survey found that 72 percent of the public believed that the media were more interested in creating controversy than in reporting the news on such stories, and 39 percent—up from 17 percent in a 1985 poll—thought that press criticism was keeping political leaders from doing their jobs. Simultaneously, media critics stepped up their complaints about the "gotcha" journalism practiced by a prosecutorial press. Sabato even put forth a "fairness doctrine" that spelled out which aspects of a public figure's private life should be fair game for press coverage; with some exceptions, it echoed the old rule of thumb that politicians deserve a sphere of privacy so long as their personal peccadilloes do not interfere with their public duties.

The problem is not only that there are no clear rules anymore, but that there is no longer anyone to enforce them. The rapidly growing scope of scandal news reflects a dramatic expansion of the media landscape since the 1990s, when the dominance of a few national print outlets, the three broadcast networks, and CNN was challenged by talk radio, new cable news competitors (led by the Fox News Channel), and a host of Internet Web sites and Web logs. The new media brought a more freewheeling and argumentative style, as well as more populist and partisan perspectives, to the news. They also brought the capacity to report 24 hours a day, 7 days a week—as well as the need to have something to report on. Gradually, the working definition of news expanded to fit the time that needed to be filled. Cable news and talk radio specialized in chat, commentary, and blockbuster stories that could be treated as ongoing soap operas, bringing audiences back day after day to learn the latest developments.

The competition to report the latest developments grew more furious than ever, as print and broadcast television journalists faced competitors with continuous instant access to audiences. This so-called 24-hour news cycle inevitably led journalists to cut corners in checking out stories for fear that they would be scooped by those with fewer scruples. The most notorious example of this destructive dynamic occurred when Internet gossip Matt Drudge broke the news of the Lewinsky scandal. *Newsweek* had the story but was holding it back while verifying the facts. Then someone leaked it to Drudge, who posted it on his Web site, setting off a sequence of events that would turn both him and Monica Lewinsky into household names.

If Drudge's rapid-fire online reporting helped to set the tone for the unfiltered and sometimes inaccurate information increasingly featured in scandal news, the 2004 presidential election campaign showed that this culture of scandal has become a fixture in national politics. From the attacks by Swift Boat Veterans for Truth on John Kerry to the controversy over George W. Bush's National Guard service, the campaign headline mongering demonstrated that the "new media" have made the echo chamber louder than ever.

While scholars agree that coverage of political scandals has become more pervasive and more negative, they disagree about the impact on the political system. Some argue that coverage encourages public cynicism, which drives down support for government as well as voter turnout and discourages capable people from running for office. In addition, scandal coverage pushes other important issues off the public agenda. Others believe that media negativity has little public consequence, particularly for presidents, who enjoy substantial public relations powers and command public support that is often resistant to scandal reports. For example, Bill Clinton's public approval numbers were higher after he was impeached by the House than they had been a year earlier, before the Lewinsky scandal came to light. Further, scandal coverage can help voters to evaluate a candidate's fitness for office and can discourage potential candidates who have good reason to fear greater public scrutiny.

Whatever one thinks of it, the rise of aggressive and partisan news sources online and elsewhere seems likely to increase scandal coverage in the near future. The new media allow whispered stories to remain alive until they attract the attention of the mainstream news outlets. Stories may live longer than ever, and unsubstantiated allegations may get more attention as media outlets loosen their standards and "race to the bottom" in order to be first in this highly competitive industry.

See also *Media feeding frenzies; New media.*

REFERENCES

Cappella, Joseph N., and Kathleen Hall Jamieson. *Spiral of Cynicism: The Press and the Public Good.* New York: Oxford University Press, 1997.

Davis, Richard, and Diana Owen. *New Media and American Politics.* New York: Oxford University Press, 1998.

Farnsworth, Stephen J., and S. R. Lichter. *The Mediated Presidency: Television News and Presidential Governance, 1981–2004.* Lanham, Md.: Rowman and Littlefield, 2006.

Garment, Suzanne. *Scandal: The Culture of Mistrust in American Politics.* New York: Times Books, 1991.

Kalb, Marvin. *One Scandalous Story: Clinton, Lewinsky, and 13 Days That Tarnished American Journalism.* New York: Free Press, 2001.

Kovach, Bill, and Tom Rosenstiel. *Warp Speed: America in the Age of Mixed Media.* New York: Century Foundation, 1999.

Pfiffner, James P. *The Character Factor: How We Judge America's Presidents.* College Station: Texas A & M University Press, 2004.

Sabato, Larry. *Feeding Frenzy: How Attack Journalism Has Transformed American Politics.* New York: Free Press, 1991.

Sabato, Larry, Mark Stencel, and S. Robert Lichter. *Peepshow: Media and Politics in an Age of Scandal.* Lanham, Md.: Rowman and Littlefield, 2000.

Seib, Philip. *Going Live: Getting the News Right in a Real-Time, Online World.* Lanham, Md.: Rowman and Littlefield, 2001.

Schieffer, Bob

Robert Schieffer (1937–) has been a broadcast journalist with CBS News since 1969, serving as chief Washington correspondent and host of the Sunday morning public affairs program *Face the Nation.* In March of 2005, he was appointed interim anchor of the *CBS Evening News,* succeeding Dan Rather. Although he was to surrender the anchor chair to Katie Couric in 2006, CBS was pleasantly surprised to see that the *CBS Evening News's* ratings increased when the friendly, folksy Schieffer took over.

Like his predecessor (Rather), Schieffer had worked in Texas journalism—though in his case, for the *Fort Worth Star-Telegram*—and had covered the Kennedy assassination in 1963. As a television news correspondent, Schieffer reported on the White House, Congress, the Pentagon, and the State Department, and he has covered every presidential campaign since 1972. Despite the fact that his brother, Thomas, is a former business partner of George W. Bush, both the president and Massachusetts senator John Kerry believed Schieffer to be a fair and objective journalist, and they selected him to moderate their third debate of the presidential election campaign, on October 13, 2004.

REFERENCES

CNN, http://edition.cnn.com/TRANSCRIPTS/0410/28/lkl.01.html.

Schieffer, Bob. *This Just In: What I Couldn't Tell You on TV.* New York: G. P. Putnam's Sons, 2003.

Schorr, Daniel

Daniel Louis Schorr (1916–) is a journalist, broadcaster, and commentator. Having served in U.S. Army Intelligence during World War II, Schorr began his journalism career as a foreign correspondent in Europe for the *Christian Science Monitor* in 1946 and later worked for the *New York Times.* Covering a disastrous dike breach and flood in the Netherlands in 1953, Schorr attracted the attention of Edward R. Murrow, who convinced him to join CBS News as a diplomatic correspondent in Washington, D.C.

Schorr's political coverage has spanned five decades, from the communist witch hunt conducted by Senator Joseph McCarthy in the 1950s to the impeachment of President Bill Clinton in the late 1990s. While covering the Watergate scandal for CBS from 1972 to 1973, he found himself No. 17 on President Richard Nixon's "enemies" list. When he refused to divulge sources for his reporting on freedom of the press grounds, he was investigated by the House Ethics Committee, which threatened him with contempt charges. CBS suspended him. After he was cleared, CBS asked him to return to broadcasting, but he refused and resigned in 1976. Schorr wrote of his experience in the tense affair in *Clearing the Air* (1977).

In 1979 Ted Turner asked Schorr to help him form the Cable News Network, and he served as the network's senior Washington correspondent until he resigned in a dispute over his editorial independence in 1985. Schorr continues to work as a commentator for National Public Radio. His memoir is *Staying Tuned: A Life in Journalism* (2001).

See also *CNN; First Amendment; Murrow, Edward R.; Watergate.*

REFERENCES

"The Case of Daniel Schorr." *America,* November 27, 1971, 445–446.

Powers, Thomas. "Schorr and a Free Press." *Commonweal,* April 9, 1976, 241–243.

Schorr, Daniel. "A Chilling Experience—The White House, the FBI, and Me." *Harper's Magazine,* March 1973, 92–97.

Steinfels, Peter. "The Schorr Witchhunt." *Commonweal,* March 26, 1976, 198–199ff.

"Suppressing the Newsman." Editorial. *Nation,* March 6, 1979, 260–261.

Waters, Harry F., with Tom Joyce. "What Makes Danny Run?" *Newsweek,* February 23, 1979, 49.

Scripps, E. W.

Edward Willis Scripps (1854–1926) was a journalist and newspaper entrepreneur, who founded both the Scripps newspaper chain and the United Press International (UPI). Scripps began running the family farm in 1869, and then tried being a school teacher, a druggist, and a window stenciler before beginning his journalism career in 1873, working for his half-brother James E. Scripps at the *Detroit Tribune* and at the *Detroit Evening News.* Having proved his ability there by increasing circulation and writing editorials, Edward Scripps founded, edited, and published the Cleveland *Penny Press* with financial support from his brothers in 1878. Once that newspaper was well-established, he tried to grow the *St. Louis Evening Chronicle* in the face of strong competition from Joseph Pulitzer's *Post-Dispatch.* Next, he moved to Cincinnati to edit the *Post* and joined with Milton McRae, an advertising manager, to expand their newspaper business.

In 1888 he formed the Scripps League—a collection of the Scripps family's four newspapers. However, disputes with James mounted until 1890, when the two brothers split for good; James retained the Detroit papers, while Edward Scripps built his estate, Miramar, north of San Diego and formed the Scripps-McRae League. By 1895, he began growing the newspaper chain, founding thirty-two newspapers and acquiring fifteen others.

Scripps established the Newspaper Enterprise Association (NEA) in 1902 to supply his newspapers and other subscribers with news stories and editorial material. In 1907 he founded the United Press Association—which eventually became United Press International (UPI)—as an independent news gathering service whose main competitor is the Associated Press (AP). He also created Science Service to provide science news for newspapers. The Scripps Howard News Service replaced the Scripps-McRae League in 1922.

See also *Penny press; United Press International.*

REFERENCES

Baldasty, Gerald J. *E. W. Scripps and the Business of Newspapers (The History of Communication).* Urbana and Chicago: University of Illinois Press, 1999.

Gardner, Gilson. *Lusty Scripps: The Life of E. W. Scripps.* New York: Vanguard Press, 1932.

Preece, Charles O. *Edward Willis and Ellen Browning Scripps: An Unmatched Pair.* Chelsea, Mich.: Bookcrafters, 1990.

Trimble, Vance H. *The Astonishing Mr. Scripps: The Turbulent Life of America's Penny Press Lord.* Ames: Iowa State University Press, 1992.

Sedition Act of 1918

In the midst of World War I, Congress passed the Sedition Act of 1918, imposing severe penalties on anyone who hindered the war effort by making false statements, obstructing enlistments, or speaking against the production of war materials, the U.S. system of government, the Constitution, or the flag. Eugene V. Debs, an American socialist, union organizer, and presidential candidate, received a ten-year prison sentence for violating this law when he spoke to a crowd gathered at a socialist antiwar rally in Canton, Ohio, in that same year. The Supreme Court unanimously

During World War I, American Socialist Party leader Eugene V. Debs, a pacifist, was convicted under the Sedition Act of 1918 for inciting subordination, disloyalty, mutiny, and obstructing recruitment in speaking out against war. The Supreme Court upheld his conviction. President Warren G. Harding pardoned him in 1921.

reaffirmed his conviction in *Debs v. United States* (1919), and President Woodrow Wilson rejected all appeals that he pardon Debs. In 1921 President Warren Harding, who had made a campaign pledge to grant amnesty for deserving antiwar advocates, freed Debs and commuted his sentence as a Christmas-time goodwill gesture.

The Sedition Act, an amendment to the Espionage Act of 1917, raised the question of what forms of speech the government could prohibit. The standard was set by Justice Oliver Wendell Holmes in his dissenting opinion in *Schenck v. United States* (1919), which established what became known as the "clear and present danger" doctrine. Holmes objected to government attempts to stifle critics of its policies, and his dissent would inspire a long struggle in the courts to strengthen constitutional protections for free speech and a free press.

REFERENCES

Debs v. United States, 249 U.S. 211 (1919).

Schenck v. United States, 249 U.S. 47 (1919).

Stone, Geoffrey R. *Perilous Times: Free Speech in Wartime from the Sedition Act of 1798 to the War on Terrorism.* New York: W. W. Norton, 2004.

Sevareid, Eric

Arnold Eric Sevareid (1912–1992) was a radio and television broadcast journalist whose idiosyncratic style of commentary became a staple of television news in his later years. Sevareid began his journalism career as a teenage copy boy for the *Minneapolis Journal* and worked as a freelancer for the *Minneapolis Star* during college. He became a reporter for the Paris edition of the *New York Herald Tribune* in 1938. Edward R. Murrow recruited Sevareid in 1939 to join CBS radio as one of "Murrow's Boys" to cover the war in Europe. He traveled with the French army and air force during the Battle of France, becoming the first American to report the French capitulation to Germany. Sevareid moved to the CBS News bureau in Washington, D.C., in 1941, and then served as a war correspondent in China from 1943 to 1944 and in London in 1945.

After the war, he returned to Washington as the bureau chief, and he went on to provide commentary alongside Walter Cronkite on the *CBS Evening News* from 1963 until his retirement in 1977. Sevareid's commentaries were either "praised as lucid and illuminating, or criticized for sounding profound without ever reaching a conclusive point," and the latter tendency gained him the nickname "Eric Severalsides." Sevareid wrote *Not So Wild a Dream* (1946), *In One Ear* (1952), and *This Is Eric Sevareid* (1964).

See also *Cronkite, Walter; Murrow, Edward R.*

Eric Sevareid, one of the "Murrow Boys," was the first American journalist to report on the fall of Paris to the Germans during World War II.

REFERENCES

Gates, Gary Paul. *Air Time: The Inside Story of CBS News.* New York: Harper and Row, 1978.

Schroth, Raymond A. *The American Journey of Eric Sevareid.* South Royalton, Vt.: Steerforth, 1995.

Shaw, Bernard

Bernard Shaw (1940–) is a broadcast journalist, and the first African American to hold a network anchor post. Shaw served as a marine before attending the University of Illinois-Chicago, where he began his journalism career at WNUS in Chicago in 1965, while attending college. Shaw worked for the Westinghouse Broadcasting Company as a White House reporter from 1968 to 1971, for CBS News as a reporter from 1971 to 1977, and then for ABC News from 1977 to 1979. He joined Ted Turner's fledgling Cable News Network as an anchor in 1980, becoming a regular anchor/moderator of CNN's *The International Hour, The World Today,* and *Inside Politics.*

While moderating a 1988 presidential debate between candidates George H. W. Bush and Michael Dukakis, Shaw asked the Massachusetts governor if he would change his mind about opposing the death penalty if his own wife were raped and killed. Caught off-guard, Dukakis offered a legalistic response that was widely viewed as weak and unemotional, thereby seriously hurting his campaign. In 1989 Shaw broadcast live coverage of the Tiananmen Square uprising in China, until the government shut down the CNN telecast. In 1991, along with two other colleagues, Shaw reported live from Baghdad during the air offensive of Operation Desert Storm. Shaw retired in 2001, although he continues to provide on occasional commentary for CNN.

See also *CNN.*

REFERENCES

Whittemore, Hank. *CNN, the Inside Story.* Boston: Little, Brown, 1990.

Wiener, Robert. *Live from Baghdad: Gathering News at Ground Zero.* New York: Doubleday, 1992.

Sheppard v. Maxwell (1966)

In *Sheppard v. Maxwell* (1966), the Supreme Court concluded that extensive, pretrial media coverage could unconstitutionally interfere with a defendant's right to a fair trial. After a jury found Dr. Sam Sheppard guilty of murdering his wife in 1954, he appealed to the Supreme Court, arguing that pretrial publicity had prejudiced the jury pool. The Court's decision, agreeing with Sheppard, cited numerous cases of sensational headlines and a newspaper article identifying all seventy-five potential jurors.

Although the Court was reluctant to place restrictions on the press, it reasoned that "legal trials are not like elections" and that the need for public discussion must be balanced against the need for "fair and orderly administration of justice." It concluded that "where there is a reasonable likelihood that prejudicial news ... will prevent a fair trial, the [trial] judge should continue [delay] the case until the threat abates." In addition, the Court argued that the trial judge should have sequestered the jury.

Sheppard v. Maxwell is an example of the Supreme Court's efforts to apply the general commands of the constitutional text, written in the eighteenth century, to ever-changing technological environments. Noting the increasing potential of modern mass communications to influence jurors—a development unforeseen by the framers—the Court outlined new procedures to minimize the media's effects on the justice system.

See also *Gag orders.*

REFERENCES

Neff, James. *The Wrong Man: The Final Verdict on the Dr. Sam Sheppard Murder Case.* New York: Random House, 2001.

Sheppard v. Maxwell, 384 U.S. 333 (1966).

Shield laws

Shield laws protect journalists from being compelled to reveal confidential sources of information. Although some consider shield laws as vital to the functioning of a free press in a democracy, no federal law exists because Supreme Court rulings do not regard the First Amendment as mandating such a privilege.

In *Garland v. Torre* (1958), Marie Torre, a columnist accused of libel, refused to reveal her source, claiming that provisions of the First Amendment protecting freedom of the press also shield reporters' sources; she was eventually imprisoned. Although the court of appeals acknowledged some constitutional implications, it ruled that a reporter must testify when the information sought is (1) highly material and relevant to the underlying claim, (2) necessary or critical to maintenance of the claim, and (3) unavailable from alternative sources.

The Court revisited this issue in *Branzburg v. Hayes* (1972). In seeking information for a story, Paul Branzburg observed and interviewed people using drugs, but when called to testify before grand juries investigating drug crimes, he refused to disclose the identities of those he had interviewed. The Court ruled that requiring reporters to disclose confidential information to grand juries served a "compelling" and "paramount" state interest that did not violate the First Amendment, reasoning that reporters' receipt of information in confidence does not privilege them to withhold that information from government investigations.

Despite such rulings, state courts and legislatures have interpreted the First Amendment or their state constitutions to offer protections for journalists. More than thirty states have passed shield laws protecting journalists from subpoenas, though some offer more blanket protection than others. On November 11, 2004, Sen. Chris Dodd (D-Conn.) introduced legislation protecting reporters from revealing sources except in cases of national security, stating, "A free press is the best guarantee of a knowledgeable citizenry." His attempt evolved in part as a response to the jailing of *New York Times* reporter Judith Miller for refusing to reveal her sources in the leak investigation surrounding the identification of Valerie Plame as a CIA agent.

See also *Branzburg v. Hayes (1972)*.

REFERENCES
Branzburg v. Hayes, 408 US 665 (1972).
Garland v. Torre, 259 F.2d 545 (2nd Cir.), cert. denied, 358 US 910 (1958).
Simons, Howard, and Joseph A. Califano Jr., eds. *The Media and the Law.* New York: Praeger, 1976.

Shields, Mark

Mark Shields (1937–) is a nationally syndicated newspaper columnist and television commentator. He began a political career in the 1960s as a legislative aide to Wisconsin senator William Proxmire and later helped to run political campaigns for Robert F. Kennedy in 1968 and Edmund Muskie in 1972. In 1979 he joined the *Washington Post* as an editorial writer. Within a year he began a political column, and within two years his work became nationally syndicated. In 1987 Shields began appearing on television as a commentator on PBS's *MacNeil/Lehrer NewsHour,* and a year later, he became a panelist on CNN's *Capital Gang,* bringing humor and wit to discussions of political issues.

Shields describes himself as a liberal who has been heavily influenced by his religious upbringing. He grew up regarding political activity as part of a civic and Christian duty, and his Catholicism drew him to the Democratic Party's philosophy that government can and should play a role in easing the inequalities inherent in a free-market economy.

REFERENCES
"Can Catholics Put Faith in Politics?" *U.S. Catholic,* October 2004, 12–16.
Darling, Lynn. "On the Run with Mark Shields, Political Consultant." *Washington Post,* November 6, 1978, B1.

Shrum, Bob

Robert M. Shrum (1943–) is a lawyer, speechwriter, and political media consultant. A graduate of Georgetown University and Harvard Law School, Shrum was a fellow at the John F. Kennedy School's Institute of Politics at Harvard University and taught at Yale University and Boston College. He served as a youthful assistant to Pierre Salinger during John F. Kennedy's 1960 presidential campaign, as the principal speechwriter for George McGovern's 1972 presidential campaign, and as press secretary to Senator Edward Kennedy from 1980 to 1984. Shrum founded a political media consulting firm in 1985, working on many local, state, national, and international political campaigns.

In 1999 Shrum joined with Stanley Greenberg and James Carville to found the Democracy Corps, a political research and consultancy company. He was also chief political strategist for John Kerry's 2004 presidential campaign. Despite having worked on eight losing presidential campaigns, Shrum is highly regarded within Democratic Party circles for his media savvy, populist speechwriting, and aggressive political counsel. He has written numerous articles, co-hosted CNN's *Crossfire,* and served as an "insider" political

Democratic political strategist Bob Shrum has produced advertisements or directly worked on the campaigns of more than twenty-five senators and eight presidential candidates and is well known for his media savvy and speech-writing. He was a key advisor to Democratic presidential hopefuls Al Gore in 2000 and John Kerry in 2004.

commentator. Journalist Jay Nordlinger calls Shrum "probably the most important Democratic operative of the last 20 years."

See also *Press secretaries; Salinger, Pierre.*

REFERENCES

Foer, Franklin. "The Boss—How Shrum Took over the Party." *New Republic,* August 2, 2004, 21–25.

Lizza, Ryan. "Kerry's Consigliere." *Atlantic Monthly,* May 2004, 32–36.

Nordlinger, Jay. "The Attack Man: Bob Shrum and the Democratic Style." *National Review,* July 3, 2000, 32–35.

Wolff, Michael. "Kerry's Karl Rove." *Vanity Fair,* August 2004, 146–150.

Sinclair, Upton

Upton Beall Sinclair Jr. (1878–1968)—also known as Clarke Fitch, Frederick Garrison, Uppie—was a Pulitzer Prize–winning novelist, essayist, and social reformer. Writing magazine and newspaper articles and dime novels to finance his education, Sinclair was a published writer even before he graduated from City College of New York in 1897 and enrolled at Columbia University for graduate studies. Despite the economic challenges of his early life, Sinclair steadfastly remained devoted to his chosen profession, penning a first novel, *Springtime and Harvest* (1901), which stemmed from his unhappy and poverty-ridden first marriage, and *The Journal of Arthur Stirling* (1902), which depicted the travails of a failed poet. In 1902 he joined the Socialist Party, and in 1905 he helped form the Intercollegiate Socialist Society, along with Jack London, Clarence Darrow, and Florence Kelley. Sinclair ran unsuccessfully for a congressional seat in New Jersey in the 1906 election.

He gained fame with his novel *The Jungle* (1906), which shocked the world with its portrayal of the Chicago meat packing industry. President Theodore Roosevelt invited Sinclair to the White House after reading the novel; the president was also receiving 100 letters a day demanding reformation of the meat-packing industry. Sinclair hoped that the book would improve worker conditions, but instead it stimulated Congress to pass the Pure Food and Drug Act of 1906 to protect consumers. He used royalties from *The Jungle* to establish a cooperative writer's commune—Helicon Home Colony in Englewood, New Jersey.

Influenced by investigative journalists such as Lincoln Steffens and Ida Tarbell, Sinclair published a number of muckraking probes into the abuses of the capitalist world. *The Metropolis* (1908) explored fashionable New York society. *King Coal* (1917) examined the 1914 Colorado coal miners' strike and the growing influence of union labor. *Jimmie Higgins* (1919) illuminated the conflict American leftists felt in supporting the class establishment in the United Kingdom and France during World War I. The ideological struggle between socialism and U.S. entry into the war, as well as President Wilson's foreign policy, had caused Sinclair to examine his political beliefs and to begin the process of distancing himself from the socialists. Sinclair wrote *Oil!* (1927) to explore the interaction of money, wealth, and social conscience through the lives of two men from opposite sides of the tracks amid the petroleum industry in California.

The author of more than ninety works, Upton Sinclair is most famous for The Jungle, *his exposé of the meatpacking industry that horrified consumers and prompted Congress to pass legislation on food production. He won the Pulitzer Prize for his novel* Dragon's Teeth.

He delved into the sensational Sacco-Vanzetti case in *Boston* (1928).

Having moved to California in 1915, Sinclair became prominent in that state's politics during the 1920s, running unsuccessfully for several offices as a socialist. He permanently left the Socialist Party and ran for governor as the Democratic Party candidate in 1934. During the campaign, the conservative *Los Angeles Times* portrayed Sinclair as a supporter of free love and a danger to society. Of his experience, Sinclair wrote *I, Governor of California* and *How I Ended Poverty: A True Story of the Future* to delineate his views on the End Poverty in California (EPIC) program, his campaign platform. He used the union organizing efforts at Ford Motor Company in the 1930s as the background for his novel *Flivver King* (1937).

Sinclair won the Pulitzer Prize for his novel *Dragon's Teeth* (1942), the third of the eleven-volume Lanny Budd series. This collection of contemporary historical novels took the illegitimate son of a munitions tycoon through the tumultuous events leading up to and during World War II, and into

the beginning of the cold war. Sinclair produced almost a hundred books, including two autobiographical works, *My Lifetime in Letters* (1960) and *The Autobiography of Upton Sinclair* (1962).

See also *Muckraking.*

REFERENCES

Blinderman, Abraham. *Critics on Upton Sinclair: Readings in Literary Criticism.* Coral Gables, Fla.: University of Miami Press, 1975.

Bloodworth, William A., Jr. *Upton Sinclair.* Boston: Twayne Publishers, 1977.

Dell, Floyd. *Upton Sinclair: A Study in Social Protest.* New York: George H. Doran, 1927.

Harris, Leon A. *Upton Sinclair: An American Rebel.* New York: Crowell, 1975.

Harte, James Lambert. *This Is Upton Sinclair.* Emmaus, Pa.: Rodale Press, 1938.

Scott, Ivan. *Upton Sinclair: The Forgotten Socialist.* Lewiston, N.Y.: Edwin Mellen Press, 1997.

Suh, Suk Bong. *Upton Sinclair and the Jungle: A Study of American Literature, Society, and Culture.* Seoul, Korea: American Studies Institute, Seoul National University, 1997.

Yoder, Jon A. *Upton Sinclair.* New York: Ungar, 1975.

Smith, Howard K.

Howard Kingsbury Smith (1914–2002) was a broadcast journalist and national network news anchor. He began his career as a reporter for the *New Orleans Item-Tribune* in 1936, and worked for United Press International (UPI) in Copenhagen in 1939 and in Berlin in 1940. His experiences in Berlin at the beginning of World War II inspired him to write *Last Train from Berlin* (1942).

Smith joined CBS New radio (1941) and became one of "Murrow's Boys," supporting Edward R. Murrow as they reported on the progress of the war in Europe. He remained in Europe until his return to Washington, D.C., in 1957. In 1961, when Chairman William S. Paley sided with an executive over the editing of a civil rights program he reported, Smith resigned from CBS and switched to ABC News, becoming the co-anchor of its broadcast news team.

Noted for his outspoken, often controversial, and even opinionated reporting, Smith gained the sobriquet "Howard K. Agnew" for his support of Vice President Spiro T. Agnew's bitter attack on TV news in 1969. Smith's other books included *The State of Europe* (1949) and *Events Leading Up to My Death: The Life of a Twentieth Century Reporter* (1996).

See also *Agnew, Spiro T.; Murrow, Edward R.*

REFERENCES

Bliss, Edward. *Now the News: The Story of Broadcast Journalism.* New York: Columbia University Press, 1991.

Vanocur, Sander. "Howard K. Smith: TV News' Courtly Rebel." *Electronic Media,* February 25, 2002, 10.

REFERENCES

Buckingham, David. "News Media, Political Socialization and Popular Citizenship: Towards a New Agenda." *Critical Studies in Mass Communications* 14, no. 3 (December 1997): 344–366.

Kelman, Steven. *American Democracy and the Public Good.* Fort Worth, Tex.: Harcourt Brace, 1996.

O'Sullivan, Tim, et al. *Key Concepts in Communication and Cultural Studies.* 2nd ed. London: Routledge, 1994.

Socialization

Socialization is a broad concept that refers to the ways in which people become and are made social. Early socialization is believed to be the deepest, as that is the period in which children learn how to live in society. Political socialization is the process by which people come to acquire political attitudes and values through exposure to the social environment around them.

The media, family, religion, school, community, and peers are all considered to be agents of political socialization. The study of communication factors in political socialization is multi-faceted; studies range from examining classroom texts and mass media content to examining the work of public information agencies. Because of our growing reliance on the media for entertainment and information, newspapers, magazines, radio, and television have emerged as important socialization agents for study. While their effects may be difficult to measure, the media play an important role in the socialization process.

A common example of political socialization is media coverage of the government. By joining in the celebration of national holidays and elections, the media promote popular support for government. At the same time, by airing criticisms of government as part of entertainment and news coverage, the media also erode public confidence in government. Indeed, studies in the 1970s found children to be more negative toward the political system in the wake of the Watergate scandal, and continued negative and cynical media coverage may account for such views in today's youth. Among adults, who are already socialized, the media's effects are less powerful, but they are generally most influential on new, emerging, or changing issues, such as altering Americans' perceptions toward China and Russia since the 1990s.

Social responsibility

The social responsibility theory of the press is a product of a particular moment in the history of mass media expansion, when scholars recoiled at the use of propaganda during World War II, and when libertarian assumptions of the rational citizen seemed unrealistic. This late-1940s vision of responsible media nevertheless resonated with many journalists and critics, and it has become a core rationale for an emerging ethos of global journalism.

The view of journalism that later became known as social responsibility theory was articulated in 1947 by the Hutchins Commission, a team of thirteen intellectuals directed by University of Chicago president Robert Maynard Hutchins to explore how media should function in a modern democratic system. Formally known as the Commission on Freedom of the Press, it published its report, *A Free and Responsible Press,* following two years of debate. In an almost eerily prescient critique, the commission addressed the phenomenon of monopolistic cross-media ownership, declaring that freedom of the press is in danger because "the few who are able to use the machinery of the press as an instrument of mass communication have not provided a service adequate to the needs of society." Concentration of ownership meant that a smaller portion of the citizenry could express their opinions through the press. The commission argued that freedom of the press was not itself a sufficient condition to ensure the continuation of a free press. A modern press can "debase and vulgarize mankind," stifling thought and discussion. Consequently, a free press must be an *accountable* press to remain free. Otherwise, media invite the heavy hand of government regulation.

The essence of the social responsibility doctrine is the principle that media must serve the interests of society first, as opposed to the interests of business or government. This theory is aligned with a libertarian view in its assertion that uninhibited expression constitutes the fundamental freedom that fosters all other liberties. But the Hutchins Commission report is historically significant in its recognition of corporate organization as a threat to an open marketplace of ideas. According to social responsibility theory, media should provide citizens with "a truthful, comprehensive, and intelligent account of the day's events in a context which gives them meaning," a "forum for the exchange of comment and criticism," a "means of projecting the opinions and attitudes of the groups in society to one another," a "method of presenting and clarifying the goals and values of the society," and "a way of reaching every member of the society by the currents of information, thought, and feeling."

In subsequent decades, social responsibility theory has been mostly ignored by media companies. Still, it endures as a normative framework by which activists and scholars critique news media. In fact, social responsibility provided a rationale for several twentieth-century journalistic innovations that are particularly associated with the quality big-city press, including professional codes of ethics, newspaper ombudsmen, and the reform movement known as public (or civic) journalism, whereby news organizations promote grassroots deliberation about a local issue.

In recent years, a model of interactive, citizen-based media has challenged the traditional orientation to journalism in which professionals transmit information to passive audiences. Social responsibility theory is once again at the forefront of debate as to how technological innovations may allow media to realize their potential in providing a forum for the exchange of ideas. Most important, social responsibility theory articulates journalistic principles that are arguably universal in application to democracies across the globe, in increasingly pluralistic media environments.

REFERENCES

Christians, Clifford, and Kaarle Nordenstreng. "Social Responsibility Worldwide." *Journal of Mass Media Ethics* 19, no. 1 (2004): 3–28.

Hutchins Commission. *A Free and Responsible Press.* Chicago: University of Chicago Press, 1947.

Soft news

See *Hard and soft news*

Sound bite

A sound bite is a short snippet of image and sound extracted from an interview or press conference and replayed on the nightly news to represent a politician's or officeholder's position on an issue or event. The sound bite has proved effective when there is a lot of news to cover, because it is brief and viewers are believed to have a short attention span.

Studies have shown that sound bites have been shrinking over time. From over forty seconds in the 1968 campaign, the average sound bite shriveled to a little over nine seconds in 1988 and has remained at a level even slightly below that ever since. Recognizing the sound bite's importance as one of the few ways to get on the air, politicians and their advisors now plan how to package their ideas in catchy, pithy phrases that are likely to draw coverage. The result is the use of more labels, shorter explanations, less pertinent information, and very little interpretation or reasoning on which viewers might base sound judgment. Critics argue that these snippets of thought are too short to be meaningful. As former senator and presidential candidate Gary Hart put it in a 1987 *Washington Post* article, "Is it any wonder that an age of televised sound-bites produces bite-sized policies?" But many in the media believe that voters can perceive a complex message from simple one-liners, and that sound bites can serve as a useful hook to draw audiences into the issues of governing and campaigning in a fast-paced information age.

REFERENCES

Hallin, Daniel C. "Sound Bite News: Television Coverage of Elections, 1968–1988." *Journal of Communication* 42 (spring 1992): 6.

Hellweg, Susan, Michael Pfau, and Steven Brydon. *Televised Presidential Debates: Advocacy in Contemporary America.* New York: Praeger, 1992.

Kellner, Douglas. *Television and the Crisis of Democracy.* Boulder, Colo.: Westview Press, 1990.

Special interest groups and political advertising

Organized interests have long been part of electoral politics in America. In recent years, however, interest groups appear to be playing an increasingly active role, becoming key players in elections at all levels of government. As campaigns have become progressively more expensive, interest groups' ability to help finance them has become increasingly valuable, especially in funding and creating campaign advertising through the media. Interest groups are permitted wide latitude to engage in media campaigning, even under the campaign finance regulatory reforms enacted by the Bipartisan Campaign Reform Act of 2002 (BCRA).

Interest groups try to affect electoral outcomes in a number of ways—by announcing both candidate endorsements and "hit lists" (in which they single out candidates targeted for defeat); by producing issue ratings, scorecards, and voter guides; and by promoting voter mobilization. Independent expenditures intended to express support for a candidate are an especially powerful tool. This targeted spending has been permitted since a 1976 Supreme Court ruling that allowed PACs, ideological organizations, and individuals to spend unlimited amounts of money opposing or supporting a particular candidate as long as they do not consult with or coordinate with the intended beneficiary. The impact of such independent expenditures became clear in the 1980 New Hampshire primary, in which Ronald Reagan benefited from $250,000 in assistance from a group called the Fund for a Conservative Majority. During that same presidential election cycle, the National Conservative Political Action Committee (NCPAC) spent more than $1 million to purchase advertising aimed to defeat a number of congressional Democrats who had voted for the Panama Canal Treaty in 1978. Independent expenditures have been a staple in political campaigns ever since.

Another classic example of independent expenditures occurred during the 1988 presidential campaign, when the National Security Political Action Committee (NSPAC) spent over $8 million to broadcast its notorious "Willie Horton" ads in support of Republican candidate George H.W. Bush. The ads, which were broadcast over 600 times, reaching an estimated 80 million people during the fall campaign, attacked the record of Democratic nominee Michael Dukakis, the governor of Massachusetts, by highlighting his state's prison furlough system, which had granted a weekend pass to a black convicted murderer who then proceeded to commit further violent crimes. Experts believe the "Willie Horton" ads to have had a strong impact on the election, even as they spawned allegations both of racism and of coordination between the Bush campaign and the NSPAC.

Although interest groups undertake a variety of activities in attempting to affect political races, the lion's share of resources is devoted to underwriting political advertising

campaigns on television. During the general election in 2000, over 10 percent of the ads broadcast on behalf of the presidential candidates were sponsored by interest groups. Groups supporting Al Gore spent nearly $12.6 million on television advertising during this period, and groups supporting George W. Bush spent $2.6 million nationwide. Interest groups also engage in "issue advocacy"—producing ads and public activities that take a particular position on an issue rather than a candidate. The Annenberg Center at the University of Pennsylvania found that groups spent $404 million on print and broadcast issue ads during the 108th Congress (2003–2004).

Interest groups typically target their television advertising spending at competitive races, and they tend to support incumbents over challengers. Evidence also suggests that the tone of television ads sponsored by interest groups, especially those produced on behalf of presidential candidates, is generally more negative than that of ads sponsored by candidates or parties. In the 2004 election, only 7.5 percent of television ads sponsored by interest groups offered positive messages, compared to 43.6 percent of candidate-sponsored ads, for example.

Interest group–sponsored advertising played an important role in the 2004 election cycle, in which over $600 million was spent on television advertising, more than in any other presidential campaign in history. Candidates and their allies broadcast over a million spots on television in 2004. Operating in a new regulatory environment established by BCRA, which eliminated the spending of "soft money" by groups not affiliated with a particular candidate and required that all electioneering communications broadcast within sixty days of the general election be financed by candidate-specific "hard money" only, the candidates relied more heavily on interest group spending earlier in the campaign. Estimates suggest that interest groups sponsored nearly 25 percent of television ads for presidential candidates during this period (up from 3 percent in 2000 for the same period), compared to only 8 percent of ads broadcast within sixty days of the election. Democrats relied most heavily on interest group spending for television advertising during the 2004 campaign.

The 2004 election also featured the emergence of so-called "527" organizations—groups, tax-exempt under section 527 of the tax code, that focus on grassroots activities such as voter education and get-out-the-vote drives. These groups also spent $114 million on ads during the campaign.

Perhaps the most notorious of these organizations was Swift Boat Veterans for Truth, which sponsored an ad that called into question Democratic nominee John Kerry's military service in Vietnam. The ad, which was broadcast 739 times in only seven media markets, generated substantial controversy and media coverage during the campaign. The role of these groups, which operate outside the normal campaign finance laws, continues to provoke controversy.

REFERENCES

Cigler, Allan J., and Burdett A. Loomis, eds. *Interest Group Politics.* Washington, D.C.: CQ Press, 2002.

Franz, Michael, Joel Rivkin, and Kenneth Goldstein. "Much More of the Same: Television Advertising Pre- and Post-BCRA." In *The Election After Reform,* edited by Michael Malbin. Lanham, Md.: Rowman and Littlefield, 2006.

Panagopoulos, Costas. "Vested Interests: Interest Group Resource Allocation in Presidential Campaigns." *Journal of Political Marketing* 5, nos. 1–2 (2006): 59–77.

Rozell, Mark, and Clyde Wilcox. *Interest Groups in American Campaigns: The New Face of Electioneering.* Washington, D.C.: CQ Press, 1999.

Spin

Spin, or selective interpretation, is the intentional slanting of ambiguous political events and situations to promote an interpretation favorable to one's own side. Although short of overt lying or propaganda, the term has a negative connotation akin to deceiving, twisting, or biasing in a preferred direction.

As a form of communication between politicians and the press, spin is not limited to one political party. Each side engages in spin when selectively choosing to emphasize certain facts, events, or situations while ignoring, downplaying, or deflecting others. Managing spin is critical because political phenomena rarely have a clear, objective significance, and politicians' success often hinges on framing situations to highlight points that are beneficial to them while minimizing those that are detrimental.

A good example of the use of spin can be found in debates on the issue of school vouchers: Democrats often describe proposals to shift taxpayer funds to private schools as a misuse of public funds and a violation of the separation of church and state, whereas Republicans portray them as an initiative to provide "opportunity scholarships" and school choices that would benefit students and families.

In today's media-saturated climate, it is not just politicians who spin, but interest groups and corporations, celebrities, and institutions as well. The widespread need for image control has led to the "professionalization of spin," or what scholar Jarol Manheim calls "strategic political communication." Essentially a sophisticated form of public relations, this practice employs experts in media message control and manipulation, who use polling, marketing, psychological, and media research to shape and target messages to maximize the positive and minimize the negative impact upon target populations. Politicians, press secretaries, communication directors, public relations consultants, and media figures are thus often referred to as "spin doctors." As long as there is mediated political communication, there is likely to be spin.

See also *Spin doctors.*

REFERENCES

Esser, Frank, Carsten Reinemann, and David Fan. "Spin Doctors in the United States, Great Britain, and Germany: Metacommunication about Media Manipulation." *Harvard International Journal of Press/Politics* 6, no. 1 (2001): 16–45.

Kurtz, Howard. *Spin Cycle: How the White House and the Media Manipulate the News.* New York: Simon and Schuster, 1998.

Maltese, John Anthony. *Spin Control: The White House Office of Communications and the Management of Presidential News.* Chapel Hill: University of North Carolina Press, 1992.

Manheim, Jarol. *All of the People, All the Time: Strategic Communication and American Politics.* Armonk, N.Y.: M. E. Sharpe, 1991.

Spin doctors

Professional commentators who are especially skilled in reframing or recasting information in the media are—often pejoratively—known as "spin doctors." Selectively emphasizing facts and evidence that support their opinion or viewpoint, spin doctors downplay any more contradictory details.

While spin has long been an informal part of political communication, the strategic management of external communications in the modern political arena originated with the creation of the White House Office of Communications during the Nixon administration. Presidents Ford and Carter also turned to communications specialists to assist with their respective public image problems. It was during the Reagan administration, however, that tactics to manipulate and control news stories using sound bites and "lines of the day" were perfected. Since then, the use of spin doctors has become increasingly prevalent; competing spin doctors are often featured guests on political television programs that rely on controversy and confrontation to capture viewers' attention and boost ratings.

Beyond the political environment, corporations also call upon spin doctors to manage media relations and communications, especially during crisis situations, in order to develop responses to unfavorable media coverage. These corporate spin doctors seek to contain adverse reports and counter criticism by emphasizing the positive steps being taken to alleviate a crisis.

See also *Media consultants; Spin.*

REFERENCES

Kurtz, Howard. *Spin Cycle: How the White House and the Media Manipulate the News.* New York: Simon and Schuster, 1998.
Maltese, John Anthony. *Spin Control: The White House Office of Communications and the Management of Presidential News.* 2nd rev. ed. Chapel Hill: University of North Carolina Press, 1994.

Stanley v. Georgia (1969)

The U.S. Supreme Court ruled in *Stanley v. Georgia* (1969) that mere possession of obscene matter was constitutionally protected under the First and Fourteenth Amendments. The case is important in the establishment of a constitutional right of privacy.

Law enforcement officers had searched a man's home looking for evidence of bookmaking, but instead found films deemed to be obscene. The man was arrested and convicted under a Georgia law banning the possession of obscene matter. In *Stanley,* the Court reaffirmed its ruling in *Roth v. United States* (1957) that the First Amendment did not protect obscenity, which the government had a legitimate interest in curbing. It refused, however, to assert that *Roth* eliminated all constitutional protections in this area. In *Stanley,* Justice Thurgood Marshall declared that Georgia was not simply asserting its right to stop the public distribution of obscenity but was attempting "to control the moral content of a person's thoughts." He also stated, "If the First Amendment means anything, it means that a State has no business telling a man, sitting alone in his own house, what books he may read or what films he may watch."

Although the Court thus ruled that the First and Four-

teenth Amendments prohibited the state from making mere private possession of obscene material a crime, it later upheld an Ohio law allowing prosecution for simply possessing child pornography. The 1990 decision distinguished the two cases by noting that the Georgia law sought to outlaw private possession of obscenity because of its effect on the mind of the viewer, whereas the Ohio law's purpose was to stop the market for exploiting children.

See also *Memoirs v. Massachusetts (1966); Miller v. California (1973); Obscenity and pornography; Roth v. United States (1957).*

REFERENCES

Calvert, Clay, and Don R. Pember. *Mass Media Law.* Boston: McGraw-Hill, 2005.
Stanley v. Georgia, 394 U.S. 557 (1969).

Steffens, Lincoln

Joseph Lincoln Steffens (1866–1936) was a journalist and social reformer who became a leading practitioner of the journalistic phenomenon known as "muckraking." Having studied in Europe and graduated from the University of California, Berkeley, Steffens began his journalistic career in 1892 as a reporter for the *New York Evening Post,* where he eventually rose to city editor. In 1894 his investigative work in exposing New York City police corruption helped to defeat the Tammany Hall machine's candidate for mayor and elect a reform candidate, who subsequently established a board of police commissioners. In 1898 Steffens became the city editor for the *New York Commercial Advertiser.*

His success led him to *McClure's Magazine,* where he became the managing editor in 1902. During his tenure at *McClure's,* Steffens wrote an article on city government corruption, "Tweed Days in St. Louis," initiating a successful series that was later collected and republished as *The Shame of the Cities* (1904). He expanded his exposé of governmental corruption at the state level in *The Struggle for Self-Government* (1906). He moved to a new assignment as associate editor of *The American* magazine in 1906, and of *Everybody's* magazine, where he remained until 1911.

His reformist zeal then led him abroad, where he reported on the Mexican Revolution, largely supporting the rebels and advocating revolution rather than reform as an instrument of change. After visiting postrevolutionary

A muckraking social commentator, journalist Lincoln Steffens' investigative reporting helped expose police corruption in New York and defeat the Tammany machine's mayoral candidate of 1894.

Russia from 1919 to 1921, Steffens made his famous declaration, "I have seen the future and it works." His enthusiasm for communism had, however, waned by the time he wrote *The Autobiography of Lincoln Steffens, Volume II: Muckraking/Revolution/Seeing America at Last* (1931). His correspondence covering the years 1889 to 1919 was published in *The Letters of Lincoln Steffens* (1938).

See also *Muckraking.*

REFERENCES

Horton, Russell M. *Lincoln Steffens.* New York: Twayne Publishers, 1974.

Kaplan, Justin. *Lincoln Steffens: A Biography.* New York: Simon and Schuster, 1974.

Shapiro, Herbert. *The Muckrakers and American Society.* Boston: D.C. Heath, 1968.

Stinson, Robert. *Lincoln Steffens.* New York: Frederick Ungar, 1979.

Stephanopoulos, George

George Stephanopoulos (1961–) is a political analyst, journalist, and former political and policy advisor to President Bill Clinton. After graduating from Columbia University and studying as a Rhodes Scholar at Oxford University, Stephanopoulos eventually worked as an aide to House minority leader Richard Gephardt. Based on that experience and political connection, he then joined the 1992 presidential campaign of then-governor Clinton as campaign communications director. His efforts, along with those of James Carville and other members of the Clinton campaign team, are immortalized in the 1993 film *The War Room.*

Upon Clinton's election, Stephanopoulos was appointed White House communications director—he was the youngest ever to hold that post. After his relationship with the media proved stormy in the early days of the administration, his position was changed to that of a senior advisor for policy and strategy.

Early in Clinton's second term, Stephanopoulos left politics to become a political analyst for ABC News, where, in 2002, he was selected to host the Sunday news and discussion program *This Week.* In 2005 he was named chief Washington correspondent for the network. He is author of *All Too Human* (1999), a best-selling memoir of his days in the White House. In some ways, Stephanopoulos's career exemplifies the symbiotic, revolving-door relationship between government, politics, and journalism today.

See also *Spin doctors; Sunday news shows.*

REFERENCES

ABC News, www.abcnews.com.

Stephanopoulos, George. *All Too Human.* Boston: Little, Brown, 1999.

Strategic political communication

See *Spin*

Sunday news shows

Sunday network television "news" shows are actually interview and dialogue programs between journalists and notable guests, usually Washington insiders and public officials, discussing current events. The current shows include ABC's *This Week,* CBS's *Face the Nation,* NBC's *Meet the Press,* CNN's *Late Edition,* and, most recently, FOX's *Fox News Sunday.* The precursors to the pundit shows that first appeared during the 1980s and remain popular today, these Sunday news programs address controversial topics that can help to generate attention on an otherwise slow news day, and sometimes make front-page news on Monday. Their elite guests appear in order to gain exposure and to air their positions, while the journalists gain access, opportunities for relatively open and direct questioning, and also prestige.

Replacing the earlier (and low-rated) *Issues and Answers,* which had aired since the early 1960s, *This Week* began in 1981 when star broadcast journalist David Brinkley came over from his anchor spot at NBC. The avuncular Brinkley was joined by White House correspondent Sam Donaldson and conservative columnist George Will, and, later, by National Public Radio's Cokie Roberts. Featuring lively roundtable discussions by the panelists in addition to the guests, the program quickly rose to the top of the ratings. Upon Brinkley's retirement in 1997, it continued with the other panelists until 2002, when the anchor position was awarded to political analyst and former Clinton advisor George Stephanopoulos, who added coverage of breaking news stories and feature pieces such as biographies.

Face the Nation, a similar program on CBS, started in 1954 and originally aired in the afternoon rather than late morning. George Herman hosted the program from 1969 to 1978; he was succeeded by Roger Mudd, who stepped down in 1991. Currently, the network's chief Washington correspondent, Bob Schieffer, is the host. Generally, one reporter questions the guests.

NBC's *Meet the Press* is the oldest such program on television, having debuted in 1947. On this show, three or four journalists—usually print reporters such as the *Washington Post*'s David Broder—join the host in questioning the guest(s). The program re-airs on cable partner MSNBC later in the day. Lawrence E. Spivak was the program moderator until 1975, when he was succeeded by Bill Monroe. Tim Russert, NBC political correspondent and analyst (and formerly an aide to New York governor Mario Cuomo), has been the main moderator since 1991.

CNN's *Late Edition,* which began in 1993, is the main cable show in the genre, airing in the early afternoon. The former *World Today* anchor, White House and foreign correspondent Wolf Blitzer, interviews a series of individual or paired guests on current topics. The program also mixes in some breaking news and standard reports, as befits a full-time news network.

Fox News Sunday debuted in 1997, mixing in panels of journalists quizzing notable guests with its regular Sunday morning news programs. Originally hosted by former Republican speechwriter Tony Snow (who became White House press secretary in 2006), the show continued with political correspondent Chris Wallace, who moved from ABC News to take over the seat in 2002. Like most of the other Sunday programs, it features a lively, spirited format filled with questioning, discussion, and punditry.

See also *Pundit shows.*

REFERENCES

Alterman, Eric. *Sound and Fury: The Making of the Punditocracy.* 2nd ed. Ithaca, N.Y.: Cornell University Press, 2000.

Ball, Rick. *Meet the Press: Fifty Years of History in the Making.* New York: McGraw-Hill, 1998.

Schieffer, Bob. *Face the Nation: My Favorite Stories from the First 50 Years of the Award-Winning Broadcast.* New York: Simon and Schuster, 2004.

T

Tabloids

A *tabloid* is a newspaper that is printed on a smaller sheet of paper than the more familiar daily broadsheet. The most commonly known type of tabloid in the United States is the supermarket tabloid, a weekly magazine-type publication that specializes in celebrity gossip and sensationalist, often exaggerated, entertainment pieces. As their name indicates, these mini-newspapers are typically available for purchase in drugstore and supermarket checkout lanes.

The second type of tabloid is the weekly alternative paper, which is generally free and generates all its revenue from advertisements. These papers usually focus on local events, and they often carry in-depth stories about local politics and social issues, as well as features about music, style, and entertainment. Examples include New York City's *Village Voice,* the *Boston Phoenix,* the Washington *City Paper,* and two papers in Seattle, the *Seattle Weekly* and the *Stranger.*

The third type of tabloid—a format most closely associated with New York City—is the daily newspaper that is printed in tabloid style. The first tabloid of this kind in the United States was the *New York Daily News,* which originated in 1919 and is currently owned by Mortimer Zuckerman. Its rivalry with the *New York Post,* owned by Rupert Murdoch's News Corporation, has driven both of these prominent newspapers to corner distinct niches in the local market. The *Daily News,* which is politically left-of-center, identifies itself as "New York's picture newspaper," while the *Post* is distinguished by its conservative political views and by its more sensationalist approach.

"Sensationalism" is the practice of producing news stories less for the purpose of conveying information about current events than for the sake of catching reader attention by publishing shocking or controversial stories or headlines. For example, the 1975 *New York Daily News* headline "Ford to City: 'Drop Dead'" was an exaggerated take on President Gerald Ford's reluctance to provide fiscal help to New York City. Even though Ford never actually said those words, this dramatic headline is thought to have contributed to his narrow loss in the 1976 election campaign. The same paper's front-page caricature of then Speaker of the House Newt Gingrich as a "crybaby" entirely disrupted congressional budget proceedings in Washington in 1995.

The sensationalism and generally low-quality journalism of the *New York Post* and the supermarket tabloids have made the word *tabloid* a general pejorative description for all sorts of journalism—including "tabloid TV shows," such as *Entertainment Tonight* and *Inside Edition*—that emphasizes celebrity and scandal over factual news coverage. Even so, some papers printed in tabloid form—including *Newsday* on New York's Long Island, the *Chicago Sun-Times,* and Denver's *Rocky Mountain News*—are reliable, mainstream newspapers.

Even the most notorious American supermarket tabloid, *The Enquirer,* which is known for its focus on celebrity gossip and for its willingness to pay sources for information, has increased its political clout over recent decades. Its early publication of lewd details regarding the Monica Lewinsky scandal made the issue very public very quickly. In 2001 it was the first paper to disclose the existence of the Rev. Jesse Jackson's illegitimate child, thereby severely weakening Jackson's political credibility.

Although the major tabloids largely fulfill their reputation for sensationalist stories and headlines, they do produce real political consequences. Precisely because their stories are so attention getting, tabloids have been very successful in shaping public opinion on the issues and subjects featured on their front pages, and their coverage is sometimes adopted by more "legitimate" mainstream media outlets.

See *History of American journalism; Magazines.*

REFERENCES

Editors of *National Enquirer. The* National Enquirer: *Thirty Years of Unforgettable Images.* New York: Talk Miramax Books, 2001.

Sloan, Bill. *"I Watched a Wild Hog Eat My Baby!" A Colorful History of Tabloids and Their Cultural Impact.* Amherst, N.Y.: Prometheus Books, 2001.

Stevens, John D. *Sensationalism and the New York Press.* New York: Columbia University Press, 1991.

Talk radio

Radio programs that emphasize the discussion of elections, policy issues, and other public affairs—and often feature a call-in format—are generally considered talk radio. Its origins date as far back as the 1930s and 1940s, but talk radio as we know it today began during the Reagan administration, when the fairness doctrine—a 1940s regulation that required that equal attention be paid to both sides of a political issue if discussed on the airwaves—was abolished by the Federal Communications Commission (FCC) in 1987. Although this regulation had been upheld by the Supreme Court in 1969, President Ronald Reagan successfully vetoed Congress's attempt to retain the fairness doctrine by making it law, and in 1989 the first Bush administration won a decisive victory when a federal appeals court upheld the FCC's 1987 ruling.

Since the late 1980s, talk radio has become both a potent political force and a popular programming format. More than 1,000 radio stations feature some type of talk radio programming nationwide, and the format has come to dominate AM radio. Researchers claim that somewhere between 15 and 36 percent of Americans listen to talk radio. Talk radio audiences tend to be predominantly older white males, and despite some anecdotal evidence to the contrary, the average talk radio listener is ideologically only slightly more conservative than the average non-listener. Recent research has also shown that the typical listener of programs of the popular talk radio hosts is relatively more affluent and issues-oriented than the typical non-listener. Moreover, talk radio listeners are generally better informed about political issues and are likely to participate in politics with greater frequency than non-listeners. Survey data also show that talk radio listeners consume political information from multiple mass media sources and often disagree with information presented on the radio programs they listen to.

The effect of talk radio on political behavior remains a key area of scholarly inquiry. Some researchers find that talk radio boosts participation rates among listeners, while others claim that it fails to mobilize new voters. Although talk radio hosts often make inflammatory claims about government failures and political corruption, research shows that talk radio has only marginally added to the public's distrust of governmental institutions. For instance, in the 1990s, listeners of programs with hosts such as the conservative Rush Limbaugh grew slightly more distrustful of the president, the judicial branch, and the education system (the abuses of which were staples of Limbaugh's show) but still held Congress (which in 1994 came under Republican control) in high regard.

Contemporary talk radio is perceived by many as a "pseudo-social network" that is dominated by ideological conservatives and works to reinforce core conservative values. To combat this perception, prominent liberals in 2004 established Air America, a "progressive" radio network hosted by such leftist personalities as comedian and social critic Al Franken; so far, its offerings have failed to match the ratings of shows featuring syndicated conservatives. Still, it is unlikely that talk radio, or other mass media outlets, can successfully persuade listeners to abandon their ideological predispositions. Instead, it seems that, due to listeners' selective exposure and retention, talk radio only reinforces existing beliefs.

REFERENCES

Alterman, Eric. "Conservative Talk Show Hosts Poison Political Discourse." In *Media Bias,* edited by Stuart A. Kallen. Farming Hills, Mich.: Greenhaven Press, 2004.

Barker, David C. *Rushed to Judgment: Talk Radio, Persuasion, and American Political Behavior.* New York: Columbia University Press, 2002.

Kurtz, Howard. *Hot Air: All Talk, All the Time.* New York: Times Books, 1996.

Moy, Patricia, and Michael Pfau. *With Malice Toward All? The Media and Public Confidence in Democratic Institutions.* Westport, Conn.: Praeger, 2000.

Talk shows

Political theorists generally agree that the free and unfettered ability of citizens to engage in political dialogue, discussion, and deliberation is central to democratic practice. And almost from the beginning of the television era, political talk shows—where that democratic practice is given a broadcast format—have been a programming staple. Starting with *Meet the Press* (seen on NBC since 1947) and *Face the Nation* (on CBS since 1954), citizens have regularly tuned in to watch political discussions between journalists and government officials. In what are often referred to as Sunday morning talk shows (for the time slot in which they typically appear), both broadcast and print journalists have served as public proxies to interrogate newsmakers about political events of the day.

In the late 1960s, a second form of political talk show appeared—the journalist or commentator roundtable discussion. Shows such as *Firing Line* and *Agronsky and Company*, where hosts and guests play the role of expert Washington insider, were the humble precursors of the heated political discussion and debate "pundit" shows of the 1980s and beyond.

In the 1980s and 1990s, new forms of political talk shows began to appear on cable channels and through syndicated programming. Instead of arising from network and cable news operations, these shows were centered in the entertainment arena—descendants of programs hosted by entertainers such as Merv Griffin, Mike Douglas, and Dick Cavett, dating back to the 1960s. Afternoon relationship talk shows, such as those hosted by Phil Donahue and Oprah Winfrey, became a stopping place for presidential candidates to chat with the hosts and their audience members.

The 1992 presidential campaign witnessed a virtual explosion of such appearances, as candidates discovered that they could enjoy easier access to the viewing public—and "free" airtime—without having to endure the typical grilling from journalists about their positions on issues. Indeed, Bill Clinton famously remarked to journalists, "You know why I can stiff you on the press conferences? Because Larry King liberated me by giving me the American people directly." Although criticized by some for their lack of hard-hitting questioning, these talk show interviews proved popular with audiences because the questioning by these entertainment hosts offered a glimpse of a different—perhaps more "human"—side to their subjects from what was seen in typically scripted candidate appearances. The audience participation component of these shows also created a "town hall meeting" feel that enhanced their popular appeal.

As Clinton's comment indicates, another entertainment talk show, CNN's *Larry King Live,* played an important role in the 1992 campaign. The program's stature as a legitimate forum for political conversations continued briefly after the election, when in 1993 King hosted Vice President Al Gore and H. Ross Perot in an important policy "debate" over the North American Free Trade Agreement (NAFTA). In short, the entertainment talk show had taken on a new role as an alternative forum for important political discourse.

The 1992 presidential campaign also marked a defining moment for other entertainment talk shows when Bill Clinton donned dark sunglasses and played the saxophone on the *Arsenio Hall Show.* Since that time, appearances on late-night talk shows have become de rigueur for political candidates, who now regularly turn up on shows such as *Late Night with David Letterman* and *The Tonight Show,* often engaging in self-deprecating humor to show that they don't take themselves too seriously.

Political talk on television also changed dramatically in the 1990s with the rising popularity of several talk shows that present "outsider" political voices in entertainment talk show formats (as opposed to the "insider" perspectives that have typically defined the genre). Beginning with *Politically Incorrect with Bill Maher* on Comedy Central in 1993—later to include *Dennis Miller Live* on HBO and *The Daily Show with Jon Stewart* on Comedy Central, among others—these shows feature comedians and other political amateurs discussing, arguing, satirizing, parodying, laughing, and ranting about political events and issues in an entertaining and substantive manner. These shows locate politics in a popular vernacular and offer a common sense approach to evaluating politics that has greatly broadened the appeal of political talk on television.

See also *Late night talk shows; Pundit shows; Sunday news shows; Talk radio.*

REFERENCES

Hirsch, Alan. *Talking Heads: Political Talk Shows and Their Star Pundits.* New York: St. Martin's Press, 1991.

Jones, Jeffrey P. *Entertaining Politics: New Political Television and Civic Culture.* Lanham, Md.: Rowman and Littlefield, 2005.

King, Larry, with Mark Stencel. *On the Line: The New Road to the White House.* New York: Harcourt Brace, 1993.

Nimmo, Dan, and James E. Combs. *The Political Pundits.* New York: Praeger, 1992.

Timberg, Bernard. *Television Talk: A History of the TV Talk Show.* Austin: University of Texas Press, 2002.

Telecommunications Act of 1996

The Telecommunications Act of 1996 was the first major overhaul of the landmark 1934 Communications Act and the first comprehensive attempt to reform U.S. media policy for the digital era. Passing Congress with significant bipartisan support after four years in the making, the bill was signed into law by President Bill Clinton on February 8, 1996. The complex and far-reaching legislation replaced structural regulation with market incentives for telephone, radio, broadcast television, cable television, and satellite communications. Hailed as an effort to unshackle market forces, and sold with the promise that deregulation would lead to enhanced competition, the law now offers a mixed legacy. Critics point to the ensuing "merger mania"—concentrated markets, and large, vertically integrated telecommunications corporations that occurred as a direct result—while defenders praise the act for removing outdated regulations. Nevertheless, it continues to affect the nation's media system in profound ways, and its significance looms large over Washington, D.C., ten years later as efforts to rewrite the law gather steam in Congress and the Federal Communications Commission.

Sweeping across multiple media sectors, the 1996 act consists of many complex details that defy simple summaries. Its general provisions define the parameters within which local exchange carriers can provide long-distance services, and the terms upon which local telephone carriers can compete. Furthermore, the act has removed cross-market barriers between telephone and cable companies that formerly prevented them from combining to provide network services or competing in other industry sectors. Communications scholar Patricia Aufderheide observes that the legislation helped to weaken the traditional divide between common carriers (such as telephones) and mass media (such as radio). She also notes that despite the act's deregulatory thrust, bedrock policy principles implying that media must serve the public interest remain intact, if ill-defined. The legislators also attempted to regulate Internet pornography with the Communications Decency Act, which was later defeated in the courts on constitutional (free speech) grounds.

Going beyond just telecom legislation, however, the act's broad sweep has also deregulated cable rates, mandated V-chip installation in televisions, and removed the forty-station national broadcast ownership cap. This latter provision has led to a rapid and unprecedented consolidation in national radio station ownership; after a series of acquisitions, the largest radio chain, Clear Channel, now owns well over 1,200 stations nationwide, dominating most major markets and arguably limiting the diversity of voices on the public airwaves. Robert McChesney, a critic of the act, believes that these results are predictable consequences of what he characterizes as an essentially corrupt and anti-democratic process that minimized public input. In his view, corporate lobbyists had undue political influence on the wording of the telecom bill, which did not provide adequate measures for protecting the public interest or even fair market competition.

Despite these criticisms, a commitment to deregulation continues to drive media policymaking in Washington. Although the ultimate legacy of the first telecom act is still debatable, blind spots have been identified—namely, the Internet, which the 128-page original bill barely mentioned. As Congress now debates revising the legislation, the Internet figures prominently in the discussion.

REFERENCES

Aufderheide, P. "Shifting Policy Paradigms and the Public Interest in the U.S. Telecommunications Act of 1996." *Communication Review* 2, no. 2 (1997): 259–281.

———. *Communications Policy and the Public Interest: The Telecommunications Act of 1996.* New York: Guilford Press, 1999.

McChesney, R. W. *Rich Media, Poor Democracy: Communication Politics in Dubious Times.* New York: New Press, 2000.

Telegraph

Samuel F. B. Morse is credited with the invention of the telegraph in 1837; the first public telegraph message was sent in 1844. Early in its history, telegraphy promised to be an important tool in news-gathering but was financially prohibitive. A group of newspapers in New York City, six of which established the Associated Press in 1848, realized the benefit of pooling their costs of telegraph time. Wire dispatches were concise and strictly factual, and the "lead" or first paragraph contained the most vital information to save time and expense.

Eventually, technological innovation made the use of the telegraph cheaper and resulted in more detailed dissemination of news over telegraph lines. In 1856 the first transatlantic cable was laid, speeding news between the United

States and Europe. Later, radiotelegraphy (or "wireless" telegraphy) was based on the same principles as telegraphy. The sending of messages by means of long and short clicks of a telegraph key (dots and dashes) was a precursor of today's digital transmission techniques. Although newsgathering technology has changed significantly since the 1840s, journalists still focus on factual, concise reporting that can be traced to the invention of the telegraph and the advent of the wire services.

REFERENCE

Gordon, George N. *The Communication Revolution*. New York: Hastings House, 1977, 41–45.

Television, broadcast

Broadway producer and television pioneer Worthington Miner sensed the power of merging politics and the small screen before most people had ever seen a television set. While watching an experimental broadcast from the 1940 Republican convention, Miner sat captivated for hours as the power shifted from the front-runners to a dark-horse candidate. As he put it, "The tension and restlessness kept building, until that explosive moment when the final votes that put Wendell Willkie over the top were recorded." Miner wasn't drawn by Willkie's stance on the major issues, but by the drama of politics. A decade later, broadcast television moved onto center stage in U.S. politics—no longer just transmitting political information, its powerful effects transformed the political process itself.

Television embraced politics for many reasons. First, the Federal Communications Commission (FCC) demanded more than entertainment programming in exchange for limited and extremely profitable broadcast licenses. The bulky, hard-to-move equipment of early television made the political conventions and election night coverage convenient subjects for public affairs programming in which television could compete with radio. This early emphasis on public affairs programming did not last, however. As the regulatory and market environments changed, and as political advertising became a dominant means of political communication, television's civic textbook evolved toward a very different set of messages. Politicians also quickly learned the medium's power to transmit both ideas and

emotion directly to the voter—a revelation that ultimately diminished the role of the political party.

A History of Powerful Effects

In one of the first powerful intersections of politics and television, people didn't like what they saw. In 1954 CBS's *See It Now* focused on Sen. Joseph McCarthy, who had become a powerful politician by spreading fear about communism in the United States. Edward R. Murrow and his staff presented film clips of McCarthy's speeches and then separated the senator's inflammatory charges from the facts. The next month, the Army-McCarthy hearings on live television further eroded McCarthy's credibility, and he was publicly censured by his fellow senators later in the year.

In an early instance of a politician appealing directly to the people through the camera lens, Richard M. Nixon saved his place on the 1952 Republican ticket by appearing on national television. Viewers promptly forgot his campaign funding scandal but remembered the emotional story about his kids' dog, Checkers. Although the fickle nature of television may have saved Nixon in that instance, the medium helped to destroy his chance at the presidency eight years later. In the first televised presidential debate, Nixon appeared tired and sick through the camera lens, while John F. Kennedy looked young, vigorous, and confident. Because television viewers picked Kennedy as the winner of that 1960 debate, while Nixon fared better with radio listeners, television's critics marked the occasion as proof of the medium's emphasis of style over substance. From that point forward, many a presidential candidate—among them Jimmy Carter, Ronald Reagan, Bill Clinton, and George W. Bush—could make up for a lack of national political experience, and work outside the traditional political party network, by successfully manipulating the direct appeal of television with simple messages, a good camera presence, and a strong network of supporters.

Television's power and reach have also placed issues on the national agenda by circulating memorable pictures and news coverage. In the 1950s and 1960s, as civil rights became one of the most divisive issues in the nation's history, news film of protests, riots, and violence were delivered to the American living room via the network newscasts night after night, forcing politicians to confront segregation and race issues. It was the assassination of John F. Kennedy in November 1963, however, that signaled the true power of television at conveying both information and emotion. For days, an entire nation of viewers crowded around their sets as the three networks suspended commercials and entertainment programming to concentrate on the pictures and analysis of the Kennedy murder in Dallas, the transfer of power, and the emotional funeral procession through the streets of Washington, D.C.

In the 1960s and 1970s, the Vietnam conflict was dubbed the "living room war" because of the graphic images presented on the nightly news. The stories and pictures provided by the reporters and photojournalists in Vietnam, however, increasingly contradicted official government reports. The zenith of network news power came in 1968 when CBS anchorman Walter Cronkite delivered an editorial calling the war a "stalemate" and urging peace negotiations. President Lyndon B. Johnson thereupon decided that if he had lost Cronkite, he had lost the country—a month later, he announced that he would not seek reelection and started peace talks with the North Vietnamese.

The *Washington Post* may have taken the lead role in the investigation of President Nixon and the Watergate scandal in the 1970s, but television provided the format for the public to learn about White House corruption. The congressional hearings of 1973 pushed aside popular soap operas during the daytime, becoming some of the most watched "programs" of that summer.

The Changing Communication Environment

The final two decades of the twentieth century brought about dramatic changes in the intersection of politics and network television because of increased competition and decreased regulatory pressure from the government. With the proliferation of cable and satellite stations, the broadcast networks no longer had a virtual monopoly on television viewing. Viewers could choose from dozens and dozens of channels, and the overall amount of news—and therefore of political coverage—increased dramatically. Ted Turner's CNN (Cable News Network) established the 24-hour broadcasting format in 1980, followed by CNN Headline News, and later MSNBC and the Fox News Channel.

At the same time that the networks were facing new competition, the FCC began to relax its rules regarding public affairs programming, reducing the pressure on the networks to provide programs that might cut into corporate profits. It was a new and different environment. At the local level, political stories fell into disfavor as news consultants'

research—echoing Robert Putnam's documentation of the general decline of civic involvement in *Bowling Alone*—indicated that news viewers had lost interest in public affairs. For scheduling and budgetary reasons, stations across the country shut down their state capitol and Washington bureaus and instead turned their attention to stronger coverage of health, lifestyle, and crime stories. The network evening newscasts continued to put a heavy emphasis on Washington political news, but the content changes in local news soon began to spread to the networks as well. While they were never able to expand their newscasts beyond thirty minutes, the major networks found outlets for the news during other parts of the day, particularly the morning shows and the prime-time magazines.

Broadcast news journalists are increasingly caught in a struggle to serve different masters. Social scientists see journalism as an important part of our democracy, providing political and governmental information that helps voters to make informed choices. Also, reporters serve as watchdogs on day-to-day government operations. At the same time, however, the U.S. broadcasting system was designed to operate within a market economy, which means that the owners of networks and local stations—now usually large corporations—are primarily concerned with satisfying stockholders and advertisers, usually by maximizing audience size for all programming. Therefore, broadcast journalists are increasingly forced to compete with entertainment programming for an audience. In the struggle between profit and public information, profit most often wins.

Political Advertising

Politicians do not rely only on TV news programs to get their message across—by far the most expensive part of campaigning today is television advertising. Dwight Eisenhower started the modern era of political ads in 1952 when he allowed an advertising agency to prepare thirty-second commercials with simple messages and a catchy slogan, "I Like Ike." Since then, politicians have relied ever more heavily on television ads both to define their candidacies and to attack their competitors. Although some studies suggest that people learn more about candidates and issues from political ads than from campaign news coverage, critics counter that the negative tone of campaign ads has led to disillusionment among voters and lower turnout on election day.

What Citizens Learn from Television

Because so much of what citizens learn about public affairs from television viewing is acquired casually, the scope and variety of the sources of what is learned are considerable. National and local television news programs, as well as debates among political candidates and political advertising during election campaigns, are obviously important windows on public affairs, but so also are less obvious sources, such as "breakfast TV," talk shows, and even comedy. The actual and potential value of broadcast television as a civic textbook is underscored by the huge audiences for the presidential debates, still among the largest audiences for any event on television despite a long-term declining trend. This conscious and deliberate participation in public affairs is complemented by considerable incidental learning from other kinds of television content.

What citizens learn deliberately or incidentally from broadcast television can be described by a sequence of three mass media effects: focusing attention, fostering comprehension, and shaping attitudes and opinions. The continuous, ever-shifting flow of news coverage on public issues influences citizens' awareness and concern about the most important problems facing the community and the nation. This ability of television to focus public attention on a small number of issues—the agenda-setting role of the media—is most evident in news programming because of the high level of redundancy in the news from day to day.

During political campaigns, ranging from presidential elections to the myriad local elections, television news—often reinforced by barrages of political advertising—also fosters awareness of who the candidates are. Critics have bemoaned this agenda-setting influence, contending that by focusing heavily on the front-runners in the political horse race and by excluding most minority-party candidates from coverage, television news largely controls the prospects of candidates presented to the public. Beyond elections, these agenda-setting effects also are found in terms of awareness of public officials and other political actors.

In addition to its influence in determining which issues and candidates citizens become aware of, television also is a major source of what is actually known about these salient issues and candidates. Television's agenda-setters pay unequal attention to the complexities of issues and to differing political perspectives, and because this inequality is particularly pronounced in political advertising, both print and broadcast news media have established "ad watches" to critique and even correct the inadequacies of such paid political messages. The images and knowledge that citizens receive about candidates and other public figures also derive in large part from exposure to television. From all types of programs and from the flood of political advertising at election time, the public acquires the varied bits of information that are the building blocks for the popular images of these political figures—everything from personality traits and biographical details to their stands on the issues.

Citizens process these bits of information about issues and public figures from television's civic textbook in a very strategic way. Most viewers do not typically fill their memories with vast quantities of detailed information, for understanding the broader issues, not remembering the specific details, is the goal. This store of political knowledge has significant implications for the public's attitudes and opinions—and for what happens at the ballot box. During presidential election campaigns, day-by-day shifts in the tone of television news coverage can change voters' preferences regarding the candidates. Favorable coverage of Republican campaign events on national television increases support for the Republican candidate; favorable coverage of Democratic campaign events decreases support for the Republican candidate.

Beyond the specific bits of information that citizens acquire about public affairs, television's civic textbook has a larger and more fundamental role—building political interest among the public. Because politics and public affairs have very low salience for most Americans, media effects on attention and comprehension—even on attitudes and opinions—are, arguably, not the most important political role of broadcast television. Its more basic function is to draw citizens into the public arena, to heighten the salience of public affairs and citizens' interest in learning about issues and public actors.

In the face of declining participation in public affairs—a trend especially visible in the diminishing voter turnout for presidential elections over the past fifty years and in citizens' reduced exposure to news—how much of the blame does television share? Scholars disagree. Roderick Hart's *Seducing America* assigns it much of the blame, while Michael Schudson's *The Good Citizen* suggests that broad social trends are more responsible. In any event, the political role of television remains at the center of scholarly attention and debate.

REFERENCES

Ansolabehere, Stephen, and Shanto Iyengar. *Going Negative: How Political Advertisements Shrink and Polarize the Electorate.* New York: Free Press, 1995.

Barnouw, Erik. *Tube of Plenty: The Evolution of American Television.* 2nd ed. New York: Oxford University Press, 1990.

Frank, Reuven. *Out of Thin Air: The Brief Wonderful Life of Network News.* New York: Simon and Schuster, 1991.

Gans, Herbert J. *Deciding What's News: A Study of* CBS Evening News, NBC Nightly News, Newsweek *and* Time. New York: Vintage Books, 1980.

Hart, Roderick. *Seducing America: How Television Charms the Modern Voter.* New York: Oxford University Press, 1994.

McChesney, Robert. *Rich Media, Poor Democracy: Communication Politics in Dubious Times.* New York: The New Press, 1999.

Mickelson, Sig. *From Whistle Stop to Sound Bite: Four Decades of Politics and Television.* Westport, Conn.: Praeger, 1989.

Miner, Worthington. *Worthington Miner: A Directors Guild of America Oral History, Interview with Franklin J. Schaffner.* Metuchen, N.J.: Scarecrow Press, 1985.

Putnam, Robert. *Bowling Alone: The Collapse and Revival of American Community.* New York: Simon and Schuster, 2000.

Schudson, Michael. *The Good Citizen: A History of American Civic Life.* New York: Free Press, 1998.

Sparrow, Bartholomew. *Uncertain Guardians: The News Media as a Political Institution.* Baltimore: Johns Hopkins University Press, 1999.

Terrorism and the media

Although precisely labeling terrorism can be difficult, one common denominator in most discussions of the term is the use of violence or threatened violence against non-combatants to achieve a social or political goal. Terrorism can also be viewed as a form of political communication—sending a message, through violence. Indeed, political communication scholar Brigitte Nacos points out that mass-mediated terrorism intentionally seeks out media coverage as a goal in order to attract public and government attention. The media are therefore a crucial part of how the message is created, transmitted, and received.

Terrorism and the media need and feed each other. Groups and individuals committing terrorism need coverage of their actions and publicity to send their political message to target governments or groups, to strike fear in target publics, and to recruit or retain followers to their cause. Media organizations want to inform the public and to attract audiences by exploiting the drama and excitement—and some critics might argue, play on fears—of terrorist acts. Media coverage of terrorist actions generally falls into pre-

dictable patterns, akin to coverage of other crisis events. Reports initially focus on the attack itself and on the death, destruction, or crisis it causes. Then, the investigation of the act takes center stage, as blame is laid, suspects and accomplices are sought, and eventually—perhaps, much later—they are successfully apprehended. If the attack's consequences are serious enough, and traceable, military retaliation may also become part of the story. As the *Washington Post* stated in an editorial following the 1998 U.S. embassy bombings in Africa, "There is a protocol of response in these terrible events: the grieving, the investigating, and the vowing of pursuit so that justice can be done."

In essence, coverage of terrorist actions is a combination of disaster, crime, and war reporting. The precise dynamic in a given case depends on the nature of the attack: coverage of a hijacking or hostage taking may emphasize the criminal aspect more than the other reporting genres, for example. Regardless of the nature of an attack, however, the inherent newsworthiness of terrorism almost guarantees media coverage. Some scholars believe that attacks of even a minor size and scope receive far more coverage than they deserve, relatively speaking, obliging the perpetrators in their quest for publicity. Events of the magnitude of the September 11, 2001, attacks in New York City and outside Washington, D.C., obviously merit major news status, but even those events arguably resulted in "coverage overkill," overshadowing all other news for weeks.

Much of the research on the relationships between the media, terrorism, and government concerns whether media coverage helps or hinders the attackers' goals. Three main points of view have emerged: the media are willingly or unwillingly used as tools of terrorism; the media, acting as watchdogs, fairly or unfairly hold the government accountable in its response; and although the media may exploit the drama of terrorism for their own purposes, the coverage is rarely favorable to terrorists. The lack of consensus on this issue may derive from scholars' differing expectations of the media and because the effects of media coverage vary with the circumstances of specific events.

Recent work employing the concept of framing leads to the conclusion that the media's portrayal and interpretation of terrorism depends upon a number of cultural, political, and situational factors. For example, media reporting of the September 11 attacks was heavily colored by a "war" frame: the country had been attacked by a foreign enemy, and the Bush administration characterized its response as a new "war on terrorism." Previous terrorist actions in the United States had generally been framed as crimes rather than as acts of war. Another example of the importance of framing such stories can be found in the very different portrayals of Palestinian suicide bombings in Israel in reporting by the Arab network al-Jazeera and by Fox News. Some observers criticize the media for creating a spectacle or theater out of terrorist incidents. In emphasizing the dramatic and emotional elements of the stories, media reports fail to adequately inform the public about the nature of terrorism and the issues involved.

Another concern is whether media coverage of terrorism itself contributes to more terrorism. Known as the contagion effect, this suspicion is not unlike the supposition that coverage of mass murderers may create "copy cat" killers. A number of studies have indeed found a direct relationship between the amount of media coverage of terrorism and the amount and scale of terrorist events thereafter. Although the contagion effect is largely accepted in law enforcement circles, others argue that it is mostly a conjecture that is useful as a justification for more government control of the media in terrorism situations. Contagion effect or no, there is little doubt that groups engaging in terrorism do learn from the media coverage of their actions, refining their methods to better attract coverage and to try to influence it. Indeed, such coverage is central to the goal of terrorism, which is usually to intimidate civilian populations so as to pressure governments to change policies.

Calls for media restraint or even government censorship have been made given the potential and even real power of the media to aid or even encourage terrorism. Some governments have imposed blackouts, limited contact with the press, or asked media managers to withhold information in deference to security concerns. For example, in the 1970s and 1980s, the British government banned broadcasts of the voices of Irish Republican Army and Sinn Fein members. More common, however, is a degree of self-censorship by news organizations whose responsible members do not want to aid and abet terrorism. Almost all major news organizations in the United States and many abroad have reporting guidelines. All of these restraints may fall victim, however, to time and competitive pressures.

The media can also perform a counterterrorist function, allowing governments at all levels to deliver important messages to the public. For example, following the September 11 attacks, the New York news media provided information ranging from what streets were open to traffic, to what schools were open, to whether people should report for jury duty in downtown Manhattan. Messages that reinforce safety precautions or that debunk rumors can perform a necessary public service. Media serve similarly to publicize government warnings and most-wanted alerts and appeals to be on the lookout for suspects.

Changes in information technology have helped shape the media-terrorism relationship. Such developments as the Internet, fax machines, cell phones, and satellite telephones and television networks have created more ways to communicate and spread messages. There is substantial evidence that groups involved in terrorism use the Internet for recruiting, planning and coordinating attacks, and communicating secretly, sometimes by relaying messages through postings on legitimate Web sites. Also, strategic uses of such new media outlets that play to news values can garner mainstream media attention for even minor groups, such as the live Web-cast executions of hostages by certain factions in Iraq demonstrated. In fact, it is possible that the new media have rendered government censorship and media control ineffective, as anyone can use more direct means to reach target populations. Because Web sites or other new media venues may yet be limited in their reach, mainstream media are still needed for widely disseminating messages. The rise of global and multinational news networks, such as CNN and Al-Jazeera, represents new venues and potentially larger audiences through which groups can spread news of attacks and propaganda. It is clear that groups employing terrorist methods have learned to use various outlets for spreading their messages. It is equally evident that the relationship between terrorism and the media continues to evolve.

See also *Crisis journalism; Framing; New media; Newsworthiness; Watchdog role.*

REFERENCES

Livingston, Steven. *The Terrorism Spectacle.* Boulder, Colo.: Westview, 1994.
Nacos, Brigitte. *Mass-Mediated Terrorism: The Central Role of the Media in Terrorism and Counterterrorism.* Lanham, Md.: Rowman and Littlefield, 2002.
———. *Terrorism and the Media.* New York: Columbia University Press, 1994.
Norris, Pippa, Montague Kern, and Marion Just, eds. *Framing Terrorism: The News Media, The Government, and the Public.* London: Routledge, 2003.
"Two Bombs." *Washington Post,* August 8, 1998, A20.
White, Jonathan R. *Terrorism and Homeland Security.* 5th ed. Belmont, Calif.: Thomson Wadsworth, 2006.
Wilkinson, Paul. "The Media and Terrorism: A Reassessment." *Terrorism and Political Violence* 9 (Summer 1997): 51–64.

This Week

See *Sunday news shows*

Thomas, Helen

Helen Thomas (1920–) is a pioneering journalist, well-known as the "First Lady of the Press." After beginning her journalism career as a copy girl for the *Washington Daily News,* Thomas was hired by United Press International (UPI) to write women's interest stories in 1943. She transitioned to political reporting when she covered John F. Kennedy's presidential campaign and then followed him to the White House.

By 1970 Thomas had become UPI's White House correspondent. She was the only print journalist to accompany President Richard M. Nixon on his historic trip to China in 1972, and she has traveled with every president from Nixon to George W. Bush. She became the first female White House wire service bureau chief, the first female member of the Gridiron Club, and the first female officer of the National Press Club and the White House Correspondents Association. After News World Communications (an affiliate of the Unification Church) bought UPI in 2000, Thomas left the news service and joined the Hearst Corporation as a columnist covering the White House and national affairs.

As Thomas's tenure as White House correspondent lengthened, her colleagues often referred to her as the dean of the White House press corps. Until President George W. Bush broke the tradition, she held the honor of asking the first question at presidential press conferences. Thomas is known for direct and incisive questioning—no small irritant to many presidents. Thomas's writings include *Dateline: White House* (1975), *Front Row at the White House: My Life and Times* (1999), and *Thanks for the Memories* (2001).

REFERENCES

Dawson, Victoria. "Grand Inquisitor." *Smithsonian,* June 2003, 27–29.
Fitzwater, Marlin. *Call the Briefing! Bush and Reagan, Sam and Helen: A Decade with Presidents and the Press.* Holbrook, Mass.: Adams Media Corp., 1996.
"Give 'Em Helen." *Harper's,* March 2003, 17.
Stan, Adele M. "Thank You, Helen Thomas." *Working Woman,* October 2000, 20.

Thomas confirmation hearings

The nomination of Clarence Thomas to the Supreme Court in 1991 occasioned one of the most widely covered confirmation hearings in U.S. history. President George H. W. Bush had selected Thomas to replace retiring Justice Thurgood Marshall. Days prior to the Senate's vote on the nomination, National Public Radio reported that a law professor, Anita Hill, had during an interview with the FBI charged that Thomas had sexually harassed her years earlier, when she had worked for him. The Senate, under pressure from women's groups, decided to postpone the confirmation vote to hear testimony from Thomas and Hill.

Journalist Helen Thomas, known as the "First Lady of the Press," has been a member of the White House press corps since 1970. Until President George W. Bush's administration, Thomas was traditionally allowed the first question at White House presidential press conferences. After a fifty-seven-year career with United Press International, in 2000 she began reporting for the Hearst Company.

Clarence Thomas addresses senators during his 1991 Supreme Court confirmation hearings, which focused on allegations by Professor Anita Hill that Thomas had sexually harassed her. The intense media scrutiny of the hearings was unprecedented for judicial confirmation hearings.

The media became a player in the confirmation process, televising coverage of the hearings and relaying competing claims from the Hill and Thomas camps. Hill alleged that Thomas had made references to pornographic material and gestures of a graphic sexual nature. Thomas adamantly denied the charges. Throughout the three days of questioning by senators, the public became engrossed in the salacious testimony and melodrama being played out on their television screens; many have compared the style of coverage to that of soap operas. The intensity of the media coverage made the hearings a spectacle, with a Gallup poll revealing 86 percent of the public as having watched at least part of the hearings. Despite the controversy, Thomas was confirmed by a vote of 52–48. His confirmation battle continues to influence how Court nominees are selected and presented to the public.

REFERENCES

Danforth, John. *Resurrection: The Confirmation of Clarence Thomas.* New York: Viking, 1994.

Maltese, John. *The Selling of Supreme Court Nominees.* Baltimore, Md.: Johns Hopkins University Press, 1995.

"The Hearings on Television." *New York Times,* September 13, 1991.

Time pressures

Journalists work on tight deadlines because of their professional obligation to inform the public promptly and concisely. "The clock," writes educator Melvin Mencher, "is the journalist's major obstacle." Deadlines allow media to function efficiently, but the related time pressures present journalists with psychological and sometimes physical challenges. They encourage news-gathering routines, which at the extreme may lead to formulaic reporting or to reliance on incomplete information, at least in the initial story. Time pressures in the presentation of broadcast news may lead to omissions of substance or context.

Traditionally, print reporters were used to less rigid deadlines than their broadcast colleagues, but the demands imposed by the online component now common to most media are changing that situation rapidly: deadlines for Web sites are not as much production-driven as event-driven, and many print journalists say they are straining to contribute to the Web edition as events are unfolding, often at the expense of depth and accuracy. Broadcast journalists, too, face increasing pressure to provide live coverage from anywhere, anytime, as the technology makes it possible, even if such live reporting is unnecessary to convey the information. Regardless of their effects on the quality of reporting, time pressures will remain part of journalistic practice and must be managed successfully by news organizations and journalists alike.

REFERENCES

Mencher, Melvin. *News Reporting and Writing.* 10th ed. New York: McGraw-Hill, 2006.

Stovall, Glenn J. *Writing for the Mass Media.* 6th ed. New York: Allyn and Bacon, 2006.

Wellman, Ferrell. "Standards under Pressure." *Quill* 90, no. 5 (June 2002): 10.

Town meetings

The general idea of town meetings is the creation of a communal place where group members can meet to make decisions. New England towns are famous for their annual town meetings, in which the residents gather to pass laws, elect officers, levy taxes, and deal with other local issues. The 1990s brought the idea of the "electronic town hall"—a televised public forum where politicians would appear before an audience, taking questions from its members or from viewers at home. Third-party presidential candidate H. Ross Perot, who launched his campaign via televised talk shows, argued that if elected, he would use such events to help him make decisions. President Bill Clinton actually employed them, though mainly as a means of bypassing the professional journalists of the Washington press corps by having average citizens ask him questions on live television. The popularity of the format then spread to other sectors of government, as evidenced by the U.S. Department of Health and Human Services Town Meeting on Health, which was part of Clinton's One America initiative on race, in 1998.

Technological advances now make it possible to hold town meetings on the Internet. The aim of these electronic forums is to increase deliberation among citizens, politicians, and experts; many of them also include a public opinion polling component. But electronic town halls, unlike traditional town meetings, have no binding component, and so their participants do not really make decisions. Essentially, these are public relations events, although they do allow the public some small measure of input into government.

REFERENCES

Abramson, Jeffrey B., F. Christopher Arterton, and Gary R. Orren. *The Electronic Commonwealth.* New York: Basic Books, 1988.

Becker, Ted, and Christa Daryl Slaton. *The Future of Teledemocracy.* Westport, Conn.: Praeger, 2000.

Lorch, Robert S. *State and Local Politics.* 6th ed. Englewood Cliffs, N.J.: Prentice Hall, 2001.

Rather, John. "First Town Meeting." *New York Times,* November 15, 1998, 2.

Tracking polls

See *Polls and the media*

Trippi, Joe

Joe Trippi (1956–) is a Democratic campaign manager who has run the campaigns of a variety of presidential, senatorial, and gubernatorial candidates. He is best known for his role as national campaign manager for Howard Dean's presidential race in 2004, for which Trippi and his staff are widely credited with revolutionizing the presidential campaign process by introducing innovative uses of the Internet.

At the beginning of the 2004 campaign season, many observers believed that the Dean campaign's lack of money and organizational support would keep it from being a major

Joe Trippi, former campaign manager for 2004 Democratic presidential hopeful Howard Dean, transformed campaign fundraising by using the Internet to collect more than $50 million in contributions from Dean supporters, primarily in individual amounts of less than $200.

factor in the primaries. By using the Internet initially to connect supporters in the same city, however, the campaign created a massive organizational structure in a very short time and at minimal expense. Trippi's staff then successfully used the campaign Web site as a fund-raising tool, soliciting more than $51 million from individuals—primarily through donations of less than $200—and thereby defying expectations about the campaign's ability to raise money.

REFERENCES

Scheiber, Noam. "Organization Man." *New Republic,* November 13, 2003.

Trippi, Joe. *The Revolution Will Not Be Televised.* New York: Regan Books, 2004.

Turner, Ted

Robert Edward Turner III (1938–)—also known as Captain Outrageous, the Mouth of the South, Terrible Ted—revolutionized television news programming in 1980 by creating the first 24-hour, continuous news broadcasting station, CNN (Cable News Network). A media entrepreneur, accomplished sportsman, and philanthropist, Turner attended Brown University, where he acquired his love of sailing, and served briefly in the U.S. Coast Guard before working as an account executive and later general manager of his father's billboard advertising company.

Turner was thrust into the leadership role of the struggling company after the untimely death of his father in 1963. He soon brought the company into profitability, enabling an expansion into the fledgling cable television industry with the purchase of Atlanta-based, independent Channel 17 in 1970. Turner's station became one of the first to use a communications satellite for signal transmission in 1975, thus significantly increasing his customer base. As his advertising revenue increased, he established WTBS and the Turner Broadcasting System (TBS), and created two additional network systems, CNN in 1980 and Turner Network Television (TNT) in 1988. Turner added other versions of CNN, including the thirty-minute-turnover news channel CNN Headline News in 1982 and CNN International in 1985.

Turner used his mounting wealth to purchase the Atlanta Braves professional baseball team in 1976 and the Atlanta Hawks professional basketball team in 1977. He also captained the victorious crew in the 1977 America's Cup sailing competition in his own twelve-meter racing boat, *Courageous.* Following President Jimmy Carter's controversial decision after the Soviet invasion of Afghanistan to prohibit U.S. participation in the 1980 Moscow Olympic Games and the Soviets' withdrawal from the 1984 Olympics in Los Angeles, Turner founded the Goodwill Games to restore the apolitical spirit of international sports competition, in 1986.

Turner has also experienced his share of failures. He made an abortive attempt at a hostile takeover of CBS in 1986, and he sparked considerable controversy in that same year when he purchased the MGM/UA Entertainment Company, including its enormous inventory of motion pictures, and then launched an ambitious effort to "colorize" many of its classic black-and-white films. He was eventually forced to sell MGM to retain control of TBS.

In 1990 Turner formed the Turner Foundation to manage his charitable contributions for environmental causes, and he stunned the world in 1997 when he pledged $1 billion to the United Nations for "good-work" programs—the largest single philanthropic gesture up to that point.

In 1995 Turner sold TBS to Time Warner for $7.5 billion, causing a revolution in cable industry mergers. He assumed the role of vice chairman—an unusual role for a person of his accomplishments—but he remained the largest single shareholder in the new corporate entity. Finding that the 2000 merger of America Online (AOL) and Time Warner left him with little direct responsibility, Turner resigned as vice chairman of AOL Time Warner in 2003 and announced that he would not seek reelection to its board in 2006.

In 2001, as co-chair with former Senator Sam Nunn, he launched the Nuclear Threat Initiative (NTI) to provide common ground for divergent views with a purpose of reducing the threat of nuclear, chemical, or biological warfare. Turner continues his numerous philanthropic endeavors, as well as other entrepreneurial activities including vast real estate holdings and a restaurant franchise.

See also *Cable television; CNN.*

REFERENCES

Bibb, Porter. *It Ain't as Easy as It Looks: Ted Turner's Amazing Story.* New York: Crown, 1993.

Goldberg, Robert, and Gerald Jay Goldberg. *Citizen Turner: The Wild Rise of an American Tycoon.* New York: Harcourt Brace, 1995.

Hack, Richard. *Clash of the Titans: How the Unbridled Ambition of Ted Turner and Rupert Murdoch Has Created Global Empires That Control What We Read and Watch.* Beverly Hills, Calif.: New Millennium Press, 2003.

Schonfeld, Reese. *Me and Ted against the World: The Unauthorized Story of the Founding of CNN.* New York: Cliff Street, 2001.

Twain, Mark

Samuel Langhorne Clemens (1835–1910), better known as Mark Twain, was arguably the most popular American author of his day. When his father died in 1847, Clemens began working as a printer's apprentice; later, he worked for his brother, Orion, who founded the *Hannibal Journal* in Missouri. In 1857 the *Daily Post* of Keokuk, Iowa, commissioned him to write a series of humorous travel letters, but after completing only five, he decided to become a riverboat captain instead. Receiving his pilot's license in 1859, Clemens piloted Mississippi riverboats until the Civil War halted river traffic. During this time he picked up the pen name Mark Twain—the boatman's sounding call to indicate a water depth of two fathoms, the minimum for safe navigation. He served briefly as a volunteer in the Confederate Army before rejoining his brother, now the territorial secretary in Nevada.

In 1862 Clemens returned to writing, as a reporter for the *Virginia City Territorial Enterprise* in Nevada, using his pseudonym for his byline. Moving to San Francisco in 1864, he wrote the story that made him famous—"The Celebrated Jumping Frog of Calaveras County." In 1866 he traveled to Hawaii as a reporter for the California-based *Sacramento Union* and then continued his journey around the world, writing of his experiences for other newspapers in California and New York; the reports from this period were compiled and published in book form as *The Innocents Abroad* (1869). Clemens became a popular and sought-after lecturer and storyteller, as well as a prolific author of articles, travelogs, essays, and novels, including his masterpiece, *The Adventures of Huckleberry Finn* (1885).

His unique form of country humor and his adroit combination of journalistic observation and writing skill gained him mounting fame, and his popularity in Europe and the United States gave him extraordinary access to leaders and politicians and, thus, influence on political thought. Fervently anti-racist and anti-imperialist in his political thinking, Clemens was keenly aware of the power of his experiences, words, and intellect. In 1903 Clemens and his family moved to Italy, where his wife died the following year. Her death, and the deaths of two daughters (in 1896 and 1909), left him morose and bitter. His distinctive humor turned unmistakably darker, as reflected in the works of this period,

Journalist and novelist Samuel Clemens, known popularly as Mark Twain, is most well-known for writing The Adventures of Huckleberry Finn, *but his social commentary and wit also made him extraordinarily popular in his time.*

What Is Man? (1906) and *The Mysterious Stranger* (1916). Clemens died in Redding, Connecticut, in 1910. His autobiography was published in two volumes in 1924.

REFERENCES

Brown, Don. *American Boy: The Adventures of Mark Twain.* New York: Houghton Mifflin, 2003.

De Voto, Bernard Augustine. *Mark Twain's America.* Westport, Conn.: Greenwood Press, 1978. First published 1932 by Little, Brown.

Howells, William Dean. *My Mark Twain: Reminiscences and Criticisms.* Brooklyn, N.Y.: Haskell House, 1977. First published 1910 by Harper and Bros.

Kaplan, Justin. *Mr. Clemens and Mark Twain: A Biography.* New York: Simon and Schuster, 1966.

Robinson, Forrest G. *In Bad Faith: The Dynamics of Deception in Mark Twain's America.* Cambridge, Mass.: Harvard University Press, 1986.

U

United Press International

United Press International (UPI) is a major international news service that grew out of a smaller company founded by Edward W. Scripps in 1907, when the Associated Press (AP) wire service refused to service some of Scripps's newspapers. Unlike the AP, Scripps's United Press (UP) was a for-profit institution that was financially lean, fiercely competitive, and noted for sharp writing.

The understaffed UP trained a regiment of noted journalists, and, at its high point during World War II, it performed to the highest standards amid staff and budget shortages. In 1945 the U.S. Supreme Court ruled that the Associated Press had to sell its service to any media concern that wanted it, and this ruling, by placing the two news gatherers in direct competition, ultimately gutted the United Press membership. In 1958 UP merged with Hearst's International News Service, becoming United Press International (UPI).

Although its reporting was stronger than that of its rival, UPI's losses continued. In 1982 the Scripps Howard newspaper chain sold the wire service because it was draining resources, and UPI filed for bankruptcy protection in April 1985. It then went through a series of owners before being purchased in 2000 by News World Communications, which is controlled by the Rev. Sun Myung Moon's Unification Church and is also the parent company of the *Washington Times*. This move raised questions about UPI's editorial independence, but it gave the wire service some much-needed financial stability.

See also *Associated Press; Scripps, E. W.; Wire services.*

REFERENCES

Gordon, Gregory, and Ronald E. Cohen. *Down to the Wire: UPI's Fight for Survival.* New York: McGraw-Hill, 1990.
Folkerts, Jean, and Dwight L. Teeter. *Voices of a Nation: A History of Mass Media in the United States.* 3rd ed. Boston: Allyn and Bacon, 1988.
Read, Donald. *The Power of News: The History of Reuters.* Oxford: Oxford University Press, 1992.

USA Today

USA Today became the United States' first general interest national newspaper when the Gannett Corporation launched it in 1982. Published only on weekdays, it is one of the most widely distributed newspapers in the country, with a five-day circulation of more than 2 million papers. The *USA Today* franchise now includes not only the U.S. daily newspaper, but also a worldwide edition—European and Asian editions were added in 1984—and a weekly baseball newspaper.

USA Today's format and use of color throughout are aimed at readers accustomed to the quick pace and graphic flash of television. Dismissively christening it "McPaper," the publication's critics assert that this visually oriented approach has "dumbed down" or trivialized news coverage; some elements of the paper's style have been copied by newspapers across the nation. On the other hand, its continued popularity as one of the few mass-marketed national dailies in the television and Internet age suggests that *USA Today* has found a loyal audience among today's media consumers.

See also *Gannett.*

REFERENCES

McCartney, James. "USA Today Grows Up." *American Journalism Review* 19, no. 7 (September 1997): 18–25.

Neuharth, Al. *Confessions of an S.O.B.* New York: Doubleday, 1989.

Prichard, Peter. *The Making of McPaper: The Inside Story of USA Today.* Kansas City: Andrews, McMeel, and Parker, 1987.

U.S. Information Agency

The U.S. Information Agency (USIA) was created as an independent foreign affairs agency within the executive branch in 1953, when Congress approved President Dwight D. Eisenhower's proposal for a means of employing public diplomacy to explain and promote U.S. foreign policy and national interests abroad. President John F. Kennedy defined the agency's mission as helping to achieve U.S. foreign policy objectives by influencing public attitudes in other nations, while advising the government on the implications of foreign opinion for U.S. policies, programs, and official statements.

The United States recognized the need to oversee international propaganda as early as World War I, creating the Committee on Public Information, also known as the Creel Commission, in 1917. A similar organization—the Office of War Information (OWI)—was formed during World War II; its foreign subdivision, the U.S. Information Service (USIS), was retained after OWI's postwar dissolution, providing the structure in which USIA operated overseas.

USIA oversaw a variety of educational and exchange programs in the United States and in foreign lands, including Fulbright scholarships, speakers' bureaus, and press centers. The agency distributed books, magazines, music, films, and other cultural materials to libraries at USIS posts abroad. USIA supervised broadcasts of the federally funded Voice of America, which at its peak broadcast 660 hours of radio programming weekly in fifty-three languages; the twenty-four-hour Radio Marti and TV Marti; and the satellite WORLD-NET Television. Nonprofit Radio Free Europe/Radio Liberty and Radio Free Asia received USIA grants. In April 1978 the agency's name was changed to the International Communication Agency (USICA), but the original name was restored in August 1982.

Consecutive U.S. governments used USIA to conduct opinion polls around the world, to monitor foreign media, and to pursue a variety of overt and covert propaganda efforts. During the late 1990s, the agency had 190 posts in 142 countries, employed more than 6,300 people, and operated on an annual budget of $1.1 billion. USIA was dissolved in October 1999, when its functions were integrated into the Department of State's Bureau of Public Diplomacy and Public Affairs.

See also *Public diplomacy.*

REFERENCES

Conroy, S.B. "The Last Word on USIA." *Washington Post,* October 4, 1999, C2.

Haefele, M. "John F. Kennedy, USIA and World Public Opinion." *Diplomatic History* 25, no. 1 (Winter 2001).

Henderson, J.W. *The United States Information Agency.* New York: Praeger, 1969.

V

Village Voice

The *Village Voice,* a free tabloid-format newspaper, was the nation's first and largest alternative newsweekly. Characterized by eclectic content, hard-hitting investigative reporting, and coverage of the New York scene, it has won three Pulitzer Prizes and numerous other journalistic awards.

Ed Fancher, Norman Mailer, and Dan Wolf founded the *Voice* in 1955 as a free-form alternative to mainstream major daily papers in New York City. It takes its name from Greenwich Village. Under Wolf's editorship, through the early 1970s, the paper became known for its freewheeling style, feature stories, and practice of new journalism. It attracted contributions from a variety of writers. Internal editorial and ownership battles plagued the paper in the 1970s, during which time it came under the control of media magnate Rupert Murdoch. In 1986 real estate mogul Leonard Stein purchased the paper and expanded the company, buying several similar papers in other cities. In 2006 Village Voice Media was formed through a merger of the *Voice* chain of papers and New Times Newspapers, another leading publisher of alternative newsweeklies. The *Voice* is still regarded as a leading model of alternative journalism. Its avant-garde coverage of culture, the arts, and politics continues to provide it distinction.

See also *Alternative media; New journalism.*

REFERENCES

McAuliffe, Kevin Michael. *The Great American Newspaper: The Rise and Fall of the* Village Voice. New York: Scribner, 1978.
Village Voice, www.villagevoice.com.

Voice of America

The Voice of America (VOA) is the primary federally funded international broadcast service of the United States, transmitting news and cultural programming to the world in forty-four languages via short- and medium-wave radio frequencies, satellite television, and the Internet. VOA's 1976 charter commits the agency to provide "accurate, objective, and comprehensive" news programming, but also to "present a balanced and comprehensive projection of significant American thought and institutions." The Voice of America serves primarily as a means by which to express American viewpoints to the world.

The U.S. government's first international radio broadcasts, aimed at Asia, were made under the auspices of the U.S. Foreign Information Service in December 1941. The first transmission to Europe, in February 1942, opened with the words, "Here speaks a voice from America," which, though spoken in German, gave the broadcast service its name. VOA operated under the Office of War Information during World War II, but was transferred to the State Department in the postwar years. In 1953 it was the single largest element of the new U.S. Information Agency (USIA). In 1994 VOA became the primary multimedia broadcasting service of the International Broadcasting Bureau (IBB), which was made into an independent agency with the dissolution of USIA in 1999.

Now overseen by the independent Broadcasting Board of Governors, whose members are appointed by the president, the IBB also operates the WORLDNET Television and Film Service, which provides programming to stations worldwide, as well as Radio Martí and TV Martí, two controversial services that broadcast programming targeting Cuba. The IBB also provides support to Radio Free Europe/Radio Liberty and Radio Free Asia, as well as to the Middle East Television Network, which broadcasts in Arabic as part of U.S. public diplomacy efforts in the Arab world.

See also *Public diplomacy; U.S. Information Agency.*

REFERENCES

Heil, Alan L. *Voice of America: A History.* New York: Columbia University Press, 2003.

Schulman, Holly Cowan. *The Voice of America: Propaganda and Democracy, 1941–1945.* Madison: University of Wisconsin Press, 1991.

Voice of America, www.VOANews.com.

Wall Street Journal

The *Wall Street Journal,* published daily in New York City and in four regional editions, is considered the most influential business-oriented newspaper in the country. It has been a pioneer in satellite publishing, and its objective reporting has made it one of the most generally respected papers worldwide.

Charles H. Dow (of Dow Jones & Company) founded the paper in 1889 because he believed that business news was not receiving appropriate coverage. Its accuracy, fairness, and depth of coverage made it an immediate success. Prior to the Great Depression, the *Journal* rarely covered anything but business and economic news, but the need to boost circulation led to the introduction of feature articles on topics from beyond the corporate world. By the 1960s, it was regularly carrying two such nonbusiness feature articles on its front page.

The *Journal's* editorial and op-ed pages are famous for offering a breadth of well-informed opinion on a range of topics, although its masthead editorials are known for their staunch conservatism and defense of free-market economics. Nonetheless, it is the paper's primary focus on business news that attracts the highest circulation of any national daily in the United States.

REFERENCES

Rosenberg, Jerry Martin. *Inside the* Wall Street Journal: *The History and Power of Dow Jones & Company and America's Most Influential Newspaper.* New York: Macmillan, 1982.
Scharff, Edward E. *Worldly Power: The Making of the* Wall Street Journal. New York: New American Library, 1986.

Walters, Barbara

Barbara Walters (1931–) is a television journalist and popular interviewer. Beginning her career as a secretary at an advertising agency, she next worked as an assistant to the publicity director of WRCA-TV, an NBC affiliate, and then moved to CBS, where she wrote for the network's morning show. In 1961 Walters returned to NBC to write for the *Today* show, where, after an assignment covering first lady Jacqueline Kennedy's travels to India and Pakistan brought her to prominence in front of the camera, she became a regular member of that show's broadcast team.

In 1976 Walters was lured to ABC, where she co-anchored the evening news program with Harry Reasoner, who was outspokenly critical of her position and salary. At the same time, she launched the first of the *Barbara Walters Special* programs, which featured her often candid and intimate interviews with the rich and famous as well as with notable and even notorious individuals. Critics claim that her casual yet probing style of interviewing and reporting has contributed to the transformation of broadcast news into "infotainment."

Walters joined ABC's *20/20,* a prime-time news program, as a co-host in 1979, and in the following year she obtained an exclusive interview with former president Richard Nixon—his first television interview since his 1974 resignation. She became co-executive producer and co-host of *The View,* a mid-morning talk show with four other, ethnically diverse female co-hosts, in 1997. Her exclusive, two-hour-long interview with former White House intern Monica Lewinsky in 1999 became one of the highest-rated network

Barbara Walters has worked for ABC since 1976, when she became the first woman to co-anchor the evening news on a major network. She is pictured here with co-anchor Harry Reasoner shortly after her debut.

news programs ever. Walters wrote the appropriately titled *How to Talk with Practically Anybody about Practically Anything* (1983).

REFERENCES

Oppenheimer, Jerry. *Barbara Walters: An Unauthorized Biography.* New York: St. Martin's Press, 1990.
Remstein, Henna. *Barbara Walters.* Philadelphia: Chelsea House, 1999.
Sanders, Marlene. *Waiting for Prime Time: The Women of Television News.* Urbana: University of Illinois Press, 1988.

War and the media

Since the rise of mass mobilization warfare in the nineteenth century, leaders have had to generate and maintain public support for war. As civilian populations became more involved—either directly as combatants or indirectly as workers in the industries of war—their attitudes about the merits of a conflict involving their nation assumed importance. This task requires mobilization of the media. Whether by such means as the "Uncle Sam Wants You" posters, created by the Committee on Public Information during World War I, or by broadcasting the carefully scripted military briefings of more recent years, media have played a central role in creating and maintaining public support for war. Yet the same media can also weaken that support. Images of the dead and maimed, as well as reports of casualties or blunders, can sap morale among troops and undermine confidence and support for the war at home. In short, there are two contests in war: one is fought on the battlefield; the other, as the cliché notes, is a battle for hearts and minds.

Public opinion plays a complex and somewhat ironic role in the conduct of war. On the one hand, it is deferred to, fretted over, and therefore often necessitates sophisticated public relations campaigns. On the other hand, the public is often indifferent to major upheavals that dominate the news, tending to be more interested in local events or entertainment than in foreign affairs. Although wars may be an exception in grabbing people's attention, public opinion is not always well informed, even on grave issues. For example, a University of Maryland survey conducted in the spring of 2004 found that sizable portions of the American public remained confused or held misconceptions about the arguments that the Bush administration had used to justify the 2003 U.S.-led invasion of Iraq.

Accurately founded or not, public opinion plays an important role in war. During the initial stages of a conflict, for example, American public support for the president typically increases, while toleration of dissent declines—the "rally 'round the flag" phenomenon or rally effect. In 1973 political scientist John Mueller identified three minimal

Associated Press photographer Huynh Thanh My shoots footage in 1965 during the Vietnam War. He was killed during combat on October 10, 1965. The Vietnam War was the first "television war" and the first "uncensored" war, as correspondents had the freedom and mobility to report from the front lines.

criteria for such an effect in the United States: it must be associated with an international event; the event must involve the United States; and the event must be dramatic, specific, and sharply focused. Examples of such events are the U.S. military intervention in Korea in 1950 and the abortive Bay of Pigs invasion in 1961. Major diplomatic actions, such as the announcement of the Truman Doctrine in 1947, can also induce a rally, as can technological threats, such as the launch of Sputnik in 1957. The al-Qaida attacks of September 11, 2001—which led to an increase of more than 40 percent in President George W. Bush's approval ratings over the next month—offer another dramatic example.

Rally effects produce room for leaders to maneuver, allowing them to endure the failures that will almost always be a part of war. A rally thus constitutes a temporal space or environment in which to pursue goals relatively free of criticism. The durability of a rally—how long it lasts—depends on a number of factors, but certainly one of them is the outcome of so-called framing contests. In general, framing is the interpretation of or assignment of meaning to events and processes. Phrases, signifiers, and photographs all contribute to the creation of meaning. The selection of some photographs but not others or the use of some phrases and not others frame the event and impart meaning.

Frames most commonly are selected and successfully propagated by authoritative officials. Political scientist Gadi

Wolfsfeld argues that the key determinant in whether officials dominate framing contests about war (or anything else) is whether they have control of the political environment, which, in turn, is determined by three variables: the ability to initiate and control events; the ability to regulate the flow of information; and the ability to mobilize elite support. The military's ability to control the flow of information is impressive but not complete, and it is diminishing. As a result, the ability to mobilize public support becomes more problematic. As for control of the events themselves, it is important to recognize that war is highly scripted as well as chaotic. Battle plans are meticulously prepared in an effort to achieve strategic and tactical objectives while minimizing the loss of life, at least among allies and civilians. Yet, as historian Paul Fussell has documented, mistakes are unavoidable: even precision bombs can hit the wrong targets—as happened when the United States bombed the Chinese embassy in Belgrade in 1999.

This inability to control events is the crucial issue in the relationship between war and media, because it results in an inability to control the story. When the action appears to be going according to plan, media coverage tends to accentuate the brilliance and valor of the armed forces, but when objectives are not met, and when the gap between expectations and reality becomes too great, media tend to underscore and amplify mistakes. Losing control of the political environment thus invites a cascade of uncontrolled media stories. Yet total control of events in war is impossible, particularly when communication and information technology is at hand to record the messy business of war.

Governments have historically controlled the flow of information from the battlefield by limiting access and by imposing censorship. Advances in technology, from the telegraph to videophones, however, have made this objective more difficult to achieve. Throughout most of the history of war-related journalism—and, before that, legend and rumor—physical distance determined the speed and content of news. Reports of the battles of Lexington and Concord on April 19, 1775, were printed that same day in the nearby *Boston News-Letter,* but the New York and Philadelphia papers did not offer accounts of the battle until April 24, and in Savannah, Georgia, the *Gazette* published its account on May 31, more than a month later. In an effort to shorten delays caused by distance, pony express systems were introduced as early as 1825, the same year that commercial railroads were established. Still, news of the Mexican-American War (1846–1848) remained dependent on physical transportation.

The invention and mass expansion of the telegraph finally removed the barrier of physical distance. Patented in 1840, the telegraph made the Civil War the first war with transmitted news. Though heavily used by the military, the expanding telegraph system came with a potential security threat as well, so in 1862 Congress granted President Abraham Lincoln the authority to place the telegraph system under military control. Thereafter, all war-related news carried over the lines was subject to censorship. At the same time, field commanders made a regular practice of restricting journalists' access to the front lines. These two developments led to a dependence on communiqués issued by the War Department, giving government officials a privileged position in framing news of the war. Secretary of War Edwin M. Stanton also required journalists to sign their copy in an effort to encourage accountability and discourage rumors; this practice evolved into today's bylines. The Civil War also saw the rise of another potentially unsettling new technology: photography. By war's end, 2,000 photographers had taken approximately 1 million exposures. The works of Matthew Brady and others helped to dispel the prevailing romanticized notions of war.

The Spanish-American War is often said to have been the product of the sensationalist "yellow" journalism of William Randolph Hearst's *New York Journal* and Joseph Pulitzer's *New York World.* According to the overheated coverage offered by these two highly competitive New York City newspapers, the Spanish had committed numerous atrocities in crushing a Cuban insurrection. When the U.S. battleship *Maine* was sunk in Havana harbor, the *Journal* attributed it to Spanish sabotage, setting off a wave of war fever across the country. After a quick series of victories, a peace treaty was signed in December 1898, instituting U.S. control over several Spanish colonial holdings, including the Philippines. In protest, the Philippine people launched a massive insurrection in which some 200,000 people had been killed by the end of 1902. American military authorities in the Philippines imposed strict military censorship, going so far as to restrict the use of the transpacific cable.

During World War I, the first large-scale mass mobilization war across national borders, journalists' access was again tightly restricted. Reporters were either forbidden near the front or placed under tight controls; to be accredited with U.S. forces, they were required to sign a loyalty oath, pay their own expenses, and post a $10,000 bond to be forfeited in case of unacceptable behavior. Military censors also reviewed all copy before it could be released. The carnage of the Great War was almost unimaginable and, at the time, almost unknown, as censors hid the true costs of the war from the public.

Meanwhile, in France, Britain, and the United States, propaganda efforts attempted to maintain public morale. The Committee on Public Information, headed by Progressive journalist George Creel, issued thousands of news releases, created hundreds of posters, and coordinated public speakers. The government discouraged dissent by such means as the Espionage Act of 1917, which imposed fines of up to $10,000 and imprisonment up to twenty years for those convicted of promoting disloyalty or insubordination; the Trading with the Enemy Act, passed in October 1917, which authorized the censorship of overseas communication and established the Censorship Board; and the Sedition Act of 1918, which amended the Espionage Act to make it illegal to speak or write anything deemed critical of the government, the flag, or the military. Under these circumstances, the outcome of any framing contest concerning the war was certain.

During World War II, control of wartime information fell to the Office of Censorship, established by the first War Powers Act on December 19, 1941. For the most part, the media complied with government controls, and commanders welcomed members of the press, who wore military uniforms. Gen. Douglas MacArthur took that same attitude toward journalism to the war in Korea. In the early weeks of the war, MacArthur resisted imposing censorship on the press, but by December, in part because of some journalists' belief that the voluntary system was too ambiguous and was therefore not working, the military started reviewing media reports from the front lines.

The Vietnam War is often referred to as the first "television war" and also as the "uncensored" war. As U.S. involvement escalated, the number of journalists covering it increased, from approximately forty full-time correspondents in mid-1964 to four hundred by the following year. Generally free to establish informal relations and arrangements with military units, reporters, including Malcolm Browne of the Associated Press, Neil Sheehan of UPI, and David Halberstam of the *New York Times,* began relaying information gathered from junior field commanders that was at odds with the more upbeat assessments offered by press officers in Saigon. Television also played an important role in shaping and conveying images of the war, especially as over the course of the decade camera technology improved to the point that by 1970 camera crews were carrying manageable equipment and sending back first-hand images of the conflict. Also, the time between events and broadcast diminished, as the cumbersome film used at the start of the war gave way to satellite transmissions that conveyed the news and images on the same day.

After Vietnam, the suspicion that the war had been lost because of uncontrolled media reports—and not because of failed strategies or actions on the ground —created tremendous distrust between the media and the military. Further advances in communication technology exacerbated these tensions. When U.S. forces invaded the small Caribbean island of Grenada on October 25, 1983, U.S. commanders—taking their cue from the British military's management of the media during the Falklands War—refused to allow journalists on the island for the first forty-eight hours of fighting. Given the short duration of hostilities, this ban effectively prevented media coverage of the invasion. News organizations protested, but the Pentagon argued that communications technology would have put U.S. troops at risk, as the element of surprise would be undermined by the speed of news reporting in the satellite age.

The Pentagon established a commission headed by Gen. Winant Sidle to resolve the issue. Among its recommendations, announced in August 1984, was the creation of press pools to consist of representatives from one of the wire services, an agency photojournalist, a television correspondent and two technicians, a radio reporter, three newspaper correspondents, and a national news magazine correspondent. The first test of the press pool system came in December 1989, when the United States invaded Panama. It proved to be a near-total failure, as the pool members were flown to an airport hangar several hours after the start of the invasion and spent much of the conflict there under armed guard.

After Iraq invaded Kuwait in August 1990, the UN Security Council authorized the use of "all means necessary" to force the Iraqis back across the border. Most of the visual images and many of the accounts of the war came from official briefings by the U.S. military based in Saudi Arabia because of the pace and prosecution of the war. This limited live coverage—though regarded as a technological breakthrough, in part because of such dramatic footage as Iraqi Scud missile attacks on Saudi Arabia and Israel—also underscored the limitations of the technology of the day. Because reporters' broadcasting equipment required a satellite uplink and a reliable power source, journalists were essentially tethered to one spot, usually a rooftop or hotel balcony. Also, during the ground campaign, correspondents depended on the military to physically transport copy and tape from the front to a rear area, where satellite equipment beamed it to the rest of the world. Delays in transportation were endemic.

By the time of the invasions of Afghanistan in 2001 and of Iraq in 2003, media technology had severed the media's dependence on fixed locations and military transfer. Videophones and other Inmarsat-based links offered journalists instant links for sending pictures, sounds, and text on the go. For the first time, journalists could report live from a distant, remote field of battle. The U.S. military responded to this new technical capacity by creating a new means of controlling coverage. The "embed" program matched journalists from news organizations with military units, in whose company the journalists covered a good part of the Iraq War live.

The immediacy of this live coverage came at a cost, however. Since the end of the cold war, "hot wars" have tended to be messy affairs. Rather than mass armies of two or more nation-states lined up against one another, recent conflicts have involved intrastate guerrilla armies and nonstate organizations; clearly defined front lines did not always exist. Meanwhile, technology has provided war correspondents greater mobility for reporting these wars without frontiers. The combination is dangerous, as the numbers show. According to the Committee for the Protection of Journalists, an advocacy group that monitors incidents involving journalists around the globe, 337 journalists were killed in war zones between 1995 and 2004.

If U.S. governments are to control the media and maintain popular backing, they must sustain the unifying rally effect. This may be one of the real lessons of Vietnam. A study by Daniel Hallin found that despite some misgivings by reporters, the media did not become critical of the war until certain politicians had already done so, fueling conflict and controversy at home. In short, administrations should recognize that once dissension begins among the political elite, it may spread to the media and on to the public.

See also *Censorship; Embedding; Framing; Pool journalism.*

REFERENCES

Entman, Robert M. *Projections of Power: Framing News, Public Opinion, and U.S. Foreign Policy.* Chicago: University of Chicago Press, 2004.
Gamson, William. "News as Framing." *American Behavioral Scientist* 33 (1989): 157–161.
Hallin, Daniel. *The "Uncensored" War: The Media and Vietnam.* New York: Oxford University Press, 1986.
Wolfsfeld, Gadi. *Media and Political Conflict: News From the Middle East.* Cambridge: Cambridge University Press, 1997.

Washington Post

The *Washington Post* is considered one of the most authoritative news sources on the activities of the U.S. government, particularly within Congress and the White House. A nationally prominent newspaper that also serves as a regional paper in Washington, D.C., and its Maryland and Virginia suburbs, the *Post* currently enjoys the fifth largest circulation nationally among U.S. daily newspapers. Founded in 1877 by Stilson Hutchins, it was the U.S. capital's first newspaper and by 1880 had become the first in that city to publish daily.

As of 2005, the *Post* had won eighteen Pulitzer Prizes. Among its many other journalistic achievements, the *Post* is best known for its role in breaking the Watergate scandal. From 1972 to 1976, *Post* reporters Bob Woodward and Carl Bernstein exposed the political mischief and the high-level cover-up that led not only to the indictment of forty White House officials but also to the resignation of President Richard M. Nixon days before the House of Representatives was to have voted on impeaching him. The newspaper also made history in 1963, when Katharine Graham inherited control of the Washington Post Company after the suicide of her husband, publisher Philip Graham, making the *Post* the first paper of national stature to be run by a woman. Today the paper is still owned by the Washington Post Company, which also publishes the news magazine *Newsweek* and the online magazine *Slate*.

See also *Bradlee, Ben; Graham, Katharine; Pentagon Papers; Watergate.*

REFERENCES

Babb, Laura Longley, ed. *Keeping Posted: 100 Years of News from the* Washington Post. Washington, D.C.: Washington Post, 1977.
Graham, Katharine. *Personal History.* New York: Knopf, 1997.
Roberts, Chalmers M. *In the Shadow of Power: The Story of the* Washington Post. Cabin John, Md.: Seven Locks Press, 1989.
Washington Post. Timeline of the History of the *Washington Post,* http://washpost.com/gen_info/history/timeline/index.shtml.

Watchdog role

One of the media's main roles in a democracy is to act as a "watchdog" over government, vigorously guarding the public interest against possible abuses by those in power. By monitoring governmental performance and alerting the public when officials are behaving improperly, failing to meet goals, or misusing their authority, the media act as the "fourth branch" of government, holding officials accountable and thereby giving them an extra incentive to behave ethically, to act in the public interest, and to tell the truth. Some recent examples of press performance of the watchdog role include the 1971 Pentagon Papers episode, which exposed government deception about the Vietnam War, and the Watergate scandal, which eventually drove President Richard M. Nixon from office.

Key elements of this role in practice are the use of investigative reporting and the maintenance of an adversarial posture toward government officials and their public statements, which requires careful scrutiny of their words and deeds. In practice, however, these elements are often lacking in political and governmental reporting. News-gathering routines, which rely on coverage of regular beats and ongoing access to official sources—coupled with the profit-maximizing drive of most media outlets, which promotes quick relaying of news released from official sources over expensive and risky investigative adventures—serve to prevent the media from providing effective oversight. One illustrative example was the media's failure to uncover the Iran-contra scandal during the Reagan administration. Not only did some earlier-known elements of the scandal—including the illegal funding of Nicaraguan rebels—go largely unreported, but the main story—the trading of U.S. arms to Iran in exchange for the promised release of American hostages—was "broken" initially by foreign, not American, media outlets. Furthermore, through adroit media management, President Ronald Reagan was able to effectively divert the focus of attention from official malfeasance to perceived problems with his leadership style, and, unlike Nixon, he remained in office despite the unfolding scandal.

In general, the media appear more willing to dig up sensational, scandalous tidbits about politicians' private lives—such as Gary Hart's and Bill Clinton's extramarital affairs—and to highlight sporadic cases of bureaucratic waste than to examine significant, substantive abuses of power and the enduring structural forces that cause them. As Herbert Altshull notes, "criticism of *individuals* has heightened markedly, [but] one must search long and hard to find serious criticism of the political and economic systems that have furthered public venality." Still, the media do at times succeed in providing the electorate with information that can be of use in holding government officials accountable at the ballot box.

See also *Hart, Gary; Investigative reporting; Muckraking; Pentagon Papers; Social responsibility; Watergate.*

REFERENCES

Altshull, J. Herbert. *Agents of Power: The Media and Public Policy.* 2nd ed. White Plains, N.Y.: Longman, 1995.

Ansolabehere, Stephen, Roy Behr, and Shanto Iyengar. *The Media Game: American Politics in the Television Age.* New York: Macmillan, 1993.

Bennett, W. Lance, and William Serrin. "The Watchdog Role." In *Institutions of American Democracy: The Press,* edited by Geneva Overholser and Kathleen Hall Jamieson. New York: Oxford University Press, 2005.

Watergate

The Watergate scandal began in June 1972 with a failed burglary, perpetrated by White House political operatives, at the Democratic National Committee's headquarters in the Watergate complex in Washington, D.C. It ended on August 7, 1974, with President Richard M. Nixon's announcement that he would resign from the presidency. As Carl Bernstein and Bob Woodward, two reporters on the metropolitan desk at the *Washington Post,* followed the trail of official involvement, what was initially considered to be a local story about "a third-rate burglary" mushroomed into a burgeoning scandal that would shake the foundations of the U.S. government.

Early on, the *Post* had revealed that one of the burglars was a security official for the Republican Party, that another had received a check for $25,000 from the Nixon campaign, and that the break-in was part of a broader campaign of "dirty tricks" employed by the Committee to Reelect the President (CREEP). Despite these revelations, Nixon defeated his challenger, Democratic senator George McGovern in the 1972 presidential election. Nevertheless, the scandal continued to grow. Two of the president's closest White House associates implicated in an attempt to cover up involvement in the crime were convicted of perjury in January 1973, and the Senate decided to hold hearings on the matter beginning in May of that year. Watergate had thus become a major political controversy, appearing on a Gallup poll's "most important problem" list of citizen concerns.

In the Senate hearings, telecast live and replayed in the evenings over thirty-seven days, the testimony of witnesses was scheduled to lay out the story, beginning with a "scene-setting phase," in which the circumstances surrounding the break-in were detailed, followed by an "accusatory phase," during which John Dean, former White House counsel, testified to Nixon's complicity in the cover-up. Polls showed that more Americans found Dean's account credible than believed Nixon's.

A major turning point came in July 1973, when Alexander Butterfield, an aide to the president, revealed that Nixon had a voice-activated tape recording system concealed under his desk. The existence of tapes of presidential conversations converted the issue from how to get at the truth to what the truth actually was. Watergate special prosecutor Archibald Cox promptly demanded that the tapes be turned over to his investigation. In October 1973, Nixon, determined to withhold the tapes, claimed "executive privilege" in refusing to release them and then ordered Attorney General Elliot Richardson to fire Cox. When Richardson and his deputy resigned in protest, the third in command at the Department of Justice, Solicitor General Robert Bork, carried out the order. Public indignation over the "Saturday night massacre" ran high, and the first calls for impeachment gained in volume in the face of Nixon's apparent stalling.

In the summer of 1974, the House Judiciary Committee held closed-session hearings to review the case for impeachment. Network television carried the ensuing public debate in full, including the committee's final bipartisan vote approving three articles of impeachment—for obstruction of justice, abuse of power, and contempt of Congress. In early August, a unanimous Supreme Court, in *United States v. Nixon,* ordered the release of the White House tapes. (The administration had earlier released edited transcripts of them.) In one recording, Nixon is heard urging a cover-up; this "smoking gun" convinced the ten Republicans in Congress who had held out against impeachment to change their minds. A few days later, Nixon became the first U.S. president to resign from office. The media's extensive coverage of the scandal, however, put the lie to any argument that the president had been ousted by a political coup d'état. The *Post's* coverage won the paper a Pulitzer Prize for public service.

The Watergate scandal continues to resonate, as the suffix "-gate" is regularly applied to political misdeeds, such as "Iran-gate" or "Monica-gate." In 2005 *Vanity Fair* revealed that one of Bernstein and Woodward's confidential sources, code-named "Deep Throat," had been W. Mark Felt, the deputy director of the FBI.

See also *Bernstein, Carl; Bradlee, Ben; Graham, Katharine; Investigative reporting; Nixon, Richard M.; Watchdog role; Woodward, Bob.*

REFERENCES

Bernstein, Carl, and Bob Woodward. *All the President's Men.* New York: Simon and Schuster, 1974.

Lang, Gladys Engel, and Kurt Lang. *The Battle for Public Opinion: The President, the Press, and the Polls during Watergate.* New York: Columbia University Press, 1983.

Sussman, Barry. *The Great Cover-Up.* New York: Thomas Y. Crowell, 1974.

White, William Allen

William Allen White (1868–1944), the publisher of a small Midwest daily newspaper, was an influential journalist and winner of two Pulitzer Prizes. Before completing his undergraduate education, White learned the printing and newspaper business in El Dorado, Kansas, and then began his journalism career in Lawrence before moving to the *Kansas City Star* as an editorial writer. In 1895 he borrowed $3,000 to purchase the *Emporia Gazette,* and he remained at that paper throughout his career.

In 1896, inspired by a street-corner debate centered on the McKinley-Bryan presidential campaign, White wrote "What's the Matter with Kansas?"—a sarcastic, scathing editorial excoriating Democratic Party leaders. The editorial was distributed nationally by the Republican Party, contributing both to McKinley's election and to White's rise in public recognition. After his sixteen-year-old daughter Mary died as a result of a tragic riding accident in 1921, White's poignant, passionate editorial pouring out his grief further endeared him to many readers beyond the subscribers to his newspaper. In 1923 he won a Pulitzer Prize for his editorials.

As a spokesman for small-town life and a liberal Republican who used his contacts and influence to gain access far beyond his venue, White advised presidents, governors, statesmen, and notables from the political world. In 1919 President Woodrow Wilson sent him as special envoy to confer with representatives of various Russian political factions at Princes Islands. In 1924 White ran as a candidate for governor of Kansas, waging a bitter fight against the Ku Klux Klan, which had endorsed the two other candidates; he came in third, but the Klan's influence in the state diminished rapidly thereafter. In 1936 he suspended his editorial writing to work for fellow Kansan Alf Landon's presidential campaign against President Franklin Roosevelt. Although he admired the president and supported some of his policies, White remained a loyal Republican.

White's numerous fiction and nonfiction works include *The Old Order Changeth: A View of American Democracy* (1910), *Politics: The Citizen's Business* (1924), and *Masks in a Pageant* (1928), as well as biographies of Woodrow Wilson (1924) and Calvin Coolidge (1925, 1938) and two collections of his newspaper writings, *The Editor and His People* (1924) and *Forty Years on Main Street* (1937). White's autobiography, published after his death, won him another Pulitzer Prize.

REFERENCES

Agran, Edward Gale. *Too Good a Town: William Allen White, Community, and the Emerging Rhetoric of Middle America.* Fayetteville: University of Arkansas Press, 1999.

Griffith, Sally Foreman. *Home Town News: William Allen White and the Emporia Gazette.* New York: Oxford University Press, 1989.

Jernigan, E. Jay. *William Allen White.* Boston: Twayne Publishers, 1983.

Johnson, Walter. *William Allen White's America.* New York: H. Holt, 1947.

White House press corps

The White House press corps consists of the relatively few reporters to whom a White House press pass has been issued. Currently, there are 1,700—a number almost unchanged since the Reagan administration—though only about 60 cover the president on a regular basis. Traditionally among the prestige assignments in Washington, the White House beat has slipped in status in recent years. That press pass, after all, conveys merely the privilege to wait—to attend a briefing or a press conference; to see the president, the press secretary, or other senior officials; and to have phone calls returned.

The press secretary's briefing is the central event in the daily distribution of official White House information. Whatever message the president and the president's staff want to highlight is presented in an opening statement. The press secretary then takes questions from the reporters assembled for the briefing, which may last from a half hour to an hour, depending on the day's issues. The press corps also seeks information from other members of the White House staff, and generally covers all presidential speeches and travel—though often this access is limited to a select press pool that shares its information with others.

The relationship between the White House and its press corps is shaped by the need each has for the other. The administration, for its part, seeks to provide reporters with a continual flow of news items it wants to emphasize, while reporters try to elicit from the press secretary and from others in the White House, including the president, answers to the questions they believe to be important. Each views the other as having the advantage in this contest of wills, yet each needs the other's cooperation to do an effective job. Along the way, skirmishes erupt—fueled, in part, by the mistrust that has colored the relationship since the lies and perceived manipulations of the Vietnam and Watergate eras of the 1960s and 1970s. As veteran White House reporter Helen Thomas put it, "I think we have tried to learn from the past, and the press is more probing, more skeptical, not just with the White House, but all candidates for public office."

Nevertheless, the reporters' dependency on government officials for regular, usable news and information means that there is generally more cooperation than conflict. Indeed, the White House press corps has been accused of being too "soft" and passive toward the president in every administration since that of Lyndon B. Johnson.

REFERENCES

Grossman, Michael Baruch, and Martha Joynt Kumar. *Portraying the President.* Baltimore, Md.: Johns Hopkins University Press, 1981.

Kernell, Samuel. *Going Public: New Strategies of Presidential Leadership.* 3rd ed. Washington, D.C.: CQ Press, 1997.

Walsh, Kenneth T. *Feeding the Beast: The White House versus the Press.* New York: Random House, 1996.

Will, George

George Frederick Will (1941–) is a journalist, author, editor, columnist, and Pulitzer Prize–winning commentator. Educated at Trinity College, Oxford University, and Princeton University (where he earned his doctorate), Will taught political philosophy at Michigan State University and at the University of Toronto. He then served on the staff of Sen. Gordon Allott (R-Colo.) before beginning his journalistic career as the Washington editor of *National Review* in 1973. Will joined the Washington Post Writers Group in 1974, four months after Ben Bradlee and Katharine Graham formed the syndication organization. He became a contributing editor of *Newsweek* magazine in 1976 and the following year was awarded the Pulitzer Prize for commentary. As a regular contributing analyst and commentator for ABC News, Will was a founding member of the Sunday morning news and interview program *This Week with David Brinkley.*

Will's prominence as a conservative thinker and writer has attracted critical scrutiny and some controversy. Journalistic ethics questions have arisen about his commentary on the 1996 election, when his wife worked as a staffer on the Dole campaign, and, more recently, about his undisclosed business relationship with controversial press baron Lord

Black. Will's service as an informal advisor to Ronald Reagan during the 1980 presidential campaign also produced some controversy when, twenty-four years later, former president Jimmy Carter accused Will of having delivered a stolen campaign briefing book to Reagan prior to their televised debate; Carter later retracted the charge publicly.

Will's numerous books include *The Pursuit of Happiness and Other Sobering Thoughts* (1978), *Solzhenitsyn and American Democracy* (1980), *Statecraft as Soulcraft: What Government Does* (1983), and *Restoration: Congress, Term Limits and The Recovery of Deliberative Democracy* (1992). His columns have been compiled and republished in several volumes as well.

REFERENCES

Burner, David, and Thomas R. West. *Column Right: Conservative Journalists in the Service of Nationalism.* New York: New York University Press, 1988.

Chappell, Larry W. *George F. Will.* New York: Twayne Publishers, 1997.

Willie Horton ad

In 1974 William Horton was convicted of armed robbery and first-degree murder by the Commonwealth of Massachusetts and sentenced to life in prison without parole. While incarcerated, however, Horton was allowed to participate in a weekend furlough program designed to promote good behavior among inmates. On one such furlough, he kidnapped a young couple, stabbing the man and raping the woman, thereby earning two life sentences plus eighty-five years in prison.

During the 1988 presidential campaign, an independent political action committee released an ad, approved by Republican strategist Lee Atwater, featuring Horton's mug shot and criticizing Democratic candidate Michael Dukakis, the governor of Massachusetts, for being "soft on crime," even though the furlough policy predated Dukakis's tenure as governor. Many leaders protested the seemingly racist subtext of the advertisement—Horton was black—particularly because of the promulgation of Horton's menacing mug shot, but rival candidate George H. W. Bush continued to exploit the issue, making harsh criminal penalties a central issue in his successful presidential campaign.

Being "tough on crime" has often been an effective rallying cry for candidates, but the Willie Horton ad, despite its racist overtone, was never effectively countered by Dukakis, even when moderator Bernard Shaw gave him the opportunity to take a more punitive position on criminal justice during a televised presidential debate. As a vivid example of negative campaigning, the ad centered on Willie Horton remains among the most controversial in U.S. electoral history.

See also *Atwater, Lee.*

REFERENCES

Anderson, David C. *Crime and the Politics of Hysteria.* New York: Random House, 1995.

Gest, Ted. *Crime and Politics: Big Government's Erratic Campaign for Law and Order.* New York: Oxford University Press, 2001.

Mendelberg, Tali. "Executing Hortons: Racial Crime in the 1988 Presidential Campaign." *Public Opinion Quarterly* 61, no. 1 (Spring 1997): 134–157.

Wire services

Wire services—also known as news services or news agencies—provide text and photos for print, television, and radio news to thousands of subscribers. The services either produce these news items themselves or gather them from their member news outlets and then make the news product available to other subscribers. This product is now supplied both in print and, increasingly, on Internet sites that carry some or all of the major wire services' news feeds.

The first American wire service originated in 1846, when several newspapers in the state of New York realized that they could pool their communications resources and share stories by telegraph. Their cooperative, which became known as the Associated Press (AP), is now the largest wire service in the world. The establishment of the AP led directly to the professionalization and routinization of news gathering. Because the member papers of the AP held differing political positions, stories that "moved" on the AP wire could not take an explicitly ideological slant. Instead, in order to serve papers on all sides, the AP stories were clearly focused on reporting the bare facts, and this avoidance of ideological bias remains one of the service's cornerstones. AP's writing style became known as the "inverted pyramid"—the essential facts are presented first in the story, while more detailed but less important information is relegated to later paragraphs.

AP's primary U.S. competitor, United Press International (UPI), was formed in 1958 in a merger of the United Press and International News services. Since that time, UPI has shrunk considerably; even in the 1960s it was a shoestring operation in comparison to AP. UPI is now owned by the Unification Church (also the owner of the *Washington Times*), and this affiliation has raised some questions about its editorial independence.

The world's two other major wire services are Britain's Reuters and the Paris-based Agence France-Presse. In countries where the media are publicly owned organs of the state, governments often have their own news services, such as Xinhua in China and the former TASS—or, in Russian, TACC, for Telegraph Agency of the Soviet Union—now known as ITAR-TASS, which is the state information agency for the Russian Federation.

See also *Associated Press; United Press International.*

REFERENCES

Alabiso, Vincent, Kelly Smith Tunney, Chuck Zoeller, and Associated Press. *Flash! The Associated Press Covers the World.* New York: Associated Press, in association with Harry N. Abrams, 1998.

Associated Press, www.ap.org.

Schwarzlose, Richard Allen. *The American Wire Services: a Study of their Development as a Social Institution.* New York: Arno Press, 1979.

United Press International, www.upi.com.

Women in politics and the media

Research on media coverage of women in political office and women as political candidates strongly indicates that women in politics are "others"—notable not so much for who and what they are as for who and what they are not: men. Communication scholars have long argued that by portraying women in general as others, the media make a powerful contribution to notions of sex roles. Such portrayals reinforce traditional gender identity patterns and powerfully support a tradition of imbalanced political power, in which the male is not only the relevant political voice, but also the appropriate political voice.

Studies examining the treatment of the sexes in news coverage, including network, cable, public television, and radio shows, reveal an unusual emphasis on the personal—romance or marital status, clothing and appearance, mother-

hood, sex, body parts—when women were mentioned. When women were featured in a political context, their concerns were often trivialized and portrayed as not quite "normal" or "regular."

A 2001 study conducted among the press secretaries of members of the U.S. House of Representatives suggests the depth of the problem. Those working for female representatives were considerably more likely to find media coverage unfair: Whereas 90 percent of the men's press secretaries stated that the media generally treated their bosses fairly, only 32 percent of the female members' press secretaries agreed with that sentiment. Many of those press secretaries to women suggested that their bosses received less coverage because the media afford female lawmakers less respect. One congresswoman's press secretary commented that "time and again, she is underestimated by the media," while another added that her boss "might as well be invisible for all the attention they pay to her leadership on issues." When asked if their bosses had been subject to media stereotypes, the vast majority of press secretaries to women complained specifically about categorizations having to do with gender: "[The media] see her as a woman, and they come to us when they think they have a 'woman's issue' and need to hear a woman's view." In stark contrast, press secretaries to male representatives were often hard-pressed to think of stereotypes they had encountered.

Media scholar David Niven quotes a 2003 *New York Times* article that illustrates quite well the basic pattern of media coverage of women in politics: "She went to Wal-Mart and Kmart to shop for blue jeans and sneakers for her twin sons, Reece and Bennett, who turn 7 later this month. She registered the boys for Little League and bought their uniforms. She sent checks to their school to cover two months' worth of cafeteria lunches, and paid for their summer camp." Although an account such as this one could have been written about the actions of any of millions of women in the United States, the subject here is a day in the life of U.S. senator Blanche Lincoln (D-Ark.) and four of her colleagues—all senators and all women. Analysts find significant implications for the way articles such as this one portray women in politics.

First, every article focused on a female politician's family life is an article not focused on her actual political accomplishments. Second, family life is frequently portrayed as conflicting with the personal responsibilities of a woman officeholder. The *Times* piece relates how these senators

Sen. Blanche Lincoln (D-Ark.) appears with Tom Carper (D-Del.) and Mark Pryor (D-Ark.), co-sponsors of her bill to aid small businesses in providing health insurance to their employees. Scholars have found that female politicians like Lincoln, a mother of two, often receive more press coverage for their role as a parent than do male colleagues. The women's political accomplishments tend to be shortchanged or overlooked.

"juggle pediatricians' appointments with Cub Scout meetings with fund-raisers and late-night roll call votes." The challenge can prove too much, as the *Times* noted in reporting that Sen. Kay Bailey Hutchison (R-Texas) was late to a meeting because her two-year-old had slept late and that Sen. Mary Landrieu (D-La.) refuses to work most nights because she wants to be with her two children.

Third, the association of women politicians with motherhood seems to encourage reporters to use childish language to describe them and their behavior. Senator Lincoln, who led the effort in the Senate to extend a tax credit to low-income families, was described in that same *Times* article as having "kicked up a fuss" on the tax issue. Sen. Lisa Murkowski (R-Alaska) was admonished in the article for missing a Senate vote in order to attend a son's sixth-grade graduation, a decision the *Times* labeled "a definite no-no."

Fourth, their experience as mothers seems to encourage reporters to credit women politicians with expertise in women-oriented issues while serving to limit their authority in other areas. For instance, the article mentions that Sen. Bill Frist (R-Tenn.) was a heart surgeon before winning his Senate seat and that he speaks with great credibility on issues related to medicine and health care. By contrast, the women senators "have a certain credibility on matters that affect women." The article does not mention that in addition to being a surgeon, Senator Frist is a man and a father or that

he has any special credibility on issues affecting men. It also fails to mention, for example, that in addition to being a woman and a mother, Senator Murkowski is a lawyer and therefore might have some special credibility on legal issues.

Coverage of women politicians as mothers offers a vastly different picture than does coverage of male politicians as fathers: the men in the Senate seem less apt to have to justify their ability to be senators as well as fathers and less likely to have their family roles interfere with their portrayal as political actors. Indeed, the *Times* directly states that political fatherhood is less important than political motherhood because "men do not carry precisely the same child-rearing burdens as women." What is most important about the *Times* article is not that it is unique, but that it is quite typical. Numerous studies of women officeholders have found them portrayed as outsiders with odd concerns.

Not surprisingly, it is not only women in office who are subject to unequal treatment by the media, but women running for office receive similar treatment as well. A number of scholars studying elections continue to find women receiving less coverage, more negative attention, and more horse-race coverage than men; being treated as inherently different from male candidates; being portrayed in family situations or according to their sex, age, appearance, or personality; and having more trouble getting coverage on the issues they have emphasized. In general, the portrait of women politicians that emerges from the press reinforces stereotypes and suggests that women are simply less weighty players in the political game. Men in politics, meanwhile, can expect greater attention paid to their experience and accomplishments as well as to their stands on the issues. Not only do male candidates receive more issue coverage, but that coverage is also more likely to suggest that they are prepared, are qualified, and understand the logic and evidence of the issue at hand. Ultimately, scholars do not suggest that women and men in politics agree on every issue or every tactic, but, they argue, their differences are often exaggerated by the media, while the genuine political voices of women are distorted or unheard.

Media designed specifically for women provide an interesting contrast in perspective. In women's magazines, women are not the "other," but instead are typically depicted as capable and creative. Women's magazines have long presented a more diverse picture of the American woman's life than is commonly assumed, suggesting that they were not exclusively homemakers in the past, nor are they exclusively career-oriented in the present. These magazines have fueled the aspirations of women socially and economically, communicating the empowering and the overwhelming aspects of high expectations. Nevertheless, the potential for women's future in politics appears much stronger in the pages of women's magazines than in other media outlets.

REFERENCES

Braden, Maria. *Women Politicians and the Media.* Lexington: University Press of Kentucky, 1996.
Jamieson, Kathleen Hall. *Beyond the Double Bind: Women and Leadership.* New York: Oxford University Press, 1995.
Kahn, Kim Fridkin. "The Distorted Mirror: Press Coverage of Women Candidates for Statewide Office." *Journal of Politics* 56, no. 1 (January 1994): 154–173.
Lind, Rebecca Ann, and Colleen Salo. "The Framing of Feminists and Feminism in News and Public Affairs Programs in U.S. Electronic Media." *Journal of Communication* 52, no. 1 (January 2002): 211–228.
Niven, David. "Gender Bias? Media Coverage of Women and Men in Congress." In *Gender and American Politics: Women, Men, and the Political Process,* edited by Sue Tolleson-Rinehart and Jyl Josephson. Armonk, N.Y.: M.E. Sharpe, 2005.
Niven, David, and Jeremy Zilber. "How Does She Have Time for Kids and Congress? Views on Gender and Media Coverage from House Offices." In *Women and Congress: Running, Winning, and Ruling,* edited by Karen O'Connor. Binghamton, N.Y.: Haworth Press, 2001.
Walker, Nancy. *Shaping our Mothers' World: American Women's Magazines.* Jackson: University Press of Mississippi, 2000.
Witt, Linda, Karen Paget, and Glenna Matthews. *Running as a Woman: Gender and Power in American Politics.* New York: Free Press, 1995.

Woodward, Bob

Robert Upshur Woodward (1943–) is a celebrated journalist and author who originally gained fame as half of the reporting team that broke the Watergate scandal in 1972. Having graduated from Yale University and served a stint in the navy, Woodward joined the *Washington Post* in 1971. The following year, he was teamed with another young reporter, Carl Bernstein, on assignment to investigate a break-in at the Democratic National Committee offices in the Watergate complex. Benefiting from the assistance of an anonymous source known as "Deep Throat"—later revealed to have been W. Mark Felt, then deputy director of the FBI—the two young reporters eventually linked what White House press secretary Ron Ziegler had described as a "third-rate burglary" to President Richard M. Nixon. Their reports won the newspaper the 1973 Pulitzer Prize and contributed to a parallel congressional inquiry that led to prison terms for key White House aides and to the only resignation of a sitting U.S. president. Woodward and Bernstein co-authored *All the President's Men* (1974), documenting their experience in reporting the Watergate scandal; the book was transformed into an Oscar-winning movie with the same title.

In 1978 Woodward was promoted to metropolitan editor of the *Post.* Since 1981 he has been its assistant managing editor. Leading the paper's reporting on the September 11, 2001, attacks, he again helped the *Post* win a Pulitzer Prize in 2002. Woodward's connections to governmental insiders would gain him extraordinary access to officials at the highest levels of government, allowing him to write several controversial "insider" books, including *The Brethren* (with Scott Armstrong, 1979), *Wired* (1984), *Veil* (1987), *The Commanders* (1991), *Maestro* (2000), *Bush at War* (2002), *Plan of Attack* (2004), and *State of Denial* (2006). Woodward's connections also earned him criticism from some of his journalistic colleagues who questioned his ability to report free of his sources' influence. In 2005, shortly after Felt's public self-disclosure, Woodward published his version of the Deep Throat story, *The Secret Man,* a tale largely written earlier but waiting for the day that the source's identity could be revealed.

REFERENCES

Havill, Adrian. *Deep Truth: The Lives of Bob Woodward and Carl Bernstein.* New York: Birch Lane Press, 1993.
Kempton, M. "Casey and Woodward: Who Used Whom?" *New York Review of Books,* November 5, 1987, 61.
Shepard, Alicia C. "Off the Record." *Washingtonian,* September 2003.

Y

Yellow journalism

The phrase "yellow journalism" can be traced to the Yellow Kid, a brightly dressed character introduced in the "Hogan's Alley" comic section of Joseph Pulitzer's popular *New York World* in 1896. Because non-smearing color print was new to the industry, the term became synonymous with the newspaper's sensationalist reporting style, which was developed to increase circulation among a working-class, immigrant, and female readership that had previously been ignored by publishers. Media scholars Michael Emery and Edwin Emery describe the practice as "a shrieking, gaudy, sensation-loving, devil-may-care kind of journalism which lured the reader by any possible means. . . . It made the high drama of life a cheap melodrama, and it twisted the facts of each day into whatever form seemed best suited to produce sales for the howling newsboy."

In the 1890s, Pulitzer's *New York World* and William Randolph Hearst's *New York Journal* competed ruthlessly for circulation, inventing wild promotional schemes and exploiting melodramatic, sensational, and sometimes-manufactured stories while espousing concern for "the people's right to know." Because it proved to be successful, this style of journalism soon spread to papers in Boston, Cincinnati, St. Louis, Denver, and San Francisco.

The 1898 Spanish-American War has been referred to as the first press-driven war, because Pulitzer and Hearst exaggerated, sensationalized, and misrepresented events in order to fuel passion for the war. Indeed, Hearst is famously—if, perhaps, incorrectly—said to have ordered his illustrator, Frederic Remington, to provide lurid pictures of purported

The image of the "Yellow Kid," pictured here on a book cover, is the source of the term "yellow journalism" to describe the sensationalist brand of reporting popularized during the circulation war between the New York publications of William Randolph Hearst and Joseph Pulitzer. One of the hallmarks of yellow journalism is exaggeration, and sometimes inaccuracy, to deliberately attract readers through outrageous stories.

Spanish wrongdoing in Cuba, declaring, "You furnish the pictures, and I will furnish the war." Human-interest stories portraying the mistreatment of the Cubans at the hands of Spanish troops filled both papers' columns day after day, topped by huge banner headlines. After an explosion sank the USS *Maine* in Havana harbor, the Hearst newspapers, with no evidence—and subsequent research points to an accident—unequivocally blamed the Spanish. Months later, the rising tide of nationalist sentiment drove Congress to declare war on Spain.

Although the era of yellow journalism was succeeded, for the most part, by a more toned-down, responsible press in the 1920s and thereafter, some important vestiges of the style have lingered. Today's near-instant television and Internet news broadcasts do not always reflect the double- and triple-checking scrutiny of sources necessary for objective reporting. The "tabloid" press—represented in print and on TV—continues to focus on sensational coverage of crime, scandal, and celebrity. Pressed by competition, even mainstream print media find less time to verify stories before publishing them on their Web sites.

See also *Tabloids; War and the media.*

REFERENCES

Campbell, W. Joseph. *Yellow Journalism: Puncturing the Myths, Defining the Legacies.* Westport, Conn.: Praeger, 2001.

Emery, Michael, and Edwin Emery. *The Press and America: An Interpretive History of the Mass Media.* Englewood Cliffs, N.J.: Prentice-Hall, 1988.

Mott, Frank Luther. *American Journalism: A History, 1690–1960.* New York: Macmillan, 1962.

Young v. American Mini Theatres (1976)

In *Young v. American Mini Theatres* (1976), the Supreme Court voted 5-4 to uphold a zoning ordinance restricting the location of adult movie theaters in Detroit. In 1972 the Detroit Common Council had amended an ordinance to prohibit adult movie theaters from locating within 1,000 feet of adult bookstores or another adult theater or within 500 feet of a residential area. A theater was considered an adult establishment if it showed material "depicting, describing, or relating to 'specified sexual activity' or 'specified anatomical areas.'" American Mini Theatres sued Mayor Coleman Young, arguing that the ordinance placed an undue burden on its First Amendment rights and violated its right of equal protection. The Sixth Circuit Court of Appeals sided with the theater company, so the city appealed to the Supreme Court.

Before the Court, American Mini Theatres argued that the statute was vague in its definition of an "adult establishment" and how much material emphasizing sex acts or anatomy would be required for an establishment to be labeled as such. It also asserted that its films were protected by the First Amendment. The city argued that it had a legitimate interest in the character of its neighborhoods and that the ordinance would protect against the development of a "skid row." The council was said to have based its decision on studies showing that dispersing adult establishments would reduce crime and prevent property values from declining.

Justice John Paul Stevens's majority opinion declared the ordinance reasonable. He stated that although pornographic material could not be completely suppressed, the city indeed had a legitimate interest in limiting its distribution. He asserted a distinction between the protection of pornography and of political or cultural speech. He also noted that the secondary effects of preventing the decline of neighborhoods justified regulating adult theaters. In dissent, Justice Potter Stewart accused the majority of "selective interference with protected speech whose content is thought to produce distasteful effects" and ignoring that the primary function of the First Amendment is to guard against such interference.

See also *First Amendment.*

REFERENCES

Finkelman, Paul, and Melvin I. Urofsky. *Landmark Decisions of the United States Supreme Court.* Washington, D.C.: CQ Press, 2003.

Gunther, Gerald. *Constitutional Law.* Westbury, N.Y.: Foundation Press, 1991.

Pember, Don R. *Mass Media Law.* Boston: McGraw-Hill, 1999.

Young v. American Mini Theatres, 427 U.S. 50 (1976).

Z

Zenger, John Peter

John Peter Zenger (1697–1746) was a printer and journalist whose acquittal on charges of seditious libel in prerevolutionary America set an early precedent for the First Amendment principle of freedom of the press. The German-born Zenger immigrated with his family to the American colonies in 1710. After the arduous journey, during which Zenger's father died, the family settled in New York City, where Zenger was soon obligated as an indentured apprentice to the city's only printer, William Bradford, who was also the publisher of the *New York Gazette.* Having completed his service in 1718 and then formed a printing partnership with Bradford in 1725, Zenger set out on his own the following year, becoming the only other printer in New York City.

A powerful group of local businessmen, offended by the arbitrary and capricious actions of newly appointed colonial governor William Cosby, formed an opposition party and established the *New York Weekly Journal* to represent their voice. The group hired Zenger as their printer and editor in 1733. The controversy surrounding Cosby's administration sparked Zenger to publish articles attacking the governor's actions and policies, while also defending the right of newspapers to print material critical of the government.

Peter Zenger's criticism of New York colonial governor William Cosby in the New York Weekly Journal *landed him in court as a defendant in a seditious libel case that would become a precedent for the adoption of freedom of the press in the United States. Successfully defended by attorney Andrew Hamilton, Zenger nonetheless spent eight months in jail for printing defamatory, but accurate, statements.*

Zenger was not seeking confrontation or notoriety as a champion for freedom of speech; he simply wanted to be a printer with some success. In 1734 the incensed governor issued a proclamation condemning the *Journal*'s "divers scandalous, virulent, false and seditious reflections." Zenger was arrested and charged with seditious libel.

After enduring eight difficult months in New York City's Old Jail, Zenger went on trial before the provincial supreme court, defended by prominent Philadelphia lawyer Andrew Hamilton. Because Zenger refused to bow to government pressure to identify the authors of the articles in question, he remained the focus of the government's ire. The case became a cause célèbre for a colonial citizenry growing more restless with the burdens of Crown policies and administration. Although constantly admonished by the governor's hand-picked chief justice during the trial, Hamilton pled Zenger's case directly to the jury, basing his argument on the principle that the truth is an absolute defense against libel. The jury's eventual verdict of not guilty established the first precedent for what would become an important pillar of freedom of the press—that defamatory statements cannot be considered libelous if proven accurate. *New York v. John Peter Zenger* (1735) was a lightning rod that helped to shape the sense of liberty that is enjoyed in the United States to this day.

REFERENCES

Latham, Frank Brown. *The Trial of John Peter Zenger: August 1735. An Early Fight for America's Freedom of the Press.* New York: Watts, 1970.

Putnam, William Lowell. *John Peter Zenger and the Fundamental Freedom.* Jefferson, N.C.: McFarland, 1997.

Rutherfurd, Livingston. *John Peter Zenger: His Press, His Trial, and a Bibliography of Zenger Imprints.* New York: Dodd, Mead, 1904.

Westermann, Karen T. *John Peter Zenger: Free Press Advocate.* Philadelphia: Chelsea House, 2001.

Zenger, John Peter, with Paul Finkelman (ed.). *A Brief Narrative of the Case and Tryal of John Peter Zenger: Printer of the New York Weekly Journal. Union, N.J.: Lawbook Exchange, 2000.*

Ziegler, Ron

Ronald Louis Ziegler (1939–2003) was administration spokesman during President Richard M. Nixon's historic trip to China in 1972 and throughout the turbulent Watergate era. Having first worked for Nixon during the 1962 gubernatorial campaign in California, Ziegler followed him into the White House in 1969, becoming the youngest presidential press secretary at the age of twenty-nine.

As the Watergate scandal reached its greatest intensity, Ziegler was aptly described as "the White House press corps' human pin cushion." He first tried to dismiss the initial break-in at the Democratic National Committee headquarters as a "third-rate burglary," and then, as the stone wall of political cover-up began to crumble, he struggled with the changing rationales that the administration offered to the press, remarking at one point, "This is the operative statement. The others are inoperative." After the resignations of White House counsel John Dean and Nixon aides John Ehrlichman and H. R. Haldeman in April 1973, Ziegler publicly apologized for previous disparagements of Bob Woodward, Carl Bernstein, and the *Washington Post*. In his own defense, he declared, "It's necessary to fudge sometimes ... give political answers ... give non-answers. But I never walked out on that podium and lied." History, however, does not support his claim.

After leaving government service, Ziegler worked in different positions in the private sector, finally serving as chief executive of the National Association of Chain Drug Stores from 1987 until his retirement in 1998. He remained staunchly loyal to Nixon to the end of his life.

See also *Press secretaries; Watergate.*

REFERENCES

"His Master's Voice." *Newsweek* May 14, 1973, 75.

"The Long Trail of Denials to Credibility Gap." *Newsweek,* April 30, 1973, 20.

"Nixon's Press Secretary Ziegler Dies." CNN.com/*Inside Politics,* February 11, 2003, at http://www.cnn.com/2003/ALLPOLITICS/02/ 10/ziegler.obit.ap/.

Osborne, John. "Guilty Men." *New Republic,* October 28, 1972, 11– 12.

Zuckerman, Mort

Mortimer Benjamin Zuckerman (1937–) is a real-estate entrepreneur and media owner and publisher. Having received a law degree from Harvard Law School and an MBA from the University of Pennsylvania, Zuckerman taught for nine years as an associate professor at Harvard Business School. As co-founder and chairman of Boston Properties, which controls substantial holdings in Boston,

New York, Washington, and San Francisco, he has accumulated considerable wealth in real estate.

Zuckerman turned to media acquisitions in 1980, when he purchased and became chairman of the *Atlantic Monthly*. He is currently the owner, publisher, and editor-in-chief of *U.S. News & World Report* (since 1984), as well as chairman and co-publisher of the *New York Daily News* (since 1993). Zuckerman is a hands-on owner and writes regular columns in the magazine and the newspaper, unabashedly promoting issues of importance to himself. He appears sporadically as a panelist on *The McLaughlin Group*. Zuckerman has served on various national and international boards, including the Advisory Board of the Graduate School of Journalism at the University of California, Berkeley, the Council on Foreign Relations, and the International Institute of Strategic Studies.

See also *News magazines*.

REFERENCES

Carr, David. "Zuckerman, Bound to the News." *New York Times*, March 6, 2006.
Dowd, Ann Reilly. "The New (again) U.S. News: Can This Marriage Survive?" *Columbia Journalism Review*, September/October 1998.
Leonard, Devin. "The Importance of Being Mort." *Fortune*, November 13, 2000, 150–170.

Zurcher v. Stanford Daily (1978)

In *Zurcher v. Stanford Daily*, the Supreme Court upheld the right of law enforcement to search newsrooms to obtain evidence of a crime after having obtained a warrant.

A photographer for Stanford University's student newspaper, the *Stanford Daily*, had captured images of a demonstration in which students assaulted a group of police officers. Later, police with a valid warrant entered and searched the newspaper's offices to look for photos that might allow them to identify the demonstrators involved in the attack. They did not remove items from the offices, but did read files, perhaps uncovering the names of sources.

The newspaper challenged the constitutionality of the search based on alleged violations of the First, Fourth, and Fourteenth Amendments. The *Daily* asserted that police searches of press offices would create a chilling effect on free speech and that the action represented an unreasonable search and seizure because no one at the paper had been suspected of participating in the crime. A district court ruled in favor of the paper, stating that a search for evidence when the property owner is not the suspect in a crime requires a subpoena duces tecum, not a warrant. It also held that because of First Amendment issues, newspaper offices could not be searched unless "there is a clear showing that (1) important materials will be destroyed or removed from the jurisdiction; and (2) a restraining order would be futile."

The Supreme Court rejected the lower court's ruling and the *Daily*'s logic, concluding that a warrant adequately protects the press from abuse while still allowing law enforcement to collect evidence. It stated that the issue of obtaining a warrant hinged on the probable cause of there being evidence in the location searched, not whether the property owner might be involved in the crime. Also, obtaining subpoenas ran the risk that suspects thus made aware of law enforcement's suspicions might destroy evidence. In addition, the Court rejected the argument on the chilling of free speech. In response to the ruling, Congress passed the Privacy Protection Act of 1980 preventing law enforcement from searching media offices and seizing materials before publication unless it pertains to reporters or other employees being investigated for alleged crimes.

See also *First Amendment; Privacy Protection Act of 1980*.

REFERENCES

Finkelman, Paul, and Melvin I. Urofsky. *Landmark Decisions of the United States Supreme Court*. Washington, D.C.: CQ Press, 2003.
White, Ethel S. "Protection of the Individual and the Free Exchange of Ideas: Justice Potter Stewart's Role in First and Fourth Amendment Cases." *University of Cincinnati Law Review* 54 (1985): 87–127.
Zurcher v. Stanford Daily, 436 U.S. 547 (1978).

Appendix

Constitution of the United States

We the People of the United States, in Order to form a more perfect Union, establish Justice, insure domestic Tranquility, provide for the common defence, promote the general Welfare, and secure the Blessings of Liberty to ourselves and our Posterity, do ordain and establish this Constitution for the United States of America.

ARTICLE I

Section 1. All legislative Powers herein granted shall be vested in a Congress of the United States, which shall consist of a Senate and House of Representatives.

Section 2. The House of Representatives shall be composed of Members chosen every second Year by the People of the several States, and the Electors in each State shall have the Qualifications requisite for Electors of the most numerous Branch of the State Legislature.

No Person shall be a Representative who shall not have attained to the age of twenty five Years, and been seven Years a Citizen of the United States, and who shall not, when elected, be an Inhabitant of that State in which he shall be chosen.

[Representatives and direct Taxes shall be apportioned among the several States which may be included within this Union, according to their respective Numbers, which shall be determined by adding to the whole Number of free Persons, including those bound to Service for a Term of Years, and excluding Indians not taxed, three fifths of all other Persons.]¹ The actual Enumeration shall be made within three Years after the first Meeting of the Congress of the United States, and within every subsequent Term of ten Years, in such Manner as they shall by Law direct. The Number of Representatives shall not exceed one for every thirty Thousand, but each State shall have at Least one Representative; and until such enumeration shall be made, the State of New Hampshire shall be entitled to chuse three, Massachusetts eight, Rhode-Island and Providence Plantations one, Connecticut five, New-York six, New Jersey four, Pennsylvania eight, Delaware one, Maryland six, Virginia ten, North Carolina five, South Carolina five, and Georgia three.

When vacancies happen in the Representation from any State, the Executive Authority thereof shall issue Writs of Election to fill such Vacancies.

The House of Representatives shall chuse their Speaker and other Officers; and shall have the sole Power of Impeachment.

Section 3. The Senate of the United States shall be composed of two Senators from each State, [chosen by the Legislature thereof,]² for six Years; and each Senator shall have one Vote.

Immediately after they shall be assembled in Consequence of the first Election, they shall be divided as equally as may be into three Classes. The Seats of the Senators of the first Class shall be vacated at the Expiration of the second Year, of the second Class at the Expiration of the fourth Year, and of the third Class at the Expiration of the sixth Year, so that one third may be chosen every second Year; [and if Vacancies happen by Resignation, or otherwise, during the Recess of the Legislature of any State, the Executive thereof may make temporary Appointments until the next Meeting of the Legislature, which shall then fill such Vacancies.]³

No Person shall be a Senator who shall not have attained to the Age of thirty Years, and been nine Years a Citizen of the United States, and who shall not, when elected, be an Inhabitant of that State for which he shall be chosen.

The Vice President of the United States shall be President of the Senate, but shall have no Vote, unless they be equally divided.

The Senate shall chuse their other Officers, and also a President pro tempore, in the Absence of the Vice President, or when he shall exercise the Office of President of the United States.

The Senate shall have the sole Power to try all Impeachments. When sitting for that Purpose, they shall be on Oath or Affirmation. When the President of the United States is tried, the Chief Justice shall preside: And no Person shall be convicted without the Concurrence of two thirds of the Members present.

Judgment in Cases of Impeachment shall not extend further than to removal from Office, and disqualification to hold and enjoy any Office of honor, Trust or Profit under the United States: but the Party convicted shall nevertheless be liable and subject to Indictment, Trial, Judgment and Punishment, according to Law.

Section 4. The Times, Places and Manner of holding Elections for Senators and Representatives, shall be prescribed in each State by the Legislature thereof; but the Congress may at any time by Law make or alter such Regulations, except as to the Places of chusing Senators.

The Congress shall assemble at least once in every Year, and such Meeting shall [be on the first Monday in December],[4] unless they shall by Law appoint a different Day.

Section 5. Each House shall be the Judge of the Elections, Returns and Qualifications of its own Members, and a Majority of each shall constitute a Quorum to do Business; but a smaller Number may adjourn from day to day, and may be authorized to compel the Attendance of absent Members, in such Manner, and under such Penalties as each House may provide.

Each House may determine the Rules of its Proceedings, punish its Members for disorderly Behaviour, and, with the Concurrence of two thirds, expel a Member.

Each House shall keep a Journal of its Proceedings, and from time to time publish the same, excepting such Parts as may in their Judgment require Secrecy; and the Yeas and Nays of the Members of either House on any question shall, at the Desire of one fifth of those Present, be entered on the Journal.

Neither House, during the Session of Congress, shall, without the Consent of the other, adjourn for more than three days, nor to any other Place than that in which the two Houses shall be sitting.

Section 6. The Senators and Representatives shall receive a Compensation for their Services, to be ascertained by Law, and paid out of the Treasury of the United States. They shall in all Cases, except Treason, Felony and Breach of the Peace, be privileged from Arrest during their Attendance at the Session of their respective Houses, and in going to and returning from the same; and for any Speech or Debate in either House, they shall not be questioned in any other Place.

No Senator or Representative shall, during the Time for which he was elected, be appointed to any civil Office under the Authority of the United States, which shall have been created, or the Emoluments whereof shall have been encreased during such time; and no Person holding any Office under the United States, shall be a Member of either House during his Continuance in Office.

Section 7. All Bills for raising Revenue shall originate in the House of Representatives; but the Senate may propose or concur with Amendments as on other Bills.

Every Bill which shall have passed the House of Representatives and the Senate, shall, before it become a Law, be presented to the President of the United States; If he approve he shall sign it, but if not he shall return it, with his Objections to that House in which it shall have originated, who shall enter the Objections at large on their Journal, and proceed to reconsider it. If after such Reconsideration two thirds of that House shall agree to pass the Bill, it shall be

sent, together with the Objections, to the other House, by which it shall likewise be reconsidered, and if approved by two thirds of that House, it shall become a Law. But in all such Cases the Votes of both Houses shall be determined by yeas and Nays, and the Names of the Persons voting for and against the Bill shall be entered on the Journal of each House respectively. If any Bill shall not be returned by the President within ten Days (Sundays excepted) after it shall have been presented to him, the Same shall be a Law, in like Manner as if he had signed it, unless the Congress by their Adjournment prevent its Return, in which Case it shall not be a Law.

Every Order, Resolution, or Vote to which the Concurrence of the Senate and House of Representatives may be necessary (except on a question of Adjournment) shall be presented to the President of the United States; and before the Same shall take Effect, shall be approved by him, or being disapproved by him, shall be repassed by two thirds of the Senate and House of Representatives, according to the Rules and Limitations prescribed in the Case of a Bill.

Section 8. The Congress shall have Power To lay and collect Taxes, Duties, Imposts and Excises, to pay the Debts and provide for the common Defence and general Welfare of the United States; but all Duties, Imposts and Excises shall be uniform throughout the United States;

To borrow Money on the credit of the United States;

To regulate Commerce with foreign Nations, and among the several States, and with the Indian Tribes;

To establish an uniform Rule of Naturalization, and uniform Laws on the subject of Bankruptcies throughout the United States;

To coin Money, regulate the Value thereof, and of foreign Coin, and fix the Standard of Weights and Measures;

To provide for the Punishment of counterfeiting the Securities and current Coin of the United States;

To establish Post Offices and post Roads;

To promote the Progress of Science and useful Arts, by securing for limited Times to Authors and Inventors the exclusive Right to their respective Writings and Discoveries;

To constitute Tribunals inferior to the supreme Court;

To define and punish Piracies and Felonies committed on the high Seas, and Offences against the Law of Nations;

To declare War, grant Letters of Marque and Reprisal, and make Rules concerning Captures on Land and Water;

To raise and support Armies, but no Appropriation of Money to that Use shall be for a longer Term than two Years;

To provide and maintain a Navy;

To make Rules for the Government and Regulation of the land and naval Forces;

To provide for calling forth the Militia to execute the Laws of the Union, suppress Insurrections and repel Invasions;

To provide for organizing, arming, and disciplining, the Militia, and for governing such Part of them as may be employed in the Service of the United States, reserving to the States respectively, the Appointment of the Officers, and the Authority of training the Militia according to the discipline prescribed by Congress;

To exercise exclusive Legislation in all Cases whatsoever, over such District (not exceeding ten Miles square) as may, by Cession of particular States, and the Acceptance of Congress, become the Seat of the Government of the United States, and to exercise like Authority over all Places purchased by the Consent of the Legislature of the State in which the Same shall be, for the Erection of Forts, Magazines, Arsenals, dock-Yards, and other needful Buildings;—And

To make all Laws which shall be necessary and proper for carrying into Execution the foregoing Powers, and all other Powers vested by this Constitution in the Government of the United States, or in any Department or Officer thereof.

Section 9. The Migration or Importation of such Persons as any of the States now existing shall think proper to admit, shall not be prohibited by the Congress prior to the Year one thousand eight hundred and eight, but a Tax or duty may be imposed on such Importation, not exceeding ten dollars for each Person.

The Privilege of the Writ of Habeas Corpus shall not be suspended, unless when in Cases of Rebellion or Invasion the public Safety may require it.

No Bill of Attainder or ex post facto Law shall be passed.

No Capitation, or other direct, Tax shall be laid, unless in Proportion to the Census or Enumeration herein before directed to be taken.[5]

No Tax or Duty shall be laid on Articles exported from any State.

No Preference shall be given by any Regulation of Commerce or Revenue to the Ports of one State over those of another; nor shall Vessels bound to, or from, one State, be obliged to enter, clear, or pay Duties in another.

No Money shall be drawn from the Treasury, but in Consequence of Appropriations made by Law; and a regular Statement and Account of the Receipts and Expenditures of all public Money shall be published from time to time.

No Title of Nobility shall be granted by the United States: And no Person holding any Office of Profit or Trust under them, shall, without the Consent of the Congress, accept of any present, Emolument, Office, or Title, of any kind whatever, from any King, Prince, or foreign State.

Section 10. No State shall enter into any Treaty, Alliance, or Confederation; grant Letters of Marque and Reprisal; coin Money; emit Bills of Credit; make any Thing but gold and silver Coin a Tender in Payment of Debts; pass any Bill of Attainder, ex post facto Law, or Law impairing the Obligation of Contracts, or grant any Title of Nobility.

No State shall, without the Consent of the Congress, lay any Imposts or Duties on Imports or Exports, except what may be absolutely necessary for executing it's inspection Laws: and the net Produce of all Duties and Imposts, laid by any State on Imports or Exports, shall be for the Use of the Treasury of the United States; and all such Laws shall be subject to the Revision and Controul of the Congress.

No State shall, without the Consent of Congress, lay any Duty of Tonnage, keep Troops, or Ships of War in time of Peace, enter into any Agreement or Compact with another State, or with a foreign Power, or engage in War, unless actually invaded, or in such imminent Danger as will not admit of delay.

ARTICLE II

Section 1. The executive Power shall be vested in a President of the United States of America. He shall hold his Office during the Term of four Years, and, together with the Vice President, chosen for the same Term, be elected, as follows:

Each State shall appoint, in such Manner as the Legislature thereof may direct, a Number of Electors, equal to the whole Number of Senators and Representatives to which the State may be entitled in the Congress: but no Senator or Representative, or Person holding an Office of Trust or Profit under the United States, shall be appointed an Elector.

[The Electors shall meet in their respective States, and vote by Ballot for two Persons, of whom one at least shall not be an Inhabitant of the same State with themselves. And they shall make a List of all the Persons voted for, and of the Number of Votes for each; which List they shall sign and certify, and transmit sealed to the Seat of the Government of the United States, directed to the President of the Senate. The President of the Senate shall, in the Presence of the Senate and House of Representatives, open all the Certificates, and the Votes shall then be counted. The Person having the greatest Number of Votes shall be the President, if such Number be a Majority of the whole Number of Electors appointed; and if there be more than one who have such Majority, and have an equal Number of Votes, then the House of Representatives shall immediately chuse by Ballot one of them for President; and if no Person have a Majority, then from the five highest on the list the said House shall in like Manner chuse the President. But in chusing the President, the Votes shall be taken by States, the Representation from each State having one Vote; A quorum for this Purpose shall consist of a Member or Members from two thirds of the States, and a Majority of all the States shall be necessary to a Choice. In every Case, after the Choice of the President, the Person having the greatest Number of Votes of the Electors shall be the Vice President. But if there should remain two or more who have equal Votes, the Senate shall chuse from them by Ballot the Vice President.][6]

The Congress may determine the Time of chusing the Electors, and the Day on which they shall give their Votes; which Day shall be the same throughout the United States.

No Person except a natural born Citizen, or a Citizen of the United States, at the time of the Adoption of this Constitution, shall be eligible to the Office of President; neither shall any Person be eligible to that Office who shall not have attained to the Age of thirty five Years, and been fourteen Years a Resident within the United States.

In Case of the Removal of the President from Office, or of his Death, Resignation, or Inability to discharge the Powers and Duties of the said Office,[7] the Same shall devolve on the Vice President, and the Congress may by Law provide for the Case of Removal, Death, Resignation or Inability, both of the President and Vice President, declaring what Officer shall then act as President, and such Officer shall act accordingly, until the Disability be removed, or a President shall be elected.

The President shall, at stated Times, receive for his Services, a Compensation, which shall neither be encreased nor diminished during the Period for which he shall have been elected, and he shall not receive within that Period any other Emolument from the United States, or any of them.

Before he enter on the Execution of his Office, he shall take the following Oath or Affirmation:—"I do solemnly swear (or affirm) that I will faithfully execute the Office of President of the United States, and will to the best of my Ability, preserve, protect and defend the Constitution of the United States."

Section 2. The President shall be Commander in Chief of the Army and Navy of the United States, and of the Militia of the several States, when called into the actual Service of the United States; he may require the Opinion, in writing, of the principal Officer in each of the executive Departments, upon any Subject relating to the Duties of their respective Offices, and he shall have Power to grant Reprieves and Pardons for Offences against the United States, except in Cases of Impeachment.

He shall have Power, by and with the Advice and Consent of the Senate, to make Treaties, provided two thirds of the Senators present concur; and he shall nominate, and by and with the Advice and Consent of the Senate, shall appoint Ambassadors, other public Ministers and Consuls, Judges of the supreme Court, and all other Officers of the United States, whose Appointments are not herein otherwise provided for, and which shall be established by Law: but the Congress may by Law vest the Appointment of such inferior Officers, as they think proper, in the President alone, in the Courts of Law, or in the Heads of Departments.

The President shall have Power to fill up all Vacancies that may happen during the Recess of the Senate, by granting Commissions which shall expire at the End of their next Session.

Section 3. He shall from time to time give to the Congress Information of the State of the Union, and recommend to their Consideration such Measures as he shall judge necessary and expedient; he may, on extraordinary Occasions, convene both Houses, or either of them, and in Case of Disagreement between them, with Respect to the Time of Adjournment, he may adjourn them to such Time as he shall think proper; he shall receive Ambassadors and other public Ministers; he shall take Care that the Laws be faithfully executed, and shall Commission all the Officers of the United States.

Section 4. The President, Vice President and all civil Officers of the United States, shall be removed from Office on Impeachment for, and Conviction of, Treason, Bribery, or other high Crimes and Misdemeanors.

ARTICLE III

Section 1. The judicial Power of the United States, shall be vested in one supreme Court, and in such inferior Courts as the Congress may from time to time ordain and establish. The Judges, both of the supreme and inferior Courts, shall hold their Offices during good Behaviour, and shall, at stated Times, receive for their Services, a Compensation, which shall not be diminished during their Continuance in Office.

Section 2. The judicial Power shall extend to all Cases, in Law and Equity, arising under this Constitution, the Laws of the United States, and Treaties made, or which shall be made, under their Authority;—to all Cases affecting Ambassadors, other public Ministers and Consuls;—to all Cases of admiralty and maritime Jurisdiction;—to Controversies to which the United States shall be a Party;—to Controversies between two or more States;—between a State and Citizens of another State;—between Citizens of different States;—between Citizens of the same State claiming Lands under Grants of different States, and between a State, or the Citizens thereof, and foreign States, Citizens or Subjects.[8]

In all Cases affecting Ambassadors, other public Ministers and Consuls, and those in which a State shall be Party, the supreme Court shall have original Jurisdiction. In all the other Cases before mentioned, the supreme Court shall have appellate Jurisdiction, both as to Law and Fact, with such Exceptions, and under such Regulations as the Congress shall make.

The Trial of all Crimes, except in Cases of Impeachment, shall be by Jury; and such Trial shall be held in the State where the said Crimes shall have been committed; but when not committed within any State, the Trial shall be at such Place or Places as the Congress may by Law have directed.

Section 3. Treason against the United States, shall consist only in levying War against them, or in adhering to their

Enemies, giving them Aid and Comfort. No Person shall be convicted of Treason unless on the Testimony of two Witnesses to the same overt Act, or on Confession in open Court.

The Congress shall have Power to declare the Punishment of Treason, but no Attainder of Treason shall work Corruption of Blood, or Forfeiture except during the Life of the Person attainted.

ARTICLE IV

Section 1. Full Faith and Credit shall be given in each State to the public Acts, Records, and judicial Proceedings of every other State. And the Congress may by general Laws prescribe the Manner in which such Acts, Records and Proceedings shall be proved, and the Effect thereof.

Section 2. The Citizens of each State shall be entitled to all Privileges and Immunities of Citizens in the several States.

A Person charged in any State with Treason, Felony, or other Crime, who shall flee from Justice, and be found in another State, shall on Demand of the executive Authority of the State from which he fled, be delivered up, to be removed to the State having Jurisdiction of the Crime.

[No Person held to Service or Labour in one State, under the Laws thereof, escaping into another, shall, in Consequence of any Law or Regulation therein, be discharged from such Service or Labour, but shall be delivered up on Claim of the Party to whom such Service or Labour may be due.]⁹

Section 3. New States may be admitted by the Congress into this Union; but no new State shall be formed or erected within the Jurisdiction of any other State; nor any State be formed by the Junction of two or more States, or Parts of States, without the Consent of the Legislatures of the States concerned as well as of the Congress.

The Congress shall have Power to dispose of and make all needful Rules and Regulations respecting the Territory or other Property belonging to the United States; and nothing in this Constitution shall be so construed as to Prejudice any Claims of the United States, or of any particular State.

Section 4. The United States shall guarantee to every State in this Union a Republican Form of Government, and shall protect each of them against Invasion; and on Application of the Legislature, or of the Executive (when the Legislature cannot be convened) against domestic Violence.

ARTICLE V

The Congress, whenever two thirds of both Houses shall deem it necessary, shall propose Amendments to this Constitution, or, on the Application of the Legislatures of two thirds of the several States, shall call a Convention for proposing Amendments, which, in either Case, shall be valid to all Intents and Purposes, as Part of this Constitution, when ratified by the Legislatures of three fourths of the several States, or by Conventions in three fourths thereof, as the one or the other Mode of Ratification may be proposed by the Congress; Provided [that no Amendment which may be made prior to the Year One thousand eight hundred and eight shall in any Manner affect the first and fourth Clauses in the Ninth Section of the first Article; and]¹⁰ that no State, without its Consent, shall be deprived of its equal Suffrage in the Senate.

ARTICLE VI

All Debts contracted and Engagements entered into, before the Adoption of this Constitution, shall be as valid against the United States under this Constitution, as under the Confederation.

This Constitution, and the Laws of the United States which shall be made in Pursuance thereof; and all Treaties made, or which shall be made, under the Authority of the United States, shall be the supreme Law of the Land; and the Judges in every State shall be bound thereby, any Thing in the Constitution or Laws of any State to the Contrary notwithstanding.

The Senators and Representatives before mentioned, and the Members of the several State Legislatures, and all executive and judicial Officers, both of the United States and of the several States, shall be bound by Oath or Affirmation, to support this Constitution; but no religious Test shall ever be required as a Qualification to any Office or public Trust under the United States.

ARTICLE VII

The Ratification of the Conventions of nine States, shall be sufficient for the Establishment of this Constitution between the States so ratifying the Same.

Done in Convention by the Unanimous Consent of the States present the Seventeenth Day of September in the Year of our Lord one thousand seven hundred and Eighty seven and of the Independence of the United States of America the Twelfth. IN WITNESS whereof We have hereunto subscribed our Names,

George Washington,
President and deputy from Virginia.

[The language of the original Constitution, not including the Amendments, was adopted by a convention of the states on September 17, 1787, and was subsequently ratified by the states on the following dates: Delaware, December 7, 1787; Pennsylvania, December 12, 1787; New Jersey, December 18, 1787; Georgia, January 2, 1788; Connecticut, January 9, 1788; Massachusetts, February 6, 1788; Maryland, April 28, 1788;

South Carolina, May 23, 1788; New Hampshire, June 21, 1788.

Ratification was completed on June 21, 1788.

The Constitution subsequently was ratified by Virginia, June 25, 1788; New York, July 26, 1788; North Carolina, November 21, 1789; Rhode Island, May 29, 1790; and Vermont, January 10, 1791.]

AMENDMENTS

Amendment I (First ten amendments ratified December 15, 1791)

Congress shall make no law respecting an establishment of religion, or prohibiting the free exercise thereof; or abridging the freedom of speech, or of the press; or the right of the people peaceably to assemble, and to petition the Government for a redress of grievances.

Amendment II

A well regulated Militia, being necessary to the security of a free State, the right of the people to keep and bear Arms, shall not be infringed.

Amendment III

No Soldier shall, in time of peace be quartered in any house, without the consent of the Owner, nor in time of war, but in a manner to be prescribed by law.

Amendment IV

The right of the people to be secure in their persons, houses, papers, and effects, against unreasonable searches and seizures, shall not be violated, and no Warrants shall issue, but upon probable cause, supported by Oath or affirmation, and particularly describing the place to be searched, and the persons or things to be seized.

Amendment V

No person shall be held to answer for a capital, or otherwise infamous crime, unless on a presentment or indictment of a Grand Jury, except in cases arising in the land or naval forces, or in the Militia, when in actual service in time of War or public danger; nor shall any person be subject for the same offence to be twice put in jeopardy of life or limb; nor shall be compelled in any criminal case to be a witness against himself, nor be deprived of life, liberty, or property, without due process of law; nor shall private property be taken for public use, without just compensation.

Amendment VI

In all criminal prosecutions, the accused shall enjoy the right to a speedy and public trial, by an impartial jury of the State and district wherein the crime shall have been committed, which district shall have been previously ascertained by law, and to be informed of the nature and cause of the accusation; to be confronted with the witnesses against him; to have compulsory process for obtaining witnesses in his favor, and to have the Assistance of Counsel for his defence.

Amendment VII

In Suits at common law, where the value in controversy shall exceed twenty dollars, the right of trial by jury shall be preserved, and no fact tried by a jury, shall be otherwise re-examined in any Court of the United States, than according to the rules of the common law.

Amendment VIII

Excessive bail shall not be required, nor excessive fines imposed, nor cruel and unusual punishments inflicted.

Amendment IX

The enumeration in the Constitution, of certain rights, shall not be construed to deny or disparage others retained by the people.

Amendment X

The powers not delegated to the United States by the Constitution, nor prohibited by it to the States, are reserved to the States respectively, or to the people.

Amendment XI (Ratified February 7, 1795)

The Judicial power of the United States shall not be construed to extend to any suit in law or equity, commenced or prosecuted against one of the United States by Citizens of another State, or by Citizens or Subjects of any Foreign State.

Amendment XII (Ratified June 15, 1804)

The Electors shall meet in their respective states and vote by ballot for President and Vice-President, one of whom, at least, shall not be an inhabitant of the same state with themselves; they shall name in their ballots the person voted for as President, and in distinct ballots the person voted for as Vice-President, and they shall make distinct lists of all persons voted for as President, and of all persons voted for as Vice-President, and of the number of votes for each, which lists they shall sign and certify, and transmit sealed to the seat of the government of the United States, directed to the President of the Senate;—The President of the Senate shall, in the presence of the Senate and House of Representatives, open all the certificates and the votes shall then be counted;—The person having the greatest number of votes for President, shall be the President, if such number be a majority of the whole number of Electors appointed; and if no person have such majority, then from the persons having the highest numbers not exceeding three on the list of those voted for as President, the House of Representatives shall choose immediately, by ballot, the President. But in choosing the President, the votes shall be taken by states, the representation from each state having one vote; a quorum for this purpose shall consist of a member or members from two-thirds of the states, and a majority of all the states shall be necessary to a choice. [And if the House of Representatives shall not choose a President whenever the right of choice shall devolve upon them, before the fourth day of March next following, then the Vice-President shall act as President, as in the case of the death or other constitutional disability of the President.—]¹¹ The person having the greatest number of votes as Vice-President, shall be the Vice-President, if such number be a majority of the whole number of Electors appointed, and if no person have a majority, then from the two highest numbers on the list, the Senate shall choose the Vice-President; a quorum for the purpose shall consist of two-thirds of the whole number of Senators, and a majority of the whole number shall be necessary to a choice. But no person constitutionally ineligible to the office of President shall be eligible to that of Vice-President of the United States.

Amendment XIII (Ratified December 6, 1865)

Section 1. Neither slavery nor involuntary servitude, except as a punishment for crime whereof the party shall have been duly convicted, shall exist within the United States, or any place subject to their jurisdiction.

Section 2. Congress shall have power to enforce this article by appropriate legislation.

Amendment XIV (Ratified July 9, 1868)

Section 1. All persons born or naturalized in the United States, and subject to the jurisdiction thereof, are citizens of the United States and of the State wherein they reside. No State shall make or enforce any law which shall abridge the privileges or immunities of citizens of the United States; nor shall any State deprive any person of life, liberty, or property, without due process of law; nor deny to any person within its jurisdiction the equal protection of the laws.

Section 2. Representatives shall be apportioned among the several States according to their respective numbers, counting the whole number of persons in each State, excluding Indians not taxed. But when the right to vote at any election for the choice of electors for President and Vice President of the United States, Representatives in Congress, the Executive and Judicial officers of a State, or the members of the Legislature thereof, is denied to any of the male inhabitants of such State, being twenty-one years of age,¹² and citizens of the United States, or in any way abridged, except for participation in rebellion, or other crime, the basis

of representation therein shall be reduced in the proportion which the number of such male citizens shall bear to the whole number of male citizens twenty-one years of age in such State.

Section 3. No person shall be a Senator or Representative in Congress, or elector of President and Vice President, or hold any office, civil or military, under the United States, or under any State, who, having previously taken an oath, as a member of Congress, or as an officer of the United States, or as a member of any State legislature, or as an executive or judicial officer of any State, to support the Constitution of the United States, shall have engaged in insurrection or rebellion against the same, or given aid or comfort to the enemies thereof. But Congress may by a vote of two-thirds of each House, remove such disability.

Section 4. The validity of the public debt of the United States, authorized by law, including debts incurred for payment of pensions and bounties for services in suppressing insurrection or rebellion, shall not be questioned. But neither the United States nor any State shall assume or pay any debt or obligation incurred in aid of insurrection or rebellion against the United States, or any claim for the loss or emancipation of any slave; but all such debts, obligations and claims shall be held illegal and void.

Section 5. The Congress shall have power to enforce, by appropriate legislation, the provisions of this article.

Amendment XV (Ratified February 3, 1870)

Section 1. The right of citizens of the United States to vote shall not be denied or abridged by the United States or by any State on account of race, color, or previous condition of servitude.

Section 2. The Congress shall have power to enforce this article by appropriate legislation.

Amendment XVI (Ratified February 3, 1913)

The Congress shall have power to lay and collect taxes on incomes, from whatever source derived, without apportionment among the several States, and without regard to any census or enumeration.

Amendment XVII (Ratified April 8, 1913)

The Senate of the United States shall be composed of two Senators from each State, elected by the people thereof, for six years; and each Senator shall have one vote. The electors in each State shall have the qualifications requisite for electors of the most numerous branch of the State legislatures.

When vacancies happen in the representation of any State in the Senate, the executive authority of such State shall issue writs of election to fill such vacancies: *Provided,* That the legislature of any State may empower the executive thereof to make temporary appointments until the people fill the vacancies by election as the legislature may direct.

This amendment shall not be so construed as to affect the election or term of any Senator chosen before it becomes valid as part of the Constitution.

Amendment XVIII (Ratified January 16, 1919)

[**Section 1.** After one year from the ratification of this article the manufacture, sale, or transportation of intoxicating liquors within, the importation thereof into, or the exportation thereof from the United States and all territory subject to the jurisdiction thereof for beverage purposes is hereby prohibited.

Section 2. The Congress and the several States shall have concurrent power to enforce this article by appropriate legislation.

Section 3. This article shall be inoperative unless it shall have been ratified as an amendment to the Constitution by the legislatures of the several States, as provided in the Constitution, within seven years from the date of the submission hereof to the States by the Congress.][13]

Amendment XIX (Ratified August 18, 1920)

The right of citizens of the United States to vote shall not be denied or abridged by the United States or by any State on account of sex.

Congress shall have power to enforce this article by appropriate legislation.

Amendment XX (Ratified January 23, 1933)

Section 1. The terms of the President and Vice President shall end at noon on the 20th day of January, and the terms of Senators and Representatives at noon on the 3d day of January, of the years in which such terms would have ended if this article had not been ratified; and the terms of their successors shall then begin.

Section 2. The Congress shall assemble at least once in every year, and such meeting shall begin at noon on the 3d day of January, unless they shall by law appoint a different day.

Section 3.[14] If, at the time fixed for the beginning of the term of the President, the President elect shall have died, the Vice President elect shall become President. If a President shall not have been chosen before the time fixed for the beginning of his term, or if the President elect shall have failed to qualify, then the Vice President elect shall act as President until a President shall have qualified; and the Congress may by law provide for the case wherein neither a President elect nor a Vice President elect shall have qualified, declaring who shall then act as President, or the manner in which one who is to act shall be selected, and such

person shall act accordingly until a President or Vice President shall have qualified.

Section 4. The Congress may by law provide for the case of the death of any of the persons from whom the House of Representatives may choose a President whenever the right of choice shall have devolved upon them, and for the case of the death of any of the persons from whom the Senate may choose a Vice President whenever the right of choice shall have devolved upon them.

Section 5. Sections 1 and 2 shall take effect on the 15th day of October following the ratification of this article.

Section 6. This article shall be inoperative unless it shall have been ratified as an amendment to the Constitution by the legislatures of three-fourths of the several States within seven years from the date of its submission.

Amendment XXI (Ratified December 5, 1933)

Section 1. The eighteenth article of amendment to the Constitution of the United States is hereby repealed.

Section 2. The transportation or importation into any State, Territory, or possession of the United States for delivery or use therein of intoxicating liquors, in violation of the laws thereof, is hereby prohibited.

Section 3. This article shall be inoperative unless it shall have been ratified as an amendment to the Constitution by conventions in the several States, as provided in the Constitution, within seven years from the date of the submission hereof to the States by the Congress.

Amendment XXII (Ratified February 27, 1951)

Section 1. No person shall be elected to the office of the President more than twice, and no person who has held the office of President, or acted as President, for more than two years of a term to which some other person was elected President shall be elected to the office of the President more than once. But this Article shall not apply to any person holding the office of President when this Article was proposed by the Congress, and shall not prevent any person who may be holding the office of President, or acting as President, during the term within which this Article becomes operative from holding the office of President or acting as President during the remainder of such term.

Section 2. This article shall be inoperative unless it shall have been ratified as an amendment to the Constitution by the legislatures of three-fourths of the several States within seven years from the date of its submission to the States by the Congress.

Amendment XXIII (Ratified March 29, 1961)

Section 1. The District constituting the seat of Government of the United States shall appoint in such manner as the Congress may direct:

A number of electors of President and Vice President equal to the whole number of Senators and Representatives in Congress to which the District would be entitled if it were a State, but in no event more than the least populous State; they shall be in addition to those appointed by the States, but they shall be considered, for the purposes of the election of President and Vice President, to be electors appointed by a State; and they shall meet in the District and perform such duties as provided by the twelfth article of amendment.

Section 2. The Congress shall have power to enforce this article by appropriate legislation.

Amendment XXIV (Ratified January 23, 1964)

Section 1. The right of citizens of the United States to vote in any primary or other election for President or Vice President, for electors for President or Vice President, or for Senator or Representative in Congress, shall not be denied or abridged by the United States or any State by reason of failure to pay any poll tax or other tax.

Section 2. The Congress shall have power to enforce this article by appropriate legislation.

Amendment XXV (Ratified February 10, 1967)

Section 1. In case of the removal of the President from office or of his death or resignation, the Vice President shall become President.

Section 2. Whenever there is a vacancy in the office of the Vice President, the President shall nominate a Vice President who shall take office upon confirmation by a majority vote of both Houses of Congress.

Section 3. Whenever the President transmits to the President pro tempore of the Senate and the Speaker of the House of Representatives his written declaration that he is unable to discharge the powers and duties of his office, and until he transmits to them a written declaration to the contrary, such powers and duties shall be discharged by the Vice President as Acting President.

Section 4. Whenever the Vice President and a majority of either the principal officers of the executive departments or of such other body as Congress may by law provide, transmit to the President pro tempore of the Senate and the Speaker of the House of Representatives their written declaration that the President is unable to discharge the powers and duties of his office, the Vice President shall immediately assume the powers and duties of the office as Acting President.

Thereafter, when the President transmits to the President pro tempore of the Senate and the Speaker of the House of Representatives his written declaration that no inability exists, he shall resume the powers and duties of his office unless the Vice President and a majority of either the princi-

pal officers of the executive departments or of such other body as Congress may by law provide, transmit within four days to the President pro tempore of the Senate and the Speaker of the House of Representatives their written declaration that the President is unable to discharge the powers and duties of his office. Thereupon Congress shall decide the issue, assembling within forty-eight hours for that purpose if not in session. If the Congress, within twenty-one days after receipt of the latter written declaration, or, if Congress is not in session, within twenty-one days after Congress is required to assemble, determines by two-thirds vote of both Houses that the President is unable to discharge the powers and duties of his office, the Vice President shall continue to discharge the same as Acting President; otherwise, the President shall resume the powers and duties of his office.

Amendment XXVI (Ratified July 1, 1971)

Section 1. The right of citizens of the United States, who are eighteen years of age or older, to vote shall not be denied or abridged by the United States or by any State on account of age.

Section 2. The Congress shall have power to enforce this article by appropriate legislation.

Amendment XXVII (Ratified May 7, 1992)

No law varying the compensation for the services of the Senators and Representatives shall take effect, until an election of Representatives shall have intervened.

SOURCE: U.S. Congress, House, Committee on the Judiciary, *The Constitution of the United States of America, as Amended,* 100th Cong., 1st sess., 1987, H Doc 10094.

NOTES: 1. The part in brackets was changed by Section 2 of the Fourteenth Amendment.
2. The part in brackets was changed by the first paragraph of the Seventeenth Amendment.
3. The part in brackets was changed by the second paragraph of the Seventeenth Amendment.
4. The part in brackets was changed by the second paragraph of the Seventeenth Amendment.
5. The Sixteenth Amendment gave Congress the power to tax incomes.
6. The material in brackets was superseded by the Twelfth Amendment.
7. This provision was affected by the Twenty-fifth Amendment.
8. These clauses were affected by the Eleventh Amendment.
9. This paragraph was superseded by the Thirteenth Amendment.
10. Obsolete.
11. The part in brackets was superseded by Section 3 of the Twentieth Amendment.
12. See the Nineteenth and Twenty-sixth Amendments.
13. This amendment was repealed by Section 1 of the Twenty-first Amendment.
14. See the Twenty-fifth Amendment.

Communications in the United States

The press and broadcasting media are privately owned and enjoy editorial freedom within the bounds of state libel laws. There is no legal ban on the ownership of broadcasting facilities by the press, and in 1950, 43 percent of the commercial television stations were so owned. The Federal Communications Commission (FCC) has, however, been under some pressure to deny relicensing under potentially monopolistic circumstances.

Press

There were 10,855 newspapers, excluding in-house and special-purpose publications, issued in the United States as of 2002. Weeklies and semiweeklies outnumbered dailies by more than five to one. Until recently only a few papers had sought national distribution, the most important of the dailies being the New York–based *Wall Street Journal,* published in four regional editions; the Boston-based *Christian Science Monitor,* published in three domestic editions plus an international edition; the *New York Times,* whose national edition is transmitted by satellite for printing in eight locations throughout the country; and *USA Today,* which, after a phased market-by-market expansion beginning in 1982, reached a nationwide circulation of 2.3 million in January 2005.

After a lengthy period of decline, in part because of the impact of television on the printed media, both the number and circulation of daily newspapers appeared to stabilize during 1979-1980. Remaining relatively constant for the ensuing fifteen years, their number declined from 1,710 to 1,507 during the period 1995-2002, with circulation declining from 58.2 million to 55.2 million over the same period. Significantly, some of the country's leading papers, including the *Buffalo Courier Express,* the *Cleveland Press,* the *Des Moines Tribune,* the *Minneapolis Star,* the *Philadelphia Bulletin,* the *Pittsburgh Press,* the *Richmond News Leader,* and the *Washington Star,* were among the casualties. Concurrently, an ever-growing number of formerly independent papers were brought under the control of publishing groups. Leaders in that field include Community Newspaper Holdings (107 dailies as of the fall of 2001), Gannett (102 dailies), Media News Group (40 dailies), Knight Ridder (32 dailies), Newhouse (26 dailies), Media General (25 dailies), E. W. Scripps (22 dailies), Stephens Media group (21 dailies), New York Times newspapers (19 dailies), Cox Enterprises (17 dailies), Dow Jones and Company (16 dailies), Tribune Company (14 dailies), Hearst newspapers (12 dailies), and Heartland Publications (10 dailies). Gannett newspapers have the largest combined circulation (7.6 million as of 2004), followed by the Tribune Company and Knight Ridder (3.9 million and 3.7 million, respectively).

In June 1993, the New York Times Co. acquired the *Boston Globe* for $1.1 billion, at the time the most ever paid for an American newspaper. In mid-2000 the Tribune Company (publisher of the *Chicago Tribune* and several smaller papers) purchased the Times Mirror Company (publisher of seven papers, including the *Los Angeles Times, Newsday,* and the *Baltimore Sun*) for $8 billion. Also in 2000 Gannett acquired Central Newspapers, Inc. (owner of six papers, including the *Arizona Republic* and the *Indianapolis Star*), for $2.6 billion. In addition, Gannett announced plans to purchase a number of papers from the Thomson Corporation, a Canadian publisher that had decided to divest itself of its once formidable newspaper holdings in the United States. Overall, newspaper purchases totaling more than $15 billion were reported for 2000.

A major turnover in newspaper ownership occurred on March 13, 2006, when the McClatchy Company announced that it had bought Knight Ridder for $6.5 billion. On April 26, 2006, it announced that the *San Jose Mercury News, Contra Costa Times, Monterey Herald,* and *St. Paul Pioneer Press* would be sold to MediaNews Group for $1 billion.

The principal guides to the following selection are size of circulation and extent of foreign affairs news coverage. A few newspapers with relatively low circulation are included

Adapted from *Political Handbook of the World, 2007* (Washington, D.C.: CQ Press, 2007).

because of their location, special readership character, and the like. The list is alphabetical according to city of publication, with city designations as components of formal names being omitted. Circulation figures, for the most part, are averages for the six months ending September 30, 2004, as provided by the Audit Bureau of Circulations.

Akron, Ohio: *Beacon Journal* (141,497 morning, 185,963 Sunday), formerly Knight Ridder.

Anchorage, Alaska: *Daily News* (68,078 morning, 82,179 Sunday), a subsidiary of the McClatchy Co.

Atlanta, Georgia: *Journal-Constitution* (400,893 morning, 606,246 Sunday), Cox Enterprises.

Baltimore, Maryland: *Sun* (270,113 morning, 454,045 Sunday), Tribune Co.

Birmingham, Alabama: *News* (149,982 morning, 184,036 Sunday), Newhouse.

Boston, Massachusetts: *Globe* (446,831 morning, 707,813 Sunday), retains "full editorial autonomy," despite acquisition by the New York Times Co.; *Herald* (230,802 morning, 152,813 Sunday), Herald Media; *Christian Science Monitor* (60,723 daily), published by the First Church of Christ, Scientist.

Buffalo, New York: *News* (196,429 all day, 282,618 Sunday). (Warren E. Buffet purchased the *News* in 1977.)

Charlotte, North Carolina: *Observer* (226,082 morning, 279,150 Sunday), formerly Knight Ridder.

Chicago, Illinois: *Tribune* (589,313 morning, 963,927 Sunday), Tribune Co.; *Sun-Times* (486,936 morning, 393,196 Sunday), Hollinger International, Inc.

Cincinnati, Ohio: *Enquirer* (188,940 morning, 301,126 Sunday), Gannett.

Cleveland, Ohio: *Plain Dealer* (354,309 morning, 479,131 Sunday), Newhouse.

Columbus, Ohio: *Dispatch* (251,045 daily, 361,304 Sunday).

Dallas, Texas: *Morning News* (494,890 morning, 776,387 Sunday), A. H. Belo.

Dayton, Ohio: *Daily News* (135,511 morning, 185,122 Sunday), Cox Enterprises.

Denver, Colorado: *Rocky Mountain News* (309,938 morning); *Post* (305,929 morning, 801,315 Sunday). Although the *News* and the *Post* remain editorially independent, they are both published by the Denver Newspaper Agency, which is owned 50 percent by E. W. Scripps Co. and 50 percent by Media News Group. Media General, Inc. has 20 percent ownership of the *Post*.

Des Moines, Iowa: *Register* (152,800 morning, 243,302 Sunday), Gannett.

Detroit, Michigan: *Free Press* (347,447 morning), formerly Knight Ridder; *News* (218,841 evening), Gannett. Combined editions are published on Saturday (488,012) and Sunday (682,798) as well as holidays.

Fort Worth, Texas: *Star-Telegram* (233,407 morning, 326,803 Sunday), formerly Knight Ridder.

Grand Rapids, Michigan: *Press* (138,126 evening, 189,690 Sunday).

Hartford, Connecticut: *Courant* (193,693 morning, 281,714 Sunday), Tribune Co.

Honolulu, Hawaii: *Advertiser* (141,341 morning, 161,325 Sunday).

Houston, Texas: *Chronicle* (554,783 morning, 737,580 Sunday), Hearst Corporation.

Indianapolis, Indiana: *Star* (252,021 morning, 358,261 Sunday), Gannett.

Jacksonville, Florida: *Florida Times-Union* (161,757 morning, 225,688 Sunday), Morris Communications Co.

Kansas City, Missouri: *Star* (270,335 morning, 377,938 Sunday), formerly Knight Ridder.

Little Rock, Arkansas: *Arkansas Democrat-Gazette* (182,391 morning, 280,529 Sunday), Arkansas Democrat-Gazette, Inc.

Los Angeles, California: *Times* (902,164 morning, 1,292,274 Sunday), Tribune Co.

Louisville, Kentucky: *Courier-Journal* (207,665 morning, 273,891 Sunday), Gannett.

Memphis, Tennessee: *Commercial Appeal* (171,599 morning, 235,889 Sunday), E. W. Scripps Co.

Miami, Florida: *Herald* (306,943 morning, 416,530 Sunday), formerly Knight Ridder.

Milwaukee, Wisconsin: *Journal Sentinel* (238,382 morning, 435,127 Sunday), subsidiary of Journal Communications.

Minneapolis, Minnesota: *Star and Tribune* (381,094 all day, 678,650 Sunday), subsidiary of the McClatchy Co.

Nashville, Tennessee: *Tennessean* (170,361 morning, 238,126 Sunday), Gannett.

New Orleans, Louisiana: *Times-Picayune* (252,799 morning, 281,374 Sunday), Newhouse.

New York, New York: *Daily News* (715,052 morning, 786,952 Sunday), Daily News, LP; *Newsday* (577,354 morning, 675,619 Sunday), Tribune Co.; *Post* (652,149 morning, 455,511 Sunday), News Corporation; *Times* (1,110,279 morning, 1,680,583 Sunday); *Wall Street Journal* (2,106,774 morning), Dow Jones and Co.

Newark, New Jersey: Star-Ledger (388,807 morning, 608,257 Sunday), Newhouse.

Oakland, California: Oakland Tribune (383,265 morning, 334,615 Sunday), Media News Group. (Figures include Almeda Newspaper Group.)

Oklahoma City, Oklahoma: Oklahoman (206,338 morning, 288,948 Sunday), Oklahoma Publishing Co.

Omaha, Nebraska: World-Herald (191,988 all day, 242,964 Sunday), Omaha World Herald Co.

Philadelphia, Pennsylvania: Inquirer/Daily News (Inquirer: 368,883 morning, 750,780 Sunday; *Daily News* 135,956 morning), formerly Knight Ridder.

Phoenix, Arizona: Arizona Republic (413,268 morning, 530,751 Sunday), Gannett.

Pittsburgh, Pennsylvania: Post-Gazette (236,877 morning, 402,981 Sunday), PG Publishing Co.

Portland, Oregon: Oregonian (335,561 all day, 405,295 Sunday), Newhouse.

Providence, Rhode Island: Journal (168,021 morning, 236,476 Sunday), Belo Corp.

Raleigh, North Carolina: News and Observer (166,336 morning, 211,735 Sunday), McClatchy Co.

Richmond, Virginia: Times-Dispatch (184,950 morning, 225,293 Sunday), Media General, Inc.

Rochester, New York: Democrat and Chronicle (166,727 morning, 224,408 Sunday), Gannett.

Sacramento, California: Bee (293,705 morning, 346,742 Sunday), McClatchy Co.

St. Louis, Missouri: Post-Dispatch (290,615 morning, 485,984 Sunday), Pulitzer, Inc.

St. Petersburg, Florida: Times (311,680 morning, 395,973 Sunday), Poynter Institute for Media Studies.

Salt Lake City, Utah: Tribune (133,025 morning, 152,859 Sunday), Media News Group.

San Diego, California: Union-Tribune (339,032 morning, 433,973 Sunday), Copley Press.

San Francisco, California: Chronicle (480,587 all day, 540,314 Sunday), Hearst Communications, Inc. In an initiative approved in 2000 following a protracted court case, Hearst Communications, Inc. sold its longtime paper, the *Examiner,* to purchase the *Chronicle.*

Seattle, Washington: Times (228,620 morning); *Post-Intelligencer* (143,559 morning), Hearst Corporation. Although the *Times* and the *Post-Intelligencer* remain editorially independent, they have a joint operating agreement under which the Seattle Times Co. provides most noned-

itorial services. A joint edition with a circulation of 462,920 is published on Sunday.

Toledo, Ohio: Blade (139,398 morning, 183,632 Sunday), Toledo Blade Co.

Washington, D.C.: Post (699,929 morning, 1,007,487 Sunday), Washington Post Co.; *Times* (97,274 morning, 43,660 Saturday), News World Communications, which is owned by Sun Myung Moon's Unification Church; *USA Today* ([national paper] 2,309,853 morning), Gannett.

Wichita, Kansas: Eagle (89,572 morning, 146,727 Sunday), formerly Knight Ridder.

News Agencies

The two major news agencies are the Associated Press (AP), an independent news cooperative serving more than 1,700 newspapers and 5,000 radio and television stations in the United States, and the United Press International (UPI), which was rescued from bankruptcy by Mexican publisher Mario Vázquez Raña in 1986 and whose operating rights were sold to an investment group associated with Financial News Network in early 1988 before being sold to the London-based, Saudi-controlled Middle East Broadcasting Centre Ltd. in June 1992. In 2000 News World Communications, which is controlled by Sun Myung Moon's Unification Church, purchased UPI. In addition, many important newspapers that maintain large staffs of foreign correspondents sell syndicated news services to other papers. Among the larger of these are the *New York Times,* the *Chicago Tribune,* the *Los Angeles Times,* and the *Washington Post.*

Broadcasting and Computing

Domestic radio and television broadcasting in the United States is a private function carried on under the auspices of the Federal Communications Commission (FCC), which licenses stations on the basis of experience, financial soundness, and projected program policy. Under the fairness doctrine embodied in FCC rules and upheld by the Supreme Court, radio and television broadcasters are required to present both sides of important issues. The so-called equal time legislation, which required a broadcaster who gave free time to a political candidate to do the same for his or her opponent, was amended on September 25, 1975, by the FCC, which stated that candidates' news conferences and political debates are news events and thus are not subject to the equal-time ruling (thus in 1996 Reform Party candidate

Ross Perot was barred from the presidential debates, despite having participated four years earlier). The National Association of Broadcasters (NAB) is a private body that sets operating rules for radio and television stations and networks.

There were approximately 273 million television receivers in use in the United States in 2003. Of 10,965 commercial radio stations in operation in 2002, 4,804 were AM and 6,161 were FM outlets. Approximately one-third of the total were owned by or affiliated with one of the four major commercial radio networks: American Broadcasting Company (ABC), Columbia Broadcasting System (CBS), Mutual Broadcasting System (MBS), and National Broadcasting Company (NBC). Supported primarily by paid advertising, most stations carry frequent news summaries; a few in the larger cities now devote all of their airtime to such programming. Noncommercial programming was offered by more than 1,300 additional FM outlets.

There were 1,333 commercial television stations in operation during 2002, most of them owned by or affiliated with one of three commercial television networks headquartered in New York City: American Broadcasting Company (ABC), Columbia Broadcasting System (CBS), and National Broadcasting Company (NBC), in addition to the Los Angeles–based Fox Network. Supported primarily by paid advertising, most stations present news highlights, evening news summaries, and programs of comments and analysis. There is also the nonprofit Public Broadcasting Service (PBS), which services approximately 380 affiliated noncommercial television stations. In addition, more than 9,000 commercial cable TV systems are in operation, servicing 86 million sub-scribers. An early beneficiary of the advent of cable TV was the Turner Broadcasting System, which by its tenth year of operation in 1990 was widely regarded as a "fourth major network"; by 1995 more new systems had been added, some (such as Paramount, Warner, and the now-commercial Fox) with roots in historic film companies.

Foreign radio broadcasting is conducted under governmental auspices by the Voice of America (VOA). Formerly a part of the U.S. Information Agency (USIA), it is now part of the International Broadcasting Bureau (IBB). It broadcasts in English and 44 other languages throughout the world. In addition, the IBB also supports Radio Free Europe and Radio Liberty, broadcasting to the peoples of the former Soviet Union. The Florida-based Radio Martí, a VOA affiliate, began Spanish-language transmissions to Cuba in May 1985, while a controversial counterpart, Television Martí, was subjected to electronic jamming upon its launch in March 1990. In September 1996, after lengthy congressional debate, an equally controversial Radio Free Asia was launched to "confront tyranny" in East Asia; although its Chinese-language impact from transmitters as far away as Armenia and Tajikistan appeared minimal, its sponsors nonetheless pressed ahead with a Tibetan-language program in December and scheduled future broadcasts aimed at North Korea and Vietnam.

The world leader in the development of computer technology, the United States had upward of 200 million personal computers in 2003 serving approximately 175 million Internet users.

Credits for Photographs and Illustrations

Newspapers / *The Granger Collection*
Newsworthiness / *Ric Feld, AP Images*

O

Obscenity and pornography / *David Phillip, AP Images*
Office of Communications / *Charles Dharapak, AP Images*
Ownership of media / *AP Images*

P

Pentagon Papers / *AP Images*
Phillips, David Graham / *The Granger Collection*
Political content in advertising / *AP Images*
Political participation and the media / *AP Images*
Political satire / *Chris Carlson, AP Images*
Politics and film / *AP Images*
Presidential debates / *Marcy Nighswander, AP Images*
Presidential press conferences / *Evan Vucci, AP Images*
Public diplomacy / *Mahmoud Tawil, AP Images*
Pulitzer, Joseph / *The Granger Collection*
Pundit shows / *Pablo Martinez Monsivais, AP Images*

R

Raspberry, William / *Denis Paquin, AP Images*
Religion and the media / *Patti Longmire, AP Images*
Roosevelt, Franklin D. / *M. L. Suckley, AP Images*

S

Scandal / *Marty Lederhandler, AP Images*
Sedition Act of 1918 / New York University, Tamiment Institute Library
Sevareid, Eric / *The Granger Collection*
Shrum, Bob / *Susan Walsh, AP Images*
Sinclair, Upton / *The Granger Collection*
Steffens, Lincoln / *The Granger Collection*

T

Thomas, Helen / *Greg Gibson, AP Images*
Thomas confirmation hearings / *John Duricka, AP Images*
Trippi, Joe / *Lenny Ignelzi, AP Images*
Twain, Mark / *The Granger Collection*

W

Walters, Barbara / *AP Images*
War and the media / *AP Images*
Women in politics and the media / *AP Images*

Y

Yellow journalism / *The Granger Collection*

Z

Zenger, John Peter / *The Granger Collection*

Index

Page numbers in italics reference photographs and illustrations.